ECONOMICS AND EMPIRE 1830-1914

WORLD ECONOMIC HISTORY

GENERAL EDITOR · CHARLES WILSON

Economics and
Empire 1830–1914
D. K. Fieldhouse

CORNELL UNIVERSITY PRESS
ITHACA, NEW YORK

First published 1973 by Cornell University Press

This edition is not for sale in the United Kingdom and British Commonwealth.

International Standard Book Number 0-8014-0810-5

Library of Congress Catalog Card Number 73-9511

Library of Congress Cataloging in Publication Data

(For library cataloging purposes only)

Fieldhouse, David Kenneth,   date.
    Economics and empire 1830-1914.

(World economic history)
Includes bibliographical references.
    1. Imperialism. 2. Economic history—
1750-1918. 1. Title.
JV105. F52 327'.11 73-9511
ISBN 0-8014-0810-5

Printed in Great Britain

To my mother, Hilda Fieldhouse

Contents

Tables

Figures

Maps

(between pages 480 and 490)

Foreword

The tensions of post-imperialism are a major fact – some would say the major fact – of our time. The conflicts, often violent, which they have engendered are not only economic, but economic problems are incontestably a basic element in their provenance and in a large proportion of existing historical and economic writings on imperialism it is assumed as a matter of course that economic motives and forces were the sole cause of the unprecedented imperial expansion of the nineteenth century.

In history, as in science, hypothesis has often preceded experiment and proof. So it was in the case of modern imperialism. From Marx to Lenin and beyond, theorists have postulated that the apparently inexplicable expansion of the colonial empires during the later nineteenth century must have been caused by economic forces inherent in the character of European capitalist society. They may have been right: but their hypothesis was so immediately attractive, so apparently complete and so satisfyingly explanatory that it gained wide acceptance long before the facts had been investigated. Popular text books like P. T. Moon's *Imperialism and World Politics* (1927) embodied rather than tested the economic hypothesis. Studies of imperialism in particular regions or during limited periods of time, however incompatible with the theory, were too localized and specialized to test or challenge a strongly entrenched general theory.

This book aims to fill the historiographical gap by approaching the problem on a broad front. Mr Fieldhouse starts with a survey of the main economic and non-economic theories which treat imperialism as a general phenomenon; he then tests their validity by examining the facts in a number of test cases spread throughout the world. His method has two special features: he examines the half-century before 1880 in order to place the later 'classical' period of imperialism in historical perspective; and he deals with countries or regions individually, rather than as part of a single global story, on the hypothesis that imperialism may have been a composite, and possibly contradictory, phenomenon rather than a unitary one. His conclusions are in many respects novel. In an area that is still a political, as well as an historical, battleground they will no doubt stimulate controversy and opposition. Yet it can fairly be said that he has written the first broad study of European imperialism before 1914 which subjects generalized theory to the facts recently established by historical research.

Mr Fieldhouse's methods are not polemical: they are scholarly, logical, patient and objective. Their purpose is not to score ephemeral points but to provide an enduring and fruitful contribution to one of the most vital debates of the modern world.

C.W.

Preface

This book is an attempt at historical revision in a hotly contested field. It stems from an article ('"Imperialism": an Historiographical Revision') which was published in the *Economic History Review* in 1961. In that article I was primarily concerned to underline what seemed to me to be serious defects in several deterministic explanations of European colonial expansion in the late nineteenth century, particularly those deriving from Hobson and Lenin. But I also traced the outlines of what I conceived to be an alternative and more satisfactory approach to late nineteenth-century imperialism, reaching the conclusion that the 'new imperialism' was 'a specifically political phenomenon in origin, the outcome of fears and rivalries within Europe'. Twelve years later I remain quite as dubious about the validity of Hobson and Lenin's explanations but I believe that, while late nineteenth-century imperialism was indeed fundamentally a 'political' phenomenon, the initial impulses to territorial expansion came not from the 'fevered nationalism of Europe' but rather from multiple problems arising on the frontiers of European activity in other continents. Those European phenomena on which most accepted accounts are based, including the diplomatic strategems of statesmen and the violent nationalism of patriotic groups, were secondary or even tertiary factors. Fundamentally the 'new imperialism' is shorthand for a multiplicity of diverse European responses to urgent and varied problems which happened to arise on the periphery of the world during the last quarter of the nineteenth century.

I have also modified my earlier views on the role and importance of economic factors in the imperialist process. In my article I was specifically concerned to criticize the traditional account of imperialism as the product of foreign investment, itself the expression of economic trends in the later nineteenth century; and I paid little attention to the influence of trade as a factor making for territorial acquisition. In this book I have tried to redress the balance. My eventual synthesis attempts to reinstate the economic factor in the critique of modern imperialism, though as only one among a number of forces, all of which were tending to create a disequilibrium between a 'modernized' European and an unreconstructed outer world.

I am grateful to the Australian National University, which gave me a Visiting Fellowship in the School of Advanced Studies for 1965 where work on this book began; to Yale University, where, as Visiting Professor in the Department of History for the first semester 1969–70, I had the time to revise the first draft; to the librarians of the Institute of Commonwealth Studies, Oxford, and of Rhodes House; and above all to Nuffield College, Oxford, for the unrivalled facilities it offers to its Fellows.

D. K. Fieldhouse
Oxford

Part One
Explanations of Imperialism

I *Introduction:*
Economic Explanations
of Imperialism

The debate over the nature of imperialism in the nineteenth and early twentieth centuries is firmly embedded in facts. In the 1830s the colonial empires were smaller than they had been at any time since the early seventeenth century. In America only the fragments of the one-time Spanish, Portuguese, French, British and Dutch empires survived revolutions for independence. In Africa European colonization had barely started. In Australasia and the Pacific colonization was in its earliest phase. Only in southern Asia and in Indonesia were there substantial European possessions. Yet, a century later, it was easier to list the few places which were not and had never been under European domination than to name those which were. Turkey, parts of Arabia, Persia, Afghanistan, Tibet, China, Mongolia, Siam, Japan, and a number of small islands, the Arctic and the Antarctic. Alternatively, the proportion of the world's land surface actually occupied by Europeans, whether still under direct European control as colonies or as one-time colonies, was 35 per cent in 1800, 67 per cent in 1878 and 84·4 per cent in 1914. Between 1800 and 1878 the average rate of imperial expansion was 216,000 square miles a year.

Such figures indicate that the nineteenth century, which had opened with the disintegration of the old colonial empires in America, saw a process of colonial expansion directly comparable with that of the sixteenth and seventeenth centuries which may

therefore be called the second expansion of Europe. The basic aim
of all theories of imperialism and of historians concerned with these
problems is simply to explain why this second expansion took place
on such a scale. But the problem is in fact more complex, for the
character of the empires developed after about 1850 differed substantially from those created in the first expansion of Europe. The
old empires had been mainly in the Americas: the new were in
Africa, Asia and the Pacific. The older colonies had for the most
part been 'settlement' colonies in which quasi-European societies
were created by emigrants: the new were for the most part colonies
of 'occupation' in which a small minority of European 'sojourners'
exercised some degree of political control but which remained
essentially non-European in race and culture. Again, the speed with
which the new nineteenth-century dependencies were occupied was
striking. It had taken some three hundred years for Europeans to
occupy the Atlantic seaboard of America and parts of the Pacific
littoral; and in the later eighteenth century the interior of the
American continent was still largely unoccupied by Europeans. Yet
during the sixty-odd years after 1850 Europeans imposed effective
control not only over the coastlines but also throughout the interior
of all the other continents, excluding only those indigenous states
which retained formal independence. Finally it must be noted that
the number of European powers with colonial possessions grew as
the areas under European control expanded. Before 1830 there
were only five significant colonial powers. By 1914 there were ten,
including the United States, an ex-colony turned imperial power.

Such facts constitute *a priori* evidence for thinking that the
nineteenth century was one of the two great periods of European
overseas expansion and justify the immense attention it has been
given by students of imperialism. The basic problems to be examined are why this expansion took place, why it took place primarily
in tropical areas where European settlement was improbable, and
why so many European powers were concerned in it. Beyond these
problems lies the question of historical continuity before and after
the 1870s. It has often been alleged that during the earlier part of
the century Europe was fundamentally 'anti-imperialist', that there
was no strong desire for new dependencies. Conversely, the following forty years have been designated 'the era of imperialism' when
the expansionist tide reached its climax and the restraint of the past
was thrown off. So precise a demarcation is, of course, historically
wrong. Examination will show that, in many respects, there was no

fundamental discontinuity between different periods of the century before the First World War; and even the figures quoted above indicate that the rate of territorial acquisition did not differ substantially before and after 1878. Yet there were valid grounds for regarding the 1870s as a watershed: certainly they appeared so to commentators during the following years. First, much of the colonial expansion of the previous fifty years had taken place in Canada, Australia, South Africa and around India, all of them British territories, and this expansion was partly explicable in terms of consolidating or expanding colonial settlements which had existed before 1800. By contrast, a great deal of the territory annexed after the 1870s was in regions of Africa, Asia or the Pacific which were largely new to Europeans. Unlike North America, South Africa and Australasia these regions were seldom suited to settlement by Europeans. They were closest in character to India or Dutch Indonesia and appeared to constitute a swing towards dominion over non-European peoples as the main feature of empire. Second, the intervention of European countries such as Germany, Belgium and Italy, with no colonial possessions or tradition, suggested that the aims of colonization were changing, for why otherwise should these continental states suddenly undertake forms of overseas activity which had previously been the preserve of the maritime powers? In particular, the intervention of these countries gave the impression of international competition for new colonies which had not been so obvious before, and implied that the stimulus to colonization was unprecedently strong and general. Finally, the fact that the new colonization was often associated with large-scale investment by Europeans suggested either that they had an extraordinary amount of spare capital to use in this way, or that the attraction of colonial investment was so great that it was drawing capital from alternative fields of activity within Europe.

There were, of course, other apparently novel features in late nineteenth-century imperialism. International bellicosity was the most obvious. On the whole British, French, Russian and Dutch expansion during the previous half-century had caused remarkably little friction between these powers and had excited little concern among others. Now colonial claims became the subject of intense diplomatic activity which seemed on occasions to take the powers concerned to the brink of war. In the 1890s and 1900s in particular colonial questions seemed intimately linked with the prestige and even the security of the European states and in many countries pressure groups were organized to support governments in their international bargaining, perhaps even to spur them on beyond their intentions. Such rivalries seemed closely related to a general rise in the temperature of international relations and an increase in armaments. Long before the outbreak of the First World War observers were therefore linking nationalistic jingoism with enthusiasm for colonies and suggesting that imperialism was the main source of heightened international tensions. Once war had actually begun it was possible to argue, as Lenin did in 1916, that it was at root a war between rival imperialisms and that the central issue was redivision of the colonial empires between the rival powers.

The truth of these and other interpretations of the second expansion of Europe will be considered in due course. For the moment the significant fact is that in the last two decades of the nineteenth century there were reasonable grounds for thinking that European imperialism had entered a new phase which demanded new explanations. Empires had expanded very substantially since the earlier nineteenth century, but after about 1880 the tempo and temper of expansion undoubtedly altered. Colonial questions came to occupy a significant part in international relations in somewhat the same way that they had done during the later eighteenth century. To the generation reared in the mid-Victorian period, which had regarded colonial empires as characteristic of a 'mercantilist' past which had disappeared with the independence of the American colonies and the triumph of free trade, and had assumed that colonization was now a special activity of the British because of their concentration on naval power and their world-wide trade, the 'new imperialism' was surprising and often startling. Some welcomed it because overseas expansion seemed to serve the particular interests they had at heart. Others distrusted it or regarded it as evidence of the decay of western civilization and nineteenth-century liberalism. But few denied that imperialism was one of the dominant facts of the age or that it was important to explain why it had occurred; and their concern to do this was the root from which the vast body of imperialist theories grew during the half-century after about 1880.

The more important of these explanatory theories, which provide the basis for the central argument of this book, will be examined in the following chapters, but it will be convenient briefly to categorize them at this point. Basically, all can be divided into two broad categories according to where they look for an explanation of why European expansion occurred in the late nineteenth century and why there was this apparent discontinuity with the mid-Victorian past. The first and larger category may be called 'Eurocentric' because the new trends of imperialism are explained primarily in terms of the condition, attitudes and needs of the states of Europe. That is, the novelty of imperialism stemmed from new developments within Europe. Within this broad arena the various types of explanation can be divided into economic and non-economic, and these can be further subdivided. Economic theories generally start from the premise that late nineteenth-century imperialism was a product of the changing character of European economies and more particularly of expanding industrialization. Europe found it necessary (or possibly convenient) to annex vast areas overseas because these were in some way necessary to her economic growth. The advantages obtained might take varying forms. Colonies could expand metropolitan trade and therefore production by opening up new and secure markets and by providing new sources of raw materials. This 'imperialism of trade' is examined in chapter 2. Alternatively new colonies might constitute fields for profitable investment of capital which, under conditions of monopoly or 'underconsumption' within Europe, could not find worthwhile fields of activity at home. This 'imperialism of capital investment', by far the most complex and influential of all theories of imperialism, is examined in chapter 3.

In a book mainly concerned with economic history these two interpretations of imperialism are obviously of primary importance, but there are two other important 'Eurocentric' theories which must be considered as possible alternatives or coordinates. Both can loosely be labelled 'political'[1] in that the apparent discontinuity of expansion is seen as the product of changed political and social conditions within Europe in the late nineteenth century, and colonies are said to have been demanded to serve the power, prestige or security of the nation state rather than the wealth of its citizens. The first of these may be called the imperialism of the statesman, or of 'the official mind', to use a now common term. Here emphasis is laid on the initiatives adopted by the rulers of Europe, the politicians and senior civil servants; and the basic assumption is that, given the new system of power relationships and formal alliances within Europe, these men thought it necessary to acquire overseas possessions as part of their diplomatic manoeuvring, as strategic bases, as symbols of status, or merely in order to deny geographical areas seen as important to national security to foreign rivals. A parallel and possibly complementary approach sees the genesis of expansionism in the growing bellicosity of nationalistic public opinion. This 'imperialism of the masses' (though the 'masses' may in fact have consisted of a few vocal pressure groups) is said to derive from a complex of jingoism and patriotism, sharpened in some cases by acceptance of neo-Darwinian theories about the survival of the fittest race. At a time when international disputes over colonial issues were common, nationalistic public opinion regarded each episode as a test of national strength and prestige, and therefore gave full support to governments already keen to take positive action or, alternatively, forced cautious statesmen to go well beyond the limits deemed judicious by the official mind.

In sharp contrast with each of these 'Eurocentric' explanations of the 'new imperialism' it is possible to approach the same questions from outside Europe, to look for answers in those areas of the world where dependencies were being acquired. This 'peripheral' approach – it is too general to be described as an explanation – is based on the initial assumption that it may not be necessary to find any all-embracing cause of European expansion either in Europe or elsewhere, but that colonial annexation commonly sprang from relatively localized issues which might be paralleled in several places but might equally be unique. These issues might be economic, political, religious or social in character. Their common denominator was that some difficulty existed in areas outside formal European possessions in which Europeans were involved which made it difficult or inconvenient to maintain the status quo. Given the rapidly growing involvement of Europeans in all parts of the world as communications improved, continents were explored and economic activities expanded during the later nineteenth century, such crises were inherently possible and the probability was that some at least of them might be solved by formal annexation by one or other of the European states whose nationals were directly involved. Such 'peripheral' explanations are not necessarily incompatible with theories of expansion taking account of European needs and ambitions, for the decision to annex necessarily remained a metropolitan responsibility, conditioned by patterns of thought in Europe. But conceptually at least the 'peripheral' approach is of great importance because, by starting the investigation at the point of action, it becomes possible to decide whether imperialism was a necessary product of the domestic condition of Europe – as Lenin was later to argue – or whether, in broad terms, it was a response to problems created by increasing contact between European civilization and that of other continents.

It is proposed briefly to examine these various possible explanations of the imperialist process in chapters 2 to 4, and at the same time to assess their inherent probability in general terms on their own assumptions. Thus, in the case of theories based on Europe, it should be possible to determine with some certainty whether the European phenomena alleged to have generated imperialism actually existed at the relevant times and in sufficient force to exert the effects claimed: whether, for example, there is good evidence of considerable amounts of surplus capital being invested in areas then being acquired as colonies or of embattled non-official groups campaigning for a 'forward' colonial policy. Conversely, in examining extra-European explanations, it will be necessary to consider whether there is any significant correlation between crises on the periphery and positive action by European states to meet them. No attempt will be made in these chapters to test the validity of a particular theory by examining specific events in detail: this will be done in chapters 6 to 12, in which a number of areas of obvious importance will be taken as case studies for assessing the importance of economic and other forces making for annexation. But an attempt will be made to summarize the evidence on the relative probability of different general explanations of imperialism; and finally in chapter 13 the evidence provided by the case studies will be used to assess the general importance of economic factors within Europe or elsewhere in the imperialistic process.

2   *The Imperialism of Trade*

Probably the best known dictum relating to colonial expansion in the late nineteenth century is that 'trade followed the flag'; that is, new colonies were acquired because possession secured their trade to the metropolis. But for analytical purposes the aphorism is too simple. If European expansion was indeed driven on by desire for additional markets and new sources of raw materials it is necessary to demonstrate three things. First, that European states felt a particularly urgent need to expand trading opportunities during the alleged era of the 'new imperialism' after about 1880. Second, that colonies, protectorates or exclusive spheres of influence were thought to provide better trading partners for developed states than otherwise comparable independent states. Third, that the actual process of acquiring new colonies was influenced by these economic considerations. In the present chapter it is proposed very briefly to consider the credibility of the first two of these propositions in general terms. The influence which such commercial considerations actually exerted on European expansion will then be assessed in the case studies of particular areas which constitute parts two and three of this book.

It has been conventional to explain the accelerating need felt by the states of Europe and North America for new overseas markets and sources of raw materials in terms of expanding industrialization and commercial competition. The argument can be summarized as follows. During the second half of the nineteenth century the major states of Western Europe and North America modernized their industrial systems along lines pioneered by Britain. At first the new industries were primarily concerned with import substitution; but, as they expanded, they became increasingly dependent on foreign markets to provide economies of scale. The resultant competition for limited markets, especially for textiles, iron, steel and metallurgical products, had consequences which are relevant to the growth of economic imperialism. First, there were exceptionally severe and prolonged cyclical depressions during the 1870s, 1880s and 1890s which had profound economic and social consequences and weakened belief in the efficacy of free trade. Second, governments in most European countries and the United States, though not in Britain, the Netherlands or Belgium, felt it politically necessary to raise tariff barriers to protect domestic producers. Third, since tariffs merely intensified market limitations within the developed world, the main states became increasingly interested in the markets of the less developed countries of Africa, Asia, the Pacific and Latin America, which were more than ever before accessible to European trade as a result of improvements in steamship design. Finally, manufacturers and traders engaged in cut-throat competition became frightened that rivals might obtain cheaper supplies of essential raw materials or even monopolize the world supply. From the 1870s, therefore, industrial Europe and North America showed increasing interest in the non-European world both as an expanding market and an essential source of primary products.

Granting the essential validity of this argument, the consequential question must be why such economic developments within the capitalist economies should have generated the expansion of formal empire in the last years of the nineteenth century? The conventional answers can be summarized as follows. First, because of the intensity of commercial competition, the importance of marginal markets for European manufactures rose substantially. So long as the states of Africa and the East remained politically independent and open to international trade on the same terms it was probable that their markets would be captured by the most efficient European producers and traders, or perhaps by nationals of states such as Britain with long established commercial contacts and political influence in these regions. Conversely, newly emergent and perhaps also less competitive producers and merchants from countries such as France might find themselves unable to compete. Their answer was to use political means to offset economic disabilities: ultimately to annex the new markets and surround them with preferential tariffs and other devices for excluding competition. Colonies would thus constitute an extension of the protected home market, enabling its producers to sell abroad at inflated domestic prices. In this way the metropolitan power could evade the consequences of accelerating competition between the developed states and expand production and trade to the wider limits of the imperial market.

This argument clearly relates primarily to protectionist states. But it can also be modified to relate to countries such as Britain which remained free-trading and would not impose differential tariffs on its colonies. Even in a free trade world there were obvious practical advantages in political control over trading partners in the less-developed regions, notably common language, currency and governmental institutions. But in a period of expanding tariffs, when other powers were closing metropolitan and colonial markets alike to foreign competition, the free trade case for colonization was greatly strengthened. If every annexation of territory overseas by a protectionist power meant closing that market to others, free-trading states such as Britain could only preserve their existing or potential markets in Africa and the East in one of two ways: by obtaining international agreement for a 'hands off' policy coupled with the 'open door' for trade; or by imposing whatever degree of political control was necessary to prevent annexation by some other power. Given the cost and inconvenience of administering tropical dependencies and the strong mid-nineteenth-century distaste for expanding formal empire, Britain would probably prefer the former policy. But if international agreement failed she might well fall back on preemptive annexation to save vital markets from exclusive foreign domination.

Concern to preserve access to sources of raw materials might be expected to have similar consequences, though in this case there was little difference between the interests of free-traders and protectionists. Price and availability were the two obvious grounds for acquiring political control over the producing areas. In an ideal free trade world the price of tropical raw materials would be determined by free market forces. But ownership of the sources of supply would enable the imperial power to fix prices. If its possessions had a monopoly of world production this could be done for the whole market. If not, the price to the metropolitan consumer could be reduced by restricting the producer to the metropolitan market and forcing him to accept prices below those ruling in the international market. This in turn, by cheapening the factors of production, would give metropolitan manufacturers a relative advantage over competitors and, by keeping down the cost of foodstuffs, would reduce pressure for higher wages, thus maximizing the profits of capital. Negatively, also, colonies would provide security against deprivation of tropical commodities and being forced to pay monopolistic prices by a rival imperial power. Colonization might therefore be a sensible hedge against manipulation of the international commodity market by monopolistic producers and middlemen of other nationalities.

These arguments provide the foundation of many attempts made to explain late nineteenth-century imperialism in terms of trade. As summarized above they are inherently reasonable. The real test of their historical validity must, of course, be whether the evidence shows that such considerations had a measurable influence on official policy, and this will be looked for in the case studies below. It is, nevertheless, possible to apply preliminary tests to assess the general credibility of this commercial explanation of the 'new imperialism'. Three aspects of the case invite obvious examination, two factual, the third involving assessment of attitudes. First, since the commercial hypothesis postulates serious deterioration in overseas market opportunities in the last quarter of the century, this can be tested by looking for secular or cyclical slumps in the value of exports from the industrialized states. It is proposed, therefore, to examine the official trade statistics for Britain, France and Germany from 1870 to 1900. Second, since the argument relies heavily on the growth of protective tariffs, it is proposed to survey the tariff policies of these and other major powers in this period. Finally it is proposed to review the evidence very briefly to see whether the statesmen of Britain, France and Germany consciously linked these commercial developments with the acquisition of overseas colonies. Here chronology is all-important. If, for example, it appears that any European government was convinced in the early 1880s or before that adverse trading balances and hostile tariffs made acquisition of colonies imperative, then there would be a strong *a priori* case for accepting a commercial explanation of imperialism. If, however, there is no evidence that statesmen consciously made this connection; or if it appears that the link was made later as an *ex post facto* rationalization of what had already been done then the question would remain open. It could not be assumed that imperialism was unconnected with commercial problems. On the other hand it might seem likely that the connection between macro-economic changes within Europe and colonial

expansion was less direct and universal than the explanation outlined above would indicate: that the correct relationship might lie
in tactical commercial problems evolving on the periphery rather
than in the grand strategy of metropolitan economic policy. This
in turn would help to define the specific problems to be examined
in the case studies of regional developments in the later parts of the
book.

Tables 1–3 and Figure 1 below fully support the general assumption that the last thirty years of the nineteenth century were a difficult period for the export-oriented economies of Western Europe.
British exports suffered a prolonged decline lasting from 1873 to
1890, followed by a further decline until 1898. So prolonged were
these periods that it was not unreasonable at the time to assume
that Britain was experiencing a secular rather than merely cyclical
reduction in her export trade and that the visible trade gap would
continue to increase indefinitely. This trade gap did not, of course,
create a balance of payments problem since re-exports and invisi-
bles gave Britain a net balance on current account. But for the
world's first industrialized state to run an adverse trading balance
of over £100 million a year for most of the period 1876–1900
implied a serious inability to compete in overseas markets. This
fact might well have stimulated British interest in new overseas
markets and in new colonies if these were necessary to secure a vent
for British products.

The French experience was very similar. There were three cyclical
depressions in the period: 1877–80, 1883–8 and 1892–6. But since
the value of exports did not regain the level of 1875 until 1899 and
France had a significant adverse balance on visible trade throughout these years there was every reason for French merchants and
politicians to take a pessimistic view of future prospects. Since,
moreover, French colonizing activity was particularly evident
during the second of these cyclical slumps, it is quite possible that
there may have been a correlation between declining exports and
the search for new markets overseas.

The German statistics suggest a comparable though much less
marked trend. By contrast with Britain and France, German exports continued to grow steadily, except for 1879, until 1883.
There was then a slight downturn from 1884 to 1889 followed by a
recovery and another decline from 1891 to 1894. Slight though these
cyclical depressions were in comparison with those affecting British
and French trade, German exports did not rise significantly above

Table 1

United Kingdom Overseas Trade, 1814–1901

(in £ million at current values*)

	Imports†	Domestic Exports	Re-exports		Imports	Domestic Exports	Re-exports
1854	152·4	97·2	18·6	1878	368·8	192·8	52·6
1855	143·5	95·7	21·0	1879	363·0	191·5	57·3
1856	172·5	115·8	23·4	1880	411·2	223·1	63·4
1857	187·8	122·1	24·1	1881	397·0	234·0	63·1
1858	164·6	116·6	23·2	1882	413·0	241·5	65·2
1859	179·2	130·4	25·3	1883	426·9	239·8	65·6
1860	210·5	135·9	28·6	1884	390·0	233·0	62·9
1861	217·5	125·1	34·5	1885	371·0	213·1	58·4
1862	225·7	124·0	42·2	1886	349·9	212·7	56·2
1863	248·9	146·6	50·3	1887	362·2	221·9	59·3
1864	275·0	160·4	52·2	1888	387·6	234·5	64·0
1865	271·1	165·8	53·0	1889	427·6	248·9	66·7
1866	295·3	188·9	50·0	1890	420·7	263·5	64·7
1867	275·2	181·0	44·8	1891	435·4	247·2	61·9
1868	294·7	179·7	48·1	1892	423·8	227·2	64·4
1869	295·5	190·0	47·1	1893	404·7	218·3	58·9
1870	303·3	199·6	44·5	1894	408·3	216·0	57·8
1871	331·0	223·1	60·5	1895	416·7	226·1	59·7
1872	354·7	256·3	58·3	1896	441·8	240·1	56·2
1873	371·3	255·2	55·8	1897	451·0	234·2	60·0
1874	370·1	239·6	58·1	1898	470·5	233·4	60·7
1875	373·9	223·5	58·1	1899	485·0	264·5	65·0
1876	375·2	200·6	56·1	1900	523·1	291·2	63·2
1877	394·4	198·9	53·5	1901	522·0	280·0	67·8

Source: B. R. Mitchell and P. Deane, *Abstract of British Historical Statistics* (Cambridge, 1962), 283.

* Imports are valued c.i.f., exports and re-exports f.o.b.
† The value of bullion, specie, and diamonds is excluded throughout.

Table 2

French Overseas Trade, 1871–1900 (special commerce in millions of francs at current values)

Year	Imports	Exports
1871	3,566·7	2,872·5
1872	3,570·3	3,761·6
1873	3,554·8	3,787·3
1874	3,507·7	3,701·1
1875	3,536·7	3,872·6
1876	3,998·7	3,575·6
1877	3,679·8	3,436·3
1878	4,176·2	3,179·7
1879	4,595·2	3,231·3
1880	5,033·2	3,467·9
1881	4,863·4	3,561·5
1882	4,821·8	3,574·4
1883	4,804·3	3,451·9
1884	4,343·5	3,232·5
1885	4,088·4	3,088·1
1886	4,208·1	3,248·8
1887	4,026·0	3,246·5
1888	4,107·0	3,246·7
1889	4,316·8	3,703·9
1890	4,436·9	3,753·4
1891	4,767·9	3,569·7
1892	4,188·1	3,460·7
1893	3,853·7	3,236·4
1894	3,850·4	3,078·1
1895	3,719·9	3,373·8
1896	3,798·6	3,400·9
1897	3,956·0	3,598·0
1898	4,472·5	3,510·9
1899	4,518·3	4,152·6
1900	4,697·8	4,108·7

Source: Shepard B. Clough, *France: A History of National Economics 1789–1939* (New York, 1939) 215, 218.

Table 3

German Overseas Trade, 1872–1900 (special trade, including bullion, in millions of marks at current values)*

Year	Imports	Exports
1872	3,464·6	2,492·2
1873	4,254·6	2,465·2
1874	3,670·6	2,459·6
1875	3,573·4	2,560·6
1876	3,911·4	2,604·9
1877	3,872·4	2,827·0
1878	3,715·6	2,915·3
1879	3,881·1	2,820·7
1880	2,859·9	2,946·1
1881	2,990·2	3,040·1
1882	3,164·6	3,244·1
1883	3,290·8	3,335·0
1884	3,284·9	3,269·4
1885	2,989·9	2,915·2
1886	2,944·8	3,051·3
1887	3,188·7	3,190·1
1888	3,435·8	3,352·6
1889	4,087·0	3,256·4
1890	4,272·9	3,409·5
1891	4,403·4	3,339·7
1892	4,227·0	3,150·1
1893	4,134·1	3,244·6
1894	4,285·5	3,051·5
1895	4,246·1	3,424·1
1896	4,558·0	3,753·8
1897	4,864·6	3,786·2
1898	5,439·7	4,010.6
1899	5,783·6	4,368·4
1900	6,043·0	4,752·6

Source: *Statistisches Jahrbuch für das Deutsche Reich* (Berlin), 1885, 1890, 1899, 1902.

* The basis on which these statistics were calculated changed from 1880.

18

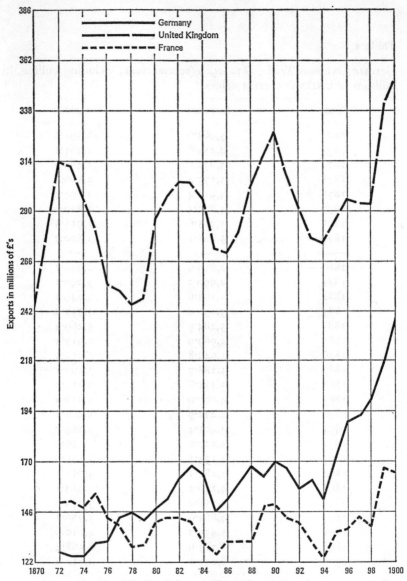

Figure 1 British, French and German Overseas Trade, 1870–1900

the level of 1883 until after 1895; and after 1888 Germany had a significant and growing adverse balance on visible trade.

How much weight should be put on these export figures? There is no doubt that British and French business interests and politicians in particular were deeply concerned at the length and severity of these trade depressions and their effects on the domestic economy; or that some of them became convinced that monopoly of the trade of existing possessions was a partial remedy. It is equally clear that they were anxious to make full use of new marketing opportunities in Africa and the East. It would however be unwise to assume on the basis of trade statistics alone that acquisition of new overseas dependencies was seen as a necessary means to expanding trade in these regions. At most it is reasonable to expect that at a time when traditional markets seemed to be contracting, the statesmen might become more ready than in the past to use political means to remove obstacles to compensating trade with other places; and that this might conceivably take the form of annexation if nothing less would serve to safeguard neutral markets from closure by some other European power or to deal with xenophobic non-Europeans. Whether or not this actually occurred on a significant scale can only be determined by examination of the evidence.

What, in the second place, is the probability that the growth of tariff protection in Europe and in existing European dependencies was a force making for colonial expansion in the later nineteenth century? There is, of course, no doubt that the last quarter of the century saw a dramatic revival of protection in several states which were also involved in the 'new imperialism', above all Germany, France, Russia and the United States. But, in briefly reviewing this development, it is important to take careful note of chronology; for tariffs could only have stimulated colonial expansion if the expansionist country or its commercial competitors had already adopted and were feeling the effects of tariffs at the time when this was taking place.

Germany and France are the key states, for in each the adoption of severe protectionist tariffs followed periods of relatively free trade. Germany had been moving towards British commercial principles in the 1860s, removing duties on imported grain in 1865 and on iron, shipbuilding materials and other goods in 1873.[1] But from about 1875 the tide turned again. Under pressure from industrialists and the agrarian interests Bismarck introduced a new tariff in 1879 which imposed relatively low duties on a wide range of imported manufactures and heavier duties on agricultural produce. No major change occurred in the 1880s, but in 1890 higher rates were imposed on many articles. The climax was reached in 1902 when new duties raised the average *ad valorem* duties on goods from Britain to 25 per cent and on those from Russia to 131 per cent.

The chronology of French protectionism was similar.[2] The Second Empire was a period of economic liberalism when France signed the Cobden Treaty with Britain in 1860, ended import prohibitions, reduced import duties across the board and made a series of commercial treaties which pointed towards virtual free trade. A reaction set in after 1870; but, after a sudden increase of many duties and denunciation of the British and Belgian commercial treaties in 1871–2, the 1870s proved to be a period of low tariffs at home and of virtually free trade in the French colonies. The turning point was 1881 when a new general tariff gave a range of manufactures effective protection while leaving agriculture and raw materials unprotected. In the same year a new shipping law revived bounties on ship-construction. During the early 1880s, therefore, when French colonial expansion was getting under way, France was still poised between free trade and a protective tariff, even though political and commercial opinion was increasingly favourable to protection. During the decade selected agricultural products were given piecemeal protection but industrial tariffs were held down by continuing commercial treaties. It was not until the Méline tariff was adopted in 1892 that France had a general protective tariff system. Grain duties were left at five francs per 100 kilos but most other agricultural duties were raised by 25 per cent. Certain raw materials were still allowed free entry but others and certain semi-manufactures which were produced in France were made dutiable for the first time since the 1860s. The tariff on foreign manufactures was stiffened and extended and bounties were adopted more widely. France had thus become one of the most severely protectionist states, though still less so than Russia or the United States.

Less need be said of these two states because they had never adopted Cobdenite principles and merely increased the severity of their tariffs in the late nineteenth century: Russia in 1881–2 and again in 1890–1; the United States by the McKinley tariff of 1890 and then, after a reduction of duties in the mid-1890s, by the Dingley tariff of 1897. The average level of American duties on specific articles thus rose from 47 per cent in 1869 to 49·5 per cent in 1890 and to 57 per cent in 1897.[3] Such high tariffs, although not radically new and therefore unlikely to affect American or Russian attitudes to empire, were bound to affect other countries in that they implied a further restriction of world markets and made it necessary to look for more readily accessible consumers elsewhere.

It is, therefore, a fact that the age of the 'new imperialism' coincided with the resurgence of protectionism in France and Germany and its intensification in Russia, the United States and other countries such as Portugal, Spain and Italy. Of the major states involved in colonial expansion only Britain, Belgium and the Netherlands were unaffected. It follows that it is perfectly possible that protectionism and imperialism may have stood as cause and effect. But one reservation must be made. The vital formative phase of imperial expansion was the 1880s. Yet this was also the period when French and German tariff levels were still relatively low and before other protectionist powers had significantly increased their general tariff levels. It may be that the limited tariff changes that had already taken place were sufficient to influence the colonial policies of the powers; yet on the figures alone one would have expected the 'new mercantilism' to make its impact in the following decade rather than in the 1880s.

It remains to consider whether there are grounds for thinking that European economists, statesmen or vested interests saw the relevance of the new protectionism for colonial policy in the way some historians have suggested: whether, on the one hand, those in protectionist states which took a leading role in the colonial partition seem to have believed that protectionism and empire were necessary bed-fellows; and whether, on the other hand, those in free trade states such as Britain reacted to the protectionism of others by adopting a policy of preemptive annexation of 'vacant' territories in order to preserve 'open door' markets. It is, of course, impossible to prove a negative. But a very brief survey of the evidence on French, German and British policy will serve as a measure of the inherent probability of this explanation of the 'new imperialism'.

The most striking feature of the French case is that, as far as can be judged, no one of importance publicized a coherent theory of colonization specifically based on protectionist tariffs before about 1890. On the other hand, it is clear that commercial considerations of a more general kind played an important role in French colonial thought from at least the mid-1870s and that it became widely accepted that existing French colonies should be made to serve metropolitan commercial needs by the imposition of differential duties. The result was an approach to imperialism which was heavily tinged with economics but was far from being a straight-forward response to the new protectionism.

Probably the typical French view of empire in the 1870s and early 1880s was that expressed by Paul Leroy-Beaulieu in his widely influential book, *De la Colonisation chez les Peuples Modernes*, which first appeared in 1874.

The most useful function which colonies perform ... is to supply the mother country's trade with a ready-made market to get its industry going and maintain it, and to supply the inhabitants of the mother country – whether as industrialists, workers or consumers – with increased profits, wages or commodities. The whole world will benefit from this, for there is no question of going back to the restrictions dating from the days of exclusive trading.[4]

This, of course, was essentially a free trade argument derived from free-trading English imperialists such as E. G. Wakefield and J. S. Mill. The striking fact is that eleven years later, on 28 July 1885, when Jules Ferry made his famous speech in the French Chamber to justify the new colonial acquisitions, he used precisely the same argument with no specific reference to protective tariffs.

But, gentlemen, there is another and more important side of this question.... The colonial question is, for countries like ours which are, by the very character of their industry, tied to large exports, vital to the question of markets.... From this point of view ... the foundation of a colony is the creation of a market.... In fact it has been stated, and there are many examples to be found in the economic history of modern peoples, that it is sufficient for the colonial link to exist between the mother country which produces and the colonies which she has founded for economic predominance to accompany and, in some degree, to depend on, political predominance.[5]

Clearly, if Ferry's expansionist policies of the early 1880s were based on economic considerations – and this will be considered in the case studies on Tunisia, West Africa and Indo-China below – he was not working from a sophisticated analysis of the actual economic consequences of the new tariff policies of France and her European rivals. It was not until 1890 that Ferry published the famous introduction to *Tonkin et la Mère Patrie*, quoted below, which provided a rational critique of imperialism based mainly on the implications of protectionism.

The impact of tariffs on imperialist ideology seems, in fact, to have grown from concern to protect the markets of existing French colonies from overwhelming British competition rather than from analysis of their theoretical implications. Thus in January 1880 Brière de L'Isle, Governor of Senegal and proponent of an expansionist policy in the Sudan, advised the Ministry of Marine that the vote of his local General Council against the differential duties he had proposed should be ignored on the ground that:

It would seem impossible that, at the very moment when France is attempting to increase her trade with Senegal, to bring the resources of the colony to light and to create for herself new markets in the very heart of Africa, all her efforts should be to the advantage of foreign industry because French industry is in some degree shut out of the Senegalese market by a few commercial houses of Bordeaux.[6]

Brière won his point. Differential duties were imposed on Senegal, Gaboon and other French dependencies from 1877; and in 1884 and 1887 respectively Algeria and Indo-China were assimilated to the full metropolitan tariff. By the mid-1880s metropolitan opinion generally was coming to the view that existing colonies were economically useful only if their markets were reserved for French exports and, consequentially, that new dependencies might be desirable if they provided a monopolistic outlet for French products. By 1887 the Bordeaux Chamber of Commerce, which had remained staunchly loyal to free trade in the previous decade, could write to the Ministry of Finance:

The revival of differential tariffs would seem justified at this stage by the need to strengthen the links, now too weak, which link France with her colonies.

Experience has proved that France, whose overseas exports are held back by ever-increasing competition, must find in colonies inhabited by her own nationals guaranteed markets for her primary and industrial products.[7]

By the later 1880s, therefore, the consensus of French official and mercantile opinion seems to have been that colonies were only useful to France if protected from foreign trade competition; and, conversely, that it might be possible to justify further imperial expansion on the grounds that every new colony could be made a monopolistic market. By 1890 such ideas had matured to the point at which Ferry, after five years in retirement from politics, could provide a rational synthesis. Although well known, the relevant passage must be quoted as perhaps the most logical exposition of the economic case for tropical colonization by a protectionist European state.

Colonial policy is the daughter of industrialization. For rich states, where capital abounds and accumulates rapidly, where the industrial system is continually growing and where it attracts, if not the majority, at least the most alert and ambitious section of the labouring class; where even the cultivation of the land must become industrialized to survive, exports are essential to political good health; and the field open for the employment of capital, like the demand for labour is controlled by the extent of the foreign market. If Europe had been able to establish something like a division of industrial labour between the manufacturing countries, based on the natural and social aptitudes and economic conditions of the different countries, securing cotton manufacturing and metallurgy in one place, reserving alcohol and sugar for one country, woollen and silks for another, Europe would not have to look outside its own boundaries for markets for what it produced. The treaties of 1860 aimed at this ideal. But today everyone wants to spin and weave, to forge and distil. All Europe makes as much sugar as possible and tries to export it. The entry of the latest countries to develop large-scale industry – the United States and Germany – the arrival in all forms of industry of little states whose peoples were asleep or exhausted – a regenerated Italy, Spain enriched by French capital, Switzerland with so much enterprise and wisdom – these events have placed the whole of the west, while it waits for Russia who is learning and growing, on a slope which it cannot climb.

On the other side of the Vosges, and across the Atlantic, the protective system has increased the number of manufactures, closed previous markets, and brought strong competition into the markets of Europe. It is something to defend oneself in turn by raising barriers, but by itself it is not enough. In his fine book on the colonization of Australia Mr Torrens has clearly shown that an increase of manufacturing capital, unless it is accompanied by a proportionate increase of foreign markets, tends to produce a general lowering of prices, profits and salaries simply as a result of domestic competition.

The protective system is a steam-engine without a safety-valve unless it is balanced and supported by a sensible and serious colonial policy. Surplus capital engaged in industry not only tends to diminish the profits of capital but also to check the rise of wages, though this is the natural and desirable tendency of all modern societies. Moreover, this is not an abstract tendency, but a reality made of flesh and bone, of passion and will, which becomes restless, complains and defends itself. The economic crisis which has pressed so hard on the European worker since 1876 or

1877, the industrial sickness which followed it, whose most depressing symptom consists in strikes – long, often unwise but always formidable – these have coincided in France, Germany and even in England with a significant and persistent decline in the volume of exports. Europe can perhaps be thought of as a business concern which sees the volume of its business declining over a certain number of years. Europe's consumption is saturated: it is essential to discover new seams of consumers in other parts of the world. The alternative is to place modern society in bankruptcy and to prepare for the dawn of the twentieth century a cataclysmic social liquidation whose consequences cannot be calculated.

It is because she was the first to foresee these distant horizons that England took the lead in the modern industrial movement. It is because she saw the potential danger to her hegemony which might, following the secession of the United States of North America, result from the separation of Australia and India that she laid seige to Africa on four fronts: in the south, by the plateau of the Cape and Bechuanaland; in the west, by the Niger and the Congo; in the north-east by the valley of the Nile; in the east by Suakim, the Somali coast and the basin of the great equatorial lakes. It is to prevent British enterprise from obtaining for its sole profit the new markets which are opening up to the products of the west that Germany meets England with her inconvenient and unexpected rivalry in all parts of the globe. Colonial policy is an international expression of the eternal laws of competition.[8]

Ferry's arguments were taken up by others in France and in other parts of Europe and passed into current usage as the true explanation of French imperialism during the 1880s and 1890s. Thus in 1890 Eugène Etienne was pressing the same argument: 'I think . . . that it is wise to look to the future and reserve to French commerce and industry those outlets which are open to her in the colonies and by the colonies.'[9] French pressure groups, such as the Comité de l'Afrique Française, formed in the same year, and similar committees set up to support French interests in Asia, Morocco, the Pacific, and Madagascar, tended to repeat and publicize Ferry's argument. The Union Coloniale Française of 1893 was set up primarily to provide co-ordination between French financial and commercial houses with interests in the colonies and exercised considerable influence both as a propaganda agency and by bringing pressure to bear on the government. Thus it is at least possible that the fervour with which France was extending her colonial territories in the 1890s, and her readiness to run considerable political dangers in confronting Britain over the Sudan in 1898 and Germany over Morocco in 1905 and 1911, may have been partly the product of a general belief that colonialism was a necessary corollary of protectionism.

But, even granting that this later orientation of French thought may, to some extent, have been responsible for subsequent expansionist policies, the significance of the protectionist argument for French imperialism as a whole remains dubious. The crucial period for French expansion lay in the years before 1885 when most of the new French Empire was acquired or projected. Annam (Vietnam) was made a protectorate in 1874. Tunis was occupied in 1881. Brazza began his occupation of the Congo in 1882. The war for Tongking began in 1883. A protectorate over Madagascar was declared in 1885. French expansion in West Africa was already under way. D'Ordega had given France the opportunity to impose a protectorate on Morocco. How do these dates fit the chronology of protection and the evolution of Ferry's theory? As has been seen, French tariffs were still low in the 1880s: the Méline tariff did not come until 1892. The German tariff dated from 1879, but was not really severe until about 1890. Russian tariffs had been further raised in 1881–2, but those of the United States were at their normal level until 1890. Hence, although it is possible that foreign tariffs were affecting French trade in the early 1880s and so gave an incentive for France to find new markets as compensation, French tariffs themselves were not yet so high as to require a 'safety-valve'. Equally there is no reason to suppose that Ferry or the other expansionist politicians and officials were consciously motivated by protectionist considerations during the early 1880s. Ferry had made no public reference to economic factors, other than the obvious interests of French financiers in Egypt and Tunis, before he left office in 1885. Neither in his speech of that year, nor in the book of 1890, did he explicitly claim, or even imply, that expansion had been deliberately undertaken to serve commercial needs. On the contrary, he spoke as if he was trying to discern a hidden hand which had been guiding him and other statesmen concerned in colonial partition along an immense steeplechase over an unknown course which had 'been in progress for hardly more than five years' but which was apparently 'gathering speed every year with the force of its own momentum. . . .'[10] These are not the words of a man explaining his own actions but of one who attempts to rationalize after the event and who wishes to lay down guidelines for future French colonial policy.

It must, therefore, be concluded that the case for interpreting

French expansion in the period after about 1875 as a direct product of the new protectionism is weak. Indeed it seems improbable that the policy-makers in Paris ever acted on their assessment of the logic of high tariffs abroad or at home. It is far more probable that the order of causation should be reversed: that the imposition of tariffs on colonial trade and the assumption that preferential tariffs were the object of imperialism were the product of expansion undertaken for complex and often non-economic reasons which had to be justified in economic terms. This at least was the interpretation put on the whole process by A. Girault, one of the leading contemporary experts on French colonial law and finance, in his explanation for the imposition of metropolitan tariffs on the dependencies which provided France with the highest possible degree of preference there.

A third reason for the tendency towards tariff assimilation is to be found in the sacrifices which France imposed upon herself at the time of Jules Ferry in order to develop her colonial empire, and in the state of mind which had resulted from these sacrifices. The policy of colonial expansion was then very much discussed and bitterly fought. The sacrifices in men and in money appeared heavy, and public opinion did not appreciate the utility of these colonies for France. 'At any rate', so it was said, 'this domain, for the acquisition of which we make so many sacrifices, ought to be made to yield some return. The markets for French products in foreign countries are in danger of being closed in consequence of the progress of protection. Might not the colonial market offer us at least a partial compensation?' Once public attention came to be fixed upon the colonies, it appeared that they did not buy enough from France. Here was a market in which French products were not protected. The adversaries of colonial expansion, who asserted that the colonies were not sufficiently profitable to the imperial state, and the supporters of the policy of expansion, who laid emphasis upon the prospective colonial markets, agreed in insisting that the colonies should be made as profitable as possible to France through the strict reservation of their market to the French producers.[11]

Girault may not have been conscious that he was inverting Ferry's arguments; but in fact his hypothesis provides an alternative interpretation of the relationship between French imperialism and the concern for economic advantages from colonization.

The precise relationship between tariff protection and colonial policy in Germany is even more difficult to establish than in France. Yet the German case is in many ways crucial, for Germany was the first power in Western Europe to revert to tariffs, in 1879, and German claims to colonies in 1884–5 were undoubtedly a major factor in the general acceleration of colonial expansion during the following years. What evidence is there that commercial arguments or more specifically the effects of German tariff policy after 1879 drove Germans on the road to empire?

One of the special features of German imperialism was the fact that Germany had no imperial tradition and no colonies before the 1880s. To a far greater extent than in France the question of whether colonies were desirable and if so, on what grounds, was therefore theoretical during the first three-quarters of the century. Those who were interested tended to be either academics or professional men, who observed the fact of the British Empire and thought Germany must have similar possessions if she was to equal Britain in prestige; or vested interests, such as merchants and shipowners in the Hanse towns, who found that the absence of German bases or forces in those parts of the world in which they were operating was an inconvenience or obstacle. Arguments in favour of empire were therefore either very theoretical or strictly limited to particular places and problems, according to whether they emanated from academics or merchants.

At the theoretical level there was a general though somewhat imprecise tradition that treated colonization as a desirable means of furthering economic development through trade. As far back as 1821 Hegel had adopted concepts from Smith and other classical economists, arguing that colonization was desirable for a bourgeois economy because it opened up new markets and relieved domestic pressures resulting from underconsumption.[12] But the real creator of a German colonial tradition of thought was Friedrich List, whose *National System of Political Economy* was first published in 1841. List's primary objective was to demonstrate that free trade was a system designed and propagated in her own interest by Britain as the first power to develop modern industries. For other countries that wished to follow the same path free trade was an obstacle because without protection their own nascent industries could not compete with the cheaper imports of the more advanced manufacturer. The solution was clearly for Germany to adopt a rigorous protectionist policy until she could compete with Britain on equal terms.

The precise role of colonies in this system is not easy to determine. Basically List favoured colonial trade (by which he meant

European trade with countries settled by Europeans, whether still dependent or now sovereign states; and also trade with 'countries of the torrid zone' such as India) on the standard lines laid down by Smith and others that they promoted specialization and enlarged the market. On this basis Germany stood to gain little from actual possession of colonies once she traded direct with those of other states in her own ships, thus saving the middleman profit then going to the British and Dutch. But List obviously felt that a great nation such as he wanted Germany to become should have her own colonies.

The highest means of development of the manufacturing power, of the internal and external commerce preceeding from it, of any considerable coast and sea navigation, of extensive sea fisheries, and consequently of a respectable naval power, are *colonies*.[13]

On this basis he definitely recommended that Germany should establish colonies at the same time as it adopted a protectionist tariff policy. But there were two peculiarities in his prescription. First, there was no attempt to provide a theoretical link between tariffs and colonies, certainly not to make them interdependent. Each was beneficial in its own right. Second, the colonization proposed was at least initially to be within existing states in Latin America, the Balkans and Australasia, with the co-operation of the governments of these countries. That is, the colonies were to be groups of settlers sticking together and retaining their German character and taste for German products, rather than genuine political dependencies. Probably too much should not be made of this, since List recognized that until Germany had a navy she could not become a true colonial power. The important point is rather that while List probably created the German tradition that colonies were economically desirable, he never made them logically integral with his proposed protectionist system.

For long after his death in 1846 his colonial theories seem to have received little support, though from time to time nationalistic writers revived his argument. For example in 1848 Roscher wrote that 'new areas for production and consumption must be secured for our national interest, be they gained by means of political or economic colonization'.[14] The tradition continued but its economic content merged with broader concepts of German nationalism. In fact most Germans who favoured colonization saw colonies as either symbols of power, evidence that Germany had caught up with England; or as places to which emigrants could go without losing their nationality.[15] More, like Bismarck himself, writing to his friend, Roon, in 1868, thought they had no commercial value.

On the one hand the advantages which may lie in the trade and industry of the colonies with the home country are based to a large extent on illusions. For the costs of founding, supporting and keeping the colonies are much bigger than the profit for the mother country, as the example of England and France proves. Another argument against colonies is that it is hardly just that the whole nation should pay for the advantage of some commercial and industrial enterprises.

On the other hand our navy is not far enough developed to fulfil the task of protecting the colonies in strange area.

Finally, the attempt to found colonies in strange area where other states claim this area, whether justifiably or not, as their spheres of influence may lead to many unwanted conflicts.[16]

It was not, therefore, surprising that when the protective tariff of 1879 was adopted no one seems to have connected it with the need or possibility of German colonization. Von Bülow asserted in that year that 'We do not wish to *found* colonies. We desire no monopoly against others. We only wish to guarantee the rights of German shipping and trade'.[17] Bismarck, who never ceased to deny that Germany needed colonies as such, apart from protecting the interests of her traders in those parts of the world where they had already established themselves, made no reference to colonies in promulgating the 1879 tariff in the Reichstag, and the question of colonies did not come up at all in the debates. Moreover, the Hanse towns, which were the main proponents of a colonial policy, were also the chief critics of protective tariffs, since much of their prosperity depended on the transit of trade through their ports. In short, there is no reason to connect the demand for German colonies in the years before 1884–5 with contemporaneous tariff policy or with the need of Germany to find new markets or sources of raw materials. No German seriously argued that imperialism was a necessary concommitant of a tariff policy, or that Germany needed colonies as markets.

This is not, of course, to suggest that commercial problems did not influence German colonial policy in the early 1880s for, as will be seen below, the specific needs and problems of German traders and entrepreneurs in several regions of Africa and the South Pacific were directly connected with Bismarck's decision in 1884 to establish German protectorates there. Moreover, it became conventional in Germany as in France during the later 1880s and 1890s to justify existing or projected colonies in terms of their general economic value. Propaganda emanating from bodies such as the Colonial Society and its Economic Committee took the line that existing colonies could be developed to provide important commercial and investment advantages; and, if these possessions ultimately proved unsatisfactory or inadequate for German needs, then new colonies should be acquired. To some extent such propaganda was defensive, for the evidence was clear that the existing colonies were of small value as markets, providing only about 0·5 per cent of Germany's total export trade; and the loss on administration was substantial. Yet vehement attacks in the Reichstag and the government's defeat on the colonial estimates naturally encouraged those supporting the colonial policy to emphasize economic compensations, just as Ferry had done in France in and after 1885. Arguments used by Bernhard Dernburg, who became the first Secretary of State for the Colonies in 1906 as part of a new deal for the German colonies, at one of a series of conferences held during the electoral campaign of 1906–7, may be summarized to illustrate the type of commercial arguments in favour of colonies being deployed in Germany at this time.[18]

Ironically, because to the British and French Germany appeared as a commercially expanding country which was threatening their own trading interests. Dernburg's central thesis was that Germany needed colonies to prevent her from losing her commercial and economic position as a result of competition from other countries. On the one hand the United States and Japan had now emerged as rivals for international markets, and, with the aid of protective tariffs, were threatening Europe in the neutral markets of Latin America and the Far East. On the other hand there was a danger that other countries might acquire a monopoly of certain vital raw materials through their colonial possessions; so that German manufacturers and consumers might have to pay extortionate prices on the open market. Concentrating on the second point, he claimed that Germany could develop the vast territories she already possessed so that they would eventually make her nearly self-sufficient in the commodities for which she had to rely on producers in tropical countries. Even if German production merely increased world supplies this would force the monopolists to reduce their prices. This in turn would increase the competitiveness of German industry and reduce prices for German workers. Germany could obtain better terms in commercial treaties and her balance of trade would be improved. All this of course would involve patience and the application of much effort and capital. The earlier dream of colonies immediately and naturally providing all the needs of trade had been proved false. Yet in the long run, colonies must be regarded as essential to any industrial nation in an age of protectionism and increasing industrialization.

Two main points in this thesis require comment. First, Dernburg was not suggesting that these arguments had been formative in German colonization twenty years before, but that these were the correct views to adopt now that the colonies existed. Second, he saw the commercial value of colonies almost entirely in terms of their production of raw materials and foodstuffs and hardly at all as markets, whereas in 1890 Ferry had taken their value as markets for manufactures to be the main thing. This inversion reflected common experience. It was now clear to all countries that the tropical colonies acquired after about 1880 had little value as markets for manufactures, except of the crudest sort, because their peoples (unlike the inhabitants of British settlement colonies) lacked the buying power or the taste for most European products. Conversely, growing demand for tropical products such as rubber, vegetable oil and cotton and the discovery in certain areas of minerals such as copper underlined the potential value of colonies as producers. This order of priorities in evaluating colonial trade was common to commentators in most countries after 1900 and remained the basis for assessing the value of colonies economically until the end of the colonial empires after 1945.

But even if France and Germany do not appear to have adopted 'forward' colonial policies as a direct or necessary concommitant of their own new protectionism, can a case be made out for seeing the 'new' British imperialism of the 1880s and 1890s as a reaction to the protectionism of others, particularly when foreign tariffs threatened exclusion of British traders from regions of Africa and the East which had hitherto offered an 'open door' to international trade? Alternatively, can one construct a rationale of British imperialism in terms of general concern for market opportunities at a time of declining domestic exports?

During the half-century before 1880 there was, of course, a strong British tradition which propounded the commercial value of colonies to the metropolis even under free trade conditions. This hypothesis was strongly supported by E. G. Wakefield, leader of the colonial reformers during the 1830s and 1840s, and can conveniently be summarized in a passage from his book, *The Art of Colonization*, published in 1849:

Colonies ... are ... naturally exporting communities: they have a large produce for exportation.
Not only have they a large produce for exportation, but that produce is peculiarly suited for exchange with old countries. In consequence of the cheapness of land in colonies, the great majority of the people are owners or occupiers of land; and their industry is necessarily in a great measure confined to the producing of what comes immediately from the soil; viz., food, and the raw materials of manufacture. In old countries, on the other hand, where the soil is fully occupied and labour abundant, it may be said that manufactured goods are their natural production for export. These are what the colonists do not produce. The colony produces what the old country wants; the old country produces what the colony wants. The old country and the colony, therefore, are, naturally, each other's best customers.[19]

Such arguments carried considerable weight in the mid-nineteenth century and served to justify the establishment and retention of the white settlement colonies in North America, South Africa and Australasia in which Wakefield and most colonial enthusiasts were most interested. Yet it cannot be said that British public or official opinion as a whole ever accepted that these arguments constituted a sufficient case for the indefinite extension of the Empire. Broadly, two factors seem to have militated against their acceptance. First, many of the existing settlement colonies invalidated the expectation of the free trade imperialists that, as Charles Buller put it in 1854, the metropolis could be sure of 'being met by no hostile tariffs on their part'.[20] After the adoption of a protective tariff by Canada in 1859, which was later copied by several Australasian colonies, it had to be assumed that self-governing colonies would eventually cease to offer special commercial advantages to the parent state. Second, although the British were aware of the great benefit to British industry of the vast unprotected market of India, as was shown by their insistence that import duties on cotton textiles should be abolished, they did not think it generally worthwhile to annex other tropical territories merely to obtain similar advantages. There were obvious reasons for this. Few if any countries open to annexation offered commercial advantages comparable with those of India. More important, experience suggested that the same commercial benefits could be obtained by negotiating 'open door' treaties with states such as China and Siam which specified low

c

ad valorem import duties and satisfactory conditions for British nationals. Isolated examples can be found in which commercial advantage was specified as the grounds for territorial annexation: Lagos in 1861, for example. But these were rare exceptions. The general view was that, while existing possessions were valuable trading partners, putative commercial advantages did not by themselves justify acquisition of new tropical dependencies.

By the later 1870s and early 1880s, however, conditions were changing dramatically. On the one hand British exports were dropping in the face of foreign competition in established markets and the rise of protectionism in Europe. On the other hand France and other powers were annexing hitherto independent territories in Africa and the East and imposing differential tariffs to exclude British trade. The question therefore arises whether British colonial expansion after about 1880 was a response to either or both of these commercial problems. Were the new colonies deliberately acquired in order to protect openings for new British trade in Africa and the East against the threat of foreign annexation coupled with exclusive tariff system?

This question cannot be answered until the evidence provided by individual case studies has been considered. At this point, however, it must be noted that, if British statesmen are taken at their public word, a strong case could be made out either way. On the one hand there were those who, like Gladstone, Harcourt and Morley, at all times refused – at least overtly – to admit that preemptive annexation could be justified on moral or practical grounds. Indeed most statesmen and civil servants took this position at some time or other. On the other hand there were an increasing number who, as time went on and competition from other powers increased, became more ready to accept the principle of preemptive annexation for commercial reasons and, more commonly, justified action already taken, whatever the actual impulsion, on commercial grounds. Thus the Foreign and Colonial Offices were seriously considering preemptive annexation in West Africa by 1883;[21] in 1886 Salisbury said in Manchester – the citadel of free trade – that encroaching foreign imperialism and protective tariffs might force Britain to annex territories to preserve trading outlets.[22] In 1885 he stated that British action in East Africa had the same objectives;[23] and in 1888 Sir Harry Johnston probably reflected Salisbury's views in a well-known article in *The Times* in which he contended that it had become a 'necessity for us to protect ourselves and forestall other

European nations in localities we desire to honestly exploit'.[24] Frederick Lugard justified a protectorate in Uganda on similar grounds in 1892,[25] Sir Edward Gray did the same in 1894[26] and Salisbury followed suit in 1895.[27] By 1896 Joseph Chamberlain, notoriously the most expansionist British statesman of the 1890s, could state categorically that if Britain had stood aside 'the greater part of Africa would have been occupied by our commercial rivals, who would have proceeded to close this great commercial market to the British empire'.[28] Such statements must be evaluated against more concrete evidence of motive and circumstance: but at least they force the historian to take seriously the proposition that British expansion after 1880 was affected, if not directly caused, by concern for overseas markets.[29]

What general conclusions can be drawn from this limited survey of evidence relating to Britain, France and Germany about the credibility of a commercial explanation of the 'new imperialism'?

First, it seems undeniable that growing competition for established markets in Europe and America, coupled with the cyclical but extended and recurrent downturn in the value of exports during the last thirty years of the century, stimulated most industrialized countries to look for new markets elsewhere. This search for markets generated greater interest than ever before in the commercial opportunities of little known regions of Africa and Asia which had not hitherto been brought fully within the orbit of international trade and whose economic possibilities were commonly over-estimated precisely because they were impossible to calculate. At the same time the growing demand for industrial raw materials and foodstuffs which could not be obtained within Europe or North America stimulated the search for new sources of supply. Together these factors ensured that Europeans would rapidly penetrate most parts of the less-developed world and that these would quickly be absorbed into the capitalist economy of the West.

Was this search for new markets likely on its own account to result in large-scale formal colonization in and after the 1880s? The evidence considered above provides no clear indication. While some theorists and men of business seem to have believed that new tropical colonies would provide desirable markets and sources of raw materials, many others, including leading political figures in most countries, remained dubious, clinging to the mid-century assumption that colonies were likely to be a nuisance and source of metropolitan expenditure. Thus while commercial depression and the search for markets may well have influenced European attitudes to the less-developed world in the 1880s and beyond, it will be necessary to look for specific evidence that these factors had a direct and measurable influence on the policies of the major states in the age of the 'new imperialism'.

Second, the importance of tariff protection as a major economic factor making for empire seems to be much less important than has sometimes been suggested. The critical years in the partition of Africa and the East were 1878–85. Yet the evidence suggests that French and German tariffs did not become really severe until the 1890s and that the first widely influential argument making colonies a necessary concomitant of protection was not propounded until 1890. It is, of course, possible that this chronological discrepancy is unimportant; that the preliminary effects of the new tariffs were being felt in the early 1880s before economists and politicians became aware of their significance for colonial policy; that they contributed to the downturn of international trade and so stimulated the search for new overseas markets. Yet, when all concessions have been made, it must remain at least dubious whether tropical colonies became or were thought to have become a necessary concomitant of protectionist tariffs early enough for these to be accepted as the prime economic cause of a 'new imperialism'.

If, however, one shifts attention from the central economic problems of Europe to commercial conditions on the periphery, a more credible *a priori* case may exist for an interpretation of late nineteenth-century imperialism based on the extension of European tariffs. Colonies may not suddenly have become an economic necessity to protectionist states, but the fear that such states might impose tariffs on hitherto 'open' regions in the less-developed world may well have stimulated defensive or preemptive imperialism on the part of other states with established or nascent interests there. The limited evidence quoted above suggests that this fear dominated British attitudes to French expansion in West Africa early in the 1880s, well before any theorist had rationalized the connection between tariffs and empire, and that the same theme recurred frequently in the public speeches of British statesmen throughout the 1880s and 1890s. Moreover, evidence to be considered below will indicate that the French, Germans and others were almost as afraid of the commercial effects of nominally nonprotective 'revenue-producing' British tariffs in tropical Africa as the British were of French or Portuguese differential tariffs. The point, of course, is that the application of alien rule by any one European power was in any case likely to harm the commercial interests of nationals of other states: differential tariffs merely made things worse. Under certain circumstances the declaration of a protectorate or a less formal 'sphere of influence' in a region apparently threatened by foreign annexation might seem a legitimate and proper defensive measure, even to European statesmen who would infinitely have preferred to avoid formal commitments in tropical Africa and the East. Here at least is a credible hypothesis linking the decline of European exports and the adoption of protective tariffs with the partition of Africa in the 1880s and 1890s. It remains to be seen whether the evidence supports this hypothesis.

3   The Imperialism of Capital

*W*ithout a doubt the most complex and influential explanation of the 'new imperialism' of the later nineteenth and early twentieth centuries is that which sees the basic cause in the necessity for capitalist Europe and North America to find satisfactory new fields for investment of surplus capital. In its simplest form the argument can be summarized as follows.

Capitalist Europe (together with the United States) was, by its very nature, preoccupied with the continued accumulation of capital, for unless its capital was continually increasing economic stagnation would inevitably set in. Accumulation was primarily achieved by the reinvestment of profits on productive activities, and the incentive to reinvest rather than to spend was the expectation of adequate profit from the increased investment. In the later nineteenth century, however, this incentive to invest within one's own country diminished because (for reasons varying with different accounts) there was a tendency for the rate of profit to decline. Capitalists with profits waiting to be invested therefore looked to other parts of the world for more rewarding fields for investment. They found them, partly at least, in areas where economic conditions differed from those of the economically advanced regions of Europe: where there were ample raw materials to exploit and where non-European labour could be employed at wage rates substantially below those demanded at home. Investment of surplus capital in such regions served a double function: it reduced the pressure of capital seeking employment and so sustained the rate of profit in Europe; and at the same time the capital invested overseas might earn a higher rate of profit than was possible at home, so providing the capitalist with a 'super profit' on his investment. Such overseas investment might be in stable independent countries such as Russia or the United States. But where political conditions were unsuitable it was preferable to annex the territory as a colony and impose satisfactory conditions. Since, moreover, a number of European countries simultaneously felt the same need for colonies as fields for investment after about 1870, a competitive rush for overseas possessions occurred which resulted in the partition of the world. Thereafter possession of these colonies of investment became increasingly necessary to capitalist states, so that they were determined to retain what they possessed and to seize the empires of rivals. Hence redivision of the colonial empires was one of the motives for the two world wars in the first half of the twentieth century.

This formulation of the theory of 'capitalist imperialism', to use Lenin's phrase, is, of course, merely a conflation of a number of distinct and in some ways conceptually incompatible arguments constructed by authors whose fundamental premises varied as widely as those of John Stuart Mill and the neo-Marxists of the early twentieth century. Space makes it impracticable to trace the evolution of this general hypothesis or even to expound it in detail; but the subject is adequately covered in a substantial body of published work and in any case it is not essential for the purposes of the present historical study to investigate the underlying theoretical assumptions.[1] Since, however, we intend to test the historical validity of certain specific aspects of this theory of capitalist imperialism it is necessary briefly to review the central arguments of four of its most influential proponents, J. A. Hobson, Rudolf Hilferding and V. I. Lenin.

Hobson's *Imperialism: a Study*, published in 1902,[2] stands as the classic expression of the attitudes of British liberals to colonial expansion in the tropics in that Hobson attempted to show that, while imperialism was a natural concomitant of the social injustice of capitalism, it was not historically inevitable because its 'taproot' could be cut by social reform. In this respect his hypothesis differed fundamentally from that of the neo-Marxists, who regarded him as a 'bourgeois revisionist' even while they borrowed many of his ideas.

Hobson's explanation of the 'new imperialism' can be summarized as follows. The paradoxical feature of British colonial expansion during the previous thirty years was that most of the new colonial possessions satisfied none of the accepted nineteenth-century criteria for useful colonization: they were seldom suited to white settlement, constituted poor markets and provided few valuable exports but cost the metropolis large sums of money. Why, then, were they annexed? Hobson's answer amounted to a conspiracy theory. The nation had been tricked into expansion by those sectional interests who stood to gain by it. These included armaments manufacturers, speculators on the stock exchange, exporters of goods in demand in tropical areas, and individuals for whom tropical colonies offered special attractions or advantages – missionaries, engineers, army officers, administrators, etc. But, although these men provided the 'motor-power' of imperialism, the decisive force lay behind them, with the men who decided whether a particular territory should be retained once these frontiersmen had created the possibility. Hobson had no hesitation in saying that these faceless men were the capitalists.

Aggressive imperialism, which costs the taxpayer so dear, which is of so little value to the manufacturer and trader, which is fraught with such grave incalculable peril to the citizen, is a source of great gain to the investor who cannot find at home the profitable use he seeks for his capital, and insists that his Government should help him to profitable and secure investments abroad.

If, contemplating the enormous expenditure on armaments, the ruinous wars, the diplomatic audacity of knavery by which modern Governments seek to extend their territorial powers, we put the plain, practical question, *Cui bono?* the first and most obvious answer is, The investor.[3]

In support of this hypothesis Hobson produced statistics which suggested that during a period when British overseas possessions had increased by some 4,754 million square miles and by a population of 88 millions, overseas capital investment had increased from £144 million in 1862 to £1,698 million in 1893 and its return as assessed for income tax from about £33 million in 1884 to £60 million in 1900.[4] Such figures seemed fully to support Hobson's main contention. Obviously capital exports and imperial expansion stood, in some degree at least, in the relation of cause and effect.

Capital export, then, was both the symptom of an unhealthy domestic economy and the cause of the 'new imperialism'. But Hobson, in common with many liberals and moderate socialists in Britain, such as H. N. Brailsford and Leonard Woolf, and a number of European socialists such as Karl Kautsky whom Lenin later labelled 'revisionists', believed that both evils could be cured by the same reformatory measures.

Let any turn in the tide of politico-economic forces divert from these owners their excess of income and make it flow, either to the workers in higher wages, or to the community in taxes, so that it will be spent instead of being saved, serving in either of these ways to swell the tide of consumption – there will be no need to fight for foreign markets or foreign areas of investment.[5]

It was on this point rather than on his basic diagnosis of the causes of imperialism that many continental neo-Marxists disagreed with Hobson. Their interest in the question was essentially a by-product of controversy over the correct interpretation of Marx's writings on the central question of when capitalist societies could be expected to collapse and whether this collapse would result automatically from structural defects in capitalist society or whether revolutionary action would be necessary to bring the proletariat to power.[6] The consensus was eventually that capitalism must be destroyed by its own inherent contradictions; and the importance of imperialism was that it provided a chronological mile-post marking the 'highest stage' reached by capitalism before its imminent collapse. Not all were agreed on the economic explanation of this apocalyptic model. Rosa Luxemburg in particular did not think that the export of capital was as important a factor in European colonization as the need of capitalist societies to realize capital gains through trade with less-developed countries.[7] But the two men whose writings did most to formulate what became the orthodox Marxist view of imperialism were Hilferding and Lenin; and it is therefore possible to concentrate attention on their central arguments.

Hilferding's contribution to the neo-Marxist debate was the concept of 'finance capital', the term he used to indicate the concentration of capital in the hands of relatively small groups of bankers and industrialists at a late state in the evolution of capitalism. Hilferding held that the historical tendency of capitalism was towards the concentration of the means of production in ever fewer hands (as Marx had said) and that this in turn led to the creation of cartels and trusts and so to monopoly in particular fields of production. This process was helped and intensified by the action of the banks which financed mergers and cartels and which themselves tended to be merged into larger banking organizations as the scale of operations grew. As banks increased their loans to industrial concerns they became closely concerned in industrial production, so that eventually the banks ceased to be merely credit organizations and became owners of industrial capital. This concentration of industrial power in the hands of banks Hilferding called finance capital, and held that it constituted the highest form of capitalism. In the end the entire industrial economy of a nation came to be controlled by a number of interlocking banks, industrial trusts and cartels. Because they operated on the largest scale and because they could establish a monopoly these organizations could obtain the highest possible return from their capital at the expense of the worker and consumer.

Monopolistic profits were, moreover, greatly increased by the application of protective tariffs, which enabled them to extract an extra profit at home in proportion to the level of protective duties. At the same time this higher price tended to reduce the size of the home market because it absorbed more of the inelastic buying capacity of the workers. Hence the need to expand the market by selling in other countries. Exports were helped by the fact that finance capitalists could afford to dump their exports at low profit margins, compensating themselves by the higher price demanded at home. Unfortunately, other countries also had protective tariffs, which obstructed imports from elsewhere and reduced the level of profit obtainable by trade. It was this factor which made the export of capital rather than of manufactures so attractive and common. The finance capitalist in Germany could export capital to the Argentine, set up a factory there, sell his products under cover of local tariffs, and re-export the profits to Germany. Thus the finance capitalist could obtain artificially high profits in each country. But a special advantage resulted from exporting capital to less economically developed countries:

The rate of interest is much higher in countries with a low capitalistic development and which are for the first time accepting credit and banking organizations than in developed capitalistic states. Added to this is the fact that parts of the wages or the profit of the employer are contained in the interest. The high rate of interest acts as an immediate stimulus for the export of loan capital. The profits of the capitalist are higher because labour is extraordinarily cheap and because the lower quality of the labour is balanced by excessively long working hours. Ground-rents are low or nominal, as there is ample land available, either naturally, or by forcible expropriation of the natives. The low price of land thus lowers the costs of production. In such places there also occurs an increase of profits as the result of privileges and monopolies.[8]

Moreover, in some cases the profits accruing from investment in these underdeveloped areas would be far greater than could be obtained by selling its products merely in the local protected market. Some products such as gold or copper commanded an international market which transcended tariff systems and so further extended the field of opportunity open to the capital of the country from which the capital originally came. And the dependent economy could further increase the profitability of industrial capital at home by producing cheap and ample supplies of raw materials. Thus export of capital had become an essential feature of economic life as the European economies developed, and as finance capitalism and tariff protection replaced free competition and free trade.

It is important to note that up to this point Hilferding's argument had no necessary connection with imperialism in the narrow sense: that is, it specified export of capital to less-developed countries but did not require that they should become formal colonies. In fact formal annexation of colonies was unnecessary to the argument, provided European states could find suitable conditions for investment of capital in independent states of the right type. Hilferding, indeed, made no distinction between colonies and what others have called 'informal' colonies or 'semi-colonies'. Formal colonies were established only when the political power of the state had to be called in to support the interests of the finance capitalists because the process of investing productive capital overseas was impeded by political obstacles or because the resistance of traditional social institutions made it impossible to create the necessary 'wage-labour proletariat' sufficiently quickly. Formal colonies were thus evidence of the haste of the finance capitalist and his ability to demand support from his own government. The result was 'colonial policy', violence, the decline of the old bourgeois belief in international harmony and the rise of nationalistic jingoism. In short, imperialism as a political phenomenon was the product of the economic needs of finance capitalism.

These assumptions were taken up and made more dogmatic by later Marxists, particularly Bukharin[9] and Lenin. Since both adopted Hilferding's concept of finance capitalism as a special historical stage of capitalism and shared the assumption that imperialism was the outcome, it is possible to save space by concentrating on Lenin's far better known exposition of the theory.

The primary contribution of Lenin to the Marxist theory of imperialism was that, building on Hilferding's principles and Hobson's argument, he made both far more precise and dogmatic. First, he gave the achievement of finance capitalism (or monopoly capitalism) a precise date: 'it was the beginning of the twentieth century'.[10] Then he refined Hilferding's explanation of why capital had to be exported by the finance capitalists. The domestic market for capital was not so much limited by its intrinsic size and the effect of tariffs as by the refusal of capitalists to invest at home because this might tend to benefit the workers rather than themselves:

It goes without saying that if capitalism could develop agriculture, which today lags far behind industry everywhere, if it could raise the standard of living of the masses, who are everywhere still poverty-stricken and underfed . . . there could be no talk of a superabundance of capital. . . . But if capitalism did these things it would not be capitalism; for unequal development and wretched conditions of the masses are fundamental and inevitable conditions and premises of this mode of production. As long as capitalism remains what it is, surplus capital will never be utilized for the purpose of raising the standard of living of the masses in a given country, for this would mean a decline in profits for the capitalists; it will be used for the purpose of increasing those profits by exporting capital abroad to the backward countries.[11]

This is, of course, a different approach from that of Hilferding, and more closely resembles that of Hobson, to whom Lenin owed rather more than he cared to acknowledge. He was, in fact, taking up an underconsumptionist position, but deriving underconsumption not, as did Hobson, merely from oversaving by capitalists, but from oversaving by finance capitalists, whose monopoly of production greatly increased their control over the home economy.

The effect, however, was much the same in each case. Europe exported her capital to 'backward countries' where 'profits are usually high, for capital is scarce, the price of land is relatively low, wages are low, raw materials are cheap'.[12] Lenin listed the capital estimated to have been exported to different parts of the world by Britain, France and Germany, showing that only Britain had invested very heavily in Asia, Africa and Australia; but, like Hobson, he made no attempt to differentiate between these three continents. Moreover, Lenin thought that the contrasting distribution of overseas investment resulted from the monopolistic finance capitalists' agreement among themselves to divide the world informally.

The capitalists divide the world, not out of any particular malice, but because the degree of concentration which has been reached forces them to adopt this method in order to get profits. And they divide it in proportion to 'capital', in proportion to 'strength', because there cannot be any other system of division under commodity production and capitalism.[13]

To some extent this division was purely economic, and produced only 'semi-colonies' (Persia, China, Turkey) and 'commercial colonies' like the Argentine. But finance capital also found it convenient to control less-organized regions which provided or promised an economic return for investment. Such areas were normally made full colonies, which had the additional advantage that 'in the colonial market it is easier to eliminate competition, to make sure of orders, to strengthen the necessary "connections", etc. by monopolist methods (and sometimes it is the only possible way)'.[14] In either case – formal or informal colonization – the power of the parent states of Europe was required to establish the claims of one monopolistic group or to establish political control. Hence a political division of the world had accompanied the economic partition, with the result that 'for the first time the world is completely divided up, so that in future *only* redivision is possible. . . .'

On this basis Lenin could produce his formal definition of imperialism.

Imperialism is capitalism in that stage of development in which the dominance of monopolies and finance capital has established itself; in which the export of capital has acquired pronounced importance; in which the division of the world among the international trusts has begun; in which the division of all territories of the globe among the great capitalist powers has been completed.[15]

The first three words are of crucial importance, for they distinguish Lenin's theory most clearly from all others. Hobson had treated imperialism as evidence of economic and social weakness in Europe, arguing that imperialism could be ended once these internal weaknesses were remedied; that is, within the structure of a reformed capitalist society. It was Lenin's main aim to reject this conclusion. Imperialism was not merely an external symptom of a curable disease of capitalism but a definition of the stage of senescence capitalism had now reached which pointed only to its grave. Once a country had become imperialist capitalism itself was within a hair's breadth of its final convulsion. All that could follow thereafter was the intensification of competition between rival imperialist states, the repartition of the world among the most powerful of them, and finally their destruction in war and revolution. Conversely, since the socio-economic conditions which had given birth to imperialism were special to capitalist countries at a particular stage of their history, it could not have occurred in the same way at any earlier time, and could not exist in a socialist world.

Since 1917 the arguments put forward by Hobson, Lenin and their contemporaries have been expanded, glossed, and in some respects made more sophisticated;[16] but little of substance has been added to their central hypotheses. It is therefore unnecessary to pursue the growth of this type of explanation of imperialism further, but to reformulate the specific questions it poses for the historian.

There are many ways in which the credibility of the imperialism of capitalism could be tested, but two stand out. First, with particular relevance to neo-Marxist assumptions, what evidence is there that the evolution of monopoly or finance capitalism actually preceded or coincided with colonial expansion? Second, and relevant to liberal and Marxist arguments alike, was there any broad geographical correlation between the export of European and North American capital in this period and the extension of colonial rule?[17]

Evidence on whether the increasing concentration of industrial concerns, coupled with the growth of monopolies, trusts, cartels and large-scale banking organizations (i.e. 'finance capitalism'), was so general a phenomenon in Europe and North America that it could operate as a primary cause of the export of capital and so of imperialism varies very considerably according to which country is examined. The two countries in which the evidence seems most likely to support the neo-Marxists were Germany and the United States, in both of which, though for rather different reasons, concentration of industrial capital and integration of industry and finance were most advanced. The United States probably provided the earliest model for concentration of industry. Normal deposit banking showed no tendency towards concentration: indeed the number of separate banks remained very great and few of them had many branches. But the big investment bank was undoubtedly central to American business growth and represented a trend towards finance capitalism. Men like J. P. Morgan developed the technique of acquiring a part interest in concerns such as railways or industrial companies, particularly when these were financially embarrassed, and gradually exerted control over company policy.

The result by about 1900 was the development of the 'trust' which was defined by the Pujo Committee of 1912 as

An established and well-defined identity and community of interest between a few leaders of finance which has been created and is held together through stock holdings interlocking directorates, and other forms of domination over banks, trust companies, railroads, public-service and industrial corporations, and which has resulted in a vast and growing concentration of control of money and credit in the hands of a comparatively few men.[18]

Thus, J. P. Morgan and his close associates held 341 directorships in 112 corporations with assets totalling more than $22,000 million. Parallel with this development of the trusts and to some extent as a result of it went growing concentration of industry in both horizontal and vertical combines. Until the early 1880s this was largely generated by technological advance which made it necessary to increase the size of the production unit. Thereafter the motives were mainly desire for greater efficiency of operation and for quasi-monopoly as a means of increasing prices. Pools – or cartels – came first as a means by which potentially rival firms could allocate the market and maintain prices. They were followed by trusts or financial mergers and then by full mergers. Horizontal combinations were most common until perhaps 1898: Standard Oil was the best example, beginning as a trust and ending in a holding company. Thereafter there was an increasing tendency towards vertical combinations, such as the American Tobacco Company and the United States Steel Corporation.

There was, moreover, evidence that the United States had 'surplus' capital in the 1890s as a result of the reluctance of institutions and individual investors to invest at home during a period of low profits and poor returns to capital. As a result American overseas investment, particularly in Canada and Latin America, expanded considerably.[19] Equally some Americans at least, such as Charles Conant, had drawn the conclusion by 1898 that

American investors are not willing to see the return upon their investments reduced to the European level. Interest rates have already declined here within the last five years. New markets and new opportunities for investment must be found if surplus capital is to be profitably employed. . . .
The writer is not an advocate of 'imperialism' from sentiment, but does not fear the name if it means only that the United States shall assert their right to free markets in all the old countries which are being

opened to the surplus resources of the capitalistic countries and thereby given the benefits of modern civilization. Whether this policy carries with it the direct government of groups of half-savage islands may be a subject for argument, but upon the economic side of the question there is but one choice – either to enter by some means upon the competition for the employment of American capital and enterprise in these countries, or to continue the needless duplication of existing means of production and communication, with the glut of unconsumed products, the convulsions followed by trade stagnation, and the steadily declining return upon investments which this policy will invoke. . . .[20]

Thus, without investigating the matter further at this point there appear to be *a priori* grounds for thinking that the United States in the later 1890s fulfilled not only Lenin's criteria for monopoly capitalism but also Hobson's for a glut of capital resulting from underconsumption.

The Marxists were also basically correct about the trends of capitalism in Germany, on which they had the best information.[21] From the start German industrialization had shown marked collectivist tendencies, and had relied very heavily on the banks for long-term capital. The great banks – the Deutsche, the Dresdener, the Diskontogesellschaft and the Darmstädter, together with a number of lesser business banks – were thus intimately connected with industry and were well represented on boards of directors. They took a direct interest in particular enterprises both within Germany and overseas, and often formed banking and industrial syndicates to set up a new venture. Cartels also emerged early in German industrial history, though they became general only from the later 1870s under the joint stimuli of economic depression and the protective tariff. By 1900 about 275 cartels were active, ranging from simple price agreements to complex regulation of production and distribution. Hardly any trade remained strictly competitive, and some of the greater cartels in fact became largely integrated *Konzerns*, like the Steel Union of 1904. Such organizations were enabled by high tariffs and their own monopoly of the home market to fix double prices – a high price for the home consumer and a low 'dumping' price for exports. Equally Germany became a substantial exporter of capital at the end of the nineteenth century. Feis estimated that in 1914 long-term foreign investment may have been some 23,500 million marks (about £1,175 million at the 1914 parity).[22] Without considering the reasons for this capital export, it is again evident that, both on grounds of monopoly capitalism and capital export, Germany conformed to Leninist and Hobsonian criteria for an imperialist state.

But these were only two of the 'imperialist' states of Lenin's definition, and these had taken a relatively small share in the partition of the world since the 1880s. What of France, Britain and Italy, and Russia, not to mention Spain, Portugal, Holland and Belgium, which also played varying roles in colonial annexation and expansion? If imperialism was necessarily or predominantly the product of evolving finance capitalism then one would expect to find finance capitalism and capital exports developing in these countries, and to find them so far advanced that the conditions associated with mature finance capitalism would apply.

In fact, however, none of these countries conformed with Lenin's conditions for monopoly capitalism before 1914, with the possible exception of Belgium which as a state took no part in colonial expansion. At first sight France might seem to qualify. She was one of the largest exporters of capital and a leading expansionist. French banks had been among the first to take a direct interest in industrial and other long-term investments: for example, the Crédit Mobilier, which failed in 1871. Moreover, during the last quarter of the century there was a marked tendency towards concentration of banks into major units – Crédit Lyonnais, Société Générale, Comptoir d'Escompte and others. But there was little tendency for these great banking combines to form close links with industry. If anything, after 1870 and the failure of several investment banks, they shunned direct industrial investment. They might be interested in share promotions but very seldom retained long-term holdings in business concerns. Thus there was nothing in France to compare with the big banking trusts of Germany and the United States. Again, although there was some tendency towards concentration of control, amalgamation and monopoly in French industry, particularly after the Méline tariff of 1892, there was nothing as large in scale as the German or American cartels and trusts. In 1914 French capitalism remained small in scale and competitive within the classical meaning of the word. On the other hand, France had large overseas investments: on Feis' estimate 28,000 million francs (some £1,000 million) in 1900 and 45,000 million francs (£1,800 million) in 1914;[23] and there were a number of important banks which specialized in overseas loans, such as the Banque Franco-Egyptienne. It is, therefore, possible that the Hobsonian interpretation of imperialism might apply to France, provided that a causal relationship could be shown between her export of capital and her expansionist policies. But it would be unrealistic to attempt to explain French expansion within the formal terms of Lenin's definition of imperialism.

Britain was the other main country with vast capital exports and colonial acquisitions which it is nevertheless impossible to describe as 'imperialist' in Lenin's definition.[24] There was, admittedly, some movement towards concentration in industry and banking and towards monopoly in certain sectors. In the 1880s and 1890s tentative steps were taken first in the direction of informal trade associations, such as the British Soap Makers Association, then towards more formal organizations. Between the mid-1880s and about 1900 there were a number of large amalgamations or mergers in industry – the Salt Union of 1888, the United Alkali Company (1891), the English Sewing–Cotton Company (1897), the Calico Printers' Association (1899). There were also some alliances, for example in the Birmingham metal trade. Some of these were successful either in increasing efficiency as a result of greater scale of operation; others merely raised prices. But none was comparable with the great German or American trusts and mergers in size or the extent of their monopolistic tendencies, and all were hampered by the absence of an external tariff and by strong prejudices against artificial elimination of competition. Nor did the banks play any major role in industrial operations. Manufacturing industry remained independent of the central banks, relying mainly on its own profits or on short-term loans by country banks to finance expansion. The London money market remained divorced from industry and also from the banks which handled overseas investment. Thus the British economy remained competitive and largely fragmented. If capital flowed overseas and colonies were acquired these could not be attributed to any structural change on the economy in the direction of finance capitalism in the later nineteenth century.

The other 'imperialist' countries must be considered even more briefly. Russia was undergoing rapid industrial growth and her banking system was developing fast between 1880 and 1914, helped by high external tariffs, foreign loans and governmental stimulation. Particularly after the financial and economic crises of 1901–3 the new industries rapidly formed associations and trusts, modelled on those of Germany: for example the 'Prodamet' metallurgical trust formed in the crisis of 1903. Indeed, it has been argued that monopoly was so far advanced in some sectors that production had been

reduced below the level of market demand by 1914.[25] To this extent
Russia may have been becoming 'imperialist' by 1914, though
certainly not during the twenty years before 1900 when colonial
expansion was at its height. Yet, even ignoring this chronological
problem, it would be ridiculous to argue that Russian finance capitalism forced the export of capital and that this was the root of
Russian territorial expansion. For Russia was a vast net importer of
capital throughout this period, in fact the largest borrower in
Europe, owing perhaps 17,500 million francs in 1914, much of it to
France.[26] In due course the evolution of Russian industry and
monopoly might have made her 'imperialist', but certainly not
before 1914.

Much the same was true of Italy.[27] There too there was superficial evidence of concentration in industry and banking and of
closer relations between the two. Before the great banking crash
of 1893 several Italian banks had taken a large share in financing
both industry and public utilities; after their failure new banks,
predominately with German or later French backing, took over the
same functions. Industrial growth was considerable, helped by
high tariffs from 1878. The size of concerns, particularly in the
textile industries, metallurgy and chemicals, grew substantially,
with considerable help from the state and the banks. In some,
particularly iron and steel, partial monopolies were created and the
ILVA combine, formed in 1905, created a cartel to control steel
prices and entered into an agreement with the German Stahlwerks-
verband to check dumping. Thus Italy also was following the
Leninist path towards finance capitalism. Yet she had certainly not
reached such a condition by 1914, for the scale of industry generally
remained non-monopolistic and cartels and trusts were weaker.
Above all, Italy remained a large net capital importer, and certainly
had no spare domestically generated capital to send overseas.
Italian imperialism clearly did not spring from the existence of an
'over-ripe' capitalist economy, or from the need to export surplus
capital.

Belgium and the Netherlands, on the other hand, though small,
do appear to have conformed in principle to the neo-Marxist definition of finance capitalism. Both were industrial states by the end of
the nineteenth century, and Belgium had become one of the leading
producers of coal, iron, steel, zinc and other metals fifty years
earlier. Both countries had advanced banking systems which developed close financial and entrepreneurial links with the industrial

concerns they financed, though a large proportion of their capital was in fact French. In Belgium cartels were well advanced as early as the 1850s, when, for example, the Vieille Montagne, Europe's leading zinc producer, either bought out or made agreements with all other European producers to sustain price levels. Both Belgium and the Netherlands, moreover, after initially depending on imported capital, became capital exporters late in the century; while at the same time Belgium acquired the Belgian Congo in 1908 and the Netherlands was consolidating and developing her vast sphere of influence in Indonesia. In all these ways both countries seemed to fit the concept of 'imperialism'. Yet certain important reservations must be made. Both countries became free-trading by the 1860s, so that in neither country did protective tariffs play the role cast for them by Hilferding. Although both became colonial powers the Belgians were so hostile to acquiring colonies in the later nineteenth century that Leopold II had to obtain the Congo in the name of an international company and financed early development out of his own purse and by private loans. Only international criticism over the Congo scandals of the first year of the twentieth century converted the political and industrial ruling groups to the necessity of taking formal responsibility for the Congo. Equally, although the Dutch were investing heavily in their East Indian possessions in this period, they did so as part of a general process of investment overseas and without showing any very strong preference for colonial investments as such. Thus, although the pattern of economic evolution in Belgium and the Netherlands before 1914 may well have created conditions favourable to economic investment overseas and may have contributed to the substantial investment both ultimately made in their own dependencies – the Congo and Netherlands East Indies – in the period before 1914, neither was formally involved in the international competition for colonies and the Belgians at least were positively hostile to the concept of a Belgian colonial empire.

Finally, neither Spain nor Portugal, who were to some degree involved in the process of colonial expansion, can in any way be fitted into the concept of 'imperialism'.[28] Spain began a belated industrial and banking development in the 1870s under cover of heavy tariff protection, which was greatly helped by shortages created by the First World War. But Spain remained largely a 'commercial colony' of the great North European countries, heavily dependent on capital from Britain, France and Germany; and Portu-

gal remained a very poor agricultural and maritime country, showing no propensity to become industrialized. Although she attempted,
with some success, to make good claims to vast areas of central
Africa, the development of these regions had to be handed over to
concessionary companies, mostly British, because she lacked any of
the financial or economic capacity to use them herself.

How, then, does the Hilferding–Lenin model of capitalist imperialism stand up to this brief survey of banking and industrial
development of capital exports in these countries most closely
involved in the expansion of European power after about 1880?
The crux of the matter is that even if we ignore Lenin's own precise
timing of the beginnings of finance capitalism in 1900, only two
countries, Germany and the United States, might reasonably be
said to fulfil the economic criteria laid down for 'imperialist' countries which also took an active part in the international partition;
while Belgium and the Netherlands would also have qualified but
took no direct part in it. Conversely, none of the other active
expansionists appear to have fulfilled these economic conditions
before 1914. On the other hand, at least four countries – Britain,
France, Germany and the United States – met Hobson's much less
rigorous conditions for capitalist imperialism in that all were actively
investing overseas in the period 1870–1914; and it is at least credible – though the point is too abstract to consider here – that this
propensity to invest overseas reflected a 'glut' of capital at home,
itself the product of maldistribution of incomes and limited pur-
chasing power among the masses.

With the question thus still very open it is possible to consider
briefly the second question relating to both Leninist and Hobsonian theories – whether the geographical distribution of the overseas
investments of the capital-exporting countries shows some correlation with the expansion of the colonial systems. This question is of
great importance, for, whatever the economic forces behind the
outflow of capital, the fact of very large outflows of capital remains,
and it is at least possible that some substantial part of this was going
to those regions of Africa, Asia and the Pacific where Europeans
were imposing formal political control or attempting to do so. If
this was so, it would be reasonable to assume, in general terms, that
imperialism was causally connected with capital investment; though
it would still be necessary to examine other evidence to make sure
that finance was the dominant cause of political action in a particular area. If, on the other hand, it appears that only a relatively

small part of European overseas investment went to the new colonial territories as a whole, the position would be reversed. It would not necessarily follow that investment played no role at all in imperialism, for on the one hand a few individual territories might have received considerable investment; and on the other hand a small overall colonial investment might merely show that many new possessions proved far less capable of absorbing large investments in the short term than optimistic capitalists at home had expected.

In point of fact the figures show relatively little correlation between investment of capital and new colonization. By far the most important capital exporters before 1914 were Britain, France, Germany and the United States. Exact figures are not and will never be available; but, taking those compiled by Herbert Feis it becomes clear that the new colonies had attracted a very small proportion of the total capital exported by any of these countries by 1914. Tables 4-9 provide the evidence in outline.

Of these four countries by far the most important overseas investor was Britain, which had been the first significant exporter of capital in the modern world and possessed the largest overseas empire. In 1914 Britain was the only colonial power which had invested a significant proportion of her capital exports in her colonies: on Feis' figures about half. This fact appears to have misled Hobson, who assumed that a significant proportion of this investment in colonies must be in new tropical colonies – the territories involved in the recent colonial expansion. Here he was quite wrong. Out of the £1,780 million invested in British colonies, all but £96·6 million was in the older colonies including the Transvaal and Orange Free State which were reannexed after the Boer War but not technically new British possessions. Hence the investment opportunities in the new colonies, although in some cases intrinsically valuable (as in Malaya) were of minimal importance in relation to those provided by the British Empire as a whole and even less significant in relation to the world market for capital. This is not to say that the economic potential of some of these new territories had not been a factor in their annexation or that none attracted substantial investments in due course. The vital point is rather that it is quite unrealistic to think that Britain had any urgent need of these new colonies simply as places in which she could dump surplus capital. The world was Britain's field of investment. Her investors, whether they were individuals wanting to place money

Table 4

British Foreign Investment, 1914

(i) Long-Term Publicly Issued British Capital Investment in Other Lands
(millions of pounds)

Within the Empire		Outside the Empire	
Canada and Newfoundland	514·9	The United States	754·6
Australia and New Zealand	416·4	Argentina	319·6
South Africa	370·2	Brazil	148·0
West Africa	37·3	Mexico	99·0
India and Ceylon	378·8	Chile	61·0
Straits Settlements	27·3	Uruguay	36·1
British North Borneo	5·8	Peru	34·2
Hong Kong	3·1	Cuba	33·2
Other colonies	26·2	Remainder Latin America	25·5
	1,780·0	Total Latin America	756·6
		Russia	110·0
		Spain	19·0
		Italy	12·5
		Portugal	8·1
		France	8·0
		Germany	6·4
		Austria	8·0
		Denmark	11·0
		Balkan States	17·0
		Rest of Europe	18·6
		Total Europe	218·6
		Egypt	44·9
		Turkey	24·0
		China	43·9
		Japan	62·8
		Rest of Foreign World	77·9
		Total	1,983·3
		Grand Total	3,763·3

Source: H. Feis, *Europe the World's Banker*, 33.

Table 5

British Foreign Investment, 1914
(ii) Fields of Employment of Capital Invested in Other Lands (millions of pounds)

Loans to national and state governments		
Dominion and colonial	675·5	
Foreign	297·0	
Total		972·5
Loans to municipal governments		152·5
Railway securities		
Dominions and colonies	306·4	
British India	140·8	
United States	616·6	
Other foreign countries	467·2	
Total		1,531·0
Mines		272·8
Financial, land and investment companies		244·2
Iron, coal, and steel industries		35·2
Commercial establishments and industrial plants		155·3
Banks		72·9
Electric light and power industries		27·3
Telegraph and telephone systems		43·7
Tramways		77·8
Gas and waterworks		29·2
Canals and docks		7·1
Oil industry		40·6
Rubber industry		41·0
Tea and coffee industry		22·4
Nitrate industry		11·7
Breweries		18·0
Miscellaneous		8·1
Total		3,763·3

Source: H. Feis, *Europe the World's Banker*, 27.

Table 6

French Foreign Investment
(i) Geographical Distribution of French Foreign Long-Term Investment,
1900 and 1914 (billions of francs)

1900		1914	
Russia	7·0	Russia	11·3
Turkey (in Asia and		Turkey (in Asia and	
Europe)	2·0	Europe	3·3
Spain and Portugal	4·5	Spain and Portugal	3·9
Austria–Hungary	2·5	Austria–Hungary	2·2
Balkan states	0·7	Balkan states	2·5
Italy	1·4	Italy	1·3
Switzerland, Belgium		Switzerland, Belgium	
and Netherlands	1·0	and Netherlands	1·5
Rest of Europe	0·8	Rest of Europe	1·5
Total Europe	19·9	Total Europe	27·5
French colonies	1·5	French colonies	4·0
Egypt, Suez and		Egypt, Suez and	
South Africa	3·0	South Africa	3·3
United States and		United States, Canada	
Canada	0·8	and Australia	2·0
Latin America	2·0	Latin America	6·0
Asia	0·8	Asia	2·2
Grand Total	28·0	Grand Total	45·0

Source: H. Feis, *Europe the World's Banker*, 51.

Table 7

French Foreign Investment
(ii) Distribution of New Investments, 1882–1914 (billions of francs)

	New Investments		Total Outstanding 1914	
	Amount	Per Cent	Amount	Per Cent
Eastern Europe	13·4	38	14·7	29
Russia			12·5	25
Balkans			2·2	4
North-West Europe	2·9	8	3·5	7
Benelux			1·0	2
Scandinavia			2·5	5
Near East	2·4	7	5·8	12
Ottoman Empire			3·3	7
Egypt and Suez			2·5	5
Central Europe	1·1	3	3·9	8
Austria–Hungary			2·4	5
Germany and Switzerland			1·5	3
Mediterranean	0·4	1	5·8	12
Italy			1·3	3
Spain and Portugal			4·5	9
Western hemisphere	7·4	21	8·0	16
Latin America			6·0	12
United States and Canada			2·0	4
Colonies	3·8	11	4·5	9
Rest of world	3·8	11	4·0	8
TOTAL	35·2	100	50·2	100

Source: Rondo E. Cameron, *France and the Economic Development of Europe, 1800–1914* (Princeton, 1961), 486.

Table 8

Geographical Distribution of German Long-Term Foreign Investment, 1914 (billions of marks)

Europe		Outside of Europe	
Austria–Hungary	3·0	Africa (including German	
Russia	1·8	colonies)	2·0
Balkan countries	1·7	Asia (including German	
Turkey (including Asiatic		colonies	1·0
Turkey)	1·8	United States and Canada	3·7
France and Great Britain	1·3	Latin America	3·8
Spain and Portugal	1·7	Other areas	0·5
Rest of Europe	1·2		
	12·5		11·0

Source: Feis, *Europe the World's Bankers*, 74.

Table 9

United States Overseas Investment, 1913 (millions of dollars)

Country	Amount
Canada	750
Cuba	100
Mexico	1,050
Central America	50
South America	100
Europe	350
China and Japan	100
Philippine Islands	75
Puerto Rico	30
Total	2,605

Source: R. W. Dunn, *American Foreign Investment* (New York, 1926), 3.

where it could provide a reasonable return or large-scale firms proposing to set up plantations, factories or utilities, did so wherever the opportunities were best. With very few exceptions it was of no importance to them whether or not the British flag flew there.

With France the case is still more striking. On Cameron's figures only about 9 per cent of total French overseas investments in 1914 were in French dependencies, and of this a substantial proportion was in Algeria, which had been receiving French investment since the 1830s. It is true that, in the period 1882–1914 French colonies absorbed some 11 per cent of total new French overseas investments, and the outstanding total in 1914 – 4,500 million francs – was substantial. Yet, by comparison both with new investment in Eastern Europe (mostly Russia) and in the Americas this was trivial; and such sums could have been invested elsewhere without difficulty. Moreover, a considerable proportion of the capital invested in the colonies had been guided there by state action: for example by provision of contracts, concessions and guaranteed rates of interest. In fact, subject to evidence of financial *affaires* playing a significant role in particular places, it must be concluded that French investors as a whole never indicated any desire for colonies as fields for investment before political annexation and thereafter largely ignored them.

German investment in the colonies acquired in the 1880s was almost ludicrously small. Feis conceals this fact by including colonial investments in larger geographical areas; but if Townsend's figure of 505 million marks total investment in the colonies in 1914 is related to Feis' total for German overseas investment of 23,500 million marks, it becomes clear how insignificant colonial investment really was. Lenin was aware of this and wrote: 'The German colonies are inconsiderable, and German capital invested abroad is divided evenly between Europe and America.'[30] It could, of course, be argued that this lack of investment merely reflected the restricted opportunities offered by the few colonies Germany originally acquired, and that German pressure for repartition of parts of Africa after 1900 indicated a continuing hunger for safe fields for further investment. But this is unrealistic. Few German banks showed any interest in colonial development, and the small amounts they invested were mostly extracted by governmental pressures and guaranteed interest rates. Had Germany acquired a really valuable territory such as Katanga or Malaya, investors would no doubt have shown as lively an interest as they did in the Rand gold mines or Ottoman territories. But this would have been on general grounds of potential profitability, for, like the British, Germans regarded the world as their field of enterprise. There is therefore no reason to think that finance capitalism, if it existed in Germany, was initially responsible for Germany's bid for colonies, or that the German economy needed dependencies as receptacles for surplus capital.

Finally, on the figures in Table 9 the American case is so clear as to require little comment. With only about 4 per cent of total overseas investment in the new dependencies – the Philippines and Puerto Rico – it is evident that, even if urgent need for new investment opportunities generated the imperialism of 1898, the need had not yet been met. Again, as with Germany, this does not necessarily invalidate Lenin's analysis of the characteristics of a trust dominated economy. Rather, it suggests that there was little causal connection between need for new outlets for capital and enterprise and formal colonization. Canada, Latin America and Europe provided America with the 'semi-colonies' or 'commercial colonies' she needed; and in none of these was formal political control needed. The most that can be said of the achievements of 1898 was that they facilitated American trade and investment in the Caribbean and Pacific and strengthened her informal control over much of Latin America. The formal colonies were as unimportant economically to her as those of Germany.

It would seem, therefore, on a cursory examination of the probabilities of the case, that the need for new openings for the profitable investment of capital made 'surplus' by the evolution of the European and North American economies is unlikely to have been the main cause of the expansion of formal colonization in the period after about 1870. This is not to deny the inherent logicality of the argument. Had the advanced economies been ready to export capital on the vast scale characteristic of the period 1870–1914 much earlier in modern history – before the Americas, Australia, Southern Africa and Southern Asia had been colonized and thus opened up to satisfactory overseas investment – then capitalistic enterprise might well have required colonization of these regions on a vast scale. As it was, Europe did not need new formal colonies in the late nineteenth century, even assuming economic conditions approximating to finance capitalism or underconsumption existed at home. The true 'capitalist imperialism' of Lenin's formula could and did operate primarily in his semi-colonies or commercial colonies generating the various types and degrees of informal empire that still existed in the second half of the twentieth century; and its really characteristic agent was the great international firm with subsidiaries throughout the non-socialist world rather than the capital-hungry colonizing adventurers typical of the age of expansive imperialism.

Yet it still remains possible that quite small amounts of invested capital may have been a significant factor in the formal annexation of particular places in the half century after 1870, however marginal to the overall needs and interests of European investors. It will therefore be necessary to look carefully for evidence of this in each case considered below, especially where there is at least some *a priori* suspicion – as in the Islamic states of the Mediterranean, in the Transvaal and China, all significantly relatively advanced areas – that what Engels called 'colonization in the interests of stock exchange swindles' may have occurred. In such cases capital might well be a factor in imperialism. Yet the scale is all-important. To repeat, in the light of what has been said above, this would constitute a local *affaire*, not part of the groundswell of the historical evolution of European capitalism.

4 *Political, Popular and Peripheral Explanations of Imperialism*

In a book explicitly concerned with the operation of economic factors in modern imperialism it is unnecessary to examine alternative non-economic explanations at length, and in any case considerations of space make this impossible. Yet a brief survey of the field is desirable on two counts. First, if, as has been suggested, most established economic interpretations of imperialism are to some extent defective, it is necessary to find an alternative hypothesis. Second, many historians have in fact attempted to account for imperialism in terms of the politico-strategic concerns of European states, the irresistible jingoism of public opinion, or problems developing outside Europe on the periphery to which European imperialism was merely a forceful reaction. It is proposed, therefore, to review these three types of evidence very briefly and then to attempt a preliminary synthesis embodying what appears to be the most credible elements in each of the approaches to imperialism so far considered.

I THE IMPERIALISM OF THE STATESMEN

There is no difficulty in constructing an elegant hypothesis which explains late nineteenth-century imperialism in terms of the rational calculations of the ministers and senior permanent officials who ruled the main powers. This would assume that these men had effective freedom of action, and that they were concerned to promote the power and security of their countries – the 'national interest' – rather than the selfish interests of private pressure groups. It would be based on analysis of the novel character of international relations in the period after about 1870. International politics were becoming more bellicose because the achievement of political unity in Germany, Italy and the United States had generated powerful nationalistic and jingoistic impulses which stimulated similar instincts in other countries. Moreover, the fact that Germany had not only defeated France in 1870–1 but also (against Bismarck's wishes) annexed Alsace and Lorraine, had produced a new bitterness in central European relations which remained intense until after 1945. In short, there were more great powers engaged in international politics than since the eighteenth century and their sense of nationality was more intense than ever before.

These factors contributed to another novel feature of this period – the growth of great power blocs and alliances. The first formal international alliance made since 1815 in peace-time – that is, as a calculated diplomatic weapon – was the Austro–German Alliance of 1879, which became the Triple Alliance in 1882 with the inclusion of Italy. This alliance was intended to be complementary to the *Dreikaiserbund* (Germany, Austria, Russia) of 1881–7 and the Reinsurance Treaty between Germany and Russia of 1887–90 in that Bismarck was concerned primarily to safeguard Germany against French resentment by isolating her from all potential allies, and at the same time to gain some control over Austro-Russian rivalries in the Balkans. In Bismarck's cautious hands such an alliance system might indeed constitute a force for international peace. But his successors did not take the same view of Germany's best interests; and in any case the very existence of such an alliance system was a challenge and possibly a threat to those excluded, notably France and Britain. It imposed new rigidities on international relations and made men think in terms of threats rather than of security. The obvious consequence was a rival alliance system once Bismarck's scheme had broken down with the end of the Reinsurance Treaty in 1890. The Franco-Russian Alliance of 1894, followed by the Anglo-French Entente of 1904 and the Anglo-Russian Convention of 1907 were the natural answer. Their effect was to divide Europe into two camps and it became natural for men on both sides to play war games on the basis of the new treaty system. This was a long cry from the facts of the international system of the 1860s and the assumptions based on it.

Although the relatively rigid alignments of the years immediately before the outbreak of war in 1914 took a long time to mature, so that in the critical period of colonial expansion before about 1890 there was still much flexibility in international relationships, this changing pattern of alliances and tensions constitutes a possible basis for constructing political interpretations of imperialism. The fundamental assumption would be that Europe had reverted to the bellicose attitudes characteristic of the Ancien Régime, with the result that any international question came to be considered in relation to accepted norms of national power and status and any change in the position of one power might be seen as a threat to the interests of others. Colonies might acquire new importance as part of this delicate balance of international forces. Even in the mid-century those few powers primarily concerned with colonies – Britain, France and Russia – were prone to strike hostile attitudes if they suspected that one of the others was encroaching on or threatening their own spheres of interest: hence Anglo-Russian hostility over Afghanistan and Anglo-French rivalries over West Africa and the South Pacific. It would not, therefore, have been surprising if after about 1870, with more powers of the first rank, with ever-increasing contacts between their nationals in Africa, Asia and the Pacific, such colonial questions should increasingly be related to the power balance within Europe. Gain for one country became loss for another. Imperialism was thus the product of hypersensitive competitiveness between all the main states of Europe and North America which in turn generated determination that no other power should be permitted to gain some advantage overseas.

But if we adopt this approach to imperialism it is necessary to define what advantages the rules of Europe hoped to obtain from new colonial possessions. Alternative answers can be provided, one specifying positive benefits, the other avoidance of inconvenience. On the positive side colonies might serve political purposes according to the character and situation of each power. They might be emotionally attractive to new states such as Germany or Italy as the culminating achievement of the rise to nationhood. But they had more practical uses. To be a world power one needed bases in all continents, for otherwise one's nationals were at the mercy of British, French or other colonial governments, consuls and war-

D

ships. Then there were the logistics of naval power. If Germany, Italy or the United States wanted to be world powers they would have to build large navies; and to operate these out of home waters they needed bases throughout the world. Another aspect of great power status in an age of international rivalry was the need for secure strategic raw materials, for it was arguable that no great industrial country could afford to depend on other and possibly hostile countries for the sinews of war. Hence the case for annexing territories which produced copper, iron ore, rubber, petroleum etc. Emigration was yet another problem. If military power depended partly on the size of the population which provided conscripts and taxes, every emigrant was a serious loss. British emigrants might remain British subjects if they went to the settlement colonies, but every Italian or German who emigrated was lost to the fatherland. Suitable colonies might solve this problem also.

Finally there was a diplomatic use for colonies. To continental states it seemed clear that the colonial powers to some extent regarded and treated their overseas possessions as an element in international relations. A threat to territories regarded by one power as a special interest could be made a bargaining point in negotiations over some other matter in dispute, as, for example, the perennial question of French fishing rights off Newfoundland or the Anglo-French Agreement of 1847 to preserve the neutrality of certain Pacific islands. In the 1870s and 1880s a number of claims to territory or influence in Africa and the East were being made by France, Britain and even Leopold of Belgium. Why should other powers not claim the right to influence these questions, to make their own claims and possibly to trade these for other advantages nearer home?

If these were some of the potential advantages which the rulers of non-colonial powers might be expected to see in staking new claims for new colonies in the later nineteenth century, what of the established imperial states? To some extent the same attractions might operate: more colonies might provide more prestige, more protection for their nationals, more bases for their navies, new sources of strategic raw materials, more homes for emigrants, more dumping grounds for convicts, more diplomatic bargaining counters. But fundamentally the problem was bound to appear different to France, the Netherlands and Russia, and, above all, to Britain. Because they were sitting tenants in many parts of the world, expansion by any other power was certain in some way to affect their existing interests, whatever these were. For example, there was virtually no area in which Britain did not possess territory or strong interests and influence. Britain might have no positive desire to make new annexations for their own sake; but the moment some other power looked like doing so in the Indian Ocean, the South Pacific or the Caribbean, British statesmen were likely to consider precautionary steps to protect British interests, real or imagined. The same was, of course, true of other established colonial or naval powers, except that none had substantive interests on the same scale. It is therefore possible to see imperialism as a cumulative precautionary process. The moment any one European state or its subjects took steps towards domination of some new territory, the cautious rulers of other states felt bound to react and either to block this move or to demand compensation, either because substantive national interests were deemed affected, or because it seemed improvident to pass over opportunities that might not recur. Thus imperialism was generated by the caution, rather than the belligerence, of the 'official mind' in its attempt to protect national interests in a period of unavoidable change.

In both these models it has been assumed that the statesmen of Europe and America had positive objectives when pursuing imperialist policies, even if these were adopted in response to a prior initiative by someone else. But it is equally possible to invert this assumption, to produce a theory of imperialism based on the anxiety of statesmen to defuse the dangerously explosive trends of late nineteenth-century international relations. Far from seeing colonies as potential weapons in diplomacy or war, they may have regarded them as red herrings to distract their own or foreign nationals from contentions within Europe that might lead to war. In terms of this theory, war was becoming all too likely and its outcome so unpredictable that no single great power, however aggressively it talked, really wanted to risk actual conflict. Colonies therefore provided a safety valve not, as Ferry said in 1890, for surplus manufactures, but for the enterprise and bellicosity of the jingoists and traditional fighting castes. Frenchmen could regain the self-respect lost at Sedan by fighting in North and West Africa and in Indo-China, far from Germans and with little but their own lives at stake. Italy, too weak to compete in Europe, could strike impressive postures in North Africa as the heir to ancient Rome. Politically ambitious soldiers could be kept far from the centres of power and the professional middle classes given satisfying administrative careers as proconsuls. In these terms imperialism was a global charade played by the statesmen as a peace-time diversion from the realities of the European power structure.

Here, then, are two alternative formulations of imperialism as a political rather than an economic phenomenon; and either, if acceptable, would solve the problem of why large-scale colonial expansion came after about 1880 rather than before or later. But how acceptable are they? The real test must lie in the evidence of motive, which will be considered in the case studies below; and space makes it impossible even to provide a preliminary survey of the general attitudes of European statesmen on these issues. But at the most general level some comments must be made on the credibility of these and similar theories which attempt to explain imperialism simply in terms of the 'official mind' of metropolitan Europe.

First, there is really no strong evidence that the politicians or senior officials of any major state drew up a prior blueprint for overseas expansion in the 1870s or 1880s on the assumption that colonies would provide political benefits of these or other varieties. The nearest approximation to planning for empire can be seen in Italy where romantically minded politicians such as Francesco Crispi regarded colonization as an essential means of satisfying the nationalistic aspirations of their weak new state. Conversely, it was only in the 1890s that statesmen in Germany began to treat colonial questions as part of a *Weltpolitik* or Frenchmen to see territorial expansion across the Sudan as necessary to French prestige as a great power. In each case these new trends were products of a decade of imperial expansion rather than the prime cause of a 'new imperialism'.

Second, it was extremely rare for any European statesman to embark on colonial expansion because of irresistible pressures from domestic political forces, or even as an electioneering device. Probably the only important example of the second of these occurred in Germany in 1884 when, it has been argued, Bismarck decided to use protectorates to protect and further German commercial enterprise overseas primarily to obtain political support at home from the National Liberals, many of whom regarded a 'colonial policy' as essential for national unity and prestige.[1]

Third, the most probable influence of strictly political considerations on European statesmen was negative: concern to protect existing overseas interests, real or conceptual, from the threat of foreign action. Such conservative attitudes were most likely to be characteristic of powers with established possessions and political interests throughout the world, Great Britain more than any other state. However opposed British statesmen might be to colonial expansion on grounds of cost and inconvenience, the official mind held that there were certain areas of major national interest which had to be protected. Many of these related to naval power – the Mediterranean, the Indian Ocean and the Cape of Good Hope in particular; others to the security of existing possessions – India and the settlement colonies. The same concern had produced recurrent military or diplomatic action in the mid-nineteenth century when Russia seemed to constitute a threat to British power in the Mediterranean and the north-west frontiers of India and when France made moves in West Africa and the South Pacific which seemed mildly dangerous. It was therefore predictable that if, for whatever reason, other powers seemed to challenge British predominance in these regions in the later nineteenth century, Britain might resort to 'preemptive' annexation, not because she wanted new territories but because she was determined to exclude others from regions deemed important to her established national interests. In different degrees the same defensive attitude was likely to influence other possessing powers at a time of rapid change.

Thus, while not closing alternative lines of interpretation, it seems initially probable that the imperialism of the statesmen in the crucial period after about 1880 would take a negative rather than a positive form. Few of the great men who presided over the initial partition of the world – Salisbury, Rosebery, Gladstone, Bismarck, Caprivi, Witte, even Ferry or Delcassé – thought that new colonies were essential as a source of political power. Yet all, under the tutelage of their permanent officials who inherited and maintained traditional concepts of what was essential to preserve national power and security, had to defend these interests overseas against evolving threats. When, therefore, a number of local crises developed on the periphery in the 1880s the governments of the great states had to act; and in many cases such actions took the form of territorial control. This at least is a reasonable hypothesis which can later be tested against the facts in individual cases.

II THE IMPERIALISM OF THE MASSES

Despite the emphasis commonly laid on economic, strategic or political factors, possibly the most popular explanation of modern

European expansion has been based on what may conveniently but loosely be described as 'the imperialism of the masses'. A short extract from W. L. Langer's article, 'A Critique of Imperialism', published in 1935, will serve to indicate the main features of this approach.

It is now fairly clear . . . that the Neo-Marxian critics have paid far too little attention to the imponderable, psychological ingredients of imperialism. The movement may, without much exaggeration, be interpreted not only as an atavism, as a remnant of the days of absolute monarchy and mercantilism . . . but also as an aberration, to be classed with the extravagances of nationalism. Just as nationalism can drive individuals to the point of sacrificing their very lives for the purposes of the state, so imperialism has driven them to the utmost exertions and the supreme sacrifice, even though the stake might be only some little known and at bottom valueless part of Africa or Asia. In the days when communication and economic interdependence have made the world one in so many ways, men still interpret international relations in terms of the old cabinet policies, they are still swayed by outmoded, feudalistic ideas of honor and prestige. . . .

Some thought they were engaged in the fulfilment of a divine mission to abolish slavery, to spread the gospel, to clothe and educate the heathen. Others thought they were protecting the new markets from dangerous competitors, securing their supplies of raw materials, or finding new fields for investment. But underlying the whole imperial outlook there was certainly more than a little misapprehension of economics, much self-delusion and self-righteousness, much misapplication of evolutionary teaching and above all much of the hoary tradition of honour, prestige, power and even plain combativeness. . . .

We shall not go far wrong, then, if we stress the psychological and political factors in imperialism as well as its economic and intellectual elements. It was, of course, connected closely with the great changes in the social structure of the western world, but it was also a projection of nationalism beyond the boundaries of Europe, a projection on a world scale of the time-honored struggle for power and a balance of power as it had existed on the Continent for centuries. The most casual perusal of the literature of imperialism will reveal the continued potency of these atavistic motives. . . .[2]

These and similar arguments raise two closely related questions which are critical for explanations of imperialism based on public opinion. First, how can one account for the alleged extreme nationalism of the last quarter of the nineteenth century, whose existence is fundamental to any theory of mass imperialism? Second, if this nationalism in fact existed, can it be demonstrated that it generated popular demands for imperial expansion, especially in the critical early years before 1890, which in turn galvanized the statesmen into action? These questions will be considered in turn.

Surveying the historiography of modern imperialism one sees a large number of conflicting hypotheses which attempt to account for the emergence of a popular nationalism which expressed itself in demands for overseas empire in the half century before 1914, each of which derives from a distinct interpretation of the character of European society. First, there is the atavistic explanation referred to by Langer, which was formulated by the economist J. A. Schumpeter in his famous essay *The Sociology of Imperialism*, first published in 1919.[3] In his view imperialism was not the product of new economic, social or political developments in Europe but the expression of an age-old 'objectless disposition on the part of the state to unlimited frontier expansion'.[4] In the modern state this disposition was not, as Lenin argued, the product of advanced capitalism, but of the surviving 'feudal substance' of pre-capitalist Europe which had fused with bourgeois-capitalism and foisted its own traditional concern with power and prestige on to the notionally peace-loving bourgeois. Imperialism would therefore end only when the 'pre-capitalist' elements in social life finally disappeared.

By contrast, others have alleged that advanced capitalism itself generated a new emotional enthusiasm for empire, particularly among the commercial bourgeoisie. Hilferding, typifying orthodox neo-Marxist thought, held that finance capital ceased to be peace-loving whenever the momentum of its overseas economic drive was obstructed by pre-capitalist societies. At this point the bourgeois discarded his conventional liberal pacificism and appealed to government to overcome indigenous resistance to his trade and investment. To justify this *volte-face* the bourgeois adopted the ideology of race and claimed the 'natural' right of his own advanced society to dominate the backward peoples of other continents. In this way popular imperialism based on racialism was an organic product of economic change.[5]

Somewhat similar arguments were produced by Hobson and other British liberals in the early twentieth century. The main difference was that, believing in the continuing rationality of the bulk of society, they claimed that popular opinion was deliberately corrupted through the cheap press by those who had a vested interest in imperial expansion. Popular imperialism, though a potent force, was therefore the product of a confidence trick played by capitalists in alliance with others with non-economic interests in colonization – soldiers, missionaries, proconsuls and jingoistic politicians. It could be dissipated by proper re-education of mass opinion.[6]

Most other interpretations of imperialism as an emotional or ideological phenomenon fall into two main categories: those which treat it as the product of intensified nationalism and those which explain it as the outcome of new theories of race.

The first and more pragmatic hypothesis is that after about 1870 pre-existing popular nationalism turned outwards and focused its ambitions on Africa and Asia. The putative reasons for this varied in each country. In Germany and Italy nationalists had achieved their aim of a unified ethnic state and instinctively looked for new worlds to conquer to increase national self-assurance. The United States, which had achieved its 'manifest destiny' by occupying the continent from sea to sea and had also surmounted the threat to internal unity, developed similar instincts in the 1890s. In France, on the other hand, nationalism expressed the determination of many patriots to rebuild national prestige and self-esteem after the disasters of 1870–1. Since war on the Rhine was for the moment inconceivable, success had to be looked for against weaker enemies in other continents. Even Britain, regarded on the continent as the least bellicose state of the mid-nineteenth century, was stimulated to assert herself overseas to match the exploits of others.[7]

Parallel with this simple 'nationalist' hypothesis is a more sophisticated theory based on the growth of racism. A striking feature of the late nineteenth century, it has been argued, was the growing belief that Europeans were racially – that is, genetically and culturally – superior to all other races. This belief stemmed partly from uncritical observation of the advantages Europeans possessed over contemporary societies in other continents in terms of technology, forms of government, social organization, etc.; partly from the growing influence among the educated of neo-Darwinian theories relating to social evolution. On these foundations a number of quasi-scientific hypotheses were publicized which for the most part fall into two categories: those which held that the principle of natural selection made the conquest of inferior peoples necessary to provide the element of struggle necessary to maintain the quality of the 'higher' races; and those which propounded the moral duty of the superior race to accept a 'civilizing mission' to the lower.

Either way, imperialism was consistent with the laws of nature as revealed by modern genetics.[8]

There are, then, a wide range of contrasting explanations of why popular demand for overseas expansion should have developed and dictated public policy in Western Europe in the later nineteenth century. How much weight should be attached to them? It would be impossible in this brief survey to measure the relative influence of each alleged source of popular imperialism; and fortunately this is quite unnecessary. The important question is not why such ideological movements developed but whether they can be shown to have had a measurable influence on the course of events. If this influence is to be demonstrated, evidence is required on at least two main points: first, that for whatever reason public demand for empire was strong before the rapid expansion of the 1880s began; second, that those statesmen with whom the power of decision rested were either persuaded or enabled by public enthusiasm to act where otherwise they might not have acted. It is, of course, harder to demonstrate a causal relationship of this kind than to allege that it must have existed. Conversely, it is difficult to prove that it did not exist. At most the historian can make a broad assessment of the general credibility of such theories by applying two tests. The first is chronological: were popular imperialist movements powerful and influential at the appropriate time? The second is causal: to examine the circumstances of any particular territorial annexation overseas and to discover how much influence popular opinion appears actually to have had. Of these the second is undoubtedly the more conclusive, just as detailed investigation of individual cases is the only true test of any all-embracing Eurocentric theory of imperialism; and where the evidence is adequate an attempt will be made in the later parts of the book to measure the impact of public demand on official policy. As a preliminary test it is proposed merely to survey the chronology of imperialist movements to see whether and where they might be expected to constitute a significant historical force.

In most states of Western Europe there was a substantial time-lag between the construction and propagation of imperialist ideologies or arguments by a handful of enthusiasts and the point at which these seem to have had any wide support; and this fact has misled some historians working from literary evidence to antedate popular imperialism as a significant force. In Germany some nationalist writers were urging colonization in the 1870s. Colonial societies date from 1878 and by 1884 there were five of some importance. In 1887 two of them – the German Colonial Association (Kolonialverein) and the Society for German Colonization – merged to form the German Colonial Society (Deutsche Kolonial-gesellschaft) which thereafter remained the most influential imperialist pressure group in Germany. All these groups issued intensive propaganda, and the Colonial Society's journal, the *Kolonial zeitung*, was particularly influential. The societies were, moreover, closely connected with National Liberal and Free Conservative parties in the Reichstag who, though in a minority, were politically important. By 1884 it is in fact clear that imperialist propaganda was having considerable success. Thus in May 1884 the British Ambassador in Berlin told Lord Granville that there was 'a growing impatience' among the electorate 'for the inauguration of a colonial policy by Prince Bismarck';[9] and in December the London *Globe* stated that:

> So deeply are the people imbued with a vague but nonetheless enticing vision of the wealth to be won in Africa that thousands of young men are longing and waiting for an opportunity to see their fortune in the new El Dorado.[10]

These enthusiasms, translated into political calculations, may have influenced Bismarck's decision to acquire colonies in 1884, as has been suggested above. Other expansionist societies developed later, notably the Navy League and the Pan-German League, and these could exert pressure on the government through the Kolonialrat, a nominated advisory council set up in 1890. In principle, therefore, German colonial enthusiasts, however few in number, were institutionally prepared to influence official policy from the early 1880s; and it is at least possible that the adoption of a German colonial policy in 1884 was the product of their pressure.

French publicists also began to preach imperialist doctrines in the 1870s and achieved a considerable public.[11] But organized pressure groups were slower to develop and until 1890 the geographical societies were the only collective expression of popular enthusiasm for expansion. The Comité de l'Afrique Française founded in 1890, was the first specifically colonial pressure group and was followed by similar committees for Asia, Morocco, Oceania and Madagascar after 1900. The Union Coloniale Française had meantime been set up in 1893 to co-ordinate the activities of all groups with substantive interests in the colonies and to disseminate propaganda. These bodies had considerable influence in the 1890s and thereafter, but they were obviously formed too late to have influenced French policy in the first and vital decade of expansion which began about 1880. During this period there were a number of deputies in the Chamber who generally supported 'forward' policies, but they were not organized in any way until 1892, when the new 'colonial group', which cut across all normal political lines, was said to number 91 in a house of 596. A short conclusion on France might therefore be that, in the words of T. F. Power,

When Ferry embarked on his colonial schemes, there was no organized colonial propaganda movement. Only a few publicists and academic writers without a following called for an empire. Colonial societies and their periodicals were rapidly appearing, but their weight was felt only in the succeeding decade. [12]

In Britain there is even less evidence of a strong popular imperialism before, at the earliest, the 1890s. All established imperialist organizations, such as the Royal Colonial Institute and the Imperial Federation League, were exclusively concerned to strengthen links with the existing settlement colonies, and showed little interest in the possibilities of new tropical dependencies. There was no organized or vocal colonialist group in Parliament and the public seemed profoundly indifferent. Public interest became evident only from about 1894, and then it was a spasmodic reaction to specific overseas issues rather than a consistent expression of nationalist or racialist idealism.

It would be possible to make similar assessments of the chronology of popular imperialism in other countries which were involved in colonial expansion. Conditions varied, yet the broad pattern is much the same. The common experience is that imperialism began as an emotive idea emanating from intellectual commitments on issues which commonly had nothing to do with overseas colonization. In the 1870s and 1880s a combination of external developments attracted the attention and excited the imagination of a small minority of European intellectuals and bourgeois, who in due course established small societies to promote their ideas. In the 1880s, however, they were too few and too politically ineffective to be able to force any government to initiate a colonial policy, though in the special political circumstances of Germany in 1884 their influence on the National Liberal Party may have affected Bismarck's decision to acquire German protectorates. For the most part their role was to give vociferous support to 'forward' policies when these were proposed by governments or to denounce what they regarded as a weak betrayal of national interests when governments refused to take a strong line. Genuine popular enthusiasm for empire as such only became evident in the 1890s and thereafter, and even so it remained spasmodic and unpredictable. In short, the case for regarding the imperialism of the masses as the genesis or driving force behind modern imperialism is inherently weak. It would be far more accurate to say that imperialism as a state of the popular mind was a shadow cast by the events of imperial expansion than that empire was the product of the imperial idea.

III   PERIPHERAL EXPLANATIONS OF IMPERIALISM

All explanations of European expansion so far considered have three common features. All were 'Eurocentric' in that they concentrated on problems and ideas within Europe and North America. All treated imperialism as a positive phenomenon: Europe deliberately acquired new colonies because she needed or wanted them. Finally, the problem was considered in the restricted context of the last quarter of the nineteenth century. Excluding Schumpeter's atavistic theory, all assumed that expansion occurred when it did because of the special character of this period, so that there was little or no continuity in the history of European imperialism before and after the 1870s.

Preliminary analysis has, however, suggested that these theories were in some degree defective precisely because of their preoccupation with Europe and the fact that they ignored longer-term historical trends. In terms of geography it was seen that in almost every case a theory based on European needs or attitudes was only viable if it took account of conditions on the periphery. As two historians have put the point in relation to Africa:

> Scanning Europe for the causes, the theorists of imperialism have been looking for the answers in the wrong places. The crucial changes that set all working took place in Africa itself.[13]

But Eurocentric theories were almost equally weak in terms of chronology. Even the most superficial examination of the imperialist process indicates that it is unwise to look for the explanation of events during the so-called 'age of imperialism' merely within the short period of time after about 1880, and this suggests that the apparent discontinuity of the historical process may be an illusion.

Dissatisfaction with these aspects of conventional explanations of late nineteenth-century European expansion is a logical reason for attempting to construct alternative hypotheses which avoid their defects by concentrating on developments on the periphery and which take a longer-term view of trends. But such an approach is not a mere *pis aller*. Any historian who begins a study of colonial history by examining evidence in the one-time colonies rather than in the archives of Europe would find it natural to regard European expansion as the product of peripheral rather than metropolitan developments.[14] How far this approach will serve varies from one region to another. In some cases what Cecil Rhodes called 'the imperial factor' became significant only at the end of the story, when a European government had to give its formal sanction to acts initiated by men on the periphery. In others Europe became directly involved at an early stage. But always the impression is that formal colonization was a response to situations which evolved far from Europe and beyond effective metropolitan control. This is a far cry from theories of imperialism in which the future colonies are regarded as lay figures in a drama which centres on the banks, warehouses, chanceries or hustings of Europe.

There would seem, therefore, to be a strong case for approaching the problem of modern imperialism from the standpoint of problems developing outside Europe and on the assumption that colonization may have constituted a response by the metropolitan powers to external stimuli rather than the expression of economic or other problems within Europe. Since this approach is generally adopted in the rest of this book it will be convenient by way of introduction to indicate some of the characteristic trends and situations on the periphery which demanded some form of action by European states. But one reservation must be made. By definition peripheral explanations are a residual category. Because they deal in specific events they cannot form the basis for any general theory of imperialism. At most, observation of recurrent patterns may justify the conclusion that since many peripheral problems stemmed from the same broad expansion of European activities they had common features and required similar remedies.

In all regional studies of situations in Africa, Asia and the Pacific which ultimately led to formal European rule during or after the nineteenth century the underlying theme is that a fundamental change took place in the relations between Europeans and other peoples. Such changes took two forms. First, the partial or total insulation of other places from Europe was ended. Second, the power relationship between Europeans and other peoples changed dramatically. These processes occurred simultaneously and stemmed from the same roots. Together they generated the peripheral problems from which European empires eventually grew.

During the nineteenth century Europe at last breached the geographical limits of its influence during the previous three centuries. European exploration, trade and settlement had expanded spectacularly since the fifteenth and sixteenth centuries, yet huge areas of the world remained unaffected and largely unknown until the nineteenth century. To some extent this was the result of deliberate choice, but far more of technical factors – the relative inefficiency of sailing ships for long-distance bulk carriage, the small marginal advantage provided by European armaments, problems of health in tropical climates, and so on. During the early nineteenth century these obstacles to European expansion were removed by economic, technical and political developments within Europe. In non-technical terms it can be said that in this period Europe underwent a 'power revolution' which had no complement in other civilizations. This was most obvious in technology and industry. In about 1750 Europe possessed practically no industrial or technical advantages over producers in the more sophisticated Asian countries. A century later this was no longer true. Mechanization of production had given the European manufacturer an immense advantage in quality and price. The evolution of the heavy iron and steel industry had revolutionized machinery and armaments and was affecting ship construction. The steam engine both contributed to industrial efficiency and provided motive power for railways and ships, thus stimulating a revolution in the means of transport. At the same time population growth provided a labour force for expanding industry and a reservoir of potential emigrants. In some states there was a comparable improvement in the efficiency of government which was reflected in the armed forces and capacity to intervene in distant parts of the world.

This power revolution was bound to affect relations between the industrialized states of Western Europe and the rest of the world. Until other societies adopted the new technology Europe was in a uniquely dominant position. She could penetrate all markets, tap all sources of raw materials and impose her will on all indigenous governments. The vital question was what precise political form the new relationship would take. Would Europe and her existing communities of white colonists be content to exploit the new economic opportunities without also imposing formal political control as had once been done in America and India? Conversely, even if Europeans were content with that degree of 'informal empire' which was inseparable from economic and military predominance, recognizing and co-operating with indigenous governments in Africa and the East, could these unreconstructed states and societies sustain the impact of accelerating European penetration?

In retrospect, of course, the general answers are clear. Though with considerable hesitation, European influence was eventually converted to empire in most, though not all, parts of Africa, Asia and the Pacific. But why did this occur and why in some places and not in others? There are two ways of approaching this question. One is to ask whether 'informal empire' eventually proved unsatisfactory to those in Europe who were active on the periphery, so that these men demanded more complete political control to serve their own economic or other interests. The other is to see whether things broke down at the periphery, so that European governments were pulled in to deal with incipient or actual crises whatever their chosen policy. How can the historian best investigate the facts along these two lines?

To consider first the question of European attitudes to peripheral problems, it is possible that an approach along these lines may make some 'Eurocentric' explanations of imperialism more credible than they would be in the form outlined above. It was seen that a major weakness of such theories was that they specified a positive demand for colonies which is difficult to substantiate. But if cause and effect are inverted and we consider whether imperialism might be a reaction to unsatisfactory conditions on the periphery, any of these hypotheses may make better sense. Thus merchants, who had not previously thought that tropical colonies were particularly valuable for trading purposes, might turn imperialist if and when existing or prospective markets in Africa or Asia were threatened by new obstacles created by indigenous governments or another European state. European capitalists, who took an entirely non-political view of the world's investment potential, might nevertheless demand political action, even colonial rule, if an indigenous government reneged on loans made by European banks. Those engaged on capitalist enterprises overseas might equally welcome the imperial factor if they could not otherwise obtain satisfactory political conditions for plantations, mines and so on. This is very different from saying that merchants and finance capitalists wanted colonies because these were the *sine qua non* for their activities; but it does suggest that business interests might on occasion come to favour formal as opposed to informal empire. Similar considerations may have affected the views of European statesmen or nationalists. Though perhaps not initially enthusiastic about imperial expansion, they might be roused by evidence that changing conditions on the periphery were threatening real or imagined national interests. In short, and without at present evaluating the hypothesis, it may be possible to rehabilitate certain elements in most 'Eurocentric' explanations of imperialism by inverting their assumptions. European imperialism may be explicable as a reaction of merchants, bankers, statesmen and jingoes to changes on the periphery which made it inconvenient or even impossible to preserve 'informal empire' during the last decades of the nineteenth century. An attempt will therefore be made in the last section of this chapter to re-formulate 'Eurocentric' hypotheses along these lines.

The obverse and complement to this modified exposition of European imperialism is to investigate why crises occurred on the periphery and why in some cases they led to alien rule. This, of course, requires detailed examination of each case, and this will be done for select territories in later chapters. It may, nevertheless, clarify the nature of the peripheral approach to imperialism to construct models of three of the more common situations which tended to destroy the existing balance between Europeans and other peoples and possibly lead to full annexation.

COLONIAL SUB-IMPERIALISM. One of the more obvious factors in the extension of formal empire was the tendency of existing European possessions to expand into their environment. Two characteristic situations can be defined, one typical of colonies of European settlement, the other of colonies in which a small minority of Europeans ruled an indigenous society. Settler expansion was as old as European overseas colonization. Any group of emigrants who established an initial settlement on the tidewater of America, South Africa or Australia regarded the hinterland as a providential endowment for its future existence and growth. In the still colonial world the most probable regions for future settler expansion were Australia, Southern and Central Africa, the South Pacific, Southern Siberia and North Africa. During the period covered by this study these tendencies were at the root of many of the problems facing metropolitan governments on the periphery and, as will be seen, were primarily responsible for territorial expansion in these regions. In this respect imperialism may be seen as a classic case of the metropolitan dog being wagged by its colonial tail.

Settler sub-imperialism is an obvious phenomenon. Less obvious was the tendency of almost all European colonies or even small trading bases in Africa and Asia to expand into their environment, irrespective of the needs or wishes of the imperial power. The reasons were as various as the character of the territories: frontier insecurity, real or imagined; the need for more customs revenues from near-by ports; desire to control areas of production or trade routes on which the colonial economy depended; the ambitions or ideals of individual administrators, soldiers, missionaries and other Europeans temporarily employed there. Equally important, it was remarkable that many if not most colonial officials came to see local problems with local rather than metropolitan eyes, responding chameleon-like to the sub-imperialism of the frontier, whatever the established policy of the imperial government. In this way the official mind of the metropolis had its parallel in virtually every petty tropical or sub-tropical dependency, each generating its own form of autochthonous imperialism.

Important though it was as a force making for the extension of formal empire, sub-imperialism in existing European colonies does not exhaust the potential stock of peripheral explanations of imperial expansion. In many cases the key to events lies in analysis of the attitudes of non-Europeans or of the effects of informal European contacts on indigenous societies and governments.

NON-EUROPEAN REACTIONS. A basic weakness of many Eurocentric theories of imperialism is that they treat non-Europeans as lay figures, whereas modern research has emphasized the vast and decisive importance of the way in which indigenous peoples reacted to the intrusion of Europeans and its associated problems. Such reactions are intrinsic to a peripheral approach to European expansion, for in many places it is clear that the main if not the only stimulus to alien occupation and formal rule was the problem of deteriorating relations with non-Europeans. Obviously such problems varied immensely and cannot be reduced to a formula. But to clarify the concept it is proposed to indicate three characteristic situations which, as will be seen in the case studies below, might well eventually lead to the imposition of formal empire by one or other of the European powers.

The first was particularly characteristic of states and societies of considerable political or ideological strength and cohesiveness: for example, most of the Islamic states of the Mediterranean and Middle East, the civilized and sophisticated states of South-East Asia and the stronger 'pagan' states of sub-Saharan Africa. In these regions almost all indigenous states sooner or later reacted strongly against the presence of Europeans, either as intrusive neighbours or as infiltrators demanding political or religious rights. In the Islamic states of North Africa resistance came late, usually after an indigenous ruler had been forced by financial or some other weakness to transfer part of his sovereign power to alien 'advisors', and it then took the form of a xenophobic popular movement or religious *jihad* to throw off foreign interference. In different circumstances comparable resistance occurred in Afghanistan, Turkestan, Burma and Indo-China; and in each case except that of Afghanistan indigenous resistance led ultimately to formal annexation. Conversely many other powerful states, including a number in sub-Saharan Africa, never willingly accepted informal European suzerainty or the need for peaceful coexistence; and in the course of time those which were thought to constitute a danger to the security of near-by European possessions or obstructed European commercial or other objectives were attacked and annexed. Thus, while by no means all indigenous states which resisted European penetration became formal dependencies, resistance was often the prelude to annexation when European interests were of sufficient importance to justify such action.

An alternative reaction to the European presence was to accept and make use of it. Indeed many non-European rulers obtained considerable short-term advantages from alliance with Europeans, acquiring money, guns or political support against indigenous rivals for power or territory in return for collaboration of many kinds. But in the end all such alliances became the kiss of death. Sooner or later the balance of local power turned against those who had treated Europeans as allies and equals. Some rulers found themselves ousted from effective power and used as puppet heads of state in a European protectorate; others were deposed when they tried to end an agreement or stand on their rights. In virtually every case indigenous collaboration ended in alien rule before 1914.

A third consequence of European informal penetration was to be found in weak indigenous states whose political and social systems could not withstand foreign pressure. In many parts of Africa and the Pacific, where political units were small and religions primitive, the presence of small numbers of European traders, planters, missionaries and beachcombers could erode indigenous institutions and social cohesion. Matters were made worse by rivalry between Europeans and by intermittent intervention by European military or naval forces. In the end such places, particularly in the Pacific, frequently reached a state of domestic disintegration which can be described as a 'crack-up'. At this point many rulers asked for formal European protection and in due course this was usually given, sometimes reluctantly, because European governments felt a responsibility both for the welfare of their nationals and for the preservation of the indigenous society. Empire was thus an un-planned product of the chronic disorder caused by informal Euro-pean penetration.

Along these and similar lines it is possible to explain many aspects of European colonization without reference to Eurocentric theories of imperialism. Empire becomes a largely self-generating organism, growing fungus-like from a multiplicity of spawns scattered round the world by the dispersion of an expanding European civilization. This is an attractive line of argument and, as will be seen below, contains substantial elements of truth. Yet two reservations must be made. First, while peripheral factors may well have been the genesis of most problems from which formal annexation actually grew, the decision to resolve these problems by formal annexation had ultimately to be taken in the metropolitan capital. In the last resort, therefore, the historian must turn back to examine the working of the official mind in Europe as it reacted to problems flowing in from the frontiers. Second, the time factor must be considered. Many of the tendencies indicated above existed long before the 1880s. Why did the climax come during the following two decades rather than before or later and why did it simul-taneously affect territories so widely different in place and circum-stance? Clearly all these peripheral developments were in some sense pulled into a single historical pattern at some period in the later nineteenth century; otherwise one could not legitimately speak of imperialism as a collective phenomenon. The onus is therefore on the historian who starts his investigation at the periphery to demonstrate how and why this happened; and again he must turn to Europe to discover why the rulers of different states should have decided to solve so many disparate questions in much the same way at the same time.

IV ECONOMIC AND OTHER EXPLANATIONS OF IMPERIALISM: A REFORMULATION

What, in the light of this brief survey of contrasting economic, political, ideological and peripheral explanations of nineteenth-century imperialism, is the most rewarding approach for the economic historian? A preliminary conclusion must be that, while none of these can stand alone as a 'total' explanation of so complex a process, each contains elements of truth. The need is clearly for a synthesis which, on the principle that correct answers flow only from proper questions, can be used as the starting point for an investigation of the precise relationship between economics and the construction of empire. It will be convenient to start with a brief recapitulation of the elements of strength and weakness evident in the two conventional economic explanations of imperialism and then to consider whether their deficiencies might be remedied by grafting on concepts deriving from political, ideological or peripheral explanations.

It was suggested in chapters 2 and 3 that the paradox of theories of imperialism based on trade or capital investment was that, while one might logically have predicted substantial appropriation of overseas territory on the basis of established economic trends after about 1880, the lines of historical causation seldom ran in a logical direction. On the one hand cyclical depressions coupled with rising tariff walls in Europe and the United States might well have stimulated merchants to demand new tropical colonies both as safe markets and as sources of cheap raw materials; while on the other hand fear of declining interest rates coupled with overproduction within trustified and protected economies was quite likely to result in larger overseas investment and concomitant acquisitions of territory to buttress productive enterprises. Yet the preliminary evidence on these basic metropolitan trends suggests that these expectations were seldom fulfilled in this precise form. European merchants showed singularly little desire for new colonies in Africa or Asia as substitute markets, but they did demand preservation of the 'open door' in independent states wherever it was threatened. For their part statesmen for long saw no necessary connection between tariff protection and colonialism, and only constructed ingenious hypotheses to link the two as cause and effect after a decade of active colonization. Investors also seemed largely blind to the potential advantages of formal colonies in the less-developed regions. With few exceptions they had previously placed no large capital sums in those territories which were subsequently annexed by European powers; and they remained notoriously reluctant to invest in colonies after annexation unless some special opportunity for profit occurred or governments guaranteed minimum profits. Yet at the same time banks, speculative companies and private investors were pouring money into the sovereign states of Europe and into a number of long-established colonial dependencies. If the new empires were built to save capitalism from the stagnation expected to accompany its maturity, they therefore proved singularly unhelpful.

Seen, then, as an expression of the needs of the European economy, territorial imperialism becomes largely irrelevant. But this does not necessarily invalidate an economic approach to imperialism. Seen as a peripheral factor in relation to specific places and events the case is quite different. The economic imperialism typical of European trade and investment created the 'semi-colonies' or 'commercial colonies' described by Lenin: yet territorial empire might still be a product of European economic activity at a micro-economic level. The copra plantations of Samoa mattered little to German industry or the investment banks, but they were important both to particular German trading firms and to Pacific islanders. British prosperity did not depend on palm oil from the Niger delta, but merchant firms in Liverpool stood to lose substantially if their trade there was obstructed by monopolistic African rulers or European rivals. The bankruptcy of an Islamic state in North Africa would not cause panic in the London and Paris money markets, but if it happened the governments of both countries would be under pressure from bond-holders to take remedial action, and intervention on their behalf might well have far-reaching consequences in Cairo, Tunis or Fez. It is at this level that one may reasonably expect to find evidence that economic factors affected European attitudes to the less-developed world of the late nineteenth century and it is quite conceivable that intrinsic-ally very small economic enterprises and parochial problems might have a disproportionate influence on the pattern of events.

This, at least, is the approach to be adopted in the following chapters. Reversing the conventional order of investigation, an attempt will be made in each overseas country considered in the case studies to analyse evidence indicating that existing or projected European economic interests may have been relevant to the ultimate decision by a European power to impose formal rule. It is at this point that specifically economic factors have to be related to other aspects of the policy-making process, the attitude of public opinion and the criteria of the official mind. This, indeed, is the hinge of historical interpretation and the main preoccupation of this book. It is one thing to demonstrate that some economic interest was at stake in some crisis on the periphery, but quite another to show that this was the main or sole determinant of official policy. To measure the balance of forces it is essential to expose the linkages through which the micro-economic problem exerted leverage on policy-making at the highest level. It is, in fact, deceptively easy to assume that when such leverage was exerted it would normally succeed. Hobson, for example, claimed that 'finance' could always exert the necessary influence in 'high politics', either directly or through 'the control which they exercise over the body of public opinion through the press. . . .'[15] Lenin equally assumed that finance capital-ists were so closely integrated with the bureaucracy, particularly in Germany, that state policy would automatically be adjusted to serve their interests.[16] Was this so? And if not invariably so, under what circumstances would a European government dance when the merchants or investors piped? Since the purpose of this intro-ductory section of the book is to pose questions rather than to answer them, it is proposed at this point merely to pinpoint the essential problem which this question poses in the form of a syl-logism whose first two propositions are based on a generalized view of the characteristic attitudes of mid-nineteenth-century Euro-pean statesmen and officials as outlined above.

(1) Use of force or formal annexation of territory overseas by a European state was a political action which, by mid-nineteenth-century convention, should only have been used to solve essentially political problems of direct importance to the nation as a whole and not to further private and non-political interests.

(2) Economic problems in the non-European world had no necessary connection with politics and, it was assumed, should have been and normally were dealt with by appropriate economic means, not including formal annexation of territory.

(3) When, therefore, armed force or formal annexation of territory was used in connection with what appear to have been fundamentally economic problems overseas, it is reasonable to assume that one of two things has happened: either that the metropolitan state had changed its attitude to such questions; or that essentially economic problems had become in some way political problems requiring a political solution.

It is not proposed at this point to elaborate or evaluate these simple propositions. They may or may not prove accurate when tested against the facts. But they do at least suggest that the fundamental question to be asked about economic imperialism can be re-formulated in the following terms: under what circumstances, in Europe or on the periphery, were European governments in the period 1830–1914 prepared to use political methods to solve economic problems? The function of the following chapters is to provide evidence for answering this question which will be reviewed in the concluding chapter.

Part Two
Case Studies in European
Expansion, 1830-80

5   *The Roots of European Expansion in the Nineteenth Century*

*I*t has been suggested above that the starting point and common denominator of most accepted interpretations of European imperialism in the period after about 1880 is the assumption that this was a 'new' phenomenon, representing a significant discontinuity in the historical process. As a result most historians have looked for new forces differentiating the later period from the mid-century, and almost all have found them within European society. Conversely, if this alleged discontinuity could be shown to be an illusion, the problem to be investigated would change. Continuity might, in fact, be shown in one of two ways. In terms of geography it might become evident that annexations occurring near the end of the century were the direct outcome not of immediate but of long-term factors in a particular place stretching back half a century or more. Alternatively, on a general view of developments throughout the world, it might be shown that the same economic or other forces were operating before as well as after about 1880. In either case the problem to be solved in the last years of the century would be sensibly altered. Imperialism would cease to be a unique phenomenon, presumably the product of a special phase of European evolution, and could be seen as part of the secular trends of modern history. The 'new imperialism' would then be different in degree but not in kind from what went before, and the historian could stop searching for first causes special to the post-1880 era. It is the function of this and the next three chapters to examine the half century before about 1880, for evidence on this point.

The essential point is that during this half century very substantial areas were annexed or brought under effective political control by European states, and the most important of these may be listed briefly to define the scope of the problem. In Mediterranean Africa, France occupied the coastal region of Algeria and was expanding into the Sahara. In West Africa, France was consolidating control in Senegal and extending her influence over the near-by coastline, while Britain retained a number of small possessions, annexed Lagos and extended informal control over adjacent coastal areas. The most striking developments were in southern Africa, where settlers under British control or suzerainty had occupied most of the region south of the Limpopo. Elsewhere, in Equatorial and East Africa, however, despite strong informal British influence in Zanzibar and Anglo-French influence in Madagascar there was little evidence of European territorial advance, and the future appeared to lie with other imperialists, Arabs, Ethiops and Egyptians.

The most spectacular achievements of mid-nineteenth-century Europe were, in fact, in Asia and the South Pacific. Within the Indian sub-continent a number of independent states were incorporated into British India, while on the north-western and eastern frontiers Punjab, Sind, Assam, Arakan, Tenasserim, Manipur and Lower Burma were annexed. In Central Asia, Russia annexed the Kazakh steppes and the Islamic khanates of Turkestan, and in the Far East she acquired Amur and the Ussuri region. In South-East Asia the British established Singapore and acquired Malacca from the Dutch; the Dutch greatly expanded their effective control within the Indonesian Archipelago; and the French established themselves in Cochin China and Cambodia. In the Far East the British took Hong Kong. In the South Pacific they extended their control over the whole of Australia, and annexed New Zealand and Fiji, while the French took Tahiti, the Marquesas and New Caledonia.

Even so short an enumeration of the main European colonial acquisitions of the period 1830–80 places the imperialism of the *fin de siècle* in a different light. Why did the empires grow in the mid-Victorian period? Was it due to any or all of the forces alleged to have operated after 1880 – the strategic planning of statesmen, the export of capital, the needs of commerce, the enthusiasm of the masses, problems on the periphery? The answers are, of course, almost as diverse as the territories involved. Yet there were inevitably common forces at work and the rest of this chapter will consist of a short analysis of the most important of these as they appear to have existed in about 1830, following the same distinction between 'Eurocentric' and 'peripheral' factors as was used in earlier chapters.

On past evidence the most likely Eurocentric motives for further colonial expansion after about 1830 fall into three categories: political objectives relating to strategy or diplomacy; economic objectives, including trade, emigration and investment; and spiritual objectives characteristic of missionary enterprise. Conversely, there was no precedent for large-scale popular demand for colonies on grounds of national prestige and no evidence of this in the second quarter of the nineteenth century. Attention will therefore be restricted to the other three categories.

Until perhaps 1815 the strictly political aspect of imperialism had been almost continually significant. From the sixteenth century statesmen had favoured colonies which provided bases from which to attack foreign rivals or which dominated important sea routes, and had used war and peace negotiations to acquire what they thought necessary. Colonies had also been used as cards at the peace tables, particularly from about 1700. But after 1815 conditions were different, Britain and France were now the only major powers with overseas colonies. So long as these states were on good terms – which was the consistent aim of both from 1830 until at least the 1870s – colonies were seldom a matter of political contention between them. If local issues arose, as in the 1840s, statesmen in both countries were quick to ensure that no damage was done to the entente. Of the other European powers only Russia had any possible political interest in the overseas possessions of others, and potential conflicts with her were limited to the common frontiers of India and Turkestan. For European diplomacy as a whole colonies were totally irrelevant, for the issues of interest to the major continental powers – France, Prussia, Austria and Russia – were still confined to continental affairs, the Mediterranean and the Ottoman Empire. The patterns of diplomacy contrived to deal with these last two areas were, indeed, to be the model on which the powers ultimately dealt with colonial questions in Africa and elsewhere; but before 1880 these distant regions lay outside the orbit of European political relationships. Thus there was no reason in the second quarter of the century to expect that the statesmen of Europe would adopt empire-building projects as a means of increasing the power of the parent state.

At a different level, however, the rulers of the maritime powers recognized a general duty to assist their nationals when engaged in legitimate enterprises overseas, and in particular to promote trade. This obligation had limits. It did not extend to active official intervention in business affairs, nor to guarantees of private contracts or loans. But the states recognized a responsibility to make commercial treaties providing the most favourable conditions for their nationals and to support bond-holders and others who had legitimate grievances against foreign governments, especially where governmental agreements or principles of international law were involved: in short, to ensure that merchants and investors had equal opportunities with foreign rivals.[1] Pursuit of these limited but important objectives would certainly involve repeated official intervention, but seldom military or naval action and still less frequently formal territorial control. British naval power might be used on occasion to protect the rights of British subjects in the period 1830–80 (in the Argentine in 1845, in Greece in 1850, in Mexico in 1861); but the only important occasion on which British naval power was used to deal with an issue falling outside these accepted limits of state action was against China in 1839–42, and this resulted in the annexation of Hong Kong. French naval power was used similarly against Cochin China in 1847 and 1858 in support of Catholic missions, and this also led to permanent occupation of territory in 1862. But these were exceptions. In general the maritime powers expected only to police treaties and agreements with non-European countries, to enforce international policies such as anti-slaving conventions, and in general to provide support for their nationals. This was political imperialism of a sort and might lead to further territorial involvement but it was not part of a project for building empires.

By 1830 there were four other specifically European forces making for greater European involvement overseas and therefore possibly for territorial expansion: Christian missions, emigration, trade and capital investment. These must be considered briefly as potential empire-building forces.

Christian missions were possibly the most characteristic of all forms of European enterprise in Africa, Asia and the East during this period. Stemming from the resurgence of all Christian churches in the early nineteenth century, they expressed at once a new or revived belief in Europe's civilizing mission and the new wealth that could support so vast an enterprise. By the 1830s there was a considerable number of missionary societies of all creeds and sects in Europe and America. One of the earliest was set up by a Lutheran sect, later called the Moravian mission. British societies included the London Missionary Society (mainly Congregational), the Society for the Propagation of the Gospel and the Church Missionary Society (both Anglican), the Methodist Missionary Society, and the Scottish Presbyterian Mission. Other Protestant societies were founded in Europe early in the nineteenth century, notably the Swiss Basel Society, and the Berlin Society. Roman Catholic organizations soon followed their lead. Some missions were created specifically for missionary work, such as the French Congregation of the Holy Ghost and later the White Fathers; others were set up by existing orders – Benedictines, Franciscans, Jesuits and Dominicans. In 1830 the missionary frontier overseas had barely formed and there was little penetration in depth; but during the next forty years the missions were to penetrate virtually every part of Africa, Asia and the Pacific. Their importance as a conduit for European influence is undoubted, but it is more difficult to assess their importance as a force making for territorial empire. Most mission headquarters in Europe had no desire to build secular empires and some deliberately opposed intervention by the metropolis or its settlers in their spheres of activity. Yet situations might arise in which the success or survival of a mission might depend on official support against an indigenous government or a rival mission. At this point the missionary society in London, Paris, Berlin or Washington might turn imperialist, demanding naval support or even outright annexation. Such demands were rare, though in Tahiti and Cochin China at least they were a significant factor leading to French annexation. But it was far more common for local missions rather than their metropolitan headquarters to think in terms of political control; and missionary imperialism can therefore best be considered as a peripheral rather than a Eurocentric factor.

It remains to consider the three economic and social forces – emigration, trade and capital investment – as possible empire-building forces. Emigration was predictably the strongest of these, for the first empires in America had been built by emigrants who almost invariably claimed the right to fly the national flag wherever they established colonies. In the nineteenth century new colonies were not required to accommodate the vast and expanding flood of emigrants from Britain, Germany, Italy and other parts of Europe, for the United States and Latin America stood open to receive them and offered the nearest and most attractive haven. Nevertheless by 1830 it was evident that some Britons at least were likely to emigrate to other regions that offered temperate climates and ample land, and in Britain there were strong supporters of planned emigration as a solution or palliative to problems of unemployment and pauperism, notably Wilmot Horton and E. G. Wakefield. In the 1820s a small stream of settlers was going to Canada, the Cape, and Australia, and in the next decade this was stimulated by colonizing companies in South Australia, Western Australia and New Zealand. In each case such corporate action led ultimately to formal action by the British government and creation of a new colony. There were limits to the possible extension of this process, for few other regions of the world were both suitable and open for white settlement; and in fact no important new settlement colonies were established after between 1840 and 1880, though Algeria and Tunis both attracted settlers. But it has been seen that the possibility of settler coloniza-tion excited imperialists in Germany and Italy during this period, and for Britain at least emigration must be regarded as a major Eurocentric force making for colonization.

In 1830 the empire-building propensity of trade and capital investment was as unpredictable as that of the missions. Trade with the tropics was, of course, as old as European contacts with Africa and the East, but in the past its effects had varied widely. Broadly, where trade could be carried on with indigenous societies as safely and profitably as within the European economic system, traders were seldom interested in political control; but when conditions were adverse or where trading commodities could only be produced by European penetration of a territory, trade had often led to formal occupation. In the 1830s the immediate prospect was that trade could expand immensely in most areas without generating formal control by Europe. The Americas were now open, as independent states, to international trade. India and other British possessions also were open to foreign traders by 1833. The Dutch had been induced to open the Netherlands Indies to foreign ships. Conditions on the coasts of Africa and South-East Asia and in the Pacific varied greatly, but very few indigenous societies closed the door to Europeans. Only China and Japan, the first partially, the second completely, refused access to foreigners. Thus, while political support might be invoked by traders against hostile local rulers or rival Europeans, the characteristic demand of the early Victorian merchants was for the 'open door', equality of opportunity and possibly a few small trading or refuelling bases from which to operate in distant regions. In rare instances such demands might lead to war and annexation of territory, as in the case of China in 1839–42. But this was exceptional. In most parts of the world conditions would have to change substantially before many merchants felt a need for formal annexation of the areas in which they traded. The question is whether this point has been reached by the 1870s in any part of the independent world.

In comparison with the commodity trades, overseas investment of European capital was relatively new in 1830 and its long-term effects therefore even more unpredictable. During the previous three centuries most of the capital required by new settler communities had either been taken overseas by the settlers or by short-lived colonizing companies, or had been accumulated after colonization from savings. Even in the East most of the capital used by trading companies was built up locally from trading profits, taxation or rapine. The British West Indies came closest to being colonies of metropolitan investment. Even so the large share of capital assets in the plantations owned by residents in Britain resulted from the amortization of short-term planters' debts and the return of successful planters to live in Britain rather than from deliberate export or capital. But in the early nineteenth century, as the rate of capital accumulation in Europe grew, long-term capital investment overseas became more common, particularly by Britain and France. For the most part this took the form either of loans made by banks or investment companies to the governments of Europe, the United States and Latin America or of enterprises established in these countries by local or expatriate companies who raised capital on the metropolitan money market. These forms of capital export remained dominant throughout the nineteenth century and were largely irrelevant to imperial expansion. But by the 1830s European finance was extending its range of activities beyond the limits of the 'civilized' world. Loans were made to Islamic governments in the Mediterranean. Speculative enterprises, ranging from plantations to railway construction, were established by Europeans in countries outside European political control. These forms of capital export were prone to lead to demands for political action by the metropolis if things went wrong and it will

E

be necessary to discover whether such demands were a significant factor making for colonial expansion before about 1880.

Reviewing the probabilities in about 1830, however, there seemed little reason to expect that specifically European activities, other than emigration to 'new' lands, would generate large-scale formal colonization. Intellectual trends, influenced by the classical economists and the revolt of American colonies, were hostile to imperialism. The rule books of the official mind largely excluded it. Traders, missionaries and investors did not require it as a pre-condition for their activities. Only emigrants expected the flag to follow them as a matter of course, and in this period settler coloniza-tion was regarded as a specifically English activity. From a European point of view, therefore, imperialism seemed largely a thing of the past, sloughed off with the aggressive mercantilism of the Ancien Régime.

But, if the viewpoint is shifted to the periphery, all the evidence of past centuries suggested that empire-building would occur on the existing frontiers of European control irrespective of the wishes and interests of the old world. In chapter 4 it was suggested that, whatever the attitude of a metropolitan government or society, almost any European living on or beyond the frontier of 'civilized' government became a compulsive empire-builder. This definition normally excludes transient traders, but might include missionaries, planters, prospectors for minerals, labour recruiters, and above all those two classical imperialists, the European settler and the civilian and military officer in tropical dependencies. It will be seen in the following chapters that by the 1870s all of these groups had made some contribution to imperial expansion; but in 1830 the most confident predictions could have been made about settlers and officials, and it is proposed briefly to surve the predictable lines of advance stemming from these two forms of sub-imperialism in each main geographical area.

In its purest classical form of the moving frontier of settlement, settler sub-imperialism could best be seen in 1830 in Canada and Australia. In each of these vast territories the first nucleus of settlers – far more numerous and better established in Canada – assumed that manifest destiny called them to expand their settlements to the geographical or political limits of their continent. In the case of Canada this meant expansion west to the Pacific and south to whatever line of demarcation Britain could arrange with the Americans. For Australia it meant occupation of the entire continent. Such expansion, though constituting a substantial part of the total colonizing achievement of the mid-Victorian British Empire, does not require detailed consideration if only because it was relatively so predictable and trouble free. Far more interesting and significant for the study of European expansion are the tendencies of Australia and Cape Colony to expand outside their frontiers into regions which were not 'vacant' for settlement and which ultimately caused very considerable imperial problems.

The significance of Australia as a growing point for further European colonization was that by the 1830s the eastern settlements had become the base for several varieties of enterprise in the South Pacific, including whaling, trading and missionary activity. At first these activities on the maritime frontier may have represented metropolitan British rather than colonial forces, for much of the early missionary effort was directed by societies in Britain, and the whaling was stimulated by bounties given by the metropolis to encourage her own long-haul shipping. Yet quite soon the missions came to be financed and run mainly by Australians; whaling and sealing became a local industry; and the trade of the South Pacific and into South-East Asia was developed by Sydney merchants. In fact the history of British enterprise in the South Pacific, beyond mere exploration, derives mainly from the settlement in Australia, for the commercial possibilities of the islands were very limited. The Pacific trade could only be carried on economically by small ships operating on a limited scale. Its products, such as copra and guano, did not attract metropolitan British merchants in the first instance; and European settlement was unlikely to develop until local traders and missionaries had made the first contacts. Thus, from the 1830s until the 1870s and beyond British involvement in the Pacific was primarily a reflection of Australian interests there. The colonization of New Zealand, which Britain formally acquired in 1840, was in the first place the result of problems created by settlers, traders and missionaries from Australia; and the large-scale immigration from Britain which followed in the 1840s was mainly a consequence of these early Australian initiatives. Thereafter these two colonies were increasingly active throughout the South Pacific, and British involvement in Pacific issues during the rest of the century was an unwelcome burden forced upon her by her own colonists. The Pacific was an excellent example of the operation of 'sub-imperialism' in a maritime environment.

In South Africa also the British found by 1830 that the possession of a single small strategic colony of European settlers involved them in undesirable imperial problems and responsibilities. The course of South African history from at least the middle of the eighteenth century had a dynamic which owed nothing to Dutch or British policy. Once a colony had been established there in the early seventeenth century and had survived its initial problems, it was certain that it would eventually expand from the narrow area round the Cape, and the geographical features of South Africa demanded that expansion should take place either along the coast to the North-East, or across the Orange River to the high veld. The nature of the country, which, as in much of Australia, dictated pastoral farming, also made large farms necessary; and this in turn resulted in a remarkably rapid movement by a very small European population. Since movement in either direction was bound in the long run to come against Bantu tribes, it was inevitable that the course of South African history should involve recurrent native wars, and that both the colonial government and its European superior would become involved in the difficult task either of attempting to restrain colonial expansion, or of assisting it with military help. This was the price the British had to pay for the strategic advantage they obtained from the possession of Cape Town and the naval base at Simonstown. It required no positive imperialist motives on their part, nor any new European influence, to produce this expansion and its concomitant problems.

Yet in 1830 India constituted a nucleus for imperial expansion as dynamic as either Australia or the Cape. India had no land-hungry European settlers, and there was no shortage of land for Indians. Expansionist tendencies therefore derived from quite different factors, some political, other commercial. The political factor related primarily to military security. By 1830 there was no external danger from the sea, for the British Navy was now un-challengeable in the Indian Ocean. But on land there were three areas of insecurity. Within the sub-continent there were a number of still powerful Indian states which were linked to Britain only by recent and unreliable treaties. Internal security might well require the further extension of British India at the expense of these Indian princes. More serious dangers existed on the North-East and North-West frontiers. On the eastern borders of Bengal lay the kingdom of Burma, a rival imperialism, whose dynasty had been expanding its territories westwards for half a century. In 1816 Burma had annexed Assam, and regarded Bengal as its next acquisition. In 1823, in apparent ignorance of the military power of a European country, the Burmese attacked the island of Shahpuri, near Chittagong. The result was the First Burmese War, which lasted until 1826. Despite extraordinary British military incompetence the Burmese were defeated and Assam, Cachar, Arakan and Tenasserim, all recent Burmese conquests, were annexed to Bengal. This decision to annex reflected a new British approach to frontier security – defence in depth. But this did not solve the problem and the North-East frontier remained insecure so long as Burma survived as an unreconstructed and politically aggressive neighbour. The search for security was to lead to two further wars and eventually the total annexation of Burma to British India.

In 1830 the North-West frontier seemed even more threatening. No natural frontier defences existed and British power stopped short at the boundaries of the Punjab and Sind. In terms of British security these regions presented contrasting problems. The Punjab was controlled by the Sikh kingdom of Ranjit Singh, which was still strong and a good neighbour. Sind was divided between five Amirs, too weak to be a threat but useless as a buffer against dangers to the West. Beyond both lay Afghanistan. In the 1820s this had been weakened by dynastic struggles for power, but by 1830 Dost Muhammad Khan had emerged as effective ruler of a temporarily weakened country. In these conditions the British faced difficult policy decisions. The problem differed according to whether these frontier states were considered in isolation or as buffer states between British India and the distant power of Russia. In the first case there was the ever-present danger that the indigenous political structure of the Punjab might collapse and the friendly régime of Ranjit Singh be replaced by another and possibly xenophobic one. If this happened the British might find it necessary to annex the region to achieve stability and protect Hindustan. The same might happen in Sind. But such action would not solve the frontier problem as such, for once these areas were annexed, only Afghanistan would lie between British and Russian spheres of influence; and if the frontier was seen in terms of the Russian threat rather than in relation to local disorders, quite different policies might seem necessary.

By about 1830, indeed, Russia was a major preoccupation for British policy both in India and Europe. In the West, Russia obtained a virtual protectorate over Turkey by the Treaty of Unkiar Skelessi in 1833, and this opened up horrifying vistas of Russian naval power in the Mediterranean. By this time also Russia was dominant in Persia, and this brought her to within striking distance of India. In Europe British diplomacy responded by attempting to prop up the Ottoman Empire as a barrier to Russian access to the Mediterranean. The question was whether Afghanistan and the other intermediate states on the North-West frontier of India could be made to serve the same purpose as a buffer against Russian influence. The alternative was for Britain to annex them all in order to create a 'natural' frontier in the mountains. In about 1830 the former policy was still possible for the Punjab and Afghanistan were both viable states not suspected of being under Russian influence, and this remained British policy in the immediate future. But within a decade conditions changed. The death of Ranjit Singh in 1839 produced disorder in the Punjab and attacks on British India which led to annexation. The British lost faith in the neutrality of Afghanistan and attempted unsuccessfully to annex it, occupying Sind in the process as a necessary means of access to the West. Thus the problems of the North-West frontier led almost inexorably to further political advance in pursuit of stability and security.

But India also possessed a maritime frontier which reflected the special interests of commerce based on India rather than of Britain. The 'country trade' with South-East Asia, China and East Africa existed long before British occupation, but had been expanded by the East India Company and by private British merchants operating from Indian ports. With the successive ending of the company's commercial monopoly in India in 1813 and in China in 1833 these firms were free to widen the scope of their operations. Their interest lay in free access to the markets of Malaya, the Archipelago and China; and, although they had no desire for British political control of these areas, political developments which obstructed trade might lead to demands for remedial state action. Here also were potential roots of a creeping sub-imperialism which might extend British influence and possibly territorial possessions in eastern seas.

These were some of the more obvious growing points within the British Empire which, in about 1830, suggested that the frontiers of British control would continue to advance whatever the preferred policy of London might be. But the British were not alone in this respect. The same sub-imperialism was predictable in other imperial systems, wherever Europeans were in direct contact with other less powerful societies. In Central Asia the frontiers between Russian

Siberia and the Islamic regions of Kazakh and Turkestan were in turmoil and there too the search for security coupled with the ambitions of local Russian officers was a potential seed-bed for territorial advance. The same was true in eastern Siberia, where Russian territories shared frontiers with China. In the Dutch East Indies the process of expanding effective control over the Outer Islands had been checked after 1795; but by 1830 the same economic and political forces that had operated in the previous two centuries might be expected to draw the Dutch into ever-increasing occupation of territories within their sphere of influence. In varying degrees the same tendencies could be expected in many other parts of the world where European possessions survived from the holocaust of the early colonial systems.

It was from these peripheral situations rather than from the needs or ambitions of the states of Europe that colonial expansion might most credibly have been expected to grow in the half-century after about 1830; and the following three chapters will examine in some detail the way in which these forces actually operated in a number of these territories. Two general questions must be borne in mind throughout. First, what was the driving force behind expansion – European or peripheral, political, spiritual or economic? Second, what were the probable consequences of earlier trends for further developments after about 1880? Such questions are, indeed, critical for a correct interpretation of the 'new imperialism', for they make it possible to isolate those factors already working in the mid-nineteenth century from others which were new in the latter period. At the same time they indicate whether the continuing trends were primarily economic in character. From this starting point it should eventually be possible to construct a valid interpretation of the real character of late nineteenth-century European imperialism.

6 Africa

The paradox of African history during the half-century before 1880 is that, while the maps reflect remarkably little expansion of European territory, this was in fact the period when forces which were to result in partition of the continent in the following twenty years were gestating. Two questions have therefore to be considered. First, how can one account for such territorial expansion of European empire as did occur before about 1880? Second, what forces were tending towards the further extension of alien rule by the end of the period, particularly if one discounts possible new needs or impulses arising within Europe? In considering these questions a 'peripheral' approach will be adopted and emphasis will be placed on the role of economic factors as a force making for and against formal empire. Space makes it impossible to examine all parts of the continent and the case studies therefore deal only with Algeria (the only entirely new European colony in this period) and with Tunisia, Egypt and West Africa, because these are of the greatest importance for interpreting the origins of imperial expansion after 1880. In the concluding section, however, a brief comment is made on developments and dominant trends in other parts of the continent.

I NORTH AFRICA

North Africa occupies a unique place in modern colonial history because special factors there conditioned European attitudes and interests. Its proximity made it an integral part of the European environment so that any significant change was certain to arouse the interest of several European states. In terms of strategy and maritime commerce it constituted a first-class political interest for Britain, France and Italy; and once the Suez canal was completed in 1869 it became the vital gateway to or guardian of the Indian Ocean. Hence the very strong reactions aroused when any one state appeared likely to annex a North African territory at any time after 1870, far stronger than any resulting from 'forward' movements in other parts of the world. Again, the states of Islamic North Africa were in many respects more 'civilized' than those in any other part of Africa, with relatively sophisticated systems of government and law. It was therefore possible for Europeans to carry on economic activities there almost as if in Europe, lending money to governments, building railways and other utilities and establishing productive enterprises. Climatically the region was relatively attractive for European settlers so that by the later nineteenth-century 'colonies' of Frenchmen, Italians, Maltese and others existed in many North African states. All these factors influenced the course of European imperialism in North Africa. The question was whether they would tend to stimulate or discourage unilateral formal control by the powers of Europe.

The main key to developments from the early nineteenth century to 1914 was the fact that all these North African states, except the independent sultanate of Morocco, were technically provinces of the Ottoman Empire, which was now too weak either to control or to protect them. Egypt was ruled by a Viceroy (later given the title of Khedive) and had achieved informal independence under Mehemet Ali before 1847. In the mid-century it was building its own empire in the horn of Africa. Tripoli, Tunis and Algeria were ruled by Deys or Beys under nominal Ottoman authority, but were in process of following Egypt into effective independence. To do so they needed European support, much as the colonies of Latin America had recently relied on British help against Spain and Portugal. They did not receive formal diplomatic recognition as sovereign states, but they could borrow money to pay for modern military equipment and to improve their economic systems; and they could import European technicians and administrators. Again, the parallel with Latin America is instructive. But there was no United States in the Mediterranean to oppose foreign intervention with a Monroe Doctrine, and inevitably the danger arose that collaboration with Europe would result in subordination to new masters. Thus the main problems posed by North Africa after

1830 are why, in the first period, none of these states except for Algeria became a formal European dependency before 1880; thereafter why all of them were occupied by France, Britain or Italy.

ALGERIA.[1] Before 1880 Algeria was the only formal European possession in North Africa apart from the small and largely derelict Spanish enclaves of Ceuta and Melilla in Morocco, both relics of the fifteenth-century crusade against Islam. Its importance for the study of nineteenth-century European imperialism is proportionately large. For France Algeria constituted the nucleus from which political control eventually spread eastwards into Tunisia, west into Morocco and south into the Sahara. It also provided a frame of reference on the problems and advantages of colonialism by which almost all emergent peripheral situations were judged, and was a training ground for generations of French soldiers and administrators who carried assumptions formulated in response to Algerian conditions into other parts of Africa and beyond. Algeria is therefore crucial for a study of French imperialism in the nineteenth century. In the wider context of European attitudes to overseas empire the French initiative of 1830 calls into question the general hypothesis that European powers did not feel any strong compulsion to acquire overseas territories in the half-century before 1880. At the same time the subsequent expansion from the coastal bases into the interior constitutes an excellent case study in the mechanisms of peripheral sub-imperialism. Yet Algeria is of almost no value for a study of the working of economic forces in nineteenth-century imperialism. Events there throw little or no light on the workings of European trade or investment as factors making for formal empire and, as will be seen, economic factors played little part in the French decision to occupy Algiers in 1830. It is proposed, therefore, to treat Algeria very briefly in terms of its general significance for European expansion in the nineteenth century rather than as an important case study in the relations between economics and empire.

The dominant feature of the conquest of 1830 was that it lacked historical roots or powerful motives. Both Louis xiv and Napoleon had considered the possibility of taking Algeria as part of larger imperial projects, but there was no continuing assumption in the official mind of Paris that Algeria was necessary to France. During the decade before 1830 two economic problems admittedly made

Algeria a problem in France. First, the endemic piracy based on Algiers had revived during the Napoleonic Wars and was an international nuisance. The concert of Europe had failed to take united action against the Dey, and the French could reasonably claim that, in view of the special interests of traders based on Marseille, they were entitled to take unilateral action. This, at least, was the official response to outraged British complaints after 1830 that France had disturbed the balance of power in the Mediterranean. Second, by ironic contrast with later situations in Tunisia and Egypt, the French government owed 13 million francs to the Dey of Algiers. This money had been borrowed during the Napoleonic Wars from the Jewish banking house of Bacri and Busnach, who were virtual rulers of Algiers, but had been assigned by them to the Dey for collection. The French acknowledged the debt in principle and in 1827 set up a commission to assess the amount due and to arrange for payment. But the Dey was understandably impatient. In 1827 he struck the French consul on the face with a fly-whisk when he tried to explain the delay, and from that date the French court considered whether to avenge this insult by an attack on Algiers.

To this point, then, it would be reasonable to conclude that the roots of French political action in Algeria were both peripheral and economic, arising from obstruction to Mediterranean trade and a dispute over a public debt. Yet it is clear that these factors were not ultimately decisive. For three years after 1827 the French government felt unable to take action in the face of British hostility to French intervention in North Africa and the absence of enthusiasm within France. The decision to attack Algiers stemmed rather from domestic political factors and was exceptional in the history of modern imperialism in that its purpose was to provide political prestige for the government of the day. In 1830, with the Restoration monarchy tottering and unpopular, it was decided to gamble on an expedition that might save the régime by giving it credit for a cheap but spectacular military success. In May the port of Algiers was captured and the Dey deposed. Nevertheless two months later Charles x was deposed and replaced by Louis Philippe. The conquest might then have been given up, but the new king and his minister, Thiers, although anxious to adopt a peaceful policy and, in particular, not to irritate Britain, feared that withdrawal might be unpopular in France. Marseille, the base for operations and main beneficiary of the suppression of piracy, was strongly in favour of keeping Algiers, and there was widespread support from both economists and agrarians who saw opportunities for land settlement. De Tocqueville, for example, was very enthusiastic, comparing Algeria with British India, and started a book on the subject which he never finished. The July Monarchy therefore decided to retain Algiers and to complete the coastal occupation by conquering Oran and Bône, which was done by 1834.

The initial conquest of Algiers can therefore best be explained in terms of French domestic politics rather than of large strategic concepts or important economic problems. It was thus 'Eurocentric' rather than 'peripheral' in origin, though characteristically the immediate stimulus to action came from Algiers rather than Paris. France was faced with the option of ignoring or reacting to a real or implied challenge to her prestige and chose to act. But from 1834 conditions changed radically. Thereafter there can be no doubt that the course of Algerian history and its effects on French policy as a whole were primarily conditioned within Algeria. Indeed these developments constitute a prime example of the growth of a peripheral imperialism and its effects on metropolitan policy.

The expansion of French occupation beyond the limits achieved by about 1834 can only be explained in terms of events in Algeria. In 1834 Abd al Kadir raised a *jihad* (holy war) against the infidel invader in the region of Oran. To defend its existing stake the French government had to send a military expedition. This was only partially successful, and the honour of the French Army required further effort. In 1839 General Bugeaud took command of an army of 100,000 and by 1847 had effectively pacified the hinterland of the ports and captured Abd al Kadir. This in effect ended the *jihad*, but it could not mean the end of conquest. Beyond the line of occupation lay the desert tribes and it seemed necessary on grounds of security to press on until they too were subdued. The Kabylie Mountains were occupied in 1857 and by 1870 the frontier of control had moved back to a line drawn from Figuig, over the Moroccan frontier, to Touggourt and Ourgla. The colony was then secure from the desert tribes but not from internal problems. A major rising in protest against many aspects of French rule broke out in the province of Constantine, and there were further local risings in 1876, 1879, 1881 and 1884. These revolts had somewhat the same impact on sections of French opinion as the Indian Mutiny of 1857 had in Britain in that they intensified fear of collusion between Algerian rebels and possible Islamic or European supporters in

Tunis and Morocco. Thus even after 1870 the logic of Algerian security made France acutely sensitive to political developments on the borders and had considerable influence on French attitudes to other parts of North Africa. To some extent at least the occupation of Tunisia in 1881 and of Morocco in 1911 were products of the quest for Algerian security.

The expansion of Algeria from the original conquests to the frontiers of the 1870s was thus primarily a peripheral process, deriving from the army's assessment of how best to safeguard the coastal region. Expansion owed little or nothing to economic development, for French and other European settlers were deliberately brought in by Bugeaud and his successors as a means of filling the vacuum left by the *refoulement* of Arabs and Berbers. They were not frontiersmen and relied entirely on the army to protect their settlements. Similarly the capitalist French land companies which acquired large estates from dispossessed Algerians in the 1850s were brought in by the government in the hope that they would encourage peasant immigration and stabilize the occupation. For the most part, however, the new landowners preferred to lease their estates back to dispossessed Algerians. Thus the main French interest in Algeria was the army and the significance of the Algerian experience for French imperialism after about 1880 lay largely in the attitudes Algeria had generated in the minds of the men who fought there.

It has been emphasized that, from 1834 onwards, Algeria was primarily a military problem. In principle Algeria was politically assimilated to France during the Second Republic in 1848. But it reverted to separate military rule in 1851; and, apart from a short period of civilian administration between 1858–60, remained a military province, controlled by the War Office and the soldiers on the spot until 1870. In this period of almost continuous peace in Europe, Algeria was the main field of French military activity and experience there shaped the views of two generations of French soldiers and administrators. In relation to later imperialist expansion this training had two formative results. First, Algeria generated the assumption among soldiers and army administrators that no permanent peace was possible with an undefeated Islamic state, and that successful colonization in tropical countries depended on initial conquest and dissolution of all indigenous political and military organizations. Second, the Algerian experience sanctified the view that military affairs in a distant province must be left to the discretion of the military and that, whatever one's assessment of the merits of their policies, once involved with an enemy, the army must be supported at all costs. Otherwise the prestige of the army and therefore of France must suffer. These two traditions were not unique to Algeria or to France. Experience in India bred similar attitudes among British soldiers and civilians who later transferred them to other colonial frontiers. But for France Algeria was the breeding ground of a brand of military imperialism that was to influence the course and character of French imperialism in many other parts of the world. Assumptions formed in Algeria were transferred to Senegal by military governors such as Louis Faidherbe, and by Brière de l'Isle, ex-Governor of Senegal, to Indo-China in the 1880s. Gallieni was one of the very few who rejected this tradition, and he belonged to a later generation and had never served in Algeria.

Algeria therefore provides important clues for understanding later French imperialism. Its initial occupation and later growth provide a model of expansion deriving primarily from political and military considerations rather than from economic problems in France or an overseas territory. In some quarters, notably on the left of French politics, it seemed to prove that colonization was necessarily wasteful and brutal. For others it provided a universal model for colonial expansion and proof that the army could sustain the prestige of France overseas even if it was defeated on the Rhine. Finally, the fact of possession of Algeria had a profound effect on French official attitudes to all near-by parts of Africa. From the 1870s it generated visionary projects for building railways across the Sahara to Senegal and thus contributed directly to the French project for occupying the Western Sudan. In the conditions of the 1880s and thereafter the requirements of Algerian security and frontier stability implied primacy or formal control first of Tunisia and eventually of Morocco. At root such attitudes were political and strategic rather than economic, and they had an immense formative influence on French policy in Africa in the period of imperial expansion.

TUNISIA.[2] There was an interval of fifty years after the initial occupation of Algiers before France or any other European state took formal control of any other North African territory; and then, in 1881 and 1882 the French and British respectively sent military forces to occupy Tunisia and Egypt. These events fall just outside the arbitrary time limits of the present chapter. It would be reasonable to include them as the direct and possibly predictable outcome of conditions in the 1870s; but it is proposed to divide the story at about 1878 on the preliminary hypothesis that essentially new forces may have come into play thereafter which determined the subsequent course of events.

Despite its small size, Tunisia provides a particularly interesting and clear-cut case study of the interaction of political and economic factors in late nineteenth-century imperialism. On the face of it an apparently strong case can be made for assuming that ultimate annexation by France was the direct consequence of economic forces. Long before 1878 France and other European states had a large stake in the Tunisian economy, as a result both of loans made to the Tunisian government and private investment by expatriates. Foreign investment produced a virtual breakdown of the Tunisian fiscal system in the early 1860s which led to international control. In due course, however, the main interested parties, Britain, France and Italy, began to compete for economic primacy; and in 1881 France occupied Tunisia in order to safeguard the existing and prospective economic interests of French nationals. Thus the annexation of Tunisia symbolizes the start of the new age of economic imperialism when European governments were, for the first time, prepared to use the full power of the state to protect or further the specifically economic interests of their subjects overseas, even to the extent of annexing independent foreign states.

This interpretation, of course, depends for its validity on evidence of the precise linkages between economic and political interests, particularly in the period 1878–81. For the moment let us look at the period 1830–78 with two main questions in mind. First, what forms did European interest and intervention in Tunisia take in this period? Second, what probability was there, before about 1878, that one European power or another would eventually take physical control of the territory?

European relations with Tunisia in this period had three main aspects. First, it was a neighbour of French Algeria. Seen from Algiers it constituted a small, politically weak territory whose frontier was a source of recurrent disorders but whose agricultural land, mostly uncomplicated by the system of collective tenures common in Algeria, would be a welcome offset to the relative poverty of most of Algeria. In short the Algerian view of Tunisia was that it must eventually be annexed to Algeria for reasons both of security and economics. Second, from the viewpoint of European statesmen, Tunisia was nominally a province of the Ottoman Empire which had become virtually independent of the Porte by the 1830s and whose future status was of considerable political and strategic importance to a number of powers. Bizerta was potentially a major naval base, and from the 1860s was significantly close to the route to Suez. More generally, control of Tunisia was obviously crucial for the balance of power in the southern Mediterranean. Beyond this Britain, France and Italy had each developed its own non-economic attitude towards Tunisia. For France it signified the security of Algeria and French predominance in North Africa. France did not necessarily want to rule it, but she would certainly oppose occupation by another power. For Italy Tunisia had a two-fold emotional significance by the 1860s. It was part of the old Roman Empire and a first objective of most imaginative enthusiasts for a revival of past Italian glories. It was also the home of some twenty thousand Italians or Italian-speaking Maltese, and a possible field for further emigration. On both counts there were strong expectations that Italy would eventually annex Tunisia. For Britain Tunisia was merely one of many autonomous non-European states with whom she had satisfactory political and economic relationships. Britain had no desire to occupy Tunisia but feared the possible effects of foreign occupation and therefore aimed to sustain the *status quo*, if necessary by combating the acquisitive tendencies of others. Finally, seen from an economic standpoint, Tunisia offered a potential source of considerable profit to any European country able to take advantage of its possibilities. Here was a relatively wealthy society, with an increasing taste for European products – capital, consumer goods, military equipment – which wanted to modernize itself and was prepared to co-operate with European finance and technology. It was therefore an attractive target for the expanding European economy, resembling Latin American countries in that economic penetration was physically easy and the indigenous government was prepared to collaborate with foreign enterprise. During the period from 1830 to the late 1870s the interaction of these three aspects of the Tunisian situation generated a classical model of mid-Victorian informal imperialism – deep economic penetration coupled with preservation of indigenous political independence. The question is whether the effect of the former tended to destroy the latter, and if so, how far this process had gone by about 1878.

To answer these questions it is necessary to distinguish between two types of European economic activity – public loans and private concessions – which had different and to some extent opposite effects on the political future of Tunisia. From the 1830s Tunisia found it necessary to borrow in the European money markets, predominantly in Paris, as well as from local Jewish and other sources both to pay for military and naval forces as a security against reconquest by Turkey and simultaneously to improve administration and provide basic economic services. Within moderation this borrowing was beneficial. In 1859 the public debt was about 12 million francs and public revenues about 11 million francs, so that there seemed no danger of insolvency. But by 1862, as a result of new loans intended mainly to re-equip the army, the debt had risen to 28 million francs with interest rates as high as 12–13 per cent. In 1863 the Bey therefore accepted the proposal of the French banking firm of Oppenheim and Erlanger to float a loan of 35 million francs at 6 per cent interest in Paris from which he could pay off the existing debt and reduce interest due in future. Unfortunately the bonds sold below par and the actual proceeds were further reduced by excessive commissions paid to European bankers and by peculation in Tunisia. As a result the Bey's situation became worse than it had been before; and during the next four years he was forced to raise further loans, and to attempt new conversions, while his revenues were pledged and repledged to pay interest. Finally in 1867 he failed to raise a new loan of 100 million francs in Paris. The outstanding debt stood at 160 million francs and the government could neither pay the interest due from revenues nor raise further loans to do so. Tunisia was bankrupt.

Up to this point it seems clear that the process was entirely economic in character. Buyers of Tunisian bonds in Europe were interested only in the relatively high rates of interest offered, well above those currently paid on European gilt-edged stock and made still higher by the bonds being bought at a discount. Bankers were out to gain substantial profits from commissions and less honourable devices. The whole thing was clearly a way of fleecing a needy and incompetent Islamic despotism and had no necessary political implications. But how would these financial interests react to the Bey's bankruptcy? On Hobson's model they might be expected to press their governments to undertake full political control; and since Frenchmen held most of the bonds, the result should have been French occupation around 1869. The French bond-holders did in fact ask the French Foreign Office to help, but it is important to note that they only wanted official pressure on the Bey either to pay his debts or to submit to financial supervision. This technique, frequently used by British and French governments in Latin America, was duly applied to Tunisia in 1869, when the French consul arranged with the Bey that all public revenues should be collected and distributed by a Joint Franco-Tunisian Commission. This, indeed, offered the best financial solution to a specifically financial problem. But political factors stood in the way: the British and Italian consuls protested that this innovation would give France political preponderance, and the Bey withdrew his agreement. The French consul then suspended diplomatic contacts and in July 1869 a new arrangement was made between the three consuls and the Bey. An international commission of nine members, representing the French, British and Italian bond-holders, became responsible for the Tunisian debts and revenues; but the original Franco-Tunisian Financial Commission was revived as the executive committee of this international body. Thus the principle of international control was coupled with the fact of French primacy to solve the debt question. The commission quickly reduced the acknowledged debt to 125 million francs and refunded it at 5 per cent interest. Since confidence among bond-holders was now restored and half the Bey's revenues could meet interest payments, the crisis seemed over.

These developments throw considerable light on the attitude of European high finance in situations of this kind. First, the financiers were happy with the security given to their capital and interest by international control of public revenue and expenditure. Formal colonization was irrelevant unless these measures failed. This did not happen in Tunisia and the public debt was not a significant factor affecting developments in 1880–1. Second, it might be argued that 1869 rather than 1881 was the critical date for Tunisia and the real culmination of economic imperialism. Thereafter Tunisia remained nominally independent, but public finance, and therefore effectively government, were now under alien control. The Bey could exercise patronage and show favours but had lost the power to take major decisions. By any normal standards this constituted partial loss of Tunisia's sovereignty. Moreover, restricted international supervision was likely to be replaced in course of time by stricter, though still probably informal, control by France as the dominant European power. This, indeed, was what the French government expected in 1869 before the disasters of the Franco-Prussian War temporarily weakened her special position in Tunisia. Even so the Bey did not regain his independence. He could merely attempt to obtain a limited freedom of action by playing one consul and national interest against the other. On this view French occupation of 1881 becomes relatively unimportant, marking only an intensification of alien control and the elimination of two of the three European states which had shared informal control since 1869.

Thus the case of Tunisia suggests that the preferred technique of mid-Victorian financial imperialism was to get a firm grip on a non-European state through loans, to invoke state help if the capital or interest were at risk, but to be content with informal methods of control. It was, of course, always possible that this system would prove transitory and might pave the way for seizure of formal power by one of the states involved. But if this happened the causes would probably lie outside the special concerns of the financier.

The network of private commercial concessions that developed in Tunisia from the 1850s and caused such vehement controversy in the 1870s may seem at first sight to have been as straightforward an expression of European economic enterprise as loans to the government, and they have therefore commonly been treated as evidence that the French occupation of 1881 was the product of international competition for favourable investment and entrepreneurial opportunities. But this interpretation assumes both that competition for such concessions between rival expatriates expressed spontaneous economic ambitions and that eventual state intervention was a response to private demands for support against foreign rivals or hostile Tunisian rulers. Conversely, if the evidence suggests that the European governments or their local representatives were in fact as much or more concerned about the political significance of the distribution of economic opportunities between competing nationals than the private interests involved, then a different conclusion would emerge. Economic enterprise would become the tool rather than the motor of political imperialism and the focus of investigation would shift from the economic means to the political ends.

This, broadly, is what seems to have happened in Tunisia before 1878. Pressure for private concessions began in the 1850s and the first big success went to France which obtained the right to build a telegraph from Algeria to Tunisia in 1857 and in 1861 got further concessions which, it was claimed, gave France a monopoly of all telegraphic communications in Tunisia. It is important to notice that these agreements were made by the French government and that the telegraphs were a state enterprise. The British consul, Sir Richard Wood, saw the political implications of these French concessions and used his own influence to extract comparable advantages for Britain. His most important success was the promise made in 1861 that a British company could build a railway from Tunis to its port La Goletta, though no British firm could be induced to make use of this opportunity until 1871 and the Tunisian Railway Company that eventually did so quickly went bankrupt. In the later 1860s interest centred temporarily on the Bey's debts rather than on economic concessions; but from 1870 the struggle between the consuls of Britain, France and Italy again became acute, and concessions were regarded as evidence of dominance at court, even if no European capitalist could be induced to take them up. Indeed, the political function of concession-hunting was obvious. In 1871 Pinna, the Italian consul, obtained a large landed estate near Jedeida for an Italian agricultural company. The company quickly withdrew in the face of difficulties which included questions of jurisdiction over Tunisian tenants; but Italy used this issue as an excuse to demand exemption from taxation and Tunisian jurisdiction for all Italian-owned property. This demand was blocked by the British and French consuls, and Wood counter-attacked by extracting concessions for a British bank to be founded in Tunisia and a British monopoly for supplying gas there. The two companies concerned were both bankrupt by 1875, but in 1874 Wood had his last big success – the option for a British firm to build a railway from Tunis to a point near the Algerian frontier, though this concession was not to be confirmed for a year. By 1875 the French consul, Roustan, was in the ascendant as ally of Khederine, the new chief minister; and in 1876 the Bey transferred this railway concession to a French company, the Société de Construction des Batignolles, which in turn gave it to a subsidiary, the Compagnie Bône-Guelma. This was clearly a political project, for the French government guaranteed 6 per cent interest on the cost of construction, and on this basis the company was able to raise money in Paris in 1877. Wood had one last success in 1877 when the Bey agreed that goods going to La Goletta must be trans-shipped from this French railway to the British line, though this was by now bankrupt. Roustan then demonstrated the current predominance of French influence by obtaining a large estate for a French resident in Tunis, the Comte de Sancy; but, when he failed to stock his property, as specified, by July 1878, the Bey, supported by the British and Italian consuls, repossessed the estate and a controversy began which lasted until 1881.

Reviewing the complicated history of foreign concessions to 1878 it seems clear that this economic penetration of Tunisia was primarily a device whereby the three contending consuls in Tunisia and, in varying degrees, their governments in Europe, attempted to assert and extend their political influence. In no case was a major concession the result primarily of individual entrepreneurial demand. Almost all were obtained by one of the consuls as a means of establishing a claim to control over some key economic function or of blocking the initiatives of a rival. Conversely, European capitalists showed very little interest in these opportunities unless, as in the case of the Compagnie Bône-Guelma, the state was prepared to underwrite its profits. Hence the significance of the struggle for concessions is not that they reflected an urgent desire among European capitalists for fields of profitable investment, but that they were a device whereby Britain, France and Italy could attempt to maintain influence or obtain predominance in Tunisia at a time when international relationships made unilateral occupation by any one of them impossible.

1878 proved a turning point in Tunisian history, marked locally by the replacement of Khederine by Mustapha ben Ismael as chief minister and by the consequential predominance of the Italian consul, Macciò; and on the international level by the Congress of Berlin, where Bismarck and Salisbury made it clear that they regarded Tunisia as a French sphere of interest. Subsequent events leading to the crisis of 1881 will be considered in a later chapter. To this point, however, the answers to the two questions posed at the beginning of this section would seem to be as follows. First, there had been two distinct types of European intervention in Tunisia, both typical of mid-Victorian imperialism: genuine economic activities, represented by loans to the Tunisian government; and essentially political activities, though sometimes taking economic forms, represented by the competition between foreign consuls for preponderance at court. Concessions might ultimately constitute genuine economic factors but in origin they were a tool of political ambitions. Whatever its form, however, European penetration sprang initially from peripheral rather than Eurocentric factors: on the one side the weakness and needs of the Tunisian government, on the other the fact of French control in Algeria and the role played by foreign consuls in Tunisian court politics. Until at least 1878 London, Paris and Rome were concerned primarily to control local developments in such a way as to protect 'national interests' – which meant primarily to prevent unilateral control by any other power – and in the case of France and Italy to lay foundations for eventual primacy without necessarily wanting formal control. These were the hallmarks of mid-nineteenth-century imperialism.

On the second question, it was still uncertain whether this informal international control would survive indefinitely, or whether one European state would eventually acquire sole power in Tunisia. Britain would certainly not do so. But if France or Italy decided to act the impulse would almost certainly spring from political or emotional factors rather than from the logic of economic imperialism. Tunisia's public debts were not a ground for political occupation. Concessions were political tools rather than economic attractions. The predictable cause of unilateral occupation by France or Italy was belief that the other was about to end the existing international control. This, essentially, was what happened in 1881.

EGYPT.[3] The case of Egypt bore a close resemblance to that of Tunisia. Egypt was another breakaway province of the Ottoman Empire, though her effective independence was completed earlier – under Mehemet Ali who ruled as Viceroy from 1811 to 1847 and obtained the Sultan's recognition of virtual independence and hereditary succession. Mehemet Ali achieved far more than this. He laid the foundations of an Egyptian territorial empire in the Eastern Sudan and the Red Sea. He undertook the modernization of Egypt, improving the structure of central government tax collection and the armed forces. He did much for the economy by construction of communications and stimulation of export commodities through state monopolies. His successors, notably Ismail, who obtained the title of Khedive from the Sultan in 1867, carried on this policy. By the 1860s Egypt was an integral part of the European economic system. In 1870 she had some hundred thousand foreign residents, all exempt from local jurisdiction and taxation under capitulations made by Turkey in the past, but making a significant contribution to economic development. Foreign trade boomed. Between 1863 and 1875 exports rose from £E4,454,000 to £E13,810,000 and imports from £E1,991,000 to £E5,410,000. By the 1870s Egypt had over 8,000 miles of irrigated canals, almost 1,000 miles of railways, 5,000 miles of telegraphs and 4,500 elementary schools. Alexandria and Cairo were centres of European civilization, with large colonies of expatriates, foreign-owned banks, trading companies, hotels and utilities.

This achievement represented an effective alliance between the Egyptian government and foreign capital and skills. It is an important fact that the bulk of foreign investment was in the form of loans to the Egyptian government, raised through flotation of Egyptian bonds, which used the proceeds to pay for the construction of publicly owned and operated utilities and other economic enterprises. Conversely, there was relatively little private direct investment or ownership of economic assets by expatriates: in 1884 public debts were some £E90 million as against investment by joint stock companies of about £E6 million.[4] Egypt therefore retained control of her own economic system. Unfortunately the government had to pay an impossibly high price for foreign capital. The big loans were floated in Europe by the international banking houses – Rothschilds, Fruhlings, Oppenheims etc. – at interest rates of 12 per cent and above; whereas the standard rate on similar loans in Europe was 6–7 per cent and in France and Britain governments could raise money at substantially lower rates. Moreover, the total debts were grossly inflated by exorbitant commissions and other charges made by the bankers and by being sold below their face value. Hence, while the nominal funded debts of Egypt rose between 1863 and 1876 from £E3 million to £E68 million and the unfunded debt to £E26 million, perhaps only about two-thirds of these sums were ever actually available to the Khedive. More serious still, the undoubted long-term benefits of this investment to the Egyptian economy were not adequately reflected in short-term expansion of public revenues. By 1875 revenues had risen from £E2 million to some £E10 million, a considerable proportionate increase, but small in absolute terms. In the mid-1870s more than two-thirds of government income had to be sent abroad as interest. In 1877, even after the preliminary financial reorganization, only some £E1 million was left for domestic expenditure, and the government had to resort to short-term loans to meet current obligations. This was obviously a desperate position, but there was little the Khedive could do about it. His liquid assets were restricted to the 177,000 shares in the Suez Canal Company – $\frac{7}{16}$ of the total – which he had received as payment for permission to build the canal and for Egypt's share in its construction. In 1875 these shares were sold to Britain for £4 million (less 2½ per cent commission to Rothschilds) to meet current interest payments; and after that the Khedive was helpless. On 8 April 1876 he suspended payment on treasury bills. Egypt had reached the same point of governmental bankruptcy as Tunisia in 1869.

On the face of it, therefore, Egypt looks like an excellent case study in economic imperialism. The Suez Canal was a relatively unimportant feature of the financial situation, since the company's profits and assets were not directly involved. But the holders of Egyptian government bonds, who included many British subjects even though the majority were French, stood to lose both their capital and high interest if the Khedive was permitted to declare himself bankrupt and evade his obligations. There is no doubt that the bond-holders appealed to the French and British governments for support, or that they received it. Although in the first instance the attempted solution took the form of a financial supervision of Egypt along Tunisian lines, it could be argued that as soon as this device broke on the refusal of Egyptians to pay almost all of its public revenues to foreigners, the British government, acting as bailiff for the bond-holders, seized Egypt as the only available asset to secure their claims. The question is whether this was indeed the way things happened between 1876 and 1882.

As in the case of Tunisia it is proposed here to consider only the immediate reactions of Britain and other European powers to the crisis of 1876 as far as the establishment of the Dual Control of 1879, which can be seen as the typical mid-Victorian reaction to a situation of this kind. Throughout this period and beyond the central issue was the relationship between, on the one hand, the economic interests and demands of British and French holders of Egyptian bonds and, on the other, the attitudes of their respective governments. What were the links between them? Could a small but powerful economic interest dictate policy to a government? Or was official policy based on the statesmen's analysis of the national interest?

A clear distinction has to be drawn between British and French official attitudes. That of Paris was relatively simple. France had a long association with Egypt, which was far more influenced by French than British language, culture and technology. French engineers had built the canal and French investors held most of the Khedive's bonds. Thus France had strong sentimental and financial interests in Egypt. On the other hand her political interests were less important than those of Britain. She had no possessions east of Suez comparable to those of Britain, nor a naval strategy which depended on freedom of access through the canal. Above all France did not want political control of Egypt. She was deeply committed in Tunisia and the French public would not have supported unilateral French military action in Egypt. French official policy was therefore based on an understanding, established between Waddington and Salisbury in 1878, whereby Britain would take the leading political role in a partnership designed to exclude third parties. On the other hand the French government felt obliged to support French holders of Egyptian bonds, so long as this did not involve military occupation. Thus Paris pressed London in 1876 for joint official control of Egyptian finances on Tunisian lines and, when this was refused, sent an official commissioner to Cairo to act with nominees of the Austro-Hungarian and Italian governments as controllers of the fund known as the Caisse de la Dette publique into which the Khedive was now to pay revenues assigned for interest on the foreign debt. Freycinet later regretted this official involvement in the private affairs of the bondholders; but it was, in fact, the tradition of French foreign policy to give such support.

British attitudes were at first very different, and from the start were based on political rather than economic or emotional considerations. Egypt was seen in terms of long-established British national interests in the eastern Mediterranean, which in turn centred on British control of the Indian Ocean. Having attempted for long to prevent the construction of the Suez Canal on the grounds that it might enable some hostile foreign power to move naval forces from the Mediterranean to the Indian Ocean, British policy was now to ensure that no foreign power had the ability to close the canal to British ships. This policy clearly lay behind Disraeli's purchase of the Khedive's shares in the Canal Company in November 1875, and he defended the purchase before Parliament in February 1876 in these terms:

I do not recommend this purchase as a financial investment. . . . I have always and do now recommend it to the country as a political transaction and one which I believe is calculated to strengthen the empire.[5]

But already many in British official circles, including Salisbury, were afraid that a holding of $\frac{7}{16}$ of the canal shares would not provide adequate security in Egypt now that Turkish suzerainty was so precarious. Rather than allow some European power to dominate Egypt Britain might be forced to do so; and in 1875 *The Times* had commented that

> Should insurrection, or aggression from without or corruption within bring a political as well as financial collapse of the Turkish Empire, it might become necessary to take measures for the security of that part of the Sultan's dominions with which we are most nearly concerned.[6]

This is not, of course, to suggest that in 1876 the British official mind seriously intended to occupy Egypt in the near future. Policy was rather to keep a close watch on events to ensure that no political threat developed. But it does suggest that in the last resort Egypt was seen as a major national interest on political grounds and that under certain circumstances British military action might therefore be justified.

By contrast, however, British economic interests in Egypt were not regarded as a significant national concern in London. British trade and private investment in Egypt were in any case small at this stage, and bond-holders had absolutely no claim on official support. As has been seen above, the Foreign Office made a fetish of refusing to support British economic activities overseas unless there was an initial commitment by the government or a breach of international law was committed. Neither of these criteria was relevant to the situation in Egypt. The bond-holders were private speculators and the Khedive had not deliberately broken his contract with them. In 1876, therefore, the government rejected applications from the British bond-holders and French government alike to intervene or even to appoint an official member of the international commission in charge of the Caisse de la Dette publique; and this attitude was sustained until, by 1879, the issues at stake were deemed no longer economic but political.

The peculiar importance of studying the evolution of French and British policy in Egypt first from 1876 to 1879 and thereafter to 1882, therefore derives largely from the curious way in which their initial assumptions changed. While the French gradually shifted their attention from the limited economic problem of the bond-holders and France's direct stake in the Egyptian economy to a

wider assessment of the national interests involved in the struggle
for power in Egypt, the British came to recognize that a limited
economic problem had developed into a major political crisis of
primary concern to British Mediterranean strategy. This evolutionary process will not be rehearsed in detail. The essential fact is that
between 1876 and 1878 the problem of interest payments on Egyptian bonds gradually undermined the Egyptian political system.
During these two years the commission in charge of the Caisse,
including Charles Rivers Wilson as a private representative of the
British bond-holders, reorganized the debt, which was funded with
interest at 6 per cent and a sinking fund of 1 per cent. Meantime the
Khedive, to show his good intentions, put his revenues and
expenditure in the hands of two expatriate Controllers of Finance,
one British, representing only the bond-holders, the other French
and representing the French government. This arrangement was a
direct precursor of the later Dual Control. Interest was duly paid to
the bond-holders; but in fact the problem was no nearer solution
because, so long as the fiscal system was unreformed, and the
economy no stronger, payment of interest overseas necessarily
meant non-payment of Egyptian civil and military officials. By
1878 the shortage of revenue was so serious that the Khedive set
up a commission of inquiry whose report, presented in August,
was so critical of his régime that he agreed to hand over power to a
responsible ministry under Nubar Pasha, an Armenian Christian
who had recently been in Britain and had attempted to persuade the
Foreign Office to impose a protectorate on Egypt. But this experiment also was doomed to failure by lack of funds. A military
demonstration in February 1878 against the government's policy of
putting 2,500 Egyptian army officers on half pay – the first real
Egyptian reaction to alien intrusion into their affairs – gave the
Khedive an excuse to dismiss the Ministry. He replaced it first by
another under his son, Tewfik Pasha, and then in April staged a
coup d'état, appointing Cherif Pasha chief minister. The European
ministers who had dominated the financial administration were
dismissed and the Khedive produced a new scheme for paying off
the national debt.

   This was the critical event which at last forced the British government to take formal action. At first sight this might seem to be
because the bond-holders' rights were endangered; and Salisbury,
now Foreign Secretary, was uncomfortably aware that British
action might be interpreted in this way. In April 1879 he wrote:

It may be quite tolerable ... to the French government to go into partnership with the bondholders; or rather to act as sheriffs' officer for them. But to us it is a new and very embarrassing sensation. ... We have no wish to part company with France: still less do we mean that France should acquire in Egypt any special ascendency [*sic*]; but subject to these two considerations I should be glad to be free of the companionship of the bondholders.[7]

The fact was that not only France but other powers were now ready to interfere more directly in Egypt, and Britain must either go along with them or forfeit influence there. On 18 May 1879 Bismarck virtually insisted on foreign intervention when he protested to the Khedive against the new political system. His motive was clearly to force Britain to act from fear that if she did not do so France, still driven by the bond-holders, might look for Russian support for military action in Egypt; and this would have been undesirable in terms of Bismarck's overall European strategy. But if Salisbury had to take some action, he could still avoid direct political occupation. Instead he organized an international approach to the Sultan of Turkey who duly deposed Khedive Ismail when he refused to abdicate.

The way was now clear for the last major attempt of the powers, including Britain, to solve the Egyptian question within the conventions of mid-nineteenth-century action – that is, by preserving nominal Egyptian sovereignty but constructing within it a system of government based on European standards and staffed at the top by Europeans. As Salisbury said:

The only form of control we have is that which is called moral influence, which in practice is a combination of nonsense, objurgation and worry. In this we are still supreme. ... We most devote ourselves to the perfecting of this weapon.[8]

In essence the chosen weapon was the system of administration already tried between 1876 and 1879. The new Khedive, Tewfik, ruled through a Ministry which nominally consisted entirely of Egyptians. But the reality of power lay with the two Controllers of Receipts and Expenditure, one British, the other French, both appointed by the Khedive, but in fact nominees of their respective governments. This was the Dual Control and the lynchpin of the system. The function of the Controllers was to undertake a radical overhaul of Egyptian finance in the hope that a reformed revenue system could afford to pay interest on the debt without starving the civil service and army. To deal with the foreign debt a new International Commission on the Liquidation of the Debt was established, consisting of two British and two French representatives and one each for Germany, Austria-Hungary and Italy. Their function was to use funds provided by the Controllers through the Egyptian Minister of Finance to pay interest as it became due and ultimately to liquidate the debt altogether. But the intended purpose of the scheme as a whole was clearly political. Britain and France could control the Egyptian government through the Controllers and dominate the Debt Commission through their majority of four members to three. If reform of administration could be undertaken while the bond-holders were kept quiet, these two powers could maintain political primacy, and ultimately it might prove possible to withdraw altogether from direct engagement within Egypt.

To a point this project was a success. By 1880 the original problem of Egyptian bankruptcy was virtually solved. The Law of Liquidation promulgated in July 1880 provided for reorganization of all debts and reduced the interest paid; but the revenue allocated to the debt was deliberately underestimated so that the expected surplus could be devoted to paying off the capital. Thereafter, with the interests of the bond-holders adequately cared for – though at substantially lower rates of interest than originally promised by the Khedive – the financial question became relatively unimportant. If changed political conditions again prevented regular payment of interest, or if repudiation seemed likely, then the bond-holders would certainly have demanded renewed action and possibly formal occupation. But this, in fact, never happened. The crisis of 1881–2 arose from quite different problems and never directly affected the interests of the bond-holders.

The first phase of European intervention in Egypt therefore ends in 1879–80. What light do these events throw on the character of British and French attitudes in the late 1870s, on the eve of the 'new imperialism'? The answer is oddly paradoxical. The French government at first reacted in the way predicted by most theories of economic imperialism, putting its weight behind the purely economic interests of its bond-holders. Yet this support stopped well short of military or political occupation. The levers used by economic interests could not move the Quai d'Orsay further because no national interest was at stake comparable in importance with maintaining good relations with Britain. Paris in fact deliberately accepted that Britain would be the dominant partner in

Egypt as France was dominant in Tunisia, even though this would adversely affect a wide range of French economic and cultural interests in Egypt. The British reaction is equally instructive. London was deeply concerned about the political status of Egypt, but felt little sympathy for the complaints of the bond-holders. Initially, therefore, the Foreign Office refused to become officially involved. In due course economic factors indirectly forced Britain to take official action, but the linkages were very complex: the Khedive's proposed new debt system of 1878 worried French bond-holders, whose government was bound to take further action and might invoke Russian support if Britain did not intervene as France's ally; and Salisbury recognized that this would seriously endanger Britain's political standing in the Middle East. Yet even so the chosen Anglo-French solution was not formal occupation but international supervision of a nominally independent Egyptian government. This was as far as either government ever wanted to go, and this reluctance indicates that the characteristic mid-Victorian solution to peripheral economic problems was still preferred in 1880. The reasons behind the British change of policy in 1882 lie beyond the present chapter; but in essence the new policy of military occupation was still intended as a temporary expedient, a stop-gap when informal supervision seemed to have failed and Britain's political pre-eminence was in danger. This was not the product of 'new' or economic imperialism but a logical outcome of events and attitudes based firmly in the past.

II WEST AFRICA

Both before and after the 1870s the character of European imperialism in West Africa[9] – as, indeed, in most other parts of that continent and in the East – was different from that in North Africa. The basic contrast stemmed from the fact, clear from analysis of European attitudes to Tunisia and Egypt, that the Mediterranean was regarded by virtually all the powers as an area of first-class political importance, whereas sub-Saharan Africa was not. Unilateral control of any part of North Africa involved complex and potentially dangerous rivalries between the powers, and every takeover was therefore preceded by an intermediate period of international supervision and in the final stage caused substantial disagreement between at least two powers. Under such conditions it is not surprising that political considerations weighed so heavily against economic interests, for private profits were dwarfed by the strategic or diplomatic objectives of the statesmen. But in this the Mediterranean was a special case. In most other parts of Africa European political interests were few and usually minor. The British had a major political interest in the Cape of Good Hope as a port of call and naval base on the route to India, and this influenced much of their thinking about southern Africa. British and French naval bases in West Africa were useful for suppressing the Atlantic slave trade until the 1860s. But neither they nor any other European power had a major national interest of any sort in any other part of sub-Saharan Africa until, in the late 1880s, the British decided that East Africa was important because of its possible relevance to Egyptian security.

Potentially, at least, this lack of major national interests in sub-Saharan Africa was likely to increase the influence of strictly economic factors on European imperialism. Compared with North Africa one would expect to find much less interest among politicians and permanent diplomatic officials in remote regions of Africa which did not impinge on their traditional concepts of international relations. Thus, to the Quai d'Orsay the Rhine mattered most, North Africa a good deal, West Africa very little and other parts of Africa hardly at all. Since the Foreign Offices of other powers applied comparable measuring rods, the course of imperialism in sub-Saharan Africa was likely to be largely and perhaps uniquely unaffected by restrictive concepts of national interest; and in this environment micro-economic factors at the periphery acquired maximum potential importance. A French trading firm operating at, for example, Porto Novo might have far more influence on Paris, which had no political blueprint for the Slave Coast, than a much larger trading interest in Cairo or Tangier, for which French officials had clear plans based on international considerations. That is not to say that a commercial interest in West Africa would necessarily demand annexation of its field of activity – in fact the Régis, who for long operated at Porto Novo, did not want French control there; nor that France would necessarily be prepared to undertake the responsibilities of government even if it was requested by private interests. But it did mean that economic issues could be assessed on their intrinsic merits rather than in terms of overriding political priorities. It is therefore arguable that the best conditions for measuring the potential influence of genuinely economic factors on European imperialism are to be found in an area such as

West Africa and during the half-century before about 1880. If formal annexation took place, the chances are that economic factors were at least partly responsible. If it did not, it is reasonable to deduce either that economic interests did not need or demand it, or, alternatively, that Paris, London and Berlin were not sufficiently impressed by the economic needs of their nationals to respond to pressures. Thus it should be possible to reach some reasonably satisfactory conclusions as to the inherent propensity of peripheral economic forces to generate imperial expansion before the end of the 1870s; and this will serve as a yardstick for interpreting the objectives of imperialism in the following quarter-century.

In approaching this problem three main questions stand out. Did such economic problems tend on their own account to generate formal control of autonomous Africa territories? What was the relative importance of peripheral and metropolitan factors in the decision-making process? Does the evidence suggest that by the early 1880s extension of existing trends would ultimately have produced substantial territorial empires?

During the half-century before about 1880 West Africa possessed almost all the classical elements which during the previous three centuries had tended to generate formal European dependencies: Christian missions, European explorers, well-organized and highly competitive African states, and rapidly growing economic links with Europe. Under these conditions it was certain that Europeans would become increasingly involved in the region. The question was whether involvement would lead to formal control and if so what role economic factors would play in this process.

The commodity trade was by far the most important aspect of Europe's economic stake in West Africa, as indeed it remained into the mid-twentieth century. It is impossible to calculate the value of fixed capital investment in the British and French territories at this period, but it must have been very small indeed, [10] and prospects for future investment were poor so long as foreign-controlled territory remained as small as it then was. Trade was therefore the dominant form of expatriate economic activity, and the most probable source of European economic imperialism was the changing needs of European traders. During this half-century the West African economic system was slowly adjusting itself to the decline of the slave trade and the growth of a 'legitimate' commerce in tropical commodities. Until early in the century European trade in the region had been virtually restricted to the exchange of manufactured imports for slaves, and the whole economy of the coast and interior, together with many aspects of African political and social structures, had been geared to this system. By the 1830s both Britain and France had renounced the slave trade, though an illicit trade in slaves continued to Brazil, Cuba and the United States until the 1860s, even growing in volume until the 1840s. During the thirty years after about 1830, therefore, the new and important legitimate export trades were developing alongside the slave trade, and this coincidence made it easier for Africans to transfer their efforts from one activity to the other and at the same time infected the new commodity trade with many of the practices characteristic of slave-trading. Of these perhaps the most important were the widespread use of truck rather than cash, European dependence on African middlemen, and the consequential limitations of European activity to the coastal towns. To a large extent the political future of the area depended on whether these traditional forms proved adaptable to a greatly expanded commodity trade.

By far the most important new African export was vegetable oils. Technical developments in Europe early in the century made it possible for the first time to use vegetable oils in the manufacture of soap and for industrial purposes; and the discovery that West Africa possessed ample supplies both of ground nuts, which were cultivated in the Gambia region, and of palm oil, the product of the uncultivated palm trees that were common in the coastal areas between the Gold Coast and the Niger Delta, opened up vast commercial possibilities. The British showed little interest in ground nuts, but began to import palm oil, obtained by crushing the outer flesh of the nut, from about 1800. In 1854, 37,631 tons of oil were imported to Britain from all sources and the volume continued to rise irregularly until about 1880 when it was 51,641 tons, after which it levelled off and remained remarkably stable into the first decade of the twentieth century. Meantime the use of the palm kernel, which yielded a higher grade oil when crushed, had begun in 1853, and by 1880 British imports had risen to nearly 50,000 tons of kernels.[11] A large proportion of these British imports came from West Africa, though significantly the majority of the palm oil did not come from the restricted areas under formal British control.[12] Meanwhile the French also had developed a substantial import of vegetable oils. Ground nut oil from the Senegal and Gambia area was used in soap production from the 1840s and in the 1850s soap manufacturers in Marseille began to

F

use palm kernel oil. Together these constituted the great bulk of French imports from West Africa which, by 1880, were not far short of the British total. Table 10 shows the growth of West African trade with France and Britain between 1854 and 1880.

These statistics suggest three main conclusions. First, although the value of the trade was considerable, it was minute in relation to the total overseas trade of either Britain or France. Total British imports in 1880 were £411,229,565 and exports £286,414,466, and her trade with West Africa was smaller than with any one of a number of Latin American republics, let alone with major trading partners in Europe, North America and the East.[13] This proportion never changed significantly. Thus the commercial value of West Africa lay not in the absolute volume of the trade but in the fact that it provided useful raw materials. In addition, imports were important only to a few specialized trading and manufacturing concerns in Britain and France, who constituted relatively small private interests rather than national needs. It was therefore not surprising that the British government at least was prepared to view the future political complexion of the area with some detachment, though with interest. Second, it is significant that, with the exception of French metropolitan exports, the bulk of both British and French trade lay outside their formal possessions on the coast. This, of course, indicated that the commodity trade did not depend on political control of the zones of production or shipment, but it also meant that both powers were sensitive to possible engrossment of these independent trading areas by another European state. Finally, while the balance of trade was always slightly against Britain – though much less in 1880 than in 1864 – the balance against France was overwhelming. The reasons for this were partly that the British export total included a proportion of re-exports carried by British ships – though only some £322,000 out of a total of £2,512,691 in 1880 – but far more that British exports could undersell French commodities in most neutral markets. Only Senegal, with its established French merchants and (after 1877) tariff preferences, was a secure market for the metropolis. It would be an oversimplification to deduce from this that French merchants were invariably anxious to extend French political control on the coast, for until the 1880s neither Marseille or Bordeaux was demanding either protective tariffs or territorial expansion. But, as has been seen above, some neo-mercantilist politicians in Paris

Table 10

British and French Trade with West Africa, 1854-80
(i) British Trade (pounds at current values)

Exports to:	1854	1864	1880
West Coast*	820,941	668,185	1,558,941
Senegal	9,141	7,462	54,444
Fernando Po	67,045	19,005	8,429
Gold Coast	134,885	134,142	502,223
Gambia	75,307	45,496 }	388,654
Sierra Leone	130,814	180,013 }	
Total	1,238,133	1,054,303	2,512,691

Imports From:	1854	1864	1880
West Coast*	1,528,896	1,037,925	1,890,599
Senegal	401	—	6,119
Fernando Po	125,801	26,248	13,923
Gold Coast	71,253	198,806	621,284
Gambia	28,002	41,720 }	157,964
Sierra Leone	153,559	54,860 }	
Total	1,907,912	1,359,559	2,689,889

* Excluding British, French and Spanish possessions.

(ii) French Trade (francs at current values)

Exports to:	1875	1880
West Africa*	—	2,591,186
Senegal	4,800,000	7,846,406
Total		10,437,592 (£416,000)

Imports from:	1875	1880
West Africa*	—	28,690,267
Senegal	9,600,000	19,783,479
Total		48,473,746 (£1,940,000)

* Including all non-French territories.

Sources: *Statistical Abstract for the United Kingdom*, no. 13 (London, 1866), table 9; *ibid.*, no. 40 (London, 1880), table 24. *Annuaire Statistique de la France*, 1878, 1882, table 3.

tended by about 1880 to draw the conclusion that France could only compete with Britain in these markets if she imposed some form of political control over them; and after 1880 the British in turn assumed that French rule meant virtual exclusion of British trade from previously established neutral markets. If not decisive, these were to be important factors in the expansion of European power after about 1880.

The growth of the commodity trade was matched and greatly stimulated by an impressive expansion of European shipping, especially steam vessels, to the coast. The first regular steamship line to West Africa was started by the British firm, MacGregor Laird, in 1852. For some years they had a virtual monopoly, but rivals appeared in 1862. In 1868 Elder Dempster began regular sailings, and they were followed by the Hamburg firm of Woermann and later by Scandinavian, Dutch and French lines. By 1881 the tonnage of steam vessels clearing from British West African ports was far greater than that of sailing ships: 294,817 against 37,277 tons from Lagos, 265,799 to 41,380 tons from the Gold Coast.[14] The effects of these regular ocean-going steamship lines on the character of West African trade was considerable. They increased the possible volume of trade, reduced the cost of transport, and improved the quality of the oil as it reached Europe. They made unnecessary the traditional off-shore hulks previously used to store the oil until a sailing ship should arrive. They made it possible for local traders and commission agents, including a number of Africans, to order European manufactures for sale in local markets; but conversely they made it virtually impossible for Africans to act as oil exporters, for the shipping companies normally dealt only with Europeans. In short, ocean-going steamships changed the character of the West African trade even if they did not immediately increase its size. But steam also had major consequences within the coastal region. Small steam vessels enabled Europeans for the first time to navigate many of the coastal lagoons, the Niger Delta and, above all, the Niger and Senegal; and in doing so they began inevitably to by-pass African middlemen who had hitherto collected the oil from the areas of production and sold it to Europeans on the coast. Particularly in the Niger region this trend implied revolutionary changes. European traders now wanted to open up a direct trade with the interior which in turn might raise major problems with African states and rival Europeans. By the 1870s it was becoming clear that the political consequences of the technological revolution in ship design would be considerable; but it was not yet certain precisely what form these would take.

These problems were not, however, new in the 1870s. From the start the commodity trade in West Africa posed a problem that had been widely experienced in previous centuries in other continents: should Europeans conduct their trade on a purely commercial basis, dealing with African traders at politically independent coastal markets as they would trade within Europe or in America; or did satisfactory trade demand formal possession of ports and perhaps also the areas of production? In about 1830 there were only three British or French colonies proper on the coast – Senegal, Gambia and Sierra Leone – plus the British and Dutch trading ports on the Gold Coast and a number of small British and French trading bases elsewhere. Should these be increased, retained or given up? Would they act as peripheral growing points for territorial empires, or become derelict survivals, as some Portuguese ports in Angola and Mozambique were becoming with the decline of the slave trade? The debate that continued over these options from the 1830s to the late 1870s is important since it reveals many of the attitudes and interests which determined the course of events both during the mid-nineteenth century and in the era of rapid territorial expansion after 1880.

The case normally made out against territorial possessions was simply that Europeans had no interests in West Africa other than trade, and that colonies were not necessary for successful trading. Neither ground nuts nor palm products were plantation crops. Both were produced by Africans within their own social and economic systems; and attempts to establish plantations in Senegal and Sierra Leone invariably failed for lack of an adequate labour force. Conversely, Africans in most parts of the coast were commercially minded, had long specialized in the Saharan trade or the slave trade, and were very willing to co-operate with Europeans. For example the Jack-Jacks on the Ivory Coast and the Brassmen in the Oil Rivers can best be described as political groups organized as professional middlemen; and elsewhere larger states, such as Dahomey and Benin, were prepared to control and profit by transit trades, whether in slaves or oil. So long as the power and efficiency of these African organizations survived it was obviously expedient for the European merchant to come to terms with them. This in turn precluded European penetration inland and made it unnecessary in most places to incur the cost of colonial bases on the coast.

This, however, had been equally true of European traders in the East before the mid-eighteenth century; yet in the end the system had broken down and was replaced by formal rule. Why had this not happened on any scale in West Africa by the 1880s? Possible answers may be found in three factors: limited Franco-British commercial competition; dissatisfaction with existing trade bases; and the trend towards free trade.

The main cause of relative harmony in West Africa between Britain and France was that commercial competition was for long limited in scope and intensity. French traders based on Goree dominated the trade of Senegal, which was in any case restricted to French ships and nationals until after 1864 by the Navigation Acts, and they effectively controlled the ground nut trade of Gambia as well. On the other hand the British had the lion's share of the palm oil trade, which lay mainly in the East, until the French began to increase their stake in this trade from the 1860s. By the end of the period harmony was, in fact, being threatened by overlapping British and French commercial interests in three main areas: north of Sierra Leone in the Scarcies and Mellacourie river region; in the region west of Lagos; and on the Niger. By 1880 such conflicts of interest were sufficiently numerous and intense to provide at least a possible motive for preemptive annexations by both parties.

A second factor was dissatisfaction in both countries with the fortified trading bases they already held. In 1843 France acquired three bases south of Senegal – Grand Bassam, Assini and Gaboon. These were largely the product of the French Navy's dislike of British naval predominance in the area, but were defended by Guizot as *points d'appui* for French trade. In the next thirty years these bases proved commercially unrewarding and expensive to maintain. Their limited trade was largely handled by British merchants, while the Régis of Marseille avoided them, preferring to operate in independent areas such as Dahomey, where customs duties were lower. By 1870 France had withdrawn its administration and military forces from Grand Bassam and Assini, retaining only Gaboon (in Equatorial West Africa) as a naval base. Paris thus seemed to have concluded that politically controlled trading bases were economically pointless.

On the whole British experience and reactions were similar. Until 1843 the small bases centred on Cape Coast Castle were administered by a committee of merchants in London as a commercial proposition and were held on lease from African rulers, not as colonies. In 1843 the British government took control over these forts, mainly because of complaints that their administrator, Captain Maclean, had exercised irregular jurisdiction over near-by Fanti rulers and was helping Portuguese slave traders. Even then the settlements did not become formal British possessions under their own governor until 1850. The aim was still to restrict British responsibility and reduce costs, and distrust of such bases was increased by the Ashanti invasion of the Gold Coast in 1863. Hence a Parliamentary Select Committee of 1865 recommended gradual withdrawal from all possessions except Sierra Leone, which was to be kept as a naval base, and that meantime, for reasons of economy, the Gold Coast forts should be placed under the Governor of Sierra Leone as between 1843 and 1850. In fact withdrawal proved impossible. Political conditions in the Gold Coast, particularly the threat of Ashanti invasion, made it impossible to withdraw without endangering British trade. Indeed the annexation of Lagos in 1861 indicated that under certain conditions new bases might have to be established. Lagos was taken for complex reasons: to solve problems of jurisdiction connected with British merchants already settled there; because Palmerston was afraid the French might take it; because Russell was convinced that annexation might promote the export of cotton; because it was alleged that slave traders were operating there and that the Régis were recruiting indentured servants for the French Antilles. But, although the annexation of Lagos was a portent in that similar situations might arise in many other places, it did not mark the beginning of a British expansionist trend. No other territories were acquired before 1880 and established British policy was still to avoid new commitments.

The third factor tending against territorial expansion was the trend of Anglo-French commercial policies. By the 1830s the British were moving towards complete free trade, and had therefore no interest in occupying parts of West Africa to gain a commercial monopoly. Their most likely motive for annexation was therefore fear that France might annex places in which British merchants had a stake, for French colonies were virtually closed to foreign trade until 1864. This was certainly a motive for annexing Lagos in 1861; but thereafter French protectionism was no real threat until after 1877. On the other side French traders showed no interest in annexation of independent territories, and by 1868 Senegal and other French possessions were open to foreigners on precisely equal terms. So long as France remained free-trading neither government had any strong commercial incentive to establish new colonies.

Limited European commercial competition, French and British metropolitan distrust of territorial possessions and the growth of free trade go far to explain why so little territorial expansion occurred in West Africa before about 1880. But this is only one side of the picture. Well before that date there was evidence of strong contrary tendencies. First, it has been seen that European territorial influence did in fact expand in this period. The French acquired the three *comptoirs* in 1843, imposed a short-lived protectorate on Porto Novo in 1863, and were extending formal or informal control in the vicinity of Senegal and on the Ivory Coast. For their part the British obtained effective control over much of the Gold Coast by acquiring the Danish forts in 1850, and Elmina, the Dutch base, in 1871 and by making treaties with African rulers. In 1861 they occupied Lagos and were similarly extending informal control over its vicinity. Why, in this period of metropolitan indifference or even hostility to territorial expansion, did this creeping imperialism occur in West Africa? Possible answers may be found in four main factors which will be considered in turn: the effects of temporarily bad relations between Britain and France; the fiscal problems of existing colonies or bases; deteriorating European relations with African states or societies; and, as a special case, the sub-imperialism of officialdom in Senegal.

The first of the factors – bad Anglo-French relations – was relatively unimportant in this period of almost continuous Franco-British entente between 1830 and 1880; yet the fact that two short lapses in the entente produced several colonial acquisitions in regions of common interest was significant for the period of relatively continuous bad relations after 1882. The first occasion was in 1840–3. Palmerston distrusted Louis Philippe and decided to exclude France from the International Conference summoned to settle the Middle East problem created by the conquests of Mehemet Ali. This caused considerable resentment in Paris and Anglo-French relations were at crisis point in 1841. Thereafter Palmerston and Thiers both left office and their successors, Aberdeen and Guizot, rapidly repaired the entente. But for the moment French political opinion was hostile to Britain; and when French naval officers, as always anxious to assert French power overseas at the expense of Britain, made a number of protectorate treaties in places where British and French interests were in close contact – Tahiti, the Comoro Islands, Diego Suarez in Madagascar, Gaboon – it was difficult for Guizot to denounce them without seeming to truckle to Britain. These protectorates were therefore ratified. Similar tensions arose between Britain and France in 1861–3, primarily over the Schleswig-Holstein question, and again Palmerston was largely responsible. Two by-products of this estrangement were British annexation of Lagos, on which France was thought to have designs in 1861, and the counter-annexation of Porto Novo by France in 1863. Again international relations improved and thereafter French-British tensions had little effect on official policy in West Africa until after 1882.

Although these two episodes were short-lived and intrinsically unimportant, they are of some significance for West African prospects after 1880. Given the close contacts and multiple causes of friction between British and French nationals in many parts of West Africa, a 'hands-off' policy depended heavily on agreement between London and Paris to restrain jingoists both on the coast and in the Ministry of Marine; and when Anglo-French relations were bad it became difficult for the most cautious officials in the two Foreign Offices to maintain this restraint. It would be wrong to suggest that Anglo-French estrangement over Egypt between 1882 and 1904 was the direct cause of French territorial expansion in West Africa or elsewhere. Yet there can be no doubt that this estrangement influenced many in Paris and that many aspects of French expansion after 1880 must, in part at least, be explained in terms of a new official readiness to sanction forward policies which would previously have been checked for fear of annoying Britain.

The second factor making for expansion of European territory or influence before 1880 was the fiscal needs of existing possessions. The problem of maintaining these poverty-stricken colonies and bases without heavy subsidies from the metropolis was as old as British and French involvement in West Africa. Since 1815 the British had been increasingly determined not to subsidize their colonies, and this desire for economy was instrumental in the transfer of the Gold Coast forts to the committee of merchants in 1828. The return to direct metropolitan control in 1843 merely revived the fiscal problem, and it became clear that the only way to make the forts financially self-supporting was to increase the area from which they could collect the customs duties on which their budgets almost entirely depended. If the area controlled by the forts was not continuous along the neighbouring coast, traders would deal direct with African states to avoid paying British customs. Hence a number of protectorate treaties were made with African rulers in the vicinity of British bases which made them liable for British customs duties and at the same time placed them under the jurisdiction of the British courts. By 1850 the Gold Coast was virtually sealed by British customs posts, and the remaining gaps were closed by the acquisition of the Danish and Dutch forts in 1851 and 1871. The same tendency occurred in the vicinity of Lagos after its annexation. The near-by ports of Palama, Lekki and Badagri were quickly annexed and the French traders in Dahomey feared that Porto Novo would soon follow. They opposed this not only because they disliked paying customs at all, but also because British customs tended to be imposed on goods normally imported by French rather than British merchants – cowries, brandy and tobacco. Thus the customs question constituted at once an incentive for Britain to occupy areas contiguous with her existing bases and a grievance for European traders of other nationalities. The French were faced with precisely the same problem in the 1860s. The French Parliament reduced the colonial vote in 1866 and it was now necessary for French bases and colonies to become more self-supporting. They too resorted to treaty-making in the Ivory Coast in 1868–9 and were anxious to extend their customs posts in other areas. There can be no doubt that the same factor would have continued to provide an important motive for local territorial expansion by both French and British for the indefinite future, irrespective of new imperialistic impulses, wherever existing bases and customs posts were being by-passed by trade with independent African states.

Difficulties arising from political relations with African states was a third and equally important factor making for further territorial expansion before and after 1880. The political situation in West Africa in this period was extremely complex and the structure of African states and politics was of great importance to Europeans. Broadly, there were three main categories of African states in the region, each of which presented special problems for Europeans. On the Ivory and Gold Coasts and on the Oil Rivers there were a large number of relatively small states or political units, many of them professional middleman organizations which lived by handling trade coming from the interior to the coast. They had little military capacity to resist European infiltration, but could be valuable allies or inconvenient enemies. Second, there were the larger inland states, such as Ashanti, Dahomey, Oyo and Benin. These were seldom in direct contact with European traders but some of them controlled areas from which vegetable oil or export commodities came; and their military power made it necessary to deal with them carefully. Finally, by the middle of the century there were two major inland empires: the Fulani, lying behind the Oil Rivers and Dahomey, and the Tokolor, on the upper reaches of the Senegal, extending to Timbuctu. Both empires were products of Islamic revivals earlier in the century and had been built up by subordinating a number of lesser kingdoms, both Islamic and pagan. By contemporary West African standards these were formidable military powers, though vulnerable to internal rebellion and the results of disputed successions. It was fortunate for the British and French that, when they came into direct conflict with these rival imperialisms after about 1880, both were in decay.

Before 1880, however, the European powers were mainly concerned with the coastal inland kingdoms of the first and second categories mentioned above. What attitudes did the British and French adopt towards them? It has been seen that, for reasons both of commerce and fiscal economy, the preferred mid-nineteenth-century policy was to avoid political responsibilities and to rely on African rulers for the functions of government outside existing colonies and bases. But this policy could only be successful, given the basic interests of Europeans, if the native states were able and willing to fulfil the role assigned to them. In practice the position was never entirely satisfactory or stable; and by about 1880 it was becoming increasingly clear that growing friction must eventually lead to the end of collaboration and the imposition of formal imperial authority.

One perennial economic problem was that alliance with small coastal states, such as the Fanti, the Jack-Jacks or the Brassmen, meant accepting also their function as monopolistic middlemen, and therefore high prices, limited quantities and low quality for export commodities. In the end unrestricted commerce would make it necessary to by-pass these coastal states and establish direct contact with the inland producers. Again, refusal to undertake political responsibility in these trade areas generated innumerable problems of jurisdiction over Europeans and Africans, primarily because there were no courts which could satisfactorily punish crime and enforce commercial agreements. Extra-territorial jurisdiction based on the coastal factories was quite inadequate in the long term, and this fact undoubtedly contributed both to the growth of British control on the Gold Coast at the expense of the small Fanti kingdoms and to French expansion around Senegal, on the Ivory Coast and in Gaboon. For half a century, from 1824 to 1874, the Ashanti kingdom was a threat to British security on the Gold Coast, since the traditional British alliance with the Fanti implied hostility from the Ashanti. Twice, in 1824 and 1863, the British on the coast suffered severely from Ashanti invasions. It was not until 1874 that Sir Garnet Wolseley at last dealt effectively with the Ashanti; and even then it was left as an independent kingdom, tied to Britain only by treaty. Similarly, the French position on the Ivory Coast, especially their short-lived protectorate over Porto Novo in 1863, was at the mercy of the King of Dahomey as suzerain of the area. In the long run the European powers would have to reach a more stable agreement with these inland powers, or impose full authority over them.

Such action, however, was not seriously in prospect before 1880. Conquest would be expensive, administration inconvenient; and the value of the trade was not thought to justify such measures. From a purely commercial viewpoint the most profitable policy was to work with a power such as Dahomey, making the best terms possible. For some twenty years after 1843, for example, the Régis found it extremely profitable to trade with Dahomey in vegetable oils without any political support from France. The basis for satisfactory collaboration was the fact that the King of Dahomey regarded the oil trade as a useful means of acquiring foreign currency with which to buy European armaments, whereas the slave trade produced non-negotiable commodities such as tobacco and rum. It is significant that the Régis, using Whydah as their port of entry, showed not the slightest desire for French political intervention and in fact feared the imposition of French customs duties on the coast. In the 1860s, however, conditions in Dahomey deteriorated. A new King began to impose less acceptable financial conditions and proved an unreliable commercial partner. This induced the Régis to accept French political intervention for the time being. They welcomed the Porto Novo protectorate of 1863 and asked for further extension of metropolitan authority. After 1868, however, political conditions in Dahomey improved again, and a satisfactory basis for collaboration between the King and the

Régis was sustained until the 1880s. But the case of Dahomey showed clearly that collaboration with an unreconstructed African kingdom was inherently unstable. At its best an admirable and inexpensive basis for a limited trade, it was very vulnerable to changing local conditions – in this case royal poverty caused by the end of the slave trade and lower market prices for oil in the 1860s. When conditions deteriorated in this way the critical question was whether the private European interests concerned would ask for metropolitan help; and, even more important, whether the parent state considered that the national interests at stake warranted state intervention. In the 1860s there was no serious chance that France would occupy Dahomey to safeguard Régis interests; but from the 1880s metropolitan reactions to similar situations were to change substantially.

Dahomey was one of many inland states of differing size and type with whom Europeans had to collaborate during the half-century before 1880. By the late 1870s almost all such relationships were under increasing strain. Europeans were increasingly dissatisfied with the political and economic conditions provided by African rulers at a time of rapid change. The volume of European trade was increasing to such an extent and rivalries between traders of different nationalities were becoming so intense – particularly on the Oil Rivers – that African states could no longer hold the balance. The result was increasing confusion and a change of attitude by some, though by no means all, foreign traders who now, for the first time, favoured formal metropolitan rule even at the cost of paying higher customs duties. The question was whether London, Paris, or some other European government would be prepared to drop the assumptions of the last half-century and set up costly political administrations to fill the void left by decaying African political systems.

If one fact stands out from this analysis of forces at work on the Gold and Ivory Coasts and in the Niger Delta before about 1880, it is that the tendency to expand European influence owed little or nothing to conscious planning by London or Paris and that most acquisitions were a reluctant response to problems arising from trade in the small coastal bases. This metropolitan indifference certainly extended to Senegal. But in the middle of the century Senegal developed its own concept of the future development of French power in the Western Sudan which is interesting not only as a classical example of a local sub-imperialism but because it proved after 1880 to be the most important single factor making for European expansion in West Africa.

Before the 1850s Senegal did not differ greatly from other European possessions in the area. Like them it was a survival from a different past, its staple exports of slaves and spirit gum dead or in decay. The French were faced with the economic problem of finding a new staple to support the economy and produce revenue and the military problem of dealing with local African states, whose demands for the conventional tribute were embarrassing to an increasingly indigent colonial Treasury. By about 1830 attempts to develop coffee, sugar and cotton plantations on the Senegal had been defeated by soil, climate and the refusal of Africans to take plantation work. The only economic prospect lay in export of ground nuts, but these were at first available only in the Gambia, Sierra Leone and the Rivers of the South, particularly the Casamance, none of which belonged to France. The French had trading bases at Albreda on the Gambia and at Sedhiou on the Casamance, and metropolitan and local merchants were thus able to turn much of the export trade through Goree and St Louis. Yet the fact that these sources of ground nuts lay outside French control created problems. Treaties made with African rulers provided inadequate security, and there was constant fear that the British might expand northwards from Sierra Leone and absorb the producing areas. In short, Senegal was economically weak because the sources of her staple commodity trade lay outside her boundaries.

This situation gave rise to a calculated imperialism unique in West Africa before the late 1870s. Its main exponent was Louis Faidherbe, Governor in 1854–61 and 1863–5. His aim was initially to make Senegal a viable colony; and for this he believed three things were necessary. First, the near-by African states must be brought to terms, if necessary by conquest, so that France effectively controlled the whole of the River Senegal. This was particularly necessary in view of the establishment of the Tokolor Empire between the Senegal and the Niger by Al-Hajj Umar, whose ambitions might well lead him on towards the Lower Senegal. Second, the production of ground nuts must be encouraged by coastal tribes within the area of French formal or informal control. Third, France must get effective control over other ground nut producing areas to the south. On this military and economic basis Senegal could become a true French colony, and the African population could be educated and fully assimilated to French civilization. It was an ambitious programme for an almost derelict colony. But by economical use of Senegalese troops and some support from Paris, Faidherbe achieved most of it by 1861. Forts had been established at Matam and Bakel in Galam and at Medina in Khasso. Umar's forces were repulsed in 1857–9, and French agents were investigating areas as far east as Segu for future action. Dakar was occupied in 1857 and the conquest of Cayor was begun. Wherever possible, ground nut production was started as new areas came under Senegalese control. By 1861 Senegal was beginning to look like a viable colony and a potential base for future expansion into the Sudan and along the Guinea Coast.

But after his return to Senegal in 1863 Faidherbe drew up far more ambitious proposals. Having secured a narrow Senegalese base, France should aim at effective control of a much larger area – the 'Senegambian triangle', stretching from St Louis along the coast to Sierra Leone and north to Bamako on the Niger. On the coast this project would involve acquisition of British Gambia and Portuguese Guinea, both by exchange with French territories in other parts of West Africa; but Bamako meant military advance into the heart of the Tokolor Empire. Thereafter the line of French advance should be down the Niger rather than along the coast. From Bamako gun boats could patrol the river as far as the Bussa rapids on the Middle Niger; and control of the Niger-Benue trading system could be completed by joint penetration of the Lower Niger with the British from the Delta. The essence of this scheme was that it combined two concepts: military conquest of the Islamic states of the Western Sudan on the Algerian premise (Faidberbe was a one-time Algerian army officer) that Europeans could not co-exist peacefully with Islamic states; and commercial enterprise on the river systems which did not necessarily involve full political control but would provide commercial prosperity for Senegal. In the context of West Africa both were revolutionary proposals, out of all proportion with the minuscule scale of existing military and commercial activity. If either was ever carried out the whole pattern of European activity in West Africa would be changed.

Between 1863 and 1879 Faidberbe's wider project remained a mere blueprint. Action was taken in the rivers of the South to promote the ground nut trade and by 1867 forts had been built at Boffa, Boke and Benty. But attempts to exchange Gambia for French bases elsewhere failed, and by the later 1860s the momentum of

French advance was lagging. Above all the great Sudan scheme hung fire. In 1864 France was deeply committed in Mexico and Indo-China. The Ministry of Marine had no interest in empire-building in West Africa and money was short. A report on the commercial prospects of the Sudan by Lieutenant Mage in 1866 was very discouraging. By 1870, when the Franco-Prussian War stopped French initiatives in all parts of the world, Paris was seriously thinking of withdrawing the garrison from Medina. In the early 1870s there seemed therefore no serious prospect that France would erupt into the hinterland of West Africa. Yet this was misleading. In Senegal and in the minds of some officials in Paris the concept of military expansion from Senegal to the Sudan was an established ultimate objective. In course of time Faidherbe's scheme was certain to be revived by Senegalese governors or soldiers, and under more favourable conditions might be accepted in France. Thus, paradoxically, the middle of the nineteenth century, which appeared to mark the lowest ebb of British and French political expansion in West Africa, generated the project which, in the twenty years after 1879, was to produce partition of the whole coast and the Sudanese interior.

By about 1880 European empire in West Africa still had little to show for the half-century of expanding economic activity since 1830. By and large, and with the important exception of Senegal, it had not been the intention of Europeans on the spot, and even less of their metropolitan governments, to build large territorial empires. The general aim was to be as little involved in political responsibilities as was compatible with the dual concern for suppressing the slave trade and developing commerce. Nevertheless, the foundations for more extensive formal rule were already laid. In Senegal there was a calculated project for expansion into the Western Sudan which only waited on support from Paris. On most other parts of the coast European involvement with African states was now so intimate and the problems so real that wider political control seemed certain to come sooner or later. In the late 1870s the omens were that competition between traders of different nationalities would lie mainly in the Niger Delta and that there would be a race between France and England for control of this most valuable oil-producing area. This region was, admittedly, exceptional. In most other parts of the coast expansion was likely to be on a much smaller scale and to develop more slowly, and it could not yet have been predicted that within twenty years virtually the whole of West Africa and the Western Sudan would have been partitioned between the powers of Europe. But at least the evidence of West Africa indicates that strictly peripheral problems in an area of relatively intense European economic activity were capable of generating territorial expansion almost irrespective of the preferred policies of European governments; and that the partition of this region after 1880 implied no basic discontinuity with the previous half-century.

III CONCLUSIONS

It is now possible to give tentative answers to the two main questions posed at the beginning of this chapter: why at least limited expansion of European territorial control in Africa occurred in the mid-Victorian period; and whether further growth of empire seemed predictable in about 1880.

The evidence indicates that there was no one common factor making for imperial expansion in this period: each area had its own distinctive pattern. In Algeria the original grounds for French action were part economic – the inconvenience of Barbary pirates and the bad political relations resulting from French debts transferred to the Dey – and part political – desire to glamorize the moribund Restoration monarchy. After 1830, however, factors making for consolidation and extension of French control were largely peripheral and had no significant economic dimension. Algeria served warning on Europe that Islamic societies did not welcome infidel occupation and the French were therefore forced to occupy ever-increasing areas in the hinterland merely to retain their initial coastal footholds. The most striking and portentious feature of this process was the substantial independence of the French Army of occupation which treated Algeria as a private fief and was able to obtain the necessary credits for apparently endless campaigning on the ground that the safety and honour of the army demanded consistent metropolitan support. This fact was ominous for later French activity in West Africa, Madagascar and Indo-China where similar arguments were used in support of largely autonomous action by the army of the Ministry of Marine. Conversely the role of strictly economic forces in the extension of French control was small. Once the coastal region had been occupied Marseille and other regional commercial interests had a stake in retaining them and thereafter consistently supported strong action.

Over time French capital acquired a stake in Algerian communications and utilities, and manufacturers, traders and settlers built
up interests there. But these were the consequence rather than
the cause of physical occupation. Basically Algeria was a military
colony which eventually became integrated into the French
economy. It cannot be regarded as the product of any form of
economic imperialism.

By contrast, although both Tunisia and Egypt had potential
political and strategic importance for the maritime powers, as had
become obvious during the French revolutionary wars, the roots
of direct European involvement were primarily economic. France
and Britain treated both countries as independent states which
offered profitable openings for trade, capital and entrepreneurial
enterprise rather than as potential dependencies; and so long as
local conditions remained unchanged there was no probability
that either would lose its political freedom. Well before 1880,
however, circumstances changed radically. Excessive overseas
borrowing reduced Tunisia and Egypt alike to the status of
Lenin's 'semi-colonies' whose finances were in pawn to European
bankers. This fact alone was not necessarily fatal to their political
freedom for the genuine financial interests of Europe had no desire
for metropolitan political control. But by the 1870s it was clear,
particularly in Tunisia, that economic tutelage was generating
political rivalries between the agents of European governments,
each anxious that the indigenous government should not become
exclusively connected with another European interest. In short,
economic factors as such led to informal European control in
Tunisia and Egypt; but their secondary consequence was to weaken
each indigenous régime and this was likely in the end to lead to
unilateral political occupation by one of the interested powers
merely to prevent that country from falling under the exclusive
control of another.

In West Africa, where European interests, apart from British and
French concern to suppress the international slave trade, were
almost entirely commercial and where capital investment was
extremely small, quite different forces were at work. The essential
point is that commerce did not, on its own account, seem likely to
generate political control outside the few small coastal bases so
long as two main conditions were satisfied: first, that the character
and volume of the commodity trade remained compatible with
existing methods of production – that is, provided independent

African producers and middlemen could supply sufficient goods of adequate quality without European penetration of the indigenous economy; and, second, that African states could and would provide a satisfactory political framework for economic activity. Despite occasional local crises, it is arguable that no major deterioration had occurred on either of these respects by the late 1870s. On commercial grounds alone there was therefore very little demand by merchants of any nationality for extension of formal empire; though the fact that direct penetration to inland markets and sources of raw materials was now beginning in certain areas meant that there would ultimately be conflict with local African interests. Conversely, the characteristic mid-nineteenth-century ground for limited extension of political control was fiscal or political: the desire of existing colonies or trading bases to extend the limits of their customs collection to raise more revenues; the problem of jurisdiction; and, in the special case of Senegal, fear of Islamic power inland coupled with desire to incorporate areas of potential ground nut production in order to increase colonial revenues. It was these peripheral political and fiscal problems, rather than strictly economic forces, which led to a limited extension of formal rule by Britain and France before the late 1870s.

Finally in South Africa, where Europeans acquired more territory than in all other parts of Africa together before 1880, the forces making for expansion had little or no connection with the economic or indeed the political interests of the metropolis. South African expansion was economic in purpose in that its primary motivation was acquisition of ever more grazing land for Boer pastoralists; and in this respect it bore a very close resemblance to the expansion of European settlement in North America and Australia. The imperial factor was involved – as it had been in America before 1783 – only because and to the extent that Boer migration and the moving frontier of settlement created acute problems of security as settlers came into conflict with African societies on the frontiers. The overriding British interest in South Africa was, and remained after 1880, political: control of the Simonstown naval base. But the price of control was responsibility for Cape Colony and therefore involvement in the complex domestic problems of South Africa. The preferred British solution was for long to restrict the area of white settlement; and once the settlers had broken through the weak barriers erected in the 1830s, London vacillated between accepting the independence of the two new Boer republics and attaching them to Cape Colony. In the early 1880s it seemed that the republics would remain independent; but radically altered circumstances during the next twenty years eventually forced the British to revert to the policy of incorporating them with Cape Colony in a single southern African confederation.

Algeria and South Africa were, therefore, the only two regions of Africa in which substantial European territorial expansion took place before about 1880. In neither case was a metropolitan economic interest the main driving force; and there was little reason to think that strictly economic forces were likely to produce dramatic changes elsewhere in the near future. Yet this general picture is to some extent misleading. With the advantage of hindsight it seems clear that developments during the previous half-century had laid foundations for a considerable expansion of European power and influence in many parts of Africa during the period after 1880. In the Mediterranean, France's position in Algeria provided a strong interest in the political future of Tunisia and Morocco and there were plans for building a trans-Saharan railway to link Algeria and Senegal. Both France and Britain were deeply involved in Egypt and either or both might be forced by changed political conditions to assert effective political control. In West Africa the French had grandiose plans for expanding from Senegal behind the small British and French enclaves on the coast to the Upper Niger. Similarly the British, now in effective control of the Gold Coast, were bound eventually to make a more stable settlement with the Ashanti. Both powers were expanding formal control along the coast in the interests of customs collection and their merchants were planning to penetrate up the Niger to the sources of palm oil. Since the Germans also were increasingly involved in trade and shipping to West Africa it was at least likely that the composite outcome would be a creeping imperialism which gradually divided West Africa into spheres of influence if not into formal colonies.

Further south, in Equatorial West and Central Africa, and in East Africa, there was still little evidence of dynamic European imperialism and almost no established colonies other than Gaboon and Angola from which sub-imperialist expansion could develop. But change was clearly under way before 1880. Exploration was virtually complete. Leopold II established the Comité d'Études du Haut Congo in 1878. European interest was aroused. No one could reasonably have expected and few wanted formal colonization of these vast regions in the near future, but informal penetration by traders and haphazard acquisition of land and mineral rights by individual speculators was clearly predictable. Penetration was likely to start from any of a number of places already under European rule or informal influence: from Gaboon, the Congo mouth, Angola, Cape Colony, the Transvaal, Mozambique, or Zanzibar. In the late 1870s the vanguard of explorers, missionaries and prospectors was on the move. The isolation of Central Africa was about to end.

At the same time there was no reason before 1880 to think that European penetration would be very rapid or that it would necessarily lead to political partition. Given the limited number and intrinsic weakness of the existing colonial nuclei, except for Algeria and South Africa, the continuing hostility of the political majority in Britain and France to new and normally expensive colonial liabilities, and the virtual absence of all other major European powers in Africa, the forces of imperialism were still weak. Given also the established traditions of commerce in tropical Africa there was every likelihood that trade and investment would for long be carried on within an indigenous political framework. Thus, while there was undoubted continuity in the fundamental forces making for expansion of European empire in North, West and South Africa, before and after about 1880, it cannot be denied that in West, Central and Equatorial East Africa the speed and character of post-1880 development was unpredictable. Thus the main problem must be why, despite these historical probabilities, only two small areas of Africa remained independent of Europe in 1914 and why seven European states then had a major stake in the continent. Was this, after all, due to structural change in the character and needs of the European economy, or were there other and perhaps more complex reasons? An attempt will be made to answer this question in later chapters of this book.

7 Asia

I INTRODUCTION

An obvious difference between the history of European imperialism in Asia and Africa during the half-century before about 1830 is that whereas in most regions of Africa this was a period of first beginnings, in much of Asia it was a time of substantial achievement. The reasons for this contrast can be seen most clearly by relating to Asia the four factors which, it has been suggested, were most significant in checking European expansion in Africa: the scarcity of European territorial possessions as possible growing points for empire; limited knowledge of the interior; lack of economic incentives to acquire territory; and the virtual absence of 'national interests' outside the Mediterranean and the Cape of Good Hope.

Four European powers played a leading role in expanding their colonial territories in Asia during this period, and three of them had large possessions there before 1830. Russian territory already stretched from the Caspian to the Bering Strait and was contiguous with Persia, Turkestan and China. Britain controlled most of the sub-continent of India, together with Ceylon and a number of smaller bases in the Indian Ocean and South-East Asia. The Dutch, regaining their Indonesian territories in 1815, had widespread political and economic interests throughout the Archipelago. In addition Spain retained the Philippines; and Portugal held Macao, near Canton, part of Timor Island, and Goa, Damao and Diu in India. Only France had no territory in the East, other than her five small trading bases in India. Thus in Asia imperialism was not an exotic new culture but could grow from established roots. Every existing territory of any size was likely to generate its own sub-imperialism. Russia's frontiers in Central Asia and Northern China were seed-beds of trouble and distant military governors had ample opportunity and incentive to extend the boundaries. For Britain every Indian frontier was a problem, and there was no reason to think that the momentum that had so far carried the East India Company from its small commercial origins to a vast empire in India was exhausted by 1830. The Dutch had no continental frontiers, but their treaty relationships with Indonesian rulers had in the past been a constant source of political involvement leading to territorial control within the Archipelago. For these three powers, at least, expansion after 1830 was predictable simply as the extension of historic trends.

Sustaining the comparison with Africa, it is also obvious that Europe knew a great deal more about the independent regions of Asia than about the African interior, for their contacts were centuries old. There were, admittedly, areas which remained virtually unknown, such as Tibet, and much of continental China. But the coastal areas of South-East Asia, and China, the Archipelago, and the regions between British India and Russian Siberia west of Tibet were all reasonably familiar. European expansion did not need to wait on the explorers.

More important, Europe already had very substantial economic interests in many parts of Asia. In the 1830s this economic stake was primarily commercial, for capital investment outside existing dependencies had scarcely begun. The special feature of European trade with Asia in the nineteenth century was that, for the first time, it was no longer controlled by a few monopolistic national trading companies nor restricted to a narrow range of commodities of small bulk but high market value. Britain was by far the largest European trader in the East; the increasing significance of her Asian commerce can be seen in Table 11. In 1860 Asia provided 13·5 per cent of total British imports and took 16·4 per cent of total exports. In 1870 the percentages were respectively 14·1 and 15·9, in 1880 13·41 and 18·11. Most of this trade was with India, China and Singapore. In comparative terms Asia was collectively as important a trading partner for Britain as the United States, whose exports to Britain in 1860 were worth £44·7 million and which imported £22·9 million of British products and re-exports.[1] Europe was far more important commercially than Asia, but the

Table 11

British Trade with Asia, 1840–1900, as a Proportion of Total British
Overseas Trade (millions of pounds at current values)

(i) Imports to UK

Date	(a) Total Imports	(b) Imports from Asia	(b) as per cent of (a)	Imports from India
1860	210·5	28·5	13·5	15·1
1870	303·3	42·9	14·1	25·1
1880	411·2	55·2	13·4	30·1
1890	420·7	51·6	12·2	32·7
1900	522·0	47·0	9·0	27·4

(ii) Exports from UK

Date	(a) Total Exports	(b) Exports to Asia	(b) as per cent of (a)	Exports to India
1840	61·4	9·3	15·1	—
1850	83·4	10·3	12·3	7·2
1860	164·5	27·1	16·4	17·7
1870	244·1	36·9	15·9	20·1
1880	286·5	51·9	18·1	32·1
1890	338·2	55·8	16·5	35·2
1900	354·4	56·2	15·8	31·0

Sources: B. R. Mitchell and P. Deane, *Abstract of British Historical Statistics* (Cambridge, 1962); *Statistical Abstract for the United Kingdom*, nos 13, 40, 50.

importance of Asian trade lay in its character as much as in its size.
India was notoriously a vital market for British cotton and metallurgical exports and a source of industrial raw materials and food
grains. China was another large market for cotton textiles and a
producer of tea, silk and other primary products. Smaller but still
valuable markets in South-East Asia were reached through
Singapore as an entrepôt. Another feature of Asian trade was that
after 1880 it gave Britain a favourable balance on visible trade, by
contrast with her increasing deficits on visible trade with other
countries, notably with the United States. No other country in
Europe had so large a trade with Asia but each had particular
interests. China was a main source of raw silk for the silk industry
centred on Lyons. The trade of Indonesia was extremely important

for the Netherlands and particularly for the Dutch merchant marine. Most other European states relied on Britain or Holland as entre-pôts for Asian trade, but the United States had a large direct trade with China.

If Asian trade was so important, was it also a potential source of empire-building? On the general assumptions concerning the relationship between commerce and formal empire outlined above it could be expected to have this effect only under two conditions. First, if the established trade were to some degree monopolized by one or more European states, others might attempt to break the ring by establishing their own colonies to rival India, Java or Singapore. Second, if indigenous states obstructed European commerce, force and possibly annexation might be used to prise open their markets. In the period after 1830 the first of these factors was relatively unimportant as a stimulus to imperialism. There were no longer any monopolistic trading companies, and British and Dutch possessions were open to international trade. A more likely commercial stimulus to European imperialism was the obstructive attitudes of indigenous governments. It was a special feature of the East in this period that the two greatest powers, China and Japan, deliberately chose not to allow direct European access to their ports, still less to their inland markets. Until 1842 China allowed foreigners to trade direct only with Canton and even there trade was canalized through an official merchant guild, the Cohong. Japan had entirely closed her ports to all but the Portu-guese. Conversely, other states in South-East Asia, such as Annam, Siam and Burma, were never entirely hostile to foreign trade, but European merchants were at the mercy of despotic régimes and unpredictable officials with virtually no legal security for their goods or persons. Thus the primary need of European commerce after 1830 was freedom of access coupled with effective security. In the first instance these might be secured by treaties similar to the capitulations made with the Ottoman Empire which permitted European trade at specified ports, restricted tariffs and provided extra-territorial jurisdiction for foreign nationals and their depend-ants. Some Asian states were ready to collaborate with Europeans on this basis. Siam signed a satisfactory treaty with Britain in 1855. Annam came to terms with France in 1862. Smaller states through-out the region seldom offered much resistance, and the rights granted to one European power were almost always extended to others. But the ports of China had to be forced open by intermittent naval wars between 1839 and the 1880s, and Japan submitted only to American naval power in 1854. By about 1880 most maritime regions of Asia were open to European trade on reasonably satisfactory terms.

Did European merchants demand or need more than freedom of access to coastal ports on satisfactory terms? Without pre-judging the evidence on particular countries it seems clear that in general they did not, at least before the 1880s. The reasons for this lay in the character of most Asian economies as well as in the typical attitudes of European traders. By contrast with many regions of sub-Saharan Africa and the Pacific, the staple export commodities in which Europeans were interested were already available. There was no need to establish rice or tea plantations, silk cultivation etc.; and up to a point existing commercial and credit systems were capable of handling the import and export trade between maritime ports and ultimate markets or producing areas. The main defects of the system, once freedom of access to a sufficient number of ports had been conceded in any country, were that primitive internal communications limited the volume and increased the overheads of trade, and that agents of European firms were, in varying degrees, prevented from establishing direct contact with consumers and producers inland. Thus, in China and South-East Asia, the characteristic pattern of European demands during the second half of the nineteenth century was for freedom of access to more ports, better conditions for expatriate residents, greater freedom of activity within the country and ultimately the right to build railways and establish enterprises inland. Provided indigenous régimes were prepared gradually to concede such demands, European states had no more incentive there than in Latin America to impose formal political control. Political problems arose only when a demand for further commercial concessions had built up over a period and Asian governments remained unmoved by diplomatic pressures. It is clear that by about 1880 such problems were accumulating. China had been forced to increase the number of treaty ports step by step, but remained adamant over railway or mining concessions and still restricted freedom of movement inland. In Burma, British enterprise was at the mercy of an increasingly xenophobic court and projects for building a railway from the Irrawaddy to Yunnan to tap the southern Chinese trade were impeded. The French had conceived a parallel notion of penetrating southern China from Tongking via the Mekong or Red Rivers but found the route obstructed both by Annamese and Chinese hostility. In each case commercial problems eventually led to demands for remedial political action, though it was by no means certain that this would necessarily involve formal political control.

There were, however, two major exceptions to the general hypothesis that in Asia trade did not require control of territory. First, European traders operating at such vast distances from home and at the mercy of local governments needed both commercial bases and also, as the use of steam vessels increased, coaling stations along the trading routes. The result during the half-century before 1880 was a string of small entrepôts in addition to existing Dutch and Portuguese bases in the Archipelago and at Macao: Rangoon, Singapore, Labuan, Saigon and Hong Kong. Second, in regions where indigenous production did not provide adequate export staples, and where indigenous governments were too weak to prevent alien penetration, formal rule might result directly from economic interests. In practice this occurred almost exclusively in the Archipelago, already recognized as a Dutch sphere of influence, where effective political control tended to expand in conjunction with the extension of expatriate productive enterprises. At first sight similar considerations may be thought to have applied in Malaya, Burma and Indo-China; but it will be necessary to consider whether in these places commercial factors were in fact the main stimulus for political control.

Finally, what major 'national interests' had the powers of Europe in Asia which might influence their attitudes to control of particular areas? As in other parts of the world such political interests – the sacred cows of official mythology – might be of two kinds: matters directly affecting metropolitan power or policy, and others primarily connected with local dependencies but regarded also as indispensable to the metropolis. It has been seen that in the Mediterranean concepts of this kind ultimately determined British policy in Egypt and French policy in Tunisia, whereas in sub-Saharan Africa the only indispensable national interest of any major power was originally the Cape of Good Hope. Had any major power interests in Asia so important that a threat by another power might be expected to produce reflex political action? Before the 1880s it is arguable that only two major powers, Britain and Russia, regarded any part of Asia in this light. The minor colonial powers – Portugal, Spain and the Netherlands – certainly took a similar view of their existing possessions or spheres of interest; but none of these could now hope to exercise political influence outside its own existing sphere, and none acquired new dependencies in this period. France is a special case, and will be considered later. Germany, Italy and the United States had not, by 1880, formulated distinctive policies towards political developments in Asia.

British concern for the security of British India had more significance for European expansion in Asia before 1880 than any other single non-economic factor. The interests of India as seen from Calcutta were clearly a potential source of sub-imperialist expansion; but the really important fact is that these interests were for the most part accepted in London as equally essential to British national interests. The British associated themselves more completely with India than with any other British possession, even the settlement colonies. They would, of course, have defended any British possession against foreign attack, but only in the case of India did they attempt to insure so completely against external dangers. Any suggestion, however improbable, that Indian security was a risk, produced instant concern. Indeed the ramifications of Indian security were almost endless because India was surrounded by relatively weak and unstable states, all of them vulnerable to European predators, and because the frontiers of India were deemed to stretch from Persia and the Red Sea in the west to the Malacca Straits in the east. By the mid-century Indian safety was thought to require British naval predominance throughout the Indian Ocean, and neutral buffer states or British possessions on all landward frontiers. By 1880 the Suez Canal had become another necessary safeguard for India, and in the next decade East Africa joined the list.

But why did India rate as a first-class British national interest? It can, of course, be argued that this was primarily on economic grounds, and that imperial expansion on account of India must qualify as economic imperialism. But although trade and investment in Indian transport and production undoubtedly increased British estimates of India's importance, there was more to it than economic interest. By the 1830s, and still more by the 1870s, India was seen as a source of political and military strength. India made Britain a great continental power east of Suez, whereas otherwise she would merely have been the greatest naval power in the East. In an era of Gladstonian budgeting the fact that the Indian Army, including British regiments seconded for Indian service, was paid for from Indian taxes was an additional advantage. There were other less easily quantifiable reasons for British concern for India: pride in possession of the second largest oriental civilization, stimulated by the romantic title 'Empress of India' which Disraeli contrived for Queen Victoria in 1876; myths associated with the near disaster of the Mutiny in 1857; institutional traditions and personal associations established by civil servants, soldiers, planters and merchants. Such factors combined with economic advantages to make India an integral part of Britain's view of world affairs and one of her greatest national interests.

East of Singapore, however, Britain had no sharply defined national interests apart from trade; and for this region Whitehall had no strategic or diplomatic scenario. The limits of British ambition were freedom of trade; and, although pursuit of trading opportunities led to successive naval wars with China and to annexation of Hong Kong, this was not regarded as an exclusively British sphere of interest. There was no attempt to maintain naval supremacy there and London raised no objections to French occupation of Cochin China. Only when French control of Tongking seemed to threaten Upper Burma and thus the security of India in the 1880s did Britain react by a precautionary occupation of Upper Burma. Thus, when eventually the powers began to hover over the corpse of imperial China, British policy was commercial rather than political: to maintain the open door and equality of opportunity.

Russia also treated peripheral problems affecting her distant provinces in Asia as a major national interest. In the middle of the nineteenth century the main area of insecurity was the southern frontier of Siberia, east of the Caspian, which adjoined the turbulent and politically anarchic Kazakh steppe and the khanates of Turkestan. Disorders in this region were a nuisance for Russian settlers and the military government of adjoining Siberian provinces; but they were regarded as important in St Petersburg mainly because it was assumed that British power was steadily advancing from Hindustan and that ultimately Britain might obtain military access to Siberia. Defence of this area in depth therefore became an official Russian political objective, a mirror-image of British concern for the security of India against the threat from Russia. In the Far East Russia acquired a national interest almost by chance when in 1858–60 Count Muraviev-Amurski took advantage of China's war with Britain and France to obtain recognition of Russian claims to territory beyond the Amur River, and established Vladivostok as a Pacific outlet for Siberian trade. This was to revive an older dream of Russian power in the Pacific; but it was not until after the check to Russian ambitions in the Balkans in 1878 that St Petersburg became seriously interested in Far Eastern possibilities. Thereafter it became established Russian policy to secure a warm water port in Korea, and the growth of Japanese territorial ambitions quickly turned this area into a major Russian national interest. Thus, although Russian objectives in the Far East were originally commercial rather than political, and Eastern Siberia was strategically useless to St Petersburg because it was beyond effective military reinforcement until the trans-Siberian railway was completed after 1900, an active proconsul was able, on his own initiative, to convert a limited economic stake into what ultimately became a prime focus of Russian foreign policy.

There remains the problem of French imperialism in South-East Asia. In 1830 France had no territory east of India, very little trade and limited naval forces. What national interest led her to establish territorial possessions in Indo-China? Merely to pose this question suggests that French imperialism in Asia may initially at least have had different roots from that of Britain, Russia and other states with an existing territorial stake in the East. Was France a state in which specific interests, such as Catholic missions, commercial groups or the navy, could masquerade as national interests? Or were the French unique in adopting an imperialistic ideology in the mid-century? Whatever the answer, it is clear that the origins of French power in South-East Asia require careful consideration and that French assessment of the proper role of state power in the East may have been different from that of Britain and other powers.

It is, in any case, clear that the course of European imperialism in Asia was likely to differ greatly from that in Africa during the half-century before 1880. Existing dependencies at many points were certain to generate peripheral problems. Expanding commerce was a probable cause of political action, though not necessarily of formal annexation. Concepts of metropolitan national interest made several major powers extremely sensitive to political change. It would be no surprise if the mid-century proved as decisive for European expansion in Asia as the thirty years after 1880 were for Africa. In the remaining sections of this chapter it is therefore proposed briefly to review the course of events in six main regions – Eastern Siberia, Central Asia, Burma, the Malay Peninsula, Indo-China and China – all significant fields of European activity. Events within India and on its North-West frontiers have been excluded for reasons of space; but since it is reasonably clear that territorial expansion in these regions derived from strictly political and strategic rather than economic considerations, it would seem unnecessary to labour the point. The consolidation of Dutch control within the Netherlands Indies had also had to be omitted, though here the interaction of economic and other factors is of considerable interest. The general function of this chapter is thus to demonstrate by select example the typical relationship between economics and other forces as a source of imperial expansion before about 1880; and in this way to provide a basis for evaluating further developments in Asia during the following thirty years.

II   RUSSIA IN THE FAR EAST AND CENTRAL ASIA

In the early nineteenth century Russian possessions in Asia already stretched in a broad band from the Urals to the Pacific.[2] Much of this vast region had been acquired before 1640 and the border with China had been roughly demarcated by the Treaty of Nerchinsk in 1689, which gave Russia a foothold on the Pacific but restricted her territory to land north of the Stanovoi Mountains. Limited territorial expansion occurred during the following century. In 1707 the Kamchatka Peninsula was occupied and a naval base constructed at Petropavlovsk. From there Russian naval expeditions and merchants investigated the Bering Strait, the Kurile, Unalaska and Kodiak Islands and Alaska. In 1797 a chartered company, the United America Company (renamed the Russian-American Company in 1799) was given a trading monopoly and administrative responsibilities for Alaska and the Kurile and Aleutian Islands. Nevertheless, despite these acquisitions, Russia was not a dynamic or expanding force in Asia before the 1830s. Indeed, Siberia increasingly gave the impression of being a relic of an earlier period of Muscovite imperialism which might possibly wither away as Portuguese power in Angola and Mozambique had declined since its heyday in the sixteenth century. The total population of Russian Siberia in the early nineteenth century was only about one and a half millions, and consisted mainly of convicts, ex-convicts, pensioned Cossack soldiers, a few free peasant settlers and nomadic Mongolian tribes. Communications were so poor that the Russian-American Company used the sea route via the Cape of Good Hope rather than the overland route across Siberia. The fact that the frontiers were almost entirely uncharted further reflected the profound lack of interest felt by St Petersburg in the future of Siberia.

The question must, therefore, be why Russian expansion into both Central Asia and Eastern Siberia began again in the mid-nineteenth century. Was this new dynamism the expression of metropolitan economic needs or, perhaps, of political, strategic or ideological ambitions? Did the momentum come from St Petersburg or from men and problems on the distant frontiers? Since conditions differed widely, it is proposed to consider events in Eastern Siberia and Central Asia in turn.

EASTERN SIBERIA AND CHINA. Although the published evidence is not conclusive, a reasonable case can be made out for treating Russian policy in the Far East, if not the actual annexation of Amur and Ussuri districts, as broadly the product of economic forces. There were two economic objectives which might be expected to have generated expansionist policies in the Far East: a general desire for improved access to Chinese markets; and a specific need for the Amur region both as a means of access to China and the Pacific and also as a source of supplies for Russian Siberia. On the first count the basic fact was that Russian trade with China was restricted by the 1689 treaty to Kiakhta, a town on the Siberian frontier east of Irkutsk. At that time the trade was so small that this limitation seemed acceptable; but by the early nineteenth century it was increasingly unsatisfactory on two counts. First, the British, French and other European states had for some time had permission to trade direct with Canton; and when four other treaty ports were opened in 1842, the Russians found themselves at a severe disadvantage. Second, industrial production in Russia increased rapidly in the first half of the nineteenth century, from 46·5 million roubles in 1824 to 159·9 million roubles in 1854. Nearly half this increased production was in textiles; and since China was virtually the only foreign country in which the relatively high-priced Russian textiles could be sold, this market seemed increasingly important. The trade with Kiakhta did in fact increase substantially in this period: exports rose by six times and imports sevenfold, producing 15 to 20 per cent of all Russian customs revenue. Thus the case for demanding freedom to trade with other parts of China, both on the Siberian frontier and at the Pacific ports, was clearly recognized in

St Petersburg and was a major element in Russian policy towards China throughout the first half of the nineteenth century.

But desire for greater freedom of trade did not necessarily imply demand for Chinese territory; and it is clear that throughout this period St Petersburg's policy closely resembled that of Britain in that its main objective was to negotiate new commercial treaties with Peking. The first step was taken in 1805–6 when the Golovkin mission was sent to China to negotiate trading conditions closely resembling those demanded by Macartney's embassy of 1792: freedom for Russians to trade at Canton, down the Amur River, and at Ili, Tarbagatai and other points on the Siberian frontier. The embassy came to nothing because the Chinese insisted on full obeisance to the Emperor; but it is very unlikely that Peking would have accepted these demands even if protocol had not caused insuperable problems. Half a century later the considered view of the imperial court remained that contact with Russia should be restricted to Kiakhta and that the 1689 treaty represented the maximum concessions that could be made. The position therefore remained unchanged in the 1840s.

By this time, however, the relative positions of Russia and China had changed considerably. Although by Western European standards still technically primitive, Russian industrial and military potential had grown fast while that of China remained virtually static. Even the balance in the Far East was changing. The population of Siberia doubled between 1815 and 1854 and its mercantile community and river trade was developing rapidly. Although St Petersburg seems to have felt little interest in the future of this region, a few individuals, such as Count Nicholas Muraviev, who became Governor General of Eastern Siberia in 1847, had visions of large-scale settlement and economic development there in the future. This enthusiasm largely explains the policies he adopted there in the 1850s. But officials in St Petersburg were far more concerned with two problems in the Far East which were the direct consequence of the Sino-British War of 1839–42. First, the defeat of China suggested that she was no longer the great power she was thought to be earlier and might therefore gradually become a British sphere of influence. British influence in China had therefore to be resisted as a threat to Russia's position as a Pacific power. Second, the Treaty of Nanking of 1842, which opened five Chinese ports to British and later French and American trade, was seen as a threat to Russian trade with China via Kiakhta. On both counts diplomatic counteraction was clearly necessary. But it is important to note that the Russian Foreign Office under Count Charles Nesselrode was throughout extremely cautious. It wanted to foster good relations with Peking on the basis of assumed common interests against third parties rather than alienate the Emperor by threats of force; and it was firmly opposed to proposals for acquiring additional territory on the Amur frontier. Nothing, therefore, was done in 1843 when Rear Admiral E. V. Putiatin proposed sending a naval expedition to the mouth of the Amur to establish a more satisfactory frontier; and when a naval expedition sent to reconnoitre the river mouth in 1846 reported unfavourably on its possibilities, St Petersburg was confirmed in its opposition to territorial claims in the area.

Muraviev, however, took a very different view. While he was interested in the commercial possibilities of the China market, his primary concern was with the future of Eastern Siberia as a field for colonization and development. He also admired the United States and hoped that Russia would colonize Siberia in the same way that the Americans were then occupying their western territories. Indeed, he wanted Russia to remain an American power and opposed proposals for ceding Alaska. The Amur region seemed crucial to both these ambitions as a source of food for Siberia, a means of commercial access to the Pacific and a base for extending informal Russian influence over China. In 1853 he wrote:

In order to preserve Siberia it is necessary now to preserve and strengthen for us Kamchatka, Sakhalin and the mouths and navigation of the Amur and to obtain solid influence over neighbouring China.[3]

Immediate action was made necessary by the growth of British influence in China, and in 1853 he wrote to Struve:

If we do not take special measures on the Eastern Ocean, then of course the results of the British war in China and the expansion of her maritime power in the seas of these regions would have increasingly harmful effects not only for our trade with China but for our very dominion over these remote countries, and could for ever put a stop to the future aspirations there of Russia.[4]

Here, then, was a clearly articulated plan for imperial expansion in the Amur–Ussuri area. But in most respects Muraviev was so far ahead of official and public opinion in Russia, that the acquisition of Amur and Ussuri in the later 1850s must be regarded as a characteristic product of sub-imperialism rather than of metropolitan policy. It was possible because circumstances were exceptionally favourable. A governor general of Eastern Siberia always had considerable freedom of action because he could act first and argue with St Petersburg afterwards. But Muraviev's claim to act from necessity was immensely strengthened by the fact that Russia was at war with Britain and France in 1854–6 and that Britain and France were fighting China in 1857–8 and again in 1860. In the first period Muraviev could justify preventive occupation of the mouth of the River Amur in case the British should seize it, while in the second China was so weak that it was possible to extract formal concessions of territory and trading rights with very little difficulty. Without these favourable circumstances it is doubtful whether even the most determined proconsul could have achieved so much.

The course of events from 1847 to 1860 can be outlined briefly. In 1849 Muraviev induced St Petersburg to set up a special committee on the Amur question which sent Captain G. I. Nevelskoy to sail up the River Amoy to show that it was navigable. Nevelskoy also demonstrated that Sakhalin was an island rather than a peninsula. In 1850 Muraviev, on his own initiative, founded Nikolayevskii as a base at the mouth of the Amur. This was contrary to his orders, but the base was retained after appeal to the Tzar on the grounds that the imperial flag, once raised, could not be hauled down. The Chinese deliberately ignored this development and in 1853 rejected a demand from St Petersburg, representing the maximum demand the Foreign Office was prepared to make, for cession of a small area near the mouth of the Amur and for the right to trade at the Chinese treaty ports. In 1854 the Tzar accepted Muraviev's case for securing the Amur region against possible British attack, though not to annex it permanently; and in 1854 and 1855 two expeditions were sent down the River Amur and a major base established at Mariinsk with seven thousand settlers. In 1855 St Petersburg at last authorized Muraviev to demand permanent cession to Russia of the whole region north of the Amur and to secure further trading rights at Chinese ports. Both requests were rejected by China and it became obvious that Peking was afraid to make any concessions to Russia for fear of arousing British hostility. Nevertheless the Russians were now in effective occupation of the whole territory north of the Amur and it was only a matter of time before Peking was forced to recognize this diplomatically.

The outbreak of war between China, Britain and France in 1857 provided the Russians with the chance to extract formal recognition of the *status quo*. Negotiations with Russia began on two fronts. Admiral Putiatin with a small Russian naval force joined the British and French fleets and negotiated with Peking over trading concessions, adopting the role of neutral friend of China. In June 1858 he extracted the Treaty of Tientsin by which all existing commercial demands were conceded. Russia was made free to trade with the treaty ports – now increased to seven – on the same terms as other European powers and also at any point on the Siberian frontier. Territorial questions were left to be settled later. Meantime Muraviev negotiated with local Chinese authorities at Aigun, and by the Treaty of Aigun in 1858 obtained provisional recognition of Russian ownership of all land on the left (Western) bank of the Amur from the junction with the River Aigun to the sea. This left two questions unsettled: whether Peking would ratify this arrangement; and whether Russia could also obtain the land east of the River Ussuri. In 1859 Peking refused both concessions; but in 1860 the Chinese were again weakened by British and French attacks and by the Taiping Rebellion. Count N. P. Ignatyev was then able to extract the Treaty of Peking which ratified the Treaty of Aigun and in addition conceded to Russia all land between the River Ussuri and the Gulf of Tartary, where Muraviev had already established a new base which he gave the significant name of Vladivostok – 'Rule over the East'.

Apart from the occupation of Sakhalin Island in 1875, ceded by Japan in exchange for the Kurile Islands (a relic of the Russian-American Company which sold its rights in Alaska to the United States in 1867) this marked the end of Russian expansion in the Far East until the late 1890s. What significance have these isolated developments in the 1850s for a study of Russian imperialism? Two main points stand out. First, territorial expansion was inconsistent with the long-term official aims of St Petersburg, which considered that Russian interests in the Far East were almost entirely commercial and was satisfied with the concessions contained in the Treaty of Tientsin. The total lack of interest shown in the new provinces between 1860 and the 1880s, when very little settlement, investment or development occurred, underline this attitude. The second point follows logically. Muraviev was reluctantly allowed to go ahead with his territorial projects because in the political conditions of the 1850s there seemed a genuine danger that Britain and perhaps also France would establish political predominance over China and might even gain control over the mouth of the River Amur. Since this would have constituted a permanent threat to Siberia and to Russian power in the Pacific, it was almost impossible to denounce Muraviev's *de facto* acquisitions. Thus the annexation of Amur and Ussuri may perhaps be regarded as the chance product of the exceptional political and military circumstances of the 1850s. While Russian interests in the Far East remained essentially economic and while Muraviev himself saw Eastern Siberia largely in economic terms, the grounds on which he was allowed to achieve his territorial ambitions were essentially political. Even so it seems clear that St Petersburg was divided on the issue. The Foreign Office remained unconvinced of the political necessity of action, aware that territorial possessions in the Far East might involve political and military obligations which Russia could not then support; while the Tzar and a small group of nationalistically minded officials and service officers were attracted by the prestigious aspects of acquiring new territory, particularly after the disasters of the Crimean War, and gave Muraviev the support he needed. Thus it is misleading to regard the acquisition of Amur and Ussuri as evidence that Russia was now set on political dominance in the Far East. The aggressive policies of the 1890s sprang from largely new impulses and circumstances which became important only in the 1880s; and these will be considered below in chapter 12.

CENTRAL ASIA. Factors influencing Russian policy in Central Asia were necessarily different from those in the Far East. Central Asia was far nearer to Russia in Europe. It was close to the Caucasus, where the Russians were establishing effective control during the first half of the nineteenth century, and to some extent constituted a common problem. The Kazakh steppe lands lay immediately to the south of a region of established Russian settlement and were a likely field for peasant settlement in course of time. Thus occupation of the region east of the Caspian was predictable as part of the long-term thrust of Russian expansion, whereas occupation of the Amur region was not so probable until effective occupation of Eastern Siberia was far more advanced. But there were other distinctive features in Central Asia. In the Far East there was as yet no well-established European power constituting a threat to Russian territory, and the Russians had therefore no ground, except momentarily in 1854–6, for making precautionary annexations to protect existing possessions in depth. But Central Asia was becoming a meeting place of rival imperialisms during the first half of the nineteenth century. South of the khanates of Turkestan and Afghanistan lay British India which appeared to St Petersburg to be a dynamic imperialism likely in the long run to extend its influence over the Himalayas into Persia and Turkestan. It was, therefore, at least likely that the Russians would feel the need to make precautionary annexations east of the Caspian, irrespective of the intrinsic value of this territory, merely to preclude British penetration.

Forces making for a Russian advance into Central Asia therefore differed substantially from those operating in Eastern Siberia at the same period; but there were at least two common factors. First, there were substantial and long-established trading routes running from India through Turkestan to Russia and it is possible that concern to safeguard and increase this commerce was a ground for territorial annexation in Central Asia as in the Amur district. Second, Russian soldiers and administrators in Central Asia seem to have enjoyed almost as much freedom from effective control by St Petersburg as those in the Far East. Expansion in this area might therefore be affected by proconsular ambitions as it undoubtedly was in Eastern Siberia. What, then, were the dominant forces making for territorial expansion in Central Asia: metropolitan planning or frontier sub-imperialism; concern to protect strategic positions or desire for areas of settlement and trade?

In the early nineteenth century the southern limits of Russian territory ran from the northern shore of the Caspian up the River Ural to Omsk, Semipalatinsk and then to the boundaries of China. To the south lay the thinly populated Kazakh steppe, and beyond the powerful and warlike khanates of Khiva, Bokhara and Kokand, whose raiding and slaving expeditions disturbed a wide area to the north. Given the character and limitations of government in St Petersburg it is probably impossible to analyse official attitudes to this region with the precision possible for West European governments, but at least three motives for expansion seem to have existed. The most important throughout the period from the 1830s to the 1870s was anxiety to solve the characteristic frontier problems of settlers, merchants and administrators whose safety and prosperity were constantly at risk. Indeed, Russian policy in this region was similar to British policy in the Cape of Good Hope – to push the frontier back until some defensible line could be established. Given the character both of the country and its indigenous societies this search for secure frontiers led on inexorably until the khanates of Turkestan had been subdued in the 1870s. Second, there was a more specifically economic interest in Central Asia as a field for settlement and trade. In the period of conquest, however, settler colonization was not so much an object of policy as a means of stabilizing areas once they were annexed. As General K. P. Von Kaufman, Governor General of Turkestan, stated in a report to the Czar in 1882:

During the final subjugation of the Kirgiz Steppe the government did not have colonization aims in view. The occupation of the Semirechie and the Trans-Ili regions from one direction and the founding of the Syr-Daria forts on the other was impelled by the need to secure our border lines and to protect Kirgiz subjects from the attacks of hostile natives who had submitted to Russia, and along with this the desire to guarantee the safety of our trade routes from Russian territory into Middle Asia and Western China.[5]

In fact St Petersburg did not positively encourage peasant colonization of this region until the late 1860s, and it was not until after 1884 that large-scale settlement became accepted policy. Meantime governors of this steppe region had harnessed the unplanned immigration of Cossacks to form military colonies to defend frontiers and to supply food and other provisions for the army. Security of trade routes was a more immediate economic objective; but by itself this was certainly not the reason for the Russian advance. Finally, from the time of the British attack on Afghanistan in 1842 St Petersburg began to fear British expansion into Turkestan. Preemptive annexation to exclude Britain from an area regarded as a Russian sphere of interest became a Russian objective.

But Russian policy in Central Asia was hesitant and the military advance spasmodic. Until about 1864 the momentum seems to have come mainly from St Petersburg, thereafter largely from military commanders on the spot. An early expedition in 1839 against the khanate of Khiva, south of the Aral Sea, intended to check slave trading and to counter the British advance into Afghanistan, was a military failure, but it indicated the need for military bases in the area. During the later 1840s forts were set up in the steppe region south of Orenburg; and in the 1850s major advance began southwards from Orenburg in the west and Semipalatinsk in the east. The Crimean War checked this movement, but it was rapidly completed by a campaign in 1864. By the end of that year the whole Kazakh steppe had been occupied and the frontier lay on the boundaries of Turkestan, with a line of bases running from Aralsk on the northern tip of the Aral Sea, along the River Syr to Perovsk, thence to Lake Issyk Kul, on the borders of Chinese Mongolia.

In St Petersburg this seemed to satisfy the needs and interests of Southern Siberia, and in 1864 Gourchakov made his famous assertion that:

> We must halt, because . . . any further extension of our rule meeting henceforth, not with unstable communities, like independent nomad tribes, but with more regularly constituted states, would exact considerable efforts, and would draw us from annexation to annexation into infinite complications . . .[6]

There could be no better example of the characteristic metropolitan point of view on frontier questions in a distant colony. Gourchakov was saying the same thing as the British House of Commons Committee were to say on West Africa the following year, and as had been said so often before in London. But for Russia, as for Britain, it proved impossible to maintain such a position; always there were urgent local reasons for further advance, and generals whose career or honour depended on military conquest. There was the very real fact, also, that the three main khanates to the south of the new frontier were strong, and that they lived by violence. Whatever St Petersburg said, Russian military commanders on the spot found it necessary to deal with each of them and to force them to accept Russian authority.

The new move forward began in 1865, when the Russian general, Cherniaev, disobeyed his instructions and captured Tashkent, which he had failed to take the previous year, on the grounds that if he did not do so, Bokhara would conquer it first. Cherniaev was recalled; but his successor Romanovski resumed the same policy, this time with official support. In 1866 he defeated the khanate of Kokand, which recognized Russia as protector. Bokhara was dealt with next, both because of its influence throughout Turkestan and also because it was feared that Britain would step in if Russia held back. After numerous defeats, Bokhara came to terms in 1868. She ceded such vital points as Samarkand and Katta-Kurgan, guaranteed freedom of trade, and became a political vassal state, though nominally still independent. By 1870 the rest of the khanate was effectively pacified, largely by co-operation with the emirs, and

Russia developed a technique of indirect rule which avoided both the cost of administration and probable native resentment at alien and infidel rule. In the next four years the process of subduing the neighbouring khanates was completed. In 1871 a new and dangerous state set up by Yakup Beg in Chinese territory, centred on Kashgar, was conquered and subordinated, though it remained nominally part of China until after 1881. In 1873 Khiva was conquered, after vast military preparations. The khanate ceded all lands to the east of the Oxus, allowed Russians to settle and trade, paid a large indemnity, and was put under loose military rule. Finally Kokand, which had become restive again after dynastic troubles, was occupied in 1875–6, and fully annexed to the Russian province of Kazakh since it seemed impossible to sort out the various claimants to the khanate.

Thus, in the twelve years after 1864, Russia had pacified the whole area to the south of her new province of Kazakh. The forces which had led her on to the borders of Persia and Afghanistan were not primarily a desire for new territory, or economic resources. Nor was Russia consumed with imperialist fervour for expansion and prestige. There were traces of all these elements in the forward movement of the previous forty years; but the dominant force behind this last push was the problem of frontiers in an area where the natural boundaries lay on the borders of Persia, Afghanistan and China. Under such conditions the concepts and ambitions of army commanders on the spot had greater force than plans made in St Petersburg. In this respect Russia had much in common with the British in India.

By the 1870s, indeed, the Russians had many problems in common with British India, of which the most serious was the fact that the double advance towards this same critical area had made them near neighbours. In the 1870s and early 1880s the two frontiers came still closer together. The Russians consolidated their hold in Turkmen, moving eastwards from their base of Krasnovodsk on the Caspian to Geok-Tepe and Merva. In 1880 they began to build a railway to link these places with Samarkand and Bokhara. This brought them into close contact both with Afghanistan and Persia. Meantime by 1876 the British, in the course of consolidating the North-Western frontier of British India, had occupied Baluchistan, Kalat and Quetta. Neither side could now advance without coming into direct contact with the other; neither would trust its rival with control of the weak states which lay between. The fear was mutual. The Russians, with good reason, feared that British India was likely to extend its influence, if not its boundaries, beyond the mountains, and might then compete for the loyalty of Turkmen and Uzbeck; similarly the British feared that Russian influence might weaken the tenuous loyalty of India, especially in the decade after the Mutiny of 1857. In 1874 Bartle Frere, for example, saw the Russians as 'a possible alternative claimant for empire in India'. Of the two, the British were probably the more frightened and therefore the more aggressive. There is little reason to suppose that the Russians even seriously considered annexing Afghanistan, whereas the British had tried to do so in 1839–42, and again in 1878–80.

In fact, the best solution for both sides was to delineate the inchoate frontiers to the north of Afghanistan and Persia and then to agree to preserve the independence of both countries. Between 1869 and 1873 a sensible start had been made on delineating the north of Afghanistan, but the coming to power of Disraeli in 1874 led to a more aggressive British approach. Against the advice of the retiring viceroy, Lord Northbrook, and the views of his two predecessors, Disraeli and his new viceroy, Lord Lytton, aimed at making Afghanistan a vassal state by the traditional Indian method of subsidiary alliance and a British Resident. They were foiled by two things – Afghan xenophobia and the support it received from Russia. Secure in the knowledge that a large Russian force lay on the northern boundary, Sher Ali, ruler of Afghanistan, refused a British Resident in 1877 and a British mission in 1878. When British forces entered the country in 1878 to force his hand, he fled to the Russians. His more pliant successor, Yakub Khan, paid the penalty for accepting a British treaty in 1879 by being turned out by a spontaneous Afghan rising against foreign domination. This rebellion had interesting affinities with similar xenophobic and religious risings in Tunisia (1881) and Egypt (1882). But in Afghanistan the result was not the strengthening of European control but its virtual elimination. Abdur Raman emerged as the Amir of Kabul, and soon established control over the other khanates of Kandahar and Herat. In 1880 the British had to recognize his authority in a treaty which gave them only a promise that he would have no political relations with another foreign power, and which did not establish a British Resident at Kabul.

On this basis the problem of Anglo-Russian conflict over Afghanistan was solved most satisfactorily. Although the solution

lies outside the chronological limits of the present chapter, it will
be convenient to trace events briefly to the late 1880s. The Russians
showed moderation, and made no move to occupy the country even
at the height of the crisis. After 1881 a joint Anglo-Russian commission could therefore systematically delineate the northern
frontier. A crisis arose in 1884–5 when a Russian general occupied
the town of Pendjeh, claiming that it lay within Turkmen, with the
result that the over-sensitive British immediately assumed that war
would be necessary to save Afghanistan. In fact, they were unnecessarily scared. Abdur Raman and the British Viceroy, Lord
Dufferin, were able to arrange an exchange of territory with Russia,
which gave Afghanistan control of the much more important Zul-
fiqar. The frontier was then completed without further difficulty
and this ended the period of crisis over Afghanistan. The state
retained its independence, and acted as a satisfactory buffer between
British and Russian territory. This solution was a credit both to
the Russians for their general moderation, and, above all, to
Abdul Raman, who showed considerable diplomatic skill in
satisfying both parties and preserving his independence against
both.

There remained, however, the question of the Persian frontier
with Turkmen, and of Persia's political future. Russian occupation
of Khiva had made Persia seem, in British eyes, as much in danger
of absorption by Russia as Afghanistan and less able to hold its own
militarily. In 1881 Russia and Persia negotiated a definite frontier
from the Caspian to Serakhs, but the crucial area to the east, north
of Afghanistan, was left undefined, though Persia secretly renounced
her claims to this area. By 1888 this frontier also had been fixed as
part of the Afghanistan settlement. Thereafter the question was
which power would control Tehran. The Shah, like Abdul Raman,
wanted to play one side against the other to preserve his independence. Russia wanted to avoid British penetration from the
south, which was likely to take the form of building railways from
the Persian Gulf. The British simply wanted to keep the Russians
out. A solution was made easier by the improvement of Anglo-
Russian relations in and after 1887, and took the form of creating
informal spheres of interest in Persia. The British sphere was in the
south-east, on the borders of Baluchistan; the Russian in the north,
including Tehran. Neither side developed any effective political or
economic interests in the country, and the Shah kept to the promise
he made to Russia in 1887 that no railways would be allowed. In

1907 this *de facto* division was consolidated by the Anglo-Russian entente.

Thus Persia, like Afghanistan, was neutralized in the interests of good relations between Russia and Britain. The fact that both countries survived, and that neither received any significant economic investment from either of their patrons before 1914, is evidence of the limited aims of British and Russian imperialism in these areas. Both countries had advanced to a common focal point without having any real desire for territorial expansion or concrete economic or political objectives. Neither wanted the disputed territories, nor, intrinsically, much of what they annexed on either side of them. Both were driven by a pathological fear of leaving a political vacuum to be filled by the other, and were relieved to discover that it was quite possible to delineate their respective spheres without further danger. Indeed, this meeting of European imperialisms in Central Asia was a microcosm of many similar contacts in Africa and the Far East; and the way in which it was finally settled demonstrated that, given intelligence and a viable native state on which to build, formal partition was not necessary.

Reviewing the course of Russian expansion in the Far East and in Central Asia during the mid-nineteenth century it is clearly impossible to define any one universal cause of imperialist activity. St Petersburg had no initial blueprint for empire in either region, and the dynamics of advance lay for the most part in specific situations on the periphery – in the insecurity of the southern frontier of Russian territory east of the Caspian, in the power vacuum north of Manchuria, and in the ambitions and imaginative concepts of soldiers and administrators on these distant frontiers. Conversely, the official mind had a clear view on strategic problems arising from these largely unplanned and unauthorized territorial acquisitions. In Central Asia it was from the start understood that British power must be kept at arm's length and the assumed British threat to Afghanistan and Persia was regarded as a matter of first-class national importance to Russia. Equally an apparent British threat to Russian interests on the Amur was sufficient ground for permitting the Governor General of Eastern Siberia to annex the Amur and Ussuri districts. Thus in the last resort the deciding factor in St Petersburg was defence of existing territorial interests against an assumed threat from a rival European imperialism. By contrast, economic interests played a secondary role in metropolitan planning. In the Far East official interest was limited to protection and extension of trade with China; in Central Asia to protecting the existing trade with Turkestan. In neither region was positive desire for land for settlement or economic exploitation an accepted ground for pushing back the frontier, whatever an imaginative proconsul such as Muraviev might think.

III   BRITISH EXPANSION IN ASIA

During the half-century before 1880 British power in Asia expanded in five main regions: within the geographical limits of the Indian peninsula; on the North-West frontiers of India; into Burma; in the Malay peninsula; and, in somewhat different ways, on the coasts of China. It is proposed to consider the reasons for this expansion only in the last three of these regions, because it was in these, if anywhere, that economic factors played a significant role in the formation of British policy. But a brief preliminary comment must first be made on the special position of the government of British India as a source of sub-imperialism and on the problems of Indian security which were the root of territorial expansion in all parts of Asia except China.

It was a special feature of British imperialism in Asia, whose closest parallels were to be found in Russian Eastern Siberia and the Netherlands Indies, that Calcutta, the seat of the Governor General, had its own official mind and constructed an Indian foreign policy in terms of Indian rather than specifically British objectives. In theory, of course, the British government had ample control over the Indian government from the time of Pitt's India Act of 1784, which was greatly increased by the establishment of direct Crown administration in place of the East India Company's rule in 1858 and still more by the completion of a reliable telegraphic link between London and Calcutta in 1870. Yet in practice effective control remained very difficult. The Indian government knew far more about local questions than the politicians or bureaucrats in London. More important, India had its own army which was paid for entirely by Indian taxes, and this army alone made Britain a major territorial force east of the Mediterranean. Indian official opinion did not always prevail. Calcutta was not necessarily more inclined to territorial expansion than London. Indian policies were closely linked with British diplomatic objectives in the Mediterranean and elsewhere. Yet British imperialism in the East can only properly be understood in terms of the special needs and problems of India as seen by the Indian Civil Service.

Calcutta's view of India's political and strategic needs during the half-century before 1880 was based on the dual premise that India was infinitely the most important British overseas dependency and that its safety could not be taken for granted. Dangers to the British raj lurked everywhere. Within the peninsula Indian loyalty was deeply suspect, particularly after the Mutiny of 1857, even though the government made considerable efforts to obtain and reward Indian collaborators. After 1857 the earlier policy of incorporating princely states into British India when excuse offered was dropped in the hope that the princes would be a bulwark of loyalism. On the whole this policy succeeded; but in fact the princes and the wealthy landed classes of British India could not, even if they wished, assure the loyalty of the mass of the population. The British had to assume that Indians might refuse to resist and perhaps even welcome a Russian invasion from the North-West. Thus the inherent weakness of the apparently invincible raj was a compelling reason for adopting a policy of defence in infinite depth on all potentially vulnerable frontiers; and the fact that British India was initially surrounded on all but the southern maritime frontier by weak or positively hostile Asian or European states was a main reason for the progressive annexation of regions of insecurity during the half-century after about 1830.

It is not proposed to examine developments on the North-West frontier in any detail for, although this was strategically the most important area of expansion, economic factors played virtually no part in the formulation of British policy.[7] This indeed, was a classic example of how the concept of a major national interest, innocent of all ulterior commercial considerations, could generate large-scale territorial annexation. Imperialism stemmed entirely from the need to stabilize frontiers of weakness and to build defence in depth against Russia. Beyond the Indus and Sutlej lay the Punjab and Sind; beyond them Afghanistan and Persia; and beyond these Russia. These intermediate states constituted a problem in themselves, for political disorder, such as developed in the Punjab after the death of the great Ranjit Singh in 1839, led to attacks on contiguous British possessions. Far more serious, however, was the danger that such weak indigenous states might become clients of Russia, providing her with direct access to British India. Given the chronically bad relations between Britain and Russia during most of the period 1830–1907 the British had to assume that Russia might at any time use a threat to British India as a weapon in international diplomacy or war-time strategy. Clearly, if these middle states were too weak to withstand Russia they must be brought firmly under British control. Hence the annexation of Sind in 1842–3, of the Punjab in 1846–9, attempts to annex or control Afghanistan in 1839–42 and 1878 and finally the informal division of Persia into British and Russian spheres of interest in 1887. Whether or not such expansion achieved its primary objectives, it must surely be regarded as a product of the strategic assumptions of the official minds of Calcutta and London. There is little point in searching for evidence that responsibility lay with the changing character of European capitalism, the effects of tariff protection, or even the interests of commerce in its widest sense.

The same cannot, however, be said with equal confidence of British expansion from the North-East frontiers of India into Burma or from the Straits Settlements into the Malay peninsula. It is proposed therefore to examine briefly the relative importance of strategic and other considerations in these two areas to about 1880, leaving the annexation of Upper Burma to a later chapter.

BURMA.[8] Forces making for British expansion into Burma in the fifty years after 1830 differed from those affecting British policy on the North-West frontier in three main respects. First, there was no other European power in the vicinity of British possessions until the French conquered Tongking in the mid-1880s. Earlier British expansion cannot, therefore, be explained in terms of preemptive annexation to defend India against another European predator. Second, at least during the early nineteenth century, Burma constituted a rival imperialism and a positive threat to Bengal which had no parallel in the North and West, and British policy was therefore to some extent defensive rather than aggressive. Finally British and Indian merchants and investors established important economic interests in Burma after the initial conquest which undoubtedly played some part in stimulating further annexation. Thus the progressive occupation of Burma between 1826 and 1886 provides an unusually complex study in mid-nineteenth-century imperialism in which the three classic forces making for territorial acquisition elsewhere – conflict with indigenous states, economic interests, and rivalry with another European power – all played some part. The important thing is to assess the relative importance of each factor at different periods. In the present section it is proposed to take the story only to the late 1870s and to deal with the final occupation of Upper Burma as part of imperial expansion in Asia after 1880.

The first phase of British policy on the eastern frontier was undoubtedly dominated by fear of Burma. During the first quarter of the nineteenth century Burma was an expanding and self-confident, not to say jingoistic, imperial state. From Ava, the capital city on the River Irrawaddy, the royal house of Konbaung had already made good its claims to rule the one-time Mon Kingdom of Pegu and the Shan states on the borders of China. King Bodawpaya, who ruled from 1782 to 1819, was an arch-imperialist who believed that he was the divinely inspired ruler of the world and wished to demonstrate this by expanding his territory in all directions. His first major conquest was Arakan, a decadent kingdom which had long been in a state of anarchy, and this brought Burma into close contact with the British in Bengal. Immediately afterwards the Burmese renewed their traditional struggle with Siam. They failed to crush that rival imperial power but retained the strip of coastline north of Malaya known as Tenasserim. Meantime Burmese control of Arakan was creating difficulties with Bengal. The weight of Burmese taxation imposed in this area to meet the cost of the Siamese wars was so great that the Arakans were constantly in revolt. These revolts were normally put down without difficulty, but refugees fled across the border into British occupied Chittagong, whence the Burmese frequently attempted to extract them, either by force or by demands sent to the British in Calcutta. Between 1802 and 1911 it seemed that this problem had been settled, and there was little Anglo-Burmese friction; but a new rising in Arakan under Chin Byan in 1811 led to further problems. The Burmese were convinced that the British had deliberately helped him and that they were hostile to Burma.

From this time it seems clear both that the Burmese were determined to defeat the British and annex Bengal, and that they had no conception of British military strength. Bodawpaya was too cautious to launch a major attack, but, after his death in 1819, the imperialist party at court easily persuaded his successor, Bagyidaw, that Bengal could be conquered. The immediate cause of the war was the situation in Assam and the small states on its boundary. Assam had become politically decadent. It was occupied by the Burmese in 1817 and reoccupied in 1819, after their puppet ruler had been ejected. In 1822 two pretenders to the throne of Assam staged an unsuccessful invasion of the country, and then retreated to British territory. The Burmese governor of Assam was Bandula, a leading supporter of the Burmese imperialist policy, and he demanded extradition of the two Assamese. Meantime the Burmese had also occupied Manipur, whence many refugees fled to Cachar. It seemed probably that the Burmese would follow them there; but the British, who saw that Burmese occupation of Cachar constituted a standing military threat to East Bengal, decided to call a halt to Burmese expansion, and accepted a request from the Raja of Cachar for British protection. In 1824 the Burmese attacked Cachar, and Bandula prepared an army for a full invasion of Bengal through Chittagong. To forestall this, the British declared war. Their strategy was to distract the Burmese from the Bengal area by making an attack on Rangoon and thence up the Irrawaddy. The plan was theoretically excellent, but the commissariat organization was deplorable. Not until early in 1826 were they in a position to attack Amarapura, now the capital of Burma; and immediately the Burmese court came to terms.

The Treaty of Yandabo which followed began the British occupation of Burma, but the areas ceded were only those which had been acquired by Burma since 1782 – Tenasserim, Assam, Arakan and Manipur. These had little intrinsic commercial or strategic value to the East India Company and, apart from Tenasserim, were only retained in order to establish a buffer zone between British India and Burma. Conversely Calcutta had no desire to retain Tenasserim and proposed first to cede it to Siam, then to hand it back to Burma as an inducement for satisfactory settlement of several outstanding problems. It was retained only because negotiations with both states came to nothing. In addition to territorial losses the Burmese were asked to pay an indemnity for the costs of the war, to make a commercial treaty, to accept a British Resident at the capital and to send their own diplomatic representative to Calcutta. In return the British gave up the areas they had occupied in Pegu which had the greatest economic value and clearly hoped that lenience would result in good relations for the future. The treaty was regarded as a final settlement, not a first step towards further territorial acquisition.

British policy towards Burma from 1826 to 1880 can, indeed, be regarded as a model of mid-nineteenth-century techniques for dealing with indigenous states in regions of southern Asia in which no major political or strategic interest required formal occupation; and very similar methods were used in dealing with Siam and the minor sultanates of Malaya. British influence would be brought to bear through a permanent Resident at Court on whom it was hoped the indigenous court would come to rely for advice, particularly on matters concerning international relations. The Resident would also exert some influence on domestic politics, protect the interests of British nationals in the territory, and ensure that no other European power could establish potentially dangerous influence. Commercial matters were to be dealt with by treaties providing freedom of access for British subjects on reasonable conditions. If this system worked satisfactorily – as it did in Siam after the treaty of 1855 – the British would have no grounds for wanting more formal control.

The system depended, however, on the willingness of the indigenous government to accept collaboration on terms laid down by the British; and the special feature of Burmese history between 1826 and 1852 was that the governing *élite* was never prepared to accept defeat and loss of territory as final and therefore would not collaborate on terms satisfactorily to the British. The commercial treaty eventually signed in 1826 was in many ways unsatisfactory. The court never fully accepted the loss of conquered territories. Perhaps most important, the system of diplomatic contact with Calcutta did not work properly. The Burmese never sent a permanent representative to Calcutta and for four years after 1826 made it impossible for a British Resident to establish contacts with the King. Between 1830 and 1837 Major Henry Burney had considerable success as British Resident and built up his influence over the King and senior ministers. But political changes resulting from the growing insanity of King Bagyidaw weakened the new system of influence and it was destroyed in 1837 when a palace revolution put the King's brother, Tharrawaddy, on the throne. The new King repudiated the 1826 treaty and Burney found it impossible to stay at Amarapura. He was convinced that the court intended to launch a war to recover the lost provinces and advised Calcutta to take preventive military action. It is significant of British reluctance to extend their territorial control in Burma that his advice was refused and that he was replaced. But his successors found conditions at court equally impossible and in 1840 Calcutta withdrew the Residency and broke off relations with Burma.

This marked the failure of the policy of indirect influence over

Burma adopted in 1826 and the British might well have declared war in response to repeated attacks by Burmese robber bands on British territories. But the crisis did not come for another decade. The British were deeply involved in the North-Western frontiers of India in the early 1840s, and King Tharrawaddy was shrewd enough not to start another war. Nevertheless, from the British point of view relations with Burma were now entirely unsatisfactory and could not be accepted indefinitely. Two main factors after 1840 led inexorably to another war and possibly to further territorial annexation. The first and probably less important was basically economic. Trade between Calcutta and Rangoon was growing but, as in all independent Asian states, was extremely vulnerable to obstructive action by local authorities. During the 1840s the Burmese government lost control over its provincial governors and this resulted in deteriorating conditions for British and Indian traders at Rangoon. Xenophobic or grasping local officials made increasing extortionate demands and seem deliberately to have tried to degrade British subjects. The climax came in 1851 when the Governor of Pegu allowed fines totalling just under a thousand rupees (about £200) to be extorted from the captains of two British ships on obviously frivolous charges of murder and embezzlement. On a microcosmic scale this resembled the crisis caused by seizure of British-owned property in Canton in 1839 and could not be ignored by Calcutta without endangering the whole future of India trade with Burma. On these grounds alone the British were bound to demand reparations and, if these were refused, to send at least a minatory naval expedition.

In fact, however, these incidents merely underlined the major long-term problems of unsatisfactory relations between India and Burma which, from a British point of view, turned on the fact that the Burmese government ignored rights established by the 1826 treaty and refused to regard Britain as in some degree the paramount power in the Bay of Bengal. Hitherto Calcutta had preferred, in view of complications elsewhere, to postpone a showdown. But in 1851 the Viceroy was Dalhousie who, as has been seen above, believed in taking a high line with non-European princes. His view, which characterized a new phase of official thought in India, was that the events of 1851 constituted a deliberate challenge which Calcutta could not ignore. 'The government of India', he wrote in a well-known minute, 'could never, consistently with its own safety, permit itself to stand for a single day in an attitude of inferiority towards a native power, and least of all towards the court of Ava.'[9] He therefore decided on a show of force to persuade Pagan Min, King since 1846, to make redress, and sent three naval vessels to Rangoon. The court promised amends and removed the offending Governor of Pegu; but his successor was equally xenophobic and insulted Commodore Lambert, the British naval officer in command of the squadron. Lambert responded with a blockade of Rangoon and sank Burmese naval vessels. Dalhousie had no desire for a major war or for territorial acquisitions. He reprimanded Lambert and attempted to induce the King to make compensation. Only when this failed did he declare war in April 1852.

The Second Burma War was not, therefore, primarily the result of commercial difficulties in Rangoon, which were merely symptomatic of the more fundamental problems of Anglo-Burmese political relations. Nor was the original intention to annex more territory. But once the three ports of Pegu – Rangoon, Martaban and Bassein – had been occupied as bargaining counters, it was decided to hold them permanently and also to take their hinterland, the province of Pegu, as a means of linking Tenasserim with Arakan and thus cut Burma off from the sea. Additional territory was occupied north of Prome initially as a means of inducing the new King, Mindon Min, to cede Pegu; but when negotiations failed, this area also was retained. The Burmese never formally accepted the loss of these territories and no peace treaty was ever signed.

Nevertheless during the third quarter of the century Anglo-Burmese relations came closer to the model conceived by the British in the 1820s than at any other time. The new King was peace-loving and realistic. If he could not formally admit that Lower Burma was lost for good, he recognized that he had to live with the British. Until 1875, moreover, the British also showed a desire to cultivate good relations with the court at Ava, even conforming to the rule that visitors must remove their shoes in the presence of the King. Good intentions on both sides paved the way to satisfactory commercial treaties. A treaty signed in 1862 permitted British ships and merchants to operate along the whole course of the Irrawaddy as far as Mandalay in return for freedom of navigation for Burmese ships on the lower reaches of the river. Goods could enter Lower Burma duty free and rice could be imported to Upper Burma without paying duties. Mindon Min undertook to reduce other import duties in course of time, though in fact he was never able to do so because the royal finances depended too heavily on customs revenue. Above all, a British Agent was permitted to reside at the court, so that at least close contact could be maintained. In 1867 another commercial treaty granted limited right of extra-territoriality in Upper Burma, giving the Agent full jurisdiction in civil cases between any two British subjects and establishing a joint court for cases between British and Burmese subjects. Mindon Min promised to abolish all royal monopolies except those on rubies, earth-oil and timber and to reduce frontier duties to a maximum of 5 per cent *ad valorem*. The King also agreed informally to allow British steamers to navigate the Irrawaddy as far north as Bhamo, on the Chinese frontier, and for an additional British Agent to live there. The British were to be allowed to survey the potential trade and railway routes from Bhamo to southern China.

Taken together, these commercial arrangements and the establishment of a permanent British Agent at the royal court appeared to satisfy all important British interests in Upper Burma and to provide an admirable basis for future collaboration. Yet by 1878 when Mindon Min died, relations between Rangoon and Ava had deteriorated very seriously and in 1879 Calcutta was seriously considering whether to send a military expedition to Mandalay. Seven years later the British finally occupied the whole of Upper Burma and deposed the monarchy. This final stage lies beyond the limits of the present chapter and will be considered briefly in a later chapter on developments in Asia after 1880. Nevertheless, because deteriorating relationships before 1880 throw light on the character of British imperialism in this earlier period, particularly by comparison with analogous French problems in Tongking, it is important to consider why a crisis already seemed imminent. Was this due primarily to economic factors? If so, had the British come to the view that mere freedom of commercial access and informal political influences were inadequate? Was full territorial control desired on economic grounds?

There were, in fact, two distinct sources of mistrust and friction – commercial and political – which must be considered separately. Commercial circles in Britain, India and Rangoon had two main economic interests in Upper Burma after 1852. The state was regarded both as a possible overland route to the markets of southern and western China and as a valuable field for trade in its own right. The first concept had much in common with French enthusiasm for an overland route from Tongking to Yunnan up the

Mekong or Red River. The British had seen the possibility of using the Irrawaddy or the Salween River route as early as 1795, for a substantial caravan trade already existed between Burma and China in which Burmese cotton and salt were exchanged for raw silk, silk cloth, velvets, gold leaf, bullion and tea. Nothing could then be done to enter this trade, but British interest grew steadily during the first half of the nineteenth century. In 1860 the Manchester Chamber of Commerce, always eager to see new commercial avenues opened up, pressed the British government to open the Moulmein-Salween route as a means of selling British cottons to southern China; but by 1862 Rangoon commercial opinion preferred the Irrawaddy route and during the next fifteen years considerable efforts were made to survey possible railway routes from Bhamo to Yunnan. The Burmese government was extremely co-operative over this and the problems came from the Chinese side of the border. In 1874–5 a double expedition started from Bhamo and Shanghai to survey routes for an ambitious railway project to link the two towns; but the project ended disastrously when Augustus Margery, leader of the Shanghai party, was killed by Chinese tribesmen in February 1875. British interest then shifted back to the Salween route, for a British expedition sent to investigate Margery's death reported that the Bhamo route was quite unsuitable for railway construction. After 1878 deteriorating political relations with the Burmese court were an obstacle to further investigation, but enthusiasm for the Bhamo route revived after 1885 and survived until the end of the century. Exhaustive surveys made between 1894 and 1900 showed that the railway was feasible but would be extremely expensive and Lord Curzon, as Viceroy of India, insisted that the project be finally buried.

What influence had enthusiasm for the overland route to China on British attitudes to Burma? The Rangoon Chamber of Commerce and commercial groups both in Calcutta and Britain pressed hard from the 1860s for more effective political control over Upper Burma to further this scheme and this was one of the specific grounds on which Rangoon demanded strong action in 1885. But the route to China was only a serious ground for political coercion or occupation of Upper Burma after 1878, for until then the Burmese government had been extremely co-operative. In this respect the parallel with the French in Tongking was obvious: in each case commercial interests only demanded political action when and because an indigenous régime changed its attitude and began to obstruct a strongly supported project for opening up overland communications with the assumed wealth of southern China.

What effect, then, had problems arising from trade and other economic activities within Upper Burma itself? Trade between Upper and Lower Burma increased rapidly as a result of the liberal terms of the 1862 and 1867 commercial treaties. In 1862 the total value of imports and exports of the British maritime provinces was 52,470,315 rupees. By 1866 trade with Upper Burma alone was worth nearly as much. In 1876 it had risen to 102,260,580 rupees and in 1883–4 to 160,437,070.[10] Commercial houses in Rangoon acquired a large stake in this trade and a substantial mercantile community developed there. But, by European standards, trade with Upper Burma was by no means free. Import duties were never abolished or uniformly reduced to the 5 per cent maximum promised informally in 1867. A wide range of export commodities were still royal monopolies, sold at inflated prices. The royal government attempted to import rice from Lower Burma on bulk purchase rather than through Rangoon brokers and it imported manufactured goods direct from Calcutta to bypass Rangoon middlemen. Such practices, particularly the royal monopolies, were obnoxious to European businessmen with free-trading assumptions, not least because they put British concerns, such as the Bombay Burmah Trading Corporation, which dominated the teak trade, at the mercy of Burmese officials. As a result the Rangoon commercial community was increasingly critical of the régime in Upper Burma. There were constant demands for pressures to be brought on the Burmese government to eliminate these obstacles to trade and there is no doubt that many in Rangoon would have welcomed formal annexation of Upper Burma well before 1880.

But commercial pressures did not necessarily influence British officials in Calcutta or London. What was the official viewpoint on the future of the Burmese kingdom in the period before 1880? Basically neither the Indian or British government had any desire to annex Upper Burma. Successive Viceroys of India and British Foreign Secretaries wished only to assert the principle that Burma lay within a British sphere of interest. At most they wished to reduce the King to the status of an Indian subsidiary prince whose foreign relations were controlled by the British Agent. On this there was necessarily a conflict of aims with Mindon Min, whose policy was to co-operate with the British but none the less to retain genuine political independence. His method was to establish direct diplomatic relations with other states to symbolize his freedom of action. Thus he attempted, unsuccessfully, to obtain a treaty with the United States. He cultivated relations with France, allowing a French embassy to visit Amarapura in 1856, employed French technicians, and finally made a commercial treaty with France in 1872. In 1873 he asked for a firm promise of French support for Burmese independence, though this was refused. In 1872 he also made a commercial treaty with Italy. By the later 1870s there was a substantial colony of French and Italian businessmen and technicians in Mandalay and French Catholic missions were firmly established in Upper Burma. After 1878 the new King, Thibaw, actively negotiated with French agents and it became clear that the new régime hoped to safeguard its future by using the French, now advancing in Tongking towards the Burmese frontier, as a lever against British overrule.

The British were worried by these tendencies; but their own unimaginative policies were largely the cause of Burmese diplomacy. During the 1870s Calcutta increasingly treated Burma as a client state. The importation of arms through Rangoon was restricted and in 1872 the first Burmese embassy ever sent abroad was forced to deal with the India Office in London rather than the Foreign Office, as if Burma was a dependency of India. The new trend came to a head in 1875 when British officials at the Burmese court were ordered not to take off their shoes when entering the royal presence. This not only insulted the King but destroyed the whole system of informal influence built up since 1852 which had depended on close personal contact between the Agent and Mindon Min. Nevertheless, although this procedural innovation reflected the increasing arrogance of British attitudes to non-European régimes in Asia, it did not mean that Britain had decided to replace informal influence by formal rule. There was no chance whatever before 1880 that the British government would decide to occupy Upper Burma permanently on political or economic grounds. The French were still far away; the Burmese might eventually accept more effective British overrule; and the grievances of Rangoon merchants were not regarded as a ground for annexation. The real crisis began with the accession of King Thibaw in 1878 because this led to political chaos in Upper Burma. British opinion was shocked at the massacre of political opponents of the new régime and disturbed by the insecurity of British nationals, and in 1879 Lord Lytton as Viceroy of India favoured sending a military expedition to place another and potentially more Anglophile king on the throne, though not to establish permanent British occupation. This proposal was rejected by London on the grounds of excessive commitments in Afghanistan and South Africa. But the situation in Burma was now, in British eyes, extremely unsatisfactory. The Burmese government was in chaos; the British Agency in Mandalay was closed for fear of violence; French and Italian influence was growing; British businessmen were increasingly alarmed. Indeed the situation closely resembled that in Annam at the same moment in that a system of informal European control built up over a long period was in danger of complete collapse.

It is, therefore, clear that by about 1880 the situation in Burma had reached crisis point and some form of British action was almost certain in the near future. Yet as things then stood there is no evidence that British officials in London or Calcutta seriously wanted to annex Upper Burma for political or economic reasons. Their objective remained what it had been since the 1820s – informal control through properly observed treaties and a British Resident with the ear of the King. This formula had worked well between 1862 and 1875 and British policy was to revive it, if necessary by a military demonstration to assert their claim to informal paramountcy. The invasion of 1885 was the product of changed political conditions in South-East Asia, yet even so the initial objective was not annexation but restoration of the old order.

MALAYA.[11] The origins of British political power in the Malay peninsula were very different from those in Burma. Here the strategic factor – concern for the security of India as an existing possession – was for long relatively unimportant, though it is true that the first significant step taken in the Malay region, the acquisition of Penang in 1786, was intended to increase the naval security of India by providing a port for repairs to British naval vessels operating in the Bay of Bengal. The original motive for establishing British influence in this region was clearly economic – the fact that the China trade had to pass through the straits, and that the economic organization of the trade required an entrepôt for the collection of the products of the Archipelago, which in turn could be traded at Canton. In short, the British needed a commercial centre in the Archipelago. Once they had acquired one they discovered that its prosperity required stable political conditions in the region. Since no other local power, European or Asian, seemed capable of supplying this political infrastructure, the British were forced by slow degrees to do so themselves.

The true starting point of this process was the acquisition of Singapore in 1819. This in itself was, of course, only the final result of a search for a naval and commercial centre in the Archipelago which began in the mid-eighteenth century. The absence of a safe harbour to shelter the British fleet against the monsoon had been felt severely in the successive Anglo-French Wars of the eighteenth century, more particularly in 1756–63 and 1780–3. At the same time the economic problems associated with the China tea trade, arising from the difficulty of finding commodities other than bullion with which to pay for the tea, produced recurrent attempts to acquire a base to which traders from China and the Archipelago could come freely, despite the Dutch monopoly of the trade of this area. The difficulty was that no one place satisfied both strategic and commercial requirements. Attempts were made in the 1760s and 1770s to establish a British commercial centre in Balambangan, an island off the north coast of Borneo, but this factory was wiped out by pirates in 1775. It would in any case have been useless as a naval base. Penang was chosen only as a substitute after the Sultan of Acheh, in Northern Sumatra, had refused any concessions. But although Penang was useful for naval purposes, it was too far to the north of the Straits, and isolated by the piracy prevalent there, to attract much of the local trade. It had a prosperous career during the Napoleonic wars; but after 1812 its trade declined rapidly and it was even decided not to retain a naval base there.

It had long been recognized that the ideal place to fulfil both naval and commercial functions would be Riau, an island off the south tip of Malaya, and the British had cast eyes on it in 1784, 1788 and 1790. Unfortunately it was well within the Dutch sphere, and its ruler felt unable to risk the wrath of the Dutch by accepting a British presence. After the Napoleonic Wars the situation was changed. Although the Dutch were given back their Indonesian possessions, the British no longer hesitated to impinge on their sphere of interest. In 1817–18 Raffles wanted to acquire Riau or Banka as compensation for returning Java to the Dutch, but was forestalled by Dutch treaties which were forced on the rulers of these islands before he could act. Singapore was therefore acquired for two reasons. It could satisfy the requirements of a trading centre and naval base in the same way as Riau, and the Dutch had not occupied it already. Raffles made a treaty with the local chief, Dato Temenggong, who was also a hereditary high official under the Sultan of Johore; and then, to secure his treaty, supported one of two claimants to the sultanate, Hussein, against a rival who had Dutch support. To obtain British support, Hussein signed a treaty in 1819 granting the British the right to plant factories at Singapore in return for allowances for himself and the Temenggong.

But British possession of Singapore as a permanent trading base was still conditional on three factors: the success of Hussein in securing the sultanate; agreement by the British East India Company, in whose monopolistic trading area the island lay; and acquiescence by Holland. These conditions were fulfilled by 1824 when an Anglo-Dutch treaty was signed. The Dutch recognized British possession of Singapore and Hussein's claim to Johore. They ceded Malacca to Britain and acknowledged that Malaya was a British sphere of interest. In return Britain ceded the moribund East India Company base at Bencoolen in Western Sumatra and recognized Dutch preponderance in the Archipelago south of Singapore. This treaty was a turning point in the history of South-East Asia and determined the political pattern of the Archipelago for the rest of the colonial period. But its obvious short-term result was that Singapore became the centre of British interests in the region. Originally only a trading base occupied mainly by Chinese colonists and administered informally by a British Resident and a committee of merchants, it soon became rich and overshadowed Penang. In 1826 Singapore, Penang and Malacca were amalgamated for administrative convenience as the Straits Settlements with its capital in Penang. In 1832 Singapore became the capital and the focal point of British activity in Malaya and the Archipelago.

The essential problem facing the British in and after the 1820s was to decide how far their interests required intervention in Malaya itself. Raffles had defined what he took to be the correct principles in 1819. His first premise was that

The extent and high value of our possessions in India renders the acquisition of further territory ... comparatively unimportant, and perhaps objectionable.

It followed that British bases in the Archipelago must be run on 'purely commercial principles'; that is, as economically as possible. Yet he recognized that even trade could not operate in a political vacuum. British bases would have

... political duties of a more extensive and different nature. They will comprise the maintenance of a due influence among the native states, and such an interference in each, as may tend to secure the British interests and remove obstructions in the way of a free commercial intercourse with them. It will be an object to avoid all interference which may involve our Government in their internal disputes, at the same time that we cultivate and improve our connection with them by all the influence and support that they can reasonably look for from a powerful ally and protecting authority.[12]

These were sensible principles, and may be taken to represent basic British policy in Malaya throughout most of the nineteenth century. The difficulty was to know where to draw the line between 'interference' and the maintenance of proper 'influence'. For half a century the British acted on the first principle by avoiding all responsibility for the political condition of the mainland, but after 1867 they were forced to recognize that 'influence' forced them to take more direct political responsibility.

The difficulty in maintaining a 'hands off' policy was that Malaya was not politically viable. Whereas in Siam, and to a large extent in China and other oriental states, European traders could rely on indigenous governments to maintain order, the sultanates of Malaya were for the most part too small and weak to do so. The problem was complicated by the presence of large-scale maritime piracy, carried on by fleets coming from as far away as Borneo, and also by the claims of Siam to be suzerain of the Malay states. If Siam had been able to make good her claims and had maintained order, the British might have been satisfied; but only in the two eastern states of Kelantan and Trengganu was this so. Elsewhere Siam tended to interfere spasmodically, without taking full control, as in Kedah in the 1820s. Moreover, if the British had been truly independent of the mainland, they might, to some extent, have been able to tolerate disorder but inevitably they had economic interests there. Penang itself depended heavily for food on Kedah, and having acquired a strip of the coast in 1800, could not ignore political conditions in the state. More generally, the development of trade with the mainland, particularly in tin, which was being extracted by Chinese colonists, led to demands for action in the Straits Settlements during periods of political crises. In the end, therefore, Britain as the dominant power in the area was bound to become involved in Malayan affairs.

But until about 1867, the British made great efforts to avoid political involvement. In 1826 a treaty was made recognizing Siamese occupation of Kedah, which they had invaded in 1821, and removing the Sultan from Penang, whence he had been stimulating rebellion. On the other hand, the same treaty established the independence of Perak which Siam had tried to occupy the previous year. In the following year a treaty, which was never in fact ratified by the East India Company, was made with Perak, guaranteeing its independence in return for a promise that it would not have political relations with any other state. Britain was thus tending to secure the independence of Malayan states against Siam in order to prevent interminable wars, but without taking control herself. Inevitably, given the political weakness of these states, this absence of external control led to chaos. By the 1860s there were frequent complaints both from British and Chinese merchants in the Straits Settlements and from Chinese tin miners in Perak, Selangor and Sungei Ujong, that political disorder was preventing economic prosperity. Yet, so long as the Settlements remained part of the East India Company's possessions – that is, until 1858 – and even after they had come under the new India Office, the principle of non-intervention was adhered to. Only after 1867, with their transference to the Colonial Office, was a new approach possible.

The critical date proved to be 1873–4, when informal British control was established over three west coast states, Perak, Selangor and Sungei Ujong, which in turn led ultimately to British authority throughout the peninsula. Why was the established policy of non-intervention dropped? On the face of it, economic factors seem the most likely explanation, for in retrospect Malaya stands out as one of the most important fields of British capital investment in the dependent Empire. By 1914 fixed investment in the Straits Settlements and the peninsula were at least £27·3 million;[13] and even though investment on the mainland only began seriously in the mid-1890s, it might reasonably be assumed that political control was imposed two decades earlier as a necessary pre-condition. Indeed, strong demands for political intervention, though not for formal annexation, were made by a number of economic interests based on Singapore between 1870 and 1874, and it is therefore necessary to examine their character and importance as a potential cause of the new British policy.

There were three main grounds on which economic interests might have been expected to or actually did demand political intervention in Malaya in these years; declining trade between the

Straits Settlements and other parts of Asia, leading to a desire for better commercial conditions in the peninsula; concern for the safety of existing investments; and desire for conditions favourable to new enterprises. The first of these is not convincing as an explanation of the new trends.[14] It is true that in the early 1870s political chaos in the west coast states was damaging trade, and that in March 1873 a group of Chinese merchants based on the Straits Settlements complained to the Colonial Office that, since their trade with the Netherlands Indies and China was decayed,

... it became necessary for us to seek elsewhere openings for Commerce, and our eyes anxiously turned to the Malayan Peninsula which affords the finest fields for the enterprise of British Subjects and from whence we may hope to reinvigorate that mercantile prosperity which our industry has hitherto secured for us.[15]

But this cannot be taken very seriously either as a statement of fact or as the general view of Singapore traders. The trade of Singapore was booming, and only the much less important trade of Penang and Malacca was temporarily depressed in 1873. At most this complaint represented the difficulties of a small section of Chinese traders based on Penang; though it may have been supported by more prosperous traders elsewhere who welcomed any improvement in commercial conditions in the region. Thus, if there was a demand for intervention in Malaya to provide trading opportunities, it did not reflect any serious secular deterioration in the commercial position of the Straits Settlements. Certainly the petition of 1873 was not taken seriously in London.

Alternatively, were political disorders threatening the safety of British capital already invested in the Malay states? It is impossible to estimate precisely the amounts of capital involved but they were very small by later standards. In the Selangor tin mines there may have been between $500,000 and $1 million (perhaps £100,000 to £200,000, with the Mexican or Hong Kong dollar at 4s. 3d. sterling), most of it lent to Chinese miners by Chinese or British merchants in Singapore, plus an unknown amount lent to political leaders to finance civil wars.[16] In addition there was a small amount of direct investment, notably by W. H. Read, the leading Singapore merchant, and his partner, J. G. Davidson, a Singapore lawyer, who in 1873 launched the Selangor Tin Company to exploit a mining concession there. There may also have been some investment in Perak and Sungeo Ujong. Clearly the Straits Settlements had already a substantial financial stake in the coastal states, and their demand for British action in 1873 reflected this. Conversely, there is no evidence that substantial amounts of metropolitan capital were directly involved in Malaya at this time: the investment boom came in the 1890s under very different conditions. If political control was an *affaire* to protect vested interests, these were not metropolitan concerns.

Finally, did demands for intervention reflect desire for future investment and economic penetration? If so, it must have been in terms of tin production, for the possibility of rubber plantations was still unknown and no attempt was made to develop other commercial products until after 1900. It is arguable that the rapid rise of tin prices between 1866 and 1872 may have stimulated interest in Malayan mines. But this interest seems again to have been confined to Singapore, for there is no evidence of any metropolitan British or European attempt to acquire concessions or to float mining companies before the 1890s. Two mining companies were indeed floated in Singapore, possibly stimulated by high international prices, and in 1873 the Selangor Tin Company was attempting to raise capital in London. This company certainly needed rapid political action to end civil war in Selangor, for its initial concession from the Sultan ran only for ten years, after which it could obtain a ninety-nine year lease of the land actually taken up only if its working capital amounted to £100,000. To raise this sum in London it was necessary to demonstrate that political instability would not endanger investments, and for this reason the company was actively canvassing the Colonial Office in 1873 for political intervention, with results which will be considered below.

The economic forces making for British political control of Malaya in the early 1870s were therefore substantial. There was considerable indirect investment and Singapore entrepreneurs were attempting to begin direct exploitation of tin. Chinese traders were interested in commercial prospects. There was almost no direct British economic stake or interest in the peninsula, but Singapore interests were exerting pressure on London to take political action and it is reasonable to assume some connection between their demands and the action authorized by Lord Kimberley, the Colonial Secretary, late in 1873. The question, as always, is what form this connection actually took: whether political action was adopted primarily to assist economic enterprise.

Rather surprisingly, the answer is that the system adopted in and after 1874 by which British Residents controlled the states of Western Malaya was not directly or simply the outcome of these economic problems, but of three other factors. First, there was growing awareness in London from 1868 that rigid non-intervention could not be sustained for ever. Second, Kimberley's decision in 1873 was ultimately based on fear of foreign political intervention in the straits, rather than on concern to further economic enterprise. Finally, the steps actually taken in 1873–4 were not approved or precisely intended by the Colonial Office. These points may be considered briefly in turn.

It seems clear that the Colonial Office was aware from at least 1868 that it could not afford indefinitely to ignore the implications of Britain's position as the recognized paramount power in the Malay Straits. If this was in any way challenged the policy of non-intervention on the mainland must be modified. In April 1868 the Governor, Sir H. Ord, was given permission to negotiate direct with all the Malay States, not merely those not under Siamese suzerainty as hitherto; and it was recognized that 'circumstances may not infrequently arise in which you may be called to act absolutely on your own judgement. . . .' He was not, however, to 'enter into formal negotiations with native princes . . . except in pursuance of an object or a policy approved of by H. M.'s government'. This has been called 'the first modification to the policy of non-intervention in Malaya'.[17] By June 1868 a further, though unpublicized, change in Colonial Office opinion can be established. In response to a request from the London agents of a Singapore mining company whose property had been confiscated during a civil war in Penang, the Colonial Secretary, Lord Buckingham, while maintaining the conventional view that the government would not intervene to help private interests in foreign states, admitted that 'there may be cases in which it might be right and proper to take strong measures', and on the same day he indicated to Ord what these conditions might be. Ord was to keep clear of disorders in the states 'which do not directly affect or threaten the peace of the Settlements themselves'.[18]

These two qualifications to a policy of uncompromising non-intervention – discretion for the Governor consistent with approved lines of policy and action if the peace of the Settlements was endangered – did not indicate any desire for positive action in the peninsula. Yet, given that London could not exercise effective control over Singapore, these concessions almost inevitably led to further British involvement before 1873. It would be impossible and inappropriate to describe developments in this period in detail. Broadly, political order in Perak, Selangor and Sungei Ujong was virtually destroyed by the interaction of two factors: the traditional dynastic struggles for power within the Malay governing class, and faction fights between clans or secret societies of immigrant Chinese tin miners. These two factors became inextricably intertwined in each state and produced endemic civil wars which, in Selangor and Sungei Ujong, turned on control of the rivers on which both the revenue of the Malay rulers and the activities of tin miners entirely depended. In 1873 no one in Singapore or London really understood the complexities of these local conflicts, but the resultant chaos was obvious enough. The question was whether Britain should stand aloof or attempt to impose order.

It is clear that until 1873 the Colonial Office was not moved by political disorder or its effect on economic life to intervene, for no serious threat could be said to arise to the peace of the Settlements or British paramountcy in the area as a whole. But by 1873 these criteria were themselves in doubt. Sir Robert Herbert had replaced Sir Frederic Rogers as Permanent Under-Secretary and Lord Kimberley succeeded Lord Granville as Colonial Secretary. Neither wanted to expand the Empire, but they were perhaps less committed to rigid mid-Victorian formulas than were their predecessors. Kimberley felt that some action was desirable; but, as he put it in July 1873, 'the difficulty is how to do anything without direct interference.'[19] A possible answer was provided by the Lieutenant Governor of Penang, G. W. R. Campbell, who, in a report on the Larut War in Perak, proposed the appointment of 'a British Resident or Political Agent for certain of the Malay States' who, as in the Indian princely states, might work wonders without involving the British in direct responsibility.[20] This suggestion was not itself the cause of a change of mind in London; nor was Kimberley impressed by the Selangor Tin Company's proposition that economic development required political control. Nevertheless, the company was indirectly responsible for the decision to intervene; and the way in which they did this is important because it was in many ways characteristic of the devious linkages between economic interests and imperial expansion.

What changed Kimberley's mind on Malaya between early July and later August 1873 was a suggestion thrown out by the company that if Britain would not intervene to restore order in Selangor

H

some other power might be invited to do so. This threat was taken seriously because it came not from the company, which was British-owned and could be controlled if necessary, but from the Tengku of Selangor, a leading Malayan aristocrat with considerable political power in his state, whose actions were beyond British control. As an ally of the company who had no doubt put him up to it, the Tengku sent the company's agent in London a letter which contained the following sentence:

I would ask you to ascertain if the English, or any other Government would interfere in any disturbance that might arise in the territory of Selangor from wicked persons, so that merchants desirous of opening up the country may have security for their property and capital invested.[21]

This was clearly an ultimatum. It was given added point by Seymour Clarke, the agent, who, in writing to the Colonial Office, commented that a Singapore resident had recently predicted that 'the independent sovereigns of the smaller states, in the Malay peninsula, would put themselves under the protectorate of some European Power and Germany is mentioned as most likely to be approached failing England'.[22] The effects of this rather simple-minded blackmail were extraordinary. The Colonial Office was not concerned about tin mining or disorder, but a threat to British paramountcy in the Straits was a serious matter. Slight as the danger appears in retrospect, it did not seem unreal in 1873. Earlier that year the ruler of Acheh, while attempting to throw off Dutch overlordship, had been in touch, so it was said, with the consuls of Italy and the United States, offering naval bases and commercial monopolies in exchange for political protection. But this was only one example of an apparent general tendency towards European powers establishing naval or trading bases in the East. The United States had acquired Midway in 1867 and a lease of Pago Pago harbour in Samoa in 1872. France annexed Rapa in 1867. Above all, the Germans now seemed interested in naval or trading bases in the East. In 1870 they were said to have been negotiating for a naval base in Pulo Tioman, an island off Johore. At that time the Colonial Office was not worried; but by 1873 they were less happy to accept Germany as a neighbour in the Straits. In that year the Dreikaiserbund was formed, and this seemed for the first time to link Germany with Russia, Britain's conventional rival for power in Asia. Thus even a suggestion that Selangor might use its undoubted sovereign right to negotiate for protection by a foreign power raised the spectre of a hostile naval base in the Malacca Strait, which was one of Britain's commercial lifelines with the Far East and therefore a major national interest. In terms of Buckingham's formulation in 1868, developments in the peninsula were now threatening not only the peace but the security of the Straits Settlements.

British fears should not be exaggerated. There is no evidence that in 1873 Kimberley or the Colonial Office had any evidence that a foreign power was actively interested in Selangor. Otherwise their reaction would have been far more incisive. Yet Kimberley took the potential danger seriously. On 22 July 1873 he minuted:

It would be impossible for us to consent to any European Power assuming the Protectorate of any state in the Malayan Peninsula. I think we might send this to F.O. and enquire whether they would see any objection to Sir A. Clarke being instructed to endeavour to extend the Treaties with Salangore [*sic*] and the other Malay States by a Stipulation that they should not enter into any Treaty ceding territory to a Foreign Power or giving such Power any rights or privileges not accorded to us.[23]

By 10 September he had decided to go further than treaty revision; and in sending the draft instructions to the Governor of the Straits to Gladstone, he defined his position:

The condition of the Malay Peninsula is becoming very serious. . . . This might go on without any very serious consequences except the stoppage of trade, were it not that European and Chinese capitalists, stimulated by the great riches in tin mines . . . are suggesting to the native princes that they should seek the aid of Europeans to enable them to put down the disorders which prevail. We are the paramount Power on the Peninsula up to the limit of the States, tributary to Siam, and looking to the vicinity of India and our whole position in the East I apprehend that it would be a serious matter if any other European Power were to obtain a footing in the Peninsula. [24]

This seems conclusive evidence that Kimberley was not convinced of the need for more formal control by economic pressure groups or by concern for British trade and investment opportunities, but by fear of foreign infiltration. Although in retrospect this fear may seem exaggerated it must be remembered that insurance against so remote a danger was extremely cheap. There was to be no expensive annexation or administration. Sir A. Clarke, the new Governor, was merely told to report on the possibility of setting up a system of British Residents in the Malay States. The relevant section of the despatch is well known.

I have to request you will carefully ascertain . . . the actual condition of affairs in each state, and that you will report to me whether there are, in your opinion, any steps which can properly be taken by the Colonial Government to promote the restoration of peace and order, and to secure protection to trade and commerce with the Native Territories.

I would wish you especially to consider whether it would be advisable to appoint a British officer to reside in any of the States. Such an appointment could, of course, only be made with the full consent of the Native Government and the expenses connected with it would have to be defrayed by the Government of the Straits Settlements.[25]

Clearly there was no intention of annexing these states. British paramountcy was to be sustained by the characteristic mid-nineteenth-century device of informal influence.

Thus the fact that between 1873 and 1876 Singapore imposed what amounted to British administrations in Perak, Selangor and Sungei Ujong rather than a system based on informal influence as intended in London must be seen as the product of a sub-imperialist impulse in the Straits Settlements rather than of metropolitan policy. In brief, Sir Andrew Clarke exceeded his instructions; indeed he later admitted that he decided to 'act in the first place and to report afterwards'.[26] On arrival at Singapore he told Read that he would act at once if he were given the opportunity, and a request for intervention was duly presented by Read's ally in Perak, Raja Muda 'Abdu'llah, pretender to the sultanate. Clarke immediately called for a conference of all Perak parties at Pangkor in January 1874 and by the famous Pangkor Engagement made 'Abdu'llah Sultan at the price of his accepting a British Resident whose advice would be asked and taken on all matters except Malay religion and custom. In February 1874, a Resident was similarly imposed in Selangor, though without any formal agreement. In April the system was extended to Sungei Ujong. In no case was London informed or consulted in advance.

The Colonial Office, however, having taken its decision on principles, accepted these developments with resignation. Herbert, in particular, saw the new system as a satisfactory solution; and Lord Carnarvon, now Colonial Secretary, was not prepared to undo it. As so often happened, the man on the spot had effectively decided the precise form in which a new principle should be applied. Yet by 1874 the Colonial Office had gone as far as it was prepared to go at this stage. The foreign danger had been eliminated and better political conditions in the three Western states could be expected to satisfy the economic needs of Singapore. Despite evidence in 1875 that the specific political settlements forced on Selangor and Perak were entirely unstable, due to Clarke's ignorance of the actual issues at stake, London rejected the views of his successor, Sir William Jervois, that these states should be annexed and governed through nominated Malay aristocrats rather than the legitimate claimant to power on dynastic grounds. Carnarvon saw the force of the proposal but rejected it as premature. The original conception of the residential system was therefore given a chance to see whether it could successfully, as Carnarvon put it,

... train up some Chief or Chiefs of sufficient capacity and enlightenment to appreciate the advantages of a civilized government and to render some effectual assistance in the government of the country.[27]

As for the remaining Malay states, these could safely be left as they were. Perlis, Kedah, Kelantan and Trengganu were under Siamese suzerainty and it was British policy to bolster Siam against possible threats from France. Johore had no formal agreement or Resident, but the Maharajah lived in Singapore and acted on advice from the Governor. Pahang was too remote to be important. The remaining small states of Negri Sembilan were organized into two confederacies, one under informal control by Malacca, the other under informal control by Johore.

As a case study in the influence of economic factors on the expansion of European rule before about 1880, events in Malaya suggest three obvious conclusions. First, metropolitan policy remained throughout entirely resistant to pressures for territorial control simply as a means to private economic advantage. The resident system was not established to please merchants or tin-mining companies. Second, and paradoxically, the conditions in which British political action became a possibility were created almost entirely by economic factors. The weak political structures of the Malay states could not stand up against the pressures caused by foreign economic enterprise – in this case the feuds of Chinese tin miners. The resulting political disorder provided incentive for British economic interests based on Singapore to work for imperial control as a basis for their own proposed enterprises on the mainland. There are few clearer examples of the way in which economic forces on the periphery could lay the foundations for imperial expansion. Finally, Kimberley's decision to advance the frontier of political control in 1873 illustrates the ultimate primacy of the political concept of the national interest over apparently more immediate and substantial economic interests. Since 1824 Britain had assumed that the Straits were politically secure and therefore that the vital commercial route to China – the only major national interest in the Far East – required no further political control of South-East Asia. In 1873 the mere hint that a major European power might establish a base in Malaya was sufficient grounds for extending imperial control. This in turn indicates that preemptive political intervention, commonly regarded as characteristic of the period after about 1880, was equally possible during the previous decade and indeed earlier. The way was already open for the gradual extension of the Resident system to all the remaining Malay states, including those under Siamese suzerainty after these were ceded to Britain in 1909, and for the evolution of 'protection' into something more like conventional colonial administration. All this had occurred by 1914.[28]

IV FRANCE IN INDO-CHINA

French territorial expansion in South-East Asia[29] poses two almost distinct problems. Why, in the first instance, should France establish a territorial base in Cochin China in 1858–62? Second, why was this foothold later expanded until by about 1885 France controlled the whole Annamese Empire and part of Cambodia? At first sight French imperialism in the earlier period seems incompatible with the general proposition that in the mid-nineteenth century European powers seldom if ever deliberately acquired formal overseas possessions unless some very strong political or economic reasons compelled them to do so. What compulsions could have operated in this instance? In 1830 France had no colonies east of the five small trading bases in India. She could not, therefore, be pulled into Annam as the British were pulled into Burma or Malaya, by real or imagined security problems. Nor were there any definable national interests to defend in the region, for France was not a significant political or military force in the East. Economic explanations seem equally improbable, for French trade in Annam was minute and there was no measurable capital investment there. Was the conquest of Cochin China, and perhaps also subsequent expansion, an example of abstract desire for empire, the product perhaps of an atavistic French urge to conquer barbarians; or, like the Mexican expedition, a romantic attempt to gain cheap prestige for the Second Empire? It would seem not. Napoleon III was never keen on the Cochin China enterprise, and in the mid-century there was no popular demand in France for eastern empire. On all these grounds French imperialism in South-East Asia remains inexplicable.

Yet close examination of peripheral problems in the region discloses elements which collectively might generate French intervention in Annam, even if not permanent occupation of territory. First, there were French Catholic missions. Christian missions did not normally need or demand political support, let alone annexation of their fields of activity; but they might do so when in distress, and there were recent precedents, particularly in the South Pacific, for French naval intervention in support of French missions which were hard pressed by indigenous rulers or Protestant rivals. Moreover, if Annam is seen in its geographical context as a neighbour and fief of China, other possible grounds for French intervention become evident. The French Navy was now recurrently active in the China Sea, and in 1858–60 was waging a naval war against China in alliance with Britain. To sustain this activity the navy needed a Far Eastern base; and this might well help to explain the occupation of Saigon. Again, French merchants were increasingly interested in the China trade, particularly in the export of raw silk. French trade suffered, among other things, from lack of a commercial entrepôt in the Far East comparable with Hong Kong. Even if French economic interests in Annam itself were nugatory, a base there might help their trade with China. It is not suggested that these or other marginal French interests led necessarily to formal occupation, for the eventual decision to occupy and retain Cochin China can be understood only in terms of a largely unpredictable series of events between 1858 and 1862 which will be described below. But they do at least constitute credible grounds on which some form of French intervention in Annam can be explained without resort to belief in a largely non-existent metropolitan urge to territorial empire in South-East Asia.

How, then, did the initial occupation come about? What was the relative importance of missionary problems, naval ambitions and commercial needs? In the long term the Christian missions were by far the most influential source of French interest in South-East Asia and the primary reason for intervention in 1858. Yet, paradoxically, the likelihood that the missions would generate some form of French political control or primacy in Annam had been far greater before 1830 than thereafter. The missions dated from the seventeenth century and were always seen by Paris as a possible basis for a French political foothold in Annam to offset British influence in southern Asia. After 1763 several proposals were in fact made in France to establish a base there basically, as Choiseul put it 'pour compenser les pertes subies' in India by the peace of Paris.[30] Nothing came of these, but events in Annam soon provided further opportunities to establish closer political relations. The story is well known. In 1777 the French missionary, Pigneau de Béhaine, became friendly with Nguyen Anh, King of Annam, who was then facing a major rebellion in the districts of Tay-son which was supported by the rival kingdoms of Cambodia and Tongking. Like many other non-European rulers, Nguyen Anh thought he might obtain useful support from a friendly European power in his local struggles; and in 1785 he sent his son to Paris with de Béhaine to ask for military help. Paris was definitely interested because an alliance with Annam would fit in well with Vergennes' current policy of rebuilding French political influence in southern Asia. In 1787 a formal treaty of alliance was made and Paris promised military help against the continuing rebellion. But at this moment of domestic crisis the government of Louis xvi could give no practical help; and in 1788 de Béhaine had to raise military supplies and a small force of volunteers in India and Ile de France on his own account. These probably turned the balance in Annam, and by 1802 Nguyen Anh had not only suppressed the rebellion but added Tongking and Cochin China to the Annamese Empire.

Under different circumstances the victory of their protégé might have given France the opportunity to establish some degree of informal control over Annam and possibly to acquire a base there. But the Revolution, followed by the European wars, made it impossible for her to capitalize on the enterprise of her missionaries. So long as Nguyen Anh lived France benefited from protection for her missions and opportunities for trade, but the opportunity to exert greater political influence passed. After Nguyen Anh's death in 1820 even these benefits disappeared. His successors, Minh-Mang (1820–41), Thieu-Tri (1841–7) and Tu-Duc (1847–83) reflected a strong movement of Annamese opinion against Western influence in general and the Christian missions in particular. Annam was prepared to sustain good political relations with France and to allow trade with Tourane as specified by treaty, but regarded the missions as dangerously subversive. In 1824 they were ordered to stop work and in 1833 a serious persecution of missionaries and Annamese converts began which lasted until French intervention in 1858. By the mid-century it was reasonable to suppose that French missions were doomed and that French political interest in Annam belonged to the imperialism of the Ancien Régime.

From this point, therefore, the problem is to account for the French expedition of 1858–60 which not only reversed the decline of missionary activity but also established the first French territorial empire in South-East Asia. Which of the factors mentioned above – religion, the navy and trade, or a combination of them – was responsible?

The case for regarding the missionary factor as the main source of French action is strong. Support for Catholic missions had been growing in France from the 1820s, helped considerably by a lay organization, the Oeuvre de la Propagation de la Foi, founded in Lyon in 1822 to provide funds. French missionaries from Annam, notably fathers Huc and Pellerin, campaigned hard for political intervention to safeguard the faithful and at the same time emphasized the country's economic potential. The 1844 Treaty of Whampoa with China, which granted toleration for Catholics in the treaty ports and their hinterlands, and the Siamese treaty of 1856 which gave similar guarantees, constituted useful precedents for intervention to safeguard Catholics. It could even be argued that since Annam was a fief of Peking, the 1844 treaty was binding on the court of Hué. Moreover, if naval action alone were sufficient to force so great a power as China to concede toleration for Christians, the same technique might succeed against the much weaker Annam. In fact it seems clear that the French naval demonstrations off Tourane in 1847 and 1858 were intended only to lead to a treaty providing security for Catholic missions and their converts. In 1857–8 Napoleon III seems to have been concerned primarily to placate French Catholics who were currently very critical of his support for Cavour in Italy and were mounting an effective propaganda campaign for intervention in Annam. The brief occupation of Tourane in 1858, which was given up after strong Annamese resistance, and the subsequent occupation of Saigon in 1858–60 while the French fleet returned to attack Peking, were both entirely compatible with a policy of using force to extract a satisfactory treaty from Annam, based on the treaties with China. Indeed the treaty signed in 1862 closely followed Chinese models in that it granted toleration to Catholics throughout the Annamese Empire, opened three ports to French trade, and provided for an indemnity. All this was compatible with a French policy intended primarily to safeguard French missions and to secure existing trading rights rather than to establish a French colony in South-East Asia.

How, then, does one account for the fact that the treaty of 1862 also provided for permanent French possession of the three eastern provinces of Cochin China and the island of Pulo Condore? The answer is probably that, once Saigon and the Saigon Delta had been occupied and held for two years, primarily as a basis for bargaining with Hué, two other French interests – the navy and metropolitan traders – were in a strong position to demand permanent retention. The navy's interest was simple: it had long felt the need for a base in the East and disliked having to depend on British bases. Saigon would give it independence. Moreover, having taken and held the Delta, the navy now had a vested interest in holding it. How important were commercial interests? It is certainly possible to find evidence of interest in Cochin China stretching back for forty years. In 1817–25 Bordeaux shipping firms had established links with Annam but found them unprofitable. In 1843 the Lagrené mission to China visited Cochin China, and Jules Itier, one of the members, suggested French occupation. It could easily be captured, he said, due to 'the absence of all spirit of nationality in its inhabitants as well as profound disaffection in regard to the government as a result of its tyrannical and stupid proceedings'. Conquest would be a matter only of 'some months', because the Catholics 'would arise *en masse* against their oppressors'. Occupation would be rewarding because it was

... a country which by the fertility of its land, its ports situated at the entrance to the China Seas, its proximity to this vast country [*sc* China] which is opening to European activity, and the healthiness of its climate, seems to unite all the desirable conditions for a colonial establishment with a great future.[31]

The most important of these advantages was that Saigon might provide an entrepôt for French trade with China. The Lagrené mission reported very favourably on commercial prospects in China generally, and more specifically on those in Yunnan, which they thought might be accessible from Tongking. They were aware of France's need for a commercial entrepôt for the China trade to match Hong Kong, and attempted to obtain Basilan Island in the Philippines. When this attempt failed the mission suggested a base in the Malay Archipelago or even in Madagascar; but some, including Itier, preferred Saigon. This was perhaps the origin of French interest in a possible commercial base in Annam.

In the short term this interest remained very small. French trade with China was minute and the merchant marine showed no desire to compete with the British. After about 1852, however, the China trade acquired a new significance. French raw silk production was disastrously reduced by an outbreak of pebrine in the silk worms. Lyon, the main centre of silk manufacturing, had to look for alternative supplies, and interest centred on China. London was the main European market for Chinese silk and French industrialists believed that they could reduce costs by buying direct from the sources of supply. It might be possible also to develop new sources of silk elsewhere in Asia. From the mid-1850s, therefore, French commercial interest in Annam centred on its potential value either as an entrepôt for a direct silk trade with China, or as a place where silk could be produced; and in 1857, when an official commission representing the main government departments was considering proposals for taking action in Annam, following Hué's rejection of French demands for better conditions for Catholics there, Baron Brenier, French Minister Plenipotentiary at Naples (who happened to be in Paris), summed up current hopes that Annam could fulfil the second of these functions as follows: 'The commercial interest is evident, for one will find in Cochin China cotton, silk, sugar, rice, wood, without counting coffee. . . .'[32]

Nevertheless, despite this growing commercial interest in Annam, it would be unrealistic to regard the acquisition of Cochin China as in any sense a direct product of economic imperialism. Trade was certainly not the reason for sending the expedition. At most, growing interest in the China market and the need for new sources of raw silk may have strengthened the decision to retain Cochin China, for when, in 1863–5, Napoleon seriously considered giving up all territory there in return for further treaty rights, the Bordeaux shipping interests and the main French chambers of commerce joined the navy and the missionary organizations in opposing retrocession. Even so the decisive intervention was by Chasseloup-Laubat, the Minister of Marine, who was interested primarily in Saigon as a naval base. If Cochin China was initially occupied as a means of protecting French missions and their converts, it was retained because the navy had a vested interest there. Until 1865 at least economic factors played a very marginal role in French expansion into South-East Asia.

After 1865, however, with France firmly established in Cochin China, the issues necessarily changed. It is no longer a question of explaining why a first foothold was acquired but why this small French possession expanded until in 1884 France held the whole of Cochin China in full sovereignty and effectively controlled most of Cambodia and the whole of Tongking and Annam as protectorates. The main focus of interest, the Tongking War of 1883–5, lies outside the scope of this chapter, but the roots of this culminating stage of French policy in Indo-China lie in the previous twenty years. What drove France on to informal domination of the whole Annamese Empire after 1865? Were the dynamics in France or on the periphery? Were they political, religious, military or economic?

It is at least clear that metropolitan political forces played little part in this development before 1880. Napoleon III remained dubious of the value of Cochin China, and the Franco-Prussian War preempted political inerests from 1870 to the mid-1870s. Between 1870 and 1880 there is no evidence that any of the new generation of Republican political leaders wanted to extend French control in Indo-China for reasons of prestige, international diplomacy or naval strategy. Nor were Catholic missions any longer a source of political expansion. Missionaries frequently pressed for extended French control, but the Republican parties were less susceptible to Catholic pressures than Napoleon and showed no inclination to go beyond insistence that Hué should observe the guarantee of religious toleration provided by treaty. Thus, by elimination, the two most probable causes of further French expansion were growing metropolitan interest in the China trade and peripheral problems stemming from the occupation of Cochin China. The events of the period 1865–80 can best be explained in terms of these two factors.

It was to be expected on general grounds that the new French colony of Cochin China would develop its own sub-imperialism as a response to local problems, and this duly occurred. By 1870 Saigon had found it necessary, in the process of suppressing local resistance to French rule, to occupy the remaining provinces of Cochin China which had not been ceded by the 1862 treaty; and by the treaty signed in 1874 Hué was forced to concede French sovereignty there. France also acquired a protectorate over much of Cambodia. As early as 1853 the King of Cambodia had appealed for French help against his suzerain, the King of Siam. In 1863 Saigon made a protectorate treaty with Cambodia which gave France effective political control short of formal sovereignty or administrative responsibility; and in 1867 a treaty with Siam recognized the French protectorate excluding the two Western provinces of Battambang and Angkor, which were ceded to Siam. There remained the problems of relations with Hué. Saigon officials knew that Tu-Duc and his court deeply resented the treaty of 1862 and feared that he might eventually invoke foreign help to regain his freedom. Formal control of Annam was still out of the question, but it was desirable as a safety measure to assert French paramountcy over the whole Annamese Empire. In 1874 advantage was taken over the crisis in Hanoi, which is described below, to impose a new treaty on Tu-Duc. On its political side this recognized French sovereignty over the whole of Cochin China, reasserted freedom of worship for all Annamese Christians and made Annam a French protectorate. A French Resident was installed at Hué and all Annamese foreign relations and commercial treaties had to be approved by France. This extension of French authority was almost entirely the product of peripheral factors, the logical consequences of French possession of Cochin China. At the time the terms of the treaty of 1874 seemed to provide a satisfactory and permanent political basis for French interests in Indo-China, but in the 1880s it proved the springboard for further intensification of French control.

Equally important as a genesis of French policy after 1880 was the growth of metropolitan commercial interest in Tongking; but it is essential to recognize that Tongking was regarded almost exclusively as a possible route to the allegedly rich markets and sources of raw materials in southern China rather than as an economic objective in its own right. French trade with China increased from the 1860s and by 1875 China was the largest single source of raw silk consumed by Lyon, providing 1·5 out of 4·5 million kilos.[33] But most of this was still imported via London, for French attempts to develop a direct trade with Shanghai or to increase French shipping on the China trade had been signally unsuccessful. In the 1870s increasingly severe competition in silk manufacturing by other European countries and Japan made the price of raw silk more than ever important to Lyon, and this ensured interest by French manufacturers in any alternative route to the south China silk-producing areas which might reduce prices. In addition the extremely unfavourable French trade balance with China provided an incentive to find new markets in China for French products, ideally in regions where there was no British competition. French industrialists and merchants were therefore very interested in the possibility of penetrating southern China from Tongking, though at this stage they showed almost no interest in Tongking itself either as a market or as a source of raw materials.

This metropolitan concern with the China trade in France coincided with a strong peripheral attempt, based on Saigon, to find a route to southern China from Hanoi. In 1866 the Governor of Cochin China sent an expedition, led by Doudart de Lagrée, to investigate the Mekong River, partly as a geographical venture but also in the hope that it might be possible 'to attract towards us the major part of the products of central China'.[34] Lagrée died and command of the expedition devolved on Francis Garnier, a young naval officer. The mission had to report that the Mekong was useless as a commercial artery to China, but it discovered that the Red River flowed from Yunnan to Tongking. Thereafter Garnier devoted himself to disseminating the idea in France that this Red River route offered direct access to untold riches. In frequent speeches and publications he tried, as he said, 'to attract the attention of the government to the commercial and political importance of the river of Tong-king' (sic), which, he believed, was 'one of the shortest, most advantageous routes, which is offered us, for the penetration of China'. By this route France had 'little to fear from the competition of other European nations', and both Tongking and Yunnan had magnificent natural resources: 'incalculable quantities of metals ... copper ... zinc ... tin and lead ... numerous veins of gold, silver and mercury'.[35] The aftermath of the Franco-Prussian War was, however, an unpropitious moment to rouse France to action in Tongking. Further initiative had to come from Saigon. In 1872 Garnier made a trip up the Yangtze to Hankow to investigate its commercial possibilities and also to discover where the commercial watershed between British trade on the Yangtze and possible French trade up the Red River might lie. Further investigation of Yunnan convinced him of its immense possibilities.

But Yunnun, with its great mineral exploitations, with the blast furnaces, the hammers, the rolling mills that Europe could construct here in abundance, what will it not be? But Tibet! But the West of China, those provinces from which silk comes to us, until now by defective transport, by onerous intermediaries, who, step by step, from hand to hand, multiply the price tenfold, before it even reaches the warehouses of the coast! What will you say of a Frenchman who comes to announce to commerce: we now hold this silk from the very producer by our rapid means of communication.[36]

This was the authentic enthusiasm of the explorer and amateur economist, seeing gold in every hill. How could the cautious businessmen and frightened statesmen of France be induced to take action in Tongking to gain access to such wealth? By chance an excellent opportunity to force the issue was offered to Garnier in 1873. The story is well known. A French merchant, Jean Dupuis, who was based on Hankow and specialized in supplying Western arms to government and rebel forces alike in China, had fulfilled a contract with the Chinese Governor of Yunnan to supply him with arms, which he took up the Red River, leaving his ships and a private army at Hanoi. He returned with a load of tin which he sold in Hanoi, and then tried to buy salt for another trip to Yunnan. Coming up against the local Annamese mandarins, who had a monopoly of salt, he occupied part of Hanoi with the small army of Chinese and Filipinos he had recruited to safeguard his very dangerous venture. He had no support or encouragement from Paris or Saigon; and when he appealed to Saigon for help, the Governor, Dupré, was anxious only to extricate him without causing a crisis. Unfortunately, he sent Garnier to do this; and Garnier deliberately misinterpreted his instructions, proclaiming that he had been 'sent to Tonkin by the Admiral to open a route to commerce . . . .' He captured the whole of Hanoi and several other coastal towns but was then killed by a force of Chinese brigands, known as the Black Flags (as distinct from the rival Red and Yellow Flags) who had been hired by the local mandarins to collect customs duties.

Garnier had, however, managed to make Tongking a serious issue. A situation of this kind offered the chance for an aggressive metropolitan government, backed by enraged popular feeling, to annex Tongking on the ground that French honour must be avenged. A decade later Paris would be prepared to capitalize on this type of situation, and it is therefore extremely significant for understanding French attitudes in the 1870s, that at this stage neither the government nor commercial interests thought it desirable to do so. Dupré was ordered to avoid new territorial commitments but to take the opportunity to impose a new treaty on Hué to settle out-standing problems. He therefore sent Louis Philastre, a civilian official known to be against further territorial expansion, first to get Dupuis and his troops out of Tongking and to evacuate Hanoi and the other coastal towns; then to negotiate terms with Tu-Duc. The political aspects of the resultant treaty which was agreed in March 1874 have been outlined above. On its economic side the treaty attempted to solve the problem of Tongking by guaranteeing freedom of trade to Yunnan. Foreign merchants could trade at Hanoi, Haiphong and Qui-Nhon, but not in other parts of Tong-king; and French Consuls could be appointed to each of these towns. In principle at least these terms should have satisfied the needs of French merchants who wanted to develop a direct trade between Hanoi and southern China.

Three major points stand out from these events and the terms of the 1874 treaty. Despite increasing metropolitan commercial interest in the south China trade, all the initiatives in opening up the Red River route came from Frenchmen living and working in China or Annam rather than from France, and from merchants or junior naval officers rather than from the government in Saigon. If the metropolis stood to benefit from free trade through Hanoi, Frenchmen on the periphery saw and publicized the opportunity long before it was recognized in France. Second, the treaty of 1874 accurately defined the limits of French metropolitan ambitions in the 1870s and indeed until the mid-1880s. It provided informal political control over Annam, thus excluding possible foreign intervention; and it promised commercial access to southern China, which provided the opportunity to establish a direct silk trade with Yunnan. There is no reason to think that any important metro-politan group positively wanted or demanded more than this. Finally, however, it is equally clear that nothing less than full implementation of the terms of the 1874 treaty would now be acceptable in Saigon or Paris. If the treaty proved abortive further action would certainly be taken. The settlement was, in fact, certain from the start to fail on three counts. First, Tu-Duc was not a docile collaborator. He and the court at Hué still resented French overlordship and quickly turned to China as a possible equipoise to French overlordship. Second, China refused to accept French access to Yunnan via the Red River or by any other inland route, on the entirely correct ground that this was contrary to the terms of the Sino-French Treaty of 1858, which did not permit direct trade with Yunnan. Finally, those merchants, mostly based on Saigon, who attempted to utilize the Red River route, found that commerce was impossible so long as the area continued to be dominated by the rival armies of Chinese rebels who had been driven out of China after the Panthay rebellion. On all these counts it was clearly only a matter of time before Paris was once again forced to review France's position in South-East Asia.

It is, in fact, important to recognize that the crisis which led to further French intervention in 1883 and ultimately to French control over the whole of what became Indo-China already existed by 1880. As in Tunisia, Egypt, Burma and many other places, the imperialism of the 1880s was a response to problems arising from earlier attempts to solve problems on the periphery without formal annexation. In 1878 Hué formally invoked Chinese overlordship and invited a Chinese army to enter Tongking to deal with yet another invading army of Chinese rebels. This was incompatible with the French view of her protectorates as defined in 1874 and could not be tolerated without endangering her whole position in South-East Asia. In 1880, moreover, Peking formally warned France that, as overlord of Annam, she could not accept any change in the political status of Tongking nor permit French traders to enter Yunnan. It is possible that, given time, these problems could have been resolved without any substantial change in France's position in Annam and without formal occupation of Tongking. But by 1880 time was thought to be against France. In 1867 the British had obtained freedom of navigation up the Irrawaddy to Upper Burma and had since been prospecting for a possible railway route through the mountains to Yunnan. If France could not clear the Red River route before the British built their railway, all the glittering hopes of a French monopoly of the direct overland trade with southern China would be destroyed. Thus in Tongking, as in many other places, the speed of the French advance after about 1880 derived as much if not more from the urgency of peripheral problems inherited from the previous decades as from new imperialistic impulses generated in the metropolis.

The French reaction to these problems will be considered in a later chapter. Reviewing the course of events during the half-century before 1880 which lead directly to the imminent crisis of the next decade, it must be concluded that economic interests in general, and those of the metropolis in particular, had been relatively unimportant. The roots of French intervention lay in Annam, in the plight of Annamese Christians, not in French imperialism. The dynamic elements in the French response were entirely non-economic – the Catholic missions and the navy. Commercial forces became significant only in 1863–5 when the slight interest already felt by metropolitan merchants in an eastern entrepôt were mobilized to prevent the retrocession of Cochin China. During the next fifteen years the determinants of French policy continued to lie in Indo-China; problems of political relations with Cambodia, Siam and Hué, and the enterprise of French merchants and naval officers based on Saigon in searching for new fields of political or commercial activity. French commercial groups, primarily the silk industry of Lyon, influenced policy only in the most indirect way by showing increasing interest in Tongking as a possible means of obtaining raw silk from Yunnan without dependence on the British middleman. But as late as 1874 it was clear that neither French commerce nor the metropolitan government was prepared to achieve this at the price of a major war or having to undertake political responsibility in Tongking. Trade if possible, but not territory, remained the key to metropolitan attitudes in the 1870s; and it was still possible to believe that this could be achieved. In the 1880s, when this proved impracticable, the slogan became trade in any case and territory also if necessary to secure the trade. This, in a nutshell, was the difference between the imperialism of the mid-nineteenth century and the two decades after 1880.

V EUROPEANS IN CHINA

European relations with China[37] throughout the whole period covered by the present study had certain special characteristics, some of which were suggested in the introduction to this chapter. Two of these require further emphasis because they largely determined the pattern of European imperialism in the Far East during the mid-nineteenth century: China's position as a major power and her attitude towards foreign trade.

During the first half of the nineteenth century China was still regarded by Europeans as a major world power closely comparable in size and importance with Russia. Until the Sino-British War of 1839 she was treated with great respect and until the 1890s there was no question of any Western state acquiring substantial amount of Chinese territory, let alone imposing alien rule on Peking. On the other hand, although European naval techniques and equipment were not significantly affected by industrial technology until the second half of the century, any European maritime power was immensely superior to China in naval power provided it could concentrate sufficient resources in the Far East. It was therefore technically possible to blockade the Chinese coast in support of political or commercial demands whereas a major campaign on land would have been out of the question. Of the four European states in closest contact with China during their period, Russia was inhibited from using naval power as a lever on Peking both because she maintained no large naval force in the East and still more because her immense continental frontier with China and established trading rights from Siberia made her vulnerable to retaliation. Equally, neither France or the United States maintained a sufficient naval presence in the China Sea to take major initiatives. But Britain was in a uniquely favourable position. She had no territorial liabilities on the Chinese frontiers. She maintained a substantial naval force in the Indian Ocean. She could therefore afford to use naval power as a means of extracting concessions from Peking with relative ease and impunity in much the same way as the Portuguese had used naval blockade in the early sixteenth century to establish themselves on the west coast of India. Thus if Europe was to use political means to change its established relationship with China the chosen weapon would almost certainly be naval power and Britain was the most likely state to take the initiative.

The second special feature of European, and especially British, relations with China was that she, in common with other highly civilized Asian states including Japan, Annam and Siam, did not accept the European assumption that international trade and other forms of contact were intrinsically desirable. This caused fundamental disagreements. Despite the conventional political and dynastic rivalries of Europe and the intense commercial competitiveness inherent in 'mercantile' economics during the seventeenth and eighteenth centuries, no European state had entirely excluded foreign traders from its metropolitan ports in time of peace. Trade might be restricted in various ways: by prohibiting specified imports; by preferential tariffs; by banning direct imports from third countries; and by monopoly of the colonial trade. But British subjects could nevertheless trade with almost all the ports of Europe, deal direct with inland markets, reside in foreign states and, in most places, practice their religion freely. Matters of jurisdiction presented few problems, since European commercial law had substantially a common basis; and in some countries, notably Spain and the Ottoman Empire, foreigners had the right to be tried by special courts. During the first half of the nineteenth century the general assumption that freedom to trade was basic to international relations was further strengthened by the disruption of the American colonial systems, which opened these once closed markets to all; by the increasing acceptance of free trade as defined by the classical economists; and by the expanding network of commercial treaties, pioneered by Britain, which provided favourable commercial conditions on a reciprocal basis. It was not, therefore, surprising that most Europeans expected similar commercial opportunities throughout the rest of the world and assumed that no country was reasonably entitled to exclude foreign activities.

European policies and actions in the Far East, and particularly in China, must be interpreted in this context. Until the early nineteenth century the major Asian states had managed to avoid or restrict contact with Europe. China made no formal treaty with a European state between the Russian Treaty of 1689 and the British Treaty of 1842. Siam, apart from treaties relating only to Malaya, made no treaty until 1855. Japan refused contact until 1854. Assam made a treaty with France under special political conditions in 1787 but made no more treaties until 1862. All these states were hostile to European influence, and restricted foreign trade as narrowly as possible. France was allowed to trade with Annam only through Tourane. Japan and Siam made no formal provision for European trade. China allowed Russians to trade overland through Kiakhta from 1689, and from 1757 allowed the British and other foreigners to carry on a maritime trade with Canton, provided they dealt exclusively with an officially controlled merchant organization, the cohong. These restrictions were most inconvenient to the British, for whom the China trade in particular had become extremely important before the end of the eighteenth century, and policy in the period 1830–80 can only be understood in this context.

The special feature of British interest in the China trade was that it formed an integral part of the pattern of British economic activity in India and was in some ways fundamental to it. The essential fact before 1833 was that the East India Company could not import sufficient goods from India to Britain to provide dividends to its share-holders and enable its servants to repatriate

the private capital they had acquired in India. Most Indian manufactures, particularly calicoes, were in direct competition with
British manufactures and were subject to statutory prohibitions
until the tariff reforms of the 1820s. Conversely, India could not
provide adequate raw material exports. The problem was complicated by the extension of British political power in India, for the
main profits of the company now derived from its territorial
revenues rather than from commerce. These revenues could only
be remitted to Britain in the form of commodities because India
was not a bullion-producing country and repatriation of company
or private profits in the form of specie would quickly have de-
nuded her of currency. The need was therefore to find suitable
export commodities. During the nineteenth century the development of such export staples as rice, jute, indigo and cotton provided
a partial answer, though even so India normally ran a deficit on
trading account with Britain which was compensated by transfers
through multilateral trading. But this option was not available on a
sufficient scale during the late eighteenth and early nineteenth
centuries. Some alternative means had to be found of transmitting
company profits made in India to its share-holders in Britain.

An ingenious though incomplete solution was found in the China
tea trade. The East India Company could use its Indian revenue
surplus to purchase Indian goods which could be sold in Canton
and the proceeds used for buying tea for sale in Britain. The tea
trade had, of course, long preceeded this system, but until about
1800 Britain had found it necessary to balance her account with
China in bullion because it was impossible to sell a sufficient
quantity of British manufactures in the Chinese market. Thus the
trade between India and China solved two problems simultaneously,
making it possible for the company to remit its Indian surplus to
Britain via China and eliminating the drain of British bullion to
China. In this way China became the pivot of British trade and
finance in the Far east.

Nevertheless this system presented problems. There were only
two commodities from India that had a ready sale in China – raw
cotton and opium, and of these opium was by far the more important. In 1828 total British imports to Canton were worth
$20,364,600, of which opium accounted for $11,243,496 and raw
cotton about $5,809,000.[38] By that time the British had had a
favourable balance of trade with Canton for some twenty years and
in 1828 more than $6 million of silver were shipped from Canton

to India by private merchants. The British were, therefore, satisfied with this aspect of trade with China though, as will be seen
below, other aspects were less satisfactory. Nevertheless the system
had the disadvantage that it depended on selling opium to China.
Peking had for long tried to check its consumption. Opium smoking
was banned in 1729, though imports were permitted for use on
medicinal grounds. In 1800 imports were forbidden altogether.
This was a serious blow to the East India Company for opium was a
governmental monopoly in India, grown for the company in Bengal
and supplied in lieu of taxes in Madras. If export to China was
stopped both the Indian fiscal system and the China trade would be
ruined. The company therefore stopped selling opium in Canton
on its own account in order to avoid trouble with the Chinese
authorities but sold opium to private Indian-based traders to
smuggle into Canton and bought the credit they acquired there for
bills of exchange drawable in India or Britain. In the early 1830s the
Indian trade with Canton therefore depended on the ability of
British merchants to smuggle opium. Hitherto this had presented
little difficulty, but if Chinese officialdom were to police the
imperial ban effectively the whole pattern of British trade and
finance in the East would be seriously damaged.

By this time, however, a second and increasingly important
commercial factor had to be taken into account when considering
trade relations with China. In the past a major factor in the complex
trading patterns of the Far East was the inability of Europeans to
manufacture consumer goods of higher quality or lower price
than were produced in India and China. By the 1820s this had
ceased to be true. British cotton textiles and, to a lesser extent,
metallurgical products were capable of underselling those of any
Asian country. British manufacturers, speculating on ever-expand-
ing markets, were already flooding the Indian market with cheap
cotton and were confident that they could sell immense quantities
in China if given the opportunity. In 1833 the end of the East
India Company's monopoly of the China trade removed one
obstacle to expanded trade. There remained the refusal of Peking to
allow foreigners to trade anywhere but in Canton, which was too
far from the main markets of Central China. The British government
was therefore under strong pressure from Lancashire manufacturers, ship-owners and enthusiasts for international free trade
to negotiate better conditions for British trade in China: access to
additional ports; freedom for foreigners to deal direct with

Chinese merchants; reasonable import duties and security for the persons and property of foreign residents. These were the substance of the many commercial treaties being made contemporaneously with the states of Europe and America in this period and British opinion was increasingly insistent that the same arrangements should be made with Asian powers. Thus, when Lord Napier was sent to Canton as Superintendent of Trade in 1834, to take over the commercial functions previously undertaken by the supercargoes of the East India Company, one of his instructions was to negotiate for extension of British trading rights to other ports. For the next half-century this was to be the main British objective in all dealings with China.

But under normal circumstances it was extremely difficult for any British government to exert sufficient leverage on Peking to extract such a concession, for the imperial court remained supremely indifferent to the economic advantages of expanded foreign trade. The primary importance of the so-called Opium War of 1839–42 was that a crisis arising from the earlier problem of the India-China trade provided both the stimulus and opportunity for the British to establish a fundamentally new commercial relationship with China. The events of 1839–42 are well known and need not be rehearsed in detail. The crux of the matter was that, while the Foreign Office and Charles Elliot, then Superintendant of Trade, accepted that British nationals could not expect British protection from the Chinese authorities if they broke Chinese laws, particularly those connected with opium, it seems to have been agreed that any legitimate grievance should be used as an excuse to force the Chinese authorities to liberalize the whole commercial system. As Elliot wrote to London, 'if any man be robbed by this govert (sic) or unjusifiably killed or detained in captivity there will be an obvious cause for earnest interference.'[39]

This opportunity arose in March 1839 when the Chinese imperial commissioner, Lin, suddenly ordered that all foreign stocks of opium should be surrendered, that a list of their owners should be compiled, and that these merchants should give bonds against further opium importation on pain of death. He also barricaded the river to prevent foreign ships and nationals from leaving Canton until all the opium was handed over. The British made no formal objection to these demands and acts and it seemed that the crisis would pass. But later in 1839 a new crisis developed, partly because the Chinese insisted that someone should be handed over to be executed for the murder of a Chinese at Kowloon, partly because Lin insisted that those foreign ships which had left Canton and taken refuge first at Macao and then at Hong Kong should either return to Canton or leave Chinese waters. When these demands were ignored Chinese war junks fired on two British naval vessels, who retaliated, sinking four junks. The British now had their excuse for 'interference'.

Was the war consistent with the principle that British governments would not provide political support for private economic interests, especially when these were compromised by smuggling? Many in Britain, including W. E. Gladstone as Opposition spokesman in the Commons, thought the war could not be justified on moral or legal grounds. The Foreign Office, however, took the line that the Chinese were technically at fault because they had not given warning that a period of *de facto* tolerance of opium smuggling was to be ended before seizing the opium stock; and, more reasonably, that British subjects and ships who were not in any way connected with opium smuggling had been held under duress. In the only surviving comment in his own hand – the incomplete draft of a Foreign Office despatch dated 4 November 1839 – Palmerston defined this case.

H.M. Govt. by no means dispute the right of the Government of China to prohibit the importation of opium into China, and to seize and confiscate any opium which, in defiance of prohibition duly made, should be brought by Foreigners or by Chinese subjects into the Territories of the Empire. But these fiscal prohibitions ought to be impartially and steadily enforced; and traps ought not to be laid for Foreigners by at one time letting the prohibition remain. . . .[40]

In terms of international law as understood in Europe these were, of course, dubious arguments, and it is clear that the British, in common with other Europeans, were prepared to dispense with legal niceties when negotiating from a position of military superiority. What were the real British objectives? Clearly to use this excuse to change the general pattern of economic relations with China: to obtain commercial access to ports north of Canton and the right of residence for British nationals there, direct access by British diplomatic officials to the imperial government in Peking, extra-territorial jurisdiction to protect British subjects from Chinese courts, and an agreed import tariff. Such demands, which were incorporated in a draft peace treaty in 1840, were fully consistent with the principle of 'trade not territory'. But in addition the

British decided that a small permanent island base was needed comparable with Portuguese Macao. An obvious reason was to provide security for British ships against sudden action by the imperial authorities in future; but, in suggesting that an island in the Chusan group near the mouth of the Yangtze should be taken, Elliot expressed the wider hopes of British manufacturers and merchants:

From that point . . . British manufactures would soon find their way to millions and millions of the most trading people on the face of the earth, from whom they are entirely shut out by the present close and expensive system. And in less than ten years I have a firm belief that that station would be the seat of a flourishing trade with Japan.[41]

These conditions were defined by Palmerston; but the new Ministry of 1841 under Peel made little change in them, except to make the retention of a permanent island base negotiable, on the grounds that 'a secure and well regulated trade is all we desire; and . . . we seek no exclusive advantages and demand nothing that we shall not willingly see enjoyed by the subjects of all other states.'[42] The Treaty of Nanking, signed on 29 August 1842, therefore conformed almost exactly with the draft treaty of 1840. An indemnity of $21 million was to be paid. The five ports specified were to be open to British traders and were to have Consuls stationed in each. Hong Kong, chosen in preference to an island in the Chusan group as an entrepôt, was ceded in perpetuity, largely due to the insistence of Colonel Sir Henry Pottinger, the British Plenipotentiary. The hong system at Canton was abolished. A supplementary treaty of 1843 further defined the regulation of trade and extra-territorial jurisdiction in the treaty ports and specified that import duties should not exceed 5 per cent *ad valorem*. Nothing was said in either treaty about the opium trade, on the assumption that the Chinese were no longer interested in stopping it. But the British government vested Hong Kong in the crown rather than in the East India Company so that the opium trade could be controlled or stopped if it caused future difficulties, even if this was against the interests of the East India Company which still ruled India.

The Treaty of Nanking began a new era of relations between China and Europe which lasted until the Sino-Japanese War of 1894. The concessions it contained were initially restricted to Britain but were extended to the United States and France in 1844 by the Treaties of Wanghia and Whampoa respectively; and in addition the French extracted toleration for Catholics which was later extended to Protestants. The effect of these treaties was to end the seclusion of China and to open it up to European influence. But four main limitations on European activity remained. Foreigners were still restricted to an area within thirty miles of each of the treaty ports, so that effective penetration of the Chinese economy was impossible. Europeans could not own property, build railways or establish enterprises anywhere except in the International Settlement outside Shanghai which was established by negotiation with the local Chinese authorities after 1845 and soon became virtually an international city state with its own laws, police, militia and administration. Foreign trade was still excluded from the great majority of Chinese ports. Finally, the imperial government still refused to establish direct diplomatic contact with European governments or allow permanent foreign embassies in Peking. A Chinese commissioner at Canton, usually the Viceroy, was the only means of formal contact. Given the basic assumptions of most Western states these limitations were not acceptable as a permanent settlement of Sino-European relations, and the history of European contacts with China in the period 1844–80 turns largely on attempts made to obtain broader concessions.

Alteration of the system established in 1842–4 depended, however, on a further shift in the balance of power between China and the West, and the key to developments during the rest of the century lies in the fact that China became politically and militarily weaker while the Western powers were becoming much stronger and more resolute in their dealings with other countries. The relative decline of imperial power had two main causes: domestic rebellions and refusal to accept the need for change. The Taiping rebellion in southern China lasted from 1850 to 1964. Its support derived from population pressures, dislike of Manchu rule, especially after the humiliation of Peking in 1839–42, and religious revivalism influenced by Christian ideas. Although eventually stamped out, the rebellion seriously weakened Peking during the second Anglo-Chinese War of 1856–60. The Panthay movement in Yunnan between 1855 and 1873, and the Tungan rising in Kansu and Shensi between 1862 and 1878, both breakaway movements in Islamic provinces on the periphery of China, at once reflected the decline of central authority and accelerated it. They were both ultimately suppressed but at great cost at a time when Peking needed all the power it could muster to deal with European pressures.

Perhaps equally important, the Chinese government showed almost no desire or ability to meet the challenge of the West. If China wanted to preserve her national identity and to limit the encroachment of foreigners, it was essential to reorganize the system of government and to adopt Western technology. Japan showed this could be done successfully after 1854, but Peking refused to do so. The reason lay primarily in the resistance of almost all classes in China to radical change. Whereas in Japan the aristocracy led the reforming movement, the Chinese aristocracy remained fundamentally conservative, and made it difficult for any government to take strong action. But conservatism and xenophobia were equally strong among the peasant classes and were demonstrated in hostility to Christian missions. Only a very strong and determined government in Peking could have overcome these obstacles to change; and China lacked firm rulers in this period. Prince Kung was the leader of a progressive party at court in the 1860s but was unable to overcome the conservatism of the aristocracy in league with the Empress Dowager Tz'u Hsi. A few minor innovations occurred. A Foreign Ministry was established in 1858, under the terms of the new treaty with Britain, so that foreign governments could deal directly with the emperor and China could develop a coherent foreign policy. A college of foreign languages was created in 1862 to train diplomats. A military school was set up in 1863 to teach Western methods of warfare. After 1877 Chinese legations were established overseas for the first time. But there was no attempt to centralize government, to modernize the revenue system, to build railways or to create a modern navy until the 1880s. In 1880 China remained almost as disorganized and defenceless as in 1830.

As a result the Western powers had little difficulty in extending the concessions they had obtained in the 1840s. In 1856 the British began a second naval war, nominally over the fact that Chinese soldiers had boarded a British registered ship at Canton and removed several of her crew as part of a general attempt to check the practice of Chinese ships registering as British, French or American in order to gain immunity from Chinese custom officials and police. In fact, however, the British government saw this as an opportunity to exert further pressure on Peking and to extend the rights obtained under the Treaty of Nanking. In 1857 they were joined by the French, whose primary interest was security for Catholic missions. The Americans and Russians remained neutral; but when the Anglo-French naval forces had captured Canton and moved to Tientsin in 1858 to negotiate with Peking, their plenipotentiaries joined in the negotiations. By the treaties agreed with each of the four Western powers at Tientsin in 1858 China opened eleven additional treaty ports to foreign trade, opened the Yangtse River to trade, permitted permanent diplomatic missions at Peking, allowed Europeans to travel throughout China, and conceded full toleration for Christianity. These treaties were not ratified until 1860 because conservative elements in Peking attempted to obstruct ratification. The Anglo-French forces therefore occupied Peking and the 1858 treaties were modified to include an indemnity and the opening of Tientsin to foreign trade. Meantime, as has been seen, the Russians had made separate treaties by which China recognized Russian possession of the Amur and Ussuri regions.

With minor modifications the treaties made in 1858 and 1860 settled European relations with China until the 1890s. The British refused to ratify a proposed revision of the 1858 treaty as requested by Peking in 1870 and in 1876 used the murder of Margery in Yunnan as the excuse for a new treaty providing for additional treaty ports and other minor concessions. But these were relatively unimportant changes to what may be regarded as an established and, from a European point of view, generally satisfactory system. The maritime powers of Western Europe and North America now had many points of access to the markets of China through treaty ports covering most of the Pacific tidewater, a secure territorial base in the International Settlement at Shanghai, and formal dependencies at Hong Kong, Vladivostock and Saigon from which naval forces could operate. China was no longer dealing only with foreign merchants visiting a single port under sufferance, but with strong naval and military forces maintained on or near her frontiers to police the treaties and impose pressure at the slightest sign that the Chinese were obstructing legitimate foreign activity. There was already some evidence that further demands would eventually be made on Peking. Japan was ready to enter the field and began to make moves to control Korea in the 1870s. She took full control over the Ryukyu Islands, which had been under joint Sino-Japanese overlordship, in 1871 and nearly sent an expedition to occupy Formosa in 1873–4. German traders were increasingly active. Russia and France might be expected at some future time to demand changes on the frontiers of Siberia and Indo-China respectively. But Britain, Germany and the United States, the three most important commercial powers in the Far East, were largely content with the commercial opportunities they had already obtained and had no desire for radical change. It was generally assumed that further commercial concessions should be demanded when opportunity occurred, including access to all ports; freedom to trade directly with all inland provinces; direct overland access from Burma, Indo-China and Siberia; and opportunities for railway building and other types of capital investment, all of which were still denied. But recent events suggested that all these could be obtained in course of time by taking advantage of the type of crisis that had occurred in 1839, 1856 and 1876 to demand new treaty concessions. There was no need for any power to occupy substantial areas of China in order to obtain wider economic opportunities.

The British, who had established this system and were still the major European power in the Far East, were naturally the main beneficiaries and had no wish for radical change. In 1880 about 76 per cent of Chinese foreign trade was with Britain or British overseas possessions; and in 1883, 11,003,296 out of a total of 17,589,914 tons of shipping cleared at Chinese customs offices was British registered.[43] Moreover, the structure of the China trade improved markedly from a British point of view. The opening of new ports near the main centres of population and freedom of access up the Yangtse made it possible to sell an increasing range of British manufactures, particularly cotton textiles; and, as can be seen from table 12, the balance of trade moved steadily in favour of Britain. Until the early 1880s the Chinese normally had a substantial favourable balance on direct trade with Britain and Hong Kong which was made up by the Indian trade with China. But British exports to China rose fairly steadily from the 1850s to a plateau in the 1880s while Chinese exports to Britain, affected by growing competition from Indian tea, declined rapidly in that decade and continued to decrease after 1890, giving Britain an increasingly favourable trading balance. Thus, although the absolute value of the China trade was relatively small compared, for example, with British trade to India, Australia, the United States and several European countries, China provided an expanding market which might be expected to grow considerably once internal markets were made more accessible by improved communications. Moreover, by contrast with many British dependencies, China required no British public expenditure apart from the small cost of military and naval forces based on Hong Kong and the consular establishments at the treaty ports. From a national point of view commercial profits were a net gain and Britain had little or no incentive to undertake the expense and inconvenience of imposing political control.

Table 12

British Trade with China (including Hong Kong), 1854–90 (millions of pounds at current values)

Date	Imports	Exports
1854	9·1	1·0
1860	9·3	5·4
1865	11·4	5·3
1870	9·9	10·0
1875	18·0	6·2
1880	13·0	9·5
1885	9·6	9·6
1890	6·0	9·5

Source: *Statistical Abstract for the United Kingdom*, nos 13, 27, 40.

The history of European relations with China during the half-century before 1880 thus demonstrates clearly two typical features of mid-nineteenth-century imperialism. First, the interests of each of the four main Western powers most concerned were almost entirely economic, for even the Russian thrust on the Amur was seen by Muraviev primarily in terms of the economic development of eastern Siberia. In this case limited territorial acquisitions were necessary, partly to secure Russia's Pacific seaboard against assumed threats from Britain or France. But for the rest the maritime powers were concerned only with freedom and security for their trade; and it is significant that after 1842 no power except Russia attempted to annex Chinese territory. Conversely, however, it is also clear that Britain and France at least were prepared after 1839 to use military force to achieve these limited economic objectives. Although such action disturbed a small minority of those visionary radicals in Britain who were unconditionally against the use of force in international relations and regarded the successive Sino-British Wars as unjust, the use of force was fully consistent both with the ideology of free trade and with contemporary belief that the state should not use its resources to protect or help private vested interests overseas. Free traders accepted that the advanced states of Europe might have to blow open the doors of xenophobic non-European countries in the interests of international trade, provided that the commercial opportunities created were open to all on equal terms. The 'open door' in China precisely fulfilled this condition. Equally the Foreign Office accepted that wars for trading opportunities might constitute a justifiable use of public resources provided they were in the interest of the nation as a whole rather than of particular private groups and that at least some notional diplomatic justification based on abuse of treaty rights or international law could be put forward. Again the China wars fulfilled these conditions. This was the true 'imperialism of free trade' whose objectives were economic rather than political and could be achieved without substantial annexation of foreign territory. Until 1880 at least the results were extremely satisfactory for Britain and, to a lesser extent, for America, France and Russia. If thereafter European attitudes to China changed significantly it must be assumed that substantially new forces were at work either within Europe or in the Far East.

8 The Pacific

The paradox of European imperialism in the South
Pacific[1] throughout the nineteenth century is that while substantive
foreign interests there were minute by comparison with those in
most other parts of the world, the process of expansion was made
almost uniquely complex by the multiplicity of minute islands and
groups, each presenting distinct problems. Yet developments in the
Pacific are of considerable importance for a study of nineteenth-
century imperialism for they provide a microcosm of many of the
processes making for the extension of European control throughout the world. They also supply an unusually clear model of the
interaction of local sub-imperialisms and forces resulting from
direct European intervention.

The special feature of the Pacific was that the islands had few
obvious attractions for European empire-builders. Apart from New
Zealand they were too small for large-scale European settlement.
Most were extremely poor in factor endowment and provided very
limited scope for trade or capital investment. They were remote
from Europe and America, too poor and too thinly populated to
constitute valuable markets, and therefore extremely marginal to
the economic interests of European states. Equally no European
power had any major national interest in the Pacific. It lacked the
strategic importance of the Mediterranean, South Africa or
southern Asia, and the only significant political stake was the security of Australia and New Zealand against conceivable, but highly
improbable, naval attack by Russia or France. By the last quarter of
the century the growth of steamship routes across the Pacific, which
required coaling bases, and of submarine telegraphs, which needed

island bases on which to land cables, provided an incentive for annexation of a few suitably placed islands. But these technical requirements do not account for the majority of territories acquired by the powers during this period. Thus the main historiographical problem is to discover what forces impelled Europeans to annex a number of individual islands or groups before about 1880 and then to partition the whole Pacific by 1900.

Although 1880 will again be taken as a convenient dividing line between the two phases of European expansion, the obvious fact of European imperialism in the Pacific was its continuity. There was nothing in Pacific history to compare with the dramatic opening of the African interior in the last quarter of the century. No major sources of mineral wealth or industrial raw materials were discovered, and no major power suddenly decided that control of the islands was essential to its security or wealth. All the powers which played a significant role in later Pacific history – Britain, France, Germany and the United States – were already involved there by the 1860s. The only novelties after 1880 were that existing problems which had hitherto been allowed to hang fire became increasingly acute and that simultaneously inter-European rivalries and suspicions generated in other parts of the world made metropolitan governments more ready than before to use political means to solve these essentially non-political problems. Despite the considerable diplomatic commotion it engendered, the partition of the Pacific after 1880 was little more than a logical corollary of the trends of the previous half-century.

The half-century before 1880 falls naturally into two periods dividing at about 1860 and will be dealt with in turn. They were distinguished by the fact that during the first period the nature of European activity in most parts of the Pacific made it inherently unlikely that formal colonization would take place, though in fact some did occur; whereas during the second the proliferation of economic activity provided increasing grounds for political control if this was deemed necessary for the success of economic enterprises.

I WHALERS, MISSIONARIES, TRADERS AND SETTLERS, 1830–60

Whaling and trade in the indigenous products of the islands were the main forms of European economic enterprise in the Pacific before the 1860s and neither constituted a strong inducement to impose political control. In broad economic terms the Pacific was extremely marginal to the economic needs of Europe and North America. Distance and the limitations of sailing ships inhibited trade in bulk commodities; and, as the eighteenth-century explorers had sadly recognized, the South Pacific contained no rich *Terra Australis* endowed with bullion, spices or sophisticated manufactures. The only important Pacific exports to Europe and North America before the 1860s were whale oil and guano, neither of which required political control of island territories. The whaling fleets that came round Cape Horn admittedly needed temporary island bases for refitting and boiling whale blubber. But the fishing grounds shifted constantly; and, once the French had a port of call in Tahiti and the British had colonies in Australia and New Zealand, there was no incentive to undertake permanent control of other islands. Much the same was true of the trade in guano, the accumulated droppings of sea birds, which could be collected in vast quantities from many uninhabited islands and atolls. The trade developed as a response to the increasing demand for agricultural fertilizers in Europe and North America as part of what has been called the second agricultural revolution. In its way this bulk export constituted an economic revolution in the Pacific and brought the islands within the circuit of the European economic system. But guano was a small traders' commodity, collected by schooners based on Australia or New Zealand. No large European or American firms were directly involved, so there was no demand for extensive concessionary areas by metropolitan companies. Above all, the guano was available in very many islands, few of which had human inhabitants. Hence neither international rivalries nor problems of contact with Pacific societies constituted grounds for imposing political control on the sources of supply.

Much the same was true of less important European trading activities in the islands. Historically the first to be established, well before 1830, were the sandalwood and sea slug trades, both for the China market rather than for Europe. American and British traders began competing for these commodities with Chinese junks from the late eighteenth century and the trade brought them into contact with a number of island groups. The brutalities of the sandalwooders had important long-term effects on relations between islanders and Europeans, but in the short term neither trade provided any conceivable incentive for imposing political control.

From the 1850s coconut oil became a significant trading commodity as a result of that increasing demand in Europe for vegetable oils which, as has been seen, stimulated the ground nut and palm oil trades of West Africa. Ultimately the demand justified and required plantation methods of production by Europeans which in turn generated multiple problems that led to political control. But before about 1860 German, British and American traders were content to buy coconut oil or copra (the dried flesh of the nut from which the oil could be extracted in Europe) from islanders in small quantities. Such trade sometimes produced friction between rival traders, and between Europeans and islanders, but it certainly did not require political control of the islands.

The characteristic commercial patterns of the Pacific before about 1860 did not, therefore, provide strong incentives for any European power to create an island empire. During this period the Christian missions were, in fact, a more important expression of European interest in the Pacific and potentially the strongest force making for some degree of alien rule. It is, nevertheless, important to emphasize that missionary enterprise did not normally require or, as a rule, demand metropolitan political support. Conditions in many island groups were favourable to missionary enterprise and conversion of a chief commonly gave the mission a dominant political position in his territory. Once this was achieved the mission tended to distrust secular European intrusion because formal rule by any European state – even its own metropolis – probably meant the end of theocracy and an influx of traders and beachcombers who might debauch the islanders. There were, nevertheless, situations in which a mission might decide to invoke metropolitan political support. The most common occasion was conflict between missionaries of different creeds and nationalities, particularly when a new mission invaded an island or group already evangelized by others. At this point the vital question was whether the metropolis would accept the principle of *cuius regio, eius religio* or whether it would insist on the 'open door' for all creeds, even to the extent of territorial annexation.

Finally there was the possible effect of permanent settlement by Europeans in Pacific territories. There was no compelling reason why small colonies of European traders, beachcombers and planters should constitute a ground for territorial annexation, for similar clusters of aliens existed in many parts of the world. Yet past experience suggested that if such settlements in countries not

formally recognized as states by European diplomats were sufficiently large or caused sufficient inconvenience, the metropolitan
power might feel obliged to give them its protection or impose its
authority.

Most of the Pacific offered little attraction for direct colonization
from Europe or America; and by far the largest area brought under
formal rule before 1860 was in Australia and New Zealand. The
initial colonization of Australia falls well before the start of the
present study and will not be considered. But the occupation of
New Zealand in 1840 must be seen as an intrinsic part of European
expansion in the South Pacific and provides important evidence on
the relative importance of different factors making for territorial
control.

These then, were the main forces likely to influence European
activity in the Pacific before about 1860. To test their relative
importance as a possible source of imperial control over island
territories it is proposed to examine briefly the grounds on which
Britain annexed New Zealand in 1840 and why the French acquired
the Society Islands and other groups in the 1840s together with
New Caledonia in 1853.

The annexation of New Zealand is of considerable importance
because it provides exceptionally clear evidence on the leverage a
capitalist colonizing company, founded to embody E. G. Wakefield's argument (considered in chapter 3 above) that Britain had a
surplus both of capital and population which could best be dealt
with by establishing new overseas colonies, could exert on a British
government.[2] Was the decision to annex New Zealand an example
of the imperialism of capital of the type commonly associated with
the last twenty years of the century, or was official policy primarily
influenced by other considerations, perhaps by problems on the
periphery rather than in Britain?

During the forty years following the occupation of Sydney as a
penal settlement in 1788, New Zealand experienced much the same
forms of contact with Europeans as other South Pacific islands
during the mid-nineteenth century. The first Europeans to visit the
islands regularly were whalers and sealers, mostly British, American and French, many of whom used Sydney as their base. In due
course the seals were killed off and traders turned to bartering guns,
blankets, grog and tobacco with the Maoris for flax, kauri timber
and grain. The main centre for this trade was the Bay of Islands in the

North Island; and by the 1820s there were substantial European settlements at Kororareka and Hokianga. In the early days European visitors were almost invariably disreputable, the riff-raff of Australia and America. There were still many beachcombers of this type in the 1830s but there was also a more sober society, including substantial merchants, tradesmen and landowners. By 1840 there was a land company and bank at Kororareka and over two thousand permanent European residents in New Zealand. A further influx of settlers was expected from Australia and Sydney speculators were beginning to buy large blocks of lands from the Maoris at ludicrously low prices.

Finally there were well-established Protestant missions, including the Church Missionary Society and the Wesleyans, whose monopoly was challenged by a French Catholic mission from 1838.

The effect of this European penetration was that by the 1830s New Zealand was virtually an informal colony of New South Wales; and the test of British attitudes to empire was therefore whether *de facto* would be converted into *de jure* British control. Private attitudes varied; but there is no doubt that the Colonial Office in London, while recognizing some moral obligation to protect subjects and to protect Maoris from the worst consequences of imported firearms and liquor, was strongly opposed to annexation and tried to avoid the necessity by a series of palliatives, such as the Act of 1817 enabling British subjects accused of crimes committed in New Zealand to be taken for trial to Sydney and by the appointment of a British Resident to foster good race relations in the Bay of Islands. But by 1838 these devices had clearly failed; and the British government therefore tentatively decided to acquire full sovereignty by treaty over those few places where Europeans were concentrated but to leave the remainder of New Zealand independent. Why, then, was this limited solution not adopted? Was New Zealand totally annexed in 1840 because the government was convinced by Wakefield that the islands were a desirable field for British trade, investment and emigration? Alternatively, was the New Zealand Company, founded in 1838, able to use the sort of levers described later by Hobson to force the government to act in its interests?

The short answer appears to be that, while the Colonial Office and government were never convinced that it was desirable to annex New Zealand on economic grounds or as a field for emigration, they were blackmailed by Wakefield into annexing the whole of both islands rather than only a few districts in the North Island. The decisive consideration was that, so long as New Zealand remained independent, London could not prevent private British settlements there nor regulate predictable conflicts with the Maoris over land and with France over the projected French settlement at Akaroa. The Colonial Office therefore reluctantly decided to acquire full sovereignty by treaty with the Maoris in order to cope with these essentially politically and moral problems. Sovereignty over part of the North Island was therefore declared on 5 February 1840 on the basis of the Treaty of Waitangi which was made with a number of North Island chiefs; but in May this was suddenly extended by proclamation to the rest of both islands to forestall French claims to sovereignty deriving from the Akaroa settlement.

British annexation of New Zealand is, therefore, important to the present study because it demonstrates with unusual clarity three characteristic features of imperial expansion in the mid-nineteenth century which might and did occur also after 1880. First, despite Wakefield's colonizing company based on Britain, the problem was essentially peripheral, resulting mainly from the activities of Australians and others based on Sydney. Second the British government never accepted that New Zealand was needed by Britain to provide economic opportunities or a field for emigration. Finally, however, the official mind recognized an obligation to act when the activities of British subjects generated political and moral problems which could not otherwise be solved or restricted. Circumstances such as these were relatively rare in the mid-nineteenth century. But the case of New Zealand is important because it demonstrates not only that peripheral questions were a potent source of imperial expansion but also that economic ventures such as a capitalist colonizing company were most likely to lead to formal rule if they raised otherwise insoluble political problems on the periphery. Thirty-four years later very similar considerations were to result in the annexation of Fiji.

The forces leading to formal French colonization in the Pacific during the 1840s were in some ways more complex than those operating in New Zealand. France possessed no territory in the Pacific in 1830 to generate a local sub-imperialism. There was no enthusiasm for colonizing adventures and no demand for colonies of settlement. Why, then, did France impose protectorates over the Marquesas and Society Islands in 1842, come near to acquiring the

Wallis, Gambier and Leeward Islands in the following years and finally annex New Caledonia in 1853?

The roots of French action lay in attempts made after 1815 to investigate the commercial possibilities of the Pacific. By the early 1820s it was recognized that successful trade would require small bases for repairing and revictualling ships, a concept which was known as 'la politique des points de relâche'. Possible sites were examined on the Swan River in Western Australia, in New Zealand and Hawaii. No action had been taken by 1830 but some interest had been raised in France which resulted in the founding of a Catholic mission in Hawaii in 1827 and projects for establishing a penal colony elsewhere. The concept of 'points de relache', however, remained largely theoretical so long as there was virtually no French trade in the Pacific; but in the early 1830s French whaling vessels had entered the Pacific and by the end of the decade provided a genuine economic argument for the acquisition of a few bases. Yet, when action eventually came, it was due less to French official planning to meet this need than to unauthorized action by Anglo-phobe French naval officers whose concern was to help French missions struggling to compete with established British missions and thus to demonstrate the power and prestige of France.

The grounds for naval intervention of this type were that French missions had been ejected from Hawaii in 1831 and from Tahiti in 1836, in each case by indigenous rulers on the prompting of established Protestant missions. Two unauthorized visits to Hawaii in 1836–7 by the French naval officer, Du Petit-Thouars, had no effect; but in 1838 he was authorized to exact compensation from Queen Pomare of Tahiti for the eviction of Father Caret in 1836. Going further, Du Petit-Thouars forced the Queen to sign a convention allowing free access by all Frenchmen; and this was extended in 1839 by another naval officer, Laplace, to include freedom of worship for Catholics and the right of residence for Catholic priests. A similar convention was then imposed on Hawaii. Thus, largely without official authorization, French naval officers had established the principle that France could dictate to independent island governments in support of private French interests.

By 1839 reports of these developments had aroused some interest among Catholic and anti-British elements in France and the government reluctantly found itself committed to a tripartite policy of supporting French missions when necessary, providing naval protection and ports of call for whalers and merchants and making commercial treaties with island rulers. It was also under pressure to acquire colonies for free settlement and as penitentiaries. But the first attempt to acquire territory failed. A Nanto-Bordelaise company was founded, with official approval, in 1839 to establish a settlement at Akaroa, in New Zealand, both as a port of call for whalers and a base for Bishop Pompellier's struggling Catholic mission. This, as has been seen, was thwarted by the British annexation of New Zealand in 1840. Failure there forced the government to save face by acting elsewhere. Du Petit-Thouars was therefore instructed to impose a protectorate in the Marquesas where there was already a flourishing French mission, and this was done in May 1842. France now had her port of call, honour was satisfied and the government wanted to go no further.

What happened subsequently therefore constitutes an excellent example of how a European government might be forced to acquire territory overseas by the unauthorized action of its own officers. Du Petit-Thouars went on from the Marquesas to Tahiti and, without any authority, forced Queen Pomare to sign a protectorate treaty. This put Guizot, the French Prime Minister, in a serious dilemma. He did not want the protectorate and was anxious not to weaken his informal entente with Britain. Yet it was politically dangerous to denounce the protectorate outright for this would alienate French nationalists and the clerical party. Fortunately the British Foreign Secretary, Lord Aberdeen, felt unable, in view of Pomare's formal request for French protection, to deny the French claim and rejected demands for counter-action from British interests in Tahiti and Australia. He recognized the protectorate and in 1844 did not insist that the British Consul, Pritchard, who had been deported by the French on allegations of plotting against them, should be allowed to return. But moderation over Tahiti entitled Britain to compensation in other ways and places. Guizot had to denounce a proclamation issued by Du Petit-Thouars in November 1843 which converted the Tahiti protectorate into annexation as a colony and offered an apology and indemnity for the deportation of Pritchard. In November 1843 Guizot moreover accepted the independence of Hawaii, which was guaranteed in a joint declaration by the two governments. Indeed France had to pay for British recognition of her control over the Marquesas and Tahiti by giving up projects for further extension of empire in the

Pacific. French protectorates declared by naval officers in the Wallis and Gambier Islands in New Caledonia were rejected by Paris. Finally France agreed, by the Declaration of London in 1847, that the Leeward Islands (Huahine, Raiatea and Borabora), which had considerable importance as ports of call and had been claimed by the French government of Tahiti on the ground that they were dependencies of Queen Pomare, should remain independent.

The Declaration of London ended a crucial phase of imperial expansion in the Pacific, though the annexation by France of New Caledonia in 1853 as a penal settlement and naval base, which had been held up by the negotiation with Britain and then by the French Revolution of 1848, was a logical completion of earlier designs. To what extent was French policy in this period determined by economic factors? There can be no doubt that its roots were economic. French metropolitan interest in the Pacific stemmed from a generalized desire to open up new markets and sources of raw materials and the early naval voyages of exploration were intended to reconnoitre these possibilities. Little conventional trade in fact developed because of French maritime and industrial weakness, but the special problems of French whalers established the need for several ports of call in the Pacific. In addition there were projects for establishing settlement colonies to New Zealand which can reasonably be regarded as economic enterprises. To this extent French colonization in the South Pacific had clear economic objectives.

Yet the actual course of events was determined by largely non-economic forces and by actions taken on the periphery without metropolitan authority. The most that Paris wanted at any stage, or formally authorized, was a single port of call in New Zealand or the Marquesas to serve the navy and the whalers. All further developments were due to initiatives taken by French naval officers, for once the French flag had been raised in these islands it was extremely embarrassing for the French government, whatever its preference, to denounce protectorate treaties already made, primarily because this would be interpreted as submission to British protests. In the last resort, therefore, French imperialism in the Pacific owed far more to the nationalism of French naval officers and the genuine problems of French Catholic missions than to the specifically economic objectives of metropolitan France.

For thirty years after the settlement of Anglo-French differences in 1847 it seemed possible that neither power, nor any other

European state, would seriously disturb the status quo in the Pacific. Neither country really wanted a large formal empire in the Pacific and both realized that competition was endangering the entente. Agreement did not prevent occasional crises in the Pacific and elsewhere, but it provided a frame of reference within which both countries could achieve specific objectives without inciting the other to counter-action. Thus the French could annex New Caledonia in 1853 and the British Fiji in 1874 without complaint from the other side. Since no third power showed any serious political interests in the Pacific until the Samoan treaties of 1877-9 Britain and France were free to restrict their activities to a minimum level consistent with protection of existing economic and missionary interests. Throughout the mid-century informal influence seemed infinitely preferable to formal empire.

II PLANTERS, TRADERS AND THE PROBLEM OF GOVERNMENT, 1860–80

The course of European imperialism in the Pacific in the second half of the nineteenth century was largely determined by an economic revolution which occurred in and after the 1860s. Hitherto, as had been seen, European economic enterprise had been narrowly based on whaling and a small-scale trade in indigenous island products and was carried on by small vessels based on Australia and later on New Zealand and Tahiti. There was very little European settlement except in New Zealand and almost no production of export commodities by expatriates. The Pacific therefore remained extremely marginal to the economic needs of Europe. But in the 1860s the island acquired a real, though still intrinsically very small, importance in the international economy as a source of raw materials. The most important single novelty was that the rising market price of vegetable oil and, temporarily during the 1860s, also of raw cotton, at last made it worth while for Europeans to establish plantations under European management. The Germans were undoubtedly the pioneers of this new development. The Hamburg trading firm of J. C. Godeffroy and Son, with world-wide commercial interests, was interested in the Pacific as early as 1845 but did not actually establish its first agency, at Apia in Samoa, until 1857. By 1861 it was exporting 700 tons of coconut oil. From 1865 Theodor Weber was head of the Apia agency and the rapid expansion of German activities thereafter was largely due to his enterprise. Weber considered that it would be more profitable to grow coconuts in efficiently run plantations and to ship dried copra to Europe where the oil could be extracted mechanically, than to buy coconut oil of inferior quality which had been extracted by leaving the flesh of the nut exposed to the sun. He established large coconut plantations in Samoa and, while waiting for the palms to mature, grew cotton on the firm's estates.

Godeffroys did not, however, restrict their activities to Samoa. The initial plantations required more labour than the Samoans were prepared to give; and from the start the Germans began large-scale labour-recruiting in other islands groups, notably the Gilbert and Ellice Islands, New Britain, the Solomans, Carolinas, and Palaus. They also established trading centres for copra and other island produce in these groups and in Tonga they started large copra plantations on the Samoan model. Their example was followed by other German firms, notably the Hernsheims, who were the dominant interest in the Marshall Islands by 1874.

This German initiative had very important economic and political consequences for the Pacific as a whole. Others, particularly Americans, Australians and New Zealanders, followed their example. By the early 1870s there were copra plantations owned by Germans, French, British or Americans in many islands with suitable soil and climate. Cotton had been grown in large quantities in the 1860s, stimulated by a world shortage resulting from the American Civil War, but was now declining in favour of other crops. Sugar was grown in several places, including Fiji and Hawaii. Coffee, cocoa and other crops were being introduced experimentally. These economic opportunities attracted a small but significant influx of European settlers not only to run the new estates but also to provide services such as shipping, banking, hotels and stores. There were sizeable European communities in Samoa, Fiji, Hawaii and Tonga in addition to those islands already under formal European control. Beyond these centres of production and settlement European influence was penetrating the most remote island groups. The urgent need of all plantations for more labour than individual islands could produce resulted in widespread labour recruiting elsewhere which commonly took the form of kidnapping or 'blackbirding'. In addition, earlier forms of European activity – missions, small traders and naval vessels on patrol – continued and became more intense.

The consequences of this accelerating economic revolution for the future of the Pacific were immense. In retrospect it seems obvious that European activity on so relatively large a scale was bound eventually to lead to political control and partition between those European and American states whose nationals were most concerned. Yet it is important not to misconstrue the relationship between economics and politics. In the first instance at least Europeans trading with the islands still felt virtually no need for political action by their parent states, and in the 1880s the vast majority of Pacific exports was still produced by islanders rather than on European plantations. In Fiji, Samoa, Tonga and Hawaii, as earlier in New Zealand, islanders were more than willing to sell land to would-be planters for ridicuously low sums and indigenous governments generally co-operated to the best of their ability. In some places, notably the New Hebrides and New Guinea, hostility to Europeans, born of experience of traders and labour recruiters, obstructed peaceful settlement; but in most islands the earlier work of missionaries had already prepared the way for Europe an enter-prise. Hence the major economic developments of the nineteenth century took place some time before most islands were under formal European control. Paradoxically, regulations imposed by formal European rule might, as in Fiji after 1874, prove an obstacle to the free enterprise of European settlers.

Nor, in this period before 1880, did any European government whose nationals were directly involved in Pacific trade or produc-tion show any desire to impose formal rule on the islands. European penetration was the work of private individuals and groups and did not express the political ambitions or economic necessities of their parent states. Godeffroys and other German firms represented Hamburg or Bremen, not the new imperial Germany which had no colonial tradition. Germans were accustomed to trade in distant countries without a political base and those in the Pacific asked no more than support from consuls and naval vessels. Washington also had no colonial tradition. American naval vessels cruised the Pacific and interfered in island affairs from time to time, in the same way as British and French ships. But until the late 1890s it was impossible to induce Congress to accept any cession of territory, even when this was offered. The French already had Pacific colonies. They took little part in the expanding commercial activity of the 1860s and 1870s and were coming to accept that earlier expectations of economic development in Tahiti would not be realized. They showed no desire for further territorial possessions except in the Leewards, which were seen as essential to the political security of Tahiti, and in the New Hebrides, which were a source of labour for New Caledonia and a possible additional penal colony. Finally the British government, which for half a century had acted on the assumption that new colonies meant new obligations, saw no need for further territory in the Pacific. 'British' interests were largely those of Australia and New Zealand and recurrent Australasian proposals for founding chartered colonizing companies or imposing formal rule on particular islands during the 1870s were normally rejected out of hand by London. In short, there is no evidence whatever that large imperialist designs for territorial expansion in the Pacific were formulated in any European capital before the 1880s.

Yet although the economic revolution in the Pacific was so unimportant in basic economic terms to the metropolitan powers, it had immensely significant consequences for those European firms and individuals directly concerned and for the general condition of the Pacific islands. These consequences require careful examination because they constitute a prime example of peripheral factors making for imperial expansion and, more precisely, of political difficulties arising out of economic developments which could only be solved by imposing formal rule. Such problems fall into two main categories: rivalries between Europeans of different nationalities; and the decay of law and order in island territories.

Inter-European rivalry varied greatly from one part of the Pacific to another, but in most cases resulted either from growing competition for limited physical or human resources or from fear that one national group would acquire a monopolistic position. The vital need for imported plantation labour led to competitive recruitment and fear that any state might impose political control over the areas of supply. German subjects were sensitive to the fact that they were relative newcomers and resented the preponderant influence of British and French missions and naval forces. In some places, notably Samoa, where there was a concentration of British, German and American activity, intensive rivalries developed in the 1870s which turned on primacy of influence with the indigenous government. Behind many of these rivalries lay the assumption that one European power or other would eventually impose political control over islands where its nationals had interests. The French, as has been seen, feared that the British had pretensions to the Leeward

Islands and New Hebrides. The Germans were frightened that British annexation of Fiji was the precursor of wider territorial control. But undoubtedly the most frightened and therefore imperialist group in the Pacific were the Australians and New Zealanders whose viewpoint was unique and requires special consideration.

By the 1860s Australians and New Zealanders had a dominant position in many parts of the Pacific. Sydney shipowners, merchants and bankers had a large share in the island trades. Sydney supplied the European goods bartered with islanders and acted as an entrepôt for island raw materials. Auckland duplicated many of these activities. Queensland 'blackbirders' were active in the labour traffic, providing 'kanaka' labour for the new sugar plantations of the colony. Protestant missions based in these and other Australian colonies were taking over from British pioneers. To these substantive interests the Australian colonists added imperialistic assumptions alien to contemporary Britain. While the metropolis was happy for other countries to share the trade and evangelization of the Pacific, many colonists regarded the whole Pacific as a British sphere of interest by right of prior discovery and occupation and resented subsequent foreign intrusion. Their position was entirely rational, for whereas to Britain the Pacific was an insignificant segment of a world-wide economic system, for the colonists it was a vital region for commercial activity. Again, while the Pacific had no strategic or political importance for Britain, it was the key to Australasian security. The colonies had virtually no military forces and the British naval squadron based on Australia was small and antiquated. Every French, German or American possession therefore seemed a possible base for attack on colonial ports and shipping. French New Caledonia had the additional inconvenience that convicts frequently escaped and made for Australia or New Zealand; and it was assumed that any new French dependency might also become a penal settlement. Thus to the British colonists foreign occupation of territories in the South Pacific was as unacceptable as German or French control of Ireland or the Shetlands would have been to the metropolis.

It was not, therefore, surprising that the Australians and New Zealanders protested at every stage of foreign intervention in Pacific territories. By the 1870s they were demanding precautionary British annexation of each group as it became a centre of controversy: Fiji, Samoa, the New Hebrides, Rapa, New Guinea and others. Their weakness was that they lacked the constitutional freedom to act for themselves or the fiscal resources adequate to pay the cost of British annexation when this was made contingent on colonial contributions to administrative expense. They were therefore unable to force Britain to follow an expansionist policy. Yet their known interests and the pressure they could bring to bear in London forced British governments in the 1870s and later to hesitate in recognizing foreign claims when they might otherwise have done so readily; and in the 1880s Britain's role in the partition of the Pacific was dictated almost entirely by her sensitivity to colonial views, heightened by growing metropolitan interest in imperial unity which made it important not to alienate colonial opinion. To foreign states this deference to the Australasian point of view seemed incredible, a mere cover for British greed. Yet colonial opinion was a reality and eventually forced Britain to take an active part in the partition of the Pacific.

Almost equally important as a secondary consequence of economic development in the Pacific leading eventually to formal empire was the impact of Europeans on indigenous systems of government and society. It has been seen above that the general assumption of all European governments in this period was that planters, traders and missionaries should pursue their legitimate activities without political intervention by European states. But this was only possible if the native governments of the islands could provide a framework of order, holding the balance between Europeans and islanders and between rival Europeans. During the 1860s it became increasingly apparent that, with few exceptions, the indigenous governments and societies of the Pacific were unable to fill this role once pressures resulting from more intensive economic development were felt. In most places the unit of government was too small, for few island groups managed to evolve an unchallenged sovereign authority, and their laws and social institutions were too unsophisticated. The result was disorder, conflicts between Europeans and danger of total collapse. By the 1880s it was increasingly clear that only full European control could meet these problems. But until then, and in some places for some time longer. European governments believed there was an alternative solution. This was to acknowledge the sovereign authority of a properly constituted indigenous government in each island or group, either *de facto* or *de jure*, and to bolster its stability by using European consular officials or other agents of the European governments to control the activities of foreign nationals. But this solution in turn depended on two conditions: that the indigenous rulers would adapt their institutions to new needs, employing Europeans to help to administer their states; and that European governments would give their official agents sufficient authority over their own nationals. Such a system of informal control was rarely successful, for it was vulnerable in two respects. It was extremely difficult for a would-be sovereign chief to exert effective authority over subordinate chiefs and islands who had never experienced a unitary sovereign state; and European residents were liable to refuse to obey an indigenous authority if it acted against their special interests. The experiment of recognizing and supporting independent island states was therefore always likely to fail; but the attempt had to be made for the alternative was unwanted formal rule by the powers of Europe and North America.

These were the two most obvious secondary consequences of the expansion of European economic interests during the 1860s and 1870s. How important was either of them as a cause of formal imperial expansion? In the short term at least neither had spectacular results. Between 1853 and 1883 the list of Pacific islands acquired by the powers as protectorates or colonies is very short. The French imposed a protectorate on Rapa in 1867. The United States annexed Midway in the same year. Britain annexed the Fij group in 1874. Germany annexed Neiafu and Jaluit, both in the Marshall Islands, in 1876 and 1878 respectively. Of these all but Fiji were minute territories, mere ports of call or coaling stations. Rapa and Midway were annexed to provide coaling bases for the new steamships on the trans-Pacific route. The German ports were bases used in the Marshall Island trade. Only Fiji was a significant territorial acquisition in which there were substantial European plantations. Clearly, therefore, the main feature of this period was that in the short term economic expansion did not lead to annexation. Moreover, none of these places was annexed primarily because of inter-European rivalries. But by 1880 conditions in several major island groups were deteriorating rapidly, mainly as a result of the inability of indigenous governments to provide a stable and neutral political basis for European activity. Since this process led directly to the partition of the last twenty years of the century and at the same time provides classic examples of how the 'crack-up' of indigenous societies might (as suggested above in chapter 4) be a source of peripheral imperialism, it is necessary to examine briefly the course of events in some of the main island groups during the twenty years before 1880.

During this period four indigenous states or quasi-states developed in the Pacific which were distinguished by the fact that their rulers claimed effective sovereignty over island groups and attempted to govern along European lines. In each case there were substantial European plantations and settler communities. Two of these experiments had considerable success and survived until near the end of the century or beyond. Hawaii, where the Americans were the dominant foreign interest and were developing large-scale sugar plantations, remained reasonably stable under an indigenous government organized along American constitutional lines until 1891, and even tried to intervene in the Samoan dispute of the 1880s, as a major external power. The Hawaian state fell only after a dynastic change in 1891 led to dissatisfaction among settlers. In 1894 the American residents staged a revolution and established a settler-dominated republic, appealing to the United States for incorporation. These appeals were rejected until 1898, but then, under the changed circumstances resulting from the war with Spain, President McKinley accepted another petition and incorporated Hawaii with the United States.

The other successfully reconstructed state was Tonga. Here there were both British and German plantations, but the dominant political influence was always Australian, deriving from the Wesleyan Mission. George Tupou was an able king who readily adopted European techniques and employed European officials. His state was formally recognized by Germany in 1876 and by Britain in 1879. It survived political crises in the 1880s which arose mainly from resentment among Polynesians and European settlers alike at the autocratic powers wielded by Shirley Baker, a Wesleyan missionary, who became Prime Minister. Tonga eventually became a British protected state in 1900 not because the government collapsed but as part of a final settlement of Pacific problems between Britain and Germany. Its long survival indicated both that foreign economic penetration did not require formal political control and also that the earlier European ideal of sustaining independent indigenous governments was not wholly unrealistic.

The two other important island states to emerge in the 1860s, Fiji and Samoa, were, however, less successful and provide clearer evidence of the problems resulting from intensive foreign economic activity. Fiji was the first to lose its independence; and its annexation in 1874 provides the main test of British objectives in the Pacific during this period. Was Fiji annexed on economic grounds because of the value of its cotton and sugar plantations and for fear of German rivalry?[3]

The weakness of Fiji as an independent island state lay not in international rivalry for economic resources, for this was always primarily an Australian 'colony', with German and American interests restricted to trade and a few plantations; but in the failure of Thakombau, claimant to sovereignty over the whole group, to obtain general Fijian and European acceptance of his paramount power. Thakombau was originally chief of the small island of Mbau, and his attempt to become accepted ruler of the whole group was strongly resisted by Ma'afu, a Tongan chief who had acquired a small island empire based on Vanua Mbalavu. Thakombau saw the value of European help and made great efforts to Westernize his government, at first relying heavily on the advice of W. T. C. Pritchard, the son of G. Pritchard, who became British Consul in 1857. Between 1865 and 1871 Thakombau tried five different constitutions which borrowed heavily from European models and in the end accepted a political system which was virtually run by settlers. In 1871 the British recognized Thakombau's government as *de facto* ruler of the islands, thus strengthening his claims to sovereignty and also evading the legal problem of the nationality of British subjects who acquired the nationality of a foreign state which was recognized *de jure*. Further constitutional changes were made in 1873 tending towards Fijian rather than settler political control but still run by European ministers, notably J. B. Thurston. But by 1874 Fiji was rapidly sliding into anarchy; and the blame lay largely with the European settlers who disliked the imposition of taxes and the authority of indigenous courts. Thakombau had failed to achieve effective authority over his own subjects or Europeans.

Long before this time, however, Thakombau had tried to persuade the British government to give him formal protection. His first attempt in 1858 was stimulated by the fact that the American Consul held him responsible for losses to himself and debts due to other Americans improbably assessed in 1855 at $43,531 and that American naval captains were pressing for payment under threat of bombardment. Thus began a period of sixteen years when the possibility of British annexation was recurrently raised. In 1861 the British government, having sent a commissioner to investigate, refused the offer of cession. But the pressure on Britain increased. Thakombau managed to pay off the American debt in 1868, but only by pledging himself to give 200,000 acres to a Melbourne land company which had advanced him money to do so. This contract could not, in fact, be fulfilled, for Thakombau did not own sufficient land to make so large a grant. The result was that Thakombau's state was in some sense in pawn to Australian land speculators. Moreover political conditions now deteriorated rapidly. There was growing lawlessness, Fijians were being kidnapped to work on the rapidly expanding cotton plantations, and settlers were increasingly reluctant to obey the government. Given the preponderance of British interests, the metropolitan government could not entirely deny responsibility, and between 1869 and 1874 the Colonial and Foreign Offices repeatedly considered the problem. For the most part official opinion remained hostile to annexation in that it would involve administrative expenditure without compensating advantages. At the same time it was recognized that some form of European supervision was desirable and London made several attempts to persuade an Australian government to take Fiji over at its own expense. These attempts failed for, although New South Wales and Victoria had substantial interests in Fiji and wanted British annexation, they were unwilling to meet the cost. The responsibility thus remained with Britain.

In 1873 a further petition from Thakombau made a decision necessary. The Gladstone government was divided on the issue. Kimberley, as Colonial Secretary, was in favour of annexation, Gladstone strongly against. As a compromise another commission was sent, which recommended annexation. When its report was received the Conservative government under Disraeli was in office. This in itself made little difference, for Disraeli was as hostile to annexation as Gladstone. But Carnarvon, the Colonial Secretary, was strongly in favour of annexation and better placed to persuade his chief. His basic argument was that Britain had a moral obligation to act, even against her own fiscal interests, because British nationals had created the Fijian problem. At the same time he suggested possible advantages Fiji might provide: a naval base to match that acquired on lease by the United States at Pago Pago in Samoa in 1872; and a base for the projected High Commission which would control British subjects throughout the Pacific. Fiji might thus reduce the pressure on Britain to undertake responsibilities in other islands. He also argued that Fiji need not remain a financial burden for long. Conversely, there was no mention of the economic advantages of controlling the group and there is no evidence whatever of pressure being exerted by the Melbourne land company for the British government to act as a bailiff for its debts. Disraeli accepted Carnarvon's arguments and Fiji was annexed by Britain in October 1874.

The annexation of Fiji was apparently inconsistent with the general lines of British and European policy in the Pacific during the thirty years before 1880, but in fact it demonstrated both that the official mind might be convinced on purely pragmatic grounds that territorial control was unavoidable, and that formal annexation of a Pacific island group might result from the political and social consequences of European economic penetration. Fiji remained exceptional in this period not because its problems were unique but because they were unusually intense and because a political solution did not generate serious international difficulties such as blocked unilateral action in Samoa.

Samoa, in fact, experienced the same basic problems as Fiji in this period in a still more complex form.[4] There was no one ruling family which could claim effective sovereignty and by the 1870s there were well-established plantations and a large international settler population. The main difference from Fiji was that foreign interests were fairly evenly balanced between the Australasians, Germans and Americans. The Germans had the largest share in production and trade, but the others were not far behind. The British had a strong missionary establishment, dating from the 1830s, but the American had gained a special political position by a treaty of 1872 which gave them the use of Pago Pago harbour. As a result foreign interests, led by their respective Consuls at Apia, were extraordinarily well balanced; and although this enabled indigenous rulers to play one party against another it also meant that favours granted to one group led to pressures from others. Thus a European-type government established in 1874 by Malietoa Laupepa, a leading chief who claimed paramount authority in the group, was broken up in 1876 on the insistence of the British and American Consuls who forced the King to dismiss his Prime Minister (Colonel Steinberger, an American settler), on the grounds that he was governing in his private interests. The King was further weakened by recurrent civil wars and was temporarily superseded by his uncle, Malietoa Talavou, from 1878 to 1880. Malietoa Laupepa recognized the inherent weakness of his government and authority and would have welcomed annexation by Britain or the United States. But neither power would do more than recognize Samoa as an independent state. The United States ratified the 1872 treaty in modified form in 1878. The Germans made a treaty the same year which recognized the government in return for concession for a coaling station. The British made a similar treaty in 1879 which conceded extra-territorial jurisdiction over British subjects and the right to establish a naval station.

By 1879, therefore, these three powers had made it impossible for any one of them to annex Samoa unilaterally by recognizing it as a civilized state. The only way to protect their interests was now jointly to support the indigenous government of the day. For the next four years it seemed possible that Samoa might remain at least nominally independent on this basis. In 1879 the three Consuls made a convention with Malietoa Talavou whereby Apia, the main centre of foreign activity, became virtually an international settlement on the lines of that at Shanghai, independent from the central government and administered by a municipal board and a European magistrate. After Malietoa Talavou's death in 1880, moreover, the Consuls jointly supported the restoration of Malietoa Laupepa as King and consoled the opposing Samoan party by recognizing one of their leaders, Tamasese, as vice-King. Yet stability depended on continued co-operation between the three Consuls and their respective nationals and this did not last for long. The German economic interest, already preponderant, was growing fast. Successive German Consuls and the German settlers and traders regarded Samoa as primarily a German sphere of interest and waited only for support from Berlin before staging a political coup to impose unilateral control over the Samoan government. They were acutely afraid that Britain might step in and annex Samoa because Germany refused to accept colonial responsibilities; and in 1883 a tense situation arose from a New Zealand request to the Colonial Office for British annexation.

The later history of the Samoan problem will be outlined below. Until 1880 its significance lies in the fact that although economic penetration by Europeans had virtually destroyed Samoa's independence and capacity to administer her own affairs, rivalry between foreign nationals states blocked the way to annexation by any one foreign state as a means of reimposing order. It is also significant that, whereas economic rivalry generated strong imperialistic instincts among European settlers and consuls in Samoa and also among interested groups in New Zealand and Australia, these had little influence in London, Berlin and Washington. By 1880 Samoa called for a political solution to the consequences of foreign economic activity, but this was impossible until the statesmen of Europe and North America had adopted a new approach to this type of peripheral problem in the mid-1880s. Even then the Samoan problem dragged on to 1899 because the United States, unlike Britain, would not agree to formal partition of Samoa between the powers.

The four Pacific island groups so far considered were the only places in which there was both substantial European settlement or investment and a possibility of preserving a stable indigenous government with foreign help before 1880. In two of them collaboration had clearly failed. Yet the case was far worse in most of the other inhabited island groups where, although there was little or no foreign investment or permanent settlement, the impact of traders, missionaries and labour-recruiters was none the less considerable. In many of these groups international competition for trade or labour was acute and conditions rapidly deteriorated. There were, in fact, two distinct problems: how to control European nationals and prevent the grosser abuses practised by blackbirders and traders; and how to punish islanders for attacks on Europeans. Until 1880 only the British attempted seriously to deal with these problems. The other Europen powers continued to rely on 'commodore justice' meted out by naval forces who punished islanders for attacks on Europeans but did not protect them against injustice. The British, with their existing possessions, considerable naval force and strong humanitarian tradition, had the means of providing a framework of security for their nationals and for Pacific islanders. In 1872 the Pacific Islanders Protection Act made it necessary for labour-recruiters to obtain a licence from a colonial governor and strengthened the powers of the supreme courts of Australia and New Zealand to try cases involving British subjects in the islands. The act was, however, made largely ineffective by lack of means to police it. In 1875, therefore, another act enabled the Crown to set up a High Commission, based on Fiji, which had jurisdiction over British subjects in all places 'not within the jurisdiction of any civilized power'; that is, in all places not annexed by a European state or recognized as a sovereign state by treaty. In 1878 the High Commission was given additional powers to deal with offences committed by British subjects in Pacific states with which treaties were made.

Unfortunately the High Commission was largely a failure. The British Treasury starved it of ships and commissioners to police the islands and in any case its legal powers did not extend to indigenous islanders or foreign Europeans. British subjects could evade its jurisdiction by sailing under a foreign flag. By the early 1880s it was clear to successive High Commissioners and many others that the commission could not fill the void left by Europe's refusal to take political control of the Pacific as a whole. The only remaining solution, short of formal partition between the powers, was a joint commission of Europeans with power to deal with any European criminal, to settle disputes between different nationalities, and, with the assent of indigenous rulers, to deal also with islanders. This too was quite impracticable, for no European power was prepared to act in concert with the others. The only example of international co-operation was the Joint Naval Commission set up by France and Britain in 1887 to enforce order in the New Hebrides. It lasted until 1906 but was notoriously ineffective.

What, then, was the importance of economic factors in European imperialism in the Pacific during the half century before 1880? It is clear that throughout the period trade was the main factor making for closer European contact with the islanders but that from the 1860s plantation production, the ancillary search for indigenous labour, and increasing European settlement in the major groups intensified these contacts. Whaling and collection of guano were other important economic activities in the first half of the century. The only other comparably important reasons for European involvement were the missions and naval patrols. In some degree, therefore, economic activity was influential on every decision taken by a European power to annex territory or impose a protectorate in this period. Yet, as in most other parts of the world, the link between economic factors and the political decision to impose formal rule was usually indirect. In both New Zealand and Fiji the British government decided to annex because the secondary consequence of economic activity was chronic political and social disorder. In neither place was annexation intended primarily to serve the interests of British settlers, planters, traders or even missionaries. The French case is more complex. In the 1840s the economic element in French policy was the need of ports of call for whalers and the navy; but the immediate cause of formal action was the unauthorized initiative of Anglophobe naval officers whose ground for declaring protectorates in the Marquesas and Society Islands was that French missions faced intolerable political obstacles to evangelism. In 1853 the annexation of New Caledonia had the simple object of providing a penal settlement. Neither the Germans nor Americans showed any enthusiasm for territorial possessions apart from a very few coaling, naval or trading bases.

This interpretation of economic imperialism in the Pacific before 1880 thus falls into line with that in most other parts of the world. European economic activity expanded rapidly from the mid-century and, although miniscule in relation to metropolitan trade or production, was important to the European nationals directly concerned. Many of these wanted and demanded formal control by their parent states, but private trade and investment alone were not regarded by metropolitan officials as valid grounds for establishing formal empire. So long as the islands remained open to all on equal terms, no power had a strong incentive to undertake the cost and inconvenience of formal responsibility.

Yet by about 1880 conditions were in rapid flux. Disorder was growing as a by-product of European economic activity. Relations between nationals of different foreign states were strained in Samoa and wherever else one national group feared that another might benefit from alliance with an indigenous régime. Consuls were playing politics and using naval support to browbeat island rulers. The British annexation of Fiji in 1874, which seriously harmed those German planters whose claims to have acquired land were rejected by the subsequent British commission on land purchases, seriously worried Germans, French and Americans in other islands as a portent for the future. Conversely, New Zealanders and Australians were increasingly frightened that France or Germany would annex islands in Polynesia, Micronesia or Melanesia which were thought important for their trade, missions or military security.

What were the omens for the future? It is certain that in 1880 no European power had any intention of solving current problems and gratifying its distant subjects by a general policy of annexation. The British were committed to work the West Pacific High Commission as an alternative to imperial rule. The French wanted to convert their protectorate over Tahiti into full ownership and to annex the nearby Leeward Islands as a security measure, but in the second case were prevented by the 1847 Declaration of London until Britain was prepared to waive her rights. They also wanted to annex the New Hebrides as a source of labour for New Caledonia and an additional penal settlement. German traders and settlers were anxious for greater naval and diplomatic support against the British and Americans but Berlin showed no sign of taking action. Finally the United States remained resolutely opposed to any formal responsibilities apart from those implied by its treaty with Samoa.

It is therefore impossible to assume that, had the Pacific situation been unaffected by new developments in Europe and other parts of the world, there would have been any dramatic change for a considerable time after 1880. That is, neither economic nor political arguments for general partition between the powers were sufficiently strong to produce action by any power. Yet the greater part of the South Pacific was in fact divided into spheres of influence, protectorates or colonies by 1886 and by 1900 virtually no independent territories remained. The question still to be solved is therefore whether this dramatic change was the outcome of new economic forces in Europe or the Pacific or, alternatively, merely of new attitudes to the solution of existing peripheral problems.

Part Three
Case Studies in European
Expansion, 1880–1914

9 *The Partition of Mediterranean Africa*

I INTRODUCTION: DOMINO THEORIES OF PARTITION

One of the few points on which most interpretations of late nineteenth-century imperial expansion agree is that, in contrast with events in the Mediterranean, South Africa and in the Pacific, a rapid and total partition of sub-Saharan Africa could not reasonably have been predicted in about 1880. Conversely, if this had not occurred the legend of a new imperialism might never have been born. As a result much of the debate over the 'causes' of imperialism has centred on Africa and historians have searched there for a 'first cause', which opened the floodgates of expansion not only in Africa but throughout the world.

It is not a function of this book to investigate the conceptual problem of which single event or European state 'began' the partition of Africa or the world: indeed the approach adopted assumes that, to a considerable extent at least, factors making ultimately for alien rule were, in varying degrees, peculiar to each territory or region, even if they were later caught up in a single tide of events. Nevertheless, while it is not proposed to look for a universal 'first cause' of the partition of Africa it would be unrealistic to ignore the fact that others have done so. Four of the most influential of these theories can be listed, without critical comment, as follows.

First, it has been suggested that Leopold II's initiative in the Congo, because of his vast ambition and because it affected areas of interest to several major powers, led to the Berlin Conference of

1884–5 which in turn formulated rules for claiming possessions and precipitated a general grab for the 'vacant' heart of Africa.[1] Conversely some argue that the critical fact was the sudden emergence of Germany as a claimant to colonies in 1883–4, which, because Germany was a great power, immediately raised hitherto minor and disconnected regional questions to the level of international issues.[2] Egypt also has claims to primacy. British occupation in 1882 aggrieved other powers, stimulated claims to territory elsewhere and weakened British resistance to them.[3] Although strongly challenged[4] this 'Egyptocentric' hypothesis has received much support. Finally the causal importance of French ambitions in the Western Sudan has recently been pressed on the ground that these were demonstrated before any of these other developments became significant.[5]

Each of these and other possible 'general' interpretations of the partition of Africa contain elements of truth: none, perhaps, is convincing in isolation. Some attempt will be made incidentally to evaluate each of these hypotheses in relation to the territories and European states with which each was most concerned, but the following analysis will examine problems by regions rather than as part of a single continental or global phenomenon. The treatment of different parts of Africa is necessarily uneven in length. In the present chapter a short account will be given of the last stages leading to formal control of Tunisia and Egypt in 1881–2 and events in Morocco will be considered in more detail. In chapter 10 West and East Africa are examined with some care but events in Equatorial, Central and South Africa defy proper analysis within the limits of a short case study. In order, however, to show how European imperialism in these areas might be fitted into the analytic framework of this study it is proposed to comment very briefly on the relationship between on the one hand the specifically economic objectives of Leopold II, Cecil Rhodes and economic interests in the Transvaal, and on the other the political forces that generated the Congo Free State and Rhodesia and brought about the Boer War of 1899–1902.

II TUNISIA, 1878–81[6]

It is always dangerous to explain new historical trends in terms of a single event or situation; but if the growth of formal European control in Mediterranean Africa after the 1870s is to be dated from a single point in time this must be the Berlin Congress of 1878. The primary aim of this meeting was, of course, to settle Balkan affairs after the Russo-Turkish War; but the occasion was taken by the diplomats to deal informally with other issues, among them Tunisia. The critical fact was that, for different reasons, Britain and Germany were now prepared to relax those international pressures which had hitherto prevented unilateral action on the Tunisian problem. Salisbury, in acquiring Cyprus from Turkey, recognized that France would require compensation for this shift in the Mediterranean power balance, and thought this might conveniently be given in Tunisia. Since, moreover, Italy had refused to support Britain in opposition to Russia in 1877–8 Salisbury was prepared to ignore Italian claims in Tunisia. In two conversations with Waddington, the French Foreign Minister, Salisbury was reported to have said: 'Do what you like there'; and 'you will be obliged to take it, you cannot leave Carthage in the hands of the Barbarians'.[7] Bismarck had other reasons for wanting to placate France. He wanted to reduce the force of French irridentism over Alsace-Lorraine by providing her with compensation elsewhere, a policy he followed more or less consistently throughout the following decade. He was reported to have told Disraeli in Berlin that if Britain took Egypt 'France would not be so vexed as may be imagined, and in any case, Tunis or Syria might be given her as an equivalent'.[8] In 1880 he repeated this to the French Ambassador in Berlin, adding Egypt, Greece and Morocco as alternative possibilities for French action.[9] Thus, for the time being at least, France had a free hand in Tunisia, limited only by continuing Italian competition. The Gladstonian government which came into office in Britain in 1880 was less ready than its predecessor to follow a *laissez faire* policy there, but in the end it accepted the primacy of French interests.

But did France actually want formal control of Tunisia; and if so, were her motives primarily economic or political? Waddington, at least, wanted to cash the blank cheque so surprisingly offered in 1878 by extracting immediate recognition of French protection from the Bey and from foreign powers; but even he proposed at first only to occupy a few strategic points and to expand French control gradually.[10] His views were supported by the Prime Minister, Dufaure, and by the government of Algeria; but Gambetta was strongly against action. There was no public support, recent Algerian risings had made colonialism unpopular, a Tunisian enterprise could be attacked on the grounds of weakening France on the Rhine. The outcome was that France took no overt action; yet there was a clear assumption in Paris that Tunisia belonged to France and that the way to establish her claims was by informal penetration rather than immediate action. In short, the official mind of Paris had decided in principle on eventual control, but the government felt unable to implement this for the time being.

This fact is crucial for interpreting the events of 1878–81, particularly the struggle over economic concessions. In 1881 critics of the occupation were to assert that the invasion was designed simply to protect private French interests in Tunisia. Thus Clemenceau in November 1881:

> In all these enterprises ... I see only persons who are in Paris, who wish to do business and make money on the Stock Exchange. .... In short, it is to satisfy such 'interests' that you have made war, violated the Constitution, and have placed Parliament face to face with an accomplished fact.[11]

Many accepted this view which, on the limited evidence then available, was a reasonable deduction. In fact, however, it is now clear that the occupation of 1881 was not primarily due to threats to French economic interests in Tunisia, and that the concessions on which attention was concentrated were regarded both by the French Consul in Tunisia and by the government in Paris as a means by which France could gradually establish political primacy in Tunisia rather than as the determinant of policy. This is clear both from the character of the concessions themselves and grounds on which the government eventually decided to act in 1881.

Between 1878 and 1881 there were four major and subsequently notorious conflicts in Tunisia arising out of economic concessions to Europeans. The de Sancy affair has already been mentioned. In 1879 France used the highest diplomatic weapons, coupled with threats of naval action, to force the Bey to recognize de Sancy's claims. But the official motive was not economic: Paris hoped that the Bey would refuse because, as Saint-Vallier, Ambassador in Berlin wrote, 'we will never have so good an opportunity to establish our preponderance over the Regency'.[12] The chance was missed. The Bey climbed down and Paris was unable ever to use the occasion even to extract recognition of French pre-eminence in Tunisia. The treatment of the Enfida Estate case was even more obviously political, though in origin it represented a perfectly genuine economic enterprise on the part of Marseille financiers. In 1880 a French financial group, the Société Marseillaise de Crédit, decided to move into land speculation and agricultural credit in Tunisia. In 1880 it agreed to buy the Enfida estate of 96,000 hectares between Sousse and Tunis from the ex-minister, Khederine; and at the same time it began to press the Bey for permission to establish an agricultural credit bank in Tunis with the right to issue banknotes to the value of its advances. This banking project was still in the balance in 1881, but the Enfida question came to a climax in 1880. The new Prime Minister, Mustapha ben Ismael, had himself expected to take over this estate without payment as a perquisite of power and, to block the sale, shifted his alliance from the French consul, Roustan, to the Italian, Macciò. By putting up a Jew from Malta called Levy, a British subject, as a man of straw with a notional claim on Enfida, Mustapha hoped also to get British support against France. He succeeded to the extent that until after the French occupation of April 1881 the case dragged on and Levy was left in immediate possession. But the French reaction was strictly political: here was a challenge to French preponderance which demonstrated how unsatisfactory the existing policy of peaceful penetration had become. It was to save that preponderance, not to help the Marseille bankers, that France acted in 1881.

Finally there was the railway question, and this also demonstrated the primacy of political objectives for both Italy and France. The issue turned on control of the now bankrupt Tunis-la Goletta railway, which was seen as vital to the Bône-Guelma Company's project for monopolizing railways in Tunisia. While Bône-Guelma waited for the price to drop, Macciò persuaded the Italian shipowner, Rubattino, whose shipping line already operated from Italy to Tunisia, to make an offer. He did this with the support of the Italian government as a device to obstruct French political penetration; but, before the agreement was ratified, Bône-Guelma offered a larger sum. Rubattino then appealed to the Court of Chancery in London, where the Tunisian Railway Company's affairs were under examination, and got a court order for the line to be auctioned in London. Rubattino won the auction, paying almost twice the sum previously offered, because he had been promised 6 per cent minimum interest on his expenditure by the Italian government. In fact this victory proved pointless, for Roustan was then able to extract from the Bey a counter-concession for building lines from Tunisia to Bizerta and Sousse, which made the TLM irrelevant and gave

K

France a virtual monopoly of railway business in Tunisia. This, too, had political overtones, for as has been seen, the French company also had an official guarantee of 6 per cent interest on its investments.

It seems clear, therefore, that although many of the foreign enterprises established in Tunisia between 1878 and 1881 had genuine economic functions, they were seen by Paris, Rome and their respective consuls in Tunisia primarily as means to establishing political influence. French policy was to encourage such enterprises on the assumption that economic penetration would lead to political primacy, as indeed a monopoly of Tunisian railways and telegraphic communications might well be expected to do. Italy wanted to obstruct French penetration and to establish economic foundations for her own eventual control. For both countries success in obtaining concessions was also evidence of the influence each had over the Bey and his Ministers, which was crucial politically. Indeed it was failure to sustain French predominance at the court, as demonstrated by victory in the race for concessions, that precipitated military intervention. On balance France had the best of the struggle for concessions; but the Enfida affair in particular demonstrated that the Bey was trying to retain his independence by playing one foreign power against the other. So long as Macciò and the Italian party offered him alternative political support France could not be certain of acquiring ultimate political predominance.

Thus the immediate reason for the French invasion of April 1881 was not protection of French economic interests in Tunisia but realization that economic penetration was failing to produce secure political control. In fact the growing political influence of Macciò indicated that Tunisia might eventually fall under Italian rule; and early in 1881 King Humbert made a speech in which he claimed that Tunisia should be annexed to Italy as an ancient province of Rome. Other European statesmen were reaching the conclusion that France had missed her opportunity. Thus Bismarck commented in January that

In politics as in games one has to take one's opportunity; the French have had three years to themselves to make use of their chance, and have not done so. The good cards have changed hands; it is Italy that holds them today.[13]

In Paris also this now seemed dangerously true. By January 1881 the permanent officials of the Quai d'Orsay were convinced that only invasion would now induce the Bey to accept French primacy.

The difficulty was to persuade the politicians to act. In January Baron de Courcel, Director of Political Affairs, succeeded in convincing Saint-Hilaire, but Saint-Hilaire could not convince Jules Ferry. Elections were pending and Ferry knew that military action might be political suicide, as indeed it eventually proved. But finally, on 23 March, Courcel succeeded in convincing Gambetta that France would lose Tunisia unless she acted at once, and Gambetta used his immense political influence to persuade the Ministry. A minor incident on the Algerian frontier on 30–31 March was made the excuse to obtain credits for a limited campaign to restore order, though not to occupy Tunisia; and at the end of April a French army occupied Tunisia, without bloodshed and officially as the agent of the Bey in suppressing a domestic rising.

Yet, even at this late stage, the French genuinely hoped to avoid full and permanent occupation. Once the Bey had been induced to sign the Treaty of Bardo on 12 May 1881, providing for effective but informal control of his foreign and domestic policies by French officials and for the presence of a small French military force, they began to remove the bulk of the army. Intervention would thus have achieved the limited aim of ensuring French primacy without the cost and political hazards of formal annexation. The army was in fact in process of embarkation in June when revolts broke out at Sfax and Gabes in protest against infidel control. In suppressing these the French necessarily completed the effective occupation of Tunisia. Before they had done so the Bey died in 1882 and Ferry, now back in office after his defeat in November 1881, decided to formalize French control. The Convention of La Marsa of June 1883 maintained the fiction of Tunisian independence, but provided for a French protectorate and effective control of government through the Resident. This was the end of the Tunisian question.

What, then, was the role of specifically economic factors in these events? They were important at all stages, but relatively more at the beginning than at the end. Tunisia's freedom of action was first lost through excessive overseas borrowing and could not be regained so long as she remained bankrupt. Whereas under mid-twentieth-century conditions the penalty for external bankruptcy would be discreet supervision by the International Monetary Fund, in the 1860s it was far more intrusive supervision by the International Commission in Tunisia. This control gave France, Britain and Italy a stranglehold on the Bey and facilitated the economic penetration of Tunisia through concessions of rights to build and run utilities. Thus, by the mid-1870s, Tunisia can be described as a semi-colony under informal international control; and this must be ascribed very largely to specifically economic forces.

Beyond that point, however, other factors were more important as a source of eventual French occupation. These were both Euro-centric and peripheral in character. Within Tunisia the rivalry between the three consuls, acting largely on their own initiative, coupled with the vagaries of court politics and pressures from competing groups of expatriate residents, made international control essentially unstable. Other peripheral forces making for French occupation were Algerian pressures and the Tunisian revolt of 1881. Within Europe also forces were at work. Italy definitely wanted to annex Tunisia, largely for sentimental reasons. France did not; but she was determined to obtain primacy in Tunisia as part of her system of Mediterranean influence and security. Until 1878 Britain struggled to prevent unilateral control by any one power, but thereafter accepted the inevitability of French predominance. For each power and its agents in Tunisia the struggle for concessions was thus a means to the chosen end, paving the way for annexation or preserving national influence against rivals. In the end therefore it was not economics that determined French invasion but the political fact that the course of events in Tunisia was tending away from French predominance. In 1881 the official mind of the Quai d'Orsay triumphed over the indecision of the statesmen and the hostility of public opinion, imposing a compromise political solution. Tunisia became a French protectorate not because it was crucial to the French economy, or even because vested interests insisted on governmental support against rivals, but because Paris could not accept the prospect of Italian occupation of a region deemed crucial to French power and status in the southern Mediterranean.

III EGYPT, 1880–82[14]

British military occupation of Egypt in August-September 1882 followed French occupation of Tunisia by a year and, as has been seen, had somewhat similar roots. Yet in many ways it was more surprising. The Dual Control established in 1879 had been operating with considerable success for three years. Interest on the debt was being paid regularly. In 1880 Gladstone, notoriously hostile to military or imperialist enterprises, replaced Disraeli as British Prime

Minister. Essentially two questions have therefore to be answered. Was military occupation undertaken for economic reasons? Why did the British undertake it alone?

The key to events in Egypt is that, by contrast with Tunisia, the crisis did not result from conflicts between two rival European powers unwilling to sustain a condominium, but from changed conditions within Egypt which apparently threatened any form of European control and made new European policies necessary. There are few better examples of a 'peripheral' stimulus to European imperialism.

Between 1879–81, despite the apparent success of the Dual Control, Egyptian opinion became increasingly hostile to alien rule. At a general level this was not surprising. Egypt was no primitive sub-Saharan society but an ancient state in process of rapid development which contained a large number of educated men in close touch with contemporary European civilization. More specifically there was increasing hostility to many aspects of alien domination. Civil servants resented the influx of expatriate officials. Egyptian army officers placed on half pay for reasons of economy were jealous of those Turkish and Circassian officers who were not. Peasants and landowners disliked higher levels of taxation; many informed Egyptians feared after 1881 that Egypt would go the way of Tunisia. The product of these and other forces was a strong nationalist movement, though one that lacked both ideology and precise objectives. Its first leaders were a group of Egyptian army officers, dominated by Colonel Arabi, who in September 1881 suddenly staged a military demonstration in Cairo, demanding redress of grievances and political changes. Arabi's intentions were confused. He had no specific programme. He was xenophobic yet his nominee as Chief Minister was Cherif Pasha, a Turk living in Egypt, and he never demanded the ejection of Europeans. He had no formulated plans for constitutional change. Above all, from a European point of view, he never proposed to denounce the foreign debt or to halt interest payments to bond-holders. Yet his sudden predominance and the support he received on all sides posed a problem. He was necessarily challenging the instruments chosen by the Dual Control, the Khedive and his Ministers. If he succeeded, and if Egypt regained control of its own affairs, the international solution worked out since 1876 would be at risk. This was the problem that dominated events from 1881–2 and eventually resulted in British occupation.

In 1881, however, at least three alternative solutions seemed possible and preferable. The first British reaction to Arabi's demonstration was to call on Turkey as nominal Suzerain to send troops which would operate under British and French officers to sustain the Khedive's government. This project was patently impracticable and was rejected by the French, but it was to be revived in 1882. A second alternative was to allow the Egyptians wider political freedom, relying on their internal divisions to prevent a solid front developing against foreign control. To some extent this policy was tried out in the early months of 1882; but it did not produce political stability and the xenophobic riots of June 1882 discredited the nationalist movement in European eyes. Third, it was possible that the British and French might strengthen the Dual Control by making threatening gestures, such as the naval demonstration off Alexandria in October 1881. But this achieved little; and Gambetta, coming to office in France in November 1881, wanted far more positive Anglo-French action, even joint armed intervention if necessary, to sustain the power of the Khedive, the chosen instrument of the Dual Control, against nationalist pressures. Momentarily Gambetta had his way. A joint note, drafted in Paris, was sent to the Khedive on 8 January 1882 in which the two governments stated that they proposed to secure the Khedive and maintain the *status quo* against possible attempts at constitutional innovation by the Chamber of Notables – a body of seventy-five Arab landowners which was now demanding more effective power against Khedival autocracy.

Of all possible courses open to Britain and France this proved the worst, for naval bombardments and threatening notes merely stimulated the Chamber to demand reforms. Early in 1882 it proposed major constitutional changes which included transfer to itself of effective control over the budget, though this was modified under pressure to exclude funds allocated to servicing the debt. Gladstone was satisfied by this, but Gambetta was not; and had he not fallen from power late in January 1882 the Anglo-French entente must have been severely strained. As it was his successor, Freycinet, wanted to avoid further provocation and favoured a return to international co-operation. It was therefore agreed that if a crisis developed in Egypt an international conference should be summoned and that, if possible, Turkey should be induced to act on behalf of the powers. This was to revert to the original British solution, and a conference in fact met at Constantinople in June

1882 in response to the riots in Alexandria. It achieved nothing. The Sultan refused to co-operate, and while the conference sat, the British occupied Egypt.

It is, in fact, clear that during the first half of 1882 London and Paris lost control over Egypt because they could not find an agreed and practicable solution to the problem created by Egyptian demands for greater control of their own affairs. Under these conditions the initiative naturally passed to Cairo and in July 1882 Britain was forced to react to a situation which had developed in Egypt under stress of local conditions. Developments there cannot be examined in detail, but three main factors making for a crisis must be distinguished. First, the Egyptian Ministry, dominated by Arabi and allied with the influential Chamber of Notables, increasingly asserted its freedom of action against both Khedive and Dual Control. After the Ministry had resigned on 27 May in protest against excessive foreign interference and had been reinstated on 29 May to appease embattled public opinion it had almost unrestricted power and Arabi was virtually a dictator. Thereafter the Dual Control in its earlier form was unworkable. Second, the Khedive also attempted to assert himself against the Dual Control. In particular, his rejection of Franco-British advice to legalize the meeting of the Chamber of Notables after it had been improperly summoned by the Ministry on 10 May, demonstrated that he was an unreliable tool and embarrasing ally for Britain and France. After 29 May he was in any case powerless and a refugee with the British fleet off Alexandria. Finally the views and actions of Sir Edward Malet, the British consul general, and other British officials in Egypt were also calculated to produce a critical situation. Malet seems to have believed that, despite the apparent moderation of Arabi in the spring of 1882, Egyptian nationalism must eventually make the Dual Control unworkable, and that this would destroy the debt settlement. Evelyn Baring (Lord Cromer) later put the argument in these terms:

The financial interests concerned were so great, and the risk that financial disorder would eventually have led to anarchy was so considerable, that it may well be that armed intervention of some sort would ultimately have become an unavoidable necessity.[15]

Hence, it became the aim of the British agents in Egypt to persuade London that a crisis was imminent and that when it came Britain and France would either have to use armed force or relinquish control of Egypt. These reports necessarily influenced the British cabinet and in particular gave support to that section, led by Lord Hartington, which favoured intervention if necessary. From June to July 1882 Malet's role was even more important for, by breaking off relations with the Egyptian Ministry, he precipitated a crisis. In fact, as the man on the spot, he played much the same role in Egypt as Roustan had played in Tunisia, making it almost impossible for his metropolitan government to sustain its chosen policy of non-intervention.

By the beginning of June 1882 the Dual Control was therefore for the first time in serious danger. In retrospect, however, it seems clear that the final crisis could have been avoided. Arabi and most nationalists were moderate and realistic. They accepted the unavoidable fact of foreign control of the debt, but wanted to reduce the extent of expatriate interference in other matters. But the opportunity to co-operate with Arabi was wasted by Britain and France, and by the end of May he was committed against the present system. He did not challenge the debt settlement but it was inconceivable that the Dual Control could be re-established while he remained in power. Some form of action was therefore necessary to remove him.

But why did the British act unilaterally and why did they impose full military occupation? First, because the French, who had increasingly distrusted Malet's policy and attempted to remain on good terms with Arabi, were reluctant to take any positive action. Even after Paris had been induced to send warships to Alexandria in June the French Assembly on 29 July 1882 refused credits for a military force to be sent to the canal. France simply refused to undertake military action to redress a crisis which, in its view, was the product of unwise British actions. Thus, when a riot occurred in Alexandria on 11 June in which forty-six Europeans or their dependants were killed by xenophobic mobs, the British were left to act alone or to admit that they could not control the situation. The cabinet was in a dilemma. It did not want to occupy Egypt, still less to do so without international support. Yet some repressive action was necessary to protect Europeans and preserve the Dual Control. This was decided on 3 July when Admiral Seymour was instructed to dismantle the Alexandria forts. This was the limit of the proposed action, but Seymour and Malet co-operated to make further intervention necessary. Seymour summoned Arabi to surrender the forts – which was beyond his instructions – and then bombarded them. He had no troops to occupy Alexandria, which was pillaged, possibly by withdrawing Egyptian troops. Order had then to be restored and Seymour got eight hundred British troops from Cyprus who occupied the town on 15 July. Since Arabi was bound to counter-attack, the British government was forced to send reinforcements and to undertake a general occupation. The main British Army, under General Wolseley, landed on 4 August and by 13 September the Egyptian Army had been destroyed at Tel-el-Kebir. By the end of the year the Dual Control had effectively, though not formally, been dissolved by this uni-lateral British action, for the French were not prepared to admit that their refusal to act in July forfeited their claim to a share in the control of Egypt, and the British found themselves sole rulers of the country.

What, then, was the role of economic factors in this complex process? Reviewing the course of events from the mid-1870s it is clear that at all stages the problem of the debt was of fundamental importance. Egyptian debts were the sole reason for the first informal European control established in 1875–6. Thereafter the problem of servicing the debt ensured that European control had to continue and this remained a major fact in 1882. But, as time went on, other non-economic factors became still more important. British official intervention in 1879 and the Dual Control itself were the result of British fear that France and possibly other powers would obtain a dominant political position in Egypt. To prevent this now became the main British preoccupation. Again, in 1882, the British decision to go beyond informal control was due pri-marily to belief that an independent Egypt would be a danger to basic British political interests, which in turn centred on the status of the Suez Canal. Ultimately, then it was the security of the canal rather than concern for holders of Egyptian bonds that led to British occupation. But to what extent was concern for the canal itself an economic factor? It is true that freedom of access through the canal was important to Britain partly because of her economic stake in India and the Far East; and that even the strategic argu-ment for maintaining naval predominance in the Indian Ocean was partly a reflection of these economic interests. It is also true that in 1882 there was strong support for military action in Egypt from British groups with economic interests – the eastern shipping and trading companies and the British bond-holders. Thus there was always an economic dimension to the Egyptian question, and Sir

Charles Dilke reflected this when he attempted to justify military action in the Commons on 25 July 1882:

England has a double interest [in the canal]; it has a predominant commercial interest, because 82 per cent of the trade passing through the Canal is British trade; and it has a predominant political interest caused by the fact that the Canal is the principal highway to India, Ceylon, the Straits, and British Burmah, where 250,000,000 people live under our rule; and also to China, where we have vast interests and 84 per cent of the external trade of that still more enormous Empire. It is also one of the roads to our Colonial Empire in Australia and New Zealand.[16]

This was a good argument to use in a body which was accustomed to weigh the costs of colonial ventures in relation to prospective economic advantage; and the economic stake was real enough. But the government's decision to occupy Egypt was not, in fact, taken on these specifically economic grounds. The struggle within the cabinet in the summer of 1882, as it faced up to the challenge presented by competing forces within Egypt, turned on a concept of national interest whose central feature was security and power rather than wealth.[17] From early in 1882 a group led by Lord Hartington, Secretary for India, took a stand on the basic need to preserve order in an area vital to British power and influence in the Mediterranean and the Indian Ocean. Convinced that Turkey would never again be able to control or protect Egypt, and afraid that an independent Egypt might fall under the control of a potentially hostile European state or itself prove hostile to Britain, these Whigs decided that the canal was too important to be left at risk. They would have preferred joint action with France or some other power; but in the last resort they were ready for Britain to go it alone. These arguments were also accepted by Salisbury for the Conservative party and indeed came from a common stock of assumptions on the fundamentals of British foreign policy that descended through Palmerston from the eighteenth century. But Gladstone, and Liberals such as John Bright and Morley, did not share them. They believed that naval power alone could ensure the security of the canal, and distrusted the use of military force as a tool of foreign policy on general grounds. Until 22 July Gladstone was therefore still trying to avoid unilateral military intervention by organizing concerted action with other powers. Eventually, when these attempts failed, Gladstone allowed himself to be overruled by his colleagues, falling back on the consoling thought that occupation might provide a rule of law, free institutions and 'a noble thirst . . . for the attainment of those blessings of civilized life which they see have been achieved in so many countries in Europe.'[18]

Thus the role of economic factors in the Egyptian crisis is complex. Had there been no financial crisis there would have been no foreign intervention, at least in this period. Even so, it was the secondary political consequences of limited occupation undertaken on economic grounds, rather than the problem of the bonds, that led ultimately to British occupation. Britain did not occupy Egypt in the interest of her bond-holders or traders – though both in fact benefited. In the last resort she did so because once a major political crisis had developed out of the Dual Control, the established rules of British foreign policy forced her to insure against foreign dominance of an area of first-class political importance. There are few better examples of preemptive imperialism undertaken to achieve political objectives.

But why did the British retain permanent control of Egypt? There can be no doubt that this was not Gladstone's intention, for he and most of his colleagues hoped that a successful invasion would serve to get rid of Arabi and re-establish a moderate régime in Cairo, after which British troops could be withdrawn and a remodelled system of informal control established. It is not the function of the present study to trace the later history of British policy in Egypt, but in view of the vast long-term importance of continued occupation a short comment is necessary.

The fact was that, once in occupation, the British found it almost impossible to withdraw without sacrificing what they had tried to achieve. In view of France's refusal to co-operate in 1882 the British were determined not to restore the Dual Control, which was simply allowed to die without formal burial. Being in possession the British quickly took control of all organs of government. They attempted to re-establish the authority of the Khedive and in effect to work the old Dual Control single-handed; but they found that the Khedive's authority had been destroyed and that, like the French in Tunisia, they must govern while acting through Egyptian forms and agents. Once started, moreover, the work of reforming Egyptian government and society, which was regarded as the prerequisite of withdrawal, proved absorbing and lengthy. By about 1885 the horizons were lengthening and the difficulties of withdrawal seemed ever greater. By this time also, a new military threat had developed. By 1883 the forces of the Mahdi, Mohammed

Ahmad, leading a nationalist movement against the horrors of the Egyptian occupation of the Sudan, was threatening Lower Egypt. The British had to stay to withdraw the remnants of the Egyptian Army from the Sudan and then to protect Egypt itself. By the end of the 1880s staying had become a habit. Salisbury was still convinced in 1889 that to evacuate would result in internal chaos and that this would again threaten British political interests – the canal and the Indian Ocean. Britain stayed because the dangers of withdrawal seemed greater than the inconveniences of continued occupation.

The consequences of this for the history of European imperialism were great, though difficult to measure precisely. It has been claimed that 'from start to finish the partition of tropical Africa was driven by the persistent crisis in Egypt'.[19] This is too strong: partition would very probably have taken much the same form had there been no Egyptian crisis. Yet with varying intensity, the French felt aggrieved that Britain had ended the Dual Control unilaterally, and the resultant Anglophobia stimulated many, though not all, French politicians and officials to oppose British pretensions in other parts of the world, in West Africa and the Sudan especially. Again, the fact that Germany, in alliance with France, Austro-Hungary and Italy, could block British proposals on the continuing Commission for the Liquidation of the Debt in Egypt gave Bismarck a handy 'baton' with which to influence British foreign policy. The growing British determination to stay in Egypt had an equally marked influence on her handling of affairs in East Africa. Without Egypt this region was of minimal importance to British interests, economic or political. But East Africa was the key to the Nile. By 1890 it was an established British assumption that no potentially hostile foreign power must control the upper reaches of the Nile; and this in turn led to the British protectorate over Uganda in 1894. Finally, desire to end the considerable inconvenience of French hostility and obstruction to British government in Egypt was a major and perhaps decisive reason why the British decided to reach a general colonial settlement with France in 1903-4 and, above all, to concede French primacy in Morocco. If the Egyptian crisis did not actually cause the partition of Africa, British occupation and French resentment had a significant impact on events not only in Africa but in all parts of the world where France and Britain had common or conflicting interests.

IV MOROCCO, 1880–1911[20]

Morocco has a dual importance for the study of economic factors in European expansion before 1914. First, the period of crisis came relatively late, after the partition of Africa was virtually complete, and these crises therefore provide valuable evidence on the inter-action of political and economic considerations and the impact of 'imperialist' public opinion on the making of national policy under the new circumstances of the period of the formation of the Anglo-French entente and of German *Weltpolitik*. Second, much play was made by each of the European powers concerned of their respective economic interests in Morocco and it might therefore appear at first sight that international rivalry there stemmed primarily from competition for economic opportunities. On both counts Morocco provides an important test of the relative importance of economic and other factors as a source of imperialism. Within these general categories there are specific problems relating to the objectives of each European power concerned: why France wanted to occupy Morocco and eventually declared a protectorate in 1912; why Britain, which had the largest commercial stake there, eventually acquiesced in French political control; why Germany, with limited but growing economic interests in Morocco, first challenged French claims to political primacy but finally accepted French control. These complex questions, covering a period of over thirty years, cannot be dealt with at length but require careful consideration. It is proposed first to summarize briefly the general position and economic interests of each group of Europeans in Morocco and the policies adopted by their respective governments to about 1900; then to concentrate on the patterns of political action of each of the powers between 1900 and 1911 leading to the French protectorate of 1912.

Despite obvious differences in size, character and situation between the two countries, the position of Morocco had affinities with that of China in the late nineteenth and early twentieth cen-turies. Both were sovereign states in which Europeans showed increasing interest but which for long resisted foreign political and economic penetration. In the mid-nineteenth century Morocco was an independent Islamic state, the rump of a once much larger Empire which had included Spain and much of the Sahara. It was ruled by a sultan and a small council, the *makhzen*, and had a primitive administrative system resembling that of an early medieval European feudal state. The country was divided into two main sections. The *bled makhzen*, covering the Atlantic coastline from Mogador to Tangier and extending inland to the mountains as far as Marrakesh in the south and Fez in the north-east, was more or less directly governed by the Sultan from his capital at Fez through a hierarchy of governors (*pashas*) and subordinate administrators (*caids*). The rest of the Empire, the *bled siba*, whose boundaries were indeterminate, recognized the spiritual authority of the Sultan but was not under his effective control. This was a region of largely independent Berber tribes, engaged in recurrent warfare. They were almost as remote from European influence as any part of sub-Saharan Africa before the 1870s. But because the *bled siba* was on the frontiers of Algeria, its chronic disorder was an important consideration for the French and an obvious ground for disputes with the Sultan.

The most significant feature of Morocco in terms of European economic activity in the nineteenth century was that successive Sultans attempted to isolate the country from foreign influence. Like the Manchu emperors of China they distrusted all infidels and felt no need for European trade or investment. During the first half of the century most Moroccan ports were entirely closed to foreigners, leaving only Tangier and Mogador open to foreign trade – and even in these trade was tightly restricted by high tariffs, royal monopolies and bans on a wide range of imports. Foreigners could not own property in Morocco or penetrate the interior. Yet Morocco offered tempting opportunities. It produced a wide range of export staples, including wool and cereals, and was a potential market whose value was commonly overestimated by optimistic European merchants and manufacturers. As the country's resources became better known towards the end of the century, Europeans became increasingly keen to exploit mineral deposits and to provide public utilities – railways, telegraphs, water supplies, port facilities. In short, the paradox of Morocco in the later nineteenth century was that while it was very near to Europe and was an obvious field for trade and investment, it was effectively closed to European enterprise by an Islamic government, strongly supported by public opinion, which had no desire to be 'modernized' by infidels. Given the relative strength of the two parties it was inevitable that Europeans would eventually storm these battlements. The question was whether European penetration would be restricted to economic enterprise supported by political pressures or would take the form of political control by one or more of the major European powers.

Until the early twentieth century it seemed possible that Morocco might retain nominal political independence while conceding full opportunities for foreign economic enterprise. In this respect the Anglo-Moroccan Commercial Treaty of 1856 was as significant a turning point as the Treaty of Nanking of 1842 was for China. By the early 1850s British cotton manufacturers and merchants, in conjunction with commercial interests in Gibraltar, then the main entrepôt for European trade with Morocco, were pressing hard for official action to open the door to wider trading opportunities. With qualified support from Spain and France, the only other European states seriously interested in Morocco before the 1880s, the British diplomat John Drummond Hay negotiated skilfully with the *makhzen* for three years between 1853 and 1856. The Sultan was reluctant to make concessions and almost drew back at the moment of signing the treaty. But many factors combined to overcome his resistance. High prices for cereal exports during the Crimean War were a temptation to expand foreign trade. The Anglo-French victory at Sebastopol impressed Moroccan opinion. Moroccan officials were bribed to support the proposed treaty. Finally the British threatened naval blockade. The treaty was signed in December 1856 and ratified in April 1857.

The treaty determined the character of European economic activity in Morocco for nearly half a century. It provided for freedom of trade and the abolition of all governmental monopolies except those on munitions, arms, tobacco and other herbs for smoking. The Sultan retained the right to ban exports of particular commodities, excluding goods already in foreign warehouses, but had to give six months' warning. British subjects were exempt from all taxation apart from customs duties and were permitted to trade throughout Morocco. Import duties were not to exceed 10 per cent *ad valorem* and export duties were defined in a schedule. British ships could visit several ports without paying additional customs duties. Foreign trade was, however, restricted to four Atlantic ports, Mogador, Mazagan, Casablanca and Tangier; the rest remained closed. Special arrangements were made for trying legal cases between any two British subjects or between a British and Moroccan subject. Moroccans working for British subjects retained the 'protection' from taxation and jurisdiction provided by earlier capitulations.

These concessions mark the starting point of European economic penetration of Morocco. The commercial rights obtained by Britain in 1856 were extended with minor changes to Spain in 1861, France in 1863 and to other European states in later years. Later treaties broadened European rights. Thus the Treaty of Madrid in 1880 gave the Sultan the right to tax protected Moroccan dependants of Europeans but conceded the right of Europeans to own land. Further ports, Safi, Rabat, Larache, Tetuan, were opened to foreign trade. But in essence the position changed very little between 1856 and about 1900. Morocco was effectively open to foreign trade on most favourable terms and became increasingly linked with the international market. Yet, as in China, foreign penetration of the indigenous economy remained limited. The government resolutely refused to permit construction of modern communications or public utilities and did not allow mining. Thus when the Vizier, Ba Ahmed, who had continued the xenophobic policies of Sultan Moulay Hassan after his death in 1894, himself died in 1900 and political power passed to the young Sultan Abd el-Aziz and his War Minister, Mehdi el Menebhi, both of whom were in favour of economic modernization, there was a considerable pent-up demand among European business circles for an opportunity to exploit Moroccan resources. This was a fundamental feature of the situation during the critical period between 1900 and 1911.

Despite the government's conservatism, however, freedom of trade produced a very substantial growth of European economic activity in Morocco before 1900. Before considering events in the later period it is proposed to survey these developments and in particular to estimate the relative economic stake of the four major powers concerned in the Moroccan problem, Britain, France, Germany and Spain.

BRITAIN AND MOROCCO. As in most parts of the less-developed world Britain was the pioneer of large-scale commerce with Morocco. Table 13 and figures 2, 3 and 4 indicate that, although her commercial predominance declined in the later part of the nineteenth century, Britain still had the largest single share of Moroccan trade at the start of the crisis in 1904.

These statistics are largely self-explanatory but one feature of British trade with Morocco needs to be emphasized. Whereas the absolute value of total British trade increased fairly steadily, apart from those periods when Moroccan overseas trade was reduced by

Table 13

Distribution of Moroccan Maritime Trade between the Main European States

(i) Percentage Share of Exports and Imports, 1876–82

	Exports to				Imports from			
	Britain	France	Spain	Ger-many	Britain	France	Spain	Ger-many
1860	63·9	—	—	—	77·0	—	—	—
1865	65·0	—	—	—	86·03	—	—	—
1876	61·6	28·6	5·4	—	75·4	21·5	8·9	—
1879	42·6	50·4	2·9	—	59·6	36·7	0·9	—
1882	58·0	35·4	5·0	—	65·6	32·4	1·1	—

Source: Miège, *Le Maroc et L'Europe*, vol II, 506, III, 427.

(ii) Percentage Share of Overseas Trade (exports and imports combined), 1889–1904

	Britain	France	Spain	Germany
1889	58·5	26·0	9	2·4
1891	48·3	27·0	—	5·1
1893	52·5	24·7	—	7·2
1895	49·6	22·1	—	9·9
1904	43·1	22·8	7·9	14·3

Sources: Miège, *Le Maroc et L'Europe*, IV, 340; Guillen, *L'Allemagne et le Maroc*, 423.

domestic crises (e.g. in 1878–84), the tendency was for British imports from Morocco to decline in comparison with British exports to Morocco. Table 14 indicates this trend.

Thus, while total British trade with Morocco constituted 43·1 per cent of total Moroccan maritime trade in 1904, Britain took only 35 per cent of Moroccan exports but provided 51·2 per cent of total imports.[21] Britain remained Morocco's largest trading partner, but her predominance as a source of manufactured imports to Morocco was greater than as a market for exports of Moroccan raw materials.

In 1904 Britain also retained the largest single share of the Moroccan carrying trade, but, as figure 5 shows, this predominance had disappeared during the 1890s and was insecure in 1904.

British economic interests in Morocco were primarily concerned with commerce and shipping, and by the early twentieth century

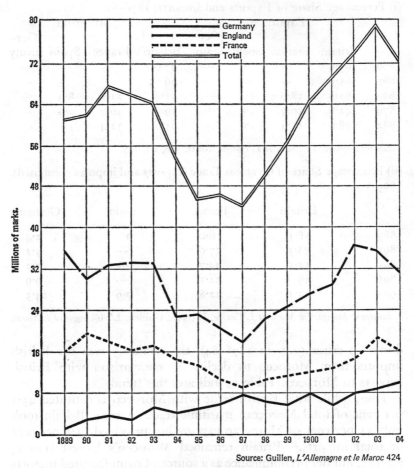

Source: Guillen, *L'Allemagne et le Maroc* 424

Figure 2   Maritime Trade of Morocco, 1889–1906

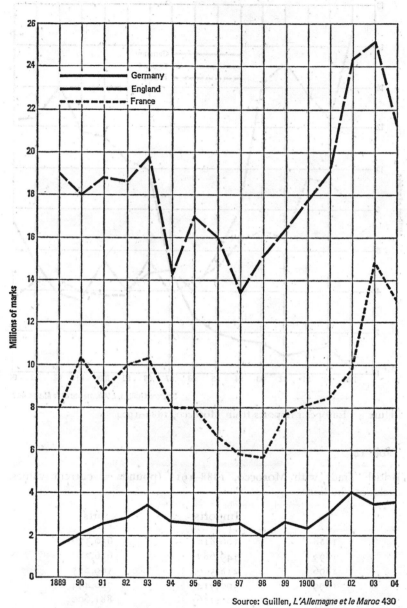

Source: Guillen, *L'Allemagne et le Maroc* 430

Figure 3   European Exports to Morocco, 1889–1904

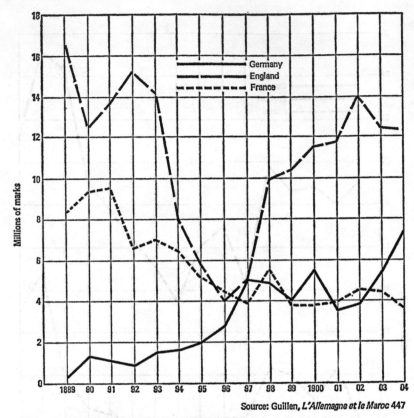

Source: Guillen, *L'Allemagne et le Maroc* 447

Figure 4   European Imports from Morocco, 1889–1904

Table 14

British Trade with Morocco, 1888–1911 (pounds at current values, excluding bullion)

	Imports	Exports
1888	506,812	630,376
1893	549,687	616,220
1896	218,309	599,255
1899	300,714	720,494
1902	700,156	881,000
1905	467,314	739,533
1908	763,903	1,270,013
1911	817,037	1,384,976

Source: *Statistical Abstract for the United Kingdom*, nos 55, 59.

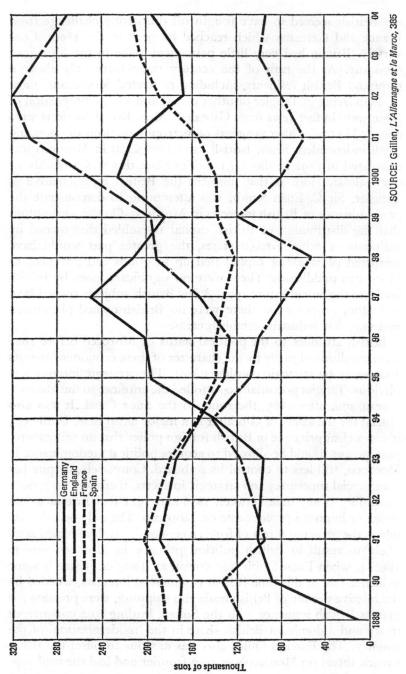

Figure 5   Foreign Ships in Moroccan Atlantic Ports, 1889–1904

the British seemed to have fought off the strong challenge from France and Germany which reached its peak in the 1890s. Conversely, Britain had very little permanent stake in the Moroccan economy. At the turn of the century there were only about a thousand British residents, including protected Moroccans, most of them living in Tangier or other ports; and a large proportion of these were in fact Jews from Gibraltar. Most British subjects were engaged in trade either as agents of metropolitan firms or operating small independent firms. British capital engaged in Morocco was calculated in 1892 at about £1 million; but this was probably an overestimate since at that moment the British representative at Tangier, Sir C. Euan Smith, was attempting to demonstrate the predominance of British interests in Morocco. On the assumption that the distribution of British capital resembled that owned by nationals of other foreign states, the greater part would have consisted of working capital tied up in goods and advances to Moroccan middlemen. There were no significant loans by British banks to the Sultan before 1902. A few British subjects owned land and other property but there were no British-owned plantations and very few industrial establishments.

British attitudes to the political status of Morocco before 1900 were conditioned partly by the character of these economic interests and partly by strategic considerations. The strategic interest was obvious. Tangier potentially controlled the entrance to the Mediterranean and, after 1869, the route to the Suez Canal. It was also crucial for the safety of Gibraltar as a major naval base. Until 1903 it was a clear principle of British foreign policy that no other European power should be allowed to acquire political predominance in Morocco, still less to control its seaboard. Conversely, despite her commercial supremacy and strategic interests, there was no serious possibility at any time between 1856 and 1911 that Britain would annex or impose a protectorate on Morocco. The only occasion on which the growing threat of foreign economic rivalry seemed at all likely to result in British political primacy in Morocco was in 1892-3, when Euan Smith was consul at Tangier. There is some evidence that at this time British commercial interests, worried by the relative decline of British trade and shipping, were pressing for greater British influence with the Sultan, leading to a commercial treaty and a dominant British share in the 'modernization' of the country. The Foreign Office also was anxious to offset the rising French threat on Morocco's eastern frontier and had the tacit support of Germany and Italy in challenging French political influence at Fez. It is clear that Salisbury did not propose to go further than this but there were others who wanted a protectorate; and it was at least conceivable that if Euan Smith could persuade the Sultan to ask for British protection, London might accept.

The enterprise in fact came to nothing. In May–July 1892 Smith made demands on the Sultan which would have given Britain effective primacy in Morocco short of an actual protectorate. On the economic side he demanded that British interests should be allowed to build and operate a telegraph from Tangier to Mogador, a railway from Tangier to Fez, a water supply in Tangier and to establish a state bank. Morocco should also be made to sign a new commercial treaty which reduced the export duty on wheat, allowed export of cattle, opened the coasting trade to British ships and allowed foreigners to acquire land freely. Slavery was to be abolished. In return Britain would drop her right to exclude 'protected' Moroccan subjects from Moroccan jurisdiction and accept mixed courts to try British subjects. In the face of these demands the Sultan prevaricated. Had Britain been the only power directly involved he must eventually have given in; but Smith was opposed at every stage by French agents at Fez who promised the Sultan French support if he resisted British demands. Smith reduced his demands but still had no success. He withdrew from Fez to Tangier in July 1892 and was recalled in January 1893. His successors made no attempt to revive his policy.

The events of 1892 thus appear in retrospect as an exception to the general pattern of British policy on Morocco. Circumstances were never again propitious for establishing informal British hegemony in Morocco, and the British government was preoccupied with problems in other parts of Africa and in the East. After 1900 British objectives in Morocco therefore remained precisely what they had been before 1890: to preserve the 'open door' and to prevent political control by France or any other European state. If opportunities for more intensive economic development should arise through a change of mind at Fez the British would certainly demand their share. But fundamentally their approach was conservative, for Britain had more to lose from radical change than any other European power. Thus the major question after 1900 is why Britain eventually accepted French primacy in Morocco which threatened both her economic interests and her Mediterranean strategy.

FRANCE AND MOROCCO. For France also Morocco constituted a major national interest; but in her case the relative importance of economic and political considerations was different. On the political side the obvious and dominant fact was that Morocco was a neighbour of Algeria, the primary focus of French attitudes to North Africa, and, by the end of the century, effectively part of metropolitan France. Contiguity generated two distinct problems. On the one hand it was entirely unacceptable that any other European power should control Morocco since this would constitute a standing threat to Algerian security. The Germans saw this and in 1870–1 seriously considered setting up a base in Morocco near the Algerian frontier from which to stimulate revolt by Algerian rebels. On the other hand the frontier between Algeria and Morocco was both indeterminate and unstable. The Sultan claimed large areas to the south of Algeria, which Algerian imperialists regarded as their natural hinterland and a possible route to Senegal. A convention of 1845 roughly delimited the boundary line as far south as Figuig but this had never been properly surveyed and the vast region to the south was beyond the jurisdiction of either country. More serious from a French point of view, the eastern zone claimed by Morocco was part of the *bled siba*, inhabited by warring Berber tribes who frequently made raids into French territory. As French occupation of southern Algeria progressed this situation became increasingly inconvenient and the case for French control of eastern Morocco seemed self-evident in Oran and Algiers. General Bugeaud did not hesitate to chase the Algerian rebel leader, Abd al Kadir, when he took refuge in Morocco and the 1845 convention permitted France to enter Moroccan territory to punish tribes for depredations within Algeria. By the 1870s, moreover, growing French interest in a possible railway between Algeria and Senegal made the political status of the Sahara potentially very important; and, as the concept of a consolidated French Empire stretching from Algeria to West Africa grew in the next quarter century, desire to control eastern Morocco became more intense.

French economic interests in Morocco were second only to those of Britain. It seems impossible to establish the volume or value of French trade with Morocco before the 1870s but it is clear that this trade centered almost entirely on Marseille and that for long France was interested in Morocco as a source of raw materials – wool, hides, almonds and grain – rather than as a market for French products. The commercial treaty of 1863 stimulated commercial development and encouraged French shipping. In 1877, 280 French ships visited Moroccan ports with a total tonnage of 137,174, 43·7 per cent of the total as against 141,509 tons of British shipping. Two years later France achieved a larger share of Moroccan maritime trade than at any time before 1911, providing 36·7 per cent of Moroccan imports and taking 50·2 per cent of Moroccan exports; but this high level could not be maintained and France's share of Moroccan trade declined to 26 per cent in 1889, 22·1 per cent in 1895, and 22·8 per cent in 1904.[22] Meantime France's share of the carrying trade, which was just above that of Britain in the early 1890s, sank to second place below Germany in 1894–5 and to third place below Britain and Germany after 1896 before rising to second place after 1901.[23]

Despite the new challenge of German trade and shipping and the recovery of British commercial enterprise, France therefore had an important commercial stake in Morocco. Like Britain, however, France had been unable to penetrate the Moroccan economy. There were only about 780 French residents in Morocco in 1904[24] and the number had declined since the 1870s. Most lived in Tangier and Casablanca and were connected with the French consulate, commercial houses or small business enterprises. Total French capital investment in Morocco was roughly estimated by the *Bulletin* of the Comité Africaine Française in 1901 at 12 million francs (c. £480,000). Proposals for building a railway from Oran had been rejected by the *makhzen* in the 1880s. Thus the real strength of the French economic position in Morocco lay in the activities of trading firms and banks. A branch of the Société des Comptoirs Maritimes de Crédit Industriel et Commercial was set up in Tangier in 1880 and in 1882 this was acquired by the Banque Transatlantique which had representatives in most Moroccan ports. The Comptoir d'Escompte and the Banque de Paris et des Pays-Bas (hereafter BPPB) were also showing interest in Morocco in the 1890s, tempted by the hope of making profitable loans to the Sultan. These great concerns played an important part in French economic penetration of the country after 1902, but until then the major role was played by commercial houses based on Tangier. The first of these was Maison Braunschvig, a Lyon firm which started business at Mogador in 1875. By the 1890s it had branches at Tangier and Casablanca and agents at Fez and Marrakesh. In addition to general import-export activities it made small loans and did business with the *makhzen*. By 1901 Braunschvig was linked with the BPPB and was well placed to act as agent for loans and concessions when and if the Sultan was ready to do business.

The other important French commercial firm was Maison Gautsch, also based on Tangier. This began as the Société Moghreb, founded in 1886 by F. Toussaint in collaboration with a group of French and Swedish traders with the double intention of trading and acquiring land concessions south of Tangier from Si Abdeslam, Cherif of Ouezzane who, as will be seen below, had promised this concession to the Comte de Chavagnac in 1883 as part of d'Ordega's scheme for French preponderance in Morocco. Toussaint and his associates were mere adventurers; but in 1887 their few assets, and particularly the rights claimed under this agreement with Si Abdeslam, were taken over by Jules Jaluzot, founder of the large French firm Grande Magazins de Printemps which already had a branch in Tangier. In 1892 he transferred his Moroccan interests to one of his subordinates, Charles Gautsch, in return for shares amounting to 100,000 francs in the new firm, Etablissements Charles Gautsch et Cie. Under the new management the firm expanded its interests rapidly. It invested in agricultural production near Tangier, and set up shops in a number of places. In 1892 the Sultan gave it a concession for a petrol depot in Tangier in return for abrogation of the original concession for Si Abdeslam's estates. A branch was established in Fez – the first permanent foreign agency there, and in 1895 the firm was allowed to establish a coaling base at Tangier. But its main asset was a network of contacts within the Sultan's court, many of whom preferred to deal with French firms rather than with British after the abortive attempt of Euan Smith to extract major concessions in 1892; and after the death of Moulay Hassan in 1894 Gautsch, like other foreign firms, confidently expected that the *makhzen* would sooner or later open the country to foreign enterprise and that established contacts would then produce immensely valuable contracts and concessions.

But in France greater concerns than Jaluzot were now considering these prospects, in particular the great metallurgical and armaments firm of Creusot, whose head was Schneider.[25] In 1902, after carefully surveying the situation in Morocco, Schneider formed a holding company, with a share capital of 1,500,000 francs, to acquire all Gautsch interests there. The function of this company, renamed Compagnie Maroccaine in 1903, was accurately defined by Delcassé: 'To prepare for the future by establishing a foothold through the small-scale activities of Gautsch, so that, at the right moment, it can use the opportunity to undertake large-scale enterprises'.[26] Other French firms showed similar interest. In 1904 a consortium led by the BPPB acquired the assets of Maison Braunschvig as a basis for large-scale commercial and investment activities. Clearly French finance and industry were mobilizing their resources for an economic drive into Morocco by the time the international crisis began in 1904. The question to be considered is therefore whether these great consortia were the determinants of French official policy or were themselves used as an instrument in the pursuit of official objectives.

Between 1879 and 1904 French official policy on Morocco had vacillated considerably. This vacillation was partly a response to external factors. On the one hand the great powers, particularly Britain, were not prepared to accept French preponderance in Morocco; on the other the *makhzen* resisted attempts by any foreign power to establish sole control. But French opinion was itself divided and hesitant. For the most part the Quai d'Orsay and successive ministers were content to preserve the *status quo* until a change in Moroccan attitudes offered the chance for more resolute French intervention. Parliamentary opinion was generally indifferent, and there was no strongly organized metropolitan interest group before 1902. Conversely, there were strong and consistent demands for French intervention from Algeria and from the small French group in Tangier: the Comte De Chavagnac, editor of the newspaper *Réveil de Maroc*, was Tangier correspondent of *La France*, and a group of French subjects and French-protected Jews who were impatient to expand their economic activities and wanted France to persuade the *makhzen*, by force if necessary, to modernize the country. This group had allies in France and in Algeria. But, until the formation of the Comité du Maroc in 1904 there was no organized political lobby in France and Morocco played little or no part in French politics.

French policy, therefore, varied from time to time according to the attitudes of the French consul at Tangier and the Ministry in Paris; but the only occasion before 1904 when it seemed at all likely that Paris would attempt to establish a protectorate was in 1883-4, and then only because the French consul at Tangier, d'Ordega, prepared the ground on his own initiative. This episode is well known but must be described briefly because it is an excellent example of how a situation generated entirely on the periphery might possibly lead to formal political control by a European state.

In 1880 the French government, under pressure from Algeria and encouraged by the temporary preponderance of French influence at Fez, adopted a policy of peaceful penetration of Morocco with four specific objectives: construction of a railway from Algeria to Oudjda, then to Fez and ultimately to Senegal; construction of a telegraph from Algeria to Morocco; establishment of agricultural enterprises, partly to provide land for French settlers in over-populated Oran; and delimitation of the Algerian frontier. But Ladislas d'Ordega, who became French consul at Tangier in 1881, had different objectives. As a friend of Gambetta and with many contacts in French political circles, he was certain that he could build up French influence in Fez as Roustan had done in Tunisia and lay the foundations for a French protectorate. The fall of Gambetta early in 1882 reduced his political support, but he persisted. He became associated with an arrangement made between the Comte de Chavagnac and Si Abdeslam, Cherif of Ouezzane and chief of the Islamic brotherhood of Taibia, whereby the Cherif would concede a large part of his vast estates together with mineral rights in return for money to pay his debts. In December 1883 the Cherif moreover asked for French protection against the Sultan, who strongly disapproved of this concession. The Italian consul at Tangier expressed the common opinion of British, German and Spanish representatives there when he wrote in January 1884 that: 'The more I observe the French government's policy in Morocco, the more I am certain that France intends to undertake a protectorate or conquest and is preparing for it by assiduous efforts.'[27]

Why did Jules Ferry, then in office, not act? Britain, Italy and Spain were certain to oppose French intervention and Italy was actively working to prevent a repetition of the Tunisian protectorate. But by 1884 France was already on bad terms with Britain over Egypt and Ferry was not held back by fear of disturbing the old entente. Moreover, he had clear though veiled support from Bismarck who was then concerned to establish an entente with France and was ready to encourage French ambitions in Morocco, as in Tunisia and West Africa, as a distraction from Alsace-Lorraine. In May 1884 Bismarck told the French Ambassador in Berlin that the best step would be for France to come to terms with Spain.

If I can be of use to you I would give you my good offices at Madrid. I am not proposing partition of Morocco, but it might be possible to agree in advance to define spheres of action which would cause no inconvenience or jealousy.[28]

Yet Ferry decided against action. Why was this? The answer appears to be that he considered that informal partition with Spain and unilateral occupation by France were both politically dangerous. On 19 June 1884 he told d'Ordega that, although his work in Morocco had been excellent, he must go no further: 'The government of the Republic does not want an affair in Morocco'.[29] When d'Ordega persisted in his intrigues he was sent as French Minister to Bucharest in December 1884.

This decision not to press on in Morocco has a double importance. First it demonstrates that the French government was not prepared to tailor its foreign policy to meet the interests of a few French subjects overseas, even though de Chavagnac had contacts with important banking and industrial interests in France. Second, it virtually determined the lines of French policy in Morocco for the next twenty years. Despite the continued activity of French adventurers in Morocco and pressure from the Algerian lobby, successive French governments concentrated on maintaining the *status quo*. So long as the *makhzen* remained hostile to foreign penetration and inter-European rivalries barred unilateral control or partition, this was in fact the most rewarding policy for France. Neither Paris nor Algeria ceased to regard Morocco as a sphere of French interest, and after 1890 it was accepted that in the long run France must acquire control of Figuig and the Touat oases to the south which were vital to the projected trans-Saharan railway and to stabilization of the Algerian frontier. But the Quai d'Orsay was prepared to wait until conditions in Morocco and Europe were ripe for a more positive approach.

GERMANY AND MOROCCO. German interest in Morocco developed much later than that of Britain, France and Spain and had one special feature. Whereas by the turn of the century German economic interests were closely comparable in type and size with those of Britain and France, Germany had no definable strategic stake in the political status of the Moroccan Empire. Germany had no possession near Morocco and she was not a Mediterranean naval power. In the early twentieth century it was important to her evolving naval strategy that she should have free access through the straits and a naval base or coaling station on the Atlantic coast would have been an asset. Yet the key to German policy after 1900 is that, in political and strategic terms, Morocco was disposable. This did not imply that German statesmen were unconcerned about its future, but that they could concentrate on two limited aspects of the Moroccan question: protection of existing and potential opportunities for German trade, investment and production in Morocco; and the diplomatic price Germany could extract for permitting France or other powers to establish political control there. For the present study the importance of Germany's role in the critical period 1904–11 turns on the interaction of these economic and diplomatic objectives in the formulation of official policy in Berlin.

The striking feature of Germany's economic activity in Morocco was the speed with which it grew from small beginnings in the twenty years before 1900. The tables and graphs above indicate the dramatic rise of German trade and shipping in this period. German economic enterprise in Morocco was negligible before about 1875, and interest was first aroused by philologists, naturalists and geographers who became active in the early 1870s. The first official German embassy was sent to Fez in 1877 on the suggestion of Krupps who thought there might be opportunities for selling armaments to the *makhzen*; and from 1878 Krupps maintained a consistent interest in Morocco both as a market and potential source of minerals. Before 1904, however, Hamburg and Bremen commercial and banking houses played the trading role. In 1878 Robert Jannasch and Otto Kersten founded the Centralverein für Handelsgeographie as a means of investigating market opportunities in many parts of the world, and this organization showed considerable interest in Morocco. In fact, German commercial activity there was part of a deliberate attempt to open up new markets and sources of raw materials and this largely accounts for its remarkable success.

The early growth rate of German trade with Morocco was, nevertheless, very slow for this was a difficult market to enter without previous experience or established local contacts. In 1878 total German trade with Morocco was only about 100,000 francs (£4,000), and in 1882 only 0·25 per cent of Moroccan imports came from Germany.[30] As late as 1889 Germany had a mere 1·5 per cent of Moroccan maritime trade,[31] and in 1885 only twenty-nine German ships sailed direct to Morocco.[32] Thereafter the scale of German commercial activity grew fast. Germans had acquired experience of the market and a network of consular and commercial agencies had been established. The Hamburg firm of Woermann, already deeply engaged in West Africa, provided a regular direct steamship line to the Atlantic ports from 1889 and in 1890 the Atlas Line was formed by the Export Bank in competition. From 1887 the Sloman Line also sent ships regularly to Tangier. In 1889 six German firms had agencies in Morocco. By 1894 there were seventeen and in 1900 thirty-four.[33] A postal service was started in 1890. Thereafter the Germans were in a position to compete effectively with European commercial rivals.

The results were striking. Germany's share of total Moroccan maritime trade rose from 2 per cent in 1888 to 4·6 per cent in 1890, 7·5 per cent in 1893 and 10 per cent in 1895. The mid-1890s, however, proved the climax of the first German commercial drive. German trade was smaller in 1900–3 than in 1898 but rose both absolutely and relatively to a total of 10·4 million marks and 14·3 per cent of total Moroccan trade in 1904.[34] Meantime German shipping was doing even better. In 1893–4 the tonnage of German ships visiting Moroccan ports was larger than that of any other nationality and this primacy was sustained until 1898, after which Germany fell to second position and then to third place in 1901–2. Meantime the pattern of German trade changed significantly. At the start German exports to Morocco were far larger than imports of Moroccan goods to Germany: 1·3 million marks against 0·2 million marks in 1890; but by 1904 exports to Morocco were worth 3·2 million marks against imports from Morocco worth 7·2 million marks. Table 15 and figure 6 indicate these trends.

Table 15

German Trade with Morocco, 1905–12 (millions of marks at current values)

Year	Imports from Morocco	Exports to Morocco
1905	5·9	1·7
1906	5·5	1·8
1907	8·5	1·2
1908	9·5	1·8
1909	7·8	3·5
1910	9·1	4·9
1911	12·5	5·5
1912	19·1	7·9

Source: *Statistisches Jahrbuch für das Deutsche Reich.*

Note: These official statistics are clearly based on different calculations from those used by Guillen before 1904, but the general trends are the same.

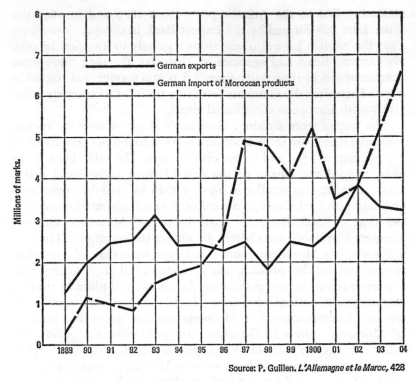

Source: P. Guillen. *L'Allemagne et le Maroc,* 428

Figure 6   German Trade with Morocco, 1889–1904

These statistics suggest two general conclusions on the character of German commercial activity in Morocco in the 1890s and 1900s. First, the sustained thrust of German enterprise lay in obtaining Moroccan raw materials rather than in exploiting the Moroccan market for German manufacturers. Germany became the largest single overseas market for Moroccan wool, taking some 58 per cent in 1904 as compared with a French share of 23 per cent and the British share of 5·2 per cent.[35] Second, although the German economic stake in Morocco after 1904 was relatively small both in relation to total German overseas trade and to Moroccan maritime trade, Germans could reasonably believe that their achievement entitled them to a fair share in the far greater economic opportunities everyone expected when Morocco became unconditionally open to foreign economic enterprise. This assumption is of great importance for interpreting German policy after 1904, and it was clearly expressed in a memorandum of the commercial section of

the German Foreign Office in April 1905, at the start of the Moroccan crisis: 'The official accounts do not give a true picture of
German trade. Taking account of what goes on at Antwerp,
Genoa, Marseille and London, German trade is at least as important
as that of France'.[36] Other indicators of German economic activity
supported this view. Although there were only about 187 German
residents in Morocco in 1904, far less than British or French,
German capital engaged there was probably as large as French
capital: 10 million marks (c. £500,000) plus 5 million used in
advances to Moroccan middlemen and 1,500,000 invested in
Moroccan enterprises, particularly agriculture.[37] As a proportion
of German capital engaged in Africa as a whole – about 1,350
million marks (c. £67,500,000) this was minute. Nevertheless it
was regarded as a mere beginning. German industrialists, banks
and mercantile interests, like those of France and Britain, considered
that Morocco, like China and Turkey, was an area of considerable
future potential and they were determined that Germany should
not be denied the reward for the efforts made before 1905. As
early as 1899 a French officer said of German interests established
in Morocco that:

They do not admit for a single moment that Germany might be
excluded from the partition which must follow the final decline [of the
Moroccan state]. They deny the historic rights of Spain and the political
claims of France and say loudly that material interests should serve as the
basis for partition.[38]

But this does not mean that economic interests in Germany
positively wanted German territorial control of Morocco. There
is no evidence that Hamburg merchants and shipowners or big
industrialists such as Krupp ever pressed the German government
to annex all or part of Morocco. In common with business concerns
in Britain and France they demanded official pressure on the
Moroccan government to permit wider commercial access, to provide opportunities for building railways and acquiring mining
concessions and to give Germans a fair share of official contracts
for providing arms and other governmental purchases. But they
were perfectly content that Morocco should remain a nominally
independent state and were aware that partition between the powers
might well exclude Germany from those areas in which the bulk of
her trade was established. Significantly, however, there was much
greater enthusiasm by the early 1900s for a German territorial stake

L

in Morocco among traditional proponents of imperialist doctrines. As usual the demand began with the geographers and academics – for example Theobald Fischer, Stümme and Pfeil. The Deutsche Kolonialgesellschaft began to show interest in Morocco in 1899 and its lead was followed by other colonial organizations, many of whom saw Morocco as a possible compensation for the admitted limitations of existing German possessions in Africa and the Pacific, and made widely exaggerated assessments of its economic potential. In 1900 the Pan-German League took up the cause and received support from the Navy League, which saw the potential value of a naval base in Morocco. How much influence had these jingo organizations on public opinion and official policy? For most of the period to about 1909 it was probably very small. The German press as a whole was unimpressed by demands for territorial control. Most papers argued that it would be politically impracticable for Germany to annex Morocco and that economic objectives could be obtained by other means. On the other hand it was generally held that Germany had a right to be consulted before any major change in Morocco's political status was made and that Germany must insist on the 'open door' and equality of opportunity for trade and investment. These attitudes were reflected by the great majority in the Reichstag, particularly in 1904–6 when German colonialism was under sustained attack by critics of the existing colonies. It was not, therefore, until after 1909, when, as will be seen below, the Mannsemann brothers allied with the Pan-German League to launch a large-scale campaign against French predominance in Morocco, that the government found itself under any strong pressure to take a hard line on the Moroccan question, beyond preservation of existing German interests there. This fact is fundamental to understanding the course of German diplomacy throughout the earlier period.

German official attitudes and policies on Morocco before 1904 were, indeed, pragmatic and in some degree vacillating. Three distinct periods can be defined. In the 1870s the government regarded Morocco in almost exclusively political terms as it affected Franco-German relations. In 1870 there was talk of using Morocco as a base for stimulating rebellion in Algeria to embarrass France during the war and a possible site for a naval base near the Algerian frontier was considered. After 1871 this interest died down and the Foreign Office showed little further interest in Morocco before 1880. During the second period, from 1880 to about 1885, however, Bismarck saw the possible diplomatic value of Morocco for his proposed rapprochement with France and, as has been seen, made it clear that he would not object to French primacy or a *de facto* partition of Morocco between France and Spain. With the waning of Franco-German co-operation in colonial questions after 1885, however, a new policy evolved. Germany would build up her political influence at Fez and play the role of a disinterested protector of Moroccan independence against French designs. If this was successful the influence gained over the Sultan might be used as a diplomatic tool against France. At the same time Germany could reach agreement with Britain and Italy to preserve Moroccan independence and thus improve relations with Britain and strengthen the Triple Alliance. By 1890 both elements in this policy seemed to have succeeded; but the apparent intention of Britain in 1892 to obtain predominant political and economic influence in Morocco, coupled with deterioration in Anglo-German diplomatic relations on other issues in the mid-1890s, led to a more independent German approach. By 1900–1 German policy was in the doldrums. Bülow was attracted by the idea of an agreement with Britain to establish a German sphere of influence in part of Morocco as part of a general agreement on international questions, including China; and in 1899–1900 Hatzfeldt indicated to Salisbury that Germany might consider partition of the Atlantic coast of Morocco, Britain to have the northern and Germany the southern half. Salisbury, however, was reluctant to move without agreement with France and the project lapsed. In 1901 Holstein refused British approaches for a firm alliance with Germany to guarantee the independence of both Morocco and China unless this formed part of a general European alliance. None of these negotiations was, in fact, very promising. It is doubtful whether the British would ever have agreed to German political control of part of Morocco or whether German opinion would have accepted an entente with Britain.

The result was that after about 1901 the German Foreign Office fell back on the essentially negative policy of sustaining German political influence at Fez with the double objective of preventing French political primacy and obtaining the best possible economic opportunities for German business. Conversely, there was no serious desire or expectation that Germany should herself acquire territory in Morocco. The Kaiser was strongly opposed to a proposal made late in 1903 that Germany should claim the southern region of the

Atlantic coast even if, as then seemed likely, France agreed to partition Morocco with Spain. In March 1904 he wrote to Bülow:

I have congratulated the King [of Spain] on his arrangement with France. It is reasonable and I approve. We do not want any territory down there, but only the opening of ports, railway concessions, importation of our manufactures. . . . The idea of annexing the South does not seem to me practicable. It is Fernando Po that we must get in return for clearly understood payment.[39]

Indeed, the Kaiser clearly hoped for a reconciliation with France on grounds similar to those held by Bismarck in 1884 and was prepared to give her satisfaction in Morocco on three conditions: that Germany should be consulted; that she should retain full freedom of commercial access; and that she might demand compensation elsewhere. It was only because in 1905 France appeared to be adopting an aggressive policy in Morocco without meeting these requirements that German policy suddenly became so aggressive.

SPAIN AND MOROCCO. Finally it is necessary briefly to survey Spanish interests in and attitudes towards Morocco before about 1904. Of all European states Spain probably felt most strongly about Moroccan questions. The fifteenth- and sixteenth-century crusades against Morocco, which had resulted in the four small Spanish enclaves, provided an emotive basis for nineteenth-century attitudes. Geographical proximity and the fact that there were about 6,400 Spanish settlers in Morocco in 1904 strengthened the belief that, if any European state was entitled to dominance in Morocco, it must be Spain. In addition Spain claimed the right to control the southern region of the Atlantic coast, the eventual protectorate of Rio de Oro, by virtue of Spanish ownership of the Canary Islands. These claims were supported by the fact that Spain had a significant share of European trade with Morocco. As can be seen from table 13 above, Spain took 5·4 per cent of Moroccan exports and provided 8·9 per cent of her imports in 1876 and in 1889 had 9 per cent of total Moroccan maritime trade. This share declined as competition increased, but was still 7·9 per cent in 1904. Spanish shipping was relatively more important. Figure 5 above (p. 277) shows that more Spanish than German ships visited Moroccan ports until 1894 and that in 1904 Spanish ships still amounted to half the number of German ships. Spain was a very weak competitor with the great industrialized countries of northern Europe but, as Morocco's fourth largest trading partner, her claim to take an active role in international decisions on the future of Morocco was undeniable.

Spanish official policy consistently reflected this national interest in Morocco. Indeed Spain was the first foreign power to attempt to acquire Moroccan territory in the nineteenth century. During the 1850s Spanish opinion was aroused by growing British commercial activity in Morocco and by the extension of French power in Algeria. Leopoldo O'Donnell, appointed Prime Minister in 1858, saw a Moroccan adventure in much the same way as the Restoration government of France had viewed the Algerian enterprise of 1830 – as a popular enterprise which would strengthen support for his government and for the Crown. Political disorder in Morocco, the capture of a Spanish ship and a series of minor issues culminating in the destruction of a new fortification built at Ceuta in 1859, provided the excuse for action. War was declared in October 1859. Spain's object was to annex the whole northern region of Morocco, including Larache, Tangier and Tetuan. Larache was easily taken and early in 1860 Tangier seemed about to fall. At this point the British, who had opposed the enterprise throughout, intervened. Madrid climbed down and peace was made in May 1860. Spain obtained clarification of the boundaries of Ceuta and Melilla and her claims to Rio de Oro were recognized. She received an indemnity, obtained the exclusive right to maintain a diplomatic representative at Fez and extracted a promise of freedom for Christian missions throughout the Moroccan Empire.

Had Spain been a major power this settlement might have led ultimately to political primacy in Morocco. But as a minor power Spain could not use her considerable advantages. Between 1860 and 1904 her policy was remarkably consistent. Madrid hoped that Spain might ultimately acquire territory in Morocco if other powers agreed to a partition. Meantime she used her diplomatic resources to ensure that Morocco would remain independent. Her reward was that Britain, France and Germany accepted Spain's right to be consulted and, whenever partition was considered, assumed that Spain would receive a share. After 1900 Madrid was virtually a lay figure in the diplomatic drama played out by the major powers, but the Franco-Spanish agreement of 1904 conceded Spanish control of

northern Morocco in principle and after 1911 this was converted
into a Spanish protectorate.

THE MOROCCAN CRISIS. The position of Morocco in about 1900
can therefore be summarized as follows. As the last important
North African territory other than Tripolitania still outside European control it was a natural focus of interest for the powers. In
economic terms Britain, France, Germany and, to a lesser extent,
Spain had established a firm commercial foothold but were prevented from deeper economic penetration by the determined
resistance of the *makhzen* to foreign influence. It was firmly believed
by industrial, banking and commercial interests in many European
countries that once this obstacle was overcome Morocco would
offer four main types of economic opportunity: an expanded field
for trade; opportunities for profitable investment in mineral extrac-
tion and possibly other forms of production; openings for construction and operation of public utilities as part of a 'modernization'
programme; and the chance to lend money to the government at
relatively high interest rates. Significantly, however, there was no
strong demand from metropolitan British, French or German
economic interests for political control of Morocco as a necessary
basis for economic activity. It was generally assumed that all these
economic objectives could be satisfactorily achieved while Morocco
remained independent, provided that the *makhzen* was induced to
co-operate with Europeans. Conversely, no one power must be
allowed to annex Morocco, especially the Atlantic seaboard where
the greater part of the trade and investment opportunities lay.

The predictable outcome of this situation in the early years of
the twentieth century was therefore that Morocco would retain
formal independence because the balance between the business and
strategic interests of the main European states was too finely
adjusted to permit the predominance of any one power. Yet in
1905 France acquired effective political primacy and in 1912 made
Morocco a protectorate. How can these developments be explained?
Three aspects of the problem require particular attention: first,
changes within Morocco after 1900 which at last made effective
economic penetration possible and at the same time opened the way
to political predominance by one or more foreign powers; second,
the reaction of public and official opinion in Britain, France and
Germany to the new situation; finally, the changing patterns of
European diplomacy which, unexpectedly, opened the way to uni-

lateral French control. Given the complexities of these developments it is impossible to give a detailed account of events; and it is proposed to consider only those aspects of the problem which directly relate to the interaction of economic and political factors.

The all-important fact which dominated the Moroccan question from 1900 to 1911 is that the crisis began in Morocco and that European policies had to be contrived to meet the new situation there. In May 1900 the Vizier, Ba Ahmed, who had governed since the death of Sultan Moulay Hassan in 1894 and had effectively blocked attempts at foreign economic or political penetration, at last died. The young Sultan Abd-el-Aziz was twenty years old and was determined to open the country to European civilization. Until 1903 his chief adviser was Mehdi el Menebhi, Minister for War, who was able to nominate an ineffectual Vizier and act as Prime Minister. Menebhi also was a convinced modernizer and wasted no time in opening negotiations in Europe for loans to pay for public works and for contracts to build railways, telegraphs and other utilities. Almost overnight Fez was opened to Europeans and the Sultan's palace was filled with European adventurers. To many in Europe it seemed that Aladdin's cave was at last open.

These developments rapidly precipitated a domestic crisis. Although in many ways desirable from the point of view of Moroccan economic development, the new policies were expensive and the Sultan had to negotiate in Europe for loans. In 1902 loans were raised from banks in Britain, France and Spain. The nominal rate of interest rate was 6 per cent but as the Moroccan bonds sold at only 62 per cent of their face value, the effective interest rate was 10 per cent.[40] The cost of servicing these loans, coupled with higher expenditure on armaments and court amenities, required higher taxation. The European powers refused to abrogate the treaty provisions which exempted Europeans and their protected Moroccan servants from taxation and the *makhzen* decided to impose a new tax on agricultural incomes which was to be collected by a new corps of professional tax collectors rather than through the caids as in the past. This caused much resentment, which was increased by conservative dislike of the new foreign influences at court. This reaction to modernization was exploited by Djilali ben Driss, better known as Bou Hamara, a wandering Islamic holyman who claimed to be the elder brother of the Sultan. On his prompting many tribes in the eastern region refused to pay the new tax and attacks were made on Sefrou and Mechnes, both near Fez. Bou Hamara established himself at Taza and claimed to be Sultan. In 1903 he occupied Oudjda on the Algerian frontier and was supported by the tribes on the lower Mouluya River. The Sultan failed to defeat him but equally his forces failed to take Fez. By the end of 1903 endemic civil war existed and it seemed probable that the Moroccan Empire would completely disintegrate.

The international crisis over Morocco sprang directly from these domestic events in the same way that the Tunisian and Egyptian crises had grown from comparable local developments twenty years before. To the major powers the new situation in Morocco presented both an opportunity and a problem. In the first stage the Sultan's readiness to invite international collaboration offered economic opportunities which no foreign government could afford to ignore; in the second chronic disorder threatened established interests and provided an excuse for political intervention by one or more power. How could these problems be dealt with? Given agreement between governments a wide range of solutions was possible. At one extreme the Sultan might be supported by loans provided by international consortia in return for concessions distributed between economic interests in each major foreign state. At the other extreme the powers might agree to partition Morocco or even to leave one state as sole protector, provided the rights and interests of all others were preserved. Conversely, inaction was impossible for if no other power acted France was certain to do so because of the effects of the Moroccan War on the Algerian frontier. The core of the problem was that it was extremely difficult to find any generally acceptable solution; and, before surveying the course of international diplomacy after 1900 it will be convenient to examine private and official attitudes in each of the three European states most immediately concerned.

French reactions were most acute because France had uniquely important interests at stake. Pressure on the government to act decisively came from two main sources, organized colonial enthusiasts and metropolitan business groups, though the action each demanded varied considerably. The crisis in Morocco stimulated all the normal enthusiasts for empire in France, in alliance with strong expansionist groups in Algeria, to demand French occupation. The Geographical Society of Algeria appropriately took the lead at the end of 1899. Eugène Etienne was at first more cautious, seeing the diplomatic difficulties ahead, and proposed a preliminary policy of 'peaceful penetration' on the lines of that undertaken in

Tunisia before 1881. But by January 1904, when negotiations with Britain seemed likely to clear the way for overt political action, he came out openly for formal French occupation in terms characteristic of thoroughgoing French expansionists in the early years of the century:

> Morocco constitutes the last imperial chance which can remain for us, having regard to the stage now reached in dividing up the globe, to use the proud expression of English policy. Everywhere else, even in the best parts of the world and even if we were called upon tomorrow to take our share in that area of vast latent wealth which is China, we can no longer hope for anything more than economic development. Only in Morocco, that country which is complementary to the territories we already govern in North Africa, do we have the possibility of enlarging our ethnic, and above all our linguistic, domain. Here we can enlarge the area of our civilization; it is here where there is to be found our last chance of compensating, albeit indeed inadequately, for the irreparable losses we suffered in North America as a result of the continental wars of Louis xiv and the apathetic levity of Louis xv.[41]

This was a trumpet-call to action and in February 1904 Etienne and others set up the Comité du Maroc as an offshoot of the Comité de l'Afrique Française. It was supported by many well-placed colonial enthusiasts, including several large industrial and banking firms which expected to benefit from opportunities in Morocco. The Comité campaigned actively for a French protectorate and received considerable success in arousing parliamentary and public interest. There was, in fact, no need to convince Delcassé of the desirability of action over Morocco and his diplomatic preparations were well under way before the public campaign was launched. But at least the imperialists were able to give colour to his claim when negotiating with Britain and Germany that French public opinion would not accept anything short of French primacy in Morocco.

The attitude of French industrial, commercial and banking interest had already been described. By 1900 and increasingly in later years they were determined to obtain a full share of whatever profitable opportunities Morocco might offer, but were content for Morocco to remain formally independent provided French interests obtained a full share of concessions and official contracts. But what, finally, was the attitude of French statesmen, and particularly of Delcassé who controlled French policy in the crucial period between 1900 and 1905? It is clear that Delcassé was from the start of the crisis in favour of taking a strong line on Morocco, primarily to offset the ignominy of Fashoda two years earlier. In May 1900, the month in which Ba Ahmed died, he commented that 'If France must seek a complement to its Algerian/Tunisian Empire, that complement lies to the west. Labourers, water and subsoil as rich as and perhaps even richer than the topsoil can be found there.'[42] But Delcassé recognized that France must act cautiously. Since 1898 his general diplomatic aim was to end French isolation in Western Europe and in particular to build better relations with Britain and Italy. Britain seemed certain to oppose unilateral French control in Morocco and Italy had obtained a secret guarantee in 1887 from her partners in the Triple Alliance that the *status quo* in North Africa would be preserved. The problem was underlined in 1900 when Britain and Germany combined to insist on the withdrawal of French troops from the Touat oases which had been occupied in response to disorder on the eastern frontier. Delcassé therefore adopted a two-pronged policy: peaceful penetration of Morocco by business firms to strengthen French claims to primacy and to counter initiatives by other powers; and at the same time diplomacy to win British, Italian and Spanish agreement to an eventual French protectorate. Meantime he was determined not to be forced into precipitate action by any French private interest. In 1899 he had told Schneider of Creusots that 'French diplomacy . . . is not at the service of private interests but is capable of co-ordinating and disciplining them as an instrument subordinate to the demands of national policy.'[43] By February 1902, however, he was convinced that peaceful penetration must be accelerated to counter British initiatives. He therefore gave Schneider full support 'to prepare for the future by establishing a foothold through the small-scale activities of Gautsch, so that at the right moment it can use the opportunity to undertake large-scale enterprises'.[44]

French official policy was to obtain primacy in Morocco, if possibly by annexation, mainly because once Morocco ceased to be a viable state after 1900 the possibility of political control by any other European state was equally unacceptable to Paris and Algeria. Morocco therefore came to be regarded as a first-class French national interest which justified determined diplomacy even to the point of war. Although means varied according to tactical requirements and political changes in Paris, this essential aim never changed between 1900 and 1911.

British policy in Morocco, however, underwent a radical change in 1903-4. Between May 1900 and the early months of 1902 it seemed likely that the British would attempt to establish informal primacy in Morocco. There was never any serious question of formal occupation and the government was under no strong pressure from imperialist popular opinion which was preoccupied with events in South Africa. But mercantile interests were anxious to protect and enlarge economic opportunities in Morocco and both the Admiralty and War Office were determined to prevent France and Germany from acquiring a naval base there. Given these requirements, the obvious and apparently feasible policy was to establish effective informal influence over the new régime at Fez and this was attempted by Sir A. Nicolson, British Minister at Tangier. During 1900 and 1901 he had considerable success. Menebhi was prepared to accept British advice and financial assistance in developing the economy and hoped for British support against the obvious threat of French encroachment on the eastern frontier. The German legation also supported Nicolson as part of Bülow's policy of attempting to seduce Britain into the Triple Alliance. At the famous Chatsworth meeting in January 1901 between Chamberlain and Eckardstein (a member of the German embassy in London), it was agreed, so Eckardstein alleged, that Morocco should be divided between the powers, Britain taking Tangier, Germany the Atlantic coast and France the eastern region.[45] Why, then, did the British initiative wither during the next two years?

The reasons appear to have been primarily diplomatic. Despite Nicolson's enthusiasm for playing the role of d'Ordega, the British Foreign Office was from the start anxious not to alienate France over Morocco, and it soon became clear to British officials that Delcassé was determined not to concede political primacy in Morocco to any other power. French troops occupied Salah and the Touat oases in 1900-1; a protocol was signed with the Sultan in January 1901 and a further agreement was made on 7 May 1902. From 1903 French troops began to move towards the Moulouya region under Lyautey. Meantime Delcassé took diplomatic steps to strengthen French claims to influence in Morocco. Italy recognized French preponderance there in December 1900 in return for French agreement that Italy should have freedom of action in Tripolitania. Prolonged negotiations with Spain from 1900-2 came to nothing but they demonstrated French determination to concede the northern region of Morocco to Spain rather than allow the British to control it. In June 1901 Delcassé negotiated with the Germans, offering Tangier and concessions in other countries – possibly Madagascar – in return for a free hand in Morocco. This also came to nothing; but in July 1901 Delcassé formally announced that France would resent foreign intrusion in Morocco without her agreement.

The British Foreign Office was impressed by this show of French determination and was particularly anxious at this moment not to drive France into giving effective support to Russia in Manchuria. In June 1901 Lansdowne, now Foreign Secretary, therefore refused to give Menebhi, who was visiting London in search of political and financial support, any guarantee that Britain would support the Sultan against French demands; and in January and February 1902 he warned Nicolson against undertaking contracts for loans to the *makhzen* or building railways unless this was done in conjunction with France. By 1903 London had concluded that Britain's weak international position – isolated in Europe, vulnerable to Russian ambitions in the Far East, unable to obtain German support any-where without subscription to the Triple Alliance – made it vital to settle all outstanding issues with France. This was the starting point of prolonged negotiations during 1903–4 which culminated in the signing of the Entente in April 1904.

It is not proposed to rehearse these well-charted negotiations. The vital facts are that each component element of the British official mind in turn – Foreign Office, Colonial Office, Admiralty, India Office – conceded that what it had once regarded as a vital national interest in Morocco might, after all, be expendable; that no one demanded formal British control of any part of Morocco; and that the only strong resistance to French primacy came from shipping and business circles who assumed that French control meant tariffs and shipping regulations which would exclude British economic enterprise. Significantly these economic pressures were ignored in the pursuit of the higher national interest. By the entente Britain accepted French political primacy, even, by implication, a protectorate, on condition of a face-saving French promise of full freedom of commercial access. There are few better examples of the primacy of political over genuine economic considerations in the history of modern imperialism.

From April 1904 it therefore seemed increasingly probable that France would gradually strengthen her political and economic hold over Morocco until eventually it became, in fact if not in name, a

French protectorate. The Spanish, no longer able to rely on British support against France, were forced in October 1904 to accept French primacy in return for agreement that Spain would have a sphere of influence stretching from Larache on the Atlantic coast to the mouth of the Moulouya River, east of Melilla, but excluding Tangier. France also agreed to Spanish control of southern Morocco beyond the Dra. Germany remained the only European power likely to oppose French designs. At the same time French penetration of Morocco accelerated. Once the entente was signed Delcassé encouraged a French banking consortium led by the BPPB to make loans to the Sultan with a face value of 62·5 million francs (though the actual yield was much less since the bonds sold at 80) which were pledged on Moroccan customs. This increased French political influence for customs collection was to be supervised by a representative of the bond-holders, who in turn was nominated by the French government, and the French banks involved were promised 'priority on equal terms for all future Moroccan Government loans'.[46] Thereafter Paris built up pressure on the Sultan to concede a French-run state bank of issue to control currency and money supply and also demanded that police in the main ports should be placed under French officers to maintain better order. Simultaneously preparations were made for the eventual occupation of Morocco. A railway was built from Oran to Colomb-Bechar, along the Algerian frontier with Morocco, and bases were established near the frontier. It seemed only a matter of time and opportunity for France to occupy Morocco.

Germany, however, remained an obstacle; and it is important to consider why German statesmen chose to create two international crises over Morocco in 1905–6 and 1911 before conceding French control. Did Germany want to control Morocco herself or merely to prevent France from doing so? Were official aims economic, strategic or diplomatic?

In the first place, how severe were domestic pressures on the German government? It is clear that by 1904 a wide range of German commercial, banking and industrial groups felt that their established business interests in Morocco entitled them to demand at the very least equality of economic opportunity with Britain and France; and, in face of the growing French threat, a campaign was mounted in November 1903 by Hamburg merchants and the Centralverein für Handelsgeographie to protect Moroccan independence. Large-scale industrialists also showed increasing interest in possible concessions from the Sultan. Philip Holzmann & Co. of Frankfurt were interested in developing the port facilities of Tangier; Felten and Guilleaume of Mülheim in telegraphs; and a consortium of electrical firms in building radio stations on the Atlantic coast as part of a system of communications extending to West Africa. The metallurgical industry was investigating possible sources of iron ore in 1901 and in 1903 a consortium was formed, including Krupps, Thyssen, Gelsenkircken and the Diskonto Gesellschaft, to acquire mining concessions. The Mannesmann brothers began looking for mining opportunities in 1904 and obtained a verbal concession in 1906.

All this indicated growing economic interest in Morocco, yet none of these groups showed any concern for German political control. The Krupps consortium showed how little finance-capitalists cared about nationalist considerations by joining a French group led by Creusot to form an international syndicate, Union Minière (not to be confused with the concern of that name in the Congo) in which the French had 50 per cent of the capital, the Germans 20 per cent. For their part German banks, while ready to co-operate with industrialists or traders, showed no enthusiasm to risk their capital in loans to the Moroccan government. In 1903–4, when the Moroccan government tried to raise loans in Germany to evade French preponderance, the German banks resolutely refused. They were happy to see France dominant in Morocco and for French banks to make loans to the Sultan, confident that they would be able to participate in any genuinely profitable loans through the international banking network.

It is, in fact, clear that with the sole exception of the Mannesmanns no major German economic interest group pressed the German government to annex Morocco or to engineer a partition at any time between 1900 and 1911. Conversely, it is also true that economic interests assumed that the government would protect existing and potential opportunities for German economic enterprise and when this was apparently threatened between 1904–6 by unconditional French predominance which might lead to adverse tariffs and a French monopoly of concessions and contracts, German business demanded official action to protect the 'open door'. This was precisely what similar economic interests in Britain were demanding in 1903–4 and what France conceded as part of the entente. That was all. There is no case whatever for regarding German diplomacy between 1904 and 1911 as the expression of a demand by German economic interests for formal partition of Morocco.

Nor can it be said that the government was forced to the point of war with France in 1905 and 1911 by the irresistible pressure of public opinion. There were, of course, bodies of organized opinion which demanded active German participation in Morocco. But these were divided in aim. The Moroccan Society, founded in 1902, was mainly interested in full economic access and therefore demanded a German share if, but only if, Morocco was partitioned. The Pan-German League on the other hand was primarily interested in obtaining part or all of Morocco for colonization and strategic bases. It campaigned hard from 1902 to 1911, after 1909 in alliance with the Mannesmann brothers, to prevent a sell-out to France. The campaign aroused little public interest before 1905 but was probably more influential by 1911. It would be too much to say that the government was at any stage forced to act by an embattled public opinion; but this publicity certainly enabled German diplomats to claim that 'popular feeling' made it imperative to obtain adequate compensation for concessions to France.

Why, then, did Bülow, after four years of virtual diplomatic inactivity over Morocco, suddenly create a crisis by sending the Kaiser to Tangier on 31 March 1905 to announce that Germany would not accept any settlement to which she was not a party? The German government had legitimate grounds for demanding international negotiations, for the French were accelerating their financial and military activities and were demanding control of banking, public works and the police force in the open ports. Moreover the Sultan formally appealed for German support and the Tangier demonstration was technically a response to his request for German intervention. Yet, behind the façade of treating Morocco as an independent state which Germany was entitled to protect against foreign attack, lay different official aims. It is improbable that these were ever clearly formulated and it is certain that there was no intention of staking a claim to annex any part of Morocco. Probably Holstein and Bülow hoped that by adopting a stance on a question of broad international concern they could repeat Bismarck's coup of 1884–5, making Germany the arbiter of international affairs and at the same time possibly shaking the Anglo-French Entente. In short the Tangier adventure was not a bid for empire or the logical consequence of a continuous line of foreign policy but a speculative diplomatic gamble whose precise objects were not calculated in advance. It falls into the same general category of events as the Kruger telegram of 1896 as an example of the peculiarities of German foreign policy in the age of *Weltpolitik*.

It is unnecessary here to trace the complex diplomacy of 1905–6 leading up to the Algeciras Conference of 16 January to 7 April 1906 and to the Algeciras Act. After the Kaiser's visit to Tangier the Germans insisted on an international conference of all twelve states which had signed the Madrid treaty of 1880, assuming that a majority of states would support them against France. In July 1905 Rouvier, the French Prime Minister, who dominated foreign policy after the resignation of Delcassé in June, agreed to hold a conference. The Germans seemed to have the upper hand for the resignation of Delcassé was a notable victory for German diplomacy and France had in effect admitted that its actions in Morocco were subject to review by a panel of interested states. But once the conference was arranged the Germans had no clear idea of what they wanted to achieve. In September 1905 Bülow rejected Holstein's suggested demands: 'all that matters is to get out of this muddle over Morocco so as to preserve our prestige in the world and to take account of German economic and financial interests as far as possible'.[47] The vital need was not to allow France to achieve a diplomatic triumph. Indeed, the Germans were so preoccupied with diplomatic considerations that they refused discreet offers by France to settle the issue by arranging a general colonial settlement, possibly on the basis of giving German territory in the French Congo for a railway from the Cameroons to Lake Chad. The fact that these proposals were ignored at least indicates that the Germans were not primarily interested in substantive economic or colonial gains. They wanted a diplomatic victory over France to consolidate their position in Europe and perhaps to demonstrate the weakness of the Anglo-French Entente.

The Algericas Conference was therefore a disaster for German policy. The German representative, Tattenbach, failed to detach the British from France and found that only Austria and Morocco would support the German demands. Germany had therefore to accept French political predominance in Morocco without the substantial safeguards and compensation offered the previous November. Her only success was in preventing the formal division of Morocco into French and Spanish spheres along the lines agreed bilaterally by these powers in 1904. By the Algeciras Act of April

1906 Morocco was to remain an independent state. France and Spain were given control of the police in the open ports in accordance with their earlier partition agreement – four ports to be controlled by France, two by Spain and two jointly – all police forces to be supervised by a Swiss officer. A state bank was to be set up in Tangier whose capital was to be subscribed equally by all twelve signatories to the Madrid treaty. Customs duties were to be redefined and to be the same for all foreign states. Contracts for public works were to be open to all. On the surface these conditions represented a defeat for French and Spanish plans to partition Morocco, for Germany had safeguarded the legitimate economic interests of other European states and had imposed a characteristic mid-nineteenth-century solution of the Moroccan problem. Yet it was a hollow victory. Algeciras demonstrated the limitations of German diplomacy. The Anglo-French Entente survived. The French and Spanish were left in a dominant position through their responsibility for maintaining order in Morocco and it was obvious that deteriorating political conditions there would provide ample excuse for consolidation of French influence. The only substantive German gain was a clearly defined right of intervention if the French should at any time contravene the terms of the settlement.

Why, then, did the Germans provoke another major international crisis five years later? Was this because German objectives changed, perhaps under pressure from economic interests who were dissatisfied with mere freedom of opportunity and demanded formal German control of all or part of Morocco?

During these five years two contrary influences affected the Moroccan situation. In the first place German policy was for the most part designed to avoid further friction over Morocco, accepting *de facto* French predominance so long as this did not overtly break the terms of the Algeciras Act. The Kaiser, always anxious to avoid friction with France over Morocco, minuted in October 1908:

> The wretched Morocco affair must be brought to a close, quickly and finally. Nothing can be done. Morocco will become French. So get out of the affair peacefully in order that we may end the friction with France now, when great questions are at stake.[48]

The Franco-German agreement of 8 February 1909 embodied this policy. Germany acknowledged French political primacy in Morocco and it was agreed to co-operate in the economic development of the country. Mining was to be undertaken by the Union Minière which, as has been seen, linked German, French and other capitalists, and by another group which included Mannesmanns and French financial houses. In 1910 the Moroccan state bank raised a loan of 100 million francs from a consortium of French, German, British and Spanish banks. Public works, however, came under exclusive French control on the understanding that France would evacuate the eastern region of Morocco as soon as the Sultan could maintain order there. The German government was genuinely anxious to make this economic collaboration a success in order to reduce political tensions with France, and it was embarrassed by the noisy protest campaign started by the Mannesmanns in alliance with the Pan-German League. The Mannesmanns were in fact merely pursuing a vendetta against Krupps and other German members of the rival consortium but their campaign had some success. By 1911 considerable German interest had for the first time been roused on the Moroccan question and, while most genuine economic interests were quite satisfied with the *status quo*, many nationalists considered that Germany had claims in Morocco which the government was unnecessarily conceding to please the French. By 1911, therefore, the German government felt that it would be dangerous in terms of domestic politics not to make at least a gesture of protest against the radically changed political position in Morocco. This was the genesis of the *Panther* incident of 1911.

But the real solvent of the international settlements of 1906 and 1909 was not the imperialism of the German official mind or of German business, but the dissolution of the Moroccan state and the consequential increase of French political control which effectively destroyed the arrangements made at Algeciras. Once again peripheral factors proved decisive. The Algeciras system depended on Morocco remaining a viable independent state. Between 1906 and 1910 it became clear that this condition could not be met. The authority of the Sultan, already in decline, steadily diminished. Islamic conservatives increasingly disliked foreign influence and there was growing opposition to the taxation necessary to pay for 'modernization'. Rebellions became endemic in the area south of Tangier, in the Atlas Mountains, in the south and near Mogador. In August 1907 Moulay Hafid, one of the Sultan's many brothers, began a civil war which ended with his becoming Sultan in August 1908. In July 1909 he was formally recognized by the powers. For a moment it seemed that he would stabilize the position, but a major revolt broke out early in 1911 and by April Fez was under siege. Morocco was no longer a viable state and the informal international control established in 1906 could only be maintained by foreign intervention.

The crisis of 1911 was the product of French reactions to this situation. In 1907 French forces occupied Casablanca and its hinterland after nine European workers employed on port development had been killed by a xenophobic mob. In the same year a French doctor was killed at Marrakesh and the French responded by occupying Oudjda. During the next two years Lyautey was authorized to occupy the region west of Oudjda to deal with Moroccan insurgents and by 1910 had reached the River Moulouya. By the terms of a Franco-German agreement of 1910 French troops were to be withdrawn from these areas as soon as the Sultan was in a position to maintain order, but this moment never came.

By the end of 1910, therefore, French forces were occupying a considerable part of western and eastern Morocco. Although this was disliked in Germany and was an obvious threat to Moroccan independence, it was diplomatically convenient for all European states to assume that the French occupation was temporary and that it was undertaken on the request of the Sultan. But in April 1911 Moulay Haif, besieged at Fez by yet another brother, Moulay ez-Zin, who claimed the sultanate, appealed for French help. At this point the correct procedure would have been for the French to consult the other signatories to the Algeciras Act, and particularly the Germans as the only power likely to disapprove. Paris considered this course but decided that immediate action was necessary. A French military column raised the siege of Fez on 21 May and took Meknes, capturing Moulay ez-Zin. A month later Rabat, also in rebel hands, was occupied by French forces. France now controlled a continuous strip of territory from Algeria to the Atlantic; and Spain, assuming that the moment of partition had arrived, occupied the northern zone provisionally allotted to her by France in 1904.

These actions were inconsistent with both the terms and the spirit of the Algeciras settlement. Germany was entitled to protest and the outcry in German colonial and nationalistic circles made it necessary for the government to do so. But the crudity of the German response made sophisticated diplomatic dealings impossible. The German gunboat, *Panther*, was sent to Agadir on the pretext of protecting German lives, though in fact this was not an open port and there were no Germans there. What was the object of this manoeuvre? To stake a claim to a share in partition of Morocco; to force France to make concessions elsewhere in return for a free hand in Morocco; to satisfy German jingos; to establish a strong diplomatic position? The answer is that, as in 1905, the government acted before the Foreign Office had worked out a rational line of policy. There was no serious intention of demanding Agadir or any other part of Morocco for Germany, though the possibility of compensation elsewhere was always in view. For her part France was only too anxious to come to terms. Compensation had been offered to Berlin before the *Panther* sailed for Agadir but had been rejected by Kiderlen, Secretary of State in the Foreign Office, on the assumption that he could obtain more if he had an actual foothold in Morocco. Since neither side was prepared to go to war over Morocco a negotiated settlement was inevitable: the difficulty was that neither side could afford to come to terms too readily for fear of losing face and displeasing the jingos. This was the reason for the apparent seriousness of the position. The British attitude was crucial. The Admiralty had no objection to German occupation of Agadir but the cabinet was determined to appear to support France and Lloyd George's famous Mansion House Speech of 21 July 1911 gave both France and Germany an exaggerated impression of British willingness to fight on the French side if necessary. Thereafter France and Germany negotiated privately and in September Kiderlen agreed to a French protectorate in Morocco if France would cede a strip of the French Congo – the same terms as those proposed by the French in 1905. An agreement signed in November embodied this agreement. In addition the two Spanish zones were to be demarcated as protectorates and the guarantee made in 1906 of an 'open door' and equal customs duties for all foreign states was renewed. Tangier was to become an international zone. Imperialists in France and Germany alike protested but economic interests were satisfied and both governments were relieved to escape from untenable diplomatic positions.

The year 1911 marked the end of the Moroccan question as an issue in European politics. The Sultan accepted French protection in March 1912 and during the next eight years French troops gradually completed the pacification of the country. The Spanish occupied their two zones. The Germans briefly annexed part of the French Congo to Kamerun and looked forward eventually to acquiring the Belgian Congo. In 1912 also the Italians, reaping the reward for the agreement they made in 1900, began the occupation of Tripolitania. The partition of Africa was virtually complete.

What is the significance of the Moroccan story for a study of European imperialism, particularly during the decade after 1900 when it was one of the few remaining territories still under dispute between the great powers? What, in particular, was the impact of economic factors on official policy?

First, it is clear from the evidence above that, while economic considerations influenced official policy at all stages, these were never the main determinant of policy. No major business interest in Europe claimed that formal political control by its own state was essential to successful economic activity in Morocco: the common aim was equality of opportunity. Politics were important only because profitable concessions had to be obtained from the Sultan and these might be given exclusively to nationals of that state which possessed political predominance at Fez. Once, therefore, it was agreed at Algeciras to apportion development opportunities on an international basis, European finance and industry were happy to arrange matters across the frontiers. Far from being anxious to annex Morocco so as to intensify economic exploitation, the great financial interests were eager to co-operate. This was the true imperialism of high finance.

Why, then, was Morocco partitioned between France and Spain? Why, in the first place, did France want formal control? The character of French interests has already been described. Basically the French wanted Morocco because it was adjacent to and closely connected with Algeria. They saw it in precisely the same terms as Tunisia. Enthusiasm for actual occupation, however, varied over time and between different groups. From the start Algerian settlers, soldiers and officials wanted nothing less than formal French control. From about 1900 metropolitan imperialists also began to demand formal occupation on the conventional grounds of national prestige, the value of Morocco as a field for settlement and the need to secure Algeria's western frontier. Morocco was, moreover, necessary to complete the imaginative project for a French Empire covering virtually the whole of North and West Africa. The Quai d'Orsay, however, was far less enthusiastic or consistent. For the most part officials were content to prevent British, Spanish and German control of Morocco and to rely on informal influence at

Fez to establish effective French primacy. Ultimately, however, French policy was determined by developments within Morocco. Once the Sultan's authority began to disintegrate after 1902 France faced the double hazard of chronic disorder on the Algerian frontier and the possibility of foreign intervention or informal preponderance. Other European powers could have afforded to stand aside while Morocco disintegrated, but France could not. From about 1902 to 1911 French policy was therefore driven by the double imperative of establishing order on the western frontier of Algeria and preventing foreign intrusion.

Why, finally, did the diplomacy of the period 1900–11 become so tense? It would be convenient to assert that international relations over Morocco were exceptionally bellicose because the statesmen were under pressure from the mass of popular imperialists and could not afford to make concessions; and there are some grounds for this assumption. After 1900 imperialist organizations were relatively well equipped to arouse public enthusiasm for pegging claims in Morocco whereas in the 1880s they were not. Statesmen certainly felt the force of public interest and were less free to make convenient diplomatic arrangements without elaborate face-saving expedients. Yet, when all allowances are made, it cannot be said that the policy of any major power was dictated by popular imperialism. The statesmen adopted positions which served the general objectives of their intricate international diplomacy. It was they who stirred up popular feeling by staging sham crises and making emotive speeches. But when it was necessary to end the crisis the diplomats invariably came to terms irrespective of popular disapproval. Morocco was not worth a war to anyone, even in the years before 1914.

Morocco can, therefore, be regarded as a classical example both of the importance of economic factors in European relations with other countries and, paradoxically, of the predominance of non-economic 'national interests' in the formulation of official policy. On the one hand genuine economic interests and expectations prevented casual allocation of Morocco to any one power and ensured that in the end the French protectorate would be conditional on preservation of the 'open door'. On the other hand the policy of the great powers was always determined by political and strategic considerations which were given greater weight than mere economic interests. At every stage private business interests were made the tool of national policy, held back or driven on as best suited the larger purposes of the statesmen. What Delcassé said of France in 1899 applied to all throughout the period: national diplomacy was not at the service of private interests but aimed to co-ordinate and discipline them to serve as instruments of national policy.

10 *The Partition of Sub-Saharan Africa*

I   WEST AFRICA

*E*uropean expansion in West Africa provides the most complex, difficult and interesting example of the interaction of economic and other factors in sub-Saharan Africa after about 1880. The basic problem derives from the proposition suggested above that, although it was predictable by the late 1870s on the basis of existing trends that formal European control would sooner or later spread throughout West Africa, there were then few grounds for expecting rapid change within the next decade and perhaps longer. Growing commodity exports and changing transport technology would eventually demand port facilities capable of handling ocean-going liners and improved inland communications to handle larger volumes at lower unit costs. Yet in fact little was done to improve the ports in the 1880s, and railways were built only in Senegal and the French Sudan. The poverty of colonial governments would lead to continued extension of coastal control to increase customs yields, but this did not necessitate occupation of distant hinterlands. Relations between Europeans and Africans were frequently unsatisfactory to both parties, yet imperial expansion cannot be explained merely in terms of intensifying race conflicts. Why, then, did events move so fast and to what extent were they the product of economic forces?

No one factor was responsible for the partition of West Africa: certainly not contemporary developments in the Congo, Egypt or

Europe, though each of these had some relevance for West Africa. At the risk of oversimplifying a very complex process it will be argued that the most important single new force was the French decision at last to implement Faidherbe's grand project for linking Senegal with the Western Sudan, the Niger river system and Algeria, which necessarily changed the political and economic geography of West Africa. At the same time rapidly growing commercial competition between British, French and German nationals on the coast intensified existing problems and eventually interacted with the new situation in the interior. Given this suggested order of priorities, it is proposed to deal first with the evolution of French policy as the main stimulus leading to change and then to treat British and German policies in turn as in some degree a reaction to this new challenge to the *status quo*.

FRANCE IN WEST AFRICA, 1880–1900.[1] The origins of French expansion in West Africa after 1880 lie in Senegal rather than in Paris and action was proposed by a colonial Governor who revived the imaginative expansionist concepts of his great predecessor, Louis Faidherbe. In 1876 Louis-Alexandre Brière de l'Isle became Governor of Senegal and found the colony in serious fiscal difficulties. To alleviate these he adopted the traditional expedient of expanding French customs control over the coastline south-east of Goree, reaffirmed control of the Guinea Coast between the Pongos and the Mellacourie, and levied customs at Benty and Fouricania. At the same time he barred the Senegal and Casamance Rivers to foreign traders and imposed differential shipping dues and tariffs. But although these actions pointed to the extension of French control on the Guinea Coast, they were a minor aspect of Brière's broad strategy. This was no less than to revive Faidherbe's grand design for French political control over the vast triangle that lay between St Louis, Bamako on the Niger and Sierra Leone, which would provide direct access to the Niger delta and a link via Timbuctu with Algeria. Like Faidherbe Brière was convinced that this project was essential to make Senegal a strong and rich colony. Politically it would not be secure so long as the great Tokolor Empire of Al-Hajj Umar, now ruled by his son, Ahmadou, dominated the hinterland of Senegal. Economically Senegal needed to tap the trade of this vast, unknown but presumed wealthy interior. Faidherbe's project had been rejected by Paris in 1864 and had since lain almost forgotten. Brière was convinced that it was now essential to disinter it. First he believed that there was a danger of Tokolor invasion into Senegal, second that the British were making contacts with Sultan Ahmadou and the chiefs of Bondu. If France did not act now the whole future of Senegal was at risk.

As always the decision lay in Paris. Brière could undertake small-scale campaigns in Futa and Upper Senegal, but beyond that Senegalese resources were too small. Why should Brière be more successful than Faidherbe had been in persuading the politicians and bureaucrats in Paris that the Western Sudan was a national interest? His success can be explained in terms of a favourable coincidence of factors and personalities. First, the project for long escaped opposition from those who normally opposed extension of French colonies because it could be explained in terms of defending existing possessions and opening up the interior of the Sudan for trade, neither of which necessarily involved territorial ownership. Second, despite Brière's fears, since no other European power was in fact interested in the area, no international complications would result. Above all the project could be publicized as a great railway-building project which would do for the African interior what railways were then doing for the Middle-West of America and Siberia. This was the great positive attraction of the scheme which ensured support from that wide cross-section of French society which was inspired by the activities of African explorers and missionaries and for whom imperialism was synonomous with Europe's civilizing mission. By 1879 there was already much support for the idea of a trans-Saharan railway from Algeria to Senegal, and in 1879 the *rapporteur* of the Budget Commission, Maurice Rouvier, had supported a vote of 200,000 francs for preliminary surveys in glowing terms. With her possessions in Algeria, Senegal and Gaboon and many trading bases in West Africa, France could not afford to stand back while Europe opened up the rich areas of the African interior. 'Le souci de la grandeur et des intérêts de notre patrie ne nous commandet-il pas de nous placer a la tête de ce mouvement'?[2] Parliament was enthusiastic and voted credits of 200,000 francs and later 600,000 francs for the surveys. Moreover by December 1879 the Prime Minister was Charles de Freycinet, an enthusiastic supporter of the trans-Saharan railway scheme. In his opening speech he stated that 'civilization can most surely be extended and secured by means of communications. We must try to link the vast regions around the Niger and the Congo'.[3]

But did this imaginative enthusiasm for railway construction imply equal enthusiasm for expansion of territorial empire, which both Faidherbe and Brière believed necessary? On this point there was a fundamental ambiguity in French attitudes. On the one hand Freycinet, Rouvier and many strong supporters of the trans-Saharan or less ambitious railway projects believed that railways were a more sophisticated means of continuing the civilizing work of mid-nineteenth-century explorers and missionaries and that they did not necessarily lead to political control of the regions through which they passed. One could thus support railways while remaining hostile to colonial expansion, and this largely explains why the Sudanese project received such wide support in its initial phase. But others thought differently. The official mind of Senegal, deriving directly from the Algerian tradition, could not believe that railways alone could transform Islamic warriors into docile collaborators. In their minds commerce and empire were firmly linked. Railway-building and military conquest must go hand in hand. This was not necessarily the view of permanent officials in the colonial department of the Ministry of Marine; but in 1879 the Minister was Admiral Jean Jauréguiberry, a former Governor of Senegal, who fully accepted this analysis; and for this reason, if only temporarily, the official mind of the Ministry was dominated by the assumptions of St Louis. Thus from the start there was an inherent tension in metropolitan intentions between those for whom railway construction and commerce were the objects of policy and those for whom they were the means to constructing a territorial empire in the Western Sudan.

Under these circumstances, and given the potential hostility of parliament to overt empire-building where no accepted French national interests were at stake, the key to events after 1879 lies in the fact that money which was obtained ostensibly to build railways was actually used to sustain an adequate army in the Western Sudan, and that this in turn became a virtually autonomous expansionist force. The Budget Commission was aware that funds were being used for military purposes in the Sudan, but, because it generally approved their objectives, it did not protest. Since, moreover, the French Treasury did not exercise such detailed control over departmental expenditure as the British Treasury, it was possible for the colonial department to provide at least minimal funds for Sudanese military activities without inconvenient publicity.

These facts largely explain why it was possible for a policy which began as a popular project for peaceful railway construction to evolve into the military conquest of the Sudan. They indicate clearly that French expansion in West Africa did not necessarily imply widespread belief in the economic necessity of formal empire. Almost equally important was the virtual independence of the Sudanese Army once launched into the interior. In December 1879 Jauréguiberry appointed Major Gustave Borgnis-Desbordes as Commandant-Supérieur du Haute Fleuve with full control over operations on the Upper Senegal. This was a crucial step, for thereafter the army became virtual master of its own actions, dependent only on receiving funds from Paris. Successive commandants – Desbordes, Combes, Gallieni and Archinard – acted on their own initiative, frequently ignoring explicit instructions from St Louis or Paris, secure in the knowledge that success would justify their actions and that in a crisis they could demand help on the principle that the military must always be supported for the honour of France. Thus, once launched in 1879, the army steadily continued its campaigns against African states until by about 1897 it had conquered virtually the whole hinterland of the west coast and had arrived at Bussa on the Middle Niger. Only then, in the face of severe British resistance, was Paris forced to call a halt.

The details of this extraordinary conquest are largely irrelevant for a study of economic factors in European expansion in West Africa, but its implications for the coastal regions and for other European powers are of primary significance. Once French forces had moved from Senegal to the Niger and became involved with indigenous states to the south and east, the whole pattern of West African history was inverted. Instead of imperial expansion moving slowly inland from the commercial centres on the coast, it descended from the northern axis of the Senegal and Niger to the hinterlands of these established colonies and bases. Thus in 1882 Futa Jalon, behind the Guinea Coast and a prospective area for British commercial expansion from Sierra Leone, became vital to French security in the Western Sudan and therefore an area of controversy. Faced by the fact of French occupation of the interior Britain recognized French predominance in this area and boundary demarcations between 1885 and 1895 tightly restricted the northern limits of Sierra Leone. A similar pattern developed in Upper Volta and Mossi, lying behind the Ivory and Gold Coasts. France had reasonable commercial claims to pre-eminence on the Ivory Coast but none in the interior. Yet both Upper Volta and Mossi were occupied by expeditions from Segu in 1896 as part of the Niger project, thus truncating the northern limits of British and German expansion from the Gold Coast and Togo. Until 1897 it looked as if the northern limits of British influence in the Niger region would be determined in the same way. Conversely, French conquest of Dahomey in 1892 was undertaken primarily to provide closer access to the Middle Niger as a means of liberating French trade on the Niger system from British customs in the Lagos Protectorate and in the Oil Rivers. Thus the logic of establishing a French axis from St Louis to Chad entailed both a vast extension of French control in the hinterlands of her old coastal possessions and a corresponding limit to the extension of British and German expansion from the coast to the interior. This, more than any other single factor, determined the eventual geography of colonial West Africa.

If, then, the French drive into the Sudan is taken as the most important single new element in West Africa after 1880, how far can it be regarded as an expression of economic imperialism? Over so long a period there were inevitably wide differences of intention between successive French governments, and disagreements between officials in the Quai d'Orsay, the Ministry of Marine, Sudanese soldiers, and civilian officials in West Africa. Two relatively distinct impulses can be distinguished, one quasi-economic and essentially metropolitan, the other mainly military and characteristic of Frenchmen in West Africa. At its inception in Paris the project was, as has been seen, primarily economic, in that the main objective of Freycinet, Rouvier, Jauréguiberry and others was the trade of the interior of West Africa. But this was not simply a desire to increase existing trade on the coast, nor a response to pressures from commercial interests in France or Senegal. The Bordeaux firm of Maurel et Prom, later of great importance in West Africa, supported the Niger railway project, set up shop at Medina and operated steamers from St Louis to Kayes by 1883. But these were exceptional in seizing a new opportunity. There is no evidence that the Sudanese scheme owed anything to the pressure of mercantile demand for new markets. Most established West African firms, although they might demand official support against British or German obstruction to their trade on the Niger or around Sierra Leone, did not at this stage want large-scale French colonization. Like many British merchants they were in fact suspicious of French officialdom and feared that empire meant customs posts. Nor is there any ground for seeing Sudanese expansion as the product of demand for new markets for French manufactures or for fields for capital investment by financiers, none of whom found the Sudan a rewarding field for enterprise until much later. In fact the scheme had little connection with the practical needs of the French business world. Its economic rationale was a visionary belief in the commercial potential of large-scale communications. This was economic imperialism of a sort, but it had little in common with the imperialism of the European merchant or manufacturer.

Yet French imperialism in West Africa had another and far more practical economic dimension. Whereas the Sudan scheme projected economic benefits for French trade at the national level there were many individual commercial problems on the coast that owed nothing to technology or imagination. From the late 1870s French merchants were increasingly and legitimately worried that first British and then German activities were tending to obstruct their trade. It has been seen above that French traders already found it difficult to compete with the British in selling goods on the coast except in protected markets. Now conditions were becoming still more unfavourable. In Sierra Leone British tariffs were rising in the 1870s and tariff control was extended to near-by regions, notably the Scarcies, where French trade predominated. The Gold Coast was by now covered by British customs posts and it was feared that the British proposed to extend customs control west of Lagos, absorbing Porto Novo, once a French protectorate, and the Slave Coast westwards to the Gold Coast. Commercial rivalry was even more intense on the Niger and in the Oil Rivers. By 1880 a new French firm, Compaigne Française de l'Afrique Equatorial (CFAE), had established trading posts at Abo, Onitsha, Lokoja and Egga, and on the Benue at Loko. Its main rival was the United Africa Company, constructed by George Goldie from four smaller British trading firms, which from 1882 was called the National African Company. Both were engaged on an essentially new project, penetration of the Niger system beyond the sphere of African middlemen to the oil-producing regions beyond. Until 1882 both companies worked together amicably, fixing buying prices and agreeing that problems of jurisdiction should be handled by their respective Consuls. But, as always happened in West Africa, the commercial alliance broke down by 1882. Thereafter war to the death was commercially inevitable for, given the highly competitive character of the oil trade at a time of declining prices, survival depended on monopoly of the inland markets. Already by 1882 Mattei had made a treaty with King Amadou of Loko giving the

French sole right to set up trading posts along his territories on the Benue and other treaties were in prospect. On equal terms the French company, which was joined by the Compagnie du Sénégal in 1882, might well be able to hold the British company. But would conditions be equal? Rightly or wrongly the French believed that the British might use political power to support their own nationals and that the Niger, like other parts of West Africa, might become a British sphere of commerce.

Here, then, were two types of genuine commercial problem on the coast, one old, the other new. Would commercial competition generate French empire-building? The answer is that Paris differentiated clearly between different areas. On the Guinea, Ivory and Slave Coasts their reaction to mercantile complaints was to peg back British control by demarcating boundaries between the respective spheres of interest and possibly to revive the old project for exchanging the Gambia for Cotonou on the Slave Coast. Thus in 1882 a frontier agreement was made which sealed off Mellacourie from Sierra Leone and gave France effective control of the Guinea Coast between Sierra Leone and Portuguese Guinea. In the same year the French protectorate over Porto Novo was renewed to block British expansion west from Lagos; and in later years France acquired control over the Slave Coast as far as Grand Popo by agreements signed with Britain and Germany. By 1889 the coast-line from St Louis to the borders of the German Cameroons had been demarcated and the eventual pattern of coastal West Africa was fixed. This was the limited but effective response of French officialdom to the specifically commercial problems facing French merchants in an area of British commercial and political preponderance.

But in the Niger region the French reaction was very different. In 1883, it is true, Jauréguiberry launched a policy of treaty making on the Oil Rivers to challenge British predominance there; and he also proposed to ratify the private agreement made by Mattei with Loko. His aim was to build up a French sphere of influence east of the Niger from the Benue to the coast which would give France freedom of access for trade on the Middle Niger and bypass the British customs system at Lagos. This scheme also fitted well with the great Senegal-Niger-Chad project by securing access to its eastern segment from the sea. Had it been pursued serious political conflict with the British might have resulted. But in 1883 Jauréguiberry was out of office and Jules Ferry, with Charles Brun at the marine, took a more realistic view of the possible limits of French policy on the Niger. He refused to give public money to either French company, though both were hard-pressed in 1883, and he did not intervene when first the Compagnie du Sénégal and then the CFAE sold out to Goldie in 1884–5. His caution indicated that the official mind of Paris had recognized that while France could stand out for freedom of access to the Lower Niger and the Delta, this would remain an area of British political predominance. At the Berlin Conference Ferry attempted to get the Lower Niger neutralized politically, but rather than accept neutralization also of the Upper Niger, now regarded as a potential French fief, he accepted British control there subject to international rights of navigation and equal customs duties for all nationalities.

Thus by 1885 the limits of French official action in support of French merchants on the coast were clearly defined. Where France had a reasonable claim to primacy French protectorates were imposed. But the aim was to prevent the imposition of unfavourable British customs duties rather than to impose differential French tariffs; and, under British pressure, France eventually agreed not to impose differential tariffs in Guinea, Ivory Coast and Dahomey. In these areas French imperialism was therefore a defensive response to genuine economic problems. In the hinterlands of these coastal regions, however, French expansion was the product of the Sudanese strategy rather than of trade, though political control there was admittedly used to divert routes from British to French coastal ports. In the Niger region, however, French policy was more complicated. Starting from a genuine attempt to safeguard French coastal commerce in the face of British political expansion, French policy after 1885 centred on the need to ensure access from the coast to the system of inland communications that led to the Middle Niger. Given the terms of the Berlin Act, France had a genuine grievance in that the Royal Niger Company (as the National African Company became in 1886) was using its right to impose customs duties merely to meet administrative costs to exclude all but its own traders from the Niger trade. The French answer was to block the northward thrust of Goldie's company, and therefore of British political control, by occupying the Niger bend at points as far south as Bussa. In this area territorial control was therefore seen as a necessary means of preserving French commercial access to the Niger river system on the assumption that eventually the British could be forced to concede genuine freedom of navigation from the Middle Niger to the sea. In this way the Niger question eventually became part of the wider problem of French preponderance in the Sudan.

The main contrast between French policy and that of Britain was that although on the coast the British acted in very much the same way as the French, they had no great plan to open up the interior of West Africa.[4] British expansion throughout this period was, in fact, largely a reaction to the initiatives first of France and then, to a lesser extent, of Germany. Official attitudes changed very slowly. Until perhaps 1895 the criteria used remained those of the period 1830–80. West African trade was important as far as it went, but it was intrinsically very small and certainly did not constitute a major national interest. Existing bases were certainly to be retained and their areas of influence extended gradually to increase their customs revenues, to counter foreign intervention or to deal with obstructive African states. But all such enterprises must be paid for from colonial resources, for Britain's interest in the area did not warrant expenditure of public funds. Private British companies were free to establish commercial empires on independent areas of the coast or inland up the rivers, but they could expect no political support beyond what a British consul or occasional naval vessel might give them. Expansion of territorial control was distrusted as an unnecessary and costly inconvenience, to be undertaken only under very pressing circumstances.

Until the end of the 1880s no significant change occurred in British attitudes to the West African coast between Lagos and Senegal because none seemed necessary. The solution to French moves on the Guinea and Slave Coasts, inconvenient as these might be to British colonies and traders, was amicable demarcation of interests and, if possible guaranteed freedom of trade. London was, of course, aware of the potential significance for British colonies of French incursions into the Sudanese interior because they threatened to cut off established trade routes to British ports and customs houses. But there was nothing London could reasonably do to check France in the Sudan, and the interests at stake certainly did not warrant counter-thrusts from the coast. But the Niger region was a more serious problem. Its trade was far more valuable than that of the western regions and the sudden incursion of French trading companies on the coast and Lower Niger, coupled with the treaties these made with African states, constituted a serious danger to established British commercial interests. Moreover, there was danger inland as well, for Gallieni made a treaty with Ahmadou at Segou and Desbordes took Bamako in 1883, which indicated that eventually France might impose formal control on the Middle Niger and possibly beyond. Thus, by about 1883 it seemed possible that access to trade on the Niger and its delta, which the British had hitherto taken for granted, might be in danger, if not immediately, then in the near future. To pinpoint the threat, an almost identical situation was simultaneously developing on the Congo, then largely a British trading preserve, where H. M. Stanley and de Brazza were making treaties which might give Leopold's International Association or France effective control over this commercial waterway. In the Cameroons, another area of established British trade, German traders were pressing Bismarck to acquire Fernando Po and a coastal strip on the mainland. Thus commercial prospects throughout the region from Lagos to the Congo were changing rapidly and for the worse. What had recently been regarded as a British commercial preserve was now threatened not only by rival traders but by possible political intervention by foreign governments. Britain's response was a real test of the character of British imperialism. Would political power be used to defend economic interests?

The important fact is that until 1884 London resolutely refused to break any new ground, certainly not to impose political control over areas at risk commercially. A proposal from Hewett, the British consul in the Oil Rivers, for a loose defensive protectorate over the delta was peremptorily rejected. Gladstone's Colonial Secretary, Lord Kimberley, not by any means a committed opponent of territorial expansion under the right circumstances, minuted that:

Such an extensive protectorate as Mr Hewett recommends would be a most serious addition to our burdens and responsibilities. The coast is pestilential; the natives numerous and unmanageable. The result of a British occupation would be almost certainly wars with the natives, heavy demands upon the British taxpayer. . . .[5]

In 1881 Goldie was refused a royal charter, comparable to that given in the same year to the North Borneo Company, which would have enabled him to impose political control over the Lower Niger on the basis of treaties made with African rulers. Farther south there was no attempt to compete with French and Belgian treaty-making on the Congo. Yet behind this façade of orthodoxy an interesting division of opinion was developing within the official mind of London. On the one hand the Foreign Office was convinced by reports from Consul Hewett and pressure from merchants, such as John Holt, operating in the Oil Rivers, that political conditions in the delta were deteriorating and that formal British control was becoming necessary.[6] At the same time the Foreign Office was aware that Paris was seriously considering political control over this area. In March 1883 the Foreign Office therefore proposed to the Colonial Office that Britain should annex the whole unoccupied region between Lagos and Gaboon as a precautionary measure. But the Colonial Office, whose conservative views contrasted strongly at this time with those of the French Marine, would have none of it, suspecting that the majority of British traders in the area did not want the cost of a British administration. The preferred alternative was to permit Hewett to make protectorate treaties to offset those made by French agents, but not to commit Britain to any form of government. On the Niger and Benue Goldie was left to compete as best he could with French firms, though London would certainly have intervened against any French attempt at political control there. On the Congo Britain exhumed a proposal made in the 1870s and recognized Portugal's prior claims to block the pretensions of France and Leopold.

Thus, by the end of 1883 the British had showed no desire whatever to solve what they regarded as essentially economic difficulties in West Africa by imposing political control. The Niger, the Delta, the Cameroons and the Congo were to remain unoccupied by all foreign powers, and local problems were dealt with pragmatically. This represented the true tradition of British economic imperialism – the rejection of political means where there was no political objectives.

During 1884, however, this position became untenable because other powers now used political weapons. In June 1884 Germany made it clear that she would not accept Portuguese possession of the Congo region, and France joined her in summoning a conference on the issue. On 14 July a German protectorate was declared over the coast of the Cameroons, and later in July over Togo, which had hitherto been regarded as within the sphere of the Gold Coast. This left only the Niger and the Delta still open to British influence, and the danger that they too might suddenly be claimed by some other power now produced rapid action. By 15 November, when the Berlin Conference met, Goldie had removed the French threat on the Lower Niger by buying out the two competing French companies; and Hewett had made sufficient treaties with African chiefs in the Delta to checkmate similar moves by other powers. At the conference these were accepted as adequate evidence of British primacy in both regions. Britain had to concede freedom of navigation on the Lower Niger but Goldie's company was conceded the right to administer areas in which it had effective control. There was no challenge in the Delta; but in June 1885 a British protectorate was declared over the coast from Lagos to the Rio del Rey, the western limit of the German Cameroons protectorate.

In the eyes of British officialdom this concession to political necessity marked the acceptable limit of political action in support of trade. The Colonial Office had been forced to accept the Niger protectorate by threats from foreigners, but it had no intention of administering the area. The coast was therefore left to informal supervision by the consul (a Foreign Office not a Colonial Office employee) who interfered from time to time, as when the Acting Consul Harry Johnston deported King Ja Ja of Opobo in 1887, because the African Association of British traders complained that he was obstructing freedom of trade. It was not until 1893 that the Niger Coast Protectorate was established with a formal administrative system to meet the growing needs for effective government in an area of expanding British trade. This too was in line with the traditional model, formal rule following a long period of creeping influence.

On the Niger also the British hoped to avoid a breach with established principles. It was now accepted that the Lower Niger must remain a British sphere of influence, and that 'effective occupation' as defined by the Berlin Act must be established there. But this could be done without cost or inconvenience to Britain by leaving the work to Goldie's company, the only potential beneficiary of British control. In 1886 he was therefore given a royal charter enabling him to exercise jurisdiction over areas in which he acquired political rights by treaty with African rulers. On this basis, and with revenues derived from customs duties which the Berlin Act permitted for administrative purposes, the newly christened Royal Niger Company could operate as a quasi-independent state, closely comparable with Leopold's new Congo Free State. This solution had its disadvantages. The company annoyed independent

British and foreign traders alike because it used customs duties and administrative devices to exclude all others from its preserves. The African Association, comprising most of the independent British firms operating west of Lagos, was afraid the company might extend its control to the Delta, and for years hovered between proposals for joining the company and attempts to destroy it. But in the end they stayed out and Goldie concentrated his efforts on the Niger rather than in the Oil Rivers. London was aware of these frictions. But the company was the only representative of British commercial interests on the Niger and had to be allowed to operate in its own way. Until the mid-1890s it seemed perfectly capable of fulfilling its role; and in 1890 Salisbury accepted French predominance north of the Say-Barruwa line on the assumption that Goldie could effectively occupy the region to the south. As Sir Percy Anderson of the Foreign Office commented: 'The Niger Company will have to protect the Central Niger and the rear of Lagos. They are aware of this'.[7]

Throughout the decade after 1885 London followed the same conservative line in all other parts of the west coast. Foreign annexations did not provoke extensive territorial claims. At most Salisbury and Rosebery were prepared to negotiate reasonable hinterlands for existing coastal possessions to counter the French advance from the Sudan. Salisbury did not hesitate to reject demands from London and Liverpool merchants trading to Gambia and Sierra Leone who demanded control of the hinterlands of the colonies to offset French movement into Futa Jalon. By the Anglo-French agreements of August 1889 and 1890 the boundaries of these colonies were drawn tightly, condemning them to remain small coastal enclaves. On the Gold Coast, whose hinterlands were similarly threatened by French and German expansion into Upper Volta, the British government was equally cautious. The 1889 and 1891 agreements with France and the 1890 agreement with Germany demarcated the Gold Coast frontiers only as far north as the ninth parallel, reserving Ashanti for Britain but leaving the hinterland open for international competition. In 1892 the London Chamber of Commerce pressed for action there, and a half-hearted attempt was made to keep open the region north of Ashanti as a possible link with the Niger Company's area by treaties with several African states. But these could not stand against the French military advance, and no treaty was ever made with Borgu, the most important state in this area. Effective action would, indeed, have required the conquest of Ashanti; and this was still deemed too expensive to contemplate. Behind Lagos it was the same. The 1889 agreement demarcated the frontier with Dahomey as far north as the ninth parallel, securing Yorubaland, and in 1893 Lagos made protectorate treaties to safeguard this region. But there was no attempt to exclude France from Nikki, the key to control of the Middle Niger.

Thus until after 1895 British official policy in West Africa remained virtually unchanged. Reviewing the period from about 1880 it is clear that, despite radically new competition from other countries, Britain had refused to peg out preemptive claims on anything like the scale which her earlier preponderance would have justified. Concessions had been made: the Niger Coast Protectorate, the Niger Company charter, even frontier demarcations inland to the ninth parallel – some 170 miles inland on the Lagos coast, more on the Gold Coast – would all have been unthinkable even in 1883. Yet overall Britain had clearly refused to adopt a policy of territorial aggrandizement to preserve commercial interests. By 1892 the extent of the failure was clear; and in West Africa as in many other parts of the world, interested parties were ruefully contemplating the consequences. In that year the Liverpool Chamber of Commerce aptly summarized mercantile opinion:

In West Africa the British governments of the last decade have been outstripped by Germany and France; the Gambia has dwindled; the Cameroons has been lost; two foreign powers have intervened between Lagos and Gold Coast Colonies – which colonies should have been coterminous – the French have spread themselves over Senegambia, and the British governments have yielded the districts of the Northern Rivers of Sierra Leone ... the Chamber is of opinion that wherever in the unappropriated territories of Africa preponderance of British trade existed, there British interests should have been secured, by proclaiming such territories spheres of British influence.[8]

But this was wisdom after the event. Had so forthright a statement been made about 1880 by any British Chamber of Commerce it would constitute strong support for theories of economic imperialism based on mercantile fear of losing markets. But, as has been seen, British merchants in West Africa were as slow as the politicians to see the danger and for long disliked the prospect of British colonial taxes more than they feared foreign intervention. British policy had thus been based on two premises, which Salisbury spelled out in 1892. First, 'Great Britain has adopted the policy of advance by commercial enterprise. She has not attempted to compete with the military operations of her neighbour'.[9] Second, the metropolis could not be expected to pay the cost of conquest and administration in regions adjacent to existing colonies:

> The colonies of the Gambia and Sierra Leone, with limited revenues barely sufficient for their administrative expenditure, would have been unable to bear any strain in the direction of military expenditure, and the sanction of Parliament was not to be expected for the employment of imperial resources adequate for the purpose.[10]

This was the epitome of mid-Victorian economic imperialism, whose criteria were genuinely economic and not territorial.

Between 1895 and 1900, however, British policy in West Africa changed radically, to meet the threat of French control on the Middle Niger. In 1892 Paris rejected proposals put up by the Anglo-French boundary commission for this area and in the same year the conquest of Dahomey at last made effective French military action in the Borgu and Mossi areas feasible. By 1894 it seemed certain that France would dominate the Middle Niger and the region north of the Benue as far east as Chad, thus depriving the Niger Company of the sphere notionally reserved for it south of the Say-Barruwa line in 1890. What were British official reactions to this military and diplomatic French activity? Until 1897 London did little more than mildly regret that the Niger Company had not been able to do better in its own interests. Rosebery made an ineffective attempt in 1893 to check French pretensions east of Lake Chad by suggesting that the Germans take this region as a buffer between French power in the Western Sudan and British interests on the Nile. But there was no prospect whatever of official intervention, diplomatic or military, to save the Middle Niger. It was the considered view both of the government and Goldie that the problem was exclusively one for the company;[11] and Goldie made no request for official help beyond asking for protection against a possible French attack on the Lower Niger from Dahomey when he proposed to attack the French forces occupying Bussa in 1897. This is important. British military intervention in 1898 was not the product of pressures exerted on the British government by a chartered company, nor was it connected with the fact that the new Colonial Secretary, Chamberlain, held shares in the Niger Company. By 1897 Chamberlain had in fact decided that the company must be bought out as soon as an alternative means of administering its territories could be evolved. British official intervention did not constitute an *affaire*.

It is in fact clear that Chamberlain's objectives in demanding governmental action to save British interests on the Middle Niger from France in 1897–8 were very different from those of the company. The contrast derived from their divergent views of the economic potential of the area and pinpoints two contrasting types of economic imperialism. To Goldie the value of the Niger was purely commercial, though he once expounded the potential value of Hausa soldiers on the analogy of British Indian troops.[12] He was not interested in formal control, still less in positive steps to develop new sources of wealth. As Chamberlain complained:

> Apparently the efforts of the Niger Company ... are confined to one matter only, namely, keeping in their hands the water-way of the Niger below the rapids. ... [They] do not profess to protect possessions which are not necessary for this one primary object. ...[13]

Chamberlain's view was quite different.[14] Although he was very concerned to promote British trade everywhere in Africa, it was not sufficient merely to tap the trade of easily accessible regions or to deal only in existing commodities, which, in this area, were uncultivated forest products. It was necessary to apply European capital and skills to develop new commodity trades, to build railways, reconstruct the indigenous economy. So positive a programme was incompatible with the old dogma that trade did not require territorial control. Territory was itself fundamental for true colonial development when defined in this way. Already, before 1897, Chamberlain had taken important steps in other parts of West Africa. Ashanti had at last been conquered in 1895 and the hinterland could now be opened up and new products established. The West African colonial governments had been authorized to start railway construction, which quickly produced the first long-term public debts in British West Africa. On these premises Chamberlain was therefore not prepared to sell out British territorial claims on the Niger. By 1897 he was prepared to act independently of the company and early in 1898 he persuaded the cabinet to establish an official military force, the West African Frontier Force, to compete with the French forces at Borgu. Salisbury was frightened by the possible effects of Anglo-French military confrontation on the Niger on the delicate diplomatic position over the Nile, and insisted on quick action. In June 1898 the Niger convention solved the problem. Britain retained Sokotu and Ilo; Borgu was divided; France kept Nikki, Mossi and Bona and the right to free navigation on the Lower Niger. The partition of West Africa was almost over.

A brief review of Britain's role in the partition suggest that from first to last economic considerations dictated policy. This was economic imperialism in its purest form, virtually untainted by considerations of national prestige or strategy and only marginally affected by other aspects of the African situation such as Egypt. Until the middle 1890s trade was the criterion of policy, and significantly trading interests generated very little territorial aggrandizement. The sudden inflation of British territory in the emirates of the Middle Niger in 1897 was also the product of economic calculations, but of a radically different type, far more akin to the concepts of French technologists than to the pedestrian calculations of British merchants and officials. Chamberlain's intervention did indeed imply an incursion of British metropolitan economic imperialism closely similar to that of Jauréguiberry and Freycinet two decades earlier. But his action was not the product of British finance capital seeking fields of investment, nor of sinister influences brought to bear by the Royal Niger Company. It derived from a new concept of 'constructive imperialism' and looked forward to forms of economic developments in tropical colonies characteristic of colonialism in the first half of the twentieth century.[15] In the context of the period 1880–1900 Chamberlain's policy in West Africa is therefore important mainly because it was a-typical. The British official mind did not believe in acquiring colonial estates for economic development, and this view virtually determined the destiny of British possessions and claims in West Africa. Had the partition been starting in 1895, British policy might have been very different, perhaps more like that of France. As the record stands Northern Nigeria was one of the very few parts of the British Empire deliberately acquired as a field for economic development.

The third European power whose policies significantly affected the growth of territorial empire in West Africa was Germany.[16] It is, however, impossible to explain German actions in this area in isolation, as, to some extent, has been done for France and Britain, because German claims to Togo, the Cameroons and part of Guinea were part of an integrated project which included claims in South-West Africa, East Africa and the South Pacific and must be considered in this broad context. Thus the question must be whether Bismarck's decision in 1884–5 to impose German protection on all these areas was the product of economic or other factors in Germany or of problems on the periphery.

Bismarck's precise motives remain one of the most debatable questions in modern imperial history. In chapter 4 above it was suggested that his decision to act in 1884 was closely related to the immediate political situation in Germany: that he took colonies in order to please imperialists in the National Liberal Party and so to strengthen his position in the Reichstag. Tactically, at least, this is probably true. But behind lies the question whether economic interests may have contributed to the decision and if so how important they were. Broadly three economic explanations of his conduct have been advanced. First, it has been suggested that as early as 1879 he had been converted by the propaganda of German imperialists to the view that, in a world of increasing tariff protection and contracting markets, Germany must acquire colonies to keep doors open for her own trade.

A great nation like Germany, in the end, could not dispense with colonies; but, as much as he was *in principle* [*sic*] in favour of the acquisition of colonies, the question appeared so complicated that he hesitated to embark on colonization without adequate preparation and a definite impulse from the nation itself.[17]

By 1884 conditions had changed. Colonial propaganda had created public support for colonies, German traders had established reasonable claims in several areas, international conditions were particularly favourable. Bismarck therefore put his long-matured scheme into effect. If this argument were sound it would certainly suggest that German imperialism derived directly from consideration of commercial needs in an era of protection. But in fact there is no evidence that Bismarck ever related his colonial enterprises to tariff questions, nor that he had formulated his policy before 1884. At most he may have felt that, in view of French, Belgian and other initiatives in Africa after 1880, doors were being closed to German trading freedom. As he said in 1889 he had earlier to ask himself:

... whether after twenty, after thirty years, people will charge that faint-hearted Chancellor back then with not having the courage to ensure for us a share of what later became such valuable property.[18]

Were there, then, more specific economic objectives? A second hypothesis is that Bismarck acted in 1884 as the tool of German bankers – finance capitalists – annexing colonies to provide fields of profitable speculation or investment.[19] Bismarck was a personal friend of the banker Adolf von Hansemann, whose brother-in-law, Heinrich von Kusserow, was the leading proponent of colonization in the German Foreign Office and advised Bismarck on African questions in 1884. Bismarck was also closely associated with Gustav Godeffroy, head of the Norddeutscher Bank; and in 1880 Bismarck had introduced an ill-fated bill into the Reichstag to save Godeffroy's bankrupt trading venture in the South Pacific from threatened acquisition by British interests. Other personal friends in high banking circles included von Bleichröder who, like Hansemann, invested in German chartered colonizing companies in and after 1884. The assumption, therefore, is that Bismarck was under pressure from these great capitalists and that he acted in 1884 to serve the interests of high finance. But again the evidence does not support this hypothesis, which is in any case inherently improbable in the light of Bismarck's position at this time and his relations with bankers and other financial interests. The bankers showed very little interest in colonial possibilities until after Bismarck had established his protectorates in West and South-West Africa. Von Hansemann in particular, despite his relationship with Kusserow, appears not to have known about the plan to annex Angra Pequena until after the protectorate was announced.[20] All the economic initiatives were taken by small entrepreneurs, such as Lüderitz in South-West Africa, or by Hamburg and Bremen trading companies, who did not propose to invest large sums in African trade. The big banks were drawn into colonization only after the protectorates had been established, when Bismarck was attempting to found chartered companies to undertake their administration. Even then most bankers subscribed to these companies only under pressure from Bismarck and did not take their investment seriously. As one banker ironically wrote to another in March 1885, these subscriptions were something 'which one could put into the savings bank of one's grandchildren'.[21] Four years later Bismarck answered complaints of inadequate official support for the colonies by saying that capitalists had failed to use opportunities offered. 'Granting money for colonial purposes' was done only as 'a favour to the government'; and in an article drafted but not published in the same year he again accused the capitalists of being excessively timid in their refusal to invest in the future prospects of the colonies without governmental guarantees.[22] In short, there is really no reason to believe that German colonization in 1884 was the product of pressure placed on Bismarck by German high finance.

But, even if explanations based on the economic policy of the state fall down, a more likely theory can be based on the individual economic problems of German traders and speculators in those regions of Africa and the South Pacific where protectorates were established in 1884–5. It can, in fact, be argued that Bismarck acted in 1884 in response to the problems and complaints of German traders for protection against the established colonial powers, notably Britain and France.[23] There can at least be no doubt about the importance of this trade or the difficulties commonly experienced by German traders overseas. German merchant houses, most of them based on Hamburg and Bremen, had built up substantial trades in West Africa, the Pacific and China, to mention only three regions involved in the politics of international imperialism. In West Africa the Hamburg firm of Woermann had established trade and steamship communications with Liberia, Gaboon and the Cameroons. Other German firms had interests in Togo and Lagos. In 1882 Hamburg alone sent ninety-six ships to West Africa and imported goods worth 8,588,000 marks (over £400,000)[24]. This was much less than the value of British or French trade on the coast, but it was a substantial stake. Like other nations, Germans in this area found their activities inconvenienced both by problems of relations with Africans and by the extension of British and French customs posts. After 1882 they were also afraid that the Anglo-Portuguese treaty on the Congo would put them at a disadvantage there. Germans were, moreover, in a worse position than Britain or France in dealing with these difficulties, for they had no local bases, no naval support and no consuls.

It is not, therefore, surprising that Hamburg's reaction to these concrete problems was to look for support from the Reich; but it is important to note that the merchants' proposed solution closely resembled that demanded by British traders in the same region and did not amount to a demand for German colonization. In March 1883 Adolf Woermann sent the German Foreign Office a memorandum asking for German naval support, a German base on Fernando Po if this could be bought from Spain, a full-time German consul in the area and rejection of the Anglo-Portuguese treaty on the Congo. In April von Kusserow also sent Bismarck a memorandum in which he alleged that the British and French were about to apply discriminatory duties against foreigners in areas under their control, though their own nationals would be mutually exempt from these. This was untrue; but as Bismarck did not know this he formally asked for the views of the Hanseatic ports. The Hamburg Chamber of Commerce, of which Woermann was Vice-President, suggested a 'trade colony' in the Cameroons, a naval station on Fernando Po, treaties with African chiefs giving Germans equal rights with other Europeans, and treaties with Britain and France to ensure that Germans could trade in their territories on an equal footing with others. Bremen merely asked for naval protection on the coast, and Lubeck did not reply. The Hamburg proposals constituted a reasonable basis for German action, but it is important to recognize that their demands stopped well short of extensive territorial acquisition. They wanted to preserve freedom of trade throughout the coast, not to found colonies in which Germans would have a monopoly. But they now recognized that under new conditions they must at least have adequate naval and consular support in dealing with Africans and with other Europeans and also a base to match Lagos. The merchants' policy was therefore far more limited than that adopted by Bismarck in 1884; yet in 1883 it was still too extensive for the Chancellor to accept. In December he announced that a naval vessel would be stationed permanently off the coast, that a special commissioner would be sent, that eventually a consul would negotiate treaties with Africans, and that he would ask Spain for the right to use a naval base in Fernando Po. But he was absolutely determined not to undertake territorial responsibilities in the Cameroons or elsewhere. Clearly, therefore, the decision to acquire protectorates in 1884 was not a direct response to mercantile pressures. Merchants had not asked for them and Bismarck had since rejected the request for a limited protectorate in the Cameroons. It is therefore necessary to look elsewhere for the origins of the system he adopted in 1884; and South-West Africa offers a possible explanation.

In South-West Africa there were already German Christian missions and German traders had a large share of the very limited trade in ivory and ostrich feathers; but the main port, Walvis Bay, was British, and the area as a whole was regarded as within the sphere of Cape Colony. But in November 1882 a Bremen merchant, F. A. E. Lüderitz, bought land from Africans south of Walvis Bay and in May 1883 acquired the harbour of Angra Pequena. This began a complicated process which led ultimately to German annexation of South-West Africa. Does it explain Bismarck's action of 1884? There can be no doubt that his views on Lüderitz changed considerably. In February 1883 Berlin informed the British Foreign

Office that, while it would give Lüderitz the normal protection provided to Germans overseas, it would not support him in any claim
to sovereignty in South-West Africa and hoped that Britain would
'extend her efficacious protection to the German settlers in those
regions'.[25] Thereafter, however, Bismarck gradually changed his
position. In September 1883 he asked London unofficially whether
Britain claimed sovereignty over Angra Pequena, and if so on what
grounds. His motive was probably not to clear the way for a
German protectorate but to see whether it was possible for Lüderitz to hold Angra Pequena without official German action, which
would only be necessary if Britain staked a prior claim. For various
reasons, but primarily because the Cape objected to admitting that
South-West Africa was open to foreign occupation, and because
the British Foreign Office failed to understand what Bismarck was
getting at, the negotiation gradually turned sour. In December
Bismarck asked formally for a British disclaimer that they had any
right to Angra Pequena; but he received no formal reply until
July 1884. During these six months it is possible that growing
irritation may have convinced him that if Britain was not prepared
to forgo dubious claims even to so unattractive a territory, sterner
measures were necessary to challenge an apparent British belief that
any unoccupied part of the world was reserved for their future
occupation. Finally, following complaints from Lüderitz that the
Cape was proposing to annex Angra Pequena, Bismarck decided
to act in South-West Africa. On 24 April he sent telegrams to the
German Ambassador in London and the Consul at Cape Town
informing both, though in obscure language, that Lüderitz' claims
'were under the protection of the Empire'.[26]

Was this the origin of Germany's protectorates not only in
South-West Africa but also in West Africa, East Africa and the
South Pacific? It may have been, though other developments early
in 1884 may have contributed to his irritation with Britain. British
refusal in January to agree to a mixed Anglo-German commission
to determine German land claims in Fiji; a false report in February
that the Gold Coast was about to annex Togo; signature of the
Anglo-Portuguese treaty on the Congo on 26 February. Peripheral
problems in other areas may also have been relevant. In March
1884 Karl Peters founded a commercial company to take up concessions to be acquired by treaty with Africans in East Africa.
Berlin gave him no support, but other Germans were negotiating
with the Sultan of Witu and knowledge that in due course the

problem caused by Lüderitz might be repeated in East Africa may have stimulated Bismarck to find a general solution. In the South Pacific also there were numerous German trading and plantation enterprises, and in New Guinea and Samoa particularly these had already caused serious political difficulties. It may be that the mere number and scale of these German commercial enterprises at last convinced Bismarck that political action was necessary to support German economic interests.

Yet two questions remain: why did Bismarck now overcome his very strong dislike of formal imperial responsibility for overseas colonies; and why did he act on so large a scale, rather than merely provide protection for Lüderitz in South-West Africa? The answer to the first is probably that on 8 April 1884 von Kusserow suggested that Lüderitz – and by extension other German entrepreneurs – could be given a charter to administer the territories he controlled on the lines of the charter given in 1881 to the British North Borneo Company. After some hesitation Bismarck seems to have seized on this as the best compromise. He refused to impose German sovereignty over Angra Pequena but offered protection (*Reichsschutz*) which would not involve the Empire in administrative responsibility or, above all, public expenditure. The concept of a protectorate administered by a chartered company thus seems to have provided Bismarck with a way to satisfy German needs on the periphery without infringing his own principles. But why simultaneously declare protectorates over three regions of West Africa – Togo, the Cameroons, and Koba Bagas (on the Rivers of the South in Guinea) – as the German Consul General at Tunis, Gustave Nachtigal, was ordered to do on 19 May, and also in New Guinea and New Britain? It may be that Bismarck was simply concerned to solve the economic difficulties of Germans in all these regions simultaneously, now that he had found a satisfactory formula for doing so. Yet at this point the political solution outlined above seems to provide a more satisfactory answer. The elections were pending. The colonial enthusiasts were demanding action, and the National Liberals would be delighted by creation of German protectorates on a large scale. It is therefore at least possible, though certainly not indisputable, that Bismarck acted on so large a scale, rather than merely over Angra Pequena, primarily because this would provide the best political return. This at least would explain why he allegedly stated in September that 'all this colonial business is a sham, but we need it for the elections',[27] and why so many contemporaries had the same impression.

Yet even if, in the last resort, German colonialism owed its birth to an election stunt, it was nevertheless conceived by genuine economic factors. Bismarck did not and would not have established protectorates in a void. In every one of the regions claimed in 1884 there were established German interests; and it has been seen that there were strong commercial grounds on which German traders and entrepreneurs in each of these places could reasonably call for political help. In this respect German intentions and techniques closely resembled those of Britain and the German protectorates in Togo and the Cameroons were almost identical in form and function with the British protectorate declared over the Niger Coast in 1885. It is significant also that the outcome of German action in West Africa was very different from that in South-West and East Africa and in the South Pacific. In each of the last three regions the German interests concerned wanted effective control of territory and chartered companies were therefore formed or authorized to take control of the new protectorates: the South-West Africa Company, established and chartered in 1885 to take over Lüderitz' concessions; the East Africa Company founded by Karl Peters in 1884 and chartered in 1885; and the New Guinea Company, chartered in 1885 as the successor to earlier colonizing ventures. But in West Africa there were no chartered companies. In Togo it proved impossible even to form a concessionary company to undertake economic development. The reason in each case is clear and important. Whereas in other areas German enterprise intended to undertake production and therefore required territorial control, in West Africa Germans were initially only interested in trade. Hamburg and Bremen, like Liverpool and London, wanted security for commerce and showed no interest in formal empire or economic development of the interior. Thus the logic of west coast economic history determined the character of German as well as British and French commercial enterprise on the coast.

How far, then, can the partition of West Africa be explained in economic terms? What light do these events throw on the attitudes of European business interests and statesmen? The evidence suggests that it is impossible to provide a single answer or formula applicable to France, Britain and Germany, nor one equally relevant to the coastal areas and their immense hinterlands. The French project in the Western Sudan stands apart as a unique phenomenon: neither the British or Germans conceived any comparably grandiose design in West Africa. Its objectives were undoubtedly economic – to establish an immense trading empire stretching from Algeria to St Louis and Lake Chad, based on a network of railways and navigable rivers. The important fact, however, is that the drive behind this project came not from French traders, railway companies or bankers, who showed remarkably little enthusiasm at any stage, but from colonial governors, soldiers and metropolitan officials. Thus the Saharan enterprise can best be seen as an example of that special brand of economic imperialism, characteristic of the 1870s and early 1880s, and found in France more than any other country, which stemmed from imaginative study of maps, newly drawn to take account of the work of the explorers, rather than from the pressure of genuine economic interests. Almost exactly the same phenomenon was at work in other 'vacant' regions of sub-Saharan Africa, notably in the Congo basin and in Central Africa. This, at least, was a novel element in the imperialism of the last quarter of the nineteenth century.

Territorial expansion on the coastal areas of West Africa stemmed from very different sources. Here the order of events is of primary importance. In the first place the motive for expanding territorial control along the coast or limited distances into the interior derived from the practical and humdrum problems of existing British and French colonies rather than from mercantile or official imperialism: the need for more customs duties, problems of jurisdiction and the need for security against African states. Territorial expansion to meet these needs began long before 1880 and followed largely predictable lines. Up to a point either power could extend its possessions without causing resentment by the other on the basis of recognized spheres of influence and plans for exchange of territories. The important fact is that, by the early 1880s, the point had been reached at which British and French coastal expansion could not continue indefinitely without encroaching on areas in which the other country had commercial interests or expectations. Moreover, the Germans and other European states which had no colonies in West Africa stood to lose by further extension of either British or French tariffs to previously independent trading zones. The problem was particularly acute to the east and west of Lagos, which were 'natural' regions for British expansion but where France and Germany had substantive trading interests. Similar difficulties were developing on the Guinea Coast and other places where the French were in the ascendant.

It was this situation which forced each European power to consider political action to preserve its commercial interests in the early 1880s. In the sphere of economics all feared that political control of these sections of the coast still outside formal European rule would exclude nationals of other states or put them at an economic disadvantage. There were only two possible answers: international agreement to neutralize these places or annexation by a single power, possibly on an undertaking not to exclude foreign traders or impose differential tariffs. What demand existed for either course among European business interests and governments? The significant fact is that almost all merchants of any nationality preferred the first alternative and that, while the French government was ready to consider annexation of coastal regions as part of the now accepted Sudanese policy, London and Berlin shared the view of the merchants and were most reluctant to undertake political responsibilities. Why, then, did both these governments claim protectorates in 1884–5? This is a crucial question for the general argument of this book. Excluding considerations relating exclusively to German domestic politics, the answer can only be that by the later months of 1884 the British and German governments were losing faith in the possibility of preserving the neutrality of these trading zones. Their pessimism was influenced by events in the Congo, where France and Leopold of Belgium seemed anxious to claim as much land as possible; and also by the initiatives of French and British firms on the Niger, which suggested that private enterprise was proposing to establish monopolistic trading spheres there. Bismarck acted first, in the summer of 1884, and the British had to choose between accepting exclusion from any region where the French and Germans might decide to claim and taking counter-action. As has been seen London decided to act, though in the most limited way possible, by imposing a skeletal protectorate on the Niger and the Oil Rivers.

Later developments in West Africa were largely the product of these two initiatives: the French thrust to the Niger, which eventually forced the British and Germans, if they wanted their coastal territories to have a commercial hinterland, to claim land in the rear, and the final occupation of the whole tidewater. It is not proposed to recapitulate these events. For the present study the steps taken by each of the powers before 1885 were the crucial ones; and the conclusions to be drawn are as follows. First, there was little positive demand in any European state in the early 1880s for extensive possessions in coastal West Africa. Traders and statesmen alike remained dubious of the possible advantages – economic, strategic and even diplomatic – of empire on the coast. Second, the main dynamic of change was the needs of existing colonies and bases. Third, the commercial interests were concerned about political control only because and to the extent that any European administration meant taxes and regulations and that foreign control might mean exclusion. Rather than lose their markets and access to raw materials merchants eventually accepted political control by their own governments. The result was the system of protectorates inaugurated in 1884–5.

These conclusions have a wider significance for analysis of the imperialism of European statesmen. After 1879 Paris was no longer seriously worried about extension of political responsibilities on the coast, provided these did not entail large expenditure or evoke strong British hostility. This in itself is important as a measure of the evolution of French imperialism. The Germans and British were less ready to drop established assumptions, holding to the view that public expenditure on territories which were of importance only to a few private merchants could not be justified in terms of the national interest. But by 1885 London and Berlin had clearly revised their views; and this must be taken as a significant turning point in official thought on the criteria on which state action in support of commerce should be based. Briefly, Bismarck and Salisbury alike reluctantly admitted that, provided the economic interests at stake could be regarded as of general importance to the nation – that is, offering trading opportunities for all rather than advantage to one or more particular concerns – and provided that no large fiscal costs were involved, the government was justified in establishing a protectorate in order to prevent closure of trading areas by a foreign power. When hedged around by so many qualifications this concession may not seem a convincing first step towards aggressive economic imperialism. Compared with the much larger conceptual stride taken by Chamberlain in the 1890s towards belief in the intrinsic advantages of political control as a basis for economic development it was small and cautious. But it was nevertheless a crucial change of position, the first reluctant retreat from the high plateau of mid-Victorian criteria for the proper use of state power towards ultimate acceptance of the general duty of government to provide a secure political base for the economic activities of its subjects overseas. This does not mean that either Britain or Germany was now prepared, as a general rule, to acquire overseas colonies to serve economic interests: merely that West Africa provided some of the first precedents for precautionary annexation to preserve commercial opportunities. From that point the descent was relatively easy.

II THE CONGO, ZAMBESIA AND SOUTH AFRICA, 1880–1900

No study of the influence of economic factors on European expansion in the late nineteenth century can ignore events in the Congo basin, in the vast region which became Bechuanaland, the Rhodesias and Nyasaland, and in South Africa. Historiographically they are important, for events in these places were the seed-bed of the theory of capitalist imperialism as it evolved in the 1890s and 1900s. To Engels, to English liberals such as Robertson and Hobson, and to European socialists such as Hilferding, Rosa Luxemburg and Lenin, one thing which suggested that the 'new imperialism' might be the product of advanced capitalism was that in these regions the engine of imperialism appeared to be the large joint-stock company. Whereas in other parts of Africa and other continents colonial expansion might be accounted for in traditional terms of the interests of traders and small settlers, the ambition of frontier administrators, soldiers and missionaries, or the strategic objectives of metropolitan governments, in Central and Equatorial Africa such explanations would not serve. The Congo and Zambesia were distinguished by the fact that the initial European occupation was the work of large capitalist organizations – Leopold II's Association Internationale du Congo and Rhodes' British South Africa Company (hereafter BSA). The subsequent growth of a multitude of inter-related investment companies to exploit these regions – Compagnie du Katanga, Comité Speciale du Kanataga, Union Minière, Tanganyika Concessions Ltd., Anglo-Belgian India-Rubber Company, the Benguela Railway Company, African Lakes Company and many others – seemed proof that in these regions at least finance capitalism had found excellent conditions for investment. Never in the history of European imperialism had so many speculative companies been spawned so rapidly to exploit such virtually unknown territories. It was little wonder that lay observers assumed that the whole movement into Equatorial and Central

Africa was a stock exchange gamble.[28] Equally events in South Africa, the Jameson Raid of December 1895, the Boer War of 1899–1902, seemed intimately related to the development of gold mining in the Transvaal in the late 1880s. On the Rand there were large alien joint stock mining companies which disliked controls imposed by the republican government which restricted their profits. Cape colonists and metropolitan Britons coveted this newly discovered El Dorado and regretted that in 1881 and 1884 the Transvaal had been allowed to slip from British control. Collusion between Rand capitalists, the BSA and the British government produced a war whose object was to incorporate the gold fields into the British Empire.

The general trend of these assumptions is that, whatever happened in other parts of the world, here at least imperialism in the period before 1914 was not only 'new' but specifically economic in character. Excluding the Congo, whose chief colonizer was head of state in Belgium, it also seems likely that in each case the policy of the metropolitan power was dictated by private economic interests – the BSA, creature of Cecil Rhodes, and the big Transvaal mining companies. If this can in fact be demonstrated it would constitute evidence that, provided an economic interest was sufficiently large, it could force a metropolitan government to obey its commands; and this in turn would have an important bearing on the central problem of the present study – the relationship between private economic interests and state policy. In the case of the Belgian Congo the problem has to be posed differently. Since Leopold was a king and because the success of his venture turned on approval by the states of Europe rather than by the Belgian government, the question must be why he thought territorial control was necessary to his economic purposes and why Germany, Britain, France and other powers were prepared to allow the Association Internationale du Congo (hereafter AIC), to establish a sovereign state covering a large part of the newly discovered and potentially very valuable heart of sub-Saharan Africa.

These problems are so important that no general interpretation of the role of economic factors in modern imperialism would be satisfactory which did not take them into account. On the other hand considerations of space make it impracticable to examine them at length in the present study. It is proposed, therefore, merely to indicate briefly how these three problems could be analysed in terms of the syllogism set out at the end of chapter 4.

Three questions must be asked. First, was the primary objective of the private interests concerned (Leopold, Rhodes, the Transvaal capitalists) financial gain? Second, why did they consider that formal control of territory was necessary to their economic objectives? Finally, why did the statesmen (the British government or the concert of powers) agree to put state authority at the disposal of these entrepreneurs? The answers to these questions should make it possible to decide whether or not imperialism in Equatorial and Southern Africa was an exception to the general assumption suggested by case studies of other parts of the world, that political action leading to formal colonial rule was normally taken either because the state considered that a national interest was directly involved or because the legitimate economic objectives of European nationals created political problems for which no specifically economic solution was adequate.

LEOPOLD II AND THE CONGO.[29] Leopold's activities in the Congo region were unique in the history of modern imperialism in one important respect: they were entirely directed at financial profit and cannot be explained in any other way. There were two obvious reasons why this was so. First, Leopold was operating not as King of Belgium but as a private individual. The Belgian government refused to support him at any stage and questions of national interest could not therefore intrude. But even if the statesmen had given formal support, the roots of colonization in the Congo necessarily differed from those of British or French colonization in Africa or elsewhere. Belgian colonies could not have grown from existing peripheral possessions, because Belgium had none, or from considerations of strategy, because Belgium was not a major power and had nothing to defend beyond her frontiers. Second, Leopold was one of the very few statesmen of the middle and late nineteenth century who unquestioningly believed that economic enterprise in undeveloped countries overseas was more profitable than investment at home. His ideas were developed long before he became King or began the Congo enterprise and were based on academic study of earlier colonial systems in America and of contemporary British and Dutch activities in India and Java.[30] In one respect he was an unreconstructed mercantilist who ignored contemporary trends of opinion towards free trade; in another a precursor of the neo-mercantilism of the later nineteenth and twentieth century. His views on colonization resembled those publicized by Leroy-Beaulieu in and after 1874, but with the difference that whereas Leroy-Beaulieu believed in free trade Leopold believed in commercial monopoly. Even before the 1870s he had made repeated attempts to put theory into practice by acquiring estates overseas, notably an island in the Spanish Philippines, but all came to nothing. The exploration of Equatorial Africa in the 1870s suggested that he might find a suitable field for a commercial colony there; and the Congo enterprise can best be seen as an attempt by a wealthy European entrepreneur to apply long-matured theories about the profitability of colonial ventures to this newly available field for European investment.

Leopold can, therefore, reasonably be regarded as the conceptual economic imperialist of the later nineteenth century whose acquisitive instincts were uncomplicated by humanitarianism, the pressure of domestic public opinion or diplomatic and strategic considerations. He had to operate as a private individual because no Belgian government would take responsibility for his actions overseas and he was therefore in virtually the same position as any private capitalist who proposed to speculate on the profitability of undeveloped property in tropical Africa. It is this characteristic which makes the history of the founding of the Congo Free State so important. Two main questions must be considered. First, does the fact that Leopold established a vast territorial state in Equatorial Africa suggest that political control was necessary for the economic exploitation of tropical countries in this period, contrary to the general trend of the evidence on the attitudes of business and finance in other countries? Second, why did the great powers allow Leopold to establish so vast a political state in this part of Africa?[31]

On the first and more important question the vital fact is that initially Leopold did not think that political control of tropical territory was necessary for economic profit. On the contrary, he shared the opinion of most European financial interests that politics were irrelevant to investment and that the profitability of a commercial enterprise might be endangered if it had to pay for administration. Until late in 1882 he therefore proposed to establish a purely commercial and investment company and chose the Congo basin because it was 'vacant' and seemed a suitable region for trade in indigenous commodities and for plantation production on the Javanese model. His projected company was to be financed by private subscription by capitalists in any country and would establish 'stations', 'agencies' and 'establishments' for trade and production. It would also build a railway to by-pass the Congo rapids and would operate a fleet of river steamers. All this was on the assumption that Equatorial Africa remained politically independent and that Leopold's company would operate as a purely commercial concern.

The facts of economic and political life, however, forced Leopold step by step to modify his plans until by 1884 he found it necessary to claim a vast territorial possession in Equatorial Africa. The first step was dictated by economic considerations. To float the company Leopold had to provide cynical capitalists with evidence that there was something to exploit. Having in 1876 founded the Association Internationale Africaine (hereafter AIA) as a philanthropic and scientific society for opening up darkest Africa and, at the same time, to pay for exploration of the Congo region, he established the Comité d'Etudes du Haut-Congo in 1879 as a private company to investigate the commercial possibilities of the area. Stanley was sent out in 1880 to make commercial agreements with African chiefs and it is important that these agreements specified only economic rights. Thus at Vivi he obtained a promise that the Comité would have the 'sole and exclusive right' to trade, cultivate, build communications, etc. There was no mention of political control. Leopold merely wanted to state in the prospectus for his proposed company that it had acquired a monopoly of economic opportunities in defined regions of the western Congo, together with the right to exploit land for mining, cultivations, etc. It was as though he was buying private estates in Latin America.

By the end of 1881 the time seemed almost ripe to launch the development company of his dreams, for Stanley had made agreements covering much of the southern bank of the Congo from Vivi to Stanley Pool. Leopold proposed to co-operate with the Rotterdam firm of Afrikaansche Handelsvereeniging, which had commercial contacts at the mouth of the Congo and had contributed heavily to the now defunct Comité. But from this point it became apparent that a purely commercial enterprise in the Congo was impossible and Leopold began to move towards territorial possession. Why was this? Was it because he decided that political control was after all essential for economic exploitation, or because his economic objectives were blocked by political obstacles?

The answer is that by this time political problems had arisen. By 1882 France was claiming political control of the northern bank of the Congo by virtue of treaties made by de Brazza, the most important being the Makoko treaty which would give France a protectorate on the site of the later Brazzaville, opposite Stanley's site for Leopoldville. France did not ratify this treaty until November 1882, but Leopold had to assume that it might be ratified and adjust his aims accordingly. If France chose to claim political control of the Congo by virtue of treaties made with Africans and imposed conventional French economic restrictions, Leopold's commercial aspirations were doomed. His only defence was to acquire countervailing political rights. From December 1881 Stanley was therefore told that treaties with Africans should in future give the Comité (whose name was still used though the body was defunct) 'suzerainty' and that all existing commercial treaties must be remodelled to include this provision. The first such treaty was not made until August 1882, and by October Leopold saw that even 'suzerainty' would not be enough if France ratified the Makoko treaty. Stanley was therefore told to negotiate the treaties yet again to include the word 'sovereignty'. Since the chiefs had no idea what this meant there was no difficulty. The effect was that by 1884 Leopold could claim that the new AIC, established in 1882 to succeed the Comité, had 'sovereignty' over its intended sphere of commercial activity.

Leopold, therefore, claimed territorial possessions on the Congo because experience showed that if he operated in a political vacuum other European powers would assert political claims to his projected field of economic action. The motives of these powers, particularly France, are not of immediate consequence here; but in brief French action resulted partly from legitimate fear that a monopolistic trading company on the Congo would destroy whatever prospects their poverty-stricken protectorate in Gaboon might have, partly from popular enthusiasm aroused by Brazza's heroic expeditions. But if France had held back others would almost certainly have objected to Leopold's claim on the grounds of commercial monopoly. The British, with the largest established trade on the Congo, were already concerned and the Portuguese, with archaic claims to the area, were outraged. Other interested states might have protested. Monopoly was essential to a nascent economic enterprise in tropical Africa when a private company had to bear all the overheads, but monopoly was not acceptable to European political and business interests who believed in the 'open door'. The answer was to acquire territorial sovereignty as a cover for commercial monopoly; and from 1884 until his death Leopold became one of the most voracious territorial imperialists of his time. The vast size of the Congo Free State was evidence of his success.

The second question, however, remains. How could Leopold, whose commercial plans were arousing hostility from European states, obtain general acceptance of his sovereignty over the greater part of the Congo basin? A full answer would require detailed analysis of international diplomacy during the twenty years after 1884; but in brief this general acceptance of the Congo Free State can be explained on three counts. First, particularly in 1884–5, when the AIC was recognized as ruler of the Congo Free State, Leopold very cleverly played down its true character and convinced many people that his aim was that of the original AIA, to bring civilization to Equatorial Africa. To many in Britain, France, Germany and the United States (the first power to recognize the sovereignty of the Free State) the AIC therefore appeared to be a benevolent and, above all, neutral agency for opening up Africa. Second, Leopold pretended that the Free State would preserve the 'open door' to all, even committing himself to the promise that there would be no customs. For many British free-traders, who disapproved of their own government's treaty of February 1884, which would have given the mouth of the Congo to Portugal – notoriously the most protectionist state in Europe – this was sufficient ground for approval. Together these two concepts convinced the major states that it would be convenient and harmless to recognize the Congo Free State and to give it a territory stretching from the Atlantic to Lake Tanganyika. As Bismarck said to the French Ambassador in Berlin in August 1884:

I do not know just what this Belgian Association is, nor what will become of it, but all the same it would not succeed in establishing itself very seriously, and it is always useful for diverting troublesome rivalries and claims that we could handle less easily ourselves. We can give it our backing to clear the way.[32]

Sustained until the beginning of the rubber scandal in the later 1890s this attitude made it possible for Leopold to broaden his territories year by year because he provided a neutral alternative to annexation by some major power.

These considerations explain why Germany recognized the Congo Free State and why Britain and other countries followed suit. But they do not account for French recognition of the Free State in February 1885; nor, looking ahead, do they explain strong British opposition to the extension of the Free State to the Nile in 1897–8. In each case the explanation is that Leopold committed himself in April 1884 to giving France first option (even, unintentionally, over Belgium) to purchase the Free State if ever the AIC should go into liquidation. He was forced to do this because otherwise France would have blocked his plans in order to preserve her interests in the hinterland of Gaboon; and he hoped also to use the French right of preemption to force Portugal, if she succeeded in getting control of the Congo mouth, to give the Free State unrestricted commercial access to the Atlantic by threatening otherwise to sell out to France. Thereafter the French had no objection to Leopold's plans for they believed the AIC would infallibly fail and that its possessions would then revert to France. The Free State was thus a convenient way of pegging out claims for future French control of Equatorial Africa which were diplomatically unacceptable in the 1880s.

But the same fact eventually set limits to Leopold's territorial possessions. The British could not block the Free State and had relatively little fear of the results of French control of Equatorial Africa if this reversion came into effect. But by the 1890s, as will be seen below, a French presence near the Nile was strategically unacceptable. Britain was prepared to give Leopold the Lado enclave in 1894, primarily to block a possible route from the French Sudan to the Nile. But in 1898, when Leopold wanted to send a force to the Upper Nile to fulfil one of his great ambitions and acquire an eastern access to the Congo, London warned him off. However slight the possibility that the AIC would go into liquidation, the British could not afford the risk that France might fall heir to Leopold's dominion on the Nile.

The history of Leopold's founding of the Congo Free State has therefore considerable significance for a study of the relations between economic and political factors in late nineteenth-century imperialism. Political control of tropical territory was not intrinsically necessary for extracting maximum economic advantage and Leopold did not initially want it. Thirty years earlier he might have been able to establish a commercial enterprise in Equatorial Africa without taking administrative responsibility; though the British would almost certainly have objected had he attempted to monopolize the region. Monopoly was, in fact, the key to what happened in the 1880s. Without it Leopold's project would have been meaningless for under free trade conditions it would not have been profitable to provide the expensive infrastructure necessary to develop the Congo. The Niger Company felt exactly the same. Twenty years later he might very well have been content to take up a large territorial concession of the sort available to private companies in the French Congo or, for that matter, in the Congo Free State, which would have given him many of the advantages he wanted without political responsibilities. But in the early 1880s this option was not open. At that time his venture had to be established in politically neutral territory and it could only be protected against French and Portuguese encroachment by establishing a state.

Does this, then, imply that political control was necessary for successful economic enterprise in the tropics under the conditions of the 1880s? The answer must be specific both to the still independent regions of Africa and to the type of enterprise Leopold had in mind, and, with this limitation, it must be concluded that it was. The reasons were, however, political not economic. Leopold needed protection against rival claimants to his field of activity for by 1884 he had nothing but paper treaties with African rulers to show for his efforts. No European state would accept these as conveying ownership unless they were recognized by the concert of powers; and the conventional basis for conceding recognition was that a claim to political sovereignty could be made good. Since he could not call on a major European power to provide this political umbrella Leopold had to provide his own, by formalizing his treaties with African chiefs into a notional sovereign state. Thus, in relation to the partition of sub-Saharan Africa as a whole, the importance of the Congo Free State is that it demonstrated the fundamental problem which resulted from the total absence of recognized European or indigenous political entities in the newly explored regions of the continent. Because there were no recognized 'civilized' states comparable with those of Islamic North Africa the heart of Africa was, by the criteria of European law, open to occupation. Because a free-for-all competition for land and mineral rights between private colonizers of all races would have produced legal and social chaos, it was seen to be necessary to establish principles by which claims could be assessed. The Berlin Conference adopted the principle of 'effective occupation' – in principle only for the tidewater but by general convention also for continental regions. Because the great powers were not in practice prepared to allow individual adventurers to establish private fiefs on the basis of treaties with African chiefs, they arrogated the right to allocate provisional spheres of influence to each other. Under such circumstances Leopold could only salvage something from his earlier commercial projects by posing as head of a sovereign African state; and he was allowed to do so because it was convenient for the powers to recognize his claims.

CECIL RHODES AND CENTRAL AFRICA.[33] The fact that in 1889 the British government gave Cecil Rhodes a royal charter to occupy and govern those areas of Zambesia which eventually became Southern and Northern Rhodesia raises important questions concerning the influence exerted by large-scale capital on European statesmen. At first sight it might appear, as it did to many at the time, that a self-made millionaire had cajoled, browbeaten or even bribed the British government of the day into giving him full authority to exploit the hoped-for mineral resources of that area, irrespective of the interests and wishes of the two main African groups concerned, the Matabele and Mashona. If this is a correct interpretation it would certainly constitute strong support for Hobson's interpretation of the characteristic relationship between government and capitalism in the age of imperialism. It is impossible in a short note to deal adequately with so large a problem and it is proposed to concentrate on two central questions: the extent to which Rhodes' aims in Central Africa were economic and the reasons for the British government's decision to give him a charter in 1889.

Rhodes' character and achievement constitute a warning that the pure economic man conjured up by those who have explained late nineteenth-century imperialism in terms of the operation of blind economic forces is largely imaginary. By the mid-1880s, when Rhodes first concentrated on the problem of Zambesia, he was already the richest man in South Africa. He had made a first fortune by acquiring the monopoly of diamond production at Kimberley, using tactics analogous to those adopted by the great American finance-capitalists of the same period. De Beers Consolidated Mines, the company which emerged from the 'amalgamation' of the smaller mining companies, was a great capitalist concern of the type described by Lenin in which banks such as Rothschilds had a major interest. Consolidated Gold Fields of South Africa which emerged from Rhodes' equally successful attempt to make a second fortune from the Rand gold discoveries after 1886 was another vast concern which demonstrated Rhodes' supreme ability to make money. In the late 1880s the two companies – though not Rhodes' personal share in them – had a market value of perhaps £20 million.[34] It was therefore natural for critics of Rhodes' policies in Central Africa to assume that his objective was to make a third fortune. The BSA began as a mining concession which Rhodes' agent, Charles Rudd, extracted from Lobenguela, King of the Matabele. The company was floated in 1889 with a nominal capital of £1 million in £1 shares, of which Rhodes and his fellow promoters held 90,000 and De Beers Consolidated 200,000. Surely this was merely another money-making project, or possibly a stock exchange gamble; and in giving the company a royal charter the British government was allowing the political authority of the metropolis to be prostituted for private profit.

However probable, this view of Rhodes and the BSA is substantially misleading. Like many very rich men Rhodes distinguished clearly between activities primarily intended to make money and those which had other purposes. He had made his money at Kimberley and in Johannesburg. He might make more in Zambesia. But this was not his primary purpose. Indeed, he had for long seen his financial success in diamonds and gold as a means to an end – the extension of British power and civilization into Central Africa which he regarded as synonymous with the expansion of the Cape of Good Hope to fill this political void. His motives were essentially romantic. He believed implicitly in the superior virtues of the British race and its imperial mission. At the same time he had a vision of the future greatness of Cape Colony, his adopted country. In the first instance he wanted to establish British colonies under Cape control in Bechuanaland and Zambesia. Ultimately he hoped to create a British dominion that stretched from South Africa to Egypt – the Cape to Cairo concept. Such a vision of empire could only have been seen on the frontiers; and, since almost no one else in Britain or South Africa shared it, Rhodes had to attempt to realize it himself. From 1885 this was his life work and everything else was a means to that end.

In the mid-1880s, however, the end seemed unobtainable. First it appeared that the Transvaal would block the route to the north by annexing two small autonomous Boer settlements, Stellaland and Goshen, in Bechuanaland. This was prevented in 1884 by the

British government under pressure from an improbable alliance of interests which included Rhodes, Sir Hercules Robinson (British Governor and High Commissioner at the Cape) the Aborigines Protection Society and British missionaries. By that time, however, there was an additional danger that the Germans, who had established a protectorate over South-West Africa in 1884, would expand their still undefined territories eastwards to Lake Tanganyika, absorbing Zambesia. This too was blocked by the declaration of a British protectorate in Bechuanaland in 1884–5. But Zambesia remained vulnerable to German penetration from East Africa and also to Portuguese thrusts from Mozambique. To most in Britain and South Africa this seemed of little consequence. There was virtually no trade and no established mineral resources in Zambesia or the Nyasa district. Cape Colony politicians were far more concerned about economic relations with the Transvaal; and London, while reluctant to see foreign control of areas in which there were British missions and which were inconveniently near to British South Africa, was not prepared to take positive preventive action.

The character and functions of the BSA must be seen in relation both to this situation and to Rhodes' general belief in the vital importance of preserving Central Africa for British occupation. He had to found a joint-stock company both to raise funds and to obtain British official support; and to attract investors he had to salt the mine. Hence the Judd concession in Matabeleland which constituted the only asset in Zambesia Rhodes could offer the investor. Indeed, in most respects both the concession and the company were a sham. It was quite unpredictable whether there were exploitable minerals in Zambesia and Rhodes must have known that it was unlikely that a company which committed itself to build a railway through Bechuanaland to a district with no established trade and would then have to conquer the Matabele and Mashona before land settlement was possible, could hope to make short-term profits. In fact the BSA distributed no dividend before 1923, thirty-four years after its creation. Moreover the head office of the company in London was a mere façade. The glittering board of directors, who included the Duke of Abercorn, the Duke of Fife (son-in-law of the Prince of Wales) and Lord Grey, was only a concession to the principle that honest companies must have aristocratic directors: Salisbury made this clear when negotiating with Rhodes early in 1889. The board had virtually no control over the company, which was run by Rhodes from South Africa.

On the other hand there was nothing shady about the flotation of the company on the London stock exchange. The majority of the shares available were bought by small investors in South Africa and Britain who were enthused by the company's objectives and who presumably hoped for speculative profits if it was successful. Conversely, the big banks showed little interest: the BSA bore little resemblance to the great trusts described by Hilferding and Lenin and was more like contemporary organizations such as the African Lakes Company and the Imperial British East Africa Company which were largely capitalized by wealthy philanthropists.

The BSA cannot, therefore, usefully be regarded as a product of European finance capitalism. But equally the British government may not have been aware of its essentially non-commercial character. Why, then, did it grant Rhodes a royal charter in October 1889? Was this because Salisbury and his colleagues in the Conservative government were convinced of the economic or perhaps the strategic importance of Zambesia to Britain? Alternatively, were they forced into compliance by pressures applied by Rhodes and his allies, perhaps through a corrupted public opinion or by underhand political manipulation?

It is clear, in the first place, that the government was never convinced that Zambesia or the Nyasa region was worth acquiring because they were economically important to Britain. By the standard economic tests the region failed to qualify as a national interest. There was no established trade, no proven minerals, no outstanding loans to an indigenous government, no prospect of capital investment by British financiers. The fact also that there was no pressure from any important British industrial, commercial or banking interest to acquire this region suggested that there was no economic case for annexation or even a sphere of interest. Conversely the indications were that, if made a protectorate under Crown administration, Zambesia would be a drain on British public revenue as Bechuanaland already was. Nor was there any conceivable strategic interest at stake. Central Africa was remote from British naval bases, sea lanes and colonies. On no conventional estate of the national interest of the metropolis could annexation of Zambesia be justified.

Was the government therefore forced to act by pressures applied by Rhodes through the medium of popular feeling, itself corrupted by an imperialist press, or through organized interest groups? There is no evidence for thinking so. No campaign was mounted for Zambesia in 1888-9 comparable with that organized to save Uganda in 1892-3 which is described in the following section of this chapter. On the contrary, once Rhodes' intentions were known, hostile pressures were applied by most organized groups with any interest in Zambesia: in particular by the Aborigines Protection Society, the South African Committee and the missionary societies, all of whom reasonably assumed that to hand over Zambesia to a mineral-exploiting company would be disastrous for indigenous Africans. Since exponents of this view included Joseph Chamberlain, Labouchère and Fowell-Buxton they carried weight. Economic interest groups and the press were divided, but on balance probably against Rhodes. The London Chamber of Commerce and the *Economist* openly opposed him, though *The Times* and the *Pall Mall Gazette* came out in his favour. With influential opinion so obviously divided the government was at least under no insuperable pressure to act and its safest and predictable line was to do nothing. Why, then, did Rhodes get his charter?

The short answer is that the government was bribed, not by money but by Rhodes' offer to solve all outstanding problems facing the British government in Central Africa at the sole expense of his company. These problems can be listed briefly. First, Salisbury wanted, if possible, to protect Zambesia from the Germans, Transvaalers and Portuguese, not for metropolitan purposes but because he knew that a substantial body of opinion in the Cape believed that this area was important to the future economic and political development of British South Africa. Equally he was anxious to please Cape colonists in order to prevent the Afrikaner Bond, which represented nascent Boer nationalism in the Cape, from forming a close alliance with the republican Transvaal because this might ultimately lead to the loss of British influence in South Africa. Bechuanaland had been taken for this reason and in July 1888 Kruger was told that the British also regarded Matabeleland as a British sphere of influence. Yet this provided no defence against the Germans and Portuguese, both of whom were known to have designs there. The need was for effective occupation; but this in turn required money which the British Treasury could not provide and which Parliament would almost certainly refuse to vote. Thus the main and perhaps only attraction of Rhodes' company for the official mind was that, like the Royal Niger Company and the Imperial British East Africa Company, it offered to establish a British presence in an area which it was desirable to preserve from

N

foreign rivals at no cost whatever to the British taxpayer. This was the primary reason why the charter was given.

But there were ancillary reasons. First, Bechuanaland urgently needed a railway if it was ever to become economically viable and able to do without the British grant in aid. The Cape government wanted to build a railway to the north through the Transvaal as being a more profitable route; but Rhodes offered to build a railway from Kimberley through Bechuanaland to Zambesia at his own expense. This was a strong attraction for the government. Second, Salisbury had a marginal desire to protect the Lake Nyasa area from the Portuguese in the interest of the three Scottish Presbyterian missions established there which feared exclusion by the Portuguese authorities. Rhodes therefore offered to include Lake Nyasa in his proposed sphere of operations or to subsidize a British protectorate administration there. Salisbury did not want the former because the missionaries and the African Lakes Company did not want to be taken over by Rhodes. But Rhodes' money enabled him to support a skeletal administration there until an imperial grant in aid was obtained in 1894. Finally Rhodes was able, by personal persuasion, to convince many in high positions that his purposes were honourable. He appears to have won over Chamberlain, Lord Grey, Lord Knutsford (the Colonial Secretary) and others; and he is alleged to have bribed Parnell and the Irish nationalists by making a contribution to their funds. By the autumn of 1889 he could begin to appear as a high-minded patriot rather than as a shady company promoter and this made the eventual grant of the charter a relatively non-controversial step.

Thus the explanation of Rhodes' success is that his speculative venture in Zambesia happened to solve a number of outstanding problems in Central Africa for which British statesmen could see no alternative solution. Equally the government was able to give Rhodes his way because there were no serious diplomatic obstacles – the German and Portuguese agreements of 1890 and 1891 cleared these away – and because British opinion was essentially neutral. The real losers were the African peoples of Zambesia who were sacrificed to the overriding need to please Cape colonists and to relieve the British taxpayer of the burden of administering Bechuanaland and Central Africa.

THE BOER WAR.[35] The origins of the Boer War of 1899 to 1902 are too complex even to be outlined in a brief note. It is proposed only to summarize the standard arguments used to demonstrate that the British decided to annex the Transvaal for economic reasons and to assess their validity in the light of recent research on the motives of British statesmen.

From the 1890s critics of British policy in South Africa alleged that the government's hostile attitude to the Transvaal was dictated primarily by economic interests, particularly the gold-mining companies and stock market speculators: Sir William Harcourt used the memorable phrase 'stock-jobbing imperialism'. For purposes of analysis it will be convenient to consider three distinct economic interests which a Marxist historian of European imperialism in Africa, Endre Sik, has defined as the grounds for British action: desire to maximize profits from the Rand goldfields; declining receipts on railways from the Cape to the Transvaal; and declining customs receipts at the Cape due to decreasing transit trade to the north.[36]

Sik has summarized the grounds for regarding the Boer War as a takeover bid for the gold of the Rand as follows:

The existence of the independent Boer republics and their endeavour to curb the insatiable appetite of British finance capital and to ensure themselves the greatest possible share of the profits from the gold business [by state monopolies and taxes] threatened to undermine the monopolistic position of rapacious British finance capital in South Africa. Thus it became a concern of immediate urgency for British imperialism to occupy the Boer republics. . . .[37]

This allegation is based on two assumptions: that the investment in the Rand goldfields was very large, and that the capitalist companies concerned wanted British rule. The first is certainly correct. In 1895 total capital invested in the Witwatersrand gold mining industry, at par value of shares, was £41·9 million plus cash and premiums worth £17·3 million. In 1900 the totals were £77·4 million and £37 million respectively. The annual distribution of dividends rose, with fluctuations, from £2·1 million in 1895 to £4·7 million in 1898.[38] This was an immense industrial complex and in 1897 was producing about 24 per cent of the world's gold supply.[39] South African gold-mining was probably the largest single capitalist development which occurred outside Europe and North America during the last two decades of the nineteenth century. Any serious threat to its prosperity would certainly have immense political repercussions.

But was there any serious threat in the 1890s; and if so, did the mine owners automatically demand British political intervention? The mines certainly had complaints against the Transvaal government. They objected to the system of state monopolies which increased costs of essential mining equipment – above all the notorious dynamite monopoly which was sold originally to a German, E. A. Lippert, and then transferred to Nobels. During the five years after 1894 Nobels and another firm which received an additional monopoly made a profit of about 100 per cent on dynamite, or about £2 a case, though the state received only about 25p of this.[40] Monopolies and other taxes on their profits, including official corruption and artificially high railway rates on the politically motivated railway to Delagoa Bay, undoubtedly irritated the mining companies and made them demand change.

But change did not necessarily imply foreign intervention, still less annexation by Britain. Many mining firms operated on German or French capital and their directors were by no means all British subjects. But whatever their origins, many firms, including A. Goerz and G. Albu, J. B. Robinson, Samuel Marks and Barney Barnato, consistently opposed British intervention at all times. As Sir Hercules Robinson wrote to Chamberlain before the Jameson Raid, neither mine owners nor Uitlanders in general wanted to see the Transvaal in the British Empire. 'They dislike the native policy of England – they dislike the meddling of the House of Commons and of the philanthropic societies. . . .'[41] What they wanted was a reformed Transvaal under their own control; and many feared that a rising organized by Rhodes would lead instead to control by Cape Town or London. After the raid the same situation continued. Despite their grievances most mine owners were confident that they could eventually come to satisfactory terms with Kruger and several major companies withdrew from the Chamber of Mines in 1896 because they disapproved of Rhodes' action. In 1898 Rhodes' own company, Consolidated Goldfields, was prepared to lend the Transvaal government £2 million but was stopped by the British government which, for reasons to be considered below, made it known to the big finance houses that it did not want them to lend money to Kruger for the purchase of armaments. In 1899 the mining companies seemed about to reach a satisfactory agreement with the government on a wide range of grievances: Werner, Beit & Co. were the only important firm to stand out. The negotiations were broken up by the British Colonial Office because, as Chamberlain put it to Lord Harris, Chairman of Consolidated Goldfields, 'public opinion would probably say that the financiers had sold their cause and their compatriots – and sold them cheap'.[42]

It is in fact clear that the big mining companies on the Rand did not at any stage unanimously or even predominately agree that British rule was desirable; and those that did so were acting as agents of Rhodes or under British political pressures. As in many other parts of the undeveloped world large-scale finance felt no need for formal political control or protection by a metropolitan government because it was confident that it would eventually secure satisfactory operating conditions by its own efforts. Moreover, it was thought that the imperial factor would have serious disadvantages which outweighed the relatively minor inconvenience of dealing with the Transvaal government. It is therefore impossible to sustain the view that the British annexed the Transvaal to please the gold-mining industry or international finance capital. On the contrary, those British statesmen who were most keen to see the Transvaal reincorporated into British South Africa, bewailed the fact that, in Lord Selborne's words, the mining magnates were 'so worthless and contemptible'.[43]

Less need be said of the other two alleged economic grounds for British annexation, railways and customs, which were closely related and can be considered together. The financial problem was real enough. Until the 1890s the only effective means of communication between the Transvaal and the outside world was the Cape railway system. In 1885 the Cape Parliament refused to extend the railway from Kimberley to Pretoria because the limited traffic would make it unprofitable. They later changed their minds when the gold boom provided ample freight, but by that time it was too late. Kruger had decided to co-operate with a company building a line from Lourenço Marques in Delagoa Bay and in 1894 this line reached Pretoria. Even before then the new railway had begun to shift the axis of Transvaal trade from the Cape. The Transvaal refused to form a customs union with the Cape and made one with Natal, which provided the third possible railway route to the coast, giving Natal railways a third of Transvaal freight. Since the Delagoa line was promised another third this left only some 33 per cent for Cape railways which had been accustomed to carrying some 80 per cent of Transvaal traffic. This was very serious, for by 1895 the Cape had invested £20·5 million in its railways out of a total public debt of £27·5 million and railway revenue at £3·4 million was almost exactly half total public revenues of £6·8 million.[44] Permanent loss of expanding Transvaal freight would be a serious blow to the Cape railways which had gambled heavily in extending their system to the Transvaal to take advantage of the gold boom. Equally, re-routing of Transvaal imports would significantly reduce the yield of Cape colony customs duties.

But was this a possible ground for Cape demands for political annexation of the Transvaal? Had the Cape railways been privately owned and run one might have expected the companies concerned to show imperialistic tendencies. But they were not. All Cape railways were publicly owned and operated. If they operated at a loss or revenues declined this would be a burden on public not private resources. If anyone was likely to demand British political action it would be the electors and ministers. But the politicians never did so. The Jameson Raid led directly to Rhodes' fall from office as Prime Minister and the two succeeding governments under Sir John Sprigg (1896–8) and the Bond leader, W. P. Schreiner (1898–1900), had no desire whatever for offensive action against the Transvaal. They negotiated hard on railway freights and customs, but had no desire to resort to military or political action when these negotiations failed. Indeed, Cape political opinion swung strongly against Rhodes and Britain after the raid and the Afrikaner Bond was either neutral or in support of the Transvaal. Although the government did not, as Kruger had hoped, support the Transvaal during the war it remained firmly neutral, refusing to accept that Britain was fighting on behalf of Cape interests. It is therefore impossible to treat the loss of railway and customs revenues as a significant cause of war with the Transvaal.

What, then, were the causes? Had these economic factors no significance? They had; but, as in so many other cases studied in the present book, the links between economic factors and imperialist action were devious. Once again the essential fact is that economic change had political implications which ultimately generated imperialist policies.[45] For the British the growth of the gold industry on the Rand, coupled with the success of the Transvaal in establishing its railway link with Delagoa Bay, implied a radical shift in the balance of political power in South Africa. From being an inconvenient but weak land-bound republic which, after 1884, was geographically contained by British control of Bechuanaland and Zambesia and was cut off from the sea by Portuguese territory which Britain hoped eventually to control, the Transvaal was now prospectively the richest and most powerful unit in southern Africa.

By the 1890s, moreover, the Germans were showing a tendency to support it against Britain and thus acquire a dangerous political lever in an area of accepted British preponderance. The British response, particularly after the formation of the Salisbury government in 1895, with Chamberlain as Colonial Secretary, was to oppose the rise of the Transvaal by every available means. They had no desire to occupy it on account of the gold mines or other economic interests, but they feared that in the end the Cape and Natal would become economic, and therefore political, satellites of the Transvaal and that British power in southern Africa would then be at risk. Lord Kimberley, Foreign Secretary in Lord Rosebery's administration, spelt out the basic assumptions of Colonial and Foreign Office policy in 1894:

> The maintenance of the Cape Colony was perhaps the most vital interest of Great Britain because by the possession of it communications with India was assured, which otherwise might be cut off any day. Cape Colony was of even greater importance to England than Malta or Gibraltar, and it was this that the German cabinet would not understand – that the English government are compelled to support the interests of Cape Colony because they do not want to lose it.[46]

But how could Cape supremacy and safety be preserved and the threatening rise of the republican Transvaal be contained? The British government tried one device after another without success. In 1894 it supported Rhodes' attempt to buy Delagoa Bay from Portugal, in the hope that this would enable Britain to control the new railway. The next hope was that Rhodes, who more than any other leading Cape politician feared the rise of the Transvaal, could engineer a rising of Uitlanders in Johannesburg which in turn might lead to political predominance by the British-speaking immigrants and so to a pro-British government. Chamberlain approved the project in general, though he did not know that the raid was actually to take place when it did. When it failed and Rhodes fell from office in Cape Town, British policy seemed to have lost its last resource. Cape opinion was now increasingly favourable to the Transvaal and the Cape government could no longer be used as an agent of imperial policy. Britain would have to take the initiative herself.

But this still did not necessarily mean war or formal annexation. In 1897–8 the majority of the British cabinet thought Chamberlain took too extreme a view of the situation and were more concerned in any case about the Sudan and China. The policy adopted after the raid was therefore to promote the Uitlander demand for reform of the franchise on the assumption that if once these predominately British immigrants could obtain political control, the Transvaal would cease to be a threat to British supremacy in South Africa. The role of the metropolis was to isolate the Transvaal from foreign support and to ensure that a minority of Uitlanders, particularly the mine owners, did not sell the pass by coming to terms with Kruger. The first objective was easily achieved. In 1898 German support for the Transvaal was bought off by a public agreement whereby Britain and Germany would make equal loans to Portugal if she approached either for financial help and by a secret agreement which allocated the southern half of Portuguese East Africa, including Delagoa Bay, together with part of Angola, to Britain if a bankrupt Portugal was ever forced to give up her colonies, while Germany was to have North Mozambique and Central Angola. Above all Germany promised not to interfere in South Africa and to oppose intervention by any third power. This ended the threat of German support for Kruger's régime which had seemed acute at the time of the Kaiser's telegram of January 1896 after the raid. In the end it enabled the British to fight the Transvaal without international complications. But Salisbury failed in his second objective, which was again to force Portugal to give up Delagoa Bay. In October 1898 Portugal rejected an Anglo-German loan whose price would have been Delagoa Bay and turned to Paris for help. The Transvaal retained its vital link with the Indian Ocean.

In 1898–9, therefore, British hopes of reasserting imperial authority throughout South Africa rested on the Uitlanders alone and Chamberlain was determined simultaneously to screw their leaders up to demand effective franchise reform and to impose strong external pressure on the Transvaal government to concede it. It was at this point that the incompatibility of British political objectives with the economic interests of the Rand mine owners became most obvious. In April 1899 Kruger offered the Uitlanders the franchise after seven years' residence but without redistribution of seats in the *Volksraad* (Parliament) or a voice in presidential elections, coupled with tax reform and modification of the monopolies. To the large mine owners this was in some ways an attractive offer but, as has been seen, Chamberlain was determined that the negotiations should fail. His view was that:

The terms will not do. It is no use for the financiers to undertake what they cannot perform and if the majority of the Uitlanders get no satisfaction the agitation must go on – even though the millionaires are satisfied.[47]

The outcome was the Bloemfontein Conference of 31 May–5 June 1899 between Kruger and Lord Milner, British High Commissioner since 1897. The conference broke on Milner's insistence on the Uitlander franchise after five years and radical reform of the Volksraad. In July, however, Chamberlain thought that Kruger's revised proposals showed that he was ready to come to terms, and, to tighten the screw, insisted that the British government should be a party to any arrangements made through a joint enquiry into the proposed reforms. In August the Transvaal offered to reduce the qualifying period for the franchise to five years, with retrospective effect, and to give not less than a quarter of the Volksraad seats to the mining constituencies. In return Britain should give up her formal right of suzerainty, promise never again to interfere in the internal affairs of the Transvaal, and refer disputes to arbitration by the other South African governments. The British were prepared to accept this last condition, but refused to concede suzerainty or the right of intervention. This marked the end of negotiations because the Boers would not accept electoral reform unless the reward was formal and real independence from Britain, while Chamberlain and Milner felt that they could not be certain that electoral reform would produce Uitlander predominance in Transvaal politics or that this would ensure permanent British control over the Transvaal. Britain had either to concede full Transvaal independence, which might well lead to Afrikaner predominance throughout South Africa, or take the still unwelcome step of using force to impose wider political changes in the Transvaal and incorporate it safely into a British federation of South African colonies. The British ultimatum, which was drafted on 8 October, outlined a programme of political and constitutional reform and insisted on limitation of armaments in return for continued Transvaal independence. But on 9 October, before these proposals were sent, a Boer ultimatum was issued which demanded that British troops should be withdrawn from the Transvaal borders. On 11 October Transvaal commandos began the fighting.

The Boer War was not, therefore, the simple outcome of economic factors in South Africa. Transvaal independence and maladministration did not inhibit British and European investment or make the mines significantly less profitable. British exports had most-favoured nation treatment in the Transvaal and London handled most of the gold exported. Few British businessmen or investors ever showed a desire for formal control of the Transvaal, though there were some in the Cape, mostly connected with Rhodes, who welcomed the chance to destroy the Transvaal's political independence for political and ideological reasons. Ultimately the British decision to force an issue to the point of war was determined neither by economics nor by Cape jingoism but by concern for British power. South Africa was a British sphere. Simonstown was a vital security for the long sea route to the East if Suez should be closed in war. Rather than see South Africa become a group of autonomous Afrikaner republics the British chose to fight. There was almost no public emotion on the question: the government took its decisions deliberately on a calculation of costs and benefits. The war was expected to be short and cheap, a small premium to pay for political security in South Africa. Ultimately, therefore, the war was an attempt to use political means to restore British political supremacy in an area where it was threatened by the secondary effects of economic change.

III   EAST AFRICA[48]

Modern European imperialism produced few more extraordinary episodes than the rapid occupation by Britain, Germany and Italy of the vast regions of East Africa, lying between Egypt in the north, Portuguese Mozambique in the south, and the line of the Nile and the Rift Valley on the west. There were two obvious grounds for surprise. First, before 1884 no European power had any territorial possessions in this part of Africa north of Portuguese Mozambique, and Portugal played very little part in the eventual scramble for ownership. There could therefore be no question of sub-imperialist expansion from an existing colony – no frontier of European settlement, no problem of security, no labour recruiting, no questions of jurisdiction. Nor, in the second place, had any of the European powers eventually involved in the partition of East Africa any major national interest there. The Italians and Belgians had no contact with this area at all before about 1880. The Germans had only a limited commercial stake. The French had a traditional interest in Madagascar. They held Réunion and occupied the islands of Nosse-bé and Mayotta in the early 1840s. During the following decade they showed considerable interest in the area around Barawa, north of Kismayu. There was a brief revival of French political interest in Zanzibar between 1860–2, but this was checked by the Anglo-French Declaration of 1862 which bound both countries to respect the independence of the Sultan of Zanzibar and his territories on the East African coast. Thereafter the French made no attempt to acquire territory in East Africa south of Ethiopia, though they were prepared after 1880 to use the right implied by this declaration for diplomatic purposes.

The British were thus the only European power with a significant political interest on the East African coast before the 1880s. This had two main elements – maintenance of British preponderance in the Indian Ocean, and suppression of the East African slave trade. The first of these was directly related to the security of British India. After 1815 the British steadily expanded informal political influence, based on naval power, throughout the Indian Ocean from the Islamic states of the Persian Gulf to the Cape of Good Hope, partly to ensure that no other power established dangerous primacy in any of these regions, partly to deal with local problems affecting Indian traders and settlers who already formed the mainstay of banking and trade in East Africa. But these aims were essentially limited and to some extent negative. They could be secured without territorial possessions by making treaties with indigenous rulers, by installing consular officials at all important points, by regular naval patrols and by diplomacy to ward off possible threats from France. Before the 1880s, in fact, the only serious external challenge to this system came from France with her bases in Madagascar and the Comoro Islands; but, as has been seen, she was persuaded to sign a joint self-denying ordinance in 1862. The Egyptians, ironically on the advice of their British *sirdar*, General Gordon, briefly laid claim to most of the East African coast in 1874–6, but were easily checked by the Foreign Office. Nevertheless, although the British regarded East Africa as an area of considerable importance, it was not seen as one of first-class national interest. Paramountcy was sustained because it was convenient and cheap. But East Africa was not directly related to Indian security in the same way as Afghanistan or Burma and at no time before the 1880s was there any serious possibility that Britain would impose formal rule over any territory there for political or strategic reasons.

Nor was humanitarian desire to suppress the slave trade likely to lead to political responsibilities. Under pressure from the anti-slavery movement at home British governments put constant pressure on successive Sultans of Zanzibar (until 1861 also rulers (Imams) of Muscat and Oman) to limit or end the trade from their dominions, and in 1822 Sultan Seyyid Said was forced to sign a treaty banning the export of slaves from his African dominions to Arabia. Finally in 1873 Sultan Barghash was induced to end the trade between the African mainland and Zanzibar and to close down the slave markets in all his dominions. This long crusade against the slave trade necessarily involved the British in the domestic affairs of Zanzibar and East Africa. In particular, the price paid for making the Sultan the reluctant agent of the British conscience was to give him effective political support against domestic rivals and foreign intruders. Thus in 1859 British intervention placed Sultan Majid on the throne over the claims of his elder brother and French intervention was blocked. In 1861 the Canning Award divided the Oman Empire into two independent parts. The Egyptian invasion was checked in 1876 and in the mid-1880s the British did their best to protect the Sultan's claims to paramountcy on the East African coast against German and other potential claimants. Yet this two-pronged policy of forcing the Sultans to end the slave trade and protecting them against rivals did not imply or lead to any desire for formal control. In this respect the contrast with West Africa was clearly marked. There, as has been seen, possession of Sierra Leone and other coastal bases was thought necessary after 1815 partly if not primarily to provide naval bases for suppressing the slave trade. But when in 1838 T. F. Buxton, leader of the anti-slavery movement, argued that Mombassa should be occupied to provide a similar base in East Africa, Palmerston refused point blank on the principle that Zanzibar already provided an adequate base for naval patrols and the Foreign Office remained loyal to this view. So long as informal control over Zanzibar provided at once a naval base and a lever to counter the slave trade in the Sultan's dominions, there was no case for undertaking the expense and inconvenience of formal territorial responsibility.

If, therefore, there is no evidence by the 1880s that more than half a century of informal British influence in East Africa was tending towards political empire, it is reasonable to wonder whether the sudden partition of the area between Britain, Germany and Italy between 1884 and 1894 may have been caused by new economic factors – expanding trade, the desire to invest, the opportunities suggested by geographical investigation of the unknown interior. The question is, indeed, of great importance to the present study because East Africa provides unusually clear evidence on the precise relations between economic factors (in this case primarily the interests of the British and German concessionary companies) and the political or strategic considerations which induced European statesmen to impose formal control over the region. Space makes detailed examination impossible, and in any case excellent work has been published, particularly on the British side. It is proposed, therefore, to concentrate attention on the character of the economic interests involved and to indicate briefly how and why these contributed to the political division of East Africa between Britain, Germany and Italy.

The conventional explanation adopted by those who saw imperialism as the inevitable product of new economic developments within Europe has been conveniently summarized by Leonard Woolf as follows.[49] The economic enterprises of the 1880s grew directly from the substantial trade carried on by both Britain and Germany from before the mid-century. In 1872 William Mackinnon, who had founded the British India Steam Navigation Co. in 1862, established a direct steamship link between Aden, Zanzibar and Natal. This gave him a direct interest in East African economic development, and in 1877-8 he induced Sultan Barghash to offer him a seventy-year concession of all his dominions, including control of administration and customs. But 'capitalist economic imperialists' such as Mackinnon were 'ahead of their times' in the late 1870s, and while the Foreign Office did not forbid him to take up the concession, it refused positive support. Mackinnon therefore turned down the concession he had engineered. In 1884, however, Carl Peters, who represented the new determination of German capitalists and merchants to control and develop African territories, formed the Gesellschaft für Deutsche Kolonisation which acquired a number of treaties on the mainland opposite Zanzibar, and immediately obtained Bismarck's protection for its claims, irrespective of the counter-claims of the Sultan. These claims were then transferred to the newly formed Deutsche-Ostafrikanische Gesellschaft (hereafter DOAG), which proceeded to consolidate and extend its concessions with the support of a German protectorate. Mackinnon's reaction to this development was to form the British East African Association, revive his earlier concessionary project, and press the British government to salvage as much of East Africa from German control as was still possible. The British government, influenced by new ideas on empire and economics and aware of the fact that the Association included distinguished men, such as the Marquis of Lorne, son-in-law of the Queen, came to terms with Germany to secure part of East Africa for Mackinnon. A preliminary territorial division was arranged with Germany; the Sultan of Zanzibar was forced to renounce his excellent claims to the mainland beyond a ten-mile strip of coastline; Mackinnon was given a charter for the newly formed Imperial British East Africa Company (hereafter IBEAC) in 1888 and was left to develop his concession.

By the early 1890s, however, both British and German companies found that it was unprofitable to govern as well as exploit their respective zones and were heading for bankruptcy. Mackinnon, having failed to persuade the British government to build or subsidize a railway from Mombassa to Uganda which might have saved his project, was able in 1893–4 to lever reluctant ministers into converting the British sphere into a formal protectorate and thus obtained compensation for the company's alleged administrative expenditure. The German company also succeeded in shifting its administrative duties onto the imperial government in 1890 and received monetary compensation together with generous rights to land, minerals and railway construction. Thus at each stage the occupation of East Africa demonstrated the ability of capitalist concessionary companies to obtain varying kinds of political support for their profit-making projects.

This account raised three main questions, all of them critical for analysis of the role of economic factors in modern imperialism. First, is it true that political intervention in East Africa sprang directly from the economic ambitions of European commercial and concessionary companies, rather than from the strategic or other aims of European governments? Second, did these economic interests reflect the need or determination of European capitalism to find new markets, sources of raw materials, or fields for investment? Finally, were the governments of Germany and Britain, at each stage from the original arrangement of spheres of interest in 1885–6 to the institution of metropolitan administration in 1890 and 1894 respectively, primarily concerned to obtain economic opportunities for their nationals or conversely to secure political, strategic or prestige objectives which had little to do with economics?

The main fact of East African economic life before the 1880s was that the limited commodity trade available on the mainland was already highly developed by Arab traders and Indian businessmen based on Zanzibar or its dependent ports along the continental coastline. Well before 1850 Zanzibar and Pemba had become entrepôts for a trading system which extended to the Great Lakes in the west and overseas to the Persian Gulf, India and even Europe. The range of export commodities was, however, limited to slaves, ivory and gum-copal, the staple exports from the mainland, which were brought to the coast by Arab caravans over very large distances. Zanzibar and Pemba specialized in production of cloves, which were grown as a compulsory crop much as similar commodities were grown in the Netherlands Indies during the period of the Culture System. Moreover, in sharp contrast with most other parts of sub-Saharan Africa, the coastal and insular possessions of the Sultan used a European type of currency, based on Maria Theresa silver dollars, Spanish crowns and Indian copper coins. In these respects at least, and within the physical limits set by problems of transportation, the commercial economy of East Africa had already been 'developed' by Arabs and Indians long before Europeans began to dominate the trade of the region.

But this did not constitute any serious obstacle to European trade. From the early 1830s a number of European states, together with the United States, had signed commercial treaties with the Sultans of Zanzibar which provided for freedom to trade at Zanzibar, Pemba and most continental ports except those immediately opposite Zanzibar and allowed consulates to be established throughout the Sultan's dominions.[50] Moreover, the French treaty of 1844 restricted import duties to a maximum of 5 per cent *ad valorem* and this right was automatically extended to all other countries whose commercial treaties contained most favoured nation clauses. Thus Zanzibar and its dominions were wide open to traders on very satisfactory terms and the pressure exerted by foreign consuls and naval commanders ensured that there would be no serious problems of jurisdiction over expatriates such as were found in West Africa, China and elsewhere. The statistics given in table 16 for trade and shipping during the twenty years before 1880 indicate that under these favourable circumstances European commerce was expanding rapidly.

What significance had these commercial developments for events in the early 1880s? Two facts stand out. First, the East African

Table 16

Zanzibar Trade and Shipping, 1860–79

(i) Total Imports to Zanzibar, 1863, 1867, 1879 (pounds at current values)

1863	261,400
1867	383,700
1879	1,300,000

(ii) Total Exports from Zanzibar, 1860, 1864, 1879 (pounds at current values)

1860	388,500
1864	437,700
1879	900,000

(iii) Number and Tonnage of Foreign Ships Putting in at Zanzibar

	1859		1871		1879	
	No.	Tons	No.	Tons	No.	Tons
British	1	493	17	10,459	69	76,265
German	17	4,428	17	7,467	13	5,940
United States	35	10,890	8	4,250	10	5,283
French	12	3,066	11	5,450	4	1,975

Note: British shipping excludes British Indian.

(iv) Main Commodity Exports from Zanzibar, 1879 (pounds)

Rubber	250,000 (approx)
Cloves	175,000
Ivory	160,000
Millet	66,000
Hides	60,000
Copra	45,000
Sesamum	43,000
Gum-copal	26,000
Orchilla	22,000

(v) Main Imports to Zanzibar, 1879 (pounds)

Cotton textiles	268,000
Rice and cereals	78,000
Guns and powder	70,000

Source: Coupland, *The Exploitation of East Africa*, 77–8, 319–22.

trade was of sufficient importance to Britain and Germany to ensure that any attempt by a single power to control Zanzibar, the entrepôt for virtually the whole trade, would be strongly resisted unless the 'open door' was firmly guaranteed. Second there is no evidence whatever that mercantile opinion in Britain or North Germany was seriously dissatisfied with trading conditions there or that there was any demand for political control on commercial grounds. Trade remained competitive for all foreigners on equal terms. Each power had a consul in Zanzibar and other coastal ports, and there were no serious problems of jurisdiction or personal security for Europeans and their possessions. Above all, although the continental trade was limited in size, it flowed smoothly to the coast in the hands of Arab traders and Indian merchants and required no investment or risk by Europeans. Had there been reason to think that there were vast sources of raw materials or rich unexploited markets inland which could be tapped only by establishing European rule and removing obstructive African middlemen, the European merchants might well have demanded or favoured alien occupation. But, despite the sometimes over-optimistic reports of explorers and missionaries, the merchants showed no interest in such possibilities. There are no grounds whatever for thinking that strictly mercantile opinion in Britain, Germany or any other foreign state was positively in favour of territorial control of East Africa in the early 1880s.

Nor, in the second place, is there any evidence that East Africa was regarded by European bankers or investors as an important field for investment at that time. No Sultan of Zanzibar had borrowed heavily in the European money market. There was no significant foreign investment in plantations, transport or public utilities, apart from a road projected by Mackinnon and Buxton from Dar-es-Salaam to Lake Tanganyika in the late 1870s. As will be seen, moreover, when the first concessionary companies were founded in Britain and Germany in the 1880s, they had great difficulty in raising capital. Clearly European business had no prior enthusiasm for investing heavily in East Africa.

By process of elimination, therefore, it seems that if economic forces lay behind European imperialism in East Africa in the 1880s these must have taken some different form. This was, in fact, the speculative land-grabbing concern, which expressed neither the commercial or investment needs of the metropolis but the opportunism and in some cases patriotism of individual British or German subjects who were encouraged by the achievements of the explorers to believe that profits could be made by acquiring large areas of 'vacant' land in those regions of darkest Africa where there were no established European commercial or other interests. Indeed, the instinct to develop trade and production and to establish colonies in East and Central Africa was as old as the exploration of these regions, and was an automatic reflex of explorers and missionaries alike. Livingstone was keen to establish British 'colonies' at the source of the Zambesi and in the Shiré highlands of Nyasa, though these would not necessarily have been formal British possessions. Indeed, he would have welcomed rule by almost any European power as a means of putting down the slave trade. Speke also believed that annexation was essential to suppress the slave trade and wrote in 1864 that:

... a few score Europeans [*sic*] ruling the country would completely transform it in a few years' time. An extensive market would be opened to the world, the present nakedness of the land would have a covering, and industry and commerce would clear the way for civilization and enlightenment.[51]

The German explorer, von der Decken, was more specific. In 1864 he wrote from Juba:

I am persuaded that in a short time a colony established here would be most successful, and after two or three years would be self-supporting. It would become of special importance after the opening of the Suez Canal. It is unfortunate that we Germans allow such opportunities of acquiring colonies to slip, especially at a time when it would be of importance to the navy.[52]

Such ideas grew naturally on the frontiers, but in the 1860s and 1870s they made no impact in Europe. The first serious attempt to colonize East Africa came from Egypt in 1875–6 when, as has been seen, Gordon, as *sirdar* of the Egyptian Army, engineered an expedition to Kismayu, on the mouth of the Juba, and the Khedive Ismail claimed possession of the whole east coast. His project came to nothing, broken by Britain's determination to preserve the patrimony of the Sultans of Zanzibar, the best guardians of the coast and effective, though reluctant, agents of British anxiety to suppress the slave trade. Yet the Egyptian enterprise proved a watershed. Its immediate outcome was that Sultan Barghash recognized that his nominal authority over the vast areas of East Africa was insecure and decided that it was better to concede restricted areas of land and limited rights of government to foreigners on his own terms rather than lose all to Egypt or some other power. Because of his close connection with Britain he tried first to obtain British collaborators. Probably in 1876 he wrote to the Foreign Office, inviting the assistance of British 'capitalists' in 'the development and civilization of Africa and the opening up of trade on the coast and in the interior'.[53]

Barghash did not lack offers of co-operation. The first came from William Mackinnon, the self-made owner of the British India Steam Navigation Co., who had established a regular steamship service from Aden to Zanzibar and was by then the dominant commercial influence in the island. In 1876 he had already, with T. F. Buxton, leader of the anti-slavery movement in Britain, begun construction of a road from Dar-es-Salaam to Lake Nyasa with the dual object of developing legitimate trade and suppressing the slave trade. In response to Barghash's invitation Mackinnon proposed in 1877 that he be given a concession covering all the Sultan's territories on the mainland. This was to run for seventy years and the Sultan would receive 20 per cent of net profits after payment of an 8 per cent dividend to the shareholders. Had this concession gone through Barghash would have remained effective ruler only of Zanzibar and Pemba and the British would have acquired an indisputable claim to the whole of continental East Africa by virtue of effective occupation. Why did the project fail? The answer, which for long baffled historians, seems to be that Salisbury, then Foreign Secretary, was hostile to it on the ground, presumably, that the concession might make the government responsible for administering the mainland. Salisbury therefore privately instructed the arabist, G. P. Badger, who went with Mackinnon to negotiate the final concession in Zanzibar, to wreck the negotiation. Whether or not this is true, Badger succeeded in offending the Sultan, who raised his demands to unacceptable heights. In May 1878 negotiations were broken off.[54]

This fiasco might have had important consequences for the economic and political future of East Africa for during the next six years European speculators, including Leopold II, E. Rabaud, a Marseille merchant and noted humanitarian, and a number of Germans, sent expeditions and negotiated with Barghash for concessions or commercial rights. Britain had a second chance only because none of these enterprises came to anything. Some foundered on evidence of limited economic possibilities but more on the pronounced hostility of the British, French and German governments to formal political involvement. In 1884 Barghash therefore remained unchallenged sovereign over the coast and presumably much of the interior and it still seemed possible that East Africa would survive as an independent Islamic Empire under informal British tutelage.

Yet, as in other parts of Africa, 1884–5 proved the years of change. By 1886 East Africa was provisionally divided into British and German spheres and two apparently dynamic concessionary companies had emerged to administer and exploit these territories. It is not proposed to trace these developments chronologically but rather to analyse the character of the two companies and to consider on what grounds both British and German governments dropped their established policies of non-intervention in continental East Africa. Was this because they were forced to do so by the irresistible pressures exerted by these finance capitalists, or were there other and possibly political interests at stake?

Although German initiatives only developed late in 1884, immediately after Gladstone had quashed a tentative move by the young British botanist, Harry Johnston, to obtain official sanction for a British colony on land he had bought near Mount Kilimanjaro, it was a German enterprise that effectively forced the political division of East Africa. This was the achievement of Karl Peters, who made a brief trip on the mainland opposite Zanzibar in November–December 1884 and obtained treaties signed by African rulers which, if valid, placed their territories under German protection. Within six months these places were German protectorates administered by the DOAG. What were Peters' motives? Was the DOAG a large-scale investment company supported by German banking capital? Why did Bismarck agree to give official support?

It is clear that in the first instance Peters acted without any support or encouragement from German banks or large-scale capital. His venture sprang from impatience with the sobriety of the Kolonialverein, which had so far failed to induce the government to found any colonies. Peters founded the Gesellschaft für Deutsche Kolonisation (hereafter GDK) in March 1884 to provide funds for patriotic colonizing ventures. This was nominally a joint-stock profit-making venture, but its initial capital of 175,000 marks (£8,750) hardly suggests substantial business backing. This was not, of course, surprising in the early stages. More significant is the lack of support for the DOAG, the GDK's successor, which was launched in 1885 to exploit land and opportunities already acquired in East Africa and had the full support of the government.[55] By November 1885 only 198,000 marks (£9,900) had been subscribed, and that mostly by small investors or well-wishers. The Hanse port merchants who were already established in the East African trade refused to join or support the company, suspecting that it would obstruct conventional trade. Indeed, the only significant support came from Karl von der Heydt, a private banker from Elberfield, whose interest clearly derived from patriotism rather than profit, for he was a noted imperialist, president of the Pan-German Association from 1890–4 and a member of the Kolonialrat. Heydt subscribed 100,000 marks (£5,000) in the first instance and later added another 300,000 marks (£15,000). Most other banks and the industrialists held back from what they regarded as an unpromising venture founded by a man of straw until Bismarck, increasingly anxious that the company should become capable of occupying and administering the new protectorate which would otherwise become an imperial responsibility, induced the Kaiser to invest 500,000 marks (£25,000) from the private Hohenzollern fortune.

From this point in 1887, however, the company began to change into a genuine business concern and to be dominated by those bankers with the largest financial stake in it. Peters was ousted from control and sent off to East Africa in 1888 to secure Uganda and possibly part of the eastern Congo under cover of organizing the Emin Pasha relief expedition. Under the new management more capital was subscribed, until in 1890 the total was 3,480,000 marks (£174,000). Apart from Heydt and the Seehandlung, 102 subscribers had bought 208 shares at 10,000 marks a share, including Mendelssohn Bank (100,000 marks – £5,000) and Krupp (40,000 marks – £2,000). After 1890, when the company was relieved of its administrative responsibilities and was compensated with 600,000 marks a year (£30,000) and wide rights to land, minerals and railway construction, it became a more attractive investment proposition; and purchase of the coastal strip from the Sultan of Zanzibar increased the opportunities for profitable trade with the interior. The capital was therefore increased by another 3 million marks to a total of 6,480,000 marks (£324,000) and the Deutsche Bank, which invested fairly heavily, shared control with the Seehandlung.

It is unnecessary for the present purpose to trace the history of the DOAG further. The important fact is that German finance capital had demonstrated its lack of interest in the investment possibilities of tropical Africa by the scale of its support. A few bankers and industrialists were prepared to support a small and highly speculative venture of this type, provided the stake was negligible, in case something of value should turn up. But serious interest was aroused only when, in 1904, the state guaranteed interest of 3 per cent on capital invested in railway construction and promised to repay the capital at 120 per cent when the government took the railways over. But this was to invest in gilt-edged government bonds rather than to speculate on the economic future of Africa. It is hardly recognizable as the out-thrust of advanced capital engaged in a desperate struggle to safeguard its profit levels by a division of the world between the great trusts.

Given this marked lack of enthusiasm on the part of finance and commerce during the twenty years after 1884 it is clearly unlikely that the business world exerted irresistible pressure on Bismarck in 1885 to reverse his earlier policy and impose German rule on East Africa. Why, then, was Peters able to obtain official recognition for his treaties and a German protectorate? The answer is simply that Peters was fortunate in his timing. By January 1885 Bismarck had committed himself by his actions in West and South-West Africa and in the Pacific to the general principle that the *bona fide* claims of German subjects to protection for established commercial or other interests in the non-European world must be accepted, provided no serious conflict of interest arose with another power. Moreover, the political motives which had influenced Bismarck's colonial policy in 1884 still operated. As a well-known patriotic imperialist who had treaties to demonstrate the reality of the territorial claims he wished the government to support, Peters clearly qualified for official protection. At some date before 23 February 1885 he sent Bismarck a memorandum describing his treaties and stated that, in view of the dangers to German trade in East Africa resulting from foreign activity on the mainland, it was desirable to stake Germany's claims. The proposed colonizing company would, moreover, co-operate with established German merchants. Kusserow explained to Bismarck that the DOAG wanted to establish a state in East Africa on the model of the British East India Company; and on 24 February Bismarck approved a provisional imperial charter giving protection for Peters' inland claims. He did not, however, want to acquire the coast round Bagamoyo for the moment, saying: 'Well, perhaps later; first only the right of transit [for trade] for without transit the thing is not manageable'.[56] On 26 February the Kaiser signed the *schutzbrief* placing the territories claimed by Peters under imperial protection and this was published on 3 March, the day after the delegates to the Berlin Conference dispersed.

Thus the origins of German East Africa can be traced directly to the enterprise of a small group of German colonial enthusiasts who, with very little support from powerful financial or commercial organizations and none from the government, took advantage of the general principles of the colonial policy Bismarck had established in 1884 to claim protection for some dubious treaties made with African chiefs in an area regarded by the British as within the dominions of the Sultan of Zanzibar. Two years earlier such treaties would probably have been ignored by Bismarck and Peters would certainly have lacked the support necessary to exert effective leverage on him. But by February 1885 such leverage was really not necessary. Within the strictly limited liability provided by a *Schutzbrief*, Berlin was now prepared to support such claims on general principles of public policy; though later events, such as the agreement of 1886 which recognized Portuguese claims to the hinterlands linking Angola and Mozambique and the arrangements made with Britain in 1886 and 1890 showed that the claims and ambitions of German subjects might still be severely curtailed where some more important national interest was at stake.

The development of British policy on East Africa from 1885 was in many ways similar to that of Germany, particularly during the first four years. Its special importance for this study lies, however, in the fact that after about 1889 new official assumptions about the importance of East Africa for the security of British power in Egypt and the Mediterranean resulted in a radical change of policy and to the subordination of private economic interests to the overriding demands of public policy. To demonstrate these trends it is proposed first to consider the character and aims of British economic interests in East Africa and then the motives of successive British governments in imposing political control there.

Apart from merchants trading to Zanzibar, who played no significant role in the establishment of British political control over East Africa, the only British economic interest directly involved was the East African Association of 1887 and its successor, the Imperial British East Africa Company of 1888. It is, however, as difficult to define the precise character of these organizations as those established by Peters. Were they genuine business concerns set up by British capitalists hoping to extract super-profits from investment in East Africa? The evidence raises doubts. First, the initiative that led to the establishment of these organizations was not taken by British capitalists or merchants, but by Frederick Holmwood, Kirk's chief consular assistant in Zanzibar, who attempted, while home on leave in April–May 1885, to revive the 1878 scheme for a British concession in East Africa. Writing to J. F. Hutton, a Manchester businessman and associate of Mackinnon in April 1885, he urged that private British enterprise should intervene to limit the extension of German claims. Since these were still thought to be restricted to the area west of Zanzibar and around Witu he proposed that a concession should be obtained from the Sultan for building a railway from Tanga to Kilimanjaro and thence to the Great Lakes, to be extended eventually to the Nile, as Gordon had proposed a decade earlier. The project should prove profitable for, in addition to the export of ivory, new plantation crops could be established and a European settlement colony might be set up in the highlands west of Mount Kenya. The best course would be to form a company, with or without a charter, to operate on the lines of the old East India Company.[57]

Holmwood's arguments were economic because he was appealing to men of business. They were also unrealistic, for Joseph Thompson, who had first explored the Kenya highlands, had been singularly unimpressed by their economic potential. But Holmwood's object was essentially political: with Kirk he wanted to salvage British influence in East Africa and to protect the nominal authority of the Sultan. Moreover, his proposals were clearly understood in these terms. Hutton and Mackinnon, supported by Lord Aberdare and five others, asked Granville to support them in a project of this kind because it was 'absolutely essential to maintain and extend British influence in East Africa, to develop British trade, and to deal in a practical manner with the Slave Trade of the interior'. But before risking their capital for these purposes they wanted an assurance of official 'countenance and support'.[58] In discussions at the Foreign Office the group made it clear that 'countenance and support' implied at least governmental approval for a concession from the Sultan similar to that projected in 1877–8 and diplomatic action to exclude the Germans from this zone. They also wanted a governmental guarantee for the costs of building a railway from Tanga to Kilimanjaro. These conditions suggest that the group had little confidence in the immediate economic prospects of East

Africa and wanted the government to share the risks in a project which was primarily intended to prevent German control of an area traditionally under British influence.

The Foreign Office was sympathetic to these aims. Sir P. Anderson, who was to be closely associated with British policy in East Africa and had formulated a general, though unadopted, British strategy for Africa,[59] was personally in favour of the scheme and tried to persuade Hutton and Mackinnon to go ahead. The government had no objection in principle and undertook preliminary negotiations with Berlin to prepare the way. But, observing the still conventional limits of state action in support of private economic interests, it refused financial guarantees, a royal charter or a formal protectorate over land to be acquired by the company. Once this was clear the whole negotiation collapsed at once. The 'capitalists' were simply not prepared to accept full liability in so highly speculative a venture. As Anderson commented, 'the truth is that we not only do not neglect the Manchester interests, but have to stir Manchester up to look after its interests'.[60] This indeed was the measure of British economic imperialism in East Africa in 1885. Large-scale capital was totally uninterested and even those merchants and shipowners with established interests were unenthusiastic. By September 1885 Salisbury was convinced that there was no real economic demand for intervention. 'Keeping every other nation out on the bare chance that some day or other our traders will pluck up heart to go in is a poor policy' he minuted on a letter from Kirk about German activities.[61]

It is not, therefore, surprising that the eventual establishment of the East African Association in 1887 and its mutation into the IBEAC in 1888 owed as much to governmental stimulus, itself resulting from a new official assessment of the East African situation, as to the economic enterprise of British business. Between May 1885 and 1887, for reasons to be considered later, the British government arranged a preliminary delimitation of East Africa into British and German spheres of influence which excluded from the German sphere only a strip of coast from Vanga to Golbanti and a hinterland running potentially to Lake Victoria Nyanza and the Kenya Highlands. This at least gave British enterprise a clear opportunity, but men of business were extremely slow to make use of it. In May 1886 Mackinnon and Hutton sent a small expedition to claim the land acquired by Johnston around Mount Kilimanjaro, though this was able to establish only a claim to Taveta. Further action was stimulated from Zanzibar. In February 1887 Sultan Barghash, probably on Holmwood's suggestion, implored Mackinnon to check German expansion by taking a concession. This time Mackinnon obliged. The British East Africa Association was formed to accept a concession which gave full administrative control over the Sultan's dominions from Kipini in the north to the River Umba in the south. To establish its claim the Association adopted Peters' technique of making treaties with African rulers to a depth of some two hundred miles inland, and planned to enlist Emin Pasha, the Governor of Equatorial province of the Egyptian Sudan, who had long been isolated by Mahdist forces there, in order to establish a claim to effective occupation of the area north of the Great Lakes. To obtain a royal charter the Association was transformed in April 1888 into a joint stock company, the IBEAC. Here, at last, was a genuine capitalist organization established to exploit the land and trade of East Africa. What were its character and aims? Did it reflect the enthusiasm of the City for investment opportunities in the tropics to relieve the pressure of surplus capital and shore up declining rates of interest?

The subscribed capital was initially £250,000, much larger than that of the DOAG before 1890, and this might imply genuine business interest. But analysis of the leading shareholders suggests that what Woolf described as 'prominent capitalists' were sheep in wolves' clothing: mostly philanthropists or old East Coast Lands. Mackinnon was the largest shareholder with £25,000 of stock. Other members of his family provided a further £25,000. Sir T. F. Buxton of the Anti-Slavery Society put up £10,000, as did Burdett-Coutts, a banker whose wife was a leading contributor to charitable causes. Other shareholders included Alexander Bruce, who was connected with David Livingstone's family; Sir John Kirk, newly retired from Zanzibar; Francis de Winton, acting consul there; and Frederick Holmwood. The list was in fact almost identical with that for the Emin Pasha Relief Fund the previous year, and the suspicion arises that most of them subscribed from humanitarian desire to suppress the slave trade or patriotic dislike of seeing Germany predominant in an area of established British commercial and political interest rather than from expectation of super-profits. The IBEAC does not, in fact, look like a genuine business venture.

Its record as a profit-making concern was, in any case, disastrous. In common with most concessionary companies operating in late nineteenth-century Africa it found that it would not be able to cover its costs, let alone make profits, until immense sums had been spent on communications and the development of suitable exports staples.[62] The IBEAC did not survive this preliminary phase. By 1892 expenditure was £80,000 and income £35,000 a year. A railway to the coast might have saved the company; but it could not afford to build one and the government put up only £20,000 for a preliminary survey. The company survived until 1894 on a gift of £40,000 raised by philanthropists and patriotic supporters in 1891–2 and its shareholders were fortunate that the government's decision to establish a protectorate in March 1894 entitled the company to compensation for administrative expenditure. After much haggling it received £250,000, gave up its charter and was dissolved in 1895. Kirk provided an epitaph for this most unbusiness-like capitalist enterprise:

> With all its failings it has been an honest concern, not a money-making one, and but for its work we should not now possess a footing in East Africa.[63]

But if, as has been suggested, the primary function of the IBEAC was not to make money but to preserve influence in East Africa and help to suppress the slave trade, and if the company lacked the power at any stage to force the hand of a reluctant government, why did British officials and politicians, who were so resistant to East Africa commitments in 1884, proceed by stages to protectorates over Uganda and the rest of British East Africa in 1894 and 1895 and begin an expensive railway from Mombassa to Uganda in 1896?

The government's readiness to establish British claims to some degree of political control in East Africa evolved after 1884 in step with Whitehall's assessment of the political and strategic importance of the area. In 1885 this was still minimal; and Salisbury was therefore prepared to negotiate a preliminary demarcation of spheres of influence with Bismarck only because it was diplomatically cheap to preserve something of the traditional British influence there in case it could be made to serve some economic or political purpose. By 1890, however, when Salisbury made the definitive Anglo-German agreement which extended the British sphere of influence westwards across Lake Victoria Nyanza to the still undefined frontiers of the Congo Free State and north to eliminate the earlier German sphere based on Witu, thus excluding the DOAG from Uganda and the northern coast, the value officially placed on East Africa had clearly risen. Did this new assessment reflect pressure from the IBEAC or perhaps a more general official concern to protect commercial opportunities for British traders? The evidence suggests otherwise. Economic considerations played virtually no part in the evolution of new official attitudes. The decisive factor was a new assessment of the importance of the Upper Nile to British control of Egypt. By 1889 Salisbury had reached the conclusion that evacuation of Egypt, which had remained British policy since 1882, could not be undertaken in the foreseeable future. Evacuation would lead to internal chaos; the French were unlikely to agree to a British right of re-entry; Egypt was the pivot of British naval power in the Mediterranean. Moreover it was now becoming accepted doctrine that control of Egypt required at least the exclusion of any other power from the Nile Valley. The Italians were moving in that direction from Eritrea; Leopold II saw the Nile as a commercial outlet from the Congo; the French might move east from Chad or the Congo and challenge British power in Egypt from the south. Improbable though it was in terms of practical engineering, it was thought that any power controlling the Upper Nile could theoretically destroy the Egyptian economy by diverting the waters of the Nile. On these grounds it had become an officially accepted British national interest by November 1890 to exclude all other powers from the Upper Nile and possibly in the end to establish effective British occupation of the region by destroying the Mahdist state in the Sudan.

The Anglo-German agreement of July 1890 which embodied these British objectives was a classic example of the diplomacy of late nineteenth-century imperialism. At the price of ceding Heligoland, making boundary adjustments in West Africa and dropping Cecil Rhodes' demand for a British corridor from Lake Nyasa to Uganda for the conceptual Cape to Cairo railway, Salisbury was able to safeguard Britain's strategic position in East Africa. Germany – that is the DOAG – was excluded from the Upper Nile and Britain was free to occupy the vast region from the coast to Lake Albert and the Egyptian Sudan. But why did British political action not stop there, leaving the IBEAC to occupy this sphere of interest? Why were formal protectorates and a railway thought necessary? Was this because the IBEAC or other economic interests demanded a more secure basis for economic exploitation and communications at government expense? Was the government forced to act by the publicity campaign run jointly by the company's agent, Frederick Lugard, missionary societies with branches in Uganda, anti-slavery groups, jingos and the IBEAC in 1891–2?

The short answer is once again that neither economic interests nor pressure groups played a significant part in the redefinition of official views on Uganda after 1890. The determinant of policy was yet another assessment of British strategic and political interests in Egypt, the Sudan and the Horn of Africa. A domestic crisis in Egypt in January 1893, when the Khedive Abbas II made a bid for greater freedom from British supervision, led to a decision to send British troops to reinforce British control. This in turn caused deep resentment in Paris, since it implied the perpetuation of British power; and a project was formulated to send French forces from West Africa and Ethiopia to reopen the Egyptian question by challenging British power on the Upper Nile. This project was held back for the moment by Paris; but almost simultaneously a Belgian force from the Congo occupied Lado on the Upper Nile, thus serving warning that this region was open for occupation by any foreign power. Early in 1894 London knew about the French project and had to prepare counter-moves. If the IBEAC had fulfilled its assigned political role and had established effective British occupation of Uganda and the region to the north, the government might have relied on the company to bar French initiatives there. But there was no British presence north of Lake Victoria Nyanza and the company was tottering to bankruptcy. The government had therefore either to leave the field to French, Belgian or possibly Ethiopian initiatives or impose formal British authority.

These were the imperatives behind the Uganda protectorate announced in August 1894 which must be seen as part of an elaborate system of diplomatic redoubts designed to keep any French raiding force from the upper waters of the Nile. By comparison with this now accepted national interest, the economic value of East Africa for the IBEAC or the British economy as a whole and the special interests of missionaries, anti-slave trade societies and jingos were of no significance. Equally, when the government decided in 1896 to start building a railway from Mombassa to Uganda, its motives were strategic not economic. Every aspect of the project points to this conclusion. It was built by the government rather than by a private company. The Treasury was not allowed to fuss about the cost and which colony would bear it. The railway had the same gauge as the Egyptian railways. It had one immediate purpose: to provide rapid access for British forces from the coast to the Upper Nile to forestall the French threat. No one could openly admit this before 1898; but in 1900 Salisbury took the Commons into his confidence:

There were considerations of a very cogent character which induced us to desire to finish, at the earliest period possible, what was practically our only access to those regions. At that time the battle of Omdurman had not been fought, the occupation of Fashoda had not taken place . . . and our position was one . . . of very considerable difficulty if any serious embarrassments with any European Power had arisen before we had done anything to make our military access to the place easier than it naturally was.[64]

The formal occupation of East Africa by Britain and Germany therefore provides two alternative and in many ways typical models of the interaction of economic and political factors in late nineteenth century imperialism. In the first instance the initiatives which disturbed the generally acceptable *status quo* in the region were private and largely economic – competition between German and British concessionary companies for land and economic opportunities in a region over which the Sultan of Zanzibar had hitherto been accepted suzerain. Why did the two governments take a first step towards political involvement by negotiating the preliminary partition of 1886? In the German case this was mainly because Bismarck felt it necessary to provide a political base for the DOAG in order to sustain the principles of colonial policy he had adopted in 1884, supporting legitimate German enterprise where it was obstructed by indigenous resistance or European rivalry. Conversely, however, DOAG and its supporters among the ranks of German imperialists had no capacity to force the government's hand. The Wilhelmstrasse regarded the East African enterprise as extremely marginal to metropolitan economic interests and had no hesitation in emasculating the company's prospects in 1890 by exchanging Uganda for Heligoland. Thus German East Africa provides evidence that private economic enterprise in the less-developed world could after 1884 expect some degree of political support; but, conversely, that it could not press the government beyond a certain point and that where no major political interest was at stake, Berlin felt no strong desire for large-scale territorial empire in tropical Africa.

The British case differed substantially. Starting from the premise that marginal commercial and political interests on the East African coast did not justify any form of political control, successive governments after 1885 felt bound at least to safeguard openings for

British economic and humanitarian enterprise by negotiating tentative spheres of interest with Germany. Whether on this basis the official mind would ever have been prepared to go as far as Bismarck had already gone in establishing formal protectorates is an open question. Certainly no British economic interest involved there possessed the leverage sufficient to force the government into action designed to bolster corporate profits. The decisive fact is that from about 1889 leading statesmen and permanent officials decided that, whatever its economic possibilities, which then seemed small, part of East Africa must be held simply as a corridor from the Indian Ocean to the Upper Nile. In this way what had started as a genuine though marginal economic question was overlaid by strategic and political considerations of the highest order. In the end, therefore, British East Africa provides an exceptionally clear model of how economic problems on the periphery could generate formal empire when and because they were transmuted into issues directly relevant to the national interest as interpreted by the official mind of a European capital.

11   *South-East Asia*

The obvious fact of European imperialism in Asia during the years 1880–1914 was that, in sharp distinction from Africa, this was a period of completion rather than of innovation. By 1880 European influence was already far advanced in each of the territories examined in chapters 7 and 8. Indeed the British had already taken the plunge in the Malay peninsula and imposed effective, though theoretically informal, political control over several west coast sultanates; and, for reasons of space, it is not proposed to trace the piecemeal extension of the Resident system to the remaining Malay states any further. But in 1880 matters were still on a knife edge in Upper Burma and much of Indo-China. In each region Britain or France might have remained content with their existing informal influence and treaty rights for an indefinite period. Yet in each there were already serious problems which were generating friction with indigenous governments and might eventually force London and Paris to review their aims and assumptions. It is proposed in this chapter to consider very briefly why Britain annexed Upper Burma to British India in 1885–6 and, in slightly more detail, why the French incorporated Annam, Tongking, Cambodia and much of Laos, along with existing territory in Cochin China, into the federation of Indo-China. It will also be necessary to consider why the French stopped there: why they did not extend their rule into southern China. In each case the primary aim will, of course, be to define the precise role of economic factors as a factor making for the extension of formal empire.

I BURMA, 1880–86

The fundamental question posed by events in Burma[1] after 1880 is whether the decision to occupy the kingdom of Upper Burma in 1885 and to annex it to British India in 1886 were the product of a new imperialist impulse in Britain or the logical outcome of events during the previous decades. In either case, was the basic motive economic? It will be convenient to examine the possible influence of economic problems first and then to consider other aspects of the situation in the early 1880s.

An apparently strong *a priori* case can be made out for the primacy of economic factors in British attitudes to Upper Burma in this period. It has been seen above that by about 1880 the relatively favourable commercial conditions of the 1860s and early 1870s were passing. Rangoon's trade was more than ever hampered by political instability in Upper Burma and by the actions of increasingly uncontrolled royal officials. The search for a trade route to China had been suspended on the same grounds. Between 1880 and 1885 conditions deteriorated still further, leading to the *cause célèbre* of the fine imposed on the Bombay Burmah Trading Corporation (hereafter BBTC) in August 1885. The Rangoon commercial community did not accept such adverse conditions quietly and repeatedly demanded effective remedial action by the British authorities. Complaints became more insistent in 1884 and in October Sir Charles Bernard, Chief Commissioner for Lower Burma, sent several petitions to Calcutta from merchants in Rangoon, commenting that the majority of British residents in Burma wanted the kingdom to be annexed. Pressure increased early in 1885 as the failure of the rice crop in Upper Burma reduced the market for imports from Rangoon. Merchants were also concerned at the reported activities of French businessmen and 'capitalists' in Mandalay, encouraged by the new French consul, Frederick Haas. When they received little sympathy in Calcutta the Rangoon Chamber of Commerce contacted chambers of commerce in Britain and induced them to bombard the India Office with petitions for action. A deputation from the London Chamber of Commerce called on Lord Kimberley at the India Office in March 1885 to deliver a memorial urging the annexation of Upper Burma. The general argument put forward in these petitions was that the government of King Thibaw was deliberately obstructing British

o

enterprise; that the people of Upper Burma desired to throw off his rule; and that annexation would make it possible to open up a direct trade with southern China. Once the expedition had been sent to Mandalay in December 1885, the Rangoon merchants pressed hard for permanent annexation rather than the replacement of Thibaw by another Burmese ruler more amenable to British influence.

There can, in fact, be no doubt that commercial interests in Rangoon were strongly in favour of political action to solve their economic difficulties in Upper Burma. This in itself is interesting and relatively unusual, for European merchants seldom wanted territorial annexation as an end in itself. The explanation is that in Burma, as in Tongking, commercial opinion had by this time reached the conclusion that, while imperial rule was not intrinsically necessary to their activities, annexation had become desirable because the Burmese government was set on a policy of non-collaboration. But the more important question is whether their pressure affected official opinion and policy in India and Britain. Was Upper Burma occupied in order to facilitate economic penetration from Rangoon?

As always, it is difficult to measure the leverage exerted by economic pressure groups; but the answer is reasonably clear. Bernard was in favour of military intervention to instal another prince in place of Thibaw. Calcutta also accepted that the merchants had a legitimate grievance and was prepared to exert pressure on their behalf. The British government was convinced that British influence in Upper Burma was declining and that this had important political implications. But there is no evidence whatever to suggest that official opinion in Rangoon, Calcutta or London was convinced by the beginning of 1885 that formal occupation was necessary primarily to provide improved conditions for British traders.

What, then was the importance of the notorious fine of Rs 23 lakhs (about £230,000) imposed on the BBTC in August 1885? Did the British government decide to occupy Upper Burma to protect the interests of this company, by far the largest foreign-owned concern operating there? The question is of general importance because the company was in many respects typical of European commercial enterprises operating outside the limits of colonial territories in the later nineteenth century. Its headquarters and timber mills were in Rangoon, though it had an office in London, and for many years it had worked the Niugyan teak forests north of Toungo under contract with the Burmese government. Its activities were highly profitable for both parties, but the company found changing political conditions in the later 1870s increasingly difficult and it was forced to rely on buying off the obstruction of local Burmese officials. New and less favourable contracts were made in 1880, 1882 and 1883 which involved larger payments to the government and caused some confusion about the basis of assessment. It was therefore easy for the Burmese court to trump up a charge that the company was extracting twice the volume of logs actually paid for, that it had failed to pay the Burmese foresters their due and that it had been bribing officials to overlook these deficiencies. The corporation denied these charges, claiming that the new contracts established bulk payments and that the volume of timber shown in their books included many worthless trees. But the government refused to review the decision and impounded several log rafts until the first instalment of the fine was paid. The British government proposed neutral arbitration and when this was refused sent an ultimatum. When an unsatisfactory reply was received a British expeditionary force set out for Mandalay on 14 November 1885.

There would therefore appear to be some causal relationship between the problems of the BBTC and the final British decision to occupy Upper Burma. If so, this is important evidence on the leverage which a large commercial organization could exert on a European government. What grounds are there for thinking that the company was able to influence high policy? There is no evidence to suggest that it was able to bring pressure to bear directly on the government of India or on the India Office, though its interests were reflected in the petitions produced by the chambers of commerce. Probably its difficulties were most effectively pressed by its agent in Mandalay, the Italian consul, Chevalier Andreino, who was also agent for the Irrawaddy Flotilla Company. Because the British agent had been withdrawn from Mandalay Andreino seems to have been the most influential source of information on developments at the Burma court available to Bernard between 1882 and 1885. Indeed Bernard wrote to Calcutta in July 1885 that Andreino 'certainly gets earlier and more accurate information concerning the intentions, discussions and doings of the King's Ministers than anybody else';[2] and his reports were passed on to the India Office by the London office of the BBTC. What influence did these reports have? Andreino certainly maintained that the company was innocent and that the Burmese government was determined to force it to give up its contract in order to transfer this to French concessionaries as part of its general policy of invoking French help against British overlordship. But Bernard, and probably also the Indian and British governments, never doubted that the BBTC was guilty of cheating the Burmese government. They accepted that the fines were excessive and thought it reasonable to press for arbitration; but they were primarily concerned with the political significance of the attack on the company as evidence of the Burmese government's intentions. In the end the fine imposed on the company was clearly a catalyst for British policy and a convenient excuse for military intervention; but there are no grounds for thinking that British policy was to any large extent determined by concern for the economic interests of the BBTC or that the company was able to force the hand of the British government or of its subordinate governments in India or Rangoon.

What, then, are the alternative explanations of British action in 1885? The commonly accepted theory is that the grounds of action were political and strategic: that the British government became convinced during 1885 that France proposed to impose some form of political control or influence over Upper Burma and that action was taken to forestall this. This is an attractive hypothesis because it fits neatly into the general pattern of Anglo-French friction during the mid-1880s over Egypt and West Africa. But before adopting it without qualification it is necessary to examine the course of French policy in Upper Burma and the view taken of it by the British and Indian governments.

Between 1883 and 1885 the Burmese certainly gave the British ample grounds for believing that they hoped to obtain French help in evading British overlordship. In 1883 a Burmese delegation was sent to Paris to negotiate a new commercial treaty and to obtain military supplies. This worried London; and Lord Lyons, British Ambassador in Paris, pressed for and obtained an official assurance that the proposed treaty would not provide for a supply of arms. But the Burmese delegation remained in Paris until January 1885, and in view of deteriorating Anglo-French relations over other issues, British suspicions deepened. In July 1884 Jules Ferry (then Prime Minister) told Lyons that the Burmese wanted a full political treaty guaranteeing Upper Burma's independence and a supply of arms; but he promised that no alliance on these terms would be concluded. In January 1885 Ferry admitted that a commercial treaty had been concluded and that a French consul was to be stationed in Mandalay, but denied that this had any political implications. This was reasonably satisfactory for Britain; but when the French consul, Frederic Haas, arrived in Mandalay in May 1885 it became clear that he was determined to build up French influence there in the same way as d'Ordega was increasing French influence in Morocco. He was said to have negotiated a railway concession by which a French concern would supply £2·5 million for constructing a railway from Mandalay to Toungo to connect with the British line from Rangoon to Toungo which was nearly completed, thus excluding the British from further penetration into Upper Burma. Another reported concession allowed the French to establish a state bank in Mandalay, also with £2·5 million capital, which would have the right of issuing currency. These loans were to be secured on the receipts of river customs and oil royalties. A Burmese delegation left for Paris in July 1885 to ratify the agreements. Then in August the text of a secret letter, sent by Ferry to the Burmese government in January 1885, was published which indicated that the French would provide arms from Tongking, even though this was not provided for in the treaty. It was also reported at this time that Haas had advised Thibaw to strengthen his diplomatic position by making treaties with other European states, thus ensuring that Britain could not occupy the country without arousing major international issues. Andreino also reported that the French were negotiating to take over management of the royal ruby and tea monopolies, to control the postal system and to run river steamers in competition with the Irrawaddy Flotilla Company. As a result, so the argument goes, the British authorities became convinced that France was obtaining a preponderant economic position in Burma and that political control would follow in due course. They therefore sent in a preemptive army of occupation. In 1906 Winston Churchill could state confidently that his father, Randolph Churchill, then Secretary for India, was forced to act because these developments 'left no room to doubt the imminence of a dominant foreign influence . . . involving the most serious and far-reaching consequences to the Indian Empire'.[3]

Although there are substantial elements of truth in this interpretation of British attitudes, it requires modification in detail. Briefly, London, Calcutta and Rangoon had all been aware for a considerable period before the crisis of October 1885 over the BBTC that the French threat was less serious and immediate than it had seemed a year earlier. In 1884 Ferry had tried to dispel British fears in discussions with Lyons; but, so long as he continued to negotiate with the Burmese delegation, London was bound to distrust him. Nevertheless, it is significant that no British action was taken or, apparently, seriously contemplated during this period of genuine mistrust. But during 1885 the situation changed radically. The war in Tongking became more serious and absorbed French attention. In March Ferry fell from office and French political opinion, appalled by the reports of military disaster in Tongking, swung against an aggressive or anti-British policy. Freycinet, the new Prime Minister, was anxious to placate the British government. Early in August Salisbury warned the French Ambassador, Waddington, that the reported railway and banking concessions 'touched us closely, that Her Majesty's Government could no more admit the existence of such a contract in Burmah than the French Government would have admitted it on [the] part of a foreigner in Tunis'. He added that 'if such an understanding were carried to any practical issue, the necessary consequences would be that the liberty and power of the King of Burmah would have to be materially restricted'.[4] But a month later Salisbury seems to have received the necessary assurances from France, and could write:

We are persuaded that the French government fully appreciates the considerations which have guided us in the case, and are aware of the precautions which it is necessary to take in order to prevent confusion arising in the affairs of semi-civilized dependent states.[5]

Indeed, the French government made every effort to placate London. Early in October Waddington assured Salisbury that his government knew nothing of 'the reported agreements between [the] Burmese government and French capitalists supported by the French Consul, and has given no kind of authority for making them'.[6] In October Haas was recalled and his projects denounced in Paris. By this time, moreover, Andreino was reporting from Mandalay that his earlier fears might have been unjustified. In September he told Rangoon that the Burmese were refusing to commit themselves to Paris: 'It is clear that M. Haas has offered his services to the government, but apparently they have not been accepted as we were at first led to believe'.[7]

It seems clear, then, that by early October 1885 officials in London, Calcutta and Rangoon were aware that the immediate threat of a French takeover in Upper Burma was over and might not be revived. This in turn makes it impossible to accept a simplistic argument that the expedition to Mandalay was sent in November as an emergency measure to preclude immediate French control. What, then, were the grounds of British action? In particular, what was the relative importance of the various factors considered above – Burmese obstruction to British commerce, the interests of the BBTC, the danger of French economic predominance and the threat of French political control?

The influence of purely economic interests was clearly limited. Calcutta and London were at no stage prepared to annex Upper Burma merely to please Rangoon merchants or the BBTC. On the other hand the reports of French commercial concessions were taken seriously, as evidence of growing French political influence; for in Burma, as in China in the later 1890s, Morocco after 1909, and in Turkey before 1914, it had to be assumed that large-scale railway, mining or banking concessions were at once the product of political influence and a potential basis for future political control. Indeed it was the report of Haas' commercial agreements with Thibaw that first convinced Bernard in July 1885 that firm action would have to be taken to pursue British political pre-eminence. Above all the fine imposed on the BBTC was rightly interpreted as evidence of Burma's desire to weaken British influence, for the Burmese council which had imposed the fine had indeed been assured that a French syndicate would take over the forest concession if the British company was evicted. Thus the specific effect of commercial problems was to convince the British authorities that Burma was attempting to throw off British paramountcy.

Conversely, although the immediate French political threat was clearly retreating during the second half of 1885, by the autumn London and Calcutta were convinced that the events of the previous two years, coming after five years of increasingly unsatisfactory political relations with Upper Burma, demonstrated that the old system of informal control had failed and could not be restored without forceful action. The Military Department at Calcutta had for some years had a plan for an invasion of Upper Burma if need arose; and by October 1885 the Viceroy was convinced that the time had come to put this plan into operation. His views were clearly expressed in a despatch to the India Office of 5 October.

There was, he admitted, 'little to complain of with regard to . . . actual treaty rights, which on the whole are respected'. Calcutta was 'in communication with the Mandalay government on the subject of their alleged ill-treatment of the Bombay-Burma Trading Corporation, but the facts of this case are not yet sufficiently clear to justify us in forming an opinion adverse to the Burmese claim.' Nevertheless, on general grounds, he thought the time had come for action.

There can be no doubt that this country is rapidly becoming a source of danger to us instead of merely an annoyance. . . . If therefore King Theebaw should give us legitimate provocation, it would probably be for our interest to annex the country. . . . At present, however, the justification for such a measure is not complete.[8]

Thus the British ultimatum to Mandalay of 22 October 1885, which was approved by the British government, was intended to provide formal justification for an invasion. The conditions demanded were arbitration on the BBTC fine; acceptance of a British Resident with the right of direct access to the King, even though wearing shoes; and control of Burma's foreign relations by the government of India. The Burmese council, dominated by the Anglophobe Queen's party, rejected the first and third of these demands and made an evasive answer about the position of a future Resident. This reply was taken by Rangoon as a rejection of the ultimatum and the invasion began on 14 November. By 28 November Mandalay had been taken. Thibaw was deposed and sent to Madras. It remained only to decide whether to install another puppet ruler or to incorporate the kingdom into British India. Bernard and others in Rangoon were in favour of the former policy on the grounds that it would be difficult and expensive to impose direct rule on so xenophobic a people. The commercial interests, however, pressed hard for full annexation. An initial attempt was made to preserve the indigenous government, but this proved impracticable, partly because Nyaung Ok, the only possible substitute for Thibaw, had been living in Pondicherry and was believed to have French sympathies; partly because it proved impossible to co-operate with the Burmese council. The India Office deputed the decision to Dufferin. He visited Burma in February 1886, became convinced that it was now impracticable to re-establish the monarchy, and declared Burma a province of British India.

The final occupation of Upper Burma was not, therefore, the

product of a new imperialist urge in Britain after 1880. Changed
political conditions in South-East Asia, particularly the dynamic
role adopted by France in Indo-China, had considerable importance; but the invasion was not in any direct sense an attempt to
forestall imminent French control. Economic factors played a
major part in the course of events, but the British government was
not primarily concerned to help British merchants or investors.
Essentially the British decision to act was the outcome of the
failure of the policy followed since 1852 of attempting to maintain
a friendly and subordinate government in Mandalay. Action came
when it did because the events of the previous two years had
underlined the fundamental insecurity of British paramountcy in
an area of increasing political and commercial importance. In
Dufferin's words, annoyance had turned into a source of danger,
even if this remained potential rather than immediate. In the last
resort Burma was occupied because it was insufferable to have even
so slight a threat to British power within the environs of British
India.

II INDO-CHINA, 1880–1900[9]

In chapter 7 above it was suggested that by 1880 the position of
France in Annam had already reached crisis point in two respects.
First, French political authority was at risk because the King, Tu-
Duc, was attempting to evade French control as established by the
treaty of 1874 by appealing to China as his overlord. If he succeeded
the French position in South-East Asia, and particularly in Tongking, would be endangered. Second, there was now considerable
optimism in France about the economic opportunities to be found
in Yunnan and to a lesser extent also in Tongking; but access to
these places was blocked by disorder in Tongking and by Peking's
refusal to allow French merchants into Yunnan. France was fully
entitled to hold Tu-Duc to the terms of the 1874 treaty and to
make Tongking safe for French trade, as specified in that treaty.
But entry to Yunnan would require a new treaty with Peking
which, on earlier precedents, would almost certainly require use of
force. In 1880 Paris seemed reluctant to take effective action on
either count. Yet by 1885 Annam and Tongking had been brought
under effective French political authority and China had been
forced to concede limited entry of French merchants to Yunnan.
Why did French policy change so completely? Is this dynamic new

approach to be explained in terms of a new metropolitan imperialism? Were its roots economic and, if so, was the primary aim
possession of Tongking as an end in itself or merely commercial
access to southern China? Such questions are crucial for an interpretation of French imperialism in the late nineteenth century.

It is clear in the first place that in the early 1880s potential support
in France for a major military campaign to annex Tongking as a
field for economic enterprise was very small indeed. French capitalists were not interested in the area. In 1882 the government of
Saigon was prospecting for coal in Tongking; but the first concession was not made until 1884, after the delta had been conquered,
and mining did not start until the end of the decade. There were
no railways in Tongking until the 1890s and no other French
investment existed or seems to have been planned in the early
1880s. The only potential financial interest was the Bank of Indo-
China, founded in 1875, which was backed by several major metropolitan banking houses; but there is no evidence that these were
intriguing for military intervention. One cannot, in short, suspect
a stock-market racket. Nor does there seem to have been any
strong pressure from industrial circles who, despite Garnier's rap-
turous vision of an industrialized Yunnan, did not wish to establish
factories in South-East Asia whose products might compete with
French goods in the metropolitan market. The strongest economic
interest in Tongking was shown by commercial groups who were
already convinced by 1880 that the Red River route would provide
a means of tapping the valuable markets of southern China. But
there is no reason to think that in 1880 Lyon or the great ports,
who together constituted the major metropolitan economic interest
in Annam and Tongking, were pressing the government for immediate action. This was not surprising. French economic interests in
Tongking and Yunnan were still mere projects, blueprints drawn
by optimists. The French economy did not depend on their
implementation.

As late as December 1882 successive French governments were
in fact keenly aware that Parliament would certainly refuse credits
for a military or naval expedition to Tongking whose express
objective was annexation to serve political or economic interests.
How then does one explain French intervention? The answer is to
be found in precisely the same factors that produced almost identical action in Senegal in the early 1880s. Despite substantial public
indifference, a succession of ministers of marine, foreign ministers

and even prime ministers became convinced that French economic and political interests alike demanded action in Tongking. Where men of business remained cautious, Jauréguiberry, Freycinet, Duclerc, Gambetta and Ferry were prepared to gamble on the glittering prospects of Yunnan just as they were gambling on the riches of the western Sudan. The risks were, in fact, small. Tongking was not Tunisia. No European power was likely to object to French intervention; and for long it was believed that very small military and naval forces could deal both with Tongking and China. But how could the necessary credits be obtained from Parliament? As in Senegal, the answer was to proceed by stages: to obtain credits for a strictly limited initial expedition to solve a local crisis; then, when the crisis deepened, to claim that national honour and interest alike demanded further support. Yet even this procedure was only possible so long as the stated objectives remained strictly limited. Parliament was prepared to accept a policy designed to open the way to trade with Yunnan, just as in earlier decades it had provided credits for naval wars to open Chinese ports to French trade. Any suggestion that the war in Tongking was intended to found another French colony there would have been violently attacked. Thus the forceful methods of the early 1880s could be justified only in terms of the limited commercial objectives of previous decades.

The first initiative was appropriately taken by Admiral Jauréguiberry as Minister of Marine who had served in Cochin China as well as in Senegal and who saw Tongking with the eyes of a Saigon administrator. Convinced that the future of French trade in the Far East depended on clearing the Red River route to Yunnan, he sent out Le Myre de Vilers as Governor of Cochin China with instructions to get things moving in Tongking. In July 1881 Ferry managed to get a small credit for suppressing brigands in the Red River Delta. Early in 1882 a convenient excuse for intervention in Tongking was provided by the Black Flags – one of the three irregular Chinese armies in the province – who obstructed two French mining engineers sent by Saigon to prospect for coal in the Delta. On instructions from Jauréguiberry, now back in office, de Vilers sent a small force of four hundred troops under Commandant Rivière to protect French interests. Rivière then did exactly what Garnier had done in 1873. He captured the fortress of Hanoi from Annamese troops and allowed himself to be beleaguered there by hostile Chinese forces. At last Saigon had managed to create a genuine crisis affecting the lives of French soldiers and French honour. How far would France be prepared to use the opportunity?

A first decision on the extent of French aims had to be taken late in 1882 when news of Rivière's position reached Paris. Duclerc, the Foreign Minister, asked for credits for a relief expedition of seven hundred men, far too few to conquer Tongking, but enough to extricate Rivière. Even this was opposed by the President, Grévy, who at the beginning of the year had prevented Gambetta from sending a far larger force to Tongking, and by many others in Parliament who feared another Algeria or Tunisia or, still worse, a disaster such as Mexico. This opposition forced those with genuine interests in the future of Tongking to show their hand; and for the first time commercial and industrial groups publicly expressed demands for political action. It seems clear that someone must have mobilized support for the proposed credits, for early in December three important commercial groups published their views on the economic advantages at stake in remarkably similar terms.[10] Their arguments nevertheless deserve careful examination as some indication of the character and limitations of metropolitan economic imperialism in the early 1880s.

First, the Chambre syndicale des Négociants-Commissionaires of Paris, who had been addressed on the subject of Tongking ten days earlier by Ernest Millot, second in command of Dupuis' Red River expedition a decade earlier, wrote to the Minister of Marine as follows:

We think . . . that the solution of this question is of a nature to procure for our country the following results: The creation of new maritime lines towards our stations in Tongkin and the surrounding countries;

Opening of new markets for French products;

Exploitation of the mineral riches and products of the soil of Tong-king; [sic].

Immediately assured commercial relations with the populations of the countries visited by M. Dupuis;

The direct importation of raw materials for which France is presently dependent on other nations.

This is why the Chambre . . . has passed the following resolutions:

That the question of Ton-king [sic] be promptly resolved by the occupation of the Red River and its customs houses, in order to ensure the security of commerce, and by the definite establishment of an effective protectorate.[11]

On the same day the *Journal des Chambres de Commerce Françaises* complained that:

In Asia we appear to be abandoning the expedition of Tongkin which would open . . . considerable markets. This abandonment would be a major mistake; let us hope that the government and our Chambers refuse to commit it.[12]

Eleven days later the Syndicat General de l'Union du Commerce et de l'Industrie passed an almost identical resolution which defined the commercial benefits to be expected, as follows:

It is principally to M. Dupuis that the honour belongs for solving the great economic problem which the English have studied for so long and which consists in the establishment of a short and easy commercial route between the sea and the western provinces of China so as to avoid the long, difficult, and costly Yangtze route.

The conquest of a new group of near to fifty million consumers which will open to our commerce markets where our manufactures will be easily exchanged for raw materials is a matter assuredly worth the trouble it entails.[13]

Commenting on these and other resolutions in favour of a forward policy in Tongking, the *Journal* emphasized that:

. . . all the regions of France are interested in the opening of this great market: Marseille from the maritime point of view, Lyon for silk, Bordeaux, Nantes, Le Havre for colonial commodities.

The *Journal* also denounced the limited territorial objectives announced by the government:

The strategic occupation of the delta of the Red River only imperfectly corresponds to the desires of French commerce. What is necessary to contribute to the ending of the economic crisis is the commercial route of the Red River and all of Tongking with its abundant resources and its fifteen million inhabitants.[14]

What light do these resolutions and editorial comments throw on French business attitudes to Tongking? First, the declared objectives were almost entirely commercial. There is no mention of investment opportunities nor of developing new resources except for mining. Second, the commercial groups expressly demanded full political control only of the delta and its customs houses, together with more efficient informal control over the court of Annam to prevent future obstruction in Tongking. The primary aim therefore remained satisfactory conditions for trade rather than possession of territory. Only the *Journal* seems to have been determined on full annexation of the whole of Tongking, though conversely there is no reason to think that any of these groups positively objected to French political control over the whole of Tongking if this was possible. How far the views of these professional associations reflected a consensus of French business opinion is impossible to say. But it is at least clear that by 1882–3 propagandists had convinced important sections of the business world as well as leading politicians that the still almost unknown economic resources of Tongking and Yunnan were so valuable that they justified use of military force and expenditure of substantial public funds. This is the main ground for regarding the events of 1883–5 as an example of French metropolitan economic imperialism. At the same time it is important to note that these economic objectives were first formulated on the periphery and that the immediate occasion for military action was obstruction of commerce by indigenous political forces. Metropolitan readiness to occupy Tongking did not stem from abstract belief that territorial empire was invariably necessary to French economic interests.

Perhaps because of the support it received from commercial groups, French governmental policy changed sharply between December 1882 and March 1883. In December 1882 Duclerc got his credits for an expeditionary force to relieve Hanoi; but his long-term objective was not conquest of the whole of Tongking, for in December 1882 the French Minister at Peking was negotiating for a partition of Tongking into French and Chinese spheres of influence, coupled with withdrawal of all official Chinese forces and freedom of access for French traders to Yunnan. This was the old programme of limited political responsibility to serve purely commercial needs. But in January 1883 Jules Ferry took office as Prime Minister, and it became clear that his aims went further than those of Duclerc or Grévy. Whether at this stage he had already decided that full and permanent occupation of Tongking was necessary is impossible to say. Probably he was certain only that the Chinese must be forced to withdraw completely and renounce any further right to interfere in Annamese territory; that Hué must be brought under proper control; and that Tongking must be cleared of Chinese brigands. Even so this policy demanded much more extensive action than Duclerc had planned. The negotiations with China were dropped and on 24 April 1883 Ferry asked for credits to provide a naval force and four thousand troops. By coincidence Rivière was killed on 19 May while these proposals were still in debate. His death was therefore not in any sense the cause of Ferry's new policy. But it did make it simpler to obtain a credit of 5·5 million francs; and it added emotional overtones to a war undertaken in defence of French commercial interests.

It is not proposed to trace the course of the Tongking War, which is largely irrelevant to analysis of its economic objectives. In brief, Hué was quickly brought to heel by naval forces and on 25 August 1883 a new treaty was signed with Annam which closely resembled the Treaty of Bardo with Tunisia. The protectorate of 1874 was reaffirmed, but was changed in character. Tongking was to be under direct French administration, though remaining part of the Annamese Empire. French sovereignty over Cochin China was reaffirmed and the province of Binh-Thuan added to it. The King was to rule the rest of Annam, but foreign affairs, customs duties, communications and public works were placed under French officials seconded to his service. In June 1884 after the Treaty of Tien-Tsin with China, a new treaty was signed with Hué, identical with that of 1883 except that Binh-Thuan was returned to Annam. This virtually ended the problem of control over Annam and constituted the basis for the federation of Indo-China which was established in 1887.

The problem of China remained. In May 1884 Peking was forced to accept the Treaty of Tien-Tsin by which China recognized French control of Annam, agreed to withdraw all imperial troops from Tongking and permitted French trade to Yunnan at specified frontier towns. This was all Ferry had hoped for, and the war was only prolonged by a genuine misunderstanding over the timetable for the withdrawal of Chinese troops. On 15 June 1884 a French force was repulsed at Bac-Le by Chinese troops who maintained that they were not yet due to evacuate the place. Peking could show from its copy of the draft treaty they were in the right, but Ferry insisted on immediate withdrawal and an indemnity of 50 million francs. Since Peking refused, a naval blockade was mounted on the China coast and by March 1885 China was ready to come to terms. In June 1885 the second Treaty of Tien-Tsin gave France almost precisely the same rights as the draft treaty of 1884 though without payment of the indemnity demanded in 1884.

This left only the task of making Tongking fit for trade by suppressing the various armies of Chinese and Annamese brigands, which was not finally completed until 1897. Indeed, the attempt was nearly given up in 1885 as a result of the ridiculous Lang-Son episode when a French army on the Chinese frontier was thought to be in serious danger from a Chinese force which in fact was already retreating. This farcical event was, however, significant because it brought about Ferry's fall from office. Equally important, the newly elected Chamber reflected a substantial public reaction against a policy which had cost immense sums of money (credits asked for in March 1885 alone were 200 million francs), had produced military disaster but had not yet opened the Red River to French trade. On 13 December 1885 it was only decided to retain Tongking by four votes and after a strong intervention by Gambetta. By this time, indeed, Tongking was losing much of its appeal in France. Committed enthusiasts such as Ulysse Pila, a Lyon silk merchant with large interests in the China silk trade, continued to defend both the Red River route and the economic prospects of Tongking itself; but in February 1885 Paul Brunet, sent by the Chambers of Commerce to investigate all Tongking's economic possibilities, reported that the Red River would be no use as a large-scale commercial artery – only a railway would give direct access to Yunnan; and that Tongking itself could only reduce French dependence on Chinese silk after a long period of preparation. French economic interests therefore concentrated increasingly on the wealth of Yunnan, the original objective of those who prospected the Red River; and the myth of an Eldorado in southern China was not in fact dispelled until after the Lyon trade mission to Yunnan in 1895–7 had demonstrated that this too was an illusion. The effects of this gradual disillusionment of French policy in southern China will be considered below.

How, then, should one define the role of economic factors in the extension of French control over Annam and Tongking between 1880 and 1885? There can be no doubt that economic interests – more precisely, economic expectations – were the main driving force throughout this period, as indeed they had been from the early 1870s. It is arguable that French political authority over Annam would in any case eventually have had to be strengthened since Hué was never prepared to accept its political subordination as defined in the 1874 treaty. Yet, without the problem of Tongking, this would have been a relatively minor problem, for it was mainly the French attempt during the 1870s to break through from Hanoi to Yunnan that led to Hué's appeal for Chinese intervention which in turn forced France to occupy Tongking. French interest in Tongking was undoubtedly economic, for France had no other

significant national interest there. But what were the precise economic objectives and did they necessarily involve political control?
Do they reflect a new type of economic imperialism in France or
merely the continuance of traditional commercial objectives?

The evidence considered above points strongly to the second of
these interpretations. French attention concentrated on southern
China rather than Tongking. The really strong and almost universal
hope, linking Lyon silk manufacturers with Bordeaux and Marseille
merchants and those few politicians concerned with the large-scale
economic problems of French overseas trade, was that the Red
River would give France a shorter, cheaper and above all monopolistic route to markets and sources of raw materials in southern
China. Although some enthusiasts undoubtedly believed that Tongking itself might be a major economic asset, to most it was merely a
transit area. Why, then, was political control of Tongking thought
necessary? In principle few thought it was, provided that Annam,
China, the Tongking mandarins and Chinese private armies did not
obstruct French trade. The preferred French solution was, therefore, to obtain freedom of access by treaty with Hué and Peking.
But when this was blocked by Annam's appeal for Chinese support
and China's refusal to allow French trade to Yunnan, France had
to make decisions; and the decision-making process provides the
best evidence on the character of French imperialism at the start
of the 1880s. Does the fact that France decided to use political
methods to achieve this essentially economic objective indicate
that the official mind of France had now adopted a new attitude to
economic problems overseas? Were the politicians now at last ready
to use the full force of the state and to impose political control over
new territories whenever merely economic interests were involved?

It is difficult to be certain whether those who committed France
to military action in Tongking – Jauréguiberry, Duclerc, Ferry –
were entirely clear about their ultimate objectives, any more than
they were in Tunisia, Egypt, Senegal or later Madagascar. The
essential point is that at the outset each of these enterprises had a
limited objective and involved strictly limited public expenditure.
The two preliminary French expeditions sent to Hanoi in 1882
were very small and cheap. Even in March 1883 Ferry asked for
only 5 million francs on the assumption that brisk naval action
and a short military campaign in the Red River would be sufficient.
On 31 October 1883, when challenged by the opposition in Parliament to define French objectives, Ferry pledged his government

to a strictly limited territorial control of the delta as a necessary means of opening the Red River route to trade.

You rightly said in your speech yesterday, Mr Perin ... that the nations of Europe long ago recognized that the conquest of China with its 400 million consumers must be carried out entirely by European products and producers. But to carry out this peaceful conquest one has to have access to this rich area! It is for this reason that I admire and am grateful for the watchfulness, the wisdom or the deep instinct that led our predecessors to the mouth of the Red River and showed them that it was necessary to control Tongking. That, gentlemen, is what gives this enterprise its great importance and lifts this debate above all questions of political office. ...

If I might read out the complete instruction (sent to our civil commissioner) you would see that they were careful to foresee, control and define everything. And as for the limits of the expedition itself you would recognize that they were fixed and restricted very precisely. This is what they say:

'The only part of Tonkin that we propose to occupy is the delta of Song-Koi: we do not intend to go beyond Bac-Ninh and Hunghoa, near the confluence of the River Claire, apart from any places on the coast that may seem necessary. It is scarcely possible at this stage to define the military posts which it may be necessary to hold. However, it is useful to mention, in addition to Hanoi and Nam-Dinh, where our flag already flies, Hai-Phong, Ninbinh, Bac-Linh, Sontay, probably Honeng-Yen and Mukoi or Vanning.'[15]

Things did not, of course, work out that way. In the end it was necessary to occupy and govern the whole of Tongking, just as it proved necessary to occupy the whole of Tunisia, the western Sudan and eventually Madagascar. Does this suggest that Ferry was dishonest in defining more limited objectives? This is possible, but unlikely. It is more probable that he and his supporters genuinely hoped that limited military action and restricted political occupation would be sufficient, but that he was also ready to go further if it proved essential. Whether he would have been ready at this stage to accept the immense expenditure of money and lives and the political consequences that resulted from escalation of the war in 1884 and thereafter is more doubtful.

It is, in fact, very important to recognize that in the early 1880s French readiness to use military and political means to solve commercial problems or to gain economic objectives overseas was conditioned by an excessively optimistic calculation of costs in relation to benefits expected. The Tongking enterprise can only be understood in these terms. The cost of the expedition in 1883 was estimated at a mere 5·5 million francs, but the potential prize – the trade of southern China – had untold value. In 1880 some 38 per cent of the raw silk used by the French silk industry came from China, either direct from Shanghai and Canton or via London.[16] Since exports of silken fabrics from Lyon alone were worth 234·2 million francs in 1880, out of total French exports of 3,500 million francs, it was clearly worth investing five million francs if it would ensure cheaper supplies of raw silk.[17] But access to southern China offered other rewards. At a time when the international depression was affecting overseas French markets, the possibility of finding a vast market in southern China to which foreign competitors would have no direct access was extremely attractive, and this was given added value by the fact that France had a very large adverse trading balance with China. In 1880 French imports from China were worth £4 million as against exports worth c. £136,000.[18] This was annoying in that the British had an adverse balance of only £3·5 million on a combined import-export trade worth £22·5 million,[19] which was entirely eliminated after 1885. Clearly the answer was to match British access to Chinese consumers via Hong Kong, Shanghai and the Yangtze by an all-French route from Hanoi to Yunnan. With such international economic interests at stake military intervention in Tongking could not be regarded as simply a concession to sectional pressure groups; and when the estimated cost was so small it was not difficult to convince the Chamber that the money would be well spent. These were the grounds on which a small campaign, leading to intensified informal control over Tongking and Annam, could be defended as a valid use of state power to serve national economic interests.

Although France's decision to conquer Tongking in 1883–5 is in many ways the most interesting aspect of French expansion in South-East Asia after 1880, it was by no means the end of the story. The war to pacify Tongking of course continued until 1897 and absorbed a large part of French resources in Indo-China. But why should French territorial expansion in this region stop with Tongking? After 1885 two main options were available: expansion westwards into the states of Laos and beyond them to Siam; expansion northwards from Tongking into southern China. To understand the character of French imperialism in this period it is necessary to consider briefly why France chose to expand into Laos but not into China.

There were obvious political and military grounds on which France might and did think it desirable to control the small states which constituted Laos, lying on the left (eastern) bank of the River Mekong.[20] The northern region of Laos, including the kingdom of Luang Prabang and several of the Shan states, occupied a strategically important position between Tongking, Upper Burma and China. Since the British had occupied Upper Burma in 1885–6 and the French were in process of occupying Tongking, northern Laos came to be regarded by the French as a necessary safeguard against British expansion into Siam and Tongking. Farther south, Laotian territories came very close to the coast of Annam and to Hué, leaving only a narrow corridor linking Cochin China with Tongking. The problem facing the French was that, although Annam, now under their effective control, had shadowy historical claims to suzerainty over these Laotian states, these were almost impossible to establish legally and in practice the Laotian rulers accepted Siamese overlordship. In the later 1880s, moreover, the King of Siam, worried by the French advance into Tongking, decided to consolidate his overlordship by effective military occupation. Having formally claimed the whole Mekong Valley in September 1884, he began a series of annual military campaigns east of the Mekong which, by 1888, had placed Siamese troops at Cam Mon, some eighty kilometres from Hué. Since Siam could still reasonably be regarded as a rival for predominance in South-East Asia and was assumed to be under strong British political and economic influence, this was a serious political threat to the new French federation of Indo-China.

French attitudes to the states of Laos in the mid-1880s were therefore essentially defensive. The British must be kept out of the region and Siamese forces must if possible be induced to withdraw to the line of the Mekong. It would be desirable to reach a general agreement with Britain which would leave France a free hand in Laos in return for British preponderance over Siamese territories in the Malay peninsula. Beyond this there were two other basic French objectives in the mid-1880s: to regain for Cambodia, now under French protection, the two provinces of Battambang and Angkor, ceded to Siam in 1867; and to guarantee the independence of Siam proper against assumed British acquisitiveness. All these were clearly political aims whose primary focus was the security of French Indo-China. But were there also economic motives for occupying Laos?

Inevitably, given the characteristic optimism of some Frenchmen, there were some who suggested that control of Laos and the Mekong would be economically advantageous. It is clear, however, that in most cases economic means were clearly intended to promote political purposes. At no stage did French commercial interests based on Saigon show marked enthusiasm for annexation of Laos as a possible commercial hinterland for Cochin China; and in fact the greater part of Saigon's trade was in the hands of British, German or Chinese merchants. But between 1885–7 the Lieutenant-Governor of Cochin China, Michel Fillipini, tried to revive the old Garnier project for penetrating Laos, and possibly southern China, via the Mekong. Fillipini's intentions were strictly political: to counter Siamese control of Laos which he regarded as a cover for British influence there. His death in 1887 effectively killed this project, which in any case had little commercial utility. From 1889 to 1893, however, somewhat similar commercial arguments were used in favour of annexation of Upper Laos. Governor General Piquet was briefly convinced by Camille Gauthier, a protégé of Pavie, French consul in Luang Prabang, that the Mekong might be used to link Tongking with Laos, and Laos in turn with Saigon, and that the Laotian market might be worth some 25 million francs a year. This hope also collapsed when it became clear – as the Lagrée mission had demonstrated in 1866–8 – that the rapids at Khone could not effectively be by-passed. Piquet nevertheless clung to the aim of establishing French trade in the extreme northern region of Laos, primarily to strengthen French claims there against those of Britain; and in this he was strongly supported by a group of French patriots and businessmen in Paris who launched two small companies to trade in Laos – the Société du Mekong and the Société du Haut Laos. Both had essentially political purposes. The Société du Haut Laos, the larger of the two, established in 1891, had a share capital of only 200,000 francs, more than half of which was subscribed by members of the Société du Géographie Commerciale de Paris, a body whose primary function was to promote French colonial expansion. None of the stockholders ever received a dividend or enquired what happened to their capital. Moreover the company's stated objects were to offset British commercial and political influence in northern Laos and to attach this area to French Indo-China. It achieved nothing commercially and stands as an example of that type of quasi-commercial organization which flourished in the 1880s and 1890s as the expression of the patriotic fervour of colonial enthusiasts who saw in commerce a means to strengthen the political claims of their metropolis to overseas territories in dispute with other European powers.

French motives for annexing Laos and eastern Cambodia were therefore clearly political rather than economic, a reaction to real or imagined frontier threats to the security of existing possessions. France had to proceed slowly, both because precipitate action might produce British counter-action and because she could not risk a major war with Siam while Tongking remained unpacified, and while metropolitan opinion was hostile to expensive campaigns in South-East Asia. In 1886 an agreement with Siam provided for a French consul to be stationed at Luang Prabang; and Pavie, the man appointed, who was already an expert on South-East Asian affairs, understood that his role was to prepare the way for later French occupation. For the time being effective action was barred by the presence of a Siamese force which was there by request of the King of Luang Prabang to deal with invading Chinese troops. But, with the support of private funds from French imperialists and general approval from Paris, Pavie was able to survey the country and strengthen French influence there as a prelude to French occupation when the time was ripe. Meantime Paris kept the issue open by refusing to delimit the frontiers of Tongking with Burma or Siam.

In 1889, however, it seemed momentarily possible that France might obtain British approval and support for occupation of Laos. The British were anxious to make a final territorial settlement of the area and accepted that Siam proper should remain an independent buffer state. Since the French also accepted this, the main obstacle to agreement lay in defining the boundaries of French and British territory in the northern region of Laos. In 1889 Paris ingeniously suggested a general agreement by which Siam would be neutralized, the Shan states between the Salween and Nam Ou Rivers would be given to Siam as a buffer between British and French possessions, and France would be allowed to occupy all territory claimed on the left (eastern) bank of the Mekong. Although this plan restricted French objectives, particularly in Battambang and Angkor, London was not prepared to give up Burmese claims to the Shan states east of the Salween nor willing to force Siam to accept the loss of Laos to help France. The negotiation therefore lapsed and the British established their own frontiers between Burma and Siam. On the other hand London did not feel able to take a stand against continuing French ambitions in Laos. Anglo-French relations were already difficult over Egypt, the Niger and the Upper Nile; and Rosebery, who became Foreign Secretary in 1892, was anxious to reach agreement with France rather than to provoke her unnecessarily. Britain was also faced with a crisis on the north-west frontier of India where a small Russian force established in Bozai Gumbaz was deemed to constitute a threat to Indian security. In such circumstances Rosebery was prepared to sacrifice Siamese imperial interests in Laos, provided that the core of Siam was preserved intact. The French were therefore able in 1893 to arrange a number of apparently provocative incidents involving French interests in various parts of Laos as a justification for intervention. On 13 July 1893 French gunboats arrived at Bangkok and delivered an ultimatum. When this was rejected a naval blockade was imposed and on 29 July Siam accepted French demands for cession of all territory on the left bank of the Mekong. On the next day an incorrect report that the French had ordered British warships to leave Bangkok produced a crisis between London and Paris; but when this had been resolved the two powers settled down amicably to arrange the permanent boundaries of Siam. Again Britain lacked the diplomatic strength to take a firm line. By the agreement of 1896 she accepted French control of Laos and the Cambodian provinces of Battambang and Angkor on condition that France jointly guaranteed the integrity of the rump of Siam. These arrangements were finalized by the Franco-Siamese treaty of 1907. French Indo-China had reached the limits of its westward expansion.

Far more important for a study of economic factors in French imperialism was the question of expansion northwards from Tongking into southern China. The main course of European intervention in China during the period after 1890 will be discussed in chapter 12. Here it is proposed to concentrate on the evolution of French attitudes to the possibility of territorial control of the southern province of China as a logical extension of their interests in Indo-China.

In the mid-1880s there were two grounds on which future French occupation of Yunnan, and possibly other southern provinces of China, might have been predicted. On political grounds these might have been thought necessary to provide defence in depth of Tongking and to ensure against annexation by Britain or some other European power. Economic factors were, however,

likely to be more significant. It has been seen that the most important single factor making for French occupation of Tongking was
desire to gain direct access to the reputed wealth of southern China.
But by the late 1880s many French imperialists were coming to
assume that, on African precedents, economic exploitation of
regions outside Europe required political control of territory rather
than mere freedom of commercial access; and genuine fear during
the early 1890s that Britain proposed to engross southern China
generated a flood of demands by imperialists in France for political
action to safeguard French economic interests there. For a decade
after 1885 French preoccupation in Tongking and Laos prevented
serious consideration of further expansion to the north; but by
1895 conditions had changed dramatically. The defeat of China by
Japan indicated that Peking was no longer militarily capable of
defending its vast empire. The near conclusion of the Tongking
War and the completion of the light military railway to Longson
in 1894 made it easier for France to make good any claim she might
wish to stake in Yunnan, Kweichow or Szechuan. Above all, the
rapid evolution of claims by other European powers to concessions
and spheres of influence in China seemed proof that France must
act or lose her chance. Yet by 1899 Paris had decided firmly against
the extension of Indo-China to the north. Why was this? What light
does eventual French endorsement of a 'hands-off' policy in China
throw on the evolution of French economic imperialism?

Between 1895 and 1898 it was by no means certain that France
would resist the temptation to impose some form of political control over southern China. From the end of 1896 the Governor
General of Indo-China was Paul Doumer, a radical politician out
of office and a convinced expansionist, who took every opportunity
to press the case for annexation of Yunnan. In 1898 he put forward
a plan for a vast railway system in Indo-China and argued that its
costs could be met 'by the annexation and exploitation of Yunnan'.
In 1899–1900 he was anxious to use any commercial local crisis –
an attack on the French consul's house at Mengtze in 1899 or the
Boxer rising of 1900 – as the occasion for military intervention;
and Paris recognized that he was quite capable of staging another
Fashoda on his own initiative. Moreover, he had some support in
the Quai d'Orsay, significantly from the political rather than the
commercial section, where it was believed that France would forfeit
political influence in China if she did not stake her claims to territory. Pichon, French Ambassador in Peking, pressed the same view

in 1899. Division of China into spheres of influence would damage some established French interests in spheres allocated to other European states, notably the French Catholic missions; but he believed that France had no alternative in view of the ambitions of other powers. Thus it was at least possible that France might stake a claim to territorial control over part of southern China in 1895–9 in pursuit of commercial objectives and to safeguard her political status in the Far East.

Why did she not do so? There appear to have been two main reasons, one economic, the other political. The really significant fact is that by the mid-1890s the largest and most specifically economic interest groups in France were almost uniformly opposed to territorial control of any part of China. Lyon, which had been a strong supporter of a forward policy in Tongking a decade earlier and had sent an important mission to southern China in 1895–7 to investigate its economic possibilities, nevertheless strongly opposed political partition of China. The basic reason was that the Lyon silk industry could see no advantage in formal territorial control by European states. Lyon was traditionally a supporter of free trade and distrusted spheres of influence intended to provide exclusive commerce. In any case the Declaration of London of 1896 provided that any commercial privileges obtained by France or Britain in China should be fully available to the other. Hence, as Auguste Isaac, representing Lyon opinion, told Doumer at a banquet given by the Chamber of Commerce in May 1901, Lyon was interested 'neither in absorption nor conquest'. They wanted only 'economic relations, the economic concourse brought by one of the civilizations to the other'. There was no advantage to be gained from political confrontation with Britain. 'The most certain way of assuring us an important role in the economic opening of Szechuan obviously is to connect by railroad the valley of the Red River with that of the Yangtze.'[22] In short, Lyon had fallen back on conventional mid-nineteenth-century attitudes. In Tongking political methods had been necessary to remove political obstacles to freedom of commercial access, but by the late 1890s there were no serious political obstacles to commerce in China and political methods were therefore irrelevant and potentially harmful. This was the authentic voice of economic imperialism, pragmatic and devoid of jingoism.

Precisely the same attitude was adopted by the big financial houses of Paris, the other important French group with economic interests in China. Their view was conditioned by the fact that existing French investments, worth perhaps 300 million francs, were widely dispersed in almost any part of China except those southern provinces which France might hope to obtain if China was partitioned: in Shanghai, Hankow and the projected Peking-Hankow railway, all of which were likely to be allocated to Britain, Russia or Germany. Conversely, the financiers were already using Russia as a satisfactory medium for investment in China, through the 1895 Franco-Russian indemnity loan to Peking, the Russo-Chinese Bank, the Trans-Siberian railway, and loans for Russian development of Manchuria. This meant that they were banking on the survival of China as an integral state under informal European supervision, for many of these investments would be at risk if Peking was unable to honour its debts. These attitudes were accepted and publicized by the immensely influential Leroy-Beaulieu family, which considered that the best role for France to play in China was to provide capital for economic development. In 1898 Paul Leroy-Beaulieu, who since 1874 had been propagating the argument that colonization was often necessary for satisfactory investment of capital overseas, stated that formal control and partition were irrelevant under the special circumstances of China. The southern provinces were not worth French attention and it followed that 'no one with good sense can have the wish or desire that the Chinese empire be materially and politically broken-up and that each great power take effective possession of one of the pieces'.[23] Pierre Leroy-Beaulieu took the same line. The southern provinces of China, in which France received commercial privileges in 1895, were overrated for they 'produced neither silk, nor tea, nor any of the great export products'. Despite the superficial optimism shown by the Lyon mission's report, their evidence in fact underlined 'the great difficulties of transport . . . the lack of population in contrast to the overabundance of the Yangtze basin and the coastal provinces'. The conclusion was inevitable: France should co-operate 'with the English, with the Germans as well as with the Belgians and Russians in order to employ our capital in a remunerative fashion in this vast market'.[24]

The second and perhaps decisive reason why France did not press for control of southern China lay in the field of international relations. From 1895 to 1898 this outcome could not have been predicted with any assurance, for Paris kept its options open. In 1895 two conventions were signed with Peking. The first gave

France additional territory on the Tongking frontier between the Mekong and Red Rivers; the second opened further frontier towns in Yunnan to French trade, reduced tariffs on the trade with Indo-China, gave France first option on mineral exploitation in southern China and permitted construction of a railway from Tongking to Yunnan. In 1897 Peking gave permission for the Longson railway to be extended to Nanning-fu and Pese. In April 1898 China promised not to alienate Yunnan, Kwangsi or Kwantung to any other power and gave France a ninety-nine-year lease on Kwang-Chow. Finally, in May 1898 Peking agreed to a railway from Pak-hoi to West River. These were all steps towards a possible French sphere of influence or protectorate over southern China. Yet Paris simultaneously left the way open for maintenance of an 'open door' policy. In 1896 Hanataux signed the Declaration of London by which Britain and France, in the tradition of Chinese treaty-making since the 1840s, pledged that they would share all commercial privileges either might obtain from China; and this immediately neutralized any special advantages France obtained in southern China while providing her with compensating opportunities on the Yangtze, where British enterprise predominated. In February 1898 Hanataux summarized the equivocating policy he had followed since 1895 in a draft of the instructions to be given to Pichon as French Ambassador to Peking: '[The] policy which we supported in 1894: the integrity of the Chinese Empire. The interest we have is that it does not disintegrate. But if it does, we claim our share'.[25] Thus, as late as the spring of 1898 Paris held its hand; and so long as it was believed that Britain was determined to establish an exclusive sphere of influence on the Yangtze France was ready to claim southern China.

From June 1898, however, when Delcassé became Foreign Minister, French policy changed. Delcassé had two major diplomatic objectives: to reduce Anglo-French tension everywhere, and to arrange a solution of the Chinese question which would protect French economic interests without alienating Britain. The new realities of the economic and political situation were fully grasped by Paul Cambon, French Ambassador in London:

Like Germany, Russia, and England, we also have to choose between the policy of spheres of influence and that of the 'open door'. It would be dangerous for us to be dominated by our experience in African conflicts. In these badly known regions, regions of uncertain future, it was natural to pursue the acquisition of considerable territories of which a portion were valuable and to adopt the theory of spheres of influence. The situation is completely different in China, and, if England is interested in encouraging Germany to support this theory, she is not less interested in encouraging us in the line of our African tradition. What sphere of influence could we claim in China? To the north, Yunnan is part of the Yangtze basin and we are engaged not to seek particular advantages there. Kwangtung is under the influence of the English of Hongkong. ... There remains Kwangsi, a mountainous and sterile country whose population furnished China with the armies with which she opposed us in Tonkin. One can think that Germany if absolutely necessary could be content with Shantung, whose wealth could compensate for the monetary sacrifices on the part of the state. For us, the conquest of our sphere of influence would lead to grave difficulties without economic compensations.[26]

Cambon's suggested solution was to co-operate with Britain to preserve the 'open door'; and in July 1899 he underlined the fact that the two countries shared common interests in China.

Our interests in China, which are considerable ... are of two sorts: some moral, those of the Catholic missions; the others material, those of our silk exporters, of our financiers engaged in railroad and mining enterprises. Neither our missionaries, nor our Lyonnais merchants, nor our financiers threaten England. Their true rivals are the Germans or the Americans. Why then should our action be strongly opposed to that of the British cabinet?

I will add that the great enterprises, which are now being undertaken in all parts of China, will lead almost necessarily to a collaboration of the nationals of the two countries at least on the level of business affairs. ... In order to execute the important works whose concessions they have obtained from China, it is very probable that the Englishmen of affairs must have recourse to the aid of the Paris [money] market.[27]

This view was accepted by the commercial section of the Quai d'Orsay but it was disputed by the political affairs section which held to the traditional view that France must control areas bordering Tongking just as Russia felt bound to control Chinese territory on the frontiers of Siberia. Delcassé and the French government had to make their choice. Delcassé at least was clear that, if French economic interests would not suffer, the right course was that which would improve Franco-British political relations. He was also clear that Russia rather than Britain was driving the powers to define spheres of influence; and, since Russia was an ally of France, her political ambitions could be restrained. The United States' 'open door' note of November 1899 gave Delcassé the opportunity to align himself with Britain without seeming to submit to British pressures; and on 24 November he committed himself before the French Chamber to preserve both the territorial integrity of China and the 'open door' for trade. With Fashoda out of the way, West African differences resolved, and France prepared to accept the British line in China, the way was now open to the entente of 1904.

What, then, is the significance of events in South-East Asia for an interpretation of economic factors in French imperialism after about 1880? The answer is to be found by contrasting French policy in Tongking in the early 1880s with that in China during the later 1890s. In each case metropolitan economic objections were the same – freedom to trade and invest in China. Different means to these ends reflected contrasting circumstances. In the 1870s and 1880s it was believed that southern China offered immense economic opportunities, and for long France hoped to gain access to these by diplomacy and informal influence. When and because these techniques failed metropolitan economic interests demanded political action to remove the political factors which obstructed the route to southern China. At first this recourse to political methods was pragmatic – there was demonstrably no other way to achieve economic objectives, and the British might reach Yunnan first if France did not take immediate action. But during the later 1880s and early 1890s the widespread use of military force and formal rule, not only in Indo-China but in Tunisia, West Africa, the Congo and elsewhere, generated belief that this was the best or even the only way to open up and safeguard overseas territories on behalf of French economic enterprise. This was certainly the typical view of French armchair imperialists, colonial administrators, frontier soldiers and even some senior officials in Paris during the 1890s; and it was further stimulated by continuing bad relations with Britain which gave every peripheral situation competitive overtones. The significant fact is, however, that the genuine economic interest groups and the more realistic politicians and officials both remained far more flexible in outlook. Formal empire was only worthwhile if it served specific functions, political or economic. By the later 1890s businessmen and some politicians and officials recognized that in China economic and political interests led away from formal control. Paul Cambon was not correct in thinking that France deliberately embarked on a general partition of Africa because no one knew which areas of that unknown continent might prove valuable; though as a retrospective comment on the partition his generalization is illuminating. But he was entirely right in thinking that formal partition was irrelevant in China if only because her economic assets were real and well-charted. For France to select territory in southern China simply because it was contiguous with Tongking would have been pointless. Nor was it worthwhile to demand partition simply to exclude Britain from certain parts of China, for France needed a political rapprochement with her. In 1899, therefore, the French government, with full support from metropolitan economic interests, rejected the conventional territorial imperialism of the 1880s and co-operated with Britain and the United States to neutralize China politically in order to provide the best conditions for economic penetration.

12 China and the Pacific

I CHINA, 1880–1905[1]

The importance of China for a study of the relations between economic and political factors in modern imperialism is that, while she had more to offer European merchants and investors than most independent countries of the non-European world, she was also one of the very few such states which, ignoring small coastal leases and the indignity of the 'unequal treaties', 'got away'. Since other states which similarly evaded alien rule – Turkey, Siam and Japan are three leading examples – are not dealt with in this book, it is doubly important to discover why this was so. The answer lies partly in the patterns of international diplomacy and partly in the specific economic interests of the many European powers involved. Since the diplomatic history of the Chinese question from about 1894 to 1905 is both complex and well documented it is not proposed to rehearse it here. Emphasis will be laid on the particular economic objectives of Russia, Britain, Germany and France and why each of these eventually decided that these objectives could best be served by preserving China as an integral state rather than by following the model of African partition.

On the assumption that late nineteenth-century imperialism was motivated by pursuit of markets and investment opportunities, China was an obvious candidate for division between the powers. To the European merchant she offered a vast market which was virtually untapped. To the manufacturer she offered raw materials, such as silk. To the capitalist investor she was even more attractive. In about 1880 China had no railways, few European-type public utilities, almost no modern industry and a very small public debt. Given the opportunity the openings for investment seemed infinite. Until the 1890s, however, all this was tantalizingly held out of reach by the continuing resistance of the imperial government in Peking to alien penetration of China beyond the treaty ports. China suddenly became an international issue in the 1890s because Japan's victory in the war of 1894–5 completely, though in fact temporarily, destroyed Peking's ability to resist. The last of the fabled Eldorados was open to exploitation.

But what form would this exploitation take? In 1895 the options were wide open. The immediate situation was that the Japanese had suddenly defeated Chinese naval and military forces in Korea and southern Manchuria. The war itself stemmed entirely from long-term rivalry between these two Asian powers for political and economic primacy in Korea, and the China question of the next decade was therefore, from a European viewpoint, a peripheral development unaffected by Western imperialism or economic needs. Yet the Japanese victory forced the government of each Western state with significant economic interests in China to adopt a line of conduct. Should Japan be allowed to keep Korea in return for territorial compensation for other powers? On Africa precedents this was at least possible. Alternatively should the powers check Japanese territorial pretensions, insist on the preservation of Chinese territorial integrity but, following earlier eastern precedents, insist on substantial economic concessions – more treaty ports, the right for the first time to build railways and factories outside the international settlements, and so on? It is proposed to consider first the immediate settlement of 1895; then the policies adopted by Russia, Britain, France and Germany to the end of 1897; next the evolution of Western policies during the years of diplomatic crisis from 1898 to 1904; finally those economic factors which, in the last resort, seem to have saved China from territorial disintegration.

It is significant that the first reaction of the Western powers to the defeat of China was to form a concert to check Japanese expansion and to preserve Chinese territorial integrity. Under the combined pressure of Britain, France, Russia and Germany peace was made in April 1895. Japan evacuated Korea and Manchuria, though temporarily retaining naval bases at Port Arthur and Wei-hai-we. She was given the Pescadores and Formosa in compensation, together with a guarantee of Korean independence and a large indemnity to be paid by China for her breach of the 1885 convention neutralizing Korea. In addition Japan was granted freedom of navigation on the Yangtze, additional treaty ports in other parts of China and the right to set up factories in any part of the country, all of which were automatically extended to the Western powers which had most favoured nation treaties with Peking.

These concessions appeared to end the crisis in the traditional way, preserving Chinese political integrity at the price of further economic concessions and marginal loss of territory. But this proved an illusion. In the first place the indemnity of about $150 million, plus a smaller amount payable for the evacuation of the Liaotung peninsula, was far greater than any indemnity previously forced on to China by the Western powers. It could not be raised within China and Peking would therefore be compelled to borrow overseas. On the precedent of Mediterranean states during the previous quarter century foreign borrowing on this scale was almost certain to entail foreign influence over Peking which in turn might disturb the general balance of European activity in China. Specifically it might endanger the established principle of parity of economic opportunity between all foreign powers which had been evolved since 1842. Second, it was now for the first time evident that China could no longer defend her territory against modern armies and that her political survival depended largely on foreign agreement that China must be preserved intact. In 1895 the concert of powers had agreed to do this rather than allow Japan to obtain a dominant position in Korea and Manchuria. But there was no guarantee that this agreement would last. If one major state fell out of line and decided to stake a claim to territory or succeeded in establishing its political predominance in Peking, the survival of China would be at risk. Every interested power would then have to choose between preserving the *status quo* and partitioning China into spheres of influence or even into formal dependencies.

The Russian reaction to the new situation must be considered first because her policies dominated events during the later 1890s.[2] Russia's interests in China were different from those of any other European power. The vital fact is that, until about 1894, St Petersburg took a defensive rather than an expansionist view of the Far East. China was regarded as a serious potential danger to the security of Eastern Siberia. There had been disputes between the two states in the 1870s over Kuldja in Central Asia and over the

Amur frontier in the early 1880s; and in each case Russian diplomacy was weakened by the virtual impossibility of transporting men and equipment across Siberia. During the 1880s Peking allowed Chinese settlement in Manchuria beyond the Great Wall, which had hitherto constituted a virtually uninhabited buffer zone between China and Amur. By 1890 there were thirty times more Chinese in northern Manchuria than there were Russians in Amur and Primorsk. In 1885 there were about 85,000 Chinese troops in Manchuria and after 1883 there was the Chinese naval base at Port Arthur. In fact all these developments were intended to strengthen Chinese control over Manchuria as a base for securing Korea against Japan. But in St Petersburg they were seen as a malign threat to Amur and therefore to Siberia.

Thus from 1884 to 1894 Russian interest in the Far East centred on providing security for existing possessions on the northern frontiers of China. The key decision, taken in principle in 1886 and formalized in 1887, was to build the trans-Siberian railway as an essential link with the West to enable Russia to send troops and equipment to defend Amur. From the start the railway therefore had a strategic rather than an economic function. This was clearly recognized in St Petersburg, for in 1887 a high-level ministerial conference stated that 'even in the future, due to the limited amount of Siberian freight, a profit can come only after some time'.[3] Construction of the railway began at both ends in 1891 and was expected to be complete in about 1903. Thereafter Russia might become a major political force in the Far East, but meantime Russian statesmen were clear that they could play only a very restricted role there. This fact conditioned Russian attitudes to the Chinese crisis throughout the 1890s, when China became the victim rather than the aggressor. Since Russia was not yet in a position to take full advantage of Chinese weakness, her interest was to defend the territorial integrity of China against all other powers until the railway was completed.

Yet conservation of the Chinese Empire was not incompatible with a policy of economic and perhaps also cultural penetration from Siberia. Indeed, the key to Russian policy after 1894 is the determination shown by the court, senior ministers led by Sergius de Witte, Finance Minister from 1892, and a group of intellectuals, including Dostoyevsky, that Russia should become the dominant political, economic and intellectual force in the Far East. What part did economic objectives play in this new drive to the East?

How far were they compatible with or even dependent on the preservation of Chinese territorial integrity?

Witte's ideas on China stemmed from his general economic policy for Russia, which may be briefly summarized as economic development through state initiative in the promotion of 'key' basic industries coupled with import of foreign capital to finance growth. China was important for Russia's economic growth because it provided a vast potential extension of the relatively limited domestic market for the products of newly established modern industries. In addition Russian enterprise might eventually be able to tap the resources of the Far East by establishing mines, factories, flour mills, etc. in potentially rich regions such as Manchuria and Korea. Ultimately China and Korea might become economic dependencies of Russia rather than, as they then were, of the Western maritime powers and Japan. But all this depended entirely on the trans-Siberian railway. Without it Russia could not export her cottons, woollens and metal goods to China at competitive prices. Once the railway was built, however, not only would Russia be able to compete with the industrialized states of Western Europe and America on equal or preferential terms, but, by building branch lines into continental China, she would be able to penetrate regions and markets effectively closed to European merchants operating from the treaty ports. As early as 1893 Witte supported a project put up by P. A. Badmaen for building a branch line from Chita in Eastern Siberia to Lanchow, capital of the province of Kansu, which was beyond the effective range of European commerce based on the Pacific coast of China; and during the next decade he consistently pressed for other branch lines from the trans-Siberian to the Yellow Sea and then to central China.

Witte did not, therefore, believe that it was necessary on economic grounds to acquire formal political control over any part of China because he assumed that in the end China would become an informal economic dependency of Russia. Indeed, he recognized after the Sino-Japanese War of 1894–5 that the real danger to his programme lay in political division of China between Japan and the Western powers. Time and geography were on the side of Russia, but in the 1890s, with the railway incomplete, she lacked military, naval, diplomatic or economic power in the Far East to compete with her rivals. In the short term Russian policy must be to avoid giving other powers any excuse to acquire exclusive political or economic claims in China. Witte therefore consistently

opposed projects evolved in St Petersburg in 1895 and 1898 for
Russia to annex Port Arthur or some ice-free port in Manchuria or
Korea on the ground that such Russian initiatives would lead to
counter-claims by other powers who might well carve China into
spheres of influence or even protectorates from which Russia would
be permanently excluded. When Russia occupied Port Arthur and
demanded a lease of the southern part of the Liaotung peninsula in
1898 this was done on the insistence of Muraviev, the Russian
Foreign Minister, with support from the Tsar, as a political response
to Germany's sudden occupation of Kiao-Chow Bay. This action
was strongly opposed by Witte; and, as he foresaw, it stimulated
other powers to stake counter-claims and seriously endangered his
long-term project for economic penetration of the whole of
China.

Until the German occupation of Kiao-Chow late in 1897, however, and in many respects much later, Witte's policy of peaceful
penetration was meticulously followed by Russia. Since this policy
in turn effectively inaugurated the international rush for economic
concessions in China and provided the model for action by other
foreign states it must be examined carefully as a model for economic
imperialism without territorial possession.

Witte's strategy was to obtain access to the heart of the Chinese
economy by persuading Peking that Russia was its best friend
against both Japan and the maritime powers. This technique had
already had some success in 1858–60 and was in sharp contrast
with the traditional Anglo-French use of naval power to impose
'unequal treaties' at the cannon's mouth. Witte was fortunate that
the Chinese experienced great difficulty in raising a loan to pay the
first instalment of the Japanese indemnity early in 1895, for this
enabled him to provide a substitute Franco-Russian loan in July
1895 on the most generous terms – 4 per cent interest and 94 per
cent of the face value of the loan received by Peking. These terms
underline the fact that this was a political not a genuinely commercial transaction. The money was raised on the Paris market as a
gilt-edged investment guaranteed by the Russian government, for
otherwise European bankers would have demanded terms consistent with a highly speculative investment. If China defaulted Russia
would be left with an expensive commitment. But St Petersburg's
immediate reward was a fund of goodwill in Peking on which
Witte immediately drew to extract agreement on the two main
instruments of his projected economic policy in China – the Russo-

Chinese Bank, whose function was to finance railway construction, banking, commerce and possibly industry; and the Manchurian section of the trans-Siberian railway which would allow the line to reach Vladivostock by the shorter southern route rather than via Russian territory north of the River Amur. These two concessions gave Russia an immense potential advantage over all foreign rivals for economic primacy in China and they were buttressed by the Treaty of Alliance signed in June 1896 which provided for mutual support if either power was attacked by any other single power. For the moment Witte failed to extract permission to build a southern branch of the Manchurian railway to the Yellow Sea, which was essential to link Russia with the main markets and producing areas of China. But time was apparently on his side. The trans-Siberian would not be completed for some years and by that time Russian influence at Peking might well be sufficient to overcome residual Chinese resistance to foreign railways in the heartlands of the Empire.

By 1896, therefore, the Russians had established a viable new model for European penetration of the Chinese economy without formal political control of any additional territory. Thereafter, despite natural suspicions in other European capitals, Russia had no good reason to want a formal partition of the Chinese Empire: indeed she could best exclude rivals by insisting on its preservation. This put the Western European states and the United States in a quandary. On the one hand few really believed that Russia, with her long tradition of territorial imperialism in the Balkans and Central Asia, could long resist the temptation to annex Manchuria and possibly Korea. Even if she did not, the concessions so far obtained might well give her effective control of the economy of northern China and result in the virtual exclusion of other European enterprises. Those powers with a significant economic stake in China – Britain, Germany, the United States and to a lesser extent France – therefore felt bound to demand compensating economic concessions; the right to build railways, establish banks and make loans to Peking. But should they also, on the assumption that Russia was proposing to occupy Manchuria and northern Korea, stake claims to spheres of interest, even if they had no intrinsic desire for formal empire?

This dilemma lies at the root of European policies on China from about 1895 to perhaps 1904 and largely explains their ambivalence. It is proposed to survey the response of each major power to the Russian challenge very briefly to the end of 1897, when the German demand for Kiao-Chow further complicated the situation, and then to consider why, under these new circumstances, no formal partition of China took place.

The collapse of China and Russia's achievements in 1894–6 posed very serious problems for Britain.[4] In economic terms Britain was the possessing foreign power in China, with some 70 per cent of Chinese overseas trade, a large share of the carrying trade to third countries, substantial capital investment in the international settlement at Shanghai and a long tradition of political primacy based on naval power. British interests therefore lay in preserving the *status quo* as far as possible while obtaining a full share of new economic opportunities. The difficulty was that defence of the 'open door' for trade and equal opportunities for foreign investors was not compatible with active participation in a struggle for regional concessions to match those likely to be acquired by Russia and France. Until the end of 1897, therefore, the British tried to keep their options open. On the one hand they supported the Sino-Japanese treaty of April 1895 which opened seven additional ports to foreign commerce and provided for European trade, investment, etc. in the Yangtze Valley because these opportunities were open on equal terms to all foreign states with most favoured nation rights. Conversely, they followed France and Russia in demanding exclusive railway building concessions which might lead to defined spheres of interest. In 1895 Peking was induced to grant a concession for a British railway from Burma to Yunnan to match the French concession for a railway from Indo-China to Lungchow. From 1896 the China Association, representing British mercantile interests based on Hong Kong and Shanghai, who feared that France or Germany might obtain exclusive railway concessions on the Yangtze, now the main field of British enterprise, pressed the government hard to acquire some form of political lien on the Yangtze Valley as a security for their interests. Here, indeed, is evidence that under certain circumstances a genuine commercial interest might demand political action to safeguard its established interests in China, not because political control was intrinsically necessary for trade or investment, but because, under the conditions of the later 1890s, it seemed quite possible that the alternative would be exclusion by some other European power.

French policy in China has already been considered in relation to

Indo-China and may be recapitulated briefly. In the mid-1890s metropolitan opinion was divided over the relative advantages of informal and formal control of southern China. It was clear that political occupation would have to form part of a general international agreement to divide China; and meantime France took the opportunity to make limited territorial gains and obtain economic concessions comparable to those gained by her ally, Russia. In June 1895 France obtained frontier adjustments on the Tongking-Yunnan frontier. She also received first option on mining and railway enterprises in the three southern provinces of China which would predictably be her share in a partition. By providing Russia with the capital to finance both the indemnity loan and the Russo-Chinese Bank, Paris also staked its claim to influence in Peking and gained a line on Russian policy. Like Britain she kept her options open.

Until late in 1897 it seemed that the Germans would follow the same cautious line. German commercial and banking groups had precisely the same economic interests in China as the British and were competing with them in the Yangtze Valley with considerable success. There is no evidence that merchants or capitalists wanted territorial control of any region of China in these years, and in 1894–5 German bankers were in close contact with British banks over loans to Peking. Berlin therefore negotiated for commercial and investment opportunities to match those conceded to other powers, and these were duly acquired in March 1898: the right for a German-Chinese company to build two railways forming a triangle in Shantung; the right to hold and develop mining properties within fifteen kilometres on each side of these railways; and the right for German nationals to be given priority in providing skills, capital and materials to the Chinese government 'for any purpose whatever within the province of Shantung'.[5] But these economic concessions, in themselves only a facsimile of those granted to other powers and not implying territorial objectives, were in fact extracted as part of a negotiation which also gave Germany the lease of Kiao-Chow harbour for ninety-nine years. Does this suggest that Germany had now decided that political control was necessary for satisfactory economic development in China and that official policy favoured partition? In fact this was not so. The Foreign Ministry, supported by leading economic interests, was still convinced that the International Settlement in Shanghai provided a perfectly adequate base for the German commercial thrust into the interior and that joint action with Britain would extract opportunities for profitable lending to Peking. The seizure of Kiao-Chow in November 1897, on the excuse that two German Catholic missionaries had been murdered in Shantung, only reflected the considered opinion of the Admiralty and the Kaiser that Germany required a naval base in the East to match the British base at Hong Kong if she was to operate successfully as a major world power. Kiao-Chow was chosen not for economic reasons but because a process of elimination suggested that this was a suitable base which lay outside any conceivable Russian, British or French sphere of interest. From Germany's point of view the lease, which was conceded under very strong pressure on Peking in March 1898, had no further implications.

Yet its effect on international policy cannot be overestimated. Kiao-Chow was the first territory other than Amur and Ussuri taken by a European state in China since the British acquired Hong Kong in 1842. At a time of intensive international rivalry for influence in China, when several powers were poised between preserving Chinese independence and adopting a policy of territorial partition, the German initiative was certain to cause general apprehension and to precipitate counter-claims. The question was whether this process could be checked before China was formally partitioned on African lines. It is therefore proposed briefly to review the reactions of the major powers in the period 1898–1902 and to consider why, in the end, China was not divided among them.

The first Russian reaction to the German demand for Kiao-Chow was to block it by exerting maximum pressure on Peking. When this attempt failed, Muraviev, the Foreign Minister, in alliance with the Tsar, insisted that Russia must acquire a rival naval base to enable her to check Germany's assumed territorial and political ambitions. Since it was diplomatically impossible to acquire a port in Korea, which the Russian Admiralty favoured, it was proposed to demand Talienwan in the Liaotung peninsula, together with the near-by Port Arthur as a naval base. Witte, together with the Ministers for the navy and army, were opposed to this, but Muraviev won out. A Russian naval squadron was sent to Port Arthur in December and Witte, accepting that he must make the best use of the situation to extract further economic concessions from Peking, presented a new list of demands: the lease of a commercial harbour on the Yellow Sea; permission for the Chinese Eastern

Railway to build the projected southern branch line from the Manchurian railway to this port; and a Russian monopoly of railway building and industrial enterprise in the three provinces of Manchuria and in Mongolia. These demands were conceded in March 1898, and Russia bought off Japanese hostility by the Nishi-Rosen Agreement concluded in April. The Germans also were persuaded not to object, and the British decided not to risk war over Port Arthur. Russia had therefore, contrary to Witte's long-term strategy, acquired effective political control of Manchuria which they consolidated in 1900 under cover of the Boxer Rising. If other powers followed suit, the partition of China seemed for the first time a serious possibility.

Outside Manchuria, however, the options still remained open and everything depended on whether Japan, France, the United States and Britain now decided to carve out their own fiefs before Russian ambitions grew still larger. Japan was for the moment satisfied with the virtually free hand she had obtained by agreement with Russia in Korea and was convinced that she could eventually destroy Russian power in Manchuria by superior military force. She was therefore content to hold her hand. But France, hitherto undecided what line to take, followed the Russian lead. In March 1898 Paris demanded a coaling base on the south coast, the right to build a railway to Yunnan-fu and a promise that Peking would not alienate the provinces of Yunnan, Kwangtung and Kwangsi to any other power. In April these were conceded, and France obtained a ninety-nine-year lease of Kwangchow as a coaling base. In May she also extracted the right to build a railway from Pakhoi to some point on the West River which, it was hoped, would draw off the trade from the interior that normally flowed to Canton and Hong Kong. If the United States and Britain also opted for informal territorial division and accepted the right of each country to regulate the trade of its sphere of influence, there was little chance that China would survive as an integral state.

The role played by the United States was very small. This was not due to lack of interest for, as has been seen, American business became increasingly anxious to expand its activities in the Far East during the 1880s and early 1890s to offset economic problems at home. Americans exports to China grew rapidly in the 1890s from about $4 million in the early years to $6·9 million in 1896, and $11·9 million in 1897.[6] In 1900 America had about 8 per cent of Chinese foreign trade. American concession hunters had little success because, as has been seen, Peking granted concessions only under political pressure and the State Department adopted precisely the same attitude as the British Foreign Office had done before 1886 in refusing to intervene on behalf of particular American firms. In April 1898, however, a new concern, the American China Development Company, was given the right to build a railway between Hankow and Canton. With American enterprise thus increasingly active in China, freedom of access was a major concern: as the *New York Commercial Advertiser* said in January 1898, it was 'supremely important that we should retain the free entry into the Chinese market which we enjoy today. . . . We cannot submit to being excluded from trade in that territory.'[7] The German occupation of Kiao-Chow and Russian occupation of Port Arthur therefore posed almost precisely the same problem for American as for British economic interests. Business circles quickly rallied to put pressure on the State Department to make a resolute stand against Russian and German ambitions and to form an alignment with Britain as the only power with common interests in China. Hence, when the British government asked formally in March 1898 whether Washington would co-operate with Britain in preserving the 'open door' in Asia, it might reasonably have been expected that the United States would provide enthusiastic co-operation.

By that time, however, the United States was embroiled in the Spanish War, and for the next two years was unable to take an active role in Chinese affairs. It was not until September 1899 that the State Department took any initiative, and then it consisted only of the famous 'Open Door' note sent to Britain, Germany and Russia which proposed that powers claiming spheres of influence in China should declare that they would:

. . . in no wise interfere with any treaty port or any vested interest within any so-called 'sphere of interest' or leased territory. . . .
. . . that the Chinese treaty tariff of the time being shall apply to all merchandise landed or shipped to all such ports . . . no matter to what nationality it may belong, and that duties so leviable shall be collected by the Chinese Government . . . that it will levy no higher harbor dues on vessels of another nationality frequenting any port in such 'sphere' than shall be levied on vessels of its own nationality, and no higher railroad charges over lines built, controlled, or operated within its 'spheres' on merchandise belonging to citizens or subjects of other nationalities transported through such 'sphere' than shall be levied on similar merchandise belonging to its own nationals transported over equal distances.[8]

This proposal accurately reflected American interests in China, which were virtually identical with those of Britain and Germany. But it had virtually no impact on the course of events. The British and Germans accepted the note, since it was in line with their own practice and interests in China. It was later accepted also by France, who thus signalized her decision not to adopt an 'African' solution in China, and by Japan and Italy. But the Russians, the only power who were seriously concerned to create a monopolistic commercial region in China, returned an evasive answer and proceeded to treat Manchuria as if it was already a Russian province. Hay's initiative therefore stood as evidence of the futility of diplomatic initiatives when unsupported by effective force.

In the last resort, therefore, the future pattern of Chinese history depended very largely on the British response to German and Russian initiatives. On general grounds the British still preferred in 1898 to preserve the 'open door' and the territorial integrity of China. The big London finance houses showed virtually no interest in the political future of the country. Railway concessions were regarded as a political device by which the government might wish to obtain *de facto* political control over particular regions, but not as a financially attractive investment proposition unless capital and interest were fully guaranteed. Bankers were able and willing to lend to Peking by forming consortia with German or French banks and did not rely on official initiatives. But, if capitalists felt little concern over political developments, commercial interests were profoundly worried by the events of 1898. Considered in relation to total overseas British trade the China trade was small in value and was declining rather than increasing during the 1890s. Table 17 indicates the trend during this decade. Despite the statistics, however, it was confidently expected that the trade would expand immensely once railways made it possible to penetrate directly to inland markets; and the business community was prepared to support special interests, including the shipping firms and managing agents, such as Jardine Matheson and Butterfield and Swire, who stood to lose most if central China fell under the control of some other European government. In the last resort, therefore, the commercial community might put strong pressure on the government to establish a British sphere or even protectorate in the Yangtze Valley if freedom of access could not be assured in any other way.

This largely explains the otherwise surprising fact that the first

428

Table 17

British Trade with China (including Hong Kong), 1890–1900 (millions of pounds)

	Exports to China	Total British Exports	Imports from China	Total British Imports
1890	9·5	328·2	6·0	420·7
1895	7·5	285·8	4·1	416·7
1898	7·4	294·0	3·4	470·5
1900	8·5	354·4	3·5	523·1

Source: *Statistical Abstract for the United Kingdom 1890–1904*, no. 52.

Note: Figures for 1890 and 1895 include Korea; those for 1898 and 1900 do not.

official British reaction to the Russian claim to Port Arthur and economic preponderance in Manchuria was to work for an agreement with Russia to divide China (and possibly also Turkey, which presented a similar problem at the same time), into 'spheres of preponderance'. Salisbury clearly and cynically defined his objectives in a letter of 15 January 1898 to the British Ambassador at St Petersburg.

Our idea was this. The two Empires of China and Turkey are so weak that in all important matters they are constantly guided by the advice of Foreign Powers. In giving this advice Russia and England are constantly opposed, neutralizing each other's efforts much more frequently than the real antagonism of their interests would justify; and this condition of things is not likely to diminish, but to increase. It is to remove or lessen this evil that we have thought that an understanding with Russia might benefit both nations.

We contemplate no infraction of existing rights. We would not admit the violation of any existing treaties, or impair the integrity of the present empires of either China or Turkey. These two conditions are vital. We aim at no partition of territory, but only a partition of preponderance. It is evident that both in respect to Turkey and China there are large portions which interest Russia much more than England and *vice versa*. Merely as an illustration, and binding myself to nothing, I would say that the portion of Turkey which drains into the Black Sea, together with the drainage valley of the Euphrates as far as Bagdad, interest Russia much more than England: whereas Turkish Africa, Arabia, and the valley of the Euphrates below Bagdad interest England much more than Russia. A similar distinction exists in China between the Valley of the Hoango with the territory north of it and the Valley of the Yangtze.

Would it be possible to arrange that where, in regard to these territories our counsels differ, the Power least interested should give way to and assist the other? I do not disguise from myself that the difficulty would be great. Is it insuperable? I have designedly omitted to deal with large tracts in each Empire, because neither Power has shown any keen interest in them.[9]

This was a purely defensive proposal. Salisbury merely wanted to obtain a Russian agreement not to penetrate central China and he did not accept Russia's right to close Manchuria to foreign trade on equal terms. But when Russia insisted on retaining Port Arthur and Talienwan (later called Dalny) and rejected demands for freedom of trade in Manchuria, Salisbury had to adopt stronger tactics. First Peking was induced to grant concessions to British firms, in some cases associated with German or Italian interests, to build railways between Canton and Kowloon and in the Yangtze basin. To match the Russian and German naval bases in the Yellow Sea Britain acquired a lease of Wei-hai-wei, which had been occupied by Japan and was due to be evacuated by her as soon as the Chinese indemnity was paid. In addition Kowloon, on the mainland opposite Hong Kong, was leased for ninety-nine years. Britain had thus followed the example of Russia and Germany, not primarily because she wanted these leased territories but because it seemed necessary to sustain British political influence in China. The real problem of preventing Russian or other foreign penetration into the Yangtze basin remained, and the award by Peking of the right to build the Peking-Hankow railway, linking the Yangtze with the Manchurian railway system as planned by Witte, to a Franco-Belgian syndicate in August 1898 underlined this danger. How could Russian expansion southwards be checked? From about August 1898 Britain tried to do so in two ways: by reaching an agreement with the Russians and by finding support from other foreign powers to hold the Russians in check and safeguard freedom of economic opportunity outside the Russian sphere in Manchuria.

Agreement with Russia was reached by an exchange of notes on 28 April 1898. Russia engaged 'not to seek for her own account or for Russian subjects any railway concessions in the basin of the Yangtze, nor to obstruct, directly or indirectly, in that region any applications for railway concessions supported by the British government'. In return Britain undertook similar obligations in the area 'north of the Great Wall'.[10]

But this agreement was really of little use. It did not block Russian expansion between Manchuria and the Yangtze Valley, possibly in conjunction with France. Nor did it safeguard the 'open door' in other regions of China against Germany, France, Japan and other powers. The dilemma therefore remained. If Britain could build an alliance system to contain Russia and also achieve a self-denying agreement among other maritime powers to preserve the 'open door' south of Manchuria, she would not need to consolidate her provisional sphere in the Yangtze and could retain freedom of access elsewhere. This was the obvious objective. But who would serve in such a concert of powers? Germany was an obvious candidate; and from 1898 to 1901 there were recurrent attempts to negotiate an agreement or even an alliance with her. Chamberlain was particularly enthusiastic about this.[11] But Germany would not commit herself to defend British interests in China unless Britain would join the Triple Alliance in Europe. Since this was inconceivable the limit of German co-operation was the so-called Yangtze Agreement of October 1900. Both powers agreed in principle to maintain the integrity of China and the 'open door' for both trade and investment in their respective spheres. If any third power made use of 'the complications in China' to obtain 'territorial advantages', Britain and Germany might reach 'a preliminary understanding as to the eventual steps to be taken for the protection of their own interests in China'.[12] The agreement was worth having as a statement of principle, but it lacked teeth for Germany was under no obligation to use military or even diplomatic force to check Russian pretensions. Indeed in March 1901 Bülow said that he viewed the fate of Manchuria with 'absolute indifference'.

In the end, therefore, the British turned to Japan as the only power whose interests for the moment coincided with those of Britain and which might be prepared to fight for common interests against Russia. Japan would obviously not be able or willing to prevent Russia or other powers from dividing China. But at least Japan might be induced not to take part in a partition and to check Russian encroachments in Korea. The Anglo-Japanese Treaty of 30 January 1902 was Britain's admission that diplomacy could not prevent an 'African' solution of the Chinese question if the maritime powers were determined on it.

Why, then, did China survive? Why did Britain, Germany, France and other powers never consolidate their notional spheres of interest into protectorates or colonies? The answer is of the greatest importance for the present study. Where diplomacy failed, economic realities succeeded. Ultimately China survived as a sovereign state partly because the one power which had already undertaken effective political occupation in Manchuria was decisively defeated by Japan in 1904–5, but still more because the maritime powers eventually recognized that, despite their previous demands for spheres of interest, their best economic interests did not lie in political division. The reasons for this can best be understood by examining the pattern of foreign trade and capital investment in China at the turn of the century when the powers had to formulate their long-term policies.

There was no possible doubt that division of China into more or less exclusive national spheres would be a disadvantage to any foreign state whose interests were genuinely commercial. By the late 1890s there were thirty-two treaty ports in China which were open to foreign trade on equal terms. Tariffs had been limited to a maximum of 5 per cent *ad valorem* since 1842; and by 1895 foreigners were free to penetrate into the heart of China down the main river systems. Thus there was absolutely no need for political control of any part of China to provide free access for European trade. In the treaty ports, moreover, Europeans had special residential and business areas, of which the international settlement in Shanghai was the largest, in which they were exempt from Chinese jurisdiction. Thus, although more treaty ports were wanted – they increased to forty-eight by 1913 – formal possession of coastal bases was quite unnecessary for any European state. There was, then, no parallel between China and, for example, West Africa in the 1870s. Indeed, the only remaining barrier to full economic penetration of continental China was inadequate communications, residual restrictions on permanent residence of Europeans outside the treaty ports and the occasional hostility of Chinese officials and others who resented foreign intrusion, all of which could be overcome. It was not necessary to pacify China by political and military means as had seemed necessary in many parts of tropical Africa.

If formal occupation was unnecessary to promote commerce, partition of China into spheres of influence or protectorates had obvious disadvantages for each Western state. The British, with something over 60 per cent of Chinese foreign trade and commercial interests in every province of China, clearly stood to lose most by fragmentations of this market; and, as has been seen, their consistent preference, even while they hedged on spheres of influence, was to preserve the 'open door' and the integrity of the whole Chinese Empire. The Germans were still far behind Britain commercially, but their trade was expanding fast in the 1890s, particularly in the Yangtze basin, and German businessmen were confident that they could compete on equal terms with the British. Possession of Shantung would be no compensation for limitation on the freedom of German enterprise in other more prosperous regions; and the Germans had therefore a fundamental common interest with Britain in preserving the 'open door'. Co-operation between the powers on this issue was difficult mainly because Berlin was not prepared to run political risks by opposing Russia in the Far East in defence of trade without compensating political advantages from a British alliance in Europe. But at no time did Berlin seriously contemplate a general partition of China or attempt to impose differential commercial regulations in its concessionary sphere.

Even more significant was the ultimate French decision not to plump for partition. As a weak commercial competitor which had attempted in most other continents to offset German and British economic preponderance by acquiring territory and ringing it with preferential tariffs, France might well have been expected to stake a claim to southern China. The reasons why she did not do so have been reviewed above: fundamentally it was recognized that France's territorial allocation would be an inadequate compensation for exclusion from other more desirable zones. Once France had decided that partition was inappropriate under Chinese conditions, it was most unlikely that any other power would want to follow African precedents there. Certainly the United States, the third largest foreign trader in China, was consistently in favour of Britain's objectives there, even though she was unable to play an active political role.

There was, therefore, a clear consensus among the dominant commercial powers that there was no case on strictly commercial grounds for formal or even semi-formal partition of China. Perhaps more surprising, the same view was taken by European and American capital about investment opportunities. The reasons for this apparent indifference to the political colour of China lay in the character of the available investment opportunities there and these can be considered under two heads: first the types of investment available, second their geographical distribution.

An essential feature of foreign lending to China in the period after 1895 was that a large proportion consisted of loans to the Chinese government: about 36·1 per cent of total foreign investment between 1895 and 1901, and 57·9 per cent of new lending between 1901 and 1913.[13] In the first period most of this was borrowed to pay off the Japanese indemnity, in the second period nearly 40 per cent was for government railway construction and 'reorganization'. Although Russia took responsibility for much of the pre-1901 indemnity loans, the capital was in fact raised on the money markets of France, Britain and Germany. Hence, although Russia reaped the short-term political reward for organizing these loans, in the long term the benefits went to European financiers and to holders of Russian and later of Chinese government bonds. The result was that foreign lending to Peking was fairly evenly divided between the three main European powers, as can be seen from table 18.

Table 18

Foreign Holdings of Government Obligations in China, 1902–31 (millions of US dollars)

	1902 Total	1902 Per Cent	1914 Total	1914 Per Cent	1931 Total	1931 Per Cent
Britain	110·3	39·4	207·5	41·8	211·6	36·1
Japan	0·0	0·0	9·6	1·9	224·1	38·2
Russia	26·4	9·4	32·8	6·6	0·0	0·0
United States	2·2	0·8	7·3	1·5	41·7	7·1
France	61·5	22·0	111·4	22·5	97·4	16·6
Germany	79·3	28·4	127·6	25·7	12·0	2·0

Source: C. F. Remer, *Foreign Investments in China* (New York, 1933), table 16, 138.

Private lending to the Chinese government, whether direct or through Russia as intermediary, thus constituted a major opportunity for European capital on very satisfactory terms. The average interest received, allowing for discount on the face value of the bonds, was about 6 per cent.[14] This was substantially higher than interest paid on most European government stock or on colonial government stock in this period, yet the security was good: the Russian government guaranteed the indemnity loans which it floated, and loans made direct to Peking were secured on Chinese customs revenues which were placed under international control. In the eyes of European capital the Chinese government therefore became an instrument for servicing very satisfactory gilt-edged investments. This was perhaps the greatest security against political action by the powers, for if the imperial government was destroyed or if China was divided into European dependencies, an excellent field for investment would disappear and existing investments would be at risk. Thus European investors interested in government lending had every reason to defend the political independence and territorial integrity of China and none in political partition.

For private direct investors in China the decisive argument against political division was the same as for the merchants – the geography of the country and the physical distribution of profitable investment opportunities. Table 19 shows the estimated total invested by each foreign country in 1902 and 1914.

Table 19

Business Investments in China by Countries, 1902–31 (millions of US dollars)

	1902 Total	1902 Per Cent	1914 Total	1914 Per Cent	1931 Total	1931 Per Cent
Britain	150·0	29·8	400·0	36·9	963·4	38·9
Japan	1·0	0·2	210·0	19·4	912·8	36·9
Russia	220·1	43·7	236·5	21·8	273·2	11·1
United States	17·5	3·5	42·0	3·9	155·1	6·3
France	29·6	5·9	60·0	5·5	95·0	3·8
Germany	85·0	16·9	136·0	12·5	75·0	3·0
	503·2		1,084·5		2,474·5	

Source: Remer, *Foreign Investments*, 99.

These figures require interpretation. First, almost all the Russian 'business' investment was in the China Eastern Railway, which was financed by the Russian government rather than by private Russian investors. Second, by far the most important European business investment outside Manchuria was also in railways, accounting for some 33 per cent of total foreign investment, including public loans, as contrasted with a mere 6·9 per cent for manufacturing. Finally, and most important, private investment was not evenly distributed throughout China, but was in fact relatively concentrated in certain areas. Table 20 gives a preliminary idea of this regional distribution in 1902 and 1914.

Table 20

Geographical Distribution of Investments in China, 1902–31 (millions of US dollars)

	1902 Total	1902 Per Cent	1914 Total	1914 Per Cent	1931 Total	1931 Per Cent
Shanghai	110·0	14·0	291·0	18·1	1,112·3	34·3
Manchuria	216·0	27·4	361·6	22·4	880·0	27·1
Rest of China	177·2	22·5	433·1	26·9	607·8	18·8
Undistributed	284·7	36·1	524·6	32·6	642·5	19·8
	787·9		1,610·3		3,242·5	

Source: Remer, *Foreign Investments*, 73.

These figures have limited value since they do not show the geographical distribution of business investment outside Shanghai and Manchuria; but, using other evidence, it is possible to construct a general pattern of distribution. A striking fact is that Shanghai alone accounted for 14 per cent of all foreign investment and 21·8 per cent of all business investment. This points to the important fact that the great majority of all business capital, other than railway investment, was put into manufacturing, commerce, shipping and banking in the treaty ports. Conversely, continuing restrictions still made it difficult or impossible for foreigners to establish factories, mines and other business establishments outside these treaty ports. Thus the pattern of foreign private investment in China can be summed up as railway construction, which was undertaken in many regions under specific concessions from Peking, and a wide variety of commercial enterprises concentrated almost entirely on the Pacific coast in the treaty ports.

The implications of this pattern of distribution are very important for European attitudes to political division of China. By about 1900 concessions for building a large number of railways had already been allocated by Peking, under intense pressure from the European governments. Many of these concessions had been taken up by international syndicates, so that, despite the nominal division of China into national concessionary spheres, railway construction outside Manchuria was barely affected by national considerations. After about 1900 moreover, Peking adopted a policy of building its own railways, raising capital through the sale of government bonds. Opportunities for further railway concessions were therefore very limited, and the main field for future business enterprise lay in manufacturing, banking, and similar activities, which were virtually restricted to the treaty ports. How did this affect the attitude of European capital and business to China's political future? Fundamentally it suggested that formal division between the powers was extremely undesirable, if only because it would have been impossible to arrange any geographical partition which would have satisfied everyone. The real plums were in southern Manchuria, Shanghai and the Yangtze basin. Under no conceivable circumstances was it possible after about 1900 that any power except Russia would control Manchuria or that Britain would be prepared to give up Shanghai and the Yangtze region. Shantung would have been no compensation for Germany or the three southern provinces for France. If partition had taken place new areas of opportunity would no doubt have developed as Chinese restrictions on foreign enterprise were removed. But in the short term, which was of immediate interest to all business groups, it was clear that China could not be satisfactorily divided. Once again, as in Tunisia, Egypt, Morocco, Turkey and many other countries, finance and business demonstrated clearly that in the undeveloped world economic realities were more important than politics.

In the last resort, then, China avoided full and formal partition mainly because the four foreign powers with the largest established economic stake there came to see that this would be contrary to their best economic interests. Indeed the apparent movement towards partition in 1898–9 was misleading. The territorial leases and concessionary areas were the outcome partly of specifically political impulses in Berlin and St Petersburg, echoed in London and Paris, which reflected anxiety to maintain or establish naval and political parity through possession of naval bases and to demonstrate political influence in Peking; partly of fear that other powers might use partition as a means to impose economic monopolies. Once the competitive spasm passed, as it had done by perhaps 1900, and the powers reviewed their substantive economic interests, all but Russia and Japan recognized that formal partition would be damaging to all concerned. China was too valuable a property to be dealt with by the crude techniques applied to tropical Africa in the 1880s. No statesman could afford to see his nationals denied reasonable opportunities to profit from trade or investment in China. Equally no one state could be permitted to monopolize any one region. Britain could not be allowed the dominant position on the Yangtze which she had obtained on the Niger nor could France be given a Chinese equivalent of her Sudanese Empire. China thus provides the clearest evidence that, where economic considerations were allowed to predominate and where an indigenous political structure could provide the essential framework of order, economic forces did not necessarily lead to formal empire.

II THE PACIFIC[15]

Imperial expansion in the Pacific during the three decades after 1880 is important for the present study, despite the very small scale of the territories concerned, because it constitutes a microcosm of many of the forces operating in this period. In particular it provides valuable evidence on the degree of continuity between the middle and later nineteenth century; on the relative importance of peripheral and metropolitan factors; and, above all on the complex interaction of economics and politics. It is not proposed to describe the course of events in detail but to examine very briefly the role of economic factors in producing the apparently dramatic change of attitude shown by Germany, France and Britain to the relative advantages of informal influence and formal rule during the last twenty years of the nineteenth century.

It was suggested above in chapter 8 that by about 1880 many parts of the Pacific were ripe, if not over-ripe, for annexation by some European power. The fundamental fact in many island groups was that European penetration, which resulted in most places from trade, plantation production, labour-recruiting and missionary activity, had already eroded the indigenous structure of society and government to a point at which the only remedy, short of total European withdrawal, was an extension of formal responsibility. Yet there seemed no serious possibility in the late 1870s that any European power would adopt this solution. Enthusiasm for formal empire was restricted almost entirely to nationals of the major powers resident in the Pacific – German traders, plantation owners and consular officials, British settlers in New Zealand and Australia, French officials and settlers in Tahiti and New Caledonia – any of whom could provide excellent arguments for territorial control. But these arguments seemed unconvincing in the metropolitan capitals. The official mind might accept the need to annex territory in particular circumstances but it was assumed that in general Pacific islands were not worth the taking.

Why, then, did metropolitan policies change so rapidly after 1880? Is the explanation to be found in Europe or in the Pacific, in economic or political considerations? In attempting to answer these questions it is proposed to look first at the reasons for German and British activity in Melanesia and Samoa and then at French and British policies in Polynesia and the New Hebrides.

ANGLO-GERMAN RIVALRY. It is in some ways paradoxical that the solvent of established German and British attitudes to Pacific empire should have been New Guinea and its neighbouring island groups – New Britain, New Ireland, the Admiralty, Solomon and smaller island groups – since these had hitherto been less affected by European penetration than many other islands in Polynesia and Micronesia. The first Christian missions were not established in the New Guinea area until 1871. Significant trades developed only in the 1870s and there were very few foreign plantations or settlements in 1880. Why, then, did the new Guinea region become an issue between Britain and Germany in the mid-1880s and precipitate an Anglo-German partition of the Pacific? The reasons are different for each country. On the German side New Guinea and its offshore islands were regarded by Godeffroys and the Deutsche Handels und Plantagen Gesellschaft (hereafter DHPG), which took over the Godeffroy interests in the Pacific in 1878, both as a necessary source of labour for their Samoan plantations and also as a potentially valuable field for trade and plantations. There were proposals in the early 1880s for a colony in New Guinea which led to the establishment of the New Guinea Company in May 1884. To that point, however, the German government had refused official support beyond that provided by naval vessels based on Samoa; and in 1880 Bismarck rejected a proposal made by his friend von Hansemann, a leading member of DHPG, that Mioko should become the centre of Pacific Island trade with a regular and state-subsidized steamer service to Germany. Clearly the economic possibilities of Melanesia were of little interest to the metropolis.

Yet by the mid-1880s German firms had a demonstrable stake in Melanesia. Between them DHPG and Hernsheims were exporting over a thousand tons of copra a year and were recruiting a considerable number of labourers there. If these firms could prove that their legitimate economic activities were threatened by the political actions of other European states, Berlin was always likely to intervene, as it had done in Samoa in 1879. After March 1884, when Bismarck seems to have accepted the general obligation of the Reich to provide full protection for German subjects overseas, this support was likely to take the form of a protectorate over any places in which Germans could demonstrate an established interest.

But why should a challenge to German economic enterprise have arisen in this period, above all from the British who were even more opposed in principle to formal empire in the Pacific than the Germans? Ironically the answer is that the British or, more precisely, the Australians, feared that political action by the Germans was imminent and that Germany would not only destroy established Australian and New Zealand interests in New Guinea and the islands – trade, labour-recruitment and Protestant missions – but that German forces established in Port Moresby would constitute a serious military threat to the security of northern Australia. Anglo-German rivalry in New Guinea therefore sprang from mutual fears on the periphery. It has virtually no connection with economic or other trends in Germany or Britain.

The story of events leading to the partition of Melanesia is well known. As early as 1874 F. P. Labillière, an Australian barrister living in London, proposed annexation of New Guinea to Australia on strategic, commercial and humanitarian grounds. The government was not entirely hostile but insisted that the Australian colonies should guarantee the costs of annexation and administration. When they refused, the matter lapsed. In 1878 Sir Arthur Gordon, Governor of Fiji and High Commissioner for the Western Pacific, recommended annexation on the ground that an expected gold rush near Port Moresby would produce disorder; but again London refused to act. Early in 1883, however, reports of the proposed German New Guinea company's intentions seriously worried Queensland, which had the largest economic and political stake. The Colonial government promised to subsidize a British administration and arranged for the British Commissioner on Thursday Island to declare British sovereignty over the whole of New Guinea east of Dutch territory and over the adjacent islands between 141° and 151° east, which included New Britain, New Ireland and the Admiralty Islands. The proclamation, which was issued on 4 April 1883, had no force in international law unless Britain as the imperial power ratified it. But this action began the political crisis in the Pacific as surely as treaties made by Leopold and France in the Congo started the crisis in Equatorial Africa in 1882. Eighteen months later Germany and Britain had staked their respective claims to territory and in 1885–6 spheres of interest were demarcated. The partition of the Pacific had begun.

What, then was the precise importance of economic factors in this process? Why should economic rivalry between Australians and Germans in this remote and extraordinarily unpromising region have induced the statesmen of London and Berlin, contrary to established conventions, to declare protectorates over New Guinea and its near-by islands? In its simplest form the answer must be that, while neither Germans nor British economic interests needed political control to pursue existing or projected economic activities, both became convinced in the early 1880s that the other was about to annex some or all of these territories. Formal empire was a precaution, not an end in itself. But why would either party have feared administration of the islands by its rivals? The reasons varied; but the central fact was that, while conventional trade might not be adversely affected by alien political control (indeed, it was not), labour-recruitment and the creation of plantations almost certainly would. Both sides assumed that the other would bar or severely curtail foreign labour-recruiting once it had established a protectorate; and the Germans could reasonably expect that British rule would, as in Fiji, mean a bar to acquisition of land for plantations. The demand for annexation therefore reflected fear of the economic consequences of foreign annexation rather than positive desire for empire.

Considerations of strategy and security also played a major part. Neither Germany nor Britain regarded the Pacific as a region of strategic importance, but to the Australians New Guinea in foreign hands would constitute a serious security risk. In 1883 an inter-colonial convention in Sydney denounced foreign annexation of any part of the Pacific as a danger to Australia and strongly advocated political control of New Guinea and adjoining islands by Britain, the colonies making permanent appropriations to provide a subsidy. The fact that by July 1884 Queensland and Victoria had promised to pay £15,000 a year if Britain would establish a protectorate demonstrated that this was meant seriously. Germany found it difficult to believe that British policy could be dictated by her colonists; but the British cabinet decision taken on 6 October 1884 to impose a protectorate was primarily a response to Australian demands and promises.

The Anglo-German partition of New Guinea and other parts of Melanesia, therefore, illustrates the complex relationship between economic and political factors during the early 1880s. Fundamentally, economic problems led to political control because British colonial settlers and German traders feared the consequences of political action by the other power. Imperialism grew from a crisis of confidence on the periphery.

August 1884 was thus the turning point for German and British policy in the Pacific as it was in West Africa. Subsequent events in the New Guinea region can be outlined briefly. The British government decided on a New Guinea protectorate on 6 August mainly because German action was clearly imminent. But it had no desire to alienate Bismarck, and after guarded negotiation with the German Ambassador on 8 August the areas to be covered by the proposed protectorate were reduced. Negotiations continued throughout the period of the Berlin Conference and a preliminary demarcation of Melanesia into spheres of influence was arranged by an exchange of notes in April 1885. Germany retained part of the north-east coast of New Guinea to the Huon Gulf and all islands to the north of the eighth parallel, including New Britain, New Ireland, the Admiralty Islands and part of the Solomons. Farther north the Caroline, Marshall and Palau Islands were agreed to lie within the German sphere. Britain retained the south-east coast of New Guinea, the small islands to the east, the southern Solomon Islands, and, farther away, the Gilbert and Ellice Islands. A final demarcation along these lines was arranged in April 1886. But neither side was committed to full political control over these island groups. The Germans did not annex the northern groups until they had bought out Spanish claims to the area in 1898. The British imposed protectorates on the Gilbert and Ellice Islands in 1892, mainly because the Germans suggested in 1891 that the British should take responsibility for order in an area where German trade predominated or give up their claim to political primary. Since the alternative was transfer of these groups to the German sphere the British reluctantly agreed.

Events in Samoa followed a somewhat similar pattern but were complicated by the presence of Americans. It has been seen above that Samoa was an established focus of European economic activity in the Pacific and the chief cockpit of local rivalry between Germans, British and Americans long before 1880. On economic grounds alone the German interest undoubtedly predominated in the 1880s. The relative size of plantations owned by nationals of each country in this decade can roughly be gauged from the recommendations of an international land commission which in 1897 awarded 75,000 acres to German claimants as compared with 36,000 acres to British subjects (mostly New Zealanders) and 21,000 acres to Americans.[16] German commercial predominance was even more marked, though since Samoa was used as an entrepôt by each foreign group, trade figures include imports to and exports from other Pacific islands. Table 21 gives the values of trade with Samoa in 1888 and figure 7 indicates the trends between 1880–4.

Table 21

Samoan Trade with Germany, the United States and British Territories, 1884 (dollars)

	Exports	Imports
Germany	323,884	77,047
United States	25,000	73,776
UK and Colonies	9,744	49,562

Source: S. Masterman, *The Origins of International Rivalry in Samoa* (London, 1934), 180, from US Consular Reports, which give lower totals for imports from Germany than German Reports which were used in Figure 7 below.

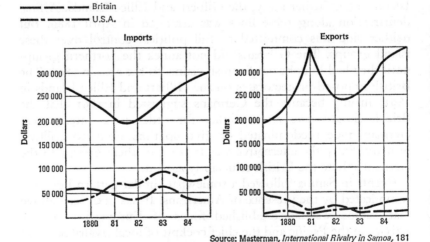

Source: Masterman, *International Rivalry in Samoa*, 181

Figure 7   Samoan Imports and Exports, 1880–4

Clearly the main difference lay in the pattern of Samoan exports rather than imports. British and American imports together were substantially larger than those from Germany, but Germany was overwhelmingly the largest overseas market for Samoan produce and re-exports from other islands. This pattern was reflected in the character of Samoa's trade with New Zealand which, of all the British colonies in the Pacific, showed the greatest interest in Samoa during the 1880s and 1890s. The Auckland firm William McArthur and Company were the main competititors of the DHPG and in 1886 claimed to own some 281,600 acres in Savaii which had been acquired in payment of debts. New Zealand imports from Samoa were very small indeed: £2,665 in 1879, £56 in 1888. But Auckland was an important entrepôt for British and New Zealand exports to Samoa, sending goods worth £15,865 in 1879, £8,239 in 1885, £41,895 in 1888, £19,415 in 1891 and £23,301 in 1894.[17] Small though these totals were in comparison with German commerce, they were regarded in Auckland as evidence that New Zealand had a substantive interest in the future of Samoa.

Nevertheless, if Samoa was predominantly a German economic colony, other countries considered that they had counter-balancing political interests there. By the treaties made in 1878 and 1879 the British and Americans had clearly defined commercial and other rights. The Americans had not made much use of the naval base at Pago Pago leased to them in 1872, but in the 1880s and 1890s American consuls were determined to play an active role in Samoan politics. Britain herself showed virtually no interest in Samoa at any stage, but the New Zealanders thought the islands were vital both to their security and to their future Pacific trade. New Zealand had petitioned London to annex Samoa as early as 1871 on economic and political grounds and had been refused. Interest and concern were again stimulated in 1879 by legitimate fear of imminent German political control and in 1883 John Lundon, a New Zealander acting as representative of the South Sea Island Produce Company, tried to stir up Samoan opinion against Germany and in favour of annexation to New Zealand. His efforts had some effect for on 19 November 1883 Malietoa Laupepa sent a petition to London asking for immediate British annexation to save him from German pressures. The petition was, of course, rejected; but it confirmed German fears that New Zealand, in league with the British consul at Apia, was determined to engineer a British takeover. This fear of British action on behalf of New Zealand was the main driving force behind German policy in Samoa during the following decade.

German attitudes to Samoa were more complex than those relating to New Guinea. The original German interest was purely commercial; but by 1883 Samoa had become in some sense a hallowed symbol of the colonial ambitions of the small but influential German imperialist movement. Paradoxically, this began in 1878 with the virtual bankruptcy of Godeffroys, the founders of German enterprise in Samoa, though the crisis arose from their European rather than their Pacific activities. A new company, the DHPG, was formed to take over the Pacific interest and assets, but the business world showed no confidence in its future and few shares were taken up. Baring Brothers, the British banking firm, had to be called in to provide a loan to meet liabilities on the security of the DHPG's shares. The danger was now that Germany's largest Pacific trading concern would fall into British hands and for this reason Bismarck, who had refused earlier requests for help, announced on 1 January 1880 that he would promote a bill in the Reichstag to provide a state guarantee of 4·5 per cent minimum return on the DHPG's capital. Since this was well above current interest rates on gilt-edged stock German investors over-subscribed the company's shares. But Bismarck's proposal was strongly attacked and defeated in the Reichstag on 27 April 1880. Many subscribers withdrew and the DHPG had to go into liquidation. The company was then reconstructed, but half the shares were held by Barings and other foreign creditors until in 1884 a Hamburg consortium, led by von Hansemann, bought out the British shareholders and saved the DHPG for Germany. The crisis of 1878–80 had a profound effect on the attitudes of many nationalistic Germans to Samoa and, more generally, to German overseas enterprises. In particular the failure of investors to take up the company's shares showed how little enthusiasm or confidence German financiers and banks had in overseas and colonial enterprises and therefore emphasized the need for public support and initiative if Germany was to compete with Britain as a great commercial and colonial power. The debate on the 1880 subsidy bill was taken up by both sides as a trial of strength for the nascent movement in favour of a positive colonial policy and after its defeat German imperialists treated Samoa as a major national objective.

It was not, therefore, surprising that the Kolonialverein and other imperialist groups in Germany reacted very strongly to the ineffective attempts made by New Zealand in 1883–4 to secure British political control of Samoa. Had the British government acted on Malietoa's petition of November 1883, or on a second petition he sent in November 1884, Samoa might have become a source of international friction, for Bismarck made it clear in December 1883 that he would not accept British annexation of Samoa and in December 1884 he again asked London for assurance that a British protectorate would not be imposed. In fact he need not have worried. The British Foreign Office was anxious only to avoid trouble. The government rejected both Samoan petitions and in December 1884 forbade the New Zealand government to send its government steamer, the *Hinemoa*, to investigate the circumstances in which the German Consul at Apia, Dr O. W. Stuebel, had forced Malietoa to sign an agreement giving the Germans effective control over his government. London was, in fact, ready to concede German primacy in Samoa, provided that its nominal independence was preserved and British subjects retained the commercial and other rights provided for in the 1879 treaty.

Once this was clear in Berlin the limited objectives of Bismarck's new imperial policy became evident. He had no intention of falling out with Britain or America over so unimportant an issue as Samoa and accepted that the treaties of 1877–9 were a bar to a formal German protectorate. Diplomatic negotiations therefore continued throughout the 1880s on the problem of maintaining order in the islands. A tripartite commission investigated the situation in 1886. A three-power conference was held in Washington in 1887 and another in Berlin in 1889. Although the Germans retained the preponderant influence acquired in 1884 and even deposed and deported Malietoa Laupepa between 1877–9, the principle of international responsibility was never seriously in question and from 1889 to 1898 the neutrality of the law as between different groups of expatriates was buttressed by a Chief Justice nominated by the King of Sweden.

Until the late 1890s it therefore seemed that Samoa, like the New Hebrides, would avoid formal annexation because political factors blocked the logical consequences of economic predominance by a single European power. The eventual division of the Samoan islands between Germany and the United States in 1899 was the result of radically changed circumstances.[18] Briefly the deadlock imposed by tripartite control was resolved by two new factors. First, the Spanish-American War of 1898 changed Washington's attitude to Pacific island problems. Congress was now prepared to accept territorial responsibilities and the navy was anxious to retain

Pago Pago harbour as a naval base. The American veto on formal partition of Samoa was therefore withdrawn and negotiations between the three powers could be resumed. Second, the death of Malietoa Laupepa in August 1898 led to a succession crisis which destroyed the precarious balance of interests between the three foreign groups. Each European colony in Apia had its own candidate for the throne and the Germans pressed the claims of Mata 'afa against those of Malietoa Tanu, who was nominated by the neutral Chief Justice. To resolve this conflict, which generated a civil war in Samoa, yet another tripartite commission was sent to investigate. The civil war was stopped by foreign intervention and the commissioners recommended that Samoa should in future be governed by a neutral administrator advised by a council representing each European interest. The kingship should be abolished and indigenous affairs should be in the hands of several regional governors. At the same time the commissioners informally suggested as an alternative solution that tripartite control should be replaced by a unilateral protectorate by one of the three powers.

From this point the destiny of Samoa was decided by international diplomacy. Each of the three powers was now clear that unilateral control was better than tripartite supervision, but as none would initially renounce its rights partition was inevitable. A logical solution was that Tutuila, which contained Pago Pago harbour, should go to the United States; Upolu, where German interests predominated, to Germany; and Savaii, in which New Zealanders had substantial land claims, to Britain, along with Tonga and Niue which had been excluded from the 1886 partition. Salisbury showed little interest in a division along these lines when it was first proposed in September 1899, since there were close connections between Upolu and Savaii and he had no desire to acquire Tonga. But at this point the Samoan question became integrated into the wider patterns of British diplomacy, whose primary aims were to secure German support for a 'hands off' policy in China and to prevent German support for the Transvaal. The Anglo-German agreement of 30 April 1898 on the future of the Portuguese colonies had reduced the likelihood of German interference in South Africa but it seemed desirable to pay an additional premium to insure against a change of policy in Berlin. These considerations persuaded the British government to pay Germany's price in Samoa, despite the certainty of protests from New Zealand, whose

substantive interests there would have to be sacrificed. Nevertheless Chamberlain was able to strike a hard bargain because the
Germans were extraordinarily keen to acquire Samoa. This
enthusiasm bore little relation to economic realities, for tripartite
control was no obstacle to successful trade and production. In fact
it stemmed from two non-economic impulses, both characteristic
of German imperialism during the twenty years before 1914 rather
than during the 1880s. On the one hand Admiral Tirpitz wanted a
naval base there as a port of call on the route from Cape Horn to the
new German base at Kiao-Chow and also as a site for landing a
projected trans-Pacific German cable. On the other hand the
colonial party in Germany had never ceased to regard Samoa as the
symbol of a successful colonial policy and nationalists treated the
negotiations as a trial of international strength. Chamberlain, who
dominated the negotiations on the British side, exploited these
German enthusiasms. By the Samoan convention of 14 November
1899 existing treaty rights and conventions were annulled. Britain
renounced all political rights and was given freedom of action in
Tonga, Niue and the German Solomon Islands east of Bougainville.
Germany also conceded areas in dispute on the borders of the
Gold Coast and Togo, renounced her extra-territorial rights in
Zanzibar (now a British protectorate) and made an agreement on
West African tariffs. Germany was thus left with Upolu and
Savaii and the United States with Tutuila, but the 'open door' for
international trade was preserved by both.

In the end, therefore, the partition and annexation of Samoa by
Germany and the United States was brought about almost entirely
by political, strategic and emotional factors. Twenty years earlier
keen European rivalries had arisen from economic and to a lesser
extent missionary activities. These did not on their own account
make it necessary for any foreign power to impose formal rule but
German fear of political action by Britain on the insistence of New
Zealand and counter-balancing New Zealand fear of the imperialistic attitudes of German agents in Apia created a situation in
1883–4 in which both parties contemplated annexation. The
balance of interests made this impracticable and the powers fell
back on the mid-nineteenth-century method of joint informal control. By the end of the century the increasing complications and
sophistication of international diplomacy made such arrangements
seem archaic and in the end a formal political solution was adopted
to resolve political problems caused originally by economic activity.

ANGLO-FRENCH RIVALRY. It has been suggested in earlier chapters that French imperialism in West Africa and Indo-China during the 1880s was strongly influenced by consideration of the commercial needs of the metropolis, even though in the last resort political action was stimulated by political obstacles to trade. It might, therefore, be reasonable to expect that French ambitions in the South Pacific stemmed from the same metropolitan anxiety to promote overseas trade and that, as in parts of West Africa, British counter-action was intended to protect established or putative commercial opportunities against the threat of French tariffs. In fact, however, this model cannot be applied to Franco-British imperialism in the Pacific after about 1880. Metropolitan France showed virtually no interest in the economic possibilities of the Pacific, where existing colonies were small and unpromising and French trade and investment were minute. Table 22 indicates the scale of French commerce between 1875 and 1891. It suggests that, if French imperialism was indeed driven on by economic factors, these were likely to be the economic interests of small-scale enterprises in Tahiti or New Caledonia rather than the economic needs of the metropolis.

But, if French interests in Polynesia are considered first, it is immediately clear that Tahiti was unlikely to constitute a dynamo of French economic expansion. Even by Pacific standards this was a lethargic economy. Attempts made during the twenty years before 1880 to develop plantations with imported labour had for the most part failed. Papeete played very little part in the commodity trades of the region and was mainly an entrepôt for foreign commerce. French expansionism in Polynesia during the early 1880s was, in fact, clearly defensive rather than aggressive, a reaction to German commercial penetration of the Leeward Islands during the 1870s. Some Huahine chiefs signed a treaty with a German naval commander in 1879 and this, coupled with the fact that the DHPG now had a trading base in Raiatea, aroused French fears that the Germans might support economic enterprise by political control. To defend a region only eighty miles from Tahiti the French imposed a protectorate on Raiatea in 1881 and also annexed Rapa, farther south in the Austral Group. If, therefore, France seemed poised in 1881 to expand her Empire in Polynesia it was not because her existing possessions there needed new markets, sources or indentured labour or fields for investment.

In Melanesia, however, economic considerations provide an

Table 22

French Trade with the Pacific, 1875–91

(i) French Trade with the Pacific excluding Australia, the Philippines and Netherlands Indies, 1875–80 (francs at current values)

Date	Imports to France	Exports from France
1875	200,000	3,300,000
1876	1,100,000	4,900,000
1877	3,500,000	4,300,000
1878	400,000	3,100,000
1879	1,500,000	2,900,000
1880	367,469	3,955,454

(ii) French Trade with New Caledonia, Tahiti, and Dependencies, 1885–91 (millions of francs at current values)

Date	Imports to France	Exports from France
1885	0·2 (Tahiti only)	6·2
1886	0·14 (Tahiti only)	3·5
1887	0·2 (N. Caledonia only)	4·2
1888	1·2 (N. Caledonia only)	4·6
1889	2·1	4·8
1890	1·6	5·9
1891	1·1	5·5

Source: *Annuaire Statistique de la France*, 1878–95/6.

Note: Imports to France consist of products of French dependencies only. Exports from France probably include goods re-exported from the dependencies.

inherently credible motive for French territorial expansion, particularly into the New Hebrides. By Pacific standards New Caledonia was a dynamic economy in the 1880s. Annexed as a penal colony in 1853, it showed no signs of its future importance until the early 1870s. During this decade, however, the economy began to grow on the basis of nickel mining, which was started in 1873 by John Higginson, an Australian who had acquired French nationality and demonstrated strong dislike of Britain. By 1893, 40,000 tons of nickel were being exported and a refinery was built at Noumea in 1908. Although attempts to exploit copper and cobalt deposits and to develop a plantation economy came to little, by 1891 there were some 20,000 French settlers, about half of them still convicts, 33,000 indigenous islanders and about 2,500 indentured

Q

immigrant labourers.[19] These immigrants were, in fact, the key to New Caledonian sub-imperialism. Most of them were recruited in the New Hebrides and from the 1870s Higginson campaigned for French annexation of this vital source of mine labour. For long he received no encouragement from Paris, but in 1881 he was given qualified assurance by Gambetta, which was later renewed by Ferry, that he might expect political support if he could establish diplomatically viable evidence of French occupation. To achieve this Higginson founded the Compagnie Calédonienne des Nouvelles-Hébrides with 500,000 francs (£20,000) capital, and bought up land from British settlers at Vila Harbour in Efate and elsewhere. In November 1882 the main chiefs at Efate accepted French protection and in November 1884 chiefs at Port Sandwich also signed a protectorate treaty.

The case for regarding French expansionist tendencies in the New Hebrides as a derivative of economic interests in New Caledonia is therefore strong, even if no similar case can be made for economic motivation in Polynesia. Yet, while France in due course annexed the Leeward Islands and Rapa, she never acquired the New Hebrides. This fact may throw some light on the priorities adopted by French policy-makers; but in order to understand these it is necessary first to consider why France faced British opposition in both areas. As in the case of New Guinea, the answer is that British metropolitan policy was primarily a response to the sub-imperialism of Australians and New Zealanders, who saw French ambitions as a major threat to their own interests. These interests varied widely in each region. There was some Australian labour-recruitment and a few settlers in the New Hebrides; but the main Australasian interest in this group was the Presbyterian missions which, it was realistically assumed, would be unable to continue under full French control. This alone constituted grounds for strong colonial opposition to French occupation; but from 1883 hostility was intensified by news that a bill was under consideration in the French Parliament which, if passed, would increase the number of *récidivistes* (lapsed criminals) which could be sent to the Pacific. Since it was also being suggested in France that the New Hebrides could serve as an additional penal colony, Australians reasonably feared that the number of escaped convicts reaching Australia would increase considerably if France was allowed to annex these islands.

Resistance to French expansion in Polynesia came mainly from

New Zealand and again derived from political as well as economic considerations. Many New Zealanders resented any French movement westwards from Tahiti on the general ground that France was a possible enemy and that French naval forces might attack New Zealand ports in time of war with Britain. New Zealand therefore demanded that the 1847 convention which neutralized many of these islands be observed as an essential bulwark of the colony's safety. But economic interests also were involved. Auckland merchants and a few politicians regarded Polynesia as the main field for future commercial activity, and in the early 1880s France appeared to threaten several islands and groups in which New Zealand had specific interests. As has been seen, the French flag was raised in the Leeward Islands and Rapa was annexed. In 1881 a French naval commander announced in Rarotonga that France proposed to establish a protectorate over the Cook Islands and that in future the group's trade would be exclusively with Tahiti. There were also rumours of French treaties with Samoa and Tonga. New Zealand objected to French annexation of Rapa because this was regarded as a possible port of call on the steamship route between Auckland and Panama; but elsewhere, New Zealand interests were primarily commercial. The Cook Islands in particular were regarded as a promising field for colonial enterprise. British missions had been there since the 1840s. There was a sizeable New Zealand settlement there. New Zealand imports from the group rose to £36,668 in 1885 and exports to £9,525.[20] There was also a considerable New Zealand trade with Tonga and Samoa. France therefore seemed to be threatening New Zealand's future as a commercial power in the South Pacific.

French imperialism in the Pacific therefore faced much the same hostility from British colonists in Australia and New Zealand as the Germans were experiencing at the same time elsewhere. Again the British government, while feeling virtually no desire to expand British possessions in this region and reluctant on general diplomatic grounds to irritate the French over trifles, felt bound to do something to placate the colonists. The Foreign Office therefore made it clear to the Quai d'Orsay that Britain could not recognize any existing or proposed French acquisition in these areas without careful scrutiny and due compensation, and this in turn forced the French to review their priorities and decide how best to use their limited diplomatic credit.

The really important fact is that France decided to stand on her claims to the Leeward Islands where, as has been suggested, she had virtually no economic ambitions or interests, and to drop claims to the New Hebrides and other places which had considerable economic potential. Control of the Leewards was regarded as the primary objective because they lay a mere eighty miles from Tahiti and were vital to its security. Paris also stood on Rapa, which had been regarded as a protectorate since 1867 and was seen as a potentially valuable port of call. To achieve these gains, which depended on British willingness to abrogate the 1847 convention, the Quai d'Orsay was ready, if necessary, to drop all other pretensions. The Cook Island protectorate was disavowed in 1882 and the projected treaties with Samoa and Tonga were suspended. In April 1884 the Quai d'Orsay ordered the suspension of all treaty-making and forward action in Polynesia 'so long as questions pending over the Leeward Islands of Tahiti have not been resolved and while we have to deal with the agitation set up by the Australian colonies'.[21] Negotiations continued over the New Hebrides and the *récidiviste* bill became law in 1885 despite Australian and New Zealand protests. But by 1886 London and Paris were clear that the British colonists would not accept French occupation of the New Hebrides even if France promised to send no more convicts or *récidivistes* to any part of the Pacific and preserved full freedom for British missions and traders in the New Hebrides.

The result was the convention signed in November 1887 and an additional declaration signed in January 1888. Britain abrogated the 1847 agreement, accepted a French protectorate over Raiatea, Huahine and other islands in the Leewards and recognized French annexation of Tahiti and Rapa. The New Hebrides were neutralized and placed under a joint Anglo-French naval commission. This virtually determined the limits of British and French territory in Polynesia and Melanesia. The French continued to work for an eventual takeover of the New Hebrides and by 1900 could reasonably claim the right to control the group on the basis of effective occupation. But once again political necessities cut across economic trends and objectives. The Anglo-French Entente made it necessary to settle all outstanding colonial issues and the New Hebrides had to be sacrificed to the needs of higher policy. Under an agreement reached in 1906 a perpetual condominium was imposed on the islands, which became a joint Franco-British protectorate. Meantime the British had attempted to satisfy Australian and New Zealand opinion by imposing protectorates on Polynesian islands safeguarded from French ambition. The Cook Islands became a protectorate in 1888 and, along with Nieu, were annexed to New Zealand in 1901. Tonga became a British protectorate in 1900. The limits of British and French expansion in the Pacific until the First World War had been reached.

It is not proposed to examine the partition of other parts of the Pacific; but, to complete the record, it may be noted that after the defeat of Spain in 1898 the United States at last became a territorial power there. Renewed petitions from Hawaii for incorporation with the United States were at last accepted, mainly because the war had emphasized the importance of Pearl Harbor, leased as a naval base since 1887. The Americans also decided to retain Guam and the Philippines, giving Spain $20,000,000 in compensation. The Germans then bought out Spanish rights in the Caroline, Mariana and other island groups, which lay within the German sphere of interest as defined by the 1886 Anglo-German agreement. The partition of the Pacific was complete.

What importance has this survey of developments in the Pacific after 1880 for interpreting the role of economic factors in modern imperialism? A first significant point is that virtually all the issues and problems which dominated the last twenty years of the century were discernible by about 1880. The economic potential of most islands was well known, the patterns of trade established and plantation production of vegetable oils already widespread. Indeed, the period of rapid economic change had occurred in the previous twenty years and there were few innovations of any kind in the 1880s and 1890s. If anything, lower world prices for vegetable oils in the 1880s might have been expected to check the growth of coconut plantations and the promising opportunities for growing raw cotton had largely disappeared with the recovery of the southern United States. Ironically the valuable phosphate deposits on Nauru were entirely unknown when the island was included in the German sphere in 1886 and their later exploitation was carried out by a company which was predominantly British. By 1880 it was also obvious that in many island groups accelerating foreign commercial activity was inconsistent in the long term with political independence. Fiji had already been annexed by Britain to prevent endemic political disorder and the need was growing for similar action by one power or another in several other island groups. Finally there is no evidence of enthusiasm among European capitalists to invest in the Pacific during this period. The difficulties facing the D HPG between 1880 and 1884 suggest that German capital regarded the Pacific as a speculative and unprofitable field for investment. John Higginson's enterprises in New Caledonia and the New Hebrides were launched on a shoestring and eventually required public help. Australian enterprises were financed almost entirely from local resources.

It is, therefore, impossible to postulate any fundamentally new economic factors making for European imperialism in the 1880s. Yet the problem remains. Why, if continuity is so obvious, did formal territorial control by foreign powers develop so rapidly after 1880 where it had not during the previous twenty years?

In the most general terms the answer is that in this later period existing problems, mostly arising from the effects of accelerating European economic activity, intensified to the point at which even the most reluctant metropolitan government felt unable to avoid political action. But was there also a positive change in European attitudes to the legitimate use of political means to solve these questions? The evidence considered above suggests that a change did take place and that the critical years were 1883–5. The German government certainly adopted a new approach in 1884 to the New Guinea area and Samoa. It is difficult to be certain how far official attitudes to the Pacific merely followed lines adopted to meet problems in South-West and West Africa; yet, in so far as German policy in the Pacific was autonomous, the new approach was a response to an assumed political threat by New Zealand and the Australian colonies to established German economic interests in New Guinea and its adjacent islands, in Samoa and in other focal points of commercial rivalry. Until 1883 Germans, both in the Pacific and at home, assumed that economic preponderance in any part of the 'uncivilized' world gave them a claim to informal political primacy without the necessity of formal annexation. But in 1883–4, when the Germans informally assumed a politically dominant role in several places, including Samoa, they were challenged by Australian and New Zealand interests who tried to offset *de facto* German preponderance with a claim that the South Pacific was a British sphere of influence. Queensland's initiative in New Guinea and New Zealand manoeuvres in Samoa were clearly designed to embody this assumption. The German response to these political threats to its established economic interests was retaliatory political action. Under the circumstances this was wholly reasonable and did not imply any sudden burst of imperialist enthusiasm. But German political action inevitably stimulated a political response from Britain, primarily to satisfy the demands of Australasian colonists. The outcome was the political partition of 1885–6 which was completed in 1899.

French policy in the Pacific after 1880 was also influenced by economic developments, though these seldom affected the metropolis itself. In Polynesia French political preponderance in the Leewards was threatened by the growing economic influence of German traders and planters. Conversely in Melanesia the main force making for change was the economic enterprise of Higginson which, though small in scale and of little interest to the metropolis, was nevertheless a potent influence on French policy. It is significant of French attitudes in the early 1880s that the Ministry of Marine did not hesitate to advise use of political means to deal with these economic problems: in Polynesia to counter German economic encroachment on islands regarded as a French sphere of influence, in Melanesia to support New Caledonian economic interests against Australian and New Zealand annexationists. By contrast the French Foreign Office was extremely hesitant. The only significant metropolitan interest at stake was the transportation of relapsed criminals and the Quay d'Orsai was far more concerned to avoid serious friction with Britain than to relieve crowded French prisons. As a result Paris took no steps without prior British approval. The Leeward Islands were not annexed until Britain agreed to abrogate the 1847 convention in 1887 and the New Hebrides had to be placed under dual control. This caution may have reflected the minute scale of French economic interests in the Pacific but it also demonstrated that the French had not suddenly become expansionists under all circumstances.

The British also showed no new enthusiasm to acquire additional Pacific territories. Their attitude remained essentially what it had been in the mid-century: Pacific islands were not worth the cost and inconvenience of administration and should only be annexed when there was an overwhelming obligation to do so. Had it not been for the interests and insistence of Australia and New Zealand, London would almost certainly have let any other power take what it wanted. British statesmen were, nevertheless, forced by their colonists to play an active diplomatic role, for the Australians and New Zealanders had genuine economic, religious and strategic interests in many island groups. There are few better examples of the primacy of peripheral forces and of the force of local sub-imperialisms in the expansion of the modern colonial empires.

Finally, the United States, with significant economic interests in the Hawaiian group, Samoa and other islands, remained resolutely opposed to political control in the Pacific until 1898. Evidently the growth of monopoly capitalism and construction of markets did not generate any strong desire to use political means to defend and expand Pacific markets and fields for investment. It is possible that growing demand for new markets and for commercial entrepôts in the 1890s paved the way to the Spanish War and there is no doubt that the Chinese commercial lobby was influential in the decision to keep the Philippines in 1898. Yet the annexation of Hawaii and eastern Samoa were mere byproducts of the war. They reflected a new American awareness of the realities of political power in the Pacific with its need for naval, coaling and cable bases, rather than a new enthusiasm for empire as a basis for economic activity.

Part Four
Conclusions

13 The Role of Economics in the Expansion of the Empires, 1830-1914

This book has been concerned with one central problem: the importance of specifically economic factors (investment, trade, etc.) as forces making for the growth of European formal empire overseas. But in approaching this historiographical summit it was found necessary to tackle two preliminary conceptual problems: first, whether there was basic discontinuity between imperialism in the middle and late nineteenth century; and, second, whether imperialism expressed the 'real' character of evolving capitalism within Europe or whether it was merely a response by Europe to changing circumstances on the periphery. It is proposed very briefly to review the evidence on these two closely connected issues before facing up to the basic question.

I CONTINUITY

It was suggested above that the question of continuity in the history of nineteenth-century imperialism was conceptually very important because of the widely held belief that the expansion which occurred between about 1880 and 1914 was generated by fundamentally 'new' factors within Europe. Doubts were thrown on the *a priori* likelihood of this assumption in the preliminary chapters and the regional case studies have shown it to be substantially incorrect for most areas which were involved in the imperial process. Without recapitulating the evidence it can be said with some confidence that in the great majority of places there were substantial European interests, whether these took economic, political, religious or other forms, well before 1880 and that in many of these places conditions were already so critical that some radical change was readily predictable. This was not, of course, invariably true. Despite limited European activity there was no reason in 1880 for thinking that much of sub-Saharan Africa would be annexed within the predictable future. Yet even there continuity can be traced from existing points of European involvement – from Senegal and the Niger Delta into the Western Sudan; from South Africa into Central Africa; from Zanzibar into East Africa; from Egypt into the Egyptian Sudan. Clearly the novelty of late nineteenth-century imperialism is to be looked for in the speed and universality of the European advance and not in the mere fact that it happened. It was the end of an old story not the start of a new one.

II CRISIS AND COINCIDENCE AT THE PERIPHERY

The need, then, is to explain why existing tendencies to overseas expansion accelerated and widened so dramatically in the years after 1880. In chapters 2–4 a number of established 'Eurocentric' explanations of this tendency were considered: the need of advanced capitalism for additional fields in which to invest 'surplus' capital; the need for new markets caused by intensified protectionism; the diplomatic consequences of new international political relationships; and the jingoism of nation states. Again each of these explanations was found to be in some degree inadequate, though each contained some valid elements. The logical alternative to all such 'Eurocentric' hypotheses was an approach based largely on coincidence at the periphery. Is 'imperialism' merely shorthand for an agglomeration of causally unrelated events which happened to occur at largely the same time in different parts of the world? If so, why did the critical period of imperialism happen to occur in these thirty years after 1880?

Again, without recapitulating the evidence, it is obvious that by about 1880 a large number of problems on the periphery, all stemming from local and dissimilar conditions, simultaneously demanded or invited action or decision by the European powers concerned. The important fact is that, for the first time in modern history, these local problems were so widespread and the European powers concerned so numerous that collectively they constituted a 'general crisis' in the relations between Europe and the less-developed world. It would be unhistorical to assert that the result could only have been rapid and universal colonization for in the past many similar local problems had been dealt with in isolation and had not stimulated a general grab for colonies. The true novelty of the early 1880s was therefore that on this occasion the statesmen of Europe adopted positive and general political solutions rather than palliatives. Why was this? Proponents of 'total' explanations of imperialism have, of course, insisted on the inevitability of this decision: that statesmen had to annex in order to satisfy the nation's need for fields of investment, sources of raw material, markets, etc. Yet the evidence suggests that the decisions of the policy-makers were much more hesitant than one would have expected from men acting under overwhelming pressures or with clear objectives. Indeed the imperialism of the early 1880s consisted rather of a number of largely unconnected *ad hoc* solutions to diverse problems, which acquired their collective significance only when seen retrospectively as a whole.

Yet one must not take refuge in obscurantism. Even though the statesmen, the merchants, the bankers, the missionaries and the explorers had no clear vision of universal empire and were fumbling for piecemeal solutions to individual problems, underlying the whole process was an undeniable element of historical determinism. These multiple crises and their timing were merely symptoms of a profound change in the pathology of international relationships. The world crisis was real and a solution had to be found. By about 1880 there was a fundamental disequilibrium between Europe and most parts of the less-developed world. Never had one continent possessed so immense a power advantage over the others or been in such close contact with them. Thesis and antithesis were bound to generate a new synthesis. It would be wrong to suggest that this must inevitably have taken the form of formal colonial rule: indeed informal tutelage based on treaties proved a satisfactory permanent alternative in many parts of the world, and was tried out in other places which subsequently became formal dependencies. But this required specially favourable circumstances. When they did not exist – where, for example, indigenous states were too weak to provide a satisfactory framework for European enterprise and where rivalry between European states was excessive – unilateral annexation seemed the best, and possibly the only, satisfactory solution.

Does this imply that formal empire was invariably imposed for the largely negative reason that the powers of Europe were unable to deal collectively with problems of common interest? Was there no positive desire to possess colonies as a necessary means to achieving particular national objectives in an overseas territory? The evidence reviewed above suggests that this desire did exist but that it was much less common or important in the early 1880s, before unilateral annexation became the accepted technique, than has commonly been supposed. The strongest positive demand for formal colonies in this period came from a small minority of intellectual imperialists on the continent who, taking the British settlement colonies and India as their model, believed that full incorporation of an overseas territory into the national estate was a prerequisite for making it serve their intended purposes – emigration, plantation production, protected markets, and so on. By the early 1890s pride of possession became an additional force making for formal control as popular feeling became intermittently jingoistic. But, in the crucial decade after 1880, when the partition was hammered out, it is difficult to find many cases in which annexation can be traced to the positive belief of a European statesman that nothing less than full possession would serve national interests. Whatever they said later to rationalize and justify their policies, most men of power and responsibility found it necessary to build formal empires because the tide of events swept them past all alternative solutions to the rapidly worsening crisis on the periphery. Colonialism was not a preference but a last resort.

It is now possible to give reasonably confident answers to the two preliminary issues raised at the start of this chapter. First, it would seem that the alleged discontinuity between the 'anti-imperialism' of the mid-nineteenth century and the 'new imperialism' of the end of the century is largely illusory, the result of concentrating attention on Europe rather than on conditions in the outside world. The conditions which produced the rapid extension of formal European empire in the 1880s and thereafter evolved over substantial periods of time, though these varied in length from one area to another. In the most general terms, the existing relationships between Europeans and many other peoples were becoming inherently unstable and it seems obvious in retrospect that some form of readjustment was necessary. At the same time the proliferation of European activities in this outer world, particularly where political structures were insufficient to hold the ring between competing Europeans, generated urgent need for effective controls. The composite effect of these and other forces was that by the beginning of the 1880s there were a substantial number of areas of tension or crisis involving an unprecedented number of European powers. These problems might have been dealt with in other ways, but in fact the powers found it convenient or necessary to solve many of them by territorial division and more or less formal possession.

If this general interpretation is adopted, there can be little question about the relative causal importance of 'Eurocentric' and 'peripheral' factors in producing imperial expansion. Although European attitudes were often influenced by domestic forces, the evidence suggests that positive action normally began as a response to existing peripheral problems or opportunities rather than as the product of calculated imperialist policy. In the 1890s this relationship between external and internal influences changed as European statesmen and public opinion began to assume that each state must stake its claims overseas or see national interests go by default. But this type of metropolitan imperialism reflected the experience of the 1880s rather than the absolute need of Europe for empire overseas. In the most general terms it must be concluded that Europe was pulled into imperialism by the magnetic force of the periphery.

III THE ROLE OF ECONOMIC FACTORS

There remains the last and most difficult question: the role of economic factors in this complex of crisis and coincidence. The evidence reviewed in this book makes it possible to provide answers at two levels: first at a high level of generality to the conventional general question 'was formal empire the necessary outcome of economic needs and ambitions'; second in the more rigorous terms defined at the end of chapter 4: 'under what circumstances were European governments prepared to use political methods to solve economic problems'. It is proposed to construct short answers to both questions.

First, a reasonable, though not in fact very useful, proposition can be made that virtually all European expansion in the whole period covered by this book was in some way and in some degree influenced by economics. Wherever one looks the profit motive is stamped on the record. Its forms were, of course, legion: bank loans in Islamic Africa; the search for vegetable oils in West Africa; greed for land and gold in southern and Central Africa; problems of timber and trade in Upper Burma; determination to use Tongking as a trade route to southern China; competition for concessions in China; problems of trade, indentured labour and land in the Pacific. To ignore these factors would make nonsense of the expansion of Europe.

But so general a conclusion is almost useless. The vital question is not whether one can find possible economic grounds for empires which is beyond doubt, but in what particular ways economic forces operated to produce formal European rule. In short, were colonies acquired because the special character of European economic interests in these territories made it necessary to govern as well as to trade or invest in them; or was it because in some, possibly devious, way economic factors created secondary problems which could best or most simply be dealt with by formal annexation? To answer this question it is necessary to re-examine the evidence with some care.

The short answer, which is the most important single conclusion to emerge from the evidence surveyed in this book, is that European governments were normally prepared to use political methods to solve problems associated with European economic enterprise on the periphery only when and because this came up against some otherwise insurmountable non-economic obstacle; or, alternatively, when economic activity gave rise to some strictly non-economic problem which again demanded political action. The link between economics and empire was not, therefore, necessary and immediate but coincidental and indirect. Economic enterprise sometimes caused political problems which might have to be resolved by political methods.

But this again is a general statement which conceals very wide variations in the relationship between 'economic' and 'political' forces in a given situation. To solve the far more important question of how and by what mechanism economic factors affected the decision-making process leading to formal empire it is proposed to divide the territories examined above into three broad categories, according to the apparent relationship between economic and other factors making for formal empire.

The first category would consist of all territories which, from the start, posed essentially political or strategic problems for European governments; were treated as matters of first-class importance to the national interest; and do not therefore, throw much light on the influence of economic factors on official policy. This group is important but very small. The borderlands of Central Asia and British India were regarded by Russia and Britain alike as security problems from first to last and any economic value they may have had was never a serious consideration. Similarly, political control of the Panama Canal zone was primarily a strategic imperative for the United States, even though it also served American shipping to the Far East. Many other examples could be added, consisting mainly of islands or small enclaves acquired as naval bases and telegraph posts: Kiao-Chow, Wei-hei-wei, Port Arthur; Guam, Rapa, Manilla.

Far larger and more interesting is the second category, consisting of territories in which European involvement arose out of some form of economic activity but which were eventually annexed because some major national interest was deemed to have developed there rather for strictly economic reasons. For France, Tunisia and possibly Morocco fall into this category. For Britain, Egypt, the Nile Valley and East Africa, the Boer republics of South Africa, Pegu and Upper Burma, New Guinea and other Pacific islands regarded by Australasians as vital for their security, and the western Malay states. For Russia the areas adjoining Amur and Ussuri and parts of Manchuria could reasonably be included in the same list. Probably no German colonies would qualify. By what process did these places in which European involvement began with some form of economic enterprise come to be regarded as vital to the national interest and to be annexed on overtly political rather than economic grounds? The answer is that this transmutation occurred when and because a European government decided that some significant political or security factor was evolving from a situation which had initially seemed to relate only or primarily to matters of trade or investment. For example, the decision to invade Tunisia was taken in 1881 because it then became unmistakably clear that the French stake there was no longer mainly economic (the security of French-owned Tunisian bonds or opportunities for acquiring economic concessions) but had become political (to prevent imminent Italian occupation of a region which bordered Algeria and had significant implications for strategic power in the southern Mediterranean). Similarly, although endemic disorder in the Malay states had not qualified them for British intervention so long as tin-mining interests alone were affected, it suddenly became an urgent political matter when, in 1873, the Colonial Office became convinced that internal disorder might lead to foreign political intrusion in an area of British paramountcy. It will be recalled that similar developments occurred in all the other territories in this list. In each case economic factors created secondary non-economic problems; and the important point is that it was only at this later stage, when economic factors had been 'politicized', that European statesmen saw any over-riding need to impose formal political control. Once this need was accepted colonization could be and commonly was justified to critics on the traditional ground of the national interest, irrespective of the specific economic issues from which the crisis had sprung.

But what of the still larger residual category – places in which the original European interest was economic, where no important political or strategic considerations were ever deemed to apply and whose annexation therefore suggests a new official readiness, perhaps even enthusiasm, to use political power in support of national or sectional economic interests? Can it still be maintained that in these cases the official mind only provided political support when and because a strictly political problem had to be solved? If so, when and for what reason did governments in Europe become more ready in the 1880s to intervene in such situations merely to facilitate economic enterprise overseas?

It will clarify the problem to rehearse the type of solution which European powers might have been expected to apply to the great variety of economic problems likely to occur on the periphery if they had clung to assumptions and techniques normally regarded as characteristic of the mid-century. The evidence surveyed in part two of this book suggests that in this period metropolitan governments would have attempted to restrict their intervention and liabilities to a minimum, but not that they would invariably have refused to act at all. When, for example, a non-European government put obstacles in the way of 'legitimate' European commercial activity in its territory, the appropriate first step before 1880 was negotiation, possibly in conjunction with other interested European governments. If this failed and the matter seemed sufficiently important, limited force might be used to produce a change of mind. Classical examples of this were the recurrent naval wars with China from 1839 to 1885, whose primary aim was to persuade

Peking to sign treaties providing freedom of access for foreign merchants, and the similar naval demonstrations made by France against Annam in 1847 and 1858, though in this case the main French stake was security for Christians. In West Africa a similar compound of treaties, consular pressures and gunboats was used from the early nineteenth century to the mid-1880s to deal with the complex problems arising from expanding European trade without recourse to territorial responsibilities. Similar techniques were used in Latin America and the South Pacific.

These methods were certainly characteristic of 'the imperialism of free trade'. The important fact is that they were not the only methods adopted by metropolitan governments. The case studies in part two show that in a considerable number of places European powers did resort to an extension of formal rule before 1880 and that by that date annexation was predictable in several others. In each case there were special reasons for territorial control; yet it is significant that in several territories acquired before 1880, notably Lagos, Malaya, Hong Kong, Fiji and New Zealand, formal rule was imposed when and because some essentially non-economic problem arose from European economic activity or projected enterprise which informal techniques appeared unable to solve. This fact suggests that there was nothing fundamentally 'new' in the approach of statesmen and officials to such economic problems and their practical consequences during the period after about 1880.

The men who made European policy in the later nineteenth century therefore inherited two alternative methods of dealing with those economic issues on the periphery which generated some non-economic difficulty and were not deemed to raise questions of major national importance. The really important fact is that they continued until 1914 and beyond to use both techniques. In the first instance most powers still preferred to use diplomatic weapons or to rely on informal influence; and in some places they never found it necessary to go further. In 1914 European and North American interests in the Ottoman Empire, the Persian Gulf, Afghanistan, Siam, Japan, China and Latin America were still for the most part based on a complex of treaties and informal influence. In other places which ultimately became colonies or protectorates the powers clung to 'spheres of influence' or relied on protectorate treaties not involving effective political control until well into the 1890s: for example in much of East and Central Africa, in Madagascar and the Pacific. When it was eventually adopted formal rule was still commonly regarded as a crude and expensive way of dealing with economic problems if they did not raise matters of strategic or political importance to the metropolis.

There was, therefore, no point in time when the official mind of European states entirely rejected the assumptions and techniques which had served mid-century governments well enough. Yet it is also undeniable that recourse to territorial control became far more frequent in the 1880s and that in the 1890s this became the accepted way of dealing with peripheral problems arising from European economic and other activities. Why was this? The evidence suggests two possible answers, complementary rather than contradictory. First, that the acceleration of existing trends on the periphery, coupled with growing international rivalries, meant that economic enterprise generated political problems more frequently than they had done previously. Second, that statesmen and permanent officials became inured to using political means to solve these problems, accepting the inevitable in a changing world – or that they gradually came to believe in the positive desirability of empire. The first hypothesis can be tested by briefly recapitulating the evidence region by region, the second by considering the changing attitudes of officials in each major 'imperialist' state.

There are, in fact, strong grounds for thinking that increasing readiness to resort to formal rule was primarily a response to the growing pressure of events after about 1880. It has been suggested above that one possible non-dogmatic explanation for the timing of the 'new imperialism' in the 1880s and 1890s is that this was a period of 'general crisis', when outstanding problems in many places on the periphery were exacerbated by the intervention of an ever-increasing number of Europeans. It may, therefore, be desirable once again to survey the field to demonstrate when and why after 1880 statesmen seem increasingly to have felt that political problems associated with alien economic enterprise required formal political solutions.

In West Africa the long-standing French project for tapping the wealth of the Sudanese interior seemed from the start to require and justify military conquest and occupation because by about 1880 officials and soldiers were convinced that the Islamic states of the region constituted an otherwise insoluble problem. In this case, however, it must be recognized that the timing reflected impatience on the part of temporary holders of office in Paris rather than radically altered circumstances on the periphery. On the west coast political action became necessary for all interested powers because the long-term fiscal and juridical problems of small existing settlements were intensified after 1880 by growing international competition and because there was mutual fear that some other power would close existing markets by imposing protectorate treaties on African rulers in key areas. In the Congo region Leopold's plans for a highly informal commercial enterprise led to formal territorial division between the Congo Free State and other powers because in the first instance the French assumed that treaty-making on Leopold's account would give him exclusive political and economic control and therefore staked defensive counter-claims; and then because other powers were not prepared to accept a protectionist French régime throughout the Congo basin. In South-West Africa Bismarck decided to protect Lüderitz' concession in 1884 partly because he could not extract a clear British assurance of political security for this private economic venture. In East Africa Bismarck similarly supported Karl Peters' enterprise because it was reasonably feared that the British might otherwise try to block German acquisition of land in an area of traditional British primacy; while the British came to regard access to the Great Lakes as a major British national interest. In Central Africa desire to satisfy Cape Colony imperialists, themselves primarily concerned with economic profit, constituted an essentially political motive for establishing a British sphere of interest and later protectorates.

In South-East Asia and the Pacific the early and mid-1880s saw a similar shift from economic to political in the character of local problems. In Upper Burma the change came in 1885; in Indo-China between 1880–5, when the French had to recognize that an almost entirely commercial project to open a trading route through Tongking to China was blocked by political obstacles and, simultaneously, that informal control over Annam had become dangerously ineffective. In China the crisis came a decade later when the effects of the Sino-Japanese War seemed to threaten the established system of commercial rights based on informal political pressure. In this case, however, the powers were eventually able to avoid formal political solutions. In the Pacific Bismarck felt obliged to declare a protectorate over part of New Guinea because Queensland's attempt to annex the whole area, itself the product of concern for Australian political security as well as interest in the labour traffic, created a political threat to German economic activity. German claims in Samoa were equally the outcome of complex political factors, including an indigenous struggle for political power, the tactical political alignments of the foreign consuls and the symbolic importance attached to Samoa by metropolitan nationalists. Again the crisis was sparked off by a New Zealand attempt in 1883 to engineer a British take-over. The British had no desire at any stage to annex Pacific islands; but they found themselves under strong pressures from Australia and New Zealand to protect a number of islands which, in the eyes of the British colonists in the region, constituted a first-class national interest on grounds of security as well as a field for colonial trade, investment and missionary enterprise. The British eventually responded to these pressures for the political reason that they did not wish to alienate the self-governing colonies at a time when Britain was attempting to reintegrate her empire. The French took a similarly defensive and political view of Pacific islands close to Tahiti; and in the New Hebrides they were anxious to forestall expected British annexation which in turn was demanded by Australia as a defence against French occupation.

In general terms, then the evidence seems very broadly to support the proposition that after about 1880 formal European rule was normally imposed by metropolitan governments in places where basic national interests were economic not because economic activity itself required formal empire but because in each case some non-economic problem existed which could not be solved by informal means. It also strengthens the hypothesis that a new willingness to take such action developed in the 1880s, and not before, because outstanding problems happened to become more intense in the first half of that decade. So far as it goes this provides a conceptually satisfactory solution to the question why European statesmen used the political weapon of formal empire in situations which did not raise questions of major national importance. Unfortunately this conclusion leads back to the second problem: why were European statesmen more ready to act in this way than during the previous half-century? The answer suggested above is that officialdom was compelled to do so by the accumulation of otherwise insoluble problems. But there may be alternative or complementary explanations. Perhaps the statesmen were after all affected by new national economic problems or inspired by ideological enthusiasm for empire. To test these possibilities it is proposed briefly to review the chronology of change in the attitudes of officials in five leading imperialist states in the decades after 1880.

It is almost undeniable that the French were prepared to increase their use of annexation as a solution to political problems arising from economic problems on the periphery earlier than any other European state and that they eventually showed greatest positive enthusiasm for doing so. Despite official hesitation over Tunisia – essentially a political rather than an economic issue – France undoubtedly took the initiative in West Africa in 1879, responded quickly to the activities of Leopold in the Congo in 1882, accepted the need for military action in Tongking by 1883, risked major crises over Siam in 1893 and over the Nile in 1898, and was prepared to occupy Madagascar in 1898 when informal methods of control failed. Why was this? Four possible explanations have been suggested. First, that the propaganda of non-official imperialists during the 1870s had a measurable impact on some politicians and officials, conditioning them to regard solution of peripheral economic problems as a worthwhile object of national concern, provided these were not of interest only to a particular private concern. Second, mercantilist assumptions remained strong, despite the free trading policy adopted in the 1860s; and the revival of tariff protection, coupled with concern for France's weak competitive position in commerce, encouraged a generalized belief that public support was necessary for economic interests. Third, republican political circles were extremely sensitive after the disaster of 1871 on questions affecting French power and prestige. Finally, the political and constitutional structure of the Third Republic enabled relatively small groups of politicians and officials, particularly those in the Colonial Department (later the Colonial Ministry) to obtain credits and undertake policies of which neither the Quai d'Orsay nor majority opinion in Parliament specifically approved. Whatever the reason, France was the first major state which was prepared to justify use of political means to deal with peripheral economic issues on the grounds that this served a general national interest, even where no major political or strategic objective was involved. Although challenged by many this doctrine was clearly enunciated by Ferry in 1885 and by the early 1890s seems to have become an accepted official principle.

It is impossible to talk of Russian imperialism in terms relevant to any of the constitutional states of Western Europe, for Russia did not possess a comparably informed or influential public opinion or Parliament, and the ministerial system was only partially developed. It is reasonably clear, moreover, that the distinction drawn in more sophisticated states between the national interest and that of private individuals had little meaning in St Petersburg. Russian expansion in Central Asia and the Balkans resulted from historic modes of thought which approximate more closely to Schumpeter's model of atavistic behaviour patterns than to the overseas policies of any advanced state in Western Europe. It is improbable, therefore, that nice distinctions were drawn in the 1880s and 1890s between specifically economic and political objectives in the Far East, for both were the concern of the government rather than of private interests and were seen as two elements in an agreed policy of preserving Russia's status as a major power in the Pacific leading to eventual predominance in China. The fact that Witte preferred to penetrate China by economic means rather than make territorial claims was due to the limited military and political resources available in the Far East until the trans-Siberian railway was completed rather than to distinctions drawn between economic and political objectives. It is therefore almost meaningless to attempt to date Russian willingness to use political means to save economic problems.

In Germany, however, this distinction was clear and important. Despite the adoption of domestic protection in 1879 and also the close personal links between many senior politicians, government officials and men of business, state power was not at the service of economic interests unless some important public interest would be served. Moreover, despite the volume of propaganda put out by imperialists, German ministers and senior officials do not, at least in the early 1880s, seem to have been convinced that colonies as such were necessary to the nation's economic interests. Hence the protectorates of 1884–5 were justified on highly conservative grounds: they provided specific solutions to otherwise insoluble problems facing German nationals on the periphery; they involved no diplomatic complications or large public expenditure; as protectorates, they could be renounced without difficulty. After about 1897, admittedly, increasing German aggressiveness in China, Morocco and the Pacific gave the impression that official attitudes had changed, that Bismarck's successors really believed in the economic importance of colonies to the metropolis and were ready to use state power to acquire territories in which no political obstacle to economic activity had arisen. But this is misleading. The evidence suggests that self-assertiveness on the periphery reflected a generally more chauvinistic foreign and naval policy, which were intended to assert the right of Germany to be consulted by other powers on all major international questions, rather than unqualified enthusiasm for colonization as an end in itself. Moreover it seems clear that the role of economic and political consideration was frequently reversed. The German state increasingly used economic weapons to further its political or military stratagems, forcing German commercial and investment interests to play a nationalistic role even against their inclinations. But the limits of political action in peripheral situations remained clear. Germany never seriously risked confrontation with any major power over a colonial issue because none was deemed to constitute a first-class national interest. The disgust of German imperialists at the Moroccan settlement of 1911 indicates that Bismarckian realism remained dominant in Berlin to the brink of the First World War.

American imperialism raises special problems of analysis and cannot be discussed at length. Fundamentally it is probable that, because of the character of the party system and the relative lack of continuity at the higher levels of the central administration, the official mind of Washington lacked those solidly established principles governing the foreign policies of all parties which could be seen in London, Berlin and to some extent at the Quai d'Orsay in Paris. Conversely, American policy was more susceptible to transient currents of public opinion. Until some point in the early 1890s it is clear that pressures from economic or other interests to acquire overseas territories for any purpose were slight, and conversely that no administration was prepared to use political methods to solve peripheral problems. Hence the refusal to partition Samoa or accept the invitation to incorporate Hawaii in 1893. Why, then, the dramatic change of policy in 1898–9 which produced formal empire in the Caribbean and Pacific? Was this due to a new consensus among politicians on the proper role of the state as protector and promoter of national economic enterprise after a period of economic hardship? It has been argued by some authors that this was so and that this change reflected both the growing political influence of the great financial corporations and pressing need during the slump of the later 1880s and early 1890s for new overseas markets. It is equally possible that concern for national security, and in particular for overseas possessions necessary for the effective exercise of naval power in an age of intensifying international naval rivalry, was partly responsible for this change of official attitude. The change must in any case not be exaggerated.

The chosen limits of American imperialism after 1900 resembled those of Britain in the mid-nineteenth century rather than those of, say, France in the 1890s. The Americans showed almost no interest in possession of territory as a protected sphere of trade or investment. It was necessary only to secure commercial entrepôts, naval bases, the site for a strategic canal and to solve existing social and economic problems, in areas of established American influence, as in Samoa and Hawaii. The state should only use political or military methods when national security was at stake or to promote expanding trade when economic methods alone were inadequate.

There can be no doubt, finally, that in Britain the mid-nineteenth-century distinction between the proper role of state action and the sphere of private economic interests were never forgotten, even in the 'age of imperialism'. Despite 'Manchester' influences earlier in the century British statesmen had never renounced the use of force or formal territorial control when dealing with political obstacles to economic enterprise. Thus the Chinese War of 1839–42 was based on the assumptions that would not have been out of period in the 1890s. Whitehall was extraordinarily unaffected by imperialist propaganda relating empire to economics until Chamberlain, in this as in many other respects a rebel against establishment assumptions, linked the two in the late 1890s. Officials and statesmen disliked the trend of events after about 1880 and were afraid that casual use of state power in connection with commercial difficulties would generate more expense and inconvenience than they warranted. Moreover, cabinet ministers and civil service mandarins distrusted the entrepreneurs of tropical empire as much as their predecessors had distrusted Wakefield fifty years earlier. Yet they could not be unaffected by the pace of events, and during the twenty years after about 1880 they gradually became inured to the fact that, when substantial British economic interests overseas were genuinely threatened by local political difficulties or by the political action of other powers, some form of political solution was inevitable. The stages of this reluctant descent from austere principles can be charted with some precision. It began in 1884–5 with the Niger Coast protectorate and the preliminary agreement with Germany over spheres of interest in East and Central Africa and the Pacific. It moved a stage further in 1886 when the Niger Company was given a charter to administer any territories it could effectively occupy. But until the early 1890s earlier principles remained almost unchanged. In each case state responsibility was kept to the minimum apparently required to secure the particular interest at stake – to preclude foreign political control of an area deemed important for British, Cape Colony or Australasian interests. The premiums Whitehall was ready to pay were, moreover, still small. A protectorate was expected to involve virtually no administration and a sphere of influence was merely a cartographical exercise. The real break came in 1897–8 when Chamberlain justified the cost of the West African Frontier Force in terms of the specific economic potential of the Middle Niger region, for this was to adopt the criteria of French and German unofficial imperialists, making imperial rule a gamble on the economic potential of semi-deserts. This was rare if not unique in the case history of British expansion after 1830; yet it is undeniable that by about 1900 British officialdom was reluctantly accepting the fact that empire had become a necessary solution to political and sometimes also economic problems on the periphery.

There were, therefore, significant differences in the time-scale of changing official attitudes to the proper role of the state when dealing with the consequences of European economic activity overseas. What determined the order of this procession? To answer the question fully, if indeed it can be answered, would require detailed analysis of many aspects of society and government in each main 'imperialist' state and is beyond the scope of the present study. Yet, when all is said, such analysis would relate only to the chronology of reactions to external events. It could not rehabilitate the basic argument that the 'new imperialism' was the product of influences operating merely within the metropolitan context. In the last resort the imperialism of the last two decades of the twentieth century must be seen as a reaction to events outside Europe which swept all governments past the solid ground of mid-nineteenth-century assumptions into deep waters where they could survive only by striking out in new directions.

To summarize the argument without making vast generalizations or indulging in high-flown hyperbole the answer to the original question – the role of economic factors in European imperialism between 1830 and 1914 – can be re-stated as a set of simple propositions.

Economic factors were present and in varying degrees influential in almost every situation outside Europe which led ultimately to formal empire; and the specific value of many of these territories to

Europeans lay in trade, investment opportunities or other forms of economic activity.

But economic factors did not, on their own account, necessarily or even commonly generate need or desire for formal empire. The true 'economic imperialism' of the European merchant and financier was frequently blind to politics. Formal ownership of territory was seldom essential or even relevant to economic activity and in some places might have positively inconvenient consequences for traders, planters, land speculators and others. Conversely the official mind of Europe for long assumed that economic interests could and should look after themselves without direct interference by the state.

The vital link between economics and formal empire was therefore neither the economic need of the metropolis for colonies nor the requirements of private economic interests, but the secondary consequence of problems created on the periphery by economic and other European enterprises for which there was no simple economic solution. At one extreme such problems directly affected what European officialdom regarded as 'first-class' national interests. At the other they raised minor political difficulties such as the instability of an indigenous political régime or obstruction by other Europeans to satisfactory trade or investment. But in virtually every case the ultimate explanation of formal annexation was that the original economic issue had to some degree become 'politicized' and therefore required a political solution.

In the crudest terms, therefore, it would seem that empire-building occurred on so large a scale in the last two decades of the nineteenth century, rather than at some previous time, and affected parts of Africa, Asia and the Pacific and not other regions, because it was in that period and in those places that relations between representatives of the advanced economies of Europe and other less-developed societies became fundamentally unstable. This fact can be explained according to initial assumptions. To the neo-Marxist it reflects the growing crisis of advanced capitalism which could only survive by absorbing and exploiting the less-developed regions of the world. To others it may suggest that, by coincidence, the activities of Europeans then became increasingly incompatible with preservation of indigenous economic, political and cultural systems in these areas. Probably, as the neo-Marxists held, though not for the economic reasons they gave, the whole process was historically inevitable. If so, it was inevitable only as a temporary expedient, to bridge the time-gap between a 'modernized' Europe and a pre-capitalist periphery. And for the same reason empire eventually provided its own solvent. Half a century after 1914 Europe could withdraw the legions with reasonable confidence that the fundamental problems of international relations which had generated the imperialism of the late nineteenth century no longer existed. In the second half of the twentieth century European merchants and investors could operate satisfactorily within the political framework provided by most reconstructed indigenous states as their predecessors would have preferred to operate a century earlier but without facing those problems which had once made formal empire a necessary expedient.

Maps

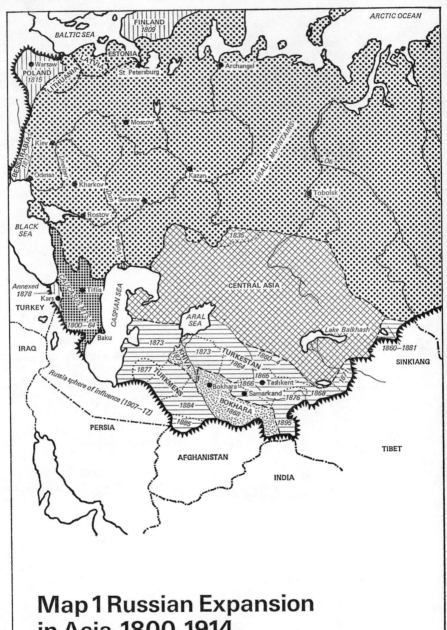

Map 1 Russian Expansion in Asia, 1800-1914

ARCTIC OCEAN

BALTIC SEA

FINLAND
1809

ESTONIA

Warsaw
POLAND
1815

LITHUANIA

LATVIA

St Petersburg

Archangel

Moscow

Kiev

Kazan

Odessa

Kharkov

Saratov

Rostov

BLACK
SEA

Tobolsk

Ob

URAL MOUNTAINS

BESSARABIA
1812

Dnieper

Don

Volga

1835

CENTRAL ASIA

Annexed
1878

Kars

Tiflis

TURKEY

1800–64

Baku

CAUCASUS

CASPIAN SEA

ARAL
SEA

Lake Balkhash

IRAQ

1873

1873

TURKESTAN
1864

1860

1860–1881

SINKIANG

Russia sphere of influence (1907–17)

1877

KHIVA

TURKMENS

1865

Tashkent

1866

Bokhara

1884

BOKHARA
1869

Samarkand

1876

1868

PERSIA

1885

1895

BUKHARA

AFGHANISTAN

INDIA

TIBET

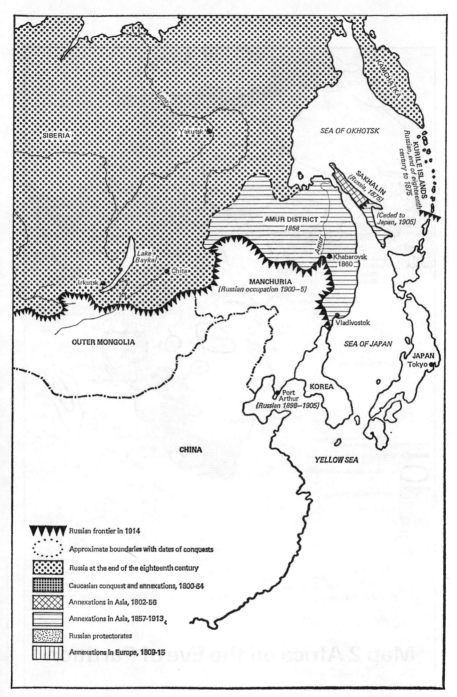

SIBERIA

Lena

Yakutsk

KAMCHATKA

SEA OF OKHOTSK

KURILE ISLANDS
Russian, end of eighteenth
century to 1875

SAKHALIN
(Russia, 1875)

AMUR DISTRICT
1858

(Ceded to
Japan, 1905)

Lake
Baykal

Chita

Amur

Khabarovsk
1860

Irkutsk

MANCHURIA
(Russian occupation 1900–5)

Vladivostok

OUTER MONGOLIA

SEA OF JAPAN

JAPAN
Tokyo

Port
Arthur
(Russian 1898–1905)

KOREA

CHINA

YELLOW SEA

Russian frontier in 1914

Approximate boundaries with dates of conquests

Russia at the end of the eighteenth century

Caucasian conquest and annexations, 1800-64

Annexations in Asia, 1802-56

Annexations in Asia, 1857-1913

Russian protectorates

Annexations in Europe, 1809-15

R

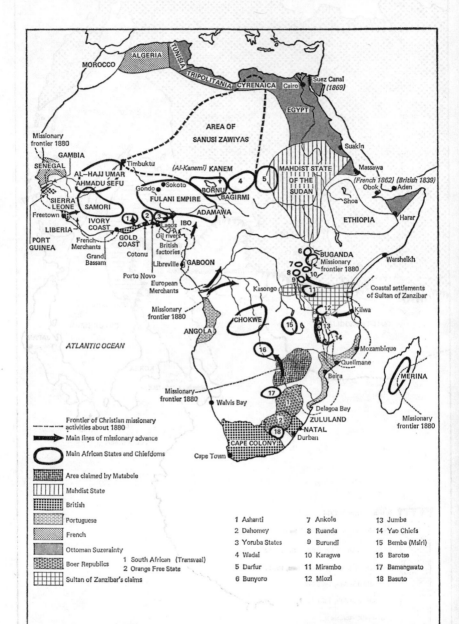

Map 2 Africa on the Eve of Partition

MOROCCO
ALGERIA
TUNISIA
TRIPOLITANIA
CYRENAICA
Cairo
Suez Canal (1869)
EGYPT

Missionary frontier 1880
GAMBIA
SENEGAL
AL-HAJJ UMAR
AHMADU SEFU
SIERRA LEONE
SAMORI
Freetown
LIBERIA
PORT GUINEA
IVORY COAST
French Merchants
Grand Bassam
GOLD COAST
Cotonu
Porto Novo
European Merchants
Timbuktu
(Al-Kanemi)
KANEM
Gondo
Sokoto
FULANI EMPIRE
BORNU
BAGIRMI
ADAMAWA
Lagos
IBO
Oil rivers
British factories
Libreville
GABOON

AREA OF SANUSI ZAWIYAS

4
5
MAHDIST STATE OF THE SUDAN

Suakin
Massawa
(French 1862) (British 1839)
Obok
Aden
Shoa
ETHIOPIA
Harar

Missionary frontier 1880
Kasongo
CHOKWE
ANGOLA

ATLANTIC OCEAN

6
BUGANDA
7
Missionary frontier 1880
8
9
10
11
12
15
13
14
Warsheikh
Coastal settlements of Sultan of Zanzibar
Kilwa
Mozambique
Quelimane
Beira
MERINA
Missionary frontier 1880

Missionary frontier 1880
Walvis Bay
16
17
18
Delagoa Bay
ZULULAND
NATAL
Durban
CAPE COLONY
Cape Town

- - - Frontier of Christian missionary activities about 1880
➤ Main lines of missionary advance
◯ Main African States and Chiefdoms

Area claimed by Matabele
Mahdist State
British
Portuguese
French
Ottoman Suzerainty
Boer Republics   1 South African (Transvaal)
                  2 Orange Free State
Sultan of Zanzibar's claims

1 Ashanti   7 Ankole   13 Jumbe
2 Dahomey   8 Ruanda   14 Yao Chiefs
3 Yoruba States   9 Burundi   15 Bemba (Msiri)
4 Wadai   10 Karagwe   16 Barotse
5 Darfur   11 Mirambo   17 Bamangwato
6 Bunyoro   12 Mlozi   18 Basuto

Map 2 Africa on the Eve of Partition

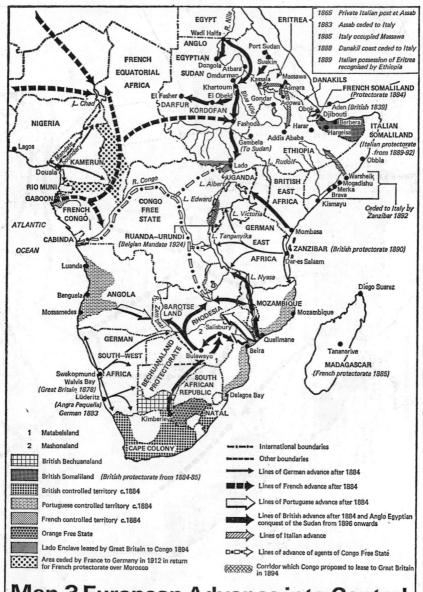

EGYPT
Wadi Halfa
R. Nile
ERITREA
Port Sudan

ANGLO
EGYPTIAN
Suakin

FRENCH
EQUATORIAL
Dongola Atbara
Massawa
DANAKILS

AFRICA
SUDAN Omdurman
Kassala
Asmara

Khartoum
Gondar
Adowa
FRENCH SOMALILAND
(Protectorate 1884)

L. Chad
El Fasher El Obeid
DARFUR
KORDOFAN
Harar
Obok
Aden *(British 1839)*
Djibouti
Berbera
ITALIAN

NIGERIA
Fashoda
Addis Ababa
Hargeisa
SOMALILAND

Mandara boundary
Gambela
(To Sudan)
ETHIOPIA
(Italian protectorate from 1889-92)

Lagos
Obbia

Douala
KAMERUN
Lado
L. Rudolf

RIO MUNI
R. Congo
UGANDA
Warsheik

GABOON
L. Albert
BRITISH
Mogadishu
Merka

FRENCH
EAST
Brava

CONGO
CONGO
L. Edward
AFRICA
Kismayu
Ceded to Italy by Zanzibar 1892

FREE
STATE

ATLANTIC
CABINDA
L. Victoria

OCEAN
RUANDA–URUNDI
(Belgian Mandate 1924)
GERMAN
Mombasa

L. Tanganyika
EAST
ZANZIBAR *(British protectorate 1890)*

Luanda
AFRICA
Dar-es-Salaam

L. Nyasa

Benguela
ANGOLA
Diego Suarez

Mossamedes
Zambezi
BAROTSE
MOZAMBIQUE

LAND
RHODESIA
Mozambique

2 Salisbury
Tananarive

GERMAN
Bulawayo 1
Quellimane
MADAGASCAR

SOUTH–WEST
Beira
(French protectorate 1885)

Swakopmund
AFRICA
BECHUANALAND
PROTECTORATE

Walvis Bay
(Great Britain 1878)
SOUTH
AFRICAN
REPUBLIC

Lüderitz
(Angra Pequeña)
German 1883
Delagoa Bay

Kimberley
NATAL

CAPE COLONY

Legend

1 Matabeleland
2 Mashonaland

British Bechuanaland
British Somaliland *(British protectorate from 1884-85)*
British controlled territory c.1884
Portuguese controlled territory c.1884
French controlled territory c.1884
Orange Free State
Lado Enclave leased by Great Britain to Congo 1894
Area ceded by France to Germany in 1912 in return for French protectorate over Morocco

International boundaries
Other boundaries
Lines of German advance after 1884
Lines of French advance after 1884
Lines of Portuguese advance after 1884
Lines of British advance after 1884 and Anglo Egyptian conquest of the Sudan from 1896 onwards
Lines of Italian advance
Lines of advance of agents of Congo Free State
Corridor which Congo proposed to lease to Great Britain in 1894

Map 3 European Advance into Central, South and East Africa, 1880-1914

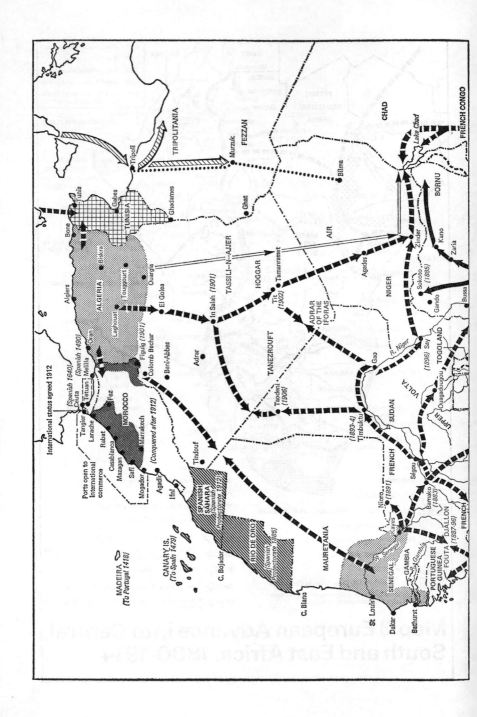

Map showing European advances into Central, South and East Africa, 1850–19—

TRIPOLITANIA

FEZZAN

CHAD

FRENCH CONGO

Tripoli

Tunis

Gabes

Bone

Ghadames

Ghat

Murzuk

Bilma

Lake Chad

BORNU

Zinder

Kano

Zaria

Algiers

Tunisia

ALGERIA

Biskra

Touggourt

Ouargla

El Golea

In Salah (1901)

TASSILI-N-AJER

HOGGAR

AIR

NIGER

Tamanrasset

Tit (1902)

Agades

Sokoto (1885)

Gando

Bussa

Laghouat

Figuig (1901)

Colomb Bechar

Beni-Abbes

Adrar

ADRAR OF THE IFORAS

TANEZROUFT

Taodeni (1906)

Gao

R. Niger

Say (1896)

TOGOLAND

VOLTA

Oran

Melilla (Spanish 1490)

Ceuta (Spanish 1640)

Tetuan

Tangier

Larache

Fez

Rabat

MOROCCO

Marrakech

Casablanca

Mazagan

Safi

Mogador

Agadir

Ifni

(Conquered after 1912)

International status agreed 1912

Ports open to International commerce

Tindouf

SPANISH SAHARA (Spanish Protectorate 1912)

RIO DE ORO (Spanish Protectorate 1885)

C. Bojador

C. Blanc

St Louis

Dakar

Bathurst

MADEIRA (To Portugal 1418)

CANARY IS. (To Spain 1479)

MAURETANIA

Timbuktu (1893-4)

SUDAN

FRENCH

Segou

Nioro (1891)

Kayes

Bamako (1883)

FRENCH

Senegal

SENEGAL

GAMBIA

R. Gambia

PORTUGUESE GUINEA

FOUTA DJALLON (1887-96)

UPPER

Ouagadougou (1896)

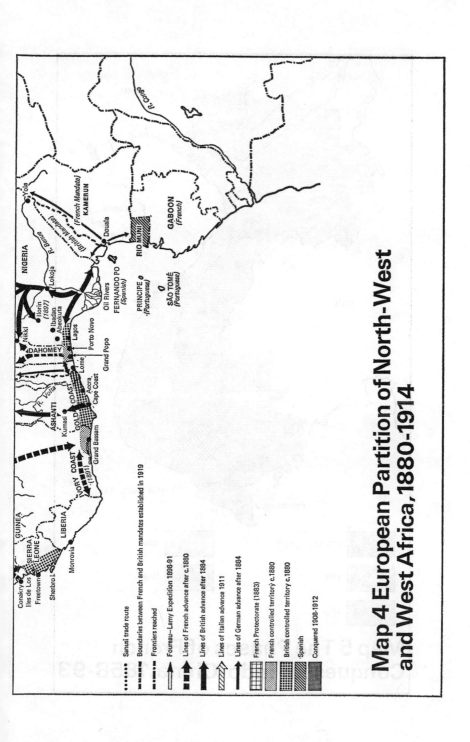

Map 4 European Partition of North-West and West Africa, 1880–1914

- •••••• Sanusi trade route
- ⋯⋯⋯ Boundaries between French and British mandates established in 1919
- ▬▬▬ Frontiers reached
- ⇨ Foureau–Lamy Expedition 1898-91
- ⬌ Lines of French advance after c.1880
- ➡ Lines of British advance after 1884
- ⇨ Lines of Italian advance 1911
- ↑ Lines of German advance after 1884
- ▦ French Protectorate (1883)
- ▩ French controlled territory c.1880
- ▤ British controlled territory c.1880
- ▨ Spanish
- ▦ Conquered 1908-1912

Map labels:

GUINEA
SIERRA LEONE
Conakry
Iles de Los
Freetown
Sherbro I.
LIBERIA
Monrovia
IVORY COAST (1891)
Grand Bassam
ASHANTI
Kumasi
GOLD COAST
Cape Coast
Accra
R. Volta
DAHOMEY
Lomé
Grand Popo
Porto Novo
Lagos
Nikki
Ilorin (1897)
Ibadan
Abeokuta
NIGERIA
Lokoja
R. Benue
Yola
(British Mandate)
(French Mandate)
KAMERUN
Douala
Oil Rivers
FERNANDO PO (Spanish)
RIO MUNI
PRINCIPE (Portuguese)
SÃO TOMÉ (Portuguese)
GABOON (French)
Fr. Congo

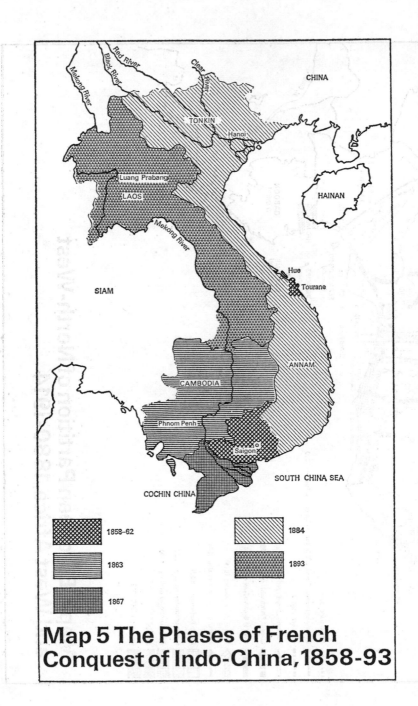

CHINA

Mekong River

Red River

Black River

Clear River

TONKIN

Hanoi

Luang Prabang

LAOS

HAINAN

Mekong River

SIAM

Hue
Tourane

ANNAM

CAMBODIA

Phnom Penh

Saigon

COCHIN CHINA

SOUTH CHINA SEA

1858–62

1863

1867

1884

1893

Map 5 The Phases of French
Conquest of Indo-China, 1858-93

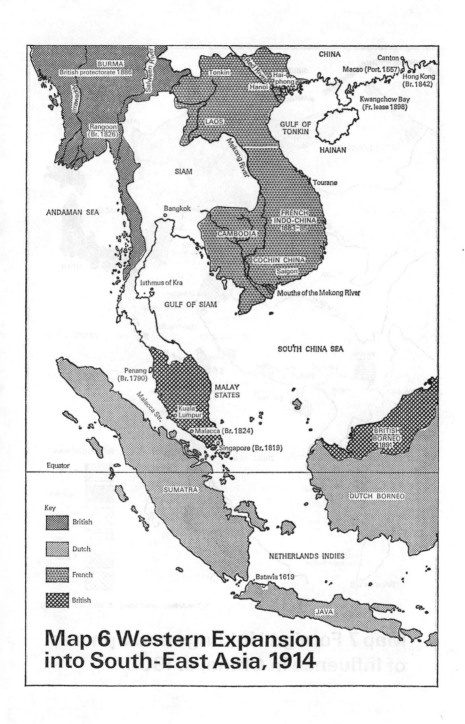

CHINA

Canton

Macao (Port. 1557)

Hong Kong (Br. 1842)

BURMA
British protectorate 1886

Tonkin

Hai-
phong

Kwangchow Bay
(Fr. lease 1898)

Hanoi

Rangoon
(Br. 1826)

LAOS

GULF OF
TONKIN

HAINAN

SIAM

Tourane

ANDAMAN SEA

Bangkok

FRENCH
INDO-CHINA
1883-85

CAMBODIA

COCHIN CHINA

Saigon

Isthmus of Kra

Mouths of the Mekong River

GULF OF SIAM

SOUTH CHINA SEA

Penang
(Br. 1790)

MALAY
STATES

Kuala
Lumpur

BRITISH
BORNEO
1891

Malacca (Br. 1824)

Singapore (Br. 1819)

Equator

SUMATRA

DUTCH BORNEO

Key

British

Dutch

NETHERLANDS INDIES

French

Batavia 1619

British

JAVA

Map 6 Western Expansion into South-East Asia, 1914

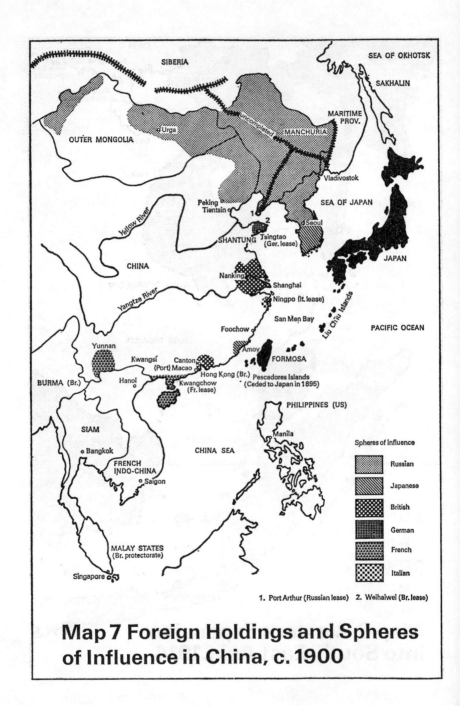

SEA OF OKHOTSK

SAKHALIN

SIBERIA

MARITIME PROV.

OUTER MONGOLIA

Urga

Uncompleted

MANCHURIA

Vladivostok

SEA OF JAPAN

Peking
Tientsin

1

2

Seoul

SHANTUNG

Tsingtao
(Ger. lease)

CHINA

Yellow River

Nanking

Shanghai

Yangtze River

Ningpo (It. lease)

San Men Bay

Foochow

PACIFIC OCEAN

Yunnan

Amoy

Kwangsí

Canton
(Port) Macao

FORMOSA

BURMA (Br.)

Hanoi

Hong Kong (Br.)

Kwangchow
(Fr. lease)

Pescadores Islands
(Ceded to Japan in 1895)

JAPAN

Liu Chiu Islands

PHILIPPINES (US)

SIAM

Bangkok

Manila

CHINA SEA

FRENCH
INDO-CHINA

Saigon

Spheres of influence

Russian

Japanese

British

German

French

Italian

MALAY STATES
(Br. protectorate)

Singapore

1. Port Arthur (Russian lease)   2. Weihaiwei (Br. lease)

Map 7 Foreign Holdings and Spheres of Influence in China, c. 1900

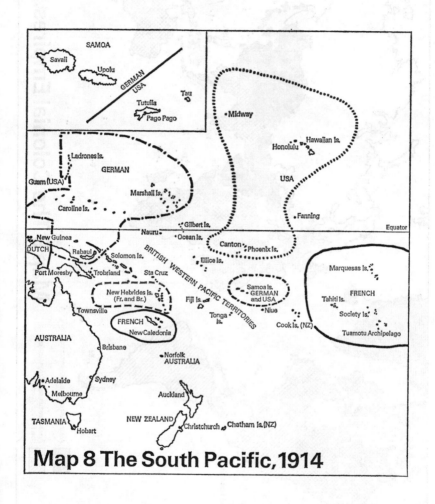

SAMOA

Savaii

Upolu

GERMAN

USA

Tutulla

Tau

Pago Pago

Midway

Hawaiian Is.

Honolulu

Ladrones Is.

GERMAN

USA

Guam (USA)

Marshall Is.

Caroline Is.

Fanning

Equator

Nauru

Gilbert Is.

Ocean Is.

Canton

Phoenix Is.

New Guinea

DUTCH

Rabaul

Solomon Is.

BRITISH WESTERN PACIFIC TERRITORIES

Ellice Is.

Marquesas Is.

Port Moresby

Trobriand

Sta Cruz

FRENCH

New Hebrides Is.
(Fr. and Br.)

Fiji Is.

Samoa Is.
GERMAN
and USA

Niue

Tahiti Is.

Society Is.

Townsville

FRENCH

New Caledonia

Tonga
Is.

Cook Is. (NZ)

Tuamotu Archipelago

AUSTRALIA

Brisbane

Norfolk

AUSTRALIA

Adelaide

Sydney

Melbourne

Auckland

TASMANIA

NEW ZEALAND

Christchurch

Chatham Is.(NZ)

Hobart

Map 8 The South Pacific, 1914

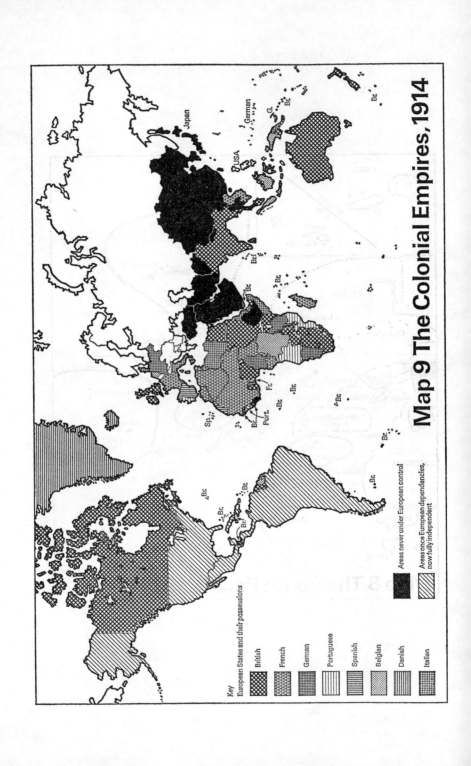

Map 9 The Colonial Empires, 1914

Key
European States and their possessions

British
French
German
Portuguese
Spanish
Belgian
Danish
Italian

Areas never under European control

Areas once European dependencies, now fully independent

Notes

CHAPTER 1: INTRODUCTION: ECONOMIC EXPLANATIONS OF IMPERIALISM

[1] The use of 'economic' and 'political' to define categories of events or motives is open to the obvious objection that neither is a precise term and that any definition may therefore be tautological. I have used both words frequently throughout this book as a shorthand to indicate differences between those situations, motives, etc. which, in the words of the *Concise Oxford Dictionary* (revised edition, Oxford, 1960) relate respectively to 'the production and distribution of wealth' and to 'the state or its government'. This makes 'political' virtually a residual category; and in practice I have used the word to indicate matters which were not necessarily related to trade, production, investment, etc. Thus, in chapter 11 I suggest that the desire of French merchants to establish a direct trade with China via the Red River was a genuinely 'economic' phenomenon; but that the military and administrative obstacles put in the way by China and Annam were 'political' factors and that French use of an army to remove these obstacles constituted 'political' action. It may be argued that if military action of this sort was intended to produce an economic benefit it is misleading to describe it as a 'political' act. Yet in my view it remains desirable to distinguish between the inherent character of the means and ends. Contemporaries certainly did so.

CHAPTER 2: THE IMPERIALISM OF TRADE

[1] For an account of the development of German tariffs see J. H. Clapham, *The Economic Development of France and Germany, 1815–1914.* (Cambridge, 1951).

[2] For French tariff history see Clapham, *ibid.*; S. B. Clough, *France – A History of National Economics 1789–1939.* (New York, 1939).

[3] *New Cambridge Modern History* XI (Cambridge, 1962), 507.

[4] H. Brunschwig, *French Colonialism, 1871-1914*. (London, 1966), 27.

[5] P. Roubiquet (ed.), *Discours et Opinions de Jules Ferry*. (7 vols, Paris, 1896-7), V. 194-6, trans. D. K. Fieldhouse.

[6] Quoted C. W. Newbury, 'The Protectionist Revival in French Colonial Trade: The Case of Senegal', *Economic History Review*, 2nd ser., XXI, 2 (1968), 343.

[7] *Ibid.*, 345.

[8] Roubiquet, *Discours*, V, 557-9, trans. D. K. Fieldhouse.

[9] Quoted S. H. Roberts, *A History of French Colonial Policy, 1870-1925* (2 vols. London, 1929), I, 21.

[10] Roubiquet, *Discours*, V, 555-6, trans. D. K. Fieldhouse.

[11] A. Girault, *The Colonial Tariff Policy of France*. (Oxford, 1916), 83.

[12] G. W. F. Hegel, *Philosophy of Right* (1821, English edition trans. T. M. Knox, Oxford 1942), 242-9.

[13] F. List, *The National System of Political Economy*. (1841: 1885 ed. reprinted New York, 1966).

[14] Quoted M. E. Townsend, *Origins of Modern German Colonialism, 1871-1885* (New York, 1921), 30.

[15] M. Walker, *Germany and the Emigration, 1816-1885* (Boston, 1964).

[16] I owe this quotation to Dr H. Pogge von Strandmann.

[17] Quoted Townsend, *Origins*, 72.

[18] Based on Brunschwig, *L'Expansion allemande d'Outre-Mer* (Paris, 1957), 167 f.

[19] *A View of the Art of Colonization* (London, 1849), 83.

[20] Charles Buller in the House of Commons, 6 April 1843. Quoted G. Bennett, *The Concept of Empire* (London, 1953), 142-3.

[21] Newbury, 'The Protectionist Revival', 348.

[22] Speech at the Free Trade Hall, Manchester, 16 April 1884. Quoted D. C. M. Platt, 'Economic Factors in British Policy during the "New Imperialism"', *Past and Present*, 39 (1968), 128.

[23] D. C. M. Platt, *Finance, Trade and Politics in British Foreign Policy, 1815-1914* (Oxford, 1968), 258.

[24] Quoted Platt, 'Economic Factors', 128.

[25] See M. Perham, *Lugard* (2 vols, London, 1956, 1960), I, 387-431.

[26] R. E. Robinson and J. A. Gallagher, *Africa and the Victorians* (London 1961), 329, n. 8.

[27] Quoted Bennett, *The Concept of Empire*, 312-13.

[28] W. K. Hancock, *Survey of British Commonwealth Affairs*, II, ii, *Problems of Economic Policy, 1918-39* (London, 1942), 82.

[29] See also William Cunningham, 'English Imperialism', *Atlantic Monthly*, July 1899, 1-6, for a favourable exposition of the case for British colonial expansion based on the danger of exclusion from areas of commercial importance by tariffs imposed by other powers.

CHAPTER 3: THE IMPERIALISM OF CAPITAL

1 For material on this subject see G. S. L. Tucker, *Progress and Profits in British Economic Thought, 1650–1850*. (Cambridge, 1960); D. K. Fieldhouse, *The Theory of Capitalist Imperialism* (London, 1967); D. Winch, *Classical Political Economy and Colonies* (London, 1965); R. N. Ghosh, *Classical Macroeconomics and the Case for Colonies* (Calcutta, 1967); and B. Semmel, *The Rise of Free Trade Imperialism* (Cambridge, 1970).

2 *Imperialism: a Study* (London, 1902). The quotations are from this first edition, which differs in some respects from later editions.

3 *Ibid.,* 62.

4 *Ibid.,* 51–63.

5 *Ibid.,* 91.

6 For a good outline of the debate see B. J. Hovde, 'Socialist Theories of Imperialism prior to the Great War'. *Journal of Political Economy,* XXXVI (1928), 713–58.

7 See Rosa Luxemburg, *The Accumulation of Capital* (1913; English translation, London, 1951).

8 R. Hilferding, *Finanzkapital* (Vienna, 1910). The English translation is taken from Fieldhouse, *Theory of Capitalist Imperialism*, 80.

9 N. I. Bukharin, *Imperialism and World Economy* (1917; English translation, New York, 1929).

10 V. I. Lenin, *Imperialism, the Highest Stage of Capitalism* (1916; English translation, Moscow, 1947), 26.

11 *Ibid.,* 77.

12 *Ibid.,* 77.

13 *Ibid.,* 91–2.

14 *Ibid.,* 103.

15 *Ibid.,* 109.

16 See for example, M. A. Dobb, *Studies in the Development of Capitalism* (London, 1946); P. M. Sweezy, *The Theory of Capitalist Development* (London, 1946): J. Strachey, *The End of Empire* (London, 1959).

17 Bernard Porter, *Critics of Empire* (London, 1968), 216, argues that this question is 'largely irrelevant' to a critique of Hobson's argument. This is true, if one is primarily concerned with Hobson's views on the domestic roots of overseas investment, but it remains critical for his explanation of tropical colonization.

18 R. M. Robertson, *History of the American Economy* (2nd ed., New York, 1964), 321.

19 See W. LaFeber, *The New Empire: an Interpretation of American Expansion, 1860–1898* (Ithaca, N.Y., 1963) 179–80 and n. 54 for further source material.

20 L. Snyder, *The Imperialist Reader* (Princeton, 1962), 86–7.

21 For an outline of these developments see Clapham, *Economic Develop-ment of France and Germany* and C. Wilson, 'Economic Conditions', in *New Cambridge Modern History*, XI, 73-4.

22 H. Feis, *Europe the World's Banker, 1870-1914* (1930; 2nd ed. New York, 1965), 74. Lenin's estimate of 35,000 million marks was sub-stantially higher, but both estimates put German overseas investment in 1914 at about half that of Britain.

23 *Ibid.,* 51.

24 The material in this paragraph is taken mainly from J. H. Clapham, *Economic History of Great Britain* (London, 1933), II; R. C. K. Ensor, *England 1870-1914* (Oxford, 1936); *New Cambridge Modern History*, XI.

25 Beloff, Renouvin, Schnabel and Valsecchi (eds), *L'Europe du XIXᵉ et du XXᵉ Siècle* (2 vols Milan, 1962), I, 260-8.

26 R. E. Cameron, *France and the Economic Development of Europe* (Prince-ton, 1961), 490 n.3.

27 This paragraph is based mainly on S. B. Clough, *The Economic History of Modern Italy* (New York, 1964), 57 f.

28 Beloff *et al.* (eds), *L'Europe*, I, 398f.

29 M. E. Townsend, *The Rise and Fall of Germany's Colonial Empire, 1884-1918* (New York, 1930), 263.

30 *Imperialism*, 79.

CHAPTER 4: POLITICAL, POPULAR AND PERIPHERAL EXPLANATIONS OF IMPERIALISM

1 H. Pogge von Strandmann, 'Domestic Origins of Germany's Colonial Expansion under Bismarck', *Past and Present*, 42 (February 1969), 140-59; M. Walker, *Germany and the Emigration, 1816-1885*; H. A. Turner, Jr, 'Bismarcks' Imperialist Venture: Anti-British in Origin', in P. Gifford and W. R. Louis (eds), *Britain and Germany in Africa* (New Haven, 1967), 47-82.

2 *Foreign Affairs*, XIV (October, 1936), 102-114. See also Langer, *The Diplomacy of Imperialism* (New York, 1935), ch. 3.

3 This essay was later published, together with an essay on 'Social Classes', as *Imperialism and Social Classes*. References are to the English translation, Oxford, 1951.

4 *Ibid.,* 7.

5 *Finanzkapital* (1910; English translation from Fieldhouse, *Theory of Capitalist Imperialism*), 83-5.

6 See *Imperialism: a Study*, 67-8.

7 Brunschwig, *French Colonialism*, 182-3.

8 B. Semmel, *Imperialism and Social Reform* (London, 1960), 41, for a general survey of these arguments and a bibliography.

9 Quoted Pogge von Strandmann, 'Domestic Origins', 146.

[10] *Ibid.*, 147.

[11] The best study of the intellectual origins of popular imperialism in France is A. Murphy, *The Ideology of French Imperialism* (Washington, 1948).

[12] T. F. Power, *Jules Ferry and the Renaissance of French Imperialism* (New York, 1944), 49.

[13] R. E. Robinson and J. Gallagher, 'The Partition of Africa'. *New Cambridge Modern History*, XI, 594.

[14] The author began his study of European expansion in the Pacific during the nineteenth century, by working on original materials in New Zealand and therefore saw these problems from a colonial and 'sub-imperialist' point of view. Since the evidence suggested that the dynamics of 'British' expansion in this region were almost exclusively peripheral rather than metropolitan, his reaction to reading Hobson and other Eurocentric exponents of imperialism was simply that their analysis was largely irrelevant in the Pacific context. Subsequent study of other regions indicated that, with considerable differences, the same was true in most places.

[15] Hobson, *Imperialism*, 67.

[16] Lenin, *Imperialism*, 51 f.

CHAPTER 5 : THE ROOTS OF EUROPEAN EXPANSION IN THE NINETEENTH CENTURY

[1] See Platt, *Finance, Trade and Politics*, parts I and II, for a fuller treatment of these questions.

[2] Space makes it impossible to deal with all the areas mentioned in this survey. In particular it has been necessary to exclude material on southern Africa, the North-West frontier and princely states of India and the Netherlands Indies.

CHAPTER: 6: AFRICA

[1] This section on Algeria is based primarily on the following: H. Brunschwig, *La Colonisation Française* (Paris, 1949); Ch.A. Julien, *Histoire de l'Algerie contemporaine: I, La Conquête et les Débuts de la Colonisation* (Paris, 1964); C. Martin, *Histoire de l'Algérie Française* (Paris, 1963); S. H. Roberts, *History of French Colonial Policy, 1870–1925* (2 vols, London, 1929).

[2] This section on Tunisia is based primarily on the following: H. Brunschwig, *French Colonialism, 1871–1914* (London, 1964) and *La Colonisation Française* J. Ganiage, *Les Origines du Protectorat Français en Tunisie* (Paris, 1959); E. Staley, *War and the Private Investor* (Chicago, 1935): L. Woolf, *Empire and Commerce in Africa* (London, 1920).

496

This section on Egypt is based primarily on the following: L. H. Jenks, *The Emigration of British Capital to 1875* (New York, 1927); W. L. Langer, *European Alliances and Alignments, 1871–1890* (New York, 1931); D. C. M. Platt, *Finance, Trade and Politics in British Foreign Policy 1815–1914* (Oxford, 1968); A. Ramm, 'Great Britain and France in Egypt, 1876–1882', in Prosser Glifford and W. Roger Louis (eds), *Britain and France in Africa* (New Haven, 1971), 73–119; R. Robinson and J. Gallagher, *Africa and the Victorians* (London, 1961); A. J. P. Taylor, *The Struggle for Mastery in Europe, 1848–1914* (Oxford, 1954).

[4] A. Crouchley, *Economic Development of Modern Egypt* (London, 1938), 273. Quoted Robinson and Gallagher, *Africa and the Victorians*, 81, n. 5.

[5] Quoted Langer, *European Alliances*, 255–6.

[6] Quoted Langer, *ibid.*, 256.

[7] Quoted Robinson and Gallagher, *Africa and the Victorians*, 84.

[8] Quoted *ibid.*, 85.

[9] This section on West Africa is based primarily on the following: K. O. Dike, *Trade and Politics in the Niger Delta* (London, 1959); J. D. Hargreaves, *Prelude to the Partition of West Africa* (London, 1963); D. Kimble, *A Political History of Ghana, 1850–1928* (London, 1963); C. W. Newbury, *The Western Slave Coast and its Rulers* (Oxford, 1961); Robinson and Gallagher, *Africa and the Victorians*; B. Schnapper, *La Politique et le Commerce Français dans le Golfe de Guinée de 1838 à 1871* (Paris, 1961); J. Suret-Canale, *Afrique Noire Occidentale et Centrale* I (Paris, 1961).

[10] As late as 1914 total British investment in West Africa was only about £37·3 million, much of which was borrowed for railway building by the colonial governments of regions not annexed until the 1880s and 1890s. There was virtually no foreign investment in industry and most capital was in trade and shipping.

[11] *Statistical Abstract for the UK*, no. 13, tables 10 and 11 and no. 40, tables 26 and 27. The price of vegetable oil declined as the supply increased. In 1880 British imports were valued at £200,000 less than in 1854 though the volume had risen by about 250,000 cwts. This adverse trend in prices may have stimulated European traders to find cheaper sources of oil by by-passing African middlemen and establishing monopolies; and in this way may have affected British and European attitudes to political control of the areas of inland production.

[12] In 1881 total British imports of palm oil were officially valued at £1,202,571. Total palm oil exports from the Gold Coast and Lagos, the only two British possessions involved, were valued at £230,572 and £147,423 respectively. Total palm kernel imports to Britain in the same year were valued at £508,906. Exports from the Gold Coast were worth £47,408 and from Lagos £221,634. *Statistical Abstract for the*

Several Colonial and Other Possessions of the UK . . . *1881–1895* (London, 1896), 102 and 104.

[13] *Statistical Abstract for the UK*, No. 40 (London, 1893), Table 25.

[14] *Statistical Abstract for the Several Colonial and other Possessions of the UK* . . . *1881–1895*, Table 11.

CHAPTER 7: ASIA

[1] *Statistical Abstract for the UK*, No. 13, Table 9.

[2] This section on Russia in the Far East and Central Asia is based primarily on the following: M. T. Florinsky, *Russia: a History and an Interpretation* (2 vols, New York, 1961); A. J. Lunger, 'The Economic Background of the Russian Conquest of Central Asia' (unpublished Ph.D. Thesis, London, 1953); A. Malozemoff, *Russian Far Eastern Policy, 1881–1904*. (Berkeley & Los Angeles, 1958); M. Mancall, 'Ignatiev's Mission to Peking, 1859–1860', *Harvard Papers on China*, No. 10, 1956; R. A. Pierce, *Russian Central Asia, 1867–1917* (Berkeley & Los Angeles, 1960); R. K. Quested, *The Expansion of Russia in East Asia, 1857–60* (Kuala Lumpur, 1967); H. Seton-Watson, *The Decline of Imperial Russia, 1855–1914* (London, 1952); B. H. Sumner, *Survey of Russian History* (London, 1944: 2nd rev. ed. 1947).

[3] Quoted Sumner, *Survey*, 299.

[4] Quoted Quested, *The Expansion of Russia*, 42.

[5] Quoted Pierce, *Russian Central Asia*, 109.

[6] Quoted Pierce, *ibid.*, 20.

[7] The main sources for British policy on the northern frontiers of India are as follows: G. J. Alder, *British India's Northern Frontier, 1865–1895* (London, 1963); C. C. Davies, *The Problem of the North-West Frontier, 1890–1908* (Cambridge, 1932); H. Dodwell (ed.), *The Cambridge History of India*, V and VI (Cambridge, 1929, 1932); D. K. Ghose, *England and Afghanistan* (Calcutta, 1960); P. C. Greaves, *Persia and the Defence of India, 1884–1892* (London, 1959); V. G. Kiernan, 'Kashgar and the Politics of Central Asia, 1868–78', *Cambridge Historical Journal*, XI, 317–42; H. A. Lamb, *Britain and Chinese Central Asia: The Road to Lhasa, 1767 to 1905* (London, 1960); B. Prasad, *The Foundations of India's Foreign Policy, 1860–82* (Calcutta, 1955); A. P. Thornton, 'Afghanistan in Anglo-Russian Diplomacy, 1869–73', *Cambridge Historical Journal*, XI, 204.

[8] This section on Burma is based primarily on the following: J. F. Cady, *A History of Modern Burma* (Ithaca, New York, 1958); H. G. Callis, *Foreign Capital in Southeast Asia* (New York, 1942); *Cambridge History of India*, V and VI; S. Deshaw, *History of the British Residency in Burma, 1826–40* (Rangoon, 1939); J. S. Furnival, 'The Fashioning of Leviathan: the Beginnings of British Rule in Burma', *Journal of the*

Burma Research Society, xxix (1939), 1–137; D. G. E. Hall, *A History of South-East Asia* (New York, 1955).

9 Hall, *South-East Asia*, 526.

10 J. G. Scott, *Burma: a Handbook of Practical Information* (London, 1911), 279. I owe this reference to Mr K. R. Sipe of Duke University.

11 This section on Malaya is based primarily on the following: C. D. Cowan: *Nineteenth Century Malaya: the Origins of British Political Control* (London, 1961); D. G. E. Hall, *A History of South-East Asia;* W. D. McIntyre, *The Imperial Frontier in the Tropics, 1865–75* (New York, 1967); C. N. Parkinson, *British Intervention in Malaya, 1867–1877* (Singapore, 1960); N. Tarling, 'British Policy in the Malay Peninsula and Archipelago, 1824–1871', *Journal of the Ceylon Branch of the Royal Asiatic Society*, XXX, 3 (1957); N. Tarling, *Piracy and Politics in the Malay World: A Study of British Imperialism in Nineteenth Century South-East Asia* (Melbourne, 1963).

12 Quoted V. Harlow and F. Madden, *British Colonial Developments 1774–1834* (Oxford, 1953), 74–6.

13 Feis, *Europe the World's Banker*, 23.

14 The following three paragraphs are based on Cowan, *Nineteenth Century Malaya*, ch. 3.

15 Quoted Cowan, 131.

16 *Ibid.*, 138–9.

17 McIntyre, 160.

18 Quoted McIntyre, 162–3.

19 Quoted Cowan, 164.

20 Quoted McIntyre, 198.

21 Quoted Cowan, 167.

22 Quoted McIntyre, 202.

23 Quoted Cowan, 168.

24 *Ibid.*, 169.

25 *Ibid.*, 175.

26 Quoted McIntyre, 209.

27 *Ibid.*, 315.

28 For the period 1880–1914 sources for Malaya, in addition to those listed above, are as follows: G. C. Allen and A. G. Donnithorne, *Western Enterprise in Indonesia and Malaya* (London, 1954); Chai Hon Chan, *The Development of British Malaya, 1896–1909* (London, 1964); L. A. Mills, *British Rule in Eastern Asia* (London, 1942); K. Sinclair, 'Hobson and Lenin in Johore: Colonial Office policy towards British concessionaires and investors, 1878–1907', *Modern Asian Studies*, I, 4 (1967), 335–52.

29 This section on Indo-China is based primarily on the following: H. Brunschwig, *La Colonisation Française* and *French Colonialism*: J. F. Cady, *The Roots of French Imperialism in Eastern Asia* (Ithaca, New York, 1954); D. G. E. Hall, *A History of South-East Asia;* J. F. Laffey,

'French Imperialism and the Lyon Mission to China' (unpublished Ph.D. thesis, Ithaca, New York 1966); T. F. Power, *Jules Ferry and the Renaissance of French Imperialism*; C. Robequain, *L'Evolution de l'Indochine Française* (Paris, 1939), S. H. Roberts, *History of French Colonial Policy 1870–1925.*

30 Quoted Hall, 365.

31 J. Itier, *Journal d'une Voyage en Chine en 1843, 1844, 1845, 1846* (Paris, 1848), quoted Laffey, 'French Imperialism', 204.

32 Quoted Laffey, 206.

33 Laffey, table III, 196–7.

34 Quoted Laffey, 209.

35 *Ibid.,* 209–10.

36 Garnier to a friend, 1872. Quoted Laffey, 211.

37 This section on China is based primarily on the following: G. C. Allen and A. G. Donnithorne, *Western Enterprise in Far Eastern Development: China and Japan* (London, 1954); W. C. Costin, *Great Britain and China, 1833–60* (Oxford, 1937); G. B. Endacott, *A History of Hong Kong* (Oxford, 1958); M. Greenberg, *British Trade and the Opening of China, 1800–42* (Cambridge, 1951); V. G. Kiernan, *British Diplomacy in China, 1880–1885* (Cambridge, 1939); *New Cambridge Modern History*, X, XI (Cambridge, 1960, 1962); C. F. Remer, *Foreign Investments in China* (New York, 1933). See also sources for Russian policy in China, n. 2 of this chapter.

38 Greenberg, 13.

39 Quoted Costin, 33.

40 *Ibid.,* 60.

41 *Ibid.,* 71.

42 *Ibid.,* 99.

43 E. M. Gull, *British Economic Interests in the Far East* (London, 1943), 56, 58.

CHAPTER 8: THE PACIFIC

1 The main sources on British, French, German and American expansion in the Pacific before about 1880 are as follows: J. I. Brookes, *International Rivalry in the Pacific Islands, 1800–1875* (Berkeley, 1941); J.-P. Faivre, *L'Expansion Française dans le Pacifique, 1800–1898* (Paris 1953); A. A. Koskinen, *Missionary Influence as a Political Factor in the Pacific Islands* (Helsinki, 1953); W. P. Morrell, *Britain in the Pacific Islands* (Oxford, 1960); A. Ross, *New Zealand Aspirations in the Pacific in the Nineteenth Century* (Oxford, 1964); O. W. Parnaby, *Britain and the Labour Traffic in the Southwest Pacific* (Durham, N. C., 1964); D. Scarr, *Fragments of Empire: a History of the Western Pacific High Commission, 1877–1914* (Canberra, A.C.T. 1967); J. M. Ward, *British Policy in the South Pacific, 1783–1893* (Sydney, 1948).

2 The following paragraphs on the annexation of New Zealand are based primarily on the following: J. C. Beaglehole, *Captain Hobson and the New Zealand Company* (Northampton, Mass, 1928); J. W. Davidson, 'New Zealand, 1820–70: An Essay in Reinterpretation', *Historical Studies Australia and New Zealand*, V (1953), 349–60; J. S. Marais, *The Colonisation of New Zealand* (London, 1927); J. Miller, *Early Victorian New Zealand* (London, 1958); W. P. Morrell, *British Colonial Policy in the Age of Peel and Russell* (Oxford, 1930); K. Sinclair, *A History of New Zealand* (Harmondsworth, 1959); F. J. Tapp, *Early New Zealand: A Dependency of New South Wales, 1788–1841* (Melbourne, 1958); T. Williams, 'James Stephen and British Intervention in New Zealand, 1838–40', *Journal of Modern History*, XIII, 1 (1941); T. Williams, 'The Treaty of Waitangi', *History*, XXV, 99.

3 The following paragraphs on the annexation of Fiji are based primarily on the following in addition to the general works listed above: E. Drus, 'The Colonial Office and the Annexation of Fiji', *Transactions of the Royal Historical Society*, 4th series, XXXII (1950); J. D. Legge, *Britain in Fiji, 1858–1880* (London, 1950); W. D. McIntyre, *The Imperial Frontier in the Tropics*.

4 The following paragraphs on Samoa are based primarily on the following in addition to the general works listed above: S. Masterman, *Origins of International Rivalry in Samoa, 1845–1884* (Stanford, 1934); G. H. Ryden, *The Foreign Policy of the United States in Relation to Samoa* (New Haven, 1933).

CHAPTER 9: THE PARTITION OF MEDITERRANEAN AFRICA

1 For example, see H. Brunschwig, *La Colonisation Française* and *French Colonialism*; R. A. Oliver and J. D. Fage, *A Short History of Africa* (Harmondsworth, 1962); M. Crowder, *West Africa under Colonial Rule* (Evanston, 1968).

2 There is not, so far as I know, a 'German' school of interpretation, though a number of writers have stressed the great importance of Bismarck's intervention in African affairs in 1884–5. For example, A. J. P. Taylor, *Germany's First Bid for Colonies, 1884–1885* (London, 1938); M. E. Townsend, *Origins of Modern German Colonialism, 1871–1885* (New York, 1921); D. K. Fieldhouse, *The Colonial Empires* (London, 1966).

3 The classic statement of the Egyptian hypothesis is in Robinson and Gallagher, *Africa and the Victorians*, though it has been echoed in a number of other books.

4 See, for example, C. W. Newbury, 'Victorians, Republicans and the Partition of West Africa', *Journal of African History*, III (1962), 493–501; J. Stengers, 'L'impérialisme coloniale de la fin du XIXe siècle:

Mythe ou réalité?', *Ibid.*, 469–91; G. Shepperson, 'Africa, the Victorians and Imperialism', *Revue Belge de Philologie et d'Histoire*, XL (1962), 2, 1228–38.

5 See C. W. Newbury and S. Kanya-Forstner, 'French Policy and the Origins of the Scramble for West Africa', *Journal of African History*, X, 2 (1969), 253–76.

6 This section on Tunisia after 1880 is based primarily on the sources listed in chapter 6, No. 20.

7 Quoted Staley, *War and the Private Investor*, 338, No. 2.

8 Quoted J. Ganiage, 'France, England and the Tunisian Affair', in Gifford and Louis (eds), *Britain and France in Africa*, 48.

9 Quoted J. Ganiage, *L'Expansion Coloniale de la France*, 69.

10 Staley, *War and the Private Investor*, 338–9.

11 Quoted Woolf, *Empire and Commerce*, 107.

12 Quoted Ganiage, 'France, England and the Tunisian Affair', *loc. cit.*, 56.

13 Quoted *ibid.* 61.

14 This section on Egypt after 1880 is based primarily on the sources listed in chapter 6, n. 3.

15 *Modern Egypt*, I, 233, quoted Langer, *European Alliances*, 269.

16 Robinson and Gallagher, *Africa and the Victorians*, 117.

17 For an analysis of this struggle, see *ibid.*, 105–11.

18 Quoted *ibid.*, 118.

19 *Ibid.*, 465.

20 This section on Morocco is based primarily on the following: H. Brunschwig, *La Colonisation Française* and *French Colonialism*; H. Feis, *Europe the World's Banker, 1870–1914* (New Haven, 1930. 2nd ed. 1965); J. Ganiage, *L'Expansion Coloniale de la France*; J. A. S. Grenville, *Lord Salisbury and Foreign Policy* (London, 1964); P. Guillen 'Les Milieux d'affaires français et le Maroc à l'aube du xxe siècle. La fondation de la Compagnie Marocaine', *Revue Historique*, CCXXIX (1963), 397–422; Guillen, *L'Allemagne et le Maroc de 1870–1905* (Paris, 1967); J.-L. Miège, *Le Maroc et l'Europe* II–IV. (Paris, 1961–3); A. J. P. Taylor, *The Struggle for Mastery in Europe*; G. Monger, *The End of Isolation: British Foreign Policy, 1900–1907* (London, 1963).

21 Guillen, *L'Allemagne et le Maroc*, 423, 447.

22 Miège, *Le Maroc et l'Europe*, III, 252, 427; IV, 370; Guillen, *L'Allemagne et le Maroc*, 423.

23 Guillen, *L'Allemagne et le Maroc*, 385.

24 *Ibid.*, 479.

25 See Guillen, 'Les Milieux d'affaires' for a full account of Creusot's activities in Morocco.

26 *Ibid.*, 417.

27 Miège, *Le Maroc et l'Europe*, IV, 52.

28 Ganiage, *L'Expansion*, 110.

[29] *Ibid.*, 111.

[30] Miège, *Le Maroc et l'Europe*, IV, 29–30.

[31] Guillen, *L'Allemagne et le Maroc*, 423.

[32] Miège, *Le Maroc et l'Europe*, IV, 31.

[33] Guillen, *L'Allemagne et le Maroc*, 393.

[34] *Ibid.*, 423.

[35] *Ibid.*, 448.

[36] *Ibid.*, 478.

[37] *Ibid.*, 489.

[38] *Ibid.*, 520.

[39] *Ibid.*, 695.

[40] Feis, *Europe the World's Banker*, 399.

[41] *Bulletin du Comité de l'Afrique Française*, January 1904. Quoted Brunschwig, *French Colonialism*, 118–19.

[42] P. Guillen, 'The Entente 1904 as a Colonial Settlement', *Britain and France in Africa*, 343, No. 3.

[43] Guillen, 'Les Milieu d'affairs', 400.

[44] *Ibid.*, 417.

[45] Theobald Fischer's cynical comment was: 'England would have the strategic part of Morocco, Germany the economic part and France the picturesque part', Ganiage, *L'Expansion*, 259, n.1.

[46] Feis, *Europe the World's Banker*, 403.

[47] Taylor, *The Struggle*, 433.

[48] Staley, *War and the Private Investor*, 179.

CHAPTER 10: THE PARTITION OF SUB-SAHARAN AFRICA

[1] In addition to the general books listed in chapter 6, n.9., this section on French policy in West Africa is based primarily on the following: J. D. Hargreaves, 'West African States and the European Conquest', in L. H. Gann and P. Duignan (eds), *Colonialism in Africa, 1870–1960*, I (Cambridge, 1969), 199–219; H. Brunschwig, 'French exploration and conquest in tropical Africa from 1865–1898', *ibid.*, 132–64; S. Kanya-Forstner, *The Conquest of the Western Sudan: A Study in French Military Imperialism* (Cambridge, 1969); Newbury and Kanya-Forstner, 'French Policy and the origins of the Scramble for West Africa'; Newbury, 'The Development of French Policy on the Lower and Upper Niger, 1880–98' *Journal of Modern History*, XXXI, 1, 1959, 16–26; Newbury, 'The Protectionist Revival in French Colonial Trade: The Case of Senegal', *Economic History Review*, second ser., XXI, 2 (1968), 337–48.

[2] Quoted Newbury and Kanya-Forstner, 'French Policy', 261.

[3] Quoted *ibid.*, 262.

[4] In addition to the general works listed in chapter 6, n. 9 this section on

British policy in West Africa is based primarily on the following: J. E. Flint, *Sir George Goldie and the Making of Nigeria* (London, 1960); Flint, 'Nigeria: the Colonial Experience', in Gann and Duignan (eds), *Colonialism in Africa*, I, 220–60; M. Perham, *Lugard* (2 vols, London, 1956–60).

5 Quoted Robinson and Gallagher, *Africa and the Victorians*, 165.

6 Dike, *Trade and Politics*, 216.

7 Quoted Flint, *Goldie*, 159.

8 Quoted Robinson and Gallagher, *Africa and the Victorians*, 382. News of the partition of Samoa between Germany and the United States evoked similar comments from R. J. Seddon, Premier of New Zealand in 1900. 'The convention made between Great Britain and Germany regarding the disposition of the Navigator Group shows that the predictions uttered about thirty years ago by the New Zealand Ministry have been verified. ... Great Britain, that civilized and Christianized them, that first traded with them, that has even now the most trade, and the most white population, and that has spent much blood and treasure in the Islands – had abandoned them to the foreign powers.' Memo to the Governor, 16 April 1900. C.O. 209/260.

9 Quoted Robinson and Gallagher, *Africa and the Victorians*, 382.

10 Quoted *ibid.*, 383.

11 See Flint, *Goldie*, chapters 10–12.

12 *Ibid.*, 263.

13 Quoted *ibid.*, 272.

14 For a lucid exposition of his economic objectives in West Africa see Robinson and Gallagher, *Africa and the Victorians*, 395–402.

15 See S. B. Saul, 'The Economic Significance of "Constructive Imperialism"', *Journal of Economic History*, XVII (1957), 173–92.

16 The following paragraphs on German policy in West Africa are based primarily on the following: W. O. Aydelotte, *Bismarck and British Colonial Policy, 1883–85* (Philadelphia, 1937); Erich Eyk, *Bismarck* (3 vols, Erlenbach-Zurich, 1941–44), III; H. Pogge von Strandmann, 'Domestic Origins'; H. R. Rudin, *Germans in the Cameroons: 1884–1919* (New Haven, 1938); A. J. P. Taylor, *Germany's First Bid for Colonies*; M. E. Townsend, *Origins of Modern German Colonialism*; H. A. Turner, 'Bismarck's Imperialist Venture: Anti-British in Origin?'; M. Walker, *Germany and the Emigration*.

17 Townsend, *Origins*, 77.

18 Quoted Turner, 'Bismarck's Imperialist Venture', 52.

19 This hypothesis is quoted by Turner, *loc. cit.*, 67, from H.-P. Jaeck, 'Die deutsche Annexion', in *Kamerun unter deutscher Kolonial herrschaft*, H. Stoecker (ed) (East Berlin, 1960) 52–3; G. W. F. Hallgarten, *Imperialismus vor 1914* (2nd ed. 2 vols, Munich, 1963), I, 211–12.

20 Turner, 'Bismarck's Imperialist Venture', 67.

21 Pogge von Strandmann, 'Domestic Origins', 150.
22 Quoted *ibid.*, 154.
23 This hypothesis is developed by Turner in 'Bismarck's Imperialist Venture'.
24 Hargreaves, *Prelude*, 316–17.
25 Quoted Turner 'Bismarck's Imperialist Venture', 57.
26 Quoted *ibid.*, 70.
27 Quoted Pogge von Strandmann, 'Domestic Origins', 146.
28 Friedrich Engels was one of many who reached this conclusion in the 1890s, and in a supplement to his 1894 edition of volume III of Marx's *Capital* commented that 'Today [colonization] is purely a subsidiary of the stock exchange, in whose interests the European powers divided Africa a few years ago. . . . Africa leased directly to companies . . . and Mashonaland and Natal [*sic*] seized by Rhodes for the stock exchange.' Quoted Fieldhouse, *Theory of Capitalist Imperialism*, 50.
29 The main printed sources, apart from general works, for the origins of the Congo Free State are as follows: R. Anstey, *Britain and the Congo in the Nineteenth Century* (Oxford, 1962); N. Ascherson, *The King Incorporated* (London, 1963); F. Bontinck, *Aux origines de l'état independant du Congo* (Louvain, 1966); S. E. Crowe, *The Berlin West African Conference, 1884–1885* (London, 1942); A. Roeykens, *Les débuts de l'oeuvre africaine de Léopold II* (Brussels, 1955); R. Slade, *English-speaking missions in the Congo Independent State, 1878–1908* (Brussels, 1959); J. Stengers, 'The Congo Free State and the Belgian Congo before 1914', in Gann and Duignan (eds), *Colonialism in Africa*, I, 261–92.
30 For the genesis of his ideas see L. Le Febve De Vivy (ed.), *Documents d'histoire précoloniale belge (1861–65)* (Brussels, 1955).
31 The argument in the following paragraphs is taken primarily from J. Stengers, 'King Leopold and Anglo-French Rivalry, 1882–1884', in Gifford and Louis (eds), *Britain and France in Africa*, 121–66.
32 Quoted *ibid.*, 163.
33 The main printed sources for the colonization of the Rhodesias are as follows: L. H. Gann, *A History of Northern Rhodesia: Early Days to 1953* (London, 1964); L. H. Gann, *A History of Southern Rhodesia: Early Days to 1934* (London, 1965); A. J. Hanna, *The Beginnings of Nyasaland and North-Eastern Rhodesia, 1859–95* (Oxford, 1956); J. G. Lockhart and C. M. Woodhouse, *Rhodes* (London, 1963); Robinson and Gallagher, *Africa and the Victorians*. There is no detailed study of the BSA.
34 S. H. Frankel, *Capital Investment in Africa* (London, 1938), 63.
35 The main printed sources for the origins of the Boer War are as follows: G. Blainey, 'Lost Causes of the Jameson Raid', *Economic History Review*, 2nd ser., XVIII (1965), 350–66; A. P. Cartwright, *The Corner House* (Cape Town, 1965), *Gold Paved the Way* (Cape Town, 1967);

T. R. H. Davenport, *The Afrikaner bond: the history of a South African political party, 1880–1911* (London, 1966); C. W. De Kiewiet, *The Imperial Factor in South Africa* (Cambridge, 1937); W. K. Hancock, *Smuts*. I. *The Sanguine Years, 1870–1919* (Cambridge, 1962); G. H. Le May, *British Supremacy in South Africa, 1899–1907* (Oxford, 1965); Lockhart and Woodhouse, *Rhodes*; R. I. Lovell, *The Struggle for South Africa, 1875–1899: A Study in Economic Imperialism* (New York, 1945); J. S. Marais, *The Fall of Kruger's Republic* (Oxford. 1961); E. Pakenham, *Jameson's Raid* (London, 1960); J. van der Poel, *Railway and Customs Policies in South Africa, 1885–1910* (London, 1933); Robinson and Gallagher, *Africa and the Victorians*.

36 E. Sik, *The History of Black Africa* (2 vols, Budapest, 1966), I, 369 f.

37 *Ibid.,* I, 372.

38 Frankel, *Capital Investment,* 95.

39 *Ibid.,* table 12.

40 Marais, *The Fall,* 31.

41 Robinson and Gallagher, *Africa and the Victorians,* 422.

42 Marais, *The Fall,* 252.

43 *Ibid.,* 162, n. 3.

44 Frankel, *Capital Investment,* 56.

45 The following argument is derived primarily from Robinson and Gallagher, *Africa and the Victorians,* ch. 14, and is only indicated briefly here.

46 *Ibid.,* 420.

47 *Ibid.,* 450.

48 This section on East Africa is based primarily on the following: W. O. Aydelotte, *Bismarck and British Colonial Policy*; H. Brunschwig, *L'Expansion allemande outre-mer du XVI siècle à nos jours* (Paris, 1957); R. Coupland, *The Exploitation of East Africa, 1856–1890* (London, 1939); R. O. Collins, 'Origins of the Nile Struggle: Anglo-German Negotiations and the Mackinnon Agreement of 1890', in Gifford and Louis (eds), *Britain and Germany in Africa;* V. Harlow and E. M. Chilver (eds), *History of East Africa,* II (Oxford, 1965); P. M. Holt, *The Mahdist State in the Sudan, 1881–1898* (Oxford, 1958); K. Ingham, *The Making of Modern Uganda* (London, 1958); D. A. Low, 'British Public Opinion and the Uganda Question, October to December 1892', *Uganda Journal,* XVIII, 2 (1954), 81–100; F. F. Müller, *Deutschland – Zanzibar – Ostafrika: Geschichte einer deutscher Kolonialeroberung, 1884–1890* (Berlin, 1959); R. A. Oliver, *The Missionary Factor in East Africa* (London, 1952), *Sir Harry Johnston and the Scramble for Africa;* R. A. Oliver and G. Mathew (eds), *History of East Africa,* I (Oxford, 1963); M. Perham, *Lugard,* I; Robinson and Gallagher, *Africa and the Victorians;* A. J. P. Taylor, *Germany's First Bid for Colonies*; G. N. Sanderson, *England, Europe and the Upper Nile, 1882–1899* (Edinburgh, 1965); M. E. Townsend, *Origins of Modern German Colonialism* and *The*

Rise and Fall of Germany's Colonial Empire, 1884-1918 (New York, 1930); L. Woolf, *Empire and Commerce in Africa.*

49 L. Woolf, *Empire and Commerce*, ch. 6 and pp. 330–6.

50 The main commercial treaties were with the United States (1833), Britain (1839), France (1844) and the Hanseatic League (1859).

51 J. H. Speke, *What Led to the Discovery of the Source of the Nile* (London, 1864), 344, quoted Coupland, *Exploitation*, 131.

52 Quoted Coupland, *Exploitation*, 131–2.

53 Quoted Coupland, *Exploitation*, 305. The original of the letter is lost but these phrases were quoted in Foreign Office instructions to Gerald Waller, an agent of Mackinnon and Buxton.

54 This explanation is given by J. Flint, 'The Wider Background to Partition and Colonial Occupation', in Oliver and Mathew (eds), *History of East Africa*, I, 360–1.

55 The following statistics are taken from Müller, *Deutschland – Zanzibar – Ostafrika*. I owe this and the following reference to Dr H. Pogge von Strandmann.

56 H. U. Wehler, *Bismarck und der Imperialismis* (Berlin, 1969), 342.

57 Coupland, *Exploitation*, 425–6.

58 Quoted *ibid.,* 427.

59 See W. R. Louis, 'Sir Percy Anderson's Grand African Strategy, 1883–1895', *English Historical Review*, LXXXI, 319 (1966), 292–314.

60 Quoted Robinson and Gallagher, *Africa and the Victorians*, 194.

61 Quoted Coupland, *Exploitation*, 433.

62 The British South Africa Company survived this first phase mainly because it had Rhodes' fortune to support it, but distributed no dividend before 1923. Other comparable companies, including the Niger Company and DOAG, were saved from bankruptcy by the compensation paid by the British and German governments respectively for 'administrative expenditure' when responsibility for administration was transferred from company to government.

63 Quoted Coupland, *Exploitation*, 486.

64 Quoted Robinson and Gallagher, *Africa and the Victorians*, 350–1.

CHAPTER 11: SOUTH-EAST ASIA

1 In addition to the source listed in chapter 7, n. 7, this section on Upper Burma is based on the following: R. H. Macaulay, *The Bombay-Burmah Trading Corporation* (London, 1934); D. P. Singhal, *The Annexation of Upper Burma* (Singapore, 1960); P. J. N. Tuck, 'Britain, France and Siam, 1885–1896' (unpublished Oxford D.Phil thesis, 1970). I am indebted to Mr Keith R. Sipe of Duke University, North Carolina, for references to several quotations from correspondence in the India

Office files which he incorporated in an unpublished paper presented to a seminar in 1969, 'The Imperialism of Free Trade: The Annexation of Upper Burma, 1885'. These have been checked and corrected where necessary.

2 Bernard to Durand, 27 July 1885, India Office, Political and Secret Department, L/P and S/7, vol. 45, 215.

3 W. S. Churchill, *Lord Randolph Churchill* (London, 1906), I, 521. See also R. Rhodes James, *Lord Randolph Churchill* (London, 1959), 205.

4 Salisbury to Walsham, 7 August 1885, *Parliamentary Papers*, 1886 (L), C.4614, 170.

5 Salisbury to Walsham, 9 September 1885, *ibid.*, 177.

6 Churchill to Dufferin, secret telegram, 6 October 1885, India Office, Political and Secret Department, L/P and S/7, vol. 45, 968.

7 Andreino to Jones, 13 September 1885, *ibid.*, 958.

8 Dufferin to Churchill, 5 October 1885, *ibid.*, 869 (a).

9 This section on France in Indo-China is based primarily on the sources listed in chapter 7, n. 1, together with the following: M. Brugière, 'Le Chemin de Fer de Yunnan: Paul Doumer et la Politique d'intervention francaise en Chine, 1889–1902', *Revue d'Histoire Diplomatique*, LXXVII (1963), 23–61, 129–62, 253–78; E. Denis, *Bordeaux et la Cochinchine* (Bordeaux, 1965); W. L. Langer, *The Diplomacy of Imperialism, 1890–1902* (2nd. ed., New York, 1951); Tuck, 'Britain, France and Siam, 1885–1896'.

10 It may also be significant that all were published in the same periodical, the *Journal des Chambres de Commerce françaises* (*JCCF*) for December 1882 and January and May 1883. See Laffey, 'French Imperialism and the Lyon Mission to China', 220–3.

11 *JCCF*, January 1883, 65, quoted Laffey, 221.

12 *JCCF*, December 1882, 4, quoted Laffey, 221.

13 *JCCF*, January 1883, 60, quoted Laffey, 222.

14 *JCCF*, May 1883, 273, 209, quoted Laffey, 222–3.

15 Quoted Roubiquet (ed), *Discours et Opinions*, V, 283, 284–5, trans D. K. Fieldhouse.

16 Laffey, *French Imperialism*, table 7, 114–15.

17 Laffey, table 8, 117; *Annuaire Statistique de la France*, 1882, table 3.

18 *Ibid.*

19 *Statistical Abstract for the UK*, 40.

20 The following paragraphs on Laos are based primarily on Tuck, 'Britain, France and Siam'.

21 Quoted Laffey, 439.

22 *Ibid.*, 445–6.

23 'La Chine, L'Europe et la France', *L'Economiste français*, March 1896, quoted Laffey, 476.

24 Quoted Laffey, 477–9.

[25] *Ibid.*, 485.
[26] Cambon to Delcassé, 11 May 1899, quoted Laffey, 489–90.
[27] *Ibid.*, 30 July 1899, quoted Laffey, 491.

CHAPTER 12: CHINA AND THE PACIFIC

[1] There is, of course, a very large literature on China in the period after 1880. In addition to the sources listed in ch. 7, n. 37, the following general studies are of particular value for studying European policies in the Far East in this period. A. E. Campbell, *Great Britain and the United States, 1895–1903* (London, 1960); H. Feis, *Europe the World's Banker*; J. A. S. Grenville, *Lord Salisbury and Foreign Policy* (London, 1964); Chi-Ming Hou, *Foreign Investment and Economic Development in China, 1840–1937* (Cambridge, Mass., 1965); W. L. Langer, *The Diplomacy of Imperialism*; C. J. Lowe, *The Reluctant Imperialists* (2 vols, London, 1967); G. W. Monger, *The End of Isolation* (London, 1963); I. H. Nish, *The Anglo-Japanese Alliance, 1894–1907* (London, 1966); N. A. Pelcovits, *Old China Hands and the Foreign Office* (New York, 1948); A. J. P. Taylor, *The Struggle for Mastery in Europe*; P. A. Varg, *The Making of a Myth: the United States and China, 1897–1912* (E. Lansing, Mich., 1968).
[2] The following paragraphs on Russian policy are based primarily on A. Malozemoff, *Russian Far Eastern Policy, 1881–1904*.
[3] Quoted *ibid.*, 39.
[4] The following paragraphs are based mainly on Grenville, *Lord Salisbury*; Lowe, *Reluctant Imperialists*; Pelcovits, *Old China Hands*; Platt, *Finance, Trade and Politics*.
[5] Langer, *Diplomacy of Imperialism*, 454.
[6] W. LaFeber, *The New Empire*, 301.
[7] Quoted *ibid.*, 354.
[8] Quoted Langer, *Diplomacy*, 686.
[9] Quoted Lowe, *Reluctant Imperialists*, II, 120–1.
[10] Quoted Langer, *Diplomacy*, 682–3.
[11] See his memorandum of 10 September 1900, printed in Lowe, II, 122.
[12] Quoted Langer, *Diplomacy*, 702.
[13] Remer, *Foreign Investments*, 117 f.
[14] Chi-Ming Hou, 25.
[15] This section on the Pacific after 1880 is based primarily on the sources listed in ch. 8, n. 1 together with general works on the diplomacy of the great powers mentioned in other sections.
[16] Morrell, *Britain in the Pacific Islands*, 301.
[17] A. Ross, 'New Zealand Aspirations in the Pacific in the Nineteenth Century (unpublished Cambridge Ph.D. thesis, 1949), appendix X (c), 475 f.

[18] For the diplomacy relating to Samoa in 1898 see Langer, Lowe, Grenville, etc.

[19] Ganiage, *L'Expansion*, 408.

[20] Ross, *New Zealand Aspirations*, 238.

[21] C. W. Newbury, 'Aspects of French Policy in the Pacific, 1853–1906', *Pacific Historical Review*, XXVII, 1 (1958), 54.

Index